UNIVERSAL KEYS
FOR WRITERS

ANN RAIMES

Hunter College, City University of New York

Houghton Mifflin Company
Boston   New York

Executive editor: Suzanne Phelps Weir
Senior development editor: Martha Bustin
Senior project editor: Rosemary Winfield
Production editorial assistant: Marlowe Shaeffer
Editorial assistant: Becky Wong
Senior production/design coordinator: Jill Haber
Manufacturing manager: Florence Cadran
Marketing manager: Cindy Graff Cohen
Marketing assistant: Sarah Donelson
Cover photo: John Wilkes

Credits   (*credits continue on p. 930, which constitutes an extension of the copyright page*)

Part I   Alvarez, Julia. "Hold the Mayonnaise." *New York Times* 12 January 1992: sec. 6: 14.
The American Heritage Dictionary of the English Language. 4th ed. Definition of "inference,"
  "Standard English." Copyright © 2000 by Houghton Mifflin Company.
Anzaldúa, Gloria. "How to Tame a Wild Tongue." *Borderlands/La Frontera: The New Mestiza.*
  2nd ed. San Francisco: Aunt Lute Books, 1999. 77–78. Copyright © 1999 by Gloria
  Anzaldúa. Reprinted by permission.
Bauman, Adrian, Neville Owen, and Eva Leslie. "Physical Activity and Health Outcomes:
  Epidemiological Evidence, National Guidelines, and Public Health Initiatives."
  Australian Journal of Nutrition and Dietetics 57 (2000): 229–232.
Bombeck, Erma. *If Life Is a Bowl of Cherries—What Am I Doing in the Pits?* New York: Fawcett,
  1971. 212.
Bordwell, David, and Kristin Thompson. *Film Art.* 3rd ed. New York: McGraw, 1990. 127.
Braithwaite, Dawn. "Viewing Persons with Disabilities as a Culture." *Intercultural
  Communication.* 6th ed. Eds. Larry Samovar and Richard E. Porter. Belmont, CA:
  Wadsworth, 1991. 36.
Burns, David D., M.D. *Feeling Good: The New Mood Therapy.* New York: Avon, 1980. 352.
Carnegie, Dale. *How to Win Friends and Influence People.* Rev. Ed. New York: Dale Carnegie &
  Associates, 1936. 121.
Caro, Robert A. *The Power Broker: Robert Moses and the Fall of New York.* New York: Knopf,
  1974. 1.
Carter, Stephen L. *Integrity.* New York: HarperCollins, 1996. 5–7.
The Columbia Encyclopedia Online. Definition of "Life." Copyright © Columbia University
  Press. Reprinted with the permission of the publisher.
Dalí, Salvador. *The Secret Life of Salvador Dalí.* Trans. Haakon M. Chevalier. New York: Dover,
  1993. 15.
Gilbert, Matthew. "All Talk, All the Time." *Boston Globe Magazine* 4 June 2000: 9. Reprinted
  courtesy of the *Boston Globe.*
Gladwell, Malcolm. "The Social Life of Paper." *New Yorker* 25 March 2002: 93. Reprinted
  with permission from The New Yorker Magazine.
Gleick, James. *Chaos.* New York: Penguin, 1987. 40–41.
Gleiser, Marcelo. *The Dancing Universe: From Creation Myths to the Big Bang.* New York:
  Plume, 1997.

Printed in the U.S.A.   Library of Congress Control Number 2002109659
Student edition: ISBN 0-618-11288-X   123456789-QV-06 05 04 03 02
Instructor's annotated edition: ISBN 0-618-11293-6   123456789-DW-06 05 04 03 02

How to Find Information in

UNIVERSAL KEYS
FOR WRITERS

 The Main Routes

▸ **Key to the Book** (*inside front cover and facing page*)
Menu-style directory to the book's ten parts.

▸ **Tabbed dividers** (*table of contents at the beginning of each part*)

■ Red tabs cover the writing process, writing in all your courses, and writing and technology issues.

■ Gold tabs cover nuts-and-bolts issues such as grammar and punctuation.

■ Blue tabs cover research and documentation.

▸ **Main Table of Contents** (*p. xix*)

▸ **Index** (*p. I–1*)
A comprehensive alphabetical list of topics and terms.

 The Alternate Routes

▸ **Common Editing and Proofreading Marks** (*inside back cover*)

▸ **Correction Guide** (*page facing inside back cover*)

▸ **Specialized Indexes** for MLA (*p. 783*), APA (*p. 838*), CBE/CSE (*p. 865*), Chicago (*p. 875*), CGOS (*p. 889*) documentation styles.

▸ **Glossary of Usage** (*p. 905*)
Clarifies the use of commonly confused words such as *affect* and *effect*, *principal* and *principle*, and *well* and *good*.

▸ **Glossary of Grammatical Terms** (*p. 919*)
Defines terms, provides examples, and gives page references of where more information can be found.

▸ **List of Boxes and Notes** (*page following Index*)
A directory to:

  Key Points boxes

  Worlds of Writing boxes

  TechNotes

  ESL Notes

Visit the Web Site for *Universal Keys for Writers*

college.hmco.com/keys.html

Resources for Students Available at Web Site

▶ **Online handbook** *Digital Keys Online*, by Ann Raimes, includes exercises, search function, and diagnostic self-tests. (Use free password provided with new copies of *Universal Keys*.)

▶ **Online tutoring** SMARTHINKING offers live online tutoring and critiques of student papers. (Passwords can be packaged for free with new copies of *Universal Keys* upon request or purchased separately.)

▶ **ESL Center**

▶ **Downloadable Templates and Editing Exercises**

▶ **eLibrary of Exercises** 700 self-quizzes help you sharpen your grammar and writing skills.

▶ *Internet Research Guide* Six tutorials help you use the Internet for research.

▶ **Usage flashcards, helpful links,** *American Heritage Dictionary's* **100 Words to Know, and more**

Resources for Instructors Available at Web Site

▶ **Instructor's Support Package**

▶ **Links to online composition journals**

▶ **ESL Center for instructors**

▶ **PowerPoint slides, diagnostic tests, online handbook access, and more.**

Preface

When I walk into a writing class, as I have for more than thirty years, I am struck by the diversity in the room. Semester after semester, the students show a stunning range of educational preparation, interests, learning styles, writing abilities, languages, cultures, and levels of technological expertise. Beyond that diversity, though, I see what students share: a desire to succeed in college and an awareness that writing well will not only help them do that but also lead to success in their future careers. So I have planned this book to be a useful and accessible tool for students, one that they will use with ease in their busy college lives—and keep on using. My goals in writing *Universal Keys for Writers* have been to offer

- recognition of students' diversity and common goals
- helpful and practical coverage of the writing process, critical thinking, and technology
- the clearest possible grammatical explanations for native speakers and ESL students alike
- handy, complete, up-to-date research and documentation guidelines

DISTINCTIVE FEATURES

Dictionary-Style Thumb Tabs Color-coded and clearly labeled, these tabs make *Universal Keys for Writers* an extraordinarily accessible and user-friendly handbook. Students can turn directly to the part of the book they need.

Internal Tables of Contents At the site of each thumb tab, students find a detailed Table of Contents for that individual part. These "part divider" reference pages are easy to consult and scan.

Key Points Boxes Eighty-six concise summary and checklist boxes highlight important information for convenient reference and class discussion. These boxes encourage students to develop and review reading, writing, editing, and critical thinking skills.

Three-Part Color-Coded Structure *Universal Keys* has comprehensive coverage, organized simply. Each of its three main divisions holds notable advantages in form and content.

DISTINCTIVE CONTENT

Writing: Communicating and Presenting Ideas
Parts I–III

Parts I to III are *rhetorical,* forming a comprehensive guide to the writing process. Advantages include:

Emphasis on Thesis Central to successful writing in college and beyond is a clear understanding of the thesis and how to build and support a good one. *Universal Keys for Writers* weaves instruction on this important topic throughout the handbook, with examples, model papers, and exercises. Stressing options, the handbook also looks at sixteen ways that writers support and develop a main idea (**5d**).

Abundance of Student Writing Drafts and papers were generously submitted by college and university instructors and by students around the country, in response to a nationwide call. Thirty papers and extracts are supported in the text with annotations, critical thinking exercises, and discussion. Together these papers convey to students that they are part of a lively, vibrant community of writers, with fresh voices and a lot to say.

Writing Arguments and Writing across the Disciplines Part II prepares students for a range of writing tasks they may meet in their college career and beyond. It especially focuses on strategies for building reasoned, logical written arguments. This part looks at genres common within the arts and humanities, social sciences, and sciences, from a literary analysis paper to a lab report, and discusses the art of writing well under pressure in exam situations.

The Latest Coverage of Writing and Technology Part III brings together the latest information on

- using computer tools in brainstorming, drafting, and editing
- using grammar-check programs—with caution
- writing for online readers and communicating online in such forums as bulletin boards and listservs
- adding charts, tables, and other visuals into one's writing
- creating a Web site and designing documents

Some students are completely at ease with technology as it relates to writing; others have less comfort and expertise. *Universal Keys* strikes a helpful balance in addressing this diverse audience and considers both what a student may need to know now and what he or she may need to know later in another course or on the job.

Full Section on Writing for Work Part III also covers job-related writing in extraordinary depth and detail, with many helpful model documents. It pays particular attention to developing résumés (print and electronic versions), job application letters, and PowerPoint presentations.

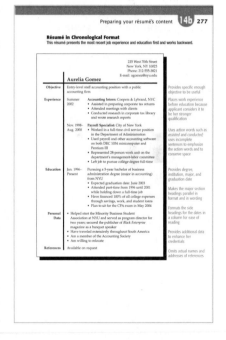

Attention to Critical Thinking and Reading Students are encouraged throughout *Universal Keys* to examine, evaluate, question, and make connections. The opening section of the handbook deals explicitly with Thinking, Reading, and Writing (**1a**) and the subject is then consistently reinforced—for example in discussions of revising (**4c**), evaluating arguments (**6a**), developing a voice (**38a**), critical reading of research sources (**49a**), and putting oneself into a paper (**51a**).

Sentences: Accuracy and Style   *Parts IV–VII*

Before, during, and after the writing process, students can easily refer to Parts IV–VII for help with sentence grammar, punctuation, style, ESL, and other language issues. Advantages include:

Neatly Clustered Grammar Coverage   Part IV gives students one convenient place to turn when they have grammar questions or need to review the Top Ten Sentence Problems, a diagnostic checklist (p. 340). Grammar coverage is not spread confusingly over a number of parts (such as Clear Sentences, Effective Sentences, or Correct Sentences), but uniquely gathered under one rubric: Common Sentence Problems.

Rich and Varied Exercise Program   *Universal Keys* contains 222 exercises, including many designed for collaborative or group work. These exercises distinguish themselves in several ways: (1) All are clearly numbered and titled, for ease of reference. (2) The topics of continuous discourse exercises are carefully drawn from a range of disciplines. Each sentence set looks at a contemporary issue, debate, development, or discovery in the humanities, social sciences, or sciences, and is so marked in the Instructor's Annotated Edition. And (3) many of the exercise passages are posted

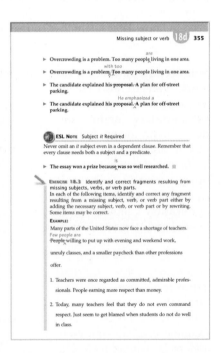

on the *Universal Keys* Web site so, if a student or instructor prefers, exercises can be downloaded for editing on a student's computer. Additional exercises are available at the Web site, in *Digital Keys Online,* and on the *Digital Keys 3.1* CD-ROM.

Comma: Yes; Comma: No   These two Key Points boxes (**26a**) and others like them summarize key information in a direct fashion.

Other unique coverage in Part V, Punctuation, Mechanics, and Spelling, includes a notable list of commonly confused words (**33h**), a section on accents, umlauts, tildes, and cedillas (**33i**), and guidelines for online punctuation (**34a–e**).

The Five C's of Style   Part VI advises students in a straightforward way to Cut, Check for Action, Connect, Commit, and Choose Your Words. Widespread class testing has proven that this easy-to-remember approach works well with students and helps them to improve their writing.

Helpful Section on Avoiding Biased Language   In a lively, supportive, coaching tone, section **39f** (pp. 627–630) discusses sensible ways to avoid divisive and exclusionary language. It looks at language issues concerning gender, race, place, age, politics, religion, health and abilities, sexual orientation, and the word *normal.*

Thorough Coverage for ESL/Multilingual Writers   *Universal Keys* features clear coverage of ESL grammar points, sample ESL student writing, and a unique opening segment that places this instruction within a supportive framework. A Language Guide to Transfer Errors chart examines the logical patterning of certain types of errors in written English if a student's original language is other than English. In addition, ESL Notes are integrated throughout the handbook, and Worlds of Writing boxes consider the interrelationship of language and culture. Topics include language and dialect variations and different style preferences across cultures.

Research: Finding, Using, and Documenting Sources *Parts VIII–X*

The third main section of *Universal Keys* guides students through the research process with expert tips, up-to-date technology coverage, and a wealth of interesting examples. Advantages include:

A Process Approach to Research, from Start to Finish For planning, formulating a thesis, finding and evaluating sources, and documenting sources, students will find everything they need in Part VIII. It covers how to do both library and Web research; how to summarize, paraphrase, and clearly indicate the boundaries of a citation; how to drive a paper's organization with ideas, not sources; and how to avoid plagiarizing.

Emphasis on Evaluating Sources A frequent obstacle for students writing a research paper is determining which sources have aca-

demic merit and which do not. With visuals, checklists, and engaging examples, *Universal Keys* helps students distinguish the useful from the useless. It includes a distinctive Key Points box, Developing Your Junk Antennae, that assists students in recognizing reliable, substantive sites and avoiding the rest.

How to Avoid Plagiarizing *Universal Keys* presents a full, timely treatment of this crucial topic (**50a–i**). It defines and discusses plagiarism, gives direct guidelines on what documentation is and what to cite; it stresses the importance of taking accurate notes and keeping track of sources during a research project; and it provides distinctive print and online templates for students to use in collecting and organizing source information and preparing a list of works cited.

Research Resources in 27 Subject Areas An invaluable list of research starting points, this feature collects frequently used reference works in print, electronic indexes, and Web sites (**51f**). Students can also go to the *Universal Keys* Web site for live and regularly updated links.

The Latest Documentation Guidelines Covering the latest guidelines of MLA, APA, CBE/CSE, *Chicago Manual of Style*, and *Columbia Guide to Online Style* (CGOS), *Universal Keys* helps students to document all types of print, electronic, and other sources and to understand that citation styles vary across disciplines. For reference, six sample student papers (complete or extracted) show the documentation styles in action. Special indexes at the beginning of the MLA, APA, and other sections make it easy for students to locate sample entries, such as a government publication, play, sound recording, or legal case.

772 **51f** Research paper resources in 27 subject areas

pointing you in the right direction for further research. Browse freely, and remember to ask a librarian for advice if you have trouble finding a source or need a specific piece of information.

TECHNOTE Links from the Web Site for *Universal Keys for Writers*

The Web site for this book at <http://www.college.hmco.com/keys.html> duplicates and expands this list, keeping it up to date and providing direct links to all the nonsubscription online reference sites. From the *Universal Keys for Writers* home page click on Web Links, then on Links across the Curriculum. From there, you can click on an online source in, say, business or engineering, and you will be taken right there. Sources with no URL given may also be available in online databases accessible in a library. Check with your librarian as to the availability of these sources. ■

ART AND ARCHITECTURE

American Museum of Photography: <http://www.photographymuseum.com>

Art Abstracts (online and CD-ROM)

Art History Resources on the Web: <http://witcombe.bcpw.sbc.edu/ARTHLinks.html>

Art Index (print, online, and CD-ROM)

Arts and Humanities Citation Index

Avery Index to Architectural Periodicals (online and CD-ROM)

Bibliography of the History of Art

Contemporary Artists

Dictionary of Art (known as *Grove's*) (print and online)

Encyclopedia of World Art

Getty Institute: <http://www.getty.edu>

Lives of the Painters

Local and Global Internet Resources for Art Historians and Art History Students: <http://www.wisc.edu/arth/otherresources.html>

Metropolitan Museum of Art Time Line: <http://www.metmuseum.org/toah/splash.htm>

Oxford Companion to Art

World Wide Arts Resources: <http://wwar.com>

Interactive Research Papers on *Digital Keys 3.1* CD-ROM Developed by Louis Molina of Miami-Dade Community College, this unique portion of the *Digital Keys 3.1* CD-ROM allows students to call up two model student research papers, one using MLA style and the other using APA style. Students click on instructional icons placed strategically throughout the papers. These icons open concise annotations on how the papers were written and documented and offer coaching for students writing their own papers.

Internet Research Guide This online guide by Jason Snart of College of DuPage presents six extended learning modules with practice exercises (tutorials) for using the Internet as a research tool. Topics include evaluating Web information, building an argument with Web research, and plagiarism and documentation.

RESOURCES FOR INSTRUCTORS

Instructor's Annotated Edition (IAE) *Universal Keys for Writers* Instructor's Annotated Edition begins with a selection of engaging and thought-provoking first-person articles by composition instructors. The complete student edition of *Universal Keys* follows, with extended margins containing commentary designed to make life easier for the composition instructor. Marginal annotations include:

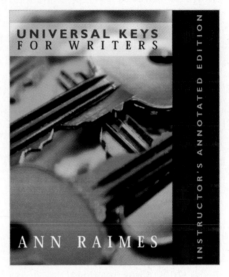

- *Answers* or suggested answers to the handbook's exercises
- *Teaching Ideas,* concise tips on approaches and activities
- *Technology in the Classroom notes,* with fresh suggestions, relevant links, and other helpful tips and resources
- *Background Notes* on quirky words or concepts mentioned in the handbook and on the text's illustrations
- *Overviews* to each part, summarizing important points
- *Slide References* indicating what material in the student text is available in PowerPoint form online at the instructor's Web site or on the ClassPrep CD-ROM
- *Quotations* about writing that can be brought into the classroom or just read for one's own enjoyment

Answer Key   This booklet contains answers or suggested answers to the exercises in *Universal Keys.* Pages can be photocopied for distribution, allowing students to correct their own or their peers' exercises.

Teaching Writing with Computers   An up-to-date resource on integrating technology into writing instruction, this book by Pamela Takayoshi and Brian Huot of University of Louisville contains seventeen rich and practical essays. The selections cover: (1) Writing Technologies for Composition Pedagogies; (2) Learning to Teach with Technology; (3) Teaching Beyond Physical Boundaries; (4)

Teaching and Learning New Media; and (5) Assigning and Assessing Student Writing.

Feeling Our Way—A Writing Teacher's Sourcebook Written by Wendy Bishop and Deborah Coxwell Teague of Florida State University in Tallahassee, this book is a unique and powerful guide for new or relatively new composition teachers. It supportively addresses many of the unvoiced questions, challenges, and seldom-discussed, yet crucial, issues that arise for those who are new to the classroom.

Writing Teacher's Companion
In this lively and practical book, Rai Peterson of Ball State University gives no-nonsense and reader-friendly advice on planning, teaching, and evaluating in the composition classroom.

Universal Keys for Writers **Web Site at <http://college .hmco.com/keys.html>** The instructor's portion of this site features the online Instructor's Support Package, with a walkthrough on using the handbook (for instructors to use with students); diagnostic tests; PowerPoint slides of many of the text's Key Points boxes, outlines, and templates; links to online composition journals and ESL sites; up-to-date coverage on using the Internet in the composition classroom, with Web tutorials for students; exercise answers; and a section on teaching composition to ESL students, with tip sheets for ten languages.

ClassPrep CD-ROM Like the instructor's portion of the *Universal Keys* Web site, this CD-ROM contains the Instructor's Support Package; diagnostic tests; PowerPoint slides, outlines, and templates; a section on using the Internet in the composition classroom, with Web tutorials; exercise answers; and material on teaching composition to ESL students.

Diagnostics and Exercises For a more intensive evaluation of your students' most frequent errors, this electronic product contains eight diagnostic tests covering a range of key writing skills.

Web/CT e-Pack A flexible, Internet-based education platform, Web/CT e-Pack contains text-specific resources to enrich students' online learning experience.

Blackboard Course Cartridge This course cartridge provides flexible, efficient, and creative ways for instructors to present materials and manage distance-learning courses. Instructors can use an electronic grade book, receive papers from students enrolled in the course via the Internet, and track student use of the communication and collaborative functions.

RESOURCES FOR STUDENTS

Digital Keys 3.1 **CD-ROM** *Digital Keys 3.1* CD-ROM contains easy-to-consult information on all handbook topics, including how to use and reference technology; grammar and punctuation exercises; and a glossary and index. Unique Interactive Research Papers showcase student papers documented in MLA and APA styles. This feature was created by Louis Molina of Miami Dade Community College.

Universal Keys for Writers **Web Site at <http://college .hmco.com/keys.html>** The student *Universal Keys* Web site contains a tutorial on how to get the most out of the handbook; a section on documentation styles at a glance, with sample research papers; a flashcard feature for reviewing commonly confused or misused words from the Glossary of Usage; Web links that review the themes of each part of *Universal Keys*; an ESL Center for English language learners with ESL self-quizzes and links to helpful ESL Web links; downloadable exercises and forms from the text, to aid in editing, planning a paper, and keeping track of source information; and the *American Heritage College Dictionary's* 100 Words to Know. The site also provides access to the eLibrary of exercises and the *Internet Research Guide* (see below).

Digital Keys Online *Digital Keys Online* offers students instant access to writing, research, and grammar support in an easy-to-use format. Every new copy of *Universal Keys* comes with a free passkey with a unique password to the online electronic handbook. Passwords, which offer twelve months of access to the online handbook, can also be purchased separately.

SMARTHINKING Available at the *Universal Keys* Web site, this online writing tutoring service connects students to qualified writing tutors, generally advanced-degree composition instructors. Tutors interact with students in real-time during prime-time afternoon and evening homework hours, five days a week, and answer questions and offer feedback on submitted papers twenty-four hours a day, seven days a week. Passwords to this service can be packaged with new copies of *Universal Keys* upon request or purchased separately.

eLibrary of Exercises This online interactive study program, available on the *Universal Keys* Web site, is designed to complement the handbook and provide more practice, as needed. It contains over seven hundred self-quizzes that give students the opportunity to sharpen their grammar writing skills in thirty areas. Students can work at their own pace wherever it is convenient for them—at home, in the computer lab, or in the classroom. Scores are available to students as they finish a test. The eLibrary is available on the *Universal Keys* Web site.

Internet Research Guide   Available on the *Universal Keys* Web site, the online *Internet Research Guide,* by Jason Snart of College of DuPage, presents six extended learning modules for using the Internet as a research tool: (1) The purpose of research; (2) E-mail, listservs, newsgroups, chat rooms; (3) Surfing and browsing; (4) Evaluating Web information; (5) Building an argument with Web research; and (6) Plagiarism and documentation.

CLAST Preparation Manual   This manual by Susan Donath Aguila, of Palm Beach Community College, contains skills-building exercises, tutorials, review, and focused instruction designed for students preparing for the English Language Skills section of the College Level Academic Skills Test in Florida.

TASP Preparation Manual   This manual by Deborah A. Johnson-Evans, of University of Texas at Arlington, helps students prepare for the Texas Academic Skill Proficiency test. It provides instruction on reading the TASP test questions, tips for taking the test, a skills review section, and practice tests.

OFFERED AT SPECIAL PRICES

American Heritage College Dictionary, **Fourth Edition**   This best-selling hardback desk reference, just out in a new edition, is an indispensable tool for students. It has more features than any other college dictionary, an accessible defining style, helpful usage guidance, and an attractive page design.

American Heritage English as a Second Language Dictionary   Specially adapted and designed to suit the needs of ESL students, this dictionary has abundant sample sentences and phrases, an easy-to-use pronunciation system, a Word Building feature, and Usage Notes.

ACKNOWLEDGMENTS

For all their help with this book, I am grateful to teachers and students, not only at my own college but across the country. When I travel to do workshops and attend conferences, faculty members have been unfailingly generous with their contributions of advice and materials. Heartfelt thanks go to my Hunter College colleagues, Anna Tomasino and Carolyn Lengel, who contributed ideas and imaginative exercises, all informed by their own classroom experiences. For his expert advice on technological matters and prompt replies to my many e-mails, I am deeply grateful to Manfred Kuechler, a colleague in the Sociology

Department at Hunter College, whose knowledge of the workings of the Internet is truly astounding. Thanks go, too, to Hunter College librarian Jean Jacques Strayer for keeping me up to date on databases and search engines; to James Allen, College of DuPage, who contributed his expertise to the section on CGOS; to Scot Ober of Ball State University, for his expertise in business communication; and to Louis Molina of Miami-Dade Community College, for his work on the Interactive Research Paper in *Digital Keys 3.1* CD-ROM.

I also offer thanks to all the students whose writing appears in this book. They were not all easy to contact (I had to go through an instructor and a registrar to find one who was working in Turkey) but once I found them they were, without exception, responsive and helpful. Instructors, too, went to great lengths to help me find student essays for inclusion: at Hunter, Jennifer Knox, Manfred Kuechler, Susan Ribner, Patricia Sokolski, Eisa Ulen, Carol Weir, and Robert White put me in touch with their students; from farther afield, James Allen, Barbara Apstein, Roberta Bernstein, Jeanne Curran, Frank Edler, and Karen Lim went out of their way to help, as did other faculty members who responded to a call for student papers.

The following reviewers and focus group participants gave the evolving manuscript the benefit of their experience, wisdom, and critical eyes. Their many excellent and tactful suggestions at each stage of development have been invaluable.

Preston L. Allen, Miami-Dade Community College
Susan Beebe, Southwest Texas State University
Marlo M. Belschner, St. Cloud State University
Mary Jane Berger, College of St. Benedict
Stuart Brown, New Mexico State University
Elizabeth Brunsvold, St. Cloud State University
Karen Carpenter, University of Maryland
David Chapman, Samford University, Alabama
Peggy Cole, Arapahoe Community College
Carolyn Dahl, St. Cloud State University
Jim Dubinsky, Virginia Polytechnic Institute
Joel English, Ball State University
Sharifa Saa Evans, Georgia Perimeter College
Evelyn M. Finklea, St. Petersburg College
Casey Gilson, Broward Community College
Susan Halter, Delgado Community College
Sandy Smith Hutchins, Belmont State University
Claudine Keenan, Pennsylvania State University
Carol Kountz, Grand Valley State University
David Lang, Golden Gate University

Scott Leonard, Youngstown State University
Loretta McBride, Southwest Tennessee Community College
Michael Morgan, Bemidji State University
W. Webster Newbold, Ball State University
Jane Opitz, College of St. Benedict
Carole Clark Papper, Ball State University
Della W. Paul, Valencia Community College
Timothy Ray, Arizona State University
Rich Rice, Ball State University

My colleagues at Houghton Mifflin have been a pleasure to work with. They are warm, supportive, responsive, and incredibly knowledgeable about textbook publishing. Special thanks go to Pat Coryell, Vice President, and Suzanne Phelps Weir, Executive Editor, for their leadership, energy, and enthusiasm for the project; to Martha Bustin, Senior Development Editor, for her keen editorial eye, contributions to the manuscript, and unfailing grace under pressure—she surely must be a textbook writer's perfect editor; to Rosemary Winfield, Senior Project Manager, for coping with challenging deadlines (and with me) during the production process; and to Cindy Graff Cohen, Marketing Manager, for keeping me attuned to market needs and adding to the fun of my trips to colleges across the U.S. (I remember wading in the Pacific in San Diego.) I also gratefully acknowledge the help and professionalism of others on the large *Universal Keys* team: Jill Haber, Henry Rachlin, Florence Cadran, Diana Coe, Sarah Helyar Smith, Becky Wong, Bruce Cantley, Janet Edmonds, Chere Bemelmans, Brian Campbell, Marlowe Shaeffer, Sarah Donelson, Ben Gould, Sara Johnson, Jodi O'Rourke, Denise Roche, Andrea Wagner, Jennifer Bixby, Ann Marie Radaskiewicz, Mark Gallaher, Todd Finley, Mary Dalton-Hoffman, Janet Young, Mary Rose Quinn, Vici Casana, Lisa Wehrle, Ellen Whalen, Deborah Prato, Deborah Karacozian, Patricia Herbst, Sherri Dietrich, John Sisson, Meg Botteon, Tom Gage, Rebecca Fagan, Bruce Carson, Karen Wise, and Sam Davison, Mike Kern, Jim Craig, Suzie Strauss, Donna Rapose, Lisa Ferry, and the other miracle workers at New England Typographic Service.

Warmest thanks to my extended circle of friends in Brooklyn and in Chatham, NY, for making sure I took time to play tennis, go to movies, eat out, and have fun. Finally, above all, thanks go to my daughters, Emily and Lucy, for their support and encouragement, and especially to my husband, James Raimes, who helped with research, typed, edited, offered advice, and cooked great meals. If I hadn't known before that writing was a collaborative effort, I would surely know it now.

Ann Raimes
Hunter College, City University of New York

Main Table of Contents

PART II Writing in All Your Courses   113

Sentences:

Accuracy and Style   303

PART V Punctuation, Mechanics, and Spelling 497

25 Periods, Question Marks, and Exclamation Points 499

26 Commas 504

27 Semicolons and Colons 526

28 Apostrophes 534

Researching:

Finding, Using, and Documenting Sources 693

Writing

Communicating and Presenting Ideas

W*riting* has two meanings, both important. It is an action and a product, a verb and a noun. Our success in our academic, professional, community, and personal lives can depend on (1) how efficiently we can perform the action of writing, either alone or in collaboration with others, and (2) how clear and effective we make the writing that we produce. Certainly the better we understand these two dimensions of the word *writing* and their interaction, the more confidently we can tackle the many writing opportunities that life presents.

As an action, writing means the setting down and rearranging of words and sentences on a page or a screen: "Stephen King is *writing* a new novel." The action of writing can be

- solitary or collaborative
- routine or creative
- spontaneous or deliberate
- inward or outward looking

It can range from jotting down a list to composing an essay on an issue you care deeply about. It can be the work of a minute or involve a great deal of revision. Writing in this sense is a dynamic process undertaken by a writer or writers actively generating words and shaping them into desired meanings for desired purposes.

On the other hand, writing is also a product: "Stephen King posted his *writing* on the Web." As a tangible product, writing invites and often needs a reader and a reader's responses. It is the presentation of a writer's work on a page or screen. It is a piece of communication.

Both these meanings of the word *writing* are equally important to a successful student's life in college and beyond, and both are central to the way we learn. Surprising as it may seem, we learn *as we write,* and we learn *from what we write.* The act of writing is not just attaching words to fully formed ideas, not just transcribing something that pops into our heads. It is a process of discovery in which we learn what we know, what we don't know, and what we need to know. The act of writing creates not just a written product, but a learning experience for the writer and, the writer hopes, for the reader, too.

Part I
Writing an Essay

4

Writing an essay for college—and in many situations beyond college—involves the following:

planning
- critical thinking and reading
- determining your purpose and audience
- generating ideas
- establishing a topic and thesis
- gathering information and support

drafting
- organizing and developing ideas
- writing drafts (preliminary versions of your finished product)

revising
- revising and checking for clarity, coherence, and unity
- editing and proofreading

These planning, drafting, and revising activities are often characterized as steps in a linear process in order to make them easier to talk about. In reality, however, virtually no one embarking on a writing project marches neatly through a series of distinct steps. In fact, the most important features to bear in mind are these:

The writing process is not linear.

Writing is a messy adventure; nothing is done according to a formula.

Few writers achieve perfection on the first draft.

The very act of writing helps you generate ideas.

This process of discovery can be exciting.

For some, writing an essay brings along with it a set of fears: of laying out our ideas, of exposing those ideas to criticism, of being judged and found wanting. Even the extraordinary Irish novelist James Joyce sometimes looked for excuses not to write: "No pen, no ink, no table, no room, no time, no quiet, no inclination."

In its favor, however, writing is less intimidating than public speaking and has distinct advantages. When expressing ourselves in writing, we will not lose our audience because we happen to have bronchitis or a bad case of nerves. Instead we write, for the most part, for an imagined audience, for readers who do not see us or know us. We can thus present to our readers an image of a person we would like to be, a person we admire and hope others will admire, too. Writing brings this freedom to invent oneself anew. As journalist Adam Gopnik says fondly of writing, "It's you there, but not quite you."

In addition to these encouraging factors, we can take comfort that our finished product will not be wrecked by poor delivery or last-minute slip-ups. Though a computer could crash or a friend's dog could chew up a vital floppy disk, such disruptive events are thankfully rare. In general, if we start early enough and allow time for thoughtful planning, drafting, and revising, the process of writing will be as satisfying as the end result.

1 Thinking, Reading, and Writing

"I wonder where she gets that from? I don't understand that point. She hasn't convinced me at all." Just as we think critically about what we read, readers think critically when they read what we write, sometimes making comments like these. Thinking is inextricably tied to reading and writing, so much so that thinking critically is essential to being a good reader and a good writer.

Thinking critically is what we all do when we ask questions about what we see, hear, or read, when we don't accept everything at face value just because someone else has thought it and expressed it and someone has seen fit to publish it. Thinking critically does not mean thinking

Auguste Rodin,
The Thinker.

negatively in order to criticize someone—unless, of course, you intend to criticize. Instead, it means questioning, discussing, and looking at an issue from a number of sides.

If you think of discussions you have with friends about movies, music, TV programs, video games, Web sites, and books, you will realize that you already have the basic tools for thinking critically as you watch, listen, read, and write. You can then develop and refine those basic tools as you do reading and writing for college courses.

For more on critical thinking, reading, and writing, see **6a, 6g, 38a,** and **49.**

1a Thinking critically, reading critically

How are you going to read what someone else has written? Imagine that you have sat down with a newspaper, comic book, poem, novel, letter from a relative, and a detailed instruction booklet on assembling a complex new grill, computer, or drum set. You will read each piece in a different way, depending on its purpose, your plans, and the response required. For instance, you may decide to skim the newspaper, admire the visual style used in the comic book's illustrations, memorize the poem, read the novel as an entertaining escape, answer immediately the letter from the relative, and study the instruction manual with an intent expression.

Now imagine that you are reading a passage that you are then going to analyze and write about, which is often the case in college. You may be looking for pieces of information, a general overview, the claim the author is making, the author's use of language, or specific details. Try the following tactics.

KEY POINTS

Tactics for Effective Reading

1. With an informational work (not a work of literature), skim when you want to know "Is this worth a detailed reading?" Look at the table of contents, any blurb or summary, preface, chapter introductions and conclusions, and index, in order to get a sense of whether the work meets your needs and how long it will take you to read and digest it.

2. Establish what background knowledge you need: what knowledge and information does the writer expect you to have? You may need to do some preliminary reading.

3. Give yourself large blocks of time for a long work, allowing yourself to become immersed. Reading quickly in short sessions will lead to a sketchy or superficial understanding of

a work. As Woody Allen puts it, "I took a course in speed reading and I've just finished *War and Peace*. It pertains to Russia."

4. Predict as you read. Literacy theorist Kenneth Goodman has called reading a "psycholinguistic guessing game." See how accurately you can predict what a writer will say next and how he or she will say it.

5. When doing focused research, read with the goal of finding a specific piece of information.

6. As you read, make inferences about what the writer intends and what assumptions the writer makes. Making an inference means "deriving conclusions that are not explicit in what is said" (*American Heritage Dictionary*).

7. Write as you read—comments, notes, questions, highlights. See the Key Points box on "Using Writing to Respond to a Reading" on page 9.

8. Read more than once, especially for a challenging text, so that you are sure you have grasped all the text's complexities and so you can review its main points.

9. Read aloud a poem, drama, short creative work, or any section of a work that you find difficult to follow; this will help you hear the writer's voice more vividly.

10. Use a dictionary to find the meanings of words you do not know.

Responding to reading with critical thinking Reading may be solitary, but it is still interactive. As a reader, you naturally interact with the writer and the ideas the writer presents. You question, consider, agree, disagree, and mentally compare what you are reading with other points or texts you know. You bring your own knowledge and experience to those marks the writer puts on a page or screen, and that knowledge and experience may cause you to read and interpret the same passage differently from the way other readers do. Here, for example, are some thoughts that may cross your mind as you read and write.

Critical thinking while reading the work of others

Hmmm. This view sounds extreme. I'll look to see if the writer provides any evidence to convince me.

Yeah. I definitely agree with this point.

What a great passage—beautifully written and makes a good point. I'll highlight it so I can later find and quote it in my paper.

I wonder if this is supposed to be ironic.

What else has this author written? I must check that.

I can't follow the logic here.

This guy's point makes an interesting contrast with what we read last week.

Similarly, when you are reading your own work, keep the same questioning attitude to evaluate what is working and what still needs revision.

Critical thinking while reading your own work

Hey, I like this part.

I think I should add some more details here.

Will readers know my reasons for saying this?

This section might alienate readers—I'd better revise.

What will readers think of my values and opinions as they read this? Is that what I want them to think?

Hmmm. Martin almost never agrees with anything I say. I wonder what he would say about this.

Do I come across as too flippant here, I wonder?

I haven't phrased this sentence very clearly. I need to revise it.

I'm not sure about the spelling of this word, but I'll mark it with an asterisk (*) and look it up later.

Responding to reading by writing When you read, annotate. Read with a pencil in hand or a keyboard along with you so you can capture and record your ideas, questions, and associations. These annotations can be helpful starting points if you need to write a response to a particular reading.

While reading the following passage about the Ultimatum Game, for example, a student annotated the passage as she read it, increasing her interaction with the article.

I like the direct approach!

Interesting that authors use feminine pronoun here

Imagine that somebody offers you $100. All you have to do is agree with some other anonymous person on how to share the sum. The rules are strict. The two of you are in separate rooms and cannot exchange information. A coin toss decides which of you will propose how to share the money. Suppose that you are the proposer. You can make a single offer of how to split the sum, and the other person—the responder—can say yes or no. The responder also knows the rules and the total amount of money at stake. If her answer is yes, the deal goes ahead. If her answer is no, neither of you gets anything. In both cases, the game is over and will not be repeated. What will you do?

Critical point

Have the authors researched this assumption?

Instinctively, <u>many people feel they should offer 50 percent</u>, because such a division is "fair" and therefore likely to be accepted. More daring people, however, think they might get away with offering somewhat less than half the sum.

Or more greedy:

But the organizers will know what I offer, so it's not entirely between two anonymous people.

Before making a decision, you should ask yourself what you would do if you were the responder. The only thing you can do as the responder is say yes or no to a given amount of money. If the offer were 10 percent, would you take $10 and let someone walk away with $90, or would you rather have nothing at all? What if the offer were only 1 percent? Isn't $1 better than no dollars? And remember, haggling is strictly forbidden. Just one offer by the proposer; the responder can take it or leave it.

So what will you offer?

—Karl Sigmund, Ernst Fehr, and Martin A. Nowak,
"The Economics of Fair Play"

It is a good idea to get into the habit of writing your responses to what you read. In this way, your critical reading becomes more systematic and helpful to you. Try the following techniques.

KEY POINTS
Using Writing to Respond to a Reading

1. Read and annotate. If you own the book or a copy of an article, read with a pencil and highlighter in hand. Highlight sparingly—only the important passages. Write comments and questions in the margins and on self-stick notes.

2. Read, pause, and make notes. Read a paragraph or a page at a time, pause, and write a brief summary and your own comments.

3. Write a summary or paraphrase of a significant work or passage on index cards or in computer files (**50g**).

4. Write questions about the writer's claims and assumptions (**6g**).

5. Write challenges to the writer's views: "But what about . . .?"

6. Record in a journal or research notebook your reactions to what you have read.

7. Use a double-entry notebook to summarize the writer's ideas and how they relate to your own ideas and experiences (**3a**).

ESL NOTE Responding to Reading in Other Languages

Attitudes to written texts are influenced by culture, such as the culture of place, language, religion, race, class, and education. Be aware that the suggestions offered in this section refer to practices common in colleges and universities in North America, which may differ from practices common in countries using other languages as the language of instruction. You may have to be flexible in responding to texts if you have been thoroughly schooled in reading and responding to texts in another culture. To get a sense of linguistic and cultural differences, think of what a native speaker of English would need to know in order to write well in your language. ■

TECHNOTE Commenting on Scanned or Downloaded Texts

Recent versions of word processing programs such as Microsoft Word and Corel WordPerfect allow you to download online material or scan print material into the program and then write comments and annotations at specific points in the text (see **10c** for an example). ■

EXERCISE 1.1 Examine your own ways of reading.
Write down five of your recent reading experiences. It could be anything you read—a newspaper, a novel, a Web page, the comics, a recipe, directions, a how-to manual on operating the DVD player, a magazine, a textbook, an assignment, a business letter, a credit card statement, a children's story. Write down how and where you read each one and why you chose that method. Bring your list to class and share the results with your classmates.

EXERCISE 1.2 Go through the critical reading process.
Read the following passage from Gloria Anzaldúa's "How to Tame a Wild Tongue" in *Borderlands: La Frontera: The New Mestiza* and the numbered questions that follow it. Use the questions to guide your critical reading of the passage. Write your responses to each question.

Chicano Spanish sprang out of the Chicano's need to identify ourselves as a distinct people. We needed a language with which we could communicate with ourselves, a secret language. For some of us, language is a homeland closer than the Southwest—for many Chicanos today live in the Midwest and the East. And because we are a complex, heterogeneous people, we speak many languages. Some of the languages we speak are:

1. Standard English
2. Working class and slang English

3. Standard Spanish

4. Standard Mexican Spanish

5. North Mexican Spanish dialect

6. Chicano Spanish (Texas, New Mexico, Arizona and California have regional variations)

7. Tex-Mex

8. *Pachuco* (called *caló*)

My "home" tongues are the languages I speak with my sister and brothers, with my friends. They are the last five listed, with 6 and 7 being closest to my heart. From school, the media and job situations, I've picked up standard and working class English. From Mamagrande Locha and from reading Spanish and Mexican literature, I've picked up Standard Spanish and Standard Mexican Spanish. From *los recién llegados,* Mexican immigrants, and *braceros,* I learned the North Mexican dialect. With Mexicans I'll try to speak either Standard Mexican Spanish or the North Mexican dialect. From my parents and Chicanos living in the Valley, I picked up Chicano Texas Spanish, and I speak it with my mom, younger brother (who married a Mexican and who rarely mixes Spanish with English), aunts and older relatives.

With Chicanas from Nuevo México or Arizona I will speak Chicano Spanish a little, but often they don't understand what I'm saying. With most California Chicanas I speak entirely in English (unless I forget). When I first moved to San Francisco, I'd rattle off something in Spanish, unintentionally embarrassing them. Often it is only with another Chicana *tejana* that I can talk freely.

—Gloria Anzaldúa, "How to Tame a Wild Tongue"

Questions

1. What is a "secret language"?

2. Why does Anzaldúa use the first person plural pronoun *we*?

3. Throughout this piece, Spanish words and phrases are interspersed. Why does Anzaldúa use both Spanish and English words?

4. How many languages does Anzaldúa speak?

5. Although this excerpt is specific to "Chicano Spanish," in what ways is it universal?

6. What are the different languages you speak?

7. At the end Anzaldúa states, "Often it is only with another Chicana *tejana* that I can talk freely." Explain.

8. To whom can you "talk freely"? Why?

Exercise 1.3 Brainstorm responses to a reading.

The following passage is a continuation of the selection from the article "The Economics of Fair Play" on pages 8–9. Read it along with the previous excerpt, and with a group of classmates brainstorm your responses. Write down your responses and compare them with those made by other groups.

You may not be surprised to learn that two thirds of offers are between 40 and 50 percent. Only four in 100 people offer less than 20 percent. Proposing such a small amount is risky because it might be rejected. More than half of all responders reject offers that are less than 20 percent. But here is the puzzle: Why should anyone reject an offer as "too small"? The responder has just two choices: take what is offered or receive nothing. The only rational option for a selfish individual is to accept any offer. Even $1 is better than nothing. A selfish proposer who is sure that the responder is also selfish will therefore make the smallest possible offer and keep the rest. This game-theory analysis, which assumes that people are selfish and rational, tells you that the proposer should offer the smallest possible share and the responder should accept it. But this is not how most people play the game. [. . .]

Werner Güth of Humboldt University in Berlin devised the Ultimatum Game some 20 years ago. Experimenters subsequently studied it intensively in many places using diverse sums. The results proved remarkably robust. Behavior in the game did not appreciably depend on the players' sex, age, schooling, or numeracy. Moreover, the amount of money involved had surprisingly little effect on results. In Indonesia, for instance, the sum to be shared was as much as three times the subjects' average monthly income—and still people indignantly refused offers that they deemed too small. Yet the range of players remained limited in some respects, because the studies primarily involved people in more developed countries, such as Western nations, China and Japan, and very often university students, at that.

Recently an ambitious cross-cultural study in 15 small-scale societies on four continents showed that there were, after all, sizable differences in the way some people play the Ultimatum Game. Within the Machiguenga tribe in the Amazon, the mean offer was considerably lower than in typical Western-type civilizations—26 instead of 45 percent. Conversely, many members of the Au tribe in Papua New Guinea offered more than half the pie. Cultural traditions in gift giving, and the strong obligations that result from accepting a gift, play a major role among some tribes, such as the Au. Indeed, the Au tended to reject excessively generous offers as well as miserly ones. Yet despite these cultural variations, the outcome was always far from what rational analysis would dictate for selfish players. In striking contrast to what selfish income maximizers ought to do, most people all over the world place a high value on fair outcomes.

—Karl Sigmund, Ernst Fehr, and Martin A. Nowak,
"The Economics of Fair Play"

EXERCISE 1.4 Respond to reading by annotating.
Annotate the following excerpt from Stephen L. Carter's "The Insufficiency of Honesty." Write your annotations on the page, on self-stick notes, or electronically. If you prefer to make annotations electronically, locate the excerpt on the *Universal Keys* Web site. Then copy and paste it into your word processing program and use the Comment feature or the Tools/Track Changes/Highlight Changes feature to make your annotations (see **4e** and **10b**). Compare your annotations to those written by your classmates. Then, as a group, conduct a brainstorming session on the topic of integrity.

A couple of years ago I began a university commencement address by telling the audience that I was going to talk about integrity. The crowd broke into applause. Applause! Just because they had heard the word "integrity"; that's how starved for it they were. . . .

When I refer to integrity, I have something very specific in mind. Integrity, as I will use the term, requires three steps: (1) *discerning* what is right and what is wrong; (2) *acting* on what you have discerned, even at personal cost; and (3) *saying openly* that you are acting on your understanding of right and wrong. The first criterion captures the idea that integrity requires a degree of moral reflectiveness. The second brings in the ideal of a person of integrity as steadfast, a quality that includes keeping one's commitments. The third reminds us that a person of integrity is unashamed of doing the right thing.

1b Writing critically

When you read critically, imagine other readers doing the same thing when they read what you write. In order to pass readers' tests, you need to examine your drafts of your writing with great care and subject them to rigorous questioning. While doing your initial drafting, do not worry too much about readers' reactions, but after you have put something down on paper, examine it from a critical reader's perspective. Try putting your draft away for a while so that you can look at it with fresh eyes and see it as a new reader might see it—warts and all.

While it is important not to stop and try to perfect every word as you write, you may find that your difficulty in choosing the right words comes from not really knowing what you are trying to say. Experiment with speaking your ideas aloud before you write them, as if explaining them to a friend.

As you write, if you feel uncertain about the information you include, the stance you take, the effectiveness of your style, or just the choice of a word, do not stop to try to get it perfect. Keep going with your train of thought, but mark the questionable passage with a symbol (such as * or #). That will remind you to return to it later and ponder it anew. You can also ask a classmate or friend to read a draft and put a question mark by anything that seems unclear or wrong.

When you read your own draft, do some role-playing. Imagine you are your professor. What is he or she likely to find fault with? What comments would he or she make?

EXERCISE 1.5 Write, read, and revise.

Write a clear set of instructions on something you know how to do well. Assume that your audience has little or no knowledge of your topic. The instructions could be on anything: how to use a computer program, how to write a résumé, how to take a nap, how to relax, how to write an essay, how to park a car, how to cut your own hair, how to procrastinate, how to turn down a date, or how to look busy at work. Don't be afraid to use humor.

Keep your audience in mind. Don't omit any steps. After writing the list of instructions, do not look at the list for several days. When you reread the list, make any necessary additions or deletions. Then bring your instructions to class and exchange papers with a classmate. After reading the papers, discuss which parts work well. Was your classmate able to follow all the steps? Did you include technical language that the other student is unfamiliar with? What did you omit? What do you need to add?

1c Weighing options: Standard English and alternatives

In an academic or business environment, the norm for written and spoken English is called Standard English. Standard English is defined by the *American Heritage Dictionary* (*AHD*) as the "variety of English that is generally acknowledged as the model for the speech and writing of educated speakers." A Usage Note in the *AHD*, however, continues, "A form that is considered standard in one region may be nonstandard in another," and points out that *standard* and *nonstandard* are relative terms, depending largely on context. The Note concludes, "Thus while the term can serve a useful descriptive purpose providing the context makes its meaning clear, it shouldn't be construed as conferring any absolute positive evaluation."

In short, the concept of Standard English is complex. It is inextricably entwined with the region, race, class, education, and gender of both the speaker (or writer) and the listener (or reader). Standard

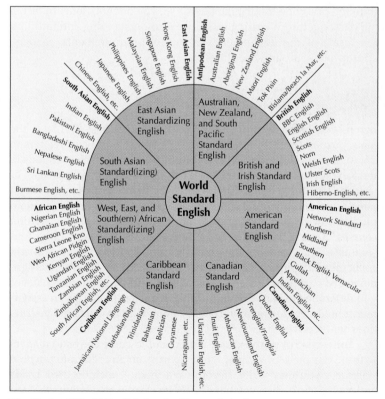

The Circle of World English (used with permission)

English, for better or for worse, is being supplemented and challenged by other ways of writing, such as those coming from the world of technology, the rap movement, and popular culture.

Some instructors may encourage you to explore alternative discourses and nonstandard language in narrative and personal writing; some may insist on Standard English and traditional rhetoric from the outset; and others may give you options depending upon the nature of the assigned task. As you read and write, keep examining and considering the context in which you are writing, what your purpose is, and what readers will expect. For the most part, in academia and business, you will be expected to know and use Standard English, the focus of this book.

2 Defining the Task

"I'm not sure what I'm supposed to be doing." "I wish I had a clearer sense of what my instructor wants." Have you often found yourself thinking or saying things like this? If so, you are not alone. In fact, a big part of getting a writing task done is understanding and fulfilling the terms of the assignment: its purpose, requirements, readers, appropriate tone, and deadlines.

2a Determining the purpose

Before you begin writing, consider these questions: "What is the main purpose of this piece of writing?" "What do I want readers to do, think, or feel as a result of reading my writing?" The questions in the Key Points box on page 17 will help guide you to an answer.

The first three items listed in the Key Points box (on expository, persuasive, and scientific or technical writing) are generally the main purposes of college writing assignments, except in creative writing courses. Among these categories, however, the overlap can be considerable. Some assignments may require you to explore and test concepts and opinions against what you already know. Other assignments may ask you to blend explanation with persuasion. Whatever you determine to be the main purpose or purposes of a given assignment should guide you as you write, along with any detailed instructions you receive.

Your sense of purpose as a writer should come across to readers within your piece of writing, quite apart from any separate purpose statement you may write. If you leave them scratching their heads and saying "So?" then you have not been clear in conveying what the readers are to think, feel, or do.

KEY POINTS

Asking about Purpose

1. Is your main purpose to explain an idea, analyze, or provide information? Writing with this purpose is called *expository writing.*

2. Is your main purpose to persuade readers to see things your way or to move readers to action? This aim leads to *persuasive writing* or *argumentation.*

3. Is your main purpose to describe an experiment or a detailed process or to report on laboratory results? Writing with this purpose is frequently referred to as *scientific* or *technical writing.*

4. Is your main purpose to record and express your own experience, observations, ideas, and feelings? In the humanities, such accounts are known as *expressive, autobiographical,* or *personal writing.*

5. Is your main purpose to create an original work of art, such as a poem, story, play, or novel? Writing with this purpose is called *creative writing.*

2b Understanding the requirements

The expectations of readers depend not only on the purpose of the piece of writing but also on the context and the specific task. Use these questions to help you establish what you need to do in any writing task in a college, community, or business setting.

- What is the assigned task?
- What directions have been supplied, if any?
- What do you already know about the type of writing required?
- Have you been given detailed instructions about content and format, or are you free to find your own topic and your own way of approaching it?
- What sources of information are appropriate for the task (for example, interviews with experts, statistics, critical essays)?
- Will you present your writing on paper or online? See **10–12.**
- Who will read what you write? See **2c.**
- How will the writing be evaluated?
- How long do you have to complete the task? See **2e.**

For more help with answering the questions and applying what you know, ask your instructor and consult **6–8** for details on some common types of writing required in college.

2c Writing for an audience

Sometimes thoughts about a reader, especially an instructor who will give you a grade based on the quality of your work, can be intimidating. Obviously readers and their expectations must be taken into account. The question is when. Writing is not just the final product or words on a page or screen. It is the process that gets you there. And because you can learn from writing, generate ideas from writing, and discover what you want to say and what you need to find out, readers do not have to play a major role from the very beginning. Consider beginning your writing for yourself alone.

Writing for yourself   Write to create a record of your thinking for your eyes only. That way, you will not worry excessively about style, accuracy, spelling, and other details. You will concentrate instead on using your writing to generate and organize your ideas. After you review your draft, think of revising that draft so that it will interest you if you pick it up in a few years' time.

Writing for others   Later in the process, of course, it is helpful to formulate a picture of readers and their expectations. A good writer connects with his or her audience and keeps readers in mind as if in a face-to-face communication. Achieving this connection, however, often proves challenging, because not all readers have the same characteristics. Readers come from different regions, communities, ethnic groups, organizations, and academic disciplines. They have different social and economic backgrounds and varied interests. Also, readers' approaches to what they are reading depend on the context or conventions of the material before them. Conventions vary, for instance, in informal letters, scholarly or scientific writing, Internet writing, newspapers and magazines, business interactions, and college papers in various disciplines.

WORLDS OF WRITING
Assessing Readers' Expectations

- Who will read your piece of writing? What will readers expect in terms of length, format, date of delivery, and content?
- Will readers expect you to write in Standard English or will they appreciate alternatives? See **1c** for more on alternatives.
- What kinds of texts do the readers usually read and write, and what are the conventions of those texts? For example, if you are writing a business letter to a company in another country, consult a business communications book to find out what readers there expect in a business letter.

- Will readers expect formal or informal language?

- Will readers expect you to use technical terms? If so, which terms are in common use?

- What characteristics do you and your readers have in common: nationality, language, culture, race, class, ethnicity, or gender? Consider what limitations writing for these readers places on your use of dialect (Australian English is different from Caribbean English, for example), punctuation (British English and American English treat quotations differently—see **29d**), vocabulary, and political and cultural expectations. Cultivate common ground, and try not to alienate readers.

- What kinds of information and evidence will readers expect to find? Some cultures value the unattributed presentation of traditional wisdom from classic texts, while others (the North American academic culture, for example) expect discussion of controversies and evidence for one position. Different approaches to writing are not necessarily better or worse—but they can be different, and you should be aware of the differences when you write.

Writing for your instructor In college, your audience is sometimes your classmates and ultimately almost always your instructor. Your instructor tends to know more than you do about the course material. However, many college instructors have developed the ability to put themselves in the shoes of other readers. In most cases, then, regard your instructor not as an expert but as a stand-in for a larger audience of general readers who are familiar with some of the basic information and the terminology of a particular discipline but not with obscure jargon, detailed facts, or the precise focus of your assigned or chosen topic. For the writing that you do in college, a unique set of conventions prevails. Even if you are certain that the reader (your instructor) knows what article, concept, or story you are writing about, the conventions of academic writing require you to identify the author and title and not simply begin by referring to "This story" or "This article."

KEY POINTS

Writing for Your Instructor

1. Ask your instructor about special guidelines for the paper: what background information should be included and what can be safely omitted. For example, for a literature paper, find out if your instructor envisions an audience that has read the

(continued)

(continued)

work of literature and so does not expect a summary of the plot or an audience that has not read the work and would benefit from a summary. For a science paper, find out if you need to include tables or charts. For a paper for an art course, determine the balance between description and analysis of a work of art.

2. Find out if your instructor is willing to look at an early outline or draft of your paper.

3. Follow carefully any instructions about length, format, organization, and date of delivery.

4. Ask your instructor if you can see model papers for the course, ideally a paper that would earn an A and a model of an unsatisfactory paper.

5. Before you begin, find out what level of formality your instructor expects. For example, how acceptable will informal language and abbreviations be?

For more on writing about literature or writing in academic disciplines, see **7** and **8**.

EXERCISE 2.1 Write for different readers.
Write three passages on the general topic of "lying"—one for your eyes alone (a diary entry or a freewrite), one for an e-mail message to a close friend (for more on writing e-mail messages, see **11b**), and one for a college instructor. Keep each version short—no more than two paragraphs each. How do the versions differ and why?

EXERCISE 2.2 Rewrite for an instructor.
A student wrote the following passage on "lying" as a journal entry in response to the previous exercise. Circle key ideas that you think could be further developed or improved. Your purpose is to help the student locate good ideas that could be developed into a formal essay about "lying."

Big lies, little lies, white lies, fibs, not truth, deception.

Lying annoys me. I hate when I'm lied to. I think it hurts the most when I am lied to by someone I care about and trust. Especially, if I don't know what I did. I can remember so many different times when friends were mad at me but didn't tell me why. They just stop taking phone calls, say they are busy and when I ask what's wrong, they don't say anything: "Nothin's wrong." But something is very wrong. I hate when I know someone is lying to me but I can't prove it. Why can't everyone just be direct? Lying is the opposite of communication; it's disconnection, building walls, distancing, and it hurts.

I don't agree with the theory that there is nothing wrong with a little white lie. There is no such thing as a little lie. Invariable, they lead to big lies. If you lie, even about a part of a story, then the entire story comes into question. The best policy is to speak your truth.

2d Choosing the right tone

Choosing the right tone means fitting the structure and language you use to the type of writing you are doing, your purpose in doing the writing, and the expectations of readers. Tone can also be explained as the attitude of the writer towards the subject and the audience. A casual e-mail message to a friend calls for a tone different from an informative business report for your boss. The content and language will be different; word choice can, in addition, determine a matter-of-fact, sarcastic, ironic, overly complex, tongue-in-cheek, formal, or informal tone. Use the chart in the Key Points box to check on how you convey tone within your draft.

KEY POINTS

Consistency of Tone

Look at each category and decide which option is most appropriate for your purpose and audience. Then check to see if your approach to tone is consistent. One instance of sarcasm, say, in an otherwise serious critical evaluation is out of place and likely to irritate readers.

Category	Which option is most appropriate?
Approach to topic	informative, humorous, serious, sarcastic, indignant, scathing, ironic, critical, judgmental, sentimental, praising
Level of formality	informal, chatty, slang, jargon, formal
Conventions	Standard English, dialect, other languages interspersed
Argument	rational, emotional, forceful, aggressive
Vocabulary	everyday, technical, community, literary, academic, ornate

Make sure your tone remains consistent throughout your piece of writing. Changes in tone can be jarring.

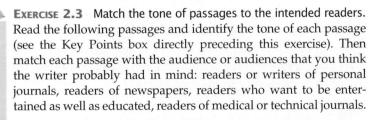

EXERCISE 2.3 Match the tone of passages to the intended readers. Read the following passages and identify the tone of each passage (see the Key Points box directly preceding this exercise). Then match each passage with the audience or audiences that you think the writer probably had in mind: readers or writers of personal journals, readers of newspapers, readers who want to be entertained as well as educated, readers of medical or technical journals.

1. It's a bit oversimplified, but substantially true: A 30-minute walk a day helps keep the doctor away. That's the gist of the 278-page *Physical Activity and Health: A Report of the Surgeon General,* issued in 1996, which urged Americans to get 30 minutes of moderate activity on most days of the week. It's also the central finding of a Harvard University study, published last August in the *New England Journal of Medicine,* which concluded that walking can reduce the risk of heart attacks in women to the same degree as vigorous exercise.
   —Carol Krucoff, "A Walk a Day"

   Tone:_____ Audience:_____

2. The health benefits of physical activity have achieved international recognition following the publication of the 1996 US Surgeon General's report on physical activity and health. Given the high prevalence of inactivity, the promotion of physical activity appears to be at least as important in coronary heart disease prevention as efforts to reduce high cholesterol or high blood pressure, and more important than these factors in contributing to the overall burden of disease. . . . Physical activity is also associated with aspects of injury prevention [and] positive mental health and reduces the risk of developing colon and probably breast and prostate cancer and possibly lung cancer. . . . Incidental [physical] activity can involve using stairs instead of lifts [elevators] or escalators, riding a bicycle rather than driving a car to do minor errands, or choosing not to use energy saving implements for domestic tasks.
   —Adrian Bauman, Neville Owen, and Eva Leslie, "Physical Activity and Health Outcomes: Epidemiological Evidence, National Guidelines and Public Health Initiatives"

   Tone:_____ Audience:_____

3. There's a reason we're born with limbs. They're supposed to move. They *need* to move. And they need to move more than just three times a week when we put on special neon-colored clothes and stand on a machine that looks like the command cabin of the Space Shuttle Atlantis.

   The active use of our physical bodies has to be more a part of our everyday lives. We need to get into the habit of using our bodies every minute by engaging our bodies in work, in play, in our errands, in all our daily rituals.

   —Loretta LaRoche, *Life Is Not a Stress Rehearsal*

   Tone:_____   Audience:_____

4. Although it's hard to actually get out there, once I'm in the park, after the first six minutes, I start to feel good. My breathing changes, and after about 15/20 minutes, I start to break a light sweat. By the time 35 minutes comes, I feel good. My mind gets clear. Sometimes I get my best ideas walking in the park. I know it's good for my body—but it's also good for my mind.

   —Suzanne Windemere, unpublished

   Tone:_____   Audience:_____

EXERCISE 2.4 Vary tone.
Pick an issue that is important to you as a college student. It could be adding more classes, avoiding long lines during registration, improving the library, adding more computers to the computer lab, or any other topic you consider important. Write a persuasive e-mail (informal) to your classmates on this issue; then write a persuasive letter (formal) to your college president on the same issue. Discuss with classmates what changes you had to make.

EXERCISE 2.5 Analyze differences in tone.
Consider the following passages.

1. I returned and saw under the sun, that the race is not to the swift, nor the battle to the strong, neither yet bread to the wise, nor yet riches to men of understanding, nor yet favour to men of skill; but time and chance happeneth to them all.

2. Objective considerations of contemporary phenomena compel the conclusion that success or failure in competitive activities exhibits no tendency to be commensurate with innate capacity,

but that a considerable element of the unpredictable must invariably be taken into account.

What is each passage saying? How does each one say it?

2e Planning the steps in the process

Radio host Ira Glass considers himself someone who thrives on deadlines, commenting, "There are people who are fundamentally lazy, who only get anything done because they put themselves under dreadful deadline pressure. Those people are all my brothers." You may agree with Glass that delaying and working in a last-minute frenzy is the only way to get anything done, but you will be pleasantly surprised at how much better you can do if you take the rush and panic out of the process. Section **47c** provides detailed guidelines for setting a schedule for a research paper, but even a much simpler writing project deserves planning.

As soon as you know what the assignment is and when the final draft is due, work backwards from that date to establish a work schedule that allows you to do what needs to be done. Here is a sample work plan for a short essay assignment in an English course with a six-day deadline.

Tuesday through Thursday	Find and narrow a topic, brainstorm ideas, make a scratch outline.
Friday	Write a first draft. Get feedback from a classmate, tutor, or study group.
Saturday	Read and analyze the draft and plan revisions.
Sunday	Find any necessary additional information. Revise, edit, and proofread.
Monday	Format, print, and hand in.

Adapt this plan to fit the requirements of the writing project, your study and work schedule, and the length of time available. If you have a heavy work and academic schedule, you may have to compress the activities into fewer segments and fewer days.

3 Generating, Shaping, and Focusing Ideas

Whether you have to generate your own idea for a topic or you already have a topic that you need to explore in detail, you need strategies other than staring at the ceiling or waiting for inspiration to fly in through the window. Professional writers use a variety of techniques to generate ideas at various stages of the process. Diane Ackerman, in her article "Oh Muse! You Do Make Things Difficult!" reports that the poet Dame Edith Sitwell used to lie in an open coffin; French novelist Colette picked fleas from her cat; statesman Benjamin Franklin soaked in the bathtub; and German dramatist Friedrich Schiller sniffed rotten apples stored in his desk.

Perhaps you have developed your own original approach to generating ideas. Perhaps you were taught a more formal way to begin a writing project, such as constructing an outline. If what you do now doesn't seem to produce good results, or if you are ready for a change, try some of the methods described in **3a–3e** and see how they work. Not every method works equally well for every project or for every writer. Experimenting is a good idea.

 TechNote Web Sites for Help with Generating Ideas

Some Web sites for writers include useful information on generating ideas and planning. Try, for example, the following:

- Purdue University Online Writing Lab at <http://owl.english.purdue.edu>
- Getting Started page of the CUNY (City University of New York) WriteSite at <http://writesite.cuny.edu/projects/stages/start/index.html>
- Paradigm Online Writing Assistant at <http://www.powa.org/whtfrms.htm> ■

 Exercise 3.1 Write about your own writing process.

Think about the most recent essay you have written. Write an account of what the assignment was, how you generated ideas, how you wrote the essay, where you did your writing, and whether you wrote it with a word processing program or not. How much time was given between the assignment and the due date, and how did you use that time? How did you feel as you wrote the essay? Be complete and frank in describing your writing process. The point is to examine the way you write. Read your account aloud to a group of classmates. Then discuss any differences from their accounts.

 3a Keeping a journal

A *journal* can be far more than a personal diary. Many writers carry a notebook and write in it every day. Journal entries can be observations, references, quotations, questions for research, notes on events, and ideas about assigned texts or topics, as well as specific pieces of writing in progress. A journal can also serve as a review for final examinations or essay tests, reminding you of areas of special interest or subjects you did not understand.

The *double-entry* or *dialectical journal* provides a formalized way for you to think critically about readings and lectures. Two pages or two columns or open windows in your word processor provide the space for interaction. On the left-hand side, write summaries, quotations, and accounts of readings, lectures, and class discussions—that is, record as exactly and concisely as you can what you read or heard. The left-hand side, in short, is reserved for information about the material. On the right-hand side, record your own comments, reactions, and questions about the material (see **1a** and **1b** on critical thinking). The right-hand side is the place to make your own connections between the reading or lecture and your own experience and knowledge.

The following example shows how a student used the Table feature in his word processing program, set at two columns and one row, to split the screen and to set up a format for a double-entry reading journal. In the left-hand column, he records a summary, quotations, and events from Louise Erdrich's short story "The Red Convertible." In the right-hand column, he comments on the context for the passage, relates it to the whole story, and reflects on its connections to his own experience and his own reading of the story.

WHAT I READ	MY COMMENTS
Lyman, a Chippewa, lives on a reservation, and, with his brother Henry, owns and loves driving a red convertible. When Lyman is sixteen, they take lots of trips together in the convertible, going even as far as Alaska with a girl they pick up. When they return home, Henry joins the Marines, and then spends three years in Vietnam while his brother fixes and looks after the car. Henry returns from the war a changed man, one day even biting through his own lip. Lyman gets Henry talking and active again by beating up the car and	I wrote this summary as I read the story the first time.

baiting Henry to fix it by saying it is a "piece of junk."

One day after Henry has fixed the car again, they take it out for a drive to the Red River, first posing for a picture for their sister, Bonita. Lyman tells us that he can't look at the picture anymore.

I wonder why. What happened? Here I wonder if something terrible is going to happen.

On the bank of the river, Henry reveals he knows what Lyman has done to the car and tells Lyman he has fixed it so that he can give it to Lyman. They drink some beers. Suddenly Henry deliberately runs into the high water and says, "My boots are filling." Lyman tries to save him but fails. The story ends with Lyman letting the car roll down the bank into the water and watching it disappear.

I marked this as I read and then found out what it meant at the end of the story. The phrase "his boots filled with water" gives an intriguing hint—I wondered about that as I read it the first time.

"Now Henry owns the whole car [. . .]"

Bonita takes a picture of the brothers. Later Lyman thinks it has changed and removes it from the wall (189).

The brothers set off for the river right after Bonita takes the picture, but in the story, we learn first about Lyman's later reaction to the picture. It provides a clue about the imminent tragedy.

Early in the story the narrator (Lyman) alerts us to the fact that he is a Chippewa Indian: "I could always make money [. . .] unusual in a Chippewa" (181).

How significant is the ethnic identity of the protagonists? What are the characteristics and history of the Chippewas? I need to find out if I am going to write about this story.

3b Freewriting

If you do not know what to write about or how to approach a broad subject, try doing from five to ten minutes of *freewriting* either on paper or on the computer. When you freewrite, you let one idea lead to another in free association, thinking only about ideas and what you can say on the topic. The important thing is to keep writing.

Zhe Chen selected the topic "name and identity" and did some exploratory work to find a focus and narrow the topic. She eventually decided to write an essay examining the effects of the Chinese Cultural Revolution on family identity. Here is her unedited freewriting that led her initially to that idea.

> I have a unusual name, Zhe. My friends in China say it's a boys name. My friends in America think it has only one letter. Most of my American friends have difficulty pronouncing my name.
>
> Some people ask me why don't I Americanize my name so it would be easier to pronounce. But I say if I change my name, it will not be me any more. What else can I write? When I was seven years old, I asked my mother what my name meant. "Ask your father," she said as she washed dishes. It was raining outside, and the room was so quiet that I could hear the rain puttering [?? Look this word up] on the #. My father's

KEY POINTS

Freewriting Tips

1. Give yourself a time limit of five or ten minutes.

2. Write as much as you can as quickly as you can on possible subjects or on a subject you have already determined.

3. As you write, concentrate on getting some ideas on the page or screen. Don't pause to check or edit. This piece of writing is for your eyes only; no one else will ever read it, let alone judge it.

4. If you get stuck, just keep repeating a promising idea or writing about why you get stuck or why the topic is difficult. Use slang, abbreviations, and the first words you think of—in any language. Try not to stop writing.

5. At the end of the time limit, read through your freewriting, highlight the best idea that has emerged, and begin writing again with that idea as the focus.

thoughts returned to another rainy day in 1967 when
the Cultural Revolution just begun. Thousands of people
had been banished to countryside and all the schools
were closed. My grandparents fled to Hong Kong but my
father and aunt stayed in China. Life was difficult.
Gangs sent them to the countryside to work. It was here
that my parents met.

Back to name again. My father named me Zhe. In
Chinese my name means remember and hope. He wanted me
remember the Cultural Revolution and he wanted me to
finish college. He didn't have that chance.

 TECHNOTE Blank Screen and Use of Symbols in Freewriting

Try this if you are a good typist. While freewriting on a computer,
turn off the monitor so that you write freely without being tempted
to scrutinize what you have written. Then you will keep writing and
not stop to edit and make changes. In addition, as you write, if you
cannot think of an appropriate word, simply put in a symbol such as
#, as Zhe Chen did when she momentarily could not recall the word
windowpanes. Use the Search command to find your symbol later,
when you can spend more time thinking about the appropriate
word.

 ESL NOTE Using Your First Language in Freewriting

Freewriting is writing for *you,* writing to discover ideas and get
words down on a page or screen. If you can't think of a phrase or
word, simply write it in your heritage language, or write a question in square brackets as Zhe Chen did, to remind yourself to get
help from a dictionary or to ask a classmate or your instructor
later. ■

EXERCISE 3.2 Freewrite on a topic.
Write down on a slip of paper two possible topics that you
would like a classmate to freewrite on. Your instructor will distribute the slips. From the slip you receive, choose one of the topics and write as much as you can as quickly as you can for five
minutes. Then read what you wrote. Is there an idea you could
develop into an essay? Discuss the ideas that came to mind with
your classmates or, if you feel comfortable, read your freewrite
to other students.

EXERCISE 3.3 Freewrite on a quotation.

Select an interesting quotation (one to three sentences long) from an article or book. Write it on a piece of paper. After collecting these quotations, your instructor will distribute one to you and each of your classmates. Write a timed five-minute freewrite on the quotation you receive. Circle any ideas that you feel you could develop into an essay. Discuss these with your classmates or group. If you feel comfortable, read your freewrite aloud.

3c Brainstorming, listing, and mapping

Another way to generate ideas is by *brainstorming*—making a free-wheeling list of ideas as you think of them. Brainstorming is enhanced if you do it collaboratively in a group, discussing and then listing or mapping your ideas. (See also **4e.**) By yourself or with the group, scrutinize the ideas, arrange them in lists or draw a map of them, and add to or eliminate them.

One group of students working collaboratively made the following brainstorming list on the topic "changing a name":

```
voluntary changes--hate name

escape from family and parents

show business

George Eliot (Mary Ann Evans)

Woody Allen (Allen Stewart Konigsberg)

P. Diddy (Sean Combs aka Puff Daddy)

writers and their pseudonyms--who?

married women: some keep own name, some change,
   some use both names and hyphenate

Hillary Clinton/Hillary Rodham Clinton

immigrants

Ellis Island

forced name changes

political name changes

name changes because of racism or oppression

criminals?
```

Once the students had made the list, they reviewed it, rejected some items, expanded on others, and grouped items. Thus, they developed a range of subcategories that led them to possibilities for new lists, further exploration, and essay organization:

Voluntary Name Changes

authors: George Eliot, Mark Twain, Isak Dinesen

show business and stage names: Woody Allen, Bob Dylan, Ringo Starr, P. Diddy, Eminem, Pink

ethnic and religious identification: Malcolm X, Muhammad Ali

Name Changes upon Marriage

reasons for changing or not changing

Hillary Clinton

problem of children's names

alternative: hyphenated name

Forced Name Changes

immigrants on Ellis Island

wartime oppression

slavery

Mapping, also called *clustering,* is a visual way of brainstorming and connecting ideas. It focuses your brainstorming, organizes the ideas as you generate them, and can be done individually or in a group. Write your topic in a circle at the center of a page, think of ideas related to the topic, and write those ideas on the page around the central topic. Draw lines from the topic to the related ideas. Then add details under each of the ideas you noted. For an assignment on "current issues in education," a student created the following map and saw that it indicated several possibilities for topics, such as school vouchers, home-schooling, and the social exclusivity of private schools.

A mind map with "education" at the center branching to: home schooling (parents' abilities and training, no organized sports, religious education, socialization? no exposure to others, study at own pace), public (common curriculum, taxes, sports teams, serving neighborhood, mix of race and class), private (exclusive, class size, cost, parochial — uniforms, religion), voucher system (survival of better schools, effect on neighborhood, beneficial to poor families, choice for parents and students)

EXERCISE 3.4 Brainstorm in a group.

With four or five classmates, choose a topic you would like to brainstorm about. Select one student to be the secretary and another student to be the spokesperson. As you brainstorm ideas, the secretary will record everything. All members of the group must contribute. Record everything. Sometimes a seemingly silly or trivial idea can lead to an excellent idea.

After brainstorming, spend some time grouping ideas and filling in any gaps. Compare your brainstorming results with other students in the class. When it is your turn to share with the class, the spokesperson will report your findings to the class.

EXERCISE 3.5 Make an ideas map.
Choose a broad topic such as the environment, heroes, immigration, or aging and construct a map of ideas. Then look at your map. What ideas does it suggest about how you could develop and organize a piece of writing on that topic?

EXERCISE 3.6 Maintain a list of topics of interest.
Keep a list of topics you would like to learn more about. Any time you come across an idea or topic that interests you, note it in your notebook. At this point, don't worry if the topic is too broad or too narrow. The point is to have access to a list of topics. Then, instead of asking yourself "What will I write about?" you can ask "How do I want to approach this topic?"

3d Joining e-mail conversations

It is often useful in developing a topic to network with others on a course electronic bulletin board, in a chat room, or in a newsgroup (see **11c**). Alternatively, you can set up your own group of students who want to work together to brainstorm over cyberspace. Daniel Kies at College of DuPage in Glen Ellyn, Illinois, set up an online threaded discussion list (**11c**) for his students in his first-year expository writing course. Here are some of the students' postings (used with permission) as they prepared to write an essay assignment on the "techno-future":

By <u>Rick Waters</u> on Thursday, April 27, 2000 - 04:09 pm:

I don't know how far along all of you are, but I wanted to offer some ideas for Essay 3. We're supposed to describe the techno-future as we see it, and I figured I would give you a reminder on what's been in the works and what's been accomplished lately.
  "Smart Homes" are being built. Bill Gates' is probably the extreme (more info at www.usnews.com/usnews/nycut/tech/billgate/gates.htm).
Microchips are being implanted in brains to reverse the effects of blindness and deafness.
The genetics industry is booming.
There's a pill for just about everything nowadays.
There are (3) cars that can actually fly.
"Lawnmower Man Technology" (the effects of virtual teaching—facts being fed into the brain via multiple stimuli at once) has been in testing since 1992.
Materials (not unlike clothing) are being developed to display video images.
Digital phones are being "blended" with Palmtop computers.
  And there's a ton more!
(continued)

(continued)

By Tabitha Schneider **on Thursday, April 27, 2000 - 04:41 pm:**

Rick, I agree with you, the list is infinite in length. By the time we finish our essays, the ideas might be obsolete.
Technology changes rapidly, we will never be right at the cutting edge, unless we are working the techno-future jobs.
 What do you all think?

By Jennifer Thomas **on Thursday, April 27, 2000 - 10:55 pm:**

Sadly enough, I haven't heard of half of the things that Rick mentioned! Am I behind or what! I think that we are far more technologically advanced than the government wants us to know. I am sitting below two skylights in my living room, and I'm pretty sure if "Big Brother" wanted to, he could probably interrupt this transmission. Scary as it is, technology is far beyond our realm. And we will be left in the dark, until the government decides we are privy to the information. The laptop I write on, although sufficient for my purposes, is an ancient artifact compared to the laptops on the market today. And my laptop can do a lot of stuff. It's far better than my parents' desktop! But yet, still out-dated. Technology scares me in certain ways. Did you also know that the purchases you make at stores are tracked by certain barcodes present on coupons? If you don't use the 25 cent ones, they will eventually send you coupons of a higher value. But if you continue to redeem the 25 cent ones, that will be all you ever get. (For the most part). Every credit card in the country is linked to a profile. I am hesitant to call it a technological age, but more of an information age. The President could probably find out how often you buy peanut butter, what brand, and whether you use a coupon for it! SCARY!
There's food for thought.

EXERCISE 3.7 Initiate an e-mail discussion.

When you next have a writing assignment, arrange with three other students in your class to communicate about the topic via e-mail. Contribute at least two postings during the discussion. Print your results and bring them to class.

 Alternatively, arrange with three other students to have an online chat. Set a time that is convenient to meet online and engage in an online dialogue about the assigned topic. Print your results and bring them to class.

3e **Using journalists' questions
 and formal prompts**

Journalists check the coverage of their stories by making sure that they answer six questions—Who? What? When? Where? Why? How?—though not in any set order. A report on a public transit strike, for example, would include details about the union leaders (who they were), the issue of working conditions and benefits (what the situation was), the date and time of the confrontation (when the strike occurred), the place (where it occurred), what caused the confrontation (why it happened), and how the people involved behaved and resolved the strike (how it evolved and ended). If you are telling the story of an event, either as a complete essay or as an example in an essay, asking the journalists' six questions will help you think comprehensively about your topic. (Note, though, that newspaper articles have different conventions from academic essays, such as shorter paragraphs and fewer or no source citations.)

Sometimes you might find it helpful to use a formal set of directions (known as *prompts*) to suggest new avenues of inquiry. Write down responses to any of the prompts that apply to your topic, and note possibilities for further exploration.

DEFINING YOUR TERMS

1. Look up key words in your topic (like *success, identity, ambition,* and *ethnicity*) in the dictionary and write down the definition you want to use.
2. What synonyms (words with similar meaning) are possible?
3. Is a brief definition adequate, or do you need a detailed definition?
4. Should your definition be illustrated with an example?
5. Has the definition changed, or is it changing?

INCLUDING DESCRIPTIONS

1. Whatever your topic, make your writing more vivid with details about color, light, location, movement, size, and shape.
2. Appeal to as many of the readers' senses as necessary or possible: tell readers not just what something looks like, but, if applicable, what it sounds, feels, smells, or tastes like.
3. Divide the object of your description into parts and describe each part in detail.
4. Help readers "see" your topic, such as a person, place, object, or scientific experiment, as exactly as you see it.

MAKING COMPARISONS

1. Help readers understand a topic by describing what it might be similar to. For example, is learning to write like learning to juggle?
2. Note what your topic is different from. For example, is learning to write different from learning to read?

ASSESSING CAUSE AND EFFECT

1. Do readers need information on what causes or produces your topic? For example, what are the causes of dyslexia? inflation? acid rain? hurricanes? asthma?
2. What effects or results emerge from your topic?

CONSIDERING WHAT OTHERS HAVE SAID

1. Can you give readers information on what others say about your topic in interviews, surveys, reading, and research?
2. What facts and statistics can you find?
3. Who supports your views?
4. Who opposes them?

EXERCISE 3.8 Look for answers to the journalists' questions. Go to a newsstand, library, or Web site and browse through current news headlines. Select a news article that grabs your attention and interest. Read the entire article. How does the journalist address the questions Who? What? When? Where? Why? How? Be specific. Then make a list of the main ideas in the article or make a map of the topic (putting the main concept the article deals with in the center).

EXERCISE 3.9 Use the formal prompts. With a group of three or four classmates, select one of the following topics and explore it by using the sets of formal prompts on pages 35–36. Keep a list of your responses to each prompt. Report to the class about the experience and whether it created any ideas that were unexpected.

study abroad programs	parenting styles
global warming	fad diets
the media	censorship
homelessness	college curriculum
sex education	the placebo effect

EXERCISE 3.10 Try different methods of generating ideas. Form a group of five students. Together, select a topic that interests you. Each of you will then explore the topic by using one of the following methods of exploration: a double-entry journal page, freewriting, mapping, asking the journalists' questions, or using a formal set of prompts. Compare your results. Which methods worked well?

3f Finding and refining an essay topic

Finding a topic "What on earth am I going to write about?" is a question frequently voiced or at least thought in college classrooms, especially in those classrooms in which students are free to write about any topic that interests them.

Using the strategies in **3a–e** will help you find topics. In addition, think about what matters to you. Reflect on issues raised in your college courses; read newspapers and magazines for current issues; consider campus, community, city, state, and nationwide issues; and look at the Library of Congress Subject Headings to get ideas (see **48e**). Sometimes, browsing an online library catalog, a Web directory, or a site such as *Researchpaper.com* at <http://www.researchpaper.com> can produce good ideas for choosing a topic, but it is usually better to begin with something that has caught your interest elsewhere and has some connection to your life.

 TECHNOTE Using Web Directories to Find a Topic

Academic Web directories assembled by librarians and academic institutions provide reliable sources for finding good academic subjects. Try, for example, Librarians' Index to the Internet at <http://lii.org>, Academic Info at <http://www.academicinfo.net>, and Voice of the Shuttle, a University of California at Santa Barbara directory for humanities research at <http://vos.ucsb.edu>. For more on using search engines and directories, see **48f–48h.** For more on evaluating online materials, see **49d–49e.** ■

In addition, general Internet search engines and directories such as Yahoo! at <http://www.yahoo.com>, AltaVista at <http://www.altavista.com>, and Google at <http://www.google.com> offer subject categories that you can explore and successively narrow down to find a topic suitable for an essay. For example, one Yahoo! search beginning with "Education" produced more than thirty different categories, as shown in the screenshot on page 38. Clicking on *reform* produced links to twenty-three site listings (such as *multicultural education reform programs, computers as tutors, guide to math and science reform,* and *no child left behind*). Many of the sites linked to Web pages on topics such as "voucher programs" and "charter schools," as well as to many other sites, some with bibliographies with further online links. Such directories can suggest a wide range of interesting topics for you to explore.

Once you have a topic in mind, discussing it with others, conducting an interview, administering a questionnaire or survey, and

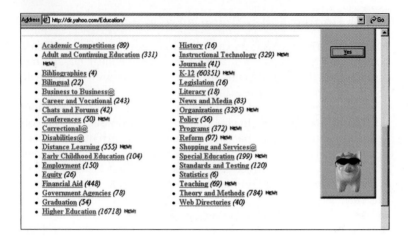

doing a preliminary library and Web search will help you determine whether enough material is available and whether what is available is relevant and interesting (see also **47** and **49**).

The strategies described in **3a–3e** can help you find a topic and ideas to include in an essay. While finding a topic is a necessary step, it is only a beginning. The topic has then to be tailored and adapted to make it appropriate for the length and type of essay you intend to write; then, for an opinion essay or an argument, you need to formulate what point of view you will express on the topic, in the form of a thesis. You also need to find specific and concrete details to use as evidence and support for the thesis; and then, if your instructor assigns it, you may have to prepare a statement of purpose, a proposal, or an outline (**3i, 47e, 51c**).

Refining a topic you find or are assigned   In college courses, you may be given any of the following types of assignments for an essay, arranged here from the broadest in scope to the narrowest:

- a free choice of subject
- a broad subject area, such as "genetic engineering" or "affirmative action"
- a focused and specific topic, such as "the city's plans to build apartments on landfill" or "the treatment of welfare recipients in California"
- an actual question to answer, such as "Is age an issue in cases of driving accidents?"

If you are given a free choice of subject, you will need to narrow your focus to a broad subject area, to a specific topic, and then to a

KEY POINTS

Subject, Topic, Question, Thesis: A Continuum

Level 1: *Broad subject area*

↓

Level 2: *Narrowed topic* for exploration within that subject area

↓

Level 3: *Key question* that concerns you

↓

Level 4: Your *thesis* (your claim or statement of opinion or your main idea in answer to the question). Often you need to do a great deal of reading and writing and trying out possible theses before you settle on an appropriate one.

specific question. After that, still more narrowing is necessary, eventually leading to a thesis. Your *thesis,* or *claim,* is your statement of opinion, main idea, or message that unifies your piece of writing, makes a connection between you and the subject area, lets readers know where you stand in relation to the topic, and answers the question posed. But you cannot move toward a good thesis if your topic is too broad or too narrow.

Here is one student's movement from subject to thesis over several days of reading, discussion, freewriting, and note-taking:

```
Subject: College admissions policies

        ↓

Narrowed Topic: College admissions for athletes

        ↓

Question: Should success in sports have any
    influence on college admissions?

        ↓

Thesis: College admissions policies should be
    based solely on academic performance and potential, not
    on athletic ability.
```

If you choose a topic and a question that are too broad, you will find it difficult to generate a thesis with focused ideas and examples. Whenever you find yourself thinking, for instance, "There's so much to say about college admissions policies—their history, goals, practice, criticisms, successes—that I don't know where to start," narrow your topic. If you begin by choosing a topic and a question that are too narrow, you probably will not find enough material, so you may have to change your topic or question because of this lack of information. Whenever you feel you have enough material to fill only a page and can't imagine how you will find more ("What else *can* I say about how my cousin got into college?"), broaden your topic or change it completely. Above all, stay flexible: you may also want to change your topic or your question as you discover more information.

EXERCISE 3.11 Find and narrow a topic in a search directory.
Access an online library database such as *InfoTrac/Expanded Academic* or *EBSCO Host/Academic Search Premier*. In the Search box, start with a subject search of any broad category: for example, "family," "health," or "music." Look at the categories until you find one you are interested in. For example, a subject search of "family" yields "family and mass media" as one of the categories. Whatever broad category you decide to search, be sure to narrow the subject to a topic you could explore in a short paper.

Click on the category and access at least two sources. Then formulate a possible question that would focus your thinking and any research.

EXERCISE 3.12 Search the Web for a focused topic.
Work with a partner, and use a search directory such as Google, AltaVista, Librarians' Index to the Internet, or Yahoo! to work your way down the levels of a subject category in order to come up with some possible focused topics for writing. Then formulate for each topic a question that will yield a thesis statement.

EXERCISE 3.13 Narrow a topic.
In groups of two or three, discuss the ways in which one of the following broad subject areas could be narrowed to a topic and a question appropriate to a seven-page essay.

small businesses	women's rights	migration
home-schooling	gambling	genetics
politics	addiction	nature vs. nurture
the death penalty	alcoholism	birth order
gun control	soap operas	the Olympics
health and physical education	the film industry	beauty pageants
	advertisements	

3g Formulating a thesis—and why you need one

Suppose someone were to ask you, "What is the main idea that you want to communicate to readers in your piece of writing?" The sentence you would give in reply is your thesis, also known as a claim. Your thesis tells readers what point you are going to make about your topic, what stand you are going to take. It is not enough to say, "I am writing about bilingual education." Are you going to address bilingual education in elementary, secondary, or higher education? Which readers do you regard as your primary audience? Which geographical areas will you discuss? Will you be concerned with the past or with the present? What do you intend to propose about the area of bilingual education you have selected? In short, what point do you want to make about which aspect of bilingual education—for which readers? It is also not enough to stop short with a question. Do not try to build an essay around a question such as "Do parents view bilingual education differently from school administrators?" You can certainly start with a question, but then you need to let your question lead you to the answer you provide, and that answer, in the form of a statement, will be your thesis.

You don't have to know where to put your thesis statement in your essay right away, nor do you need to settle immediately on the exact wording of your thesis. However, even a preliminary idea for a topic can generate a working thesis that you can then refine as you plan, read, and write. See **6c** on the thesis in an argument paper.

How to write a good thesis statement A good thesis statement may be one or more of the following:

1. a strong, thought-provoking, or controversial statement

   ▶ **Bilingual education has not fulfilled its early promise.**

2. a call to action

   ▶ **All inner-city schools should set up transitional bilingual programs.**

3. a question preceding the thesis statement as its answer, backed up with details in the essay

   ▶ **What can bilingual education accomplish for a child? It can lead to personal as well as academic development.**

4. a preview or reflection of the structure of the essay

   ▶ **Bilingual education suffers from two main problems: a shortage of trained teachers and a lack of parental involvement.**

▶ **Although bilingual education suffers from a shortage of teachers and lack of parental involvement, its theoretical principles are sound.**

KEY POINTS

Thesis Checklist

Use this list to help you work on the thesis statement of an essay. You should be able to put a checkmark next to each quality.

Your thesis

1. is worth saying

2. narrows your topic to the one main idea that you want to communicate

3. makes a claim or asserts an opinion about your topic

4. can be supported by details, facts, and examples within the assigned limitations of time and space

5. stimulates curiosity and interest in readers and prompts them to think "Why do you say that?" and then read on

6. uses exact language and concepts rather than vague generalizations

7. does not include anything that you do not intend to discuss in your essay

8. is one complete sentence, usually with only one independent clause (though you will come across many variations)

After you have formulated your thesis statement, write it on a self-stick note or an index card and keep it near you as you write. The note or card will remind you to stick to the point. If you still digress as you write, you may need to consider changing your thesis.

From working thesis to revision   An initial working thesis may be a tentative opinion statement that you formulate soon after you formulate your question—but try to move beyond it to something focused as soon as you can. As you think more, read more, learn more, and discover more specific ideas, you will usually find that you rework your thesis several times to make it more informative, less general, and more precise. You may even indicate in your thesis what main points of support you will discuss in your essay. Here are some examples of a preliminary working thesis later revised as a final draft thesis for a two- to three-page essay:

QUESTION (personal essay): What are the difficulties of starting college many years after high school?

Preliminary working thesis: Starting college at age thirty-four was difficult for me.

Revised thesis: Starting college at age thirty-four means reassessing how to balance work, family, and free time.
[This thesis indicates that the writer will deal with each of the three areas, probably in the order given.]

QUESTION (informative essay): How can people handle credit responsibly?

Preliminary working thesis: There are many ways to handle credit responsibly.

Revised thesis: It takes planning, budgeting, and controlled shopping for students to handle credit responsibly.
[Here the "many ways" have been limited to three, named specifically. In addition, the target population has been limited to students.]

QUESTION (persuasive essay): What are the benefits of affirmative action?

Preliminary working thesis: Affirmative action is a controversial policy in college admissions.

Revised thesis: Affirmative action used in the college admissions process is a good way to ensure diversity of students and equality in society.
[Here readers expect a twofold argument, one addressing the ability of affirmative action to create diversity in a student body, the other broadening the concept to the idea of affirmative action also having an equalizing effect on society.]

QUESTION (persuasive essay): Are cell phones a blessing or a curse?

Preliminary working thesis: Cell phones have many advantages.

Revised thesis: Although cell phones may cause problems when they are misused, they are a boon to working parents wanting to keep track of their children's whereabouts after school hours.
[This refined thesis statement limits discussion of the advantages of cell phones to the benefits they provide to working parents; it also indicates that the writer will acknowledge some disadvantages but will evaluate these as less important than the advantages.]

Recognizing and writing a good thesis statement A good thesis statement is a complete sentence (or, sometimes, more than one sentence), makes an interesting and debatable assertion, expresses an opinion that needs to be supported and explained, and does not simply state a fact or obvious truism. A good thesis statement also gives readers some sense of what main points will be used to support the thesis and how the essay will be organized.

Ineffective	**The desolation of shopping malls.** [This phrase lacks a verb and so is not a sentence. It is more suitable as a title than a thesis. A thesis statement is a sentence that makes an assertion.]
Ineffective	**City life and its disadvantages.** [This phrase lacks a verb and so is not a sentence. A thesis statement is a sentence that makes an assertion.]
Ineffective	**There are many kinds of exercise machines.** [This statement is a sentence, but it does not make an interesting and debatable assertion. It does not express an opinion that needs to be supported and explained. Instead, it states a fact. The reader has no incentive to read on, no notion that by reading on he or she will find out useful or necessary information about exercise machines.]
Ineffective	*Death of a Salesman* **is a play by Arthur Miller.** [This sentence states a fact. It does not make an interesting and debatable assertion. Readers, especially those who know their literature, will nod and think "Yes, I know that," and will not feel driven to read on to find out what makes you say that.]
Ineffective	**Murder is wrong.** [Almost nobody would disagree or find this an interesting statement. This sentence states a truism, a statement so obvious that it does not merit discussion or engage readers' interest.]
Ineffective	**Almost half of the students in college are adults with families and jobs.** [This sentence states a fact. It does not make an interesting comment or observation about this aspect of college life today.]
Effective	**Because so many students are older adults, colleges should allow a longer time to get a degree, provide more day-care centers, and develop more online courses.** [This thesis statement establishes a clear focus on a topic, asserts an opinion, and gives the reader some

sense of what main points will be used to support the thesis and how the essay will be organized.]

 ESL NOTE Language, Identity, and the Thesis Statement

Often writers who have developed their writing skills in one language notice distinct differences in the conventions of writing in another, particularly with respect to the explicit statement of opinion in the thesis. Fan Shen, in attempting to define how his "Chinese identity" is different from the self he assumes when writing in English, sees the explicit thesis statement favored in Western writing as "symbolic of the values of a busy people in an industrialized society, rushing to get things done." For more on this subject, see Fan Shen's article "The Classroom and the Wider Culture: Identity as a Key to Learning English Composition," *College Composition and Communication* (Dec. 1989): 462. It is difficult to determine how much of a role one's culture plays in the way one writes and to separate culture's role from the roles of gender, socioeconomic status, family background, and education. However, always consider what approaches your anticipated readers are likely to be familiar with and to value. ▪

Stating your thesis in your paper   Even though it is useful to have a working thesis as you read and write drafts and to refine your thesis as you work, you will eventually need to decide if and where you will include a thesis statement in your essay. Ask your instructor about any special requirements for thesis location. In most academic writing in the humanities and social sciences, a thesis is stated clearly in the essay, usually near the beginning. See your thesis statement as a signpost—both for you as you write your draft and, later, for readers as they read your essay. A clear thesis prepares readers well for the rest of the essay.

Sometimes, though, particularly in descriptive, narrative, and informative writing, you may choose to imply your thesis and not explicitly state it. In such a case, you make your thesis clear by the examples, details, and information you include. You may also choose to state your thesis at the end of your essay instead of the beginning. If so, you present all the evidence to build a case and then make the thesis act as a climax and logical statement about the outcome of the evidence. If you use key words from your thesis as you write, you will keep readers focused on your main idea.

On not falling in love with your working thesis   A good working thesis often takes so long to develop that you might be reluctant to change it. Be willing, however, to refine and change your thesis as you find more information and work with your material. Many writers begin with a tentative working thesis and then find that they come to a new conclusion at the end of the first draft. If that happens to you, start your second draft by focusing on the thesis that emerged during the writing of the first draft. In other words, change your thesis as you go along. Be flexible: it is easier to change a thesis statement to fit new ideas and new evidence that you discover than to find new evidence to fit a thesis.

In addition, if you do not change your thesis to accommodate new evidence, you risk failing to convince readers who may be acquainted with evidence that does not support your thesis. Note that your final revised thesis statement should take a firm stand on the issue. Flexibility during the writing process is not the same as indecision in the final product.

EXERCISE 3.14 Locate thesis statements.
In each of the following passages from essays, find and underline the thesis statement.

1. Some parents choose to educate their children themselves, using curricular materials from a home-schooling association, tutoring their children daily, and arranging other tutors and educational life experiences for their children. But what happens to these home-schooled children when they are teenagers and ready to apply to college? More than traditionally schooled students, home-schooled students need to research school policies, complete strong applications that detail their studies, submit a portfolio of their work, and furnish letters of recommendation.

2. Many people fail to make a favorable impression because they don't know how to listen. Isaac F. Marcosson, a journalist who has interviewed hundreds of celebrities, notes that many of them are "so much concerned with what they are going to say next that they do not keep their ears open[. . .]. Very important people have told me that they prefer good listeners to good talkers, but the ability to listen seems rarer than almost any other good trait." The more one tunes in to this phenomenon, the more one notices that few people in any setting or walk of life have good listening skills and that their inattentiveness reflects poorly on them. —Dale Carnegie, *How to Win Friends and Influence People*

3. During the past several decades, alternative treatments such as aromatherapy, massage, acupuncture, and herbal remedies have

become popular. Consumers no longer need to special-order items from health food stores; they can purchase them at their local supermarket and pharmacy. Although patients are often pleased with results of alternative treatments, many of these treatments are untested and not approved by the Food and Drug Administration (FDA). Rather than encourage an either/or approach, many physicians are now treating patients through an integrated approach. Integrated medicine successfully combines conventional medical treatment with alternative therapies.

4. Big chain video-rental stores use unfair practices to rid an area of competition. These chain stores drive out small mom-and-pop video stores that provide friendlier service, more diverse stock, and other conveniences, such as better store hours. Initially the big chain video-rental stores offer discounts, a large stock of new releases, store credit cards, and new employment opportunities. Once the independent stores have been put out of business, however, the chain stores cut back the selection, service, and convenient store hours and raise prices. Consumers are at their mercy, with no alternatives.

EXERCISE 3.15   Evaluate thesis statements.
Which of the following statements work well as a thesis statement to focus an essay of three to five pages in length, and which do not? Give the reasons for your assessment.

1. Adding a sixth day of classes is more effective in helping students than extending the hours of the present five-day class schedule.

2. Although the goals of the European Union (EU) are commendable, the diversity and history of European people make the EU highly unlikely to succeed.

3. Although art and music therapies differ in their approaches, there are compelling similarities between these methods.

4. In order to assist the increasing population of young homeless people, new policies are needed to improve the quality of shelters, create back-to-work employment programs, and fund medical and mental health treatment.

5. Although several studies reveal that placebos are effective in healing ill patients, physicians need to conduct more research into how and why placebos work.

6. Understanding personality types provides us with insights into ourselves and the world.

7. "Mindfulness" or "paying attention" to the world around us is a vital skill to develop because it enriches our lives, sharpens our memory skills, keeps us safe, and helps us become more aware eyewitnesses.

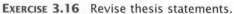

EXERCISE 3.16 Revise thesis statements.

The following thesis statements are too narrow, too broad, or too vague or are factual statements. Revise each one to make it an appropriate thesis statement for a three- to five-page essay.

1. Legalizing homosexual marriage is a controversial issue.

2. Literacy is an important issue that must be dealt with.

3. Plants enhance the beauty of a home.

4. People with disabilities can face employment discrimination in several ways.

5. Alcoholism affects children.

6. Advertisers of food products use color-enhanced images to entice consumers into purchasing their products.

7. The media are responsible for causing eating disorders, lowering self-esteem, and encouraging unrealistic ideals of beauty.

EXERCISE 3.17 Revise thesis statements.

Revise all the thesis statements on page 44 except for the last one.

EXERCISE 3.18 Write thesis statements.

Read the following list of topics and, together with a group of classmates, refine the topics into thesis statements for a three- to four-page argumentative or persuasive essay. Use the four levels outlined in the Key Points box on page 39 and in the example below:

EXAMPLE

Level 1: Subject	Survival TV shows
Level 2: Narrowed topic	Reality TV shows such as *Survivor*
Level 3: Key question	Why did they become popular?
Level 4: Tentative thesis	Reality TV shows such as *Survivor* enjoyed widespread popularity and high ratings because of the perceived originality of the series, as well as interest in individual contestants, challenging activities, and financial prizes.

1. Level 1: Subject   Your college's registration process

2. Level 1: Subject   America's system of movie ratings

   [Note: G (general audience, all ages admitted); PG (parental guidance suggested); PG 13 (parents strongly cautioned); R (restricted—under 17 requires accompanying parent or adult guardian); NC-17 (no one 17 or under admitted)]

3. Level 1: Subject   Women in combat

4. Level 1: Subject   Alternative energy sources for automobiles

3h   Providing evidence and support

Whether you are writing a paragraph or an essay, you need to show readers that your opinion or information is well founded and supported by experience, knowledge, logical arguments, the work of experts, or reasoned examples. In addition, you want to engage readers and provide vital, unique details.

Once you have come up with a good thesis for your essay, you then have to find ways to develop and support it. Readers expect to find out why you hold a certain point of view or why you regard your information as important: What are your reasons? What is your evidence? Where does the evidence come from? Your paragraphs will develop and support your thesis one point at a time.

Let's say you are writing a paper with the following thesis:

College admissions policies should be based solely on academic performance and potential, not on athletic ability.

Your job in the paper is to show readers why you think that, to provide information that backs up your case, and to write a convincing argument. You may not be able to win over a scholarship football star to your side, but you should be able to make his team recognize that sound arguments exist. Here are some strategies you might use:

- Provide information about research studies showing low academic success rate of athletes and report statistics of class rank at graduation.
- Give an account of an interview with a college admissions officer and an athletics coach.
- Give examples of credentials of students who were rejected when athletes were admitted.
- Describe details of the athletic culture on a campus, showing how the athletic culture discourages academic study.

- Compare and contrast two high school students—one athlete and one nonathlete—applying to the same college.
- Define the terms "academic performance" and "athletic ability."
- Classify athletes into types of athlete (for example, athletes who have maintained a B, C, or D average; athletes who need to practice for 7 hours a week, 15 hours, or more than 15).
- Explain the problem facing admissions officers and offer a solution.

KEY POINTS

Support for a Point in an Essay or a Paragraph

Use any one, several, or all of the following methods in your essay to support your thesis. In a paragraph, too, you can develop and support your controlling idea or topic sentence (see **5b**) by using one or several of the following:

- facts and statistics
- examples
- stories
- descriptions
- definitions
- instructions on how to do something
- classifications or analyses
- comparisons and contrasts
- discussions of causes and effects
- analysis of problems and solutions
- expert testimony

See **5d** for examples of the above types of supporting details that various writers have used within paragraphs and essays.

EXERCISE 3.19 Find details to use in support of a thesis. For each of the following thesis statements, discuss with other students which types of supporting details you would choose to support the thesis and provide evidence to make a convincing case to readers (for example, facts and statistics, examples, stories, descriptions, definitions, instructions; see the Key Points box immediately preceding this exercise). Create a list of the types of supporting details that would be effective for each thesis statement, and include any specific details that would illustrate the point.

1. The current adoption systems must be reformed so that couples seeking to adopt a child avoid long delays, unnecessary extensive paperwork, and costly fees.

2. Community centers in ethnic neighborhoods play an important role in helping new immigrants assimilate into America by providing job assistance, English language instruction classes, and interaction with other immigrants who have successfully struck a balance between assimilation and preservation of heritage.

3. "Recycle, Reduce, and Reuse" are three activities citizens can do on a daily basis to help protect our environment from the hazards of pollution and solid waste.

4. Although law enforcement authorities claim that video surveillance of neighborhood streets protects residents from crime, video surveillance infringes on our civil liberties and should not be used.

5. Internships help students explore their intended careers, make important contacts, and gain valuable work experience.

3i Preparing a proposal or outline

Proposals You may be asked to submit a proposal for a piece of writing to get approval for the topic, contents, and organization. A proposal is not necessarily as detailed or as precise as an outline, and in fact, you can view it as an exploration—something that tests out whether a topic will work for you. A proposal should indicate your audience, your thesis, and your major points. It can be written as a narrative or a numbered list, whichever fits your topic. Here is an example of a proposal for a short paper in an expository writing course. (See **47e** for a preliminary statement of purpose for a research paper, one that can be developed into a fuller proposal or outline.)

```
In this essay, I intend to persuade my classmates and my
instructor that freedom of speech does not necessarily
mean freedom from repercussions. While the Constitution
guarantees the right to freedom of speech without
imprisonment, it does not guarantee that people will not
have to pay the price of being denounced or ostracized
for expressing repugnant views. I will include the
following points relating to reactions to the terrorist
attack of September 11, 2001, and will provide specific
examples to back up each one.
```

1. Television and news personalities should be able to express their views without the censorship of corporate sponsors stifling their freedom. However, they cannot expect viewers to agree with them; they should expect outrage if outrage is warranted. Discuss the case of Bill Maher in *Politically Incorrect*.

2. College professors should be able to express their views on controversial issues. However, students have the right to refuse to attend their classes, and taxpayers have the right to react strongly and even urge dismissal. Even so, the principle of academic freedom should stand to protect jobs. Discuss examples in Texas and New York.

3. Writers have the right to express their opinions in their works. Bookstore owners have the right not to stock their books and readers have the right not to buy their books, thus denying them a living. Discuss Barbara Kingsolver.

Scratch outlines A *scratch outline* is a rough list of numbered points that you intend to cover in your essay. A scratch outline lets you see what ideas you already have, how they connect, what you can do to support and develop them, and what further planning or research you still need to do. One student in the group that made the brainstorming list on page 30 developed the following scratch outline and formulated a working thesis:

Topic: Changing a name
Question: Why do people change their names?
Tentative working thesis: People change their names because they either have to or want to.
Types of name changes:

1. Forced name changes in a new country or a new school

2. Name changes to avoid discrimination or persecution

3. Name changes upon marriage

4. Name changes in show business

5. Voluntary name changes to avoid recognition

   a. Criminals

   b. Writers

When this student began to write his draft, however, he changed direction and unified some of his points, developing a more focused thesis (see more on formal outlines, directly following).

Formal outlines A *formal outline* spells out, in order, what points and supportive details you will use to develop your thesis and arranges them to show the overall form and structure of the essay, moving from the general to the specific, using points you have generated in brainstorming, mapping (**3c**), or other methods. As you formulate an outline, keep an image of readers in mind. Imagine them asking when they read your thesis, "Why do you think that? What is the evidence?" If you have explored the question in enough depth and breadth, you should be able to identify several reasons or main points of support. These will form the structural backbone of the essay. Then for each main reason or piece of support, imagine readers again asking, "Why is this point important? What is the evidence?"

You may produce a formal outline before you begin to write, but you are likely to find that making an outline with a high level of detail is more feasible after you have written a draft. Done at this later point, the outline serves as a check on the logic and completeness of what you have written, revealing any gaps, repetition, or illogical steps in the development of your essay.

The format of an outline When you make an outline, you organize your material into sections and subsections. Use the following system:

Main ideas:	I
	II
	III
	and so on
Points under each main idea:	A
	B
	C
	and so on
Examples or reasons for each point under a main idea (A, B, C, and so on):	1
	2
	3
	and so on
Specific details illustrating and expanding each example or reason (1, 2, 3, and so on):	a
	b
	c
	and so on

KEY POINTS

Writing an Outline

1. Write a formal outline only after you have done a great deal of thinking, reading, writing, and research. Sometimes it is better to delay writing an outline until after you have a rough draft on paper; then you can outline what you have written and see if it makes sense.

2. Decide on whether items in the outline will be words and phrases (with no end punctuation) or complete sentences. If you can, go with complete sentences—you will find that doing that helps record or formulate your ideas more clearly. For a short essay, complete sentences written to indicate major points can then stand as the topic sentences of supporting paragraphs.

3. Use parallel structures for major headings—sentences or phrases, but not a mixture.

4. Organize your outline so that it moves from larger ideas to smaller, with all ideas under a similar letter or number equal in level of generality and importance.

5. Whenever you divide a point, always have at least two parts (just like dividing a cake). So whenever you have I, you must have II. Whenever you have A, you must have B, and so on.

6. Keep outline categories separate and distinct, without confusing overlap.

7. Do not include the introduction and the conclusion in your outline.

This is what a formal outline may look like:

Thesis statement
    I. First major point of support
       A. First piece of evidence for first point of support
          1. First point of discussion, reason, or example
             a. First specific illustration or detail
             b. Second specific illustration or detail (and so on)
          2. Second point of discussion, reason, or example (and so on)
       B. Second piece of evidence for first point of support

      1. First point of discussion, reason, or example

      2. Second point of discussion, reason, or example

      3. Third point of discussion, reason, or example (and so on)

  II. Second major point of support

    A. First piece of evidence for second point of support (and so on)

The student who worked with the group on brainstorming (**3c**) and made the scratch outline shown on page 52 finally settled on a thesis and made this formal sentence outline of his essay draft.

Thesis: A voluntary name change is usually motivated by a desire to avoid or gain recognition.

  I. The desire to avoid recognition by others is one motivation for a name change.

    A. Criminals change their names after serving a prison sentence.

    B. Writers often change their names.

      1. Women writers adopt men's names.

        a. Mary Ann Evans took on the name George Eliot.

        b. George Sand's real name was Amandine Aurore Lucie Dupin.

        c. The baroness Karen Blixen chose to write under the name Isak Dinesen.

      2. Writers adopt a pseudonym.

        a. Mark Twain's real name was Samuel Clemens.

        b. The writer of *Alice in Wonderland* was actually Charles Dodgson, but he hid behind the name Lewis Carroll.

        c. Crime novels by Amanda Cross are actually the work of a renowned scholar, Carolyn Heilbrun.

    C. People want to avoid ethnic identification.

  II. Some people change a name to join a group and gain recognition.

    A. Married women mark membership in a family.

      1. They want to indicate married status.

      2. They want to have the same name as their children.

B. Entertainers choose eye-catching names.
   1. Marilyn Monroe's given name was
      Norma Jean Baker.
   2. Woody Allen began life as Allen Stewart
      Konigsberg.
   3. Richard Starkey adopted the distinctively
      descriptive name Ringo Starr.
   4. Entertainers in the public eye often take
      extraordinary names: P. Diddy (Sean Combs) and
      Eminem (Marshall Mathers).

Making this outline allowed the student to see some shortcomings in his draft. He saw that, on the whole, his draft was basically well structured, but he noticed gaps: for instance, he needed to find out more about criminals and their aliases (Point I.A. in the outline) and about people who change a name to avoid ethnic identification (Point I.C.). He was pleased that he had used complete sentences for the main divisions of the outline because he was then able to transfer these sentences directly into his next draft.

For an outline of the MLA research paper in **52f**, see **51c**.

 TECHNOTE Using the Computer's Outline Function

Most word processing programs mark each paragraph of your draft with a symbol and mark levels of headings with a different symbol. (In Microsoft Word, go to the View menu and select Outline to see the outline view of your document.) You may find this helpful for seeing what shape your draft takes. Similarly, as you type, you can designate various levels of headings (1–9 in Word), and your program can format each heading for you. You can also print out an outline showing whichever levels of headings you select. ◼

 EXERCISE 3.20 Write a scratch outline and a formal outline. Choose one of the thesis statements you wrote in Exercise 3.16 or 3.17 on page 48, and write a scratch outline. Bring your outline to class and, as a group, select one scratch outline to develop together into a formal outline.

 EXERCISE 3.21 Write a formal outline for an essay assignment. Write a formal outline for an essay assignment you are currently working on. Alternatively, write a formal outline for a topic you are interested in using for your next essay assignment.

4 Drafting, Revising, and Editing an Essay

The opportunity to write drafts means the opportunity to take your time to get it right. You can keep early drafts of an important document for your critical eyes alone or you can ask friends and colleagues to offer their responses. Provided that you allow yourself enough time (a big "provided that," as we all know), you never have to give your documents to readers until you feel ready. Drafting is a crucial part of the writing process, allowing you to develop and refine your ideas.

Revising—making changes to improve a piece of writing—is another essential part of the writing process. It is not a punishment inflicted on inexperienced writers. Good finished products are the result of careful revision. Even Leo Tolstoy, author of the monumental Russian novel *War and Peace,* commented: "I cannot understand how anyone can write without rewriting everything over and over again."

As you revise and edit, you will address both "big-picture" and "little-picture" concerns. Big-picture revising involves making changes in content and organization. When you revise, you may add or delete details, sections, or paragraphs; alter your thesis statement; vary or strengthen your use of transitions; move material from one position to another; and improve clarity, logic, flow, and style. Little-picture editing involves making adjustments to improve sentence variety; vary sentence length; and correct errors in grammar, spelling, word choice, mechanics, and punctuation. Both are necessary, but most people like to focus first on the big picture and then turn to fixing up the details.

4a Tips for writing drafts

Writing provides what speech can never provide: the opportunity to revise your ideas and the way you present them without your audience's realization. The drafting process lets you make substantive changes as you progress through drafts. You can add, delete, and reorganize sections of your paper. You can rethink your thesis and support. You can change your approach to parts or all of the paper. Writing drafts allows you to work on a piece of writing until you feel you have made it meet your goals.

KEY POINTS

Tips for Drafts

1. Set a schedule. First set the deadline date; then, working backwards, establish dates for completing drafts and getting feedback. See **2e** and **47c** for sample schedules.

2. Don't automatically begin at the beginning. Begin by writing the essay parts for which you already have some specific material.

3. Write in increments of twenty to thirty minutes to take advantage of momentum.

4. Write your first draft as quickly and fluently as you can. Write notes to yourself in capitals or surrounded by asterisks to remind yourself to add or change something or do further research.

5. Print out your draft triple-spaced so that you can easily write in questions, comments, and changes.

6. Keep your topic, purpose, question, and thesis very much in mind.

7. Avoid the obvious (such as "All people have feelings"). Be specific, and include interesting supporting details.

8. Revise for ideas, interest, and logic; don't merely fix errors. It is often tempting just to correct errors in spelling and grammar and see the result as a new draft. Revising entails more than that. You need to look at what you have written, check for the logic and development of each paragraph (see **5d**), imagine readers' reactions, and rethink your approach to the topic.

TECHNOTE Adding Comments to a Word Document

Some word processing programs have a Comment function that allows you to type notes that can appear only on the screen, or on the screen and in a printout. These notes—to yourself or to your instructor—can be easily deleted from later drafts. In addition, if you use a term frequently (for example, "bilingual education"), abbreviate it (as *b.e.,* for example) and use a tool like AutoCorrect to replace the whole phrase throughout your draft as you type. ∎

EXERCISE **4.1** Use the tips; set a schedule.

Before you begin your next writing assignment, reread the Key Points box "Tips for Drafts" and use all or most of its first six tips. Then discuss with classmates what you did, how it was or was not a change from the way you usually write, and how well it worked. As you work on the first tip (to set a schedule), use or adapt the following template. Mark your calendar and use these dates as you complete your next writing assignment.

SCHEDULE FOR ESSAY #____

Due Date **(month and date)**	**Activity**
Day 1 _____	Find a topic.
Day 2 _____	Brainstorm ideas.
Day 3 _____	Make scratch outline.
Day 4 _____	Write a first draft, get feedback (for example, from a tutor, study group, or classmate).
Day 5 _____	Revise and edit.
Day 6 _____	Proofread.
Day 7 _____	Format, print, and hand in.

4b Managing drafts and files

The first draft   Don't feel that a first draft has to be perfect. Allow a set period of time, and make sure that you write as quickly as you can and as much as you can to get all your ideas on the page or screen. The first draft is for your eyes only. It lets you know what you know and don't know, what you have done and need to do. It can be a jumble of ideas, but once those ideas are there for you to look at, you can sort them out and evaluate them.

Later drafts   Save all your notes and drafts until your writing is completed and the course is over. Print out a copy of each new draft so that if something happens to the disk or the computer, you still have a copy of your work. In addition, save each new draft under a new file name, just in case you want to compare versions or return to ideas in a prior draft. If you cut out substantial passages, save them in a separate file labeled "Outtakes." Then you can easily retrieve the passages if you change your mind and want to use them. Above all, do remember to make back-up copies of all your draft files. A computer virus can crash a hard drive and wipe out all your work.

Files for notes and drafts   For a five-page essay on athletic scholarships, a student kept as many as twelve computer documents in one "Athletic Scholarships Essay" folder to handle the recording of information from sources, as well as his own notes and drafts:

Athletics notes	Athletics list of sources
Athletics freewriting	Athletics downloads from Web
Athletics plan	Athletics draft 1 with comments
Athletics draft 1	Athletics notes for revision
Athletics outtakes	Athletics draft 2
Athletics outline	Athletics draft 3

Consider the file structure you will use for every essay, report, or business letter you write.

EXERCISE 4.2   Comment on file management.
The screenshot that follows shows a student's computer files listed under "Courses Fall 2002" in My Documents. How could the student set up folders to improve the organization and accessibility? What do you suggest for the names of the folders? Would you rename any of the documents? If so, which ones, and how would you rename them?

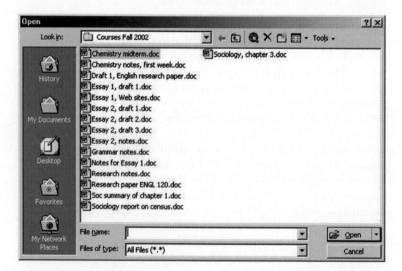

4c Analyzing and revising your drafts

For college essays and important business documents, always allow time in your writing schedule for at least a second draft—more if possible. Before writing a second draft, you need to examine a printed copy of your first draft, assess how it measures up to the assignment, evaluate it as a response to the assignment, and plan the changes you need to make. Occasionally, a few simple changes may be enough (the Band-Aid approach); more often, however, radical surgery will be necessary, in the form of cutting, rearranging, and adding—or in extreme cases, starting all over. Do any of the following to help you with your analysis.

- Create distance and space. Put a draft away for a day or two and then read it again with fresher, more critical eyes. Imagine readers' reactions to your title and your thesis.

- Highlight key words in the assignment. Mark passages in your draft that address the words. If you fail to find any, it could be a clear signal that you need to revise.

- Read your draft aloud. Mark any places where you hesitate and have to struggle to understand the point. Go back to them later. Alternatively, ask somebody else to read a copy of the draft; note where the reader hesitates or seems unclear about the meaning.

- Make an outline of what you have written (see **3i**).

KEY POINTS
Triggers for Revision

The following should alert you to consider the need for revision:

1. a weak or boring introductory paragraph (see **5f**)

2. any spot in your draft that causes a worried frown, a pause, or a thought of "Huh? Something is wrong here" as you read

3. a paragraph that never makes a point or offers support

4. a phrase, sentence, or passage that you cannot immediately and fully understand (if you have trouble grasping your own ideas, readers surely will have trouble, too)

5. excessive use of generalizations—*everyone, most people, all human beings, all students/lawyers/politicians*, and so on (better to use specific examples in their place: *the students in my political science course this semester*)

(continued)

(continued)

6. a feeling that you would have difficulty summarizing your draft (maybe it is too vague?)

7. an awareness that you have just read the same point earlier in the draft

8. a sense that you would like to turn beyond the last page in an attempt to find a definite conclusion

See **4j** for a student's annotations on her first draft.

 TECHNOTE Copy and Paste First Sentences

1. Select the first sentence of each paragraph, and use the Copy and Paste features to move the sequence of sentences into a new file. Then examine these first sentences. Do they provide a sense of logical progression of ideas? Is there any repetition? What will readers of these first sentences expect the paragraph to contain?

2. Save all new drafts and old drafts under different file names so that you can retrieve older material if you need to. If you use Microsoft Word, use the Tools/Track Changes/Compare Documents features to highlight and examine the differences between drafts. ■

 EXERCISE 4.3 Analyze a draft.

Select a paragraph from an essay you wrote earlier for this course or in another course. Read it aloud and then follow the guidelines in **4c** (p. 61) to mark places where you would consider revising. For example, you may notice a paragraph that never makes a point, an excessive use of generalizations, a vague or confusing spot, and so on. Discuss with classmates what alerted you to the places that need revising.

4d Using feedback and peer review

Sometimes, another reader can spot things that we miss, especially when we have just finished a draft and feel flush with the success of having actually finished the draft. Ask a friend, colleague, or tutor to read your draft with a critical eye and a pencil in hand, placing a checkmark next to the passages that work well and a question mark next to those that do not. Ask your reader to tell back to you what main point you made and how you supported and developed it. This process might reveal any lack of clarity or indicate gaps in the logic of your draft. Your reader does not have to be an expert English teacher to give you good feedback. If you notice worried frowns (or worse, yawns) as the person reads, you will know that something in your text is puzzling, disconcerting, or boring. Even that simple level of feedback can be valuable.

KEY POINTS
Giving Feedback to Others

1. When you are asked to give feedback to a classmate, don't think of yourself as an English teacher armed with a red pen.

2. Read for clarity and positive reactions to ideas. Look for parts that make you nod ("I agree." "I like this." "This is well done.").

3. As you read, put a light pencil mark next to one or two passages that make you pause and send you back to reread a passage.

4. Try to avoid comments that sound like accusations ("You were too vague in paragraph 3"). Instead, use "I" to emphasize your reaction as a reader ("I had a hard time visualizing the scene in paragraph 3").

Here is a sample peer response form that a classmate can use to provide you with feedback. This form is available online for downloading and printing at <http://college.hmco.com/keys.html>.

Draft by _____   Date _____
Response by _____   Date _____

1. What do you see as the writer's main point in this draft?
2. What part of the draft interests you the most? Why?
3. Where do you feel you would like more detail or explanation? Where do you need less?
4. Do you find any parts unclear, confusing, or undeveloped? Mark each spot with a pencil question mark in the margin and then write a note to the writer with questions and comments about the parts you have marked.
5. Give the writer one suggestion about one change that you think would improve the draft.

EXERCISE 4.4 Give a writer feedback.

Read the following passage written by a student. Write a response to it, using the directions in the sample peer response form in **4d**. Indicate errors with an X in the margin.

Every society has expectations of how men and women are supposed to act and what they are supposed to do. Women were wives and were expected to stay home with kids and take care of the house. The reason why women were assigned this role is biological—women give birth to babies and nurtured them. In the past, women were the caretakers. Men, on the other hand, were expected to be earners. They were often groomed in the family business. Their role was to work and financially provide for their family. Also, since men were generally financially and physically stronger than women, they became dominant and women subordinate. But the changing roles of women since the women's revolution movement has challenged these traditional notions.

4e Writing and revising collaboratively

Writing, as well as providing feedback, is not necessarily a solitary process. In the academic or business world, you might be expected to work in formal collaborative structures. Groups, teams, or committees might be formed to draft a proposal or report, or you might be expected to produce documents reflecting the consensus of your section or group. You will always want to be sure, however, that you work collaboratively only when doing so is expected. An instructor who assigns an essay may not expect or want you to work on it with anyone else.

In such group settings, make sure that you work out a way for every member of the group to contribute. You can do this by assigning each person a set of specific tasks, such as making lists of ideas, drafting, analyzing the draft, revising, editing, assembling visuals, and preparing the final document. Schedule regular meetings, and expect everyone to come with a completed written assignment. Build on strengths within the group. For example, for a business report, ask the member skilled in document design and computer graphics to prepare the visual features of the final document (**10**).

TechNote Working Collaboratively on the Computer

In networked computer labs, in distance-learning courses, and in the business world, writing collaboratively is often encouraged—and certainly the technology makes it easy. One person can post an idea or a draft and invite response; or participants can work together on an outline, research, drafting, and editing, with assigned roles. Then all the results and drafts can be posted online, with feedback from peers, the instructor, or the project leader.

Microsoft Word provides useful tools for such collaboration. Click on Tools and then Revisions or Track Changes. You can work on a text, show additions and deletions, highlight changes (see **10c**), and attach the revised text to an e-mail message to a classmate or colleague, who can then click to Accept or Reject the changes and compare the original with the revised version (using the Compare Documents feature). ■

4f Working on a title

You probably have in mind a useful working title as you write, but after you finish writing, brainstorm several titles and pick the one you like best. If titles occur to you as you write, make a note of them. A good title captures readers' attention, makes readers want to read on, and lets readers know what to expect in the essay.

Pay attention to the mechanics of a title. Do not italicize or underline your title, and do not enclose it in quotation marks unless your title is a quotation from a source. Capitalize all words except the following: prepositions (such as *in, on, of, for, with, without*), articles (*a, an, the*), coordinating conjunctions (*and, but, or, nor, so, for, yet*), and *to* in an infinitive phrase (*to laugh*). But capitalize those words if they occur at the beginning of the title or subtitle (after a colon).

WORKING TITLE	**Problems in the Fashion Industry**
REVISED TITLE	**Thin and Thinner: How the Fashion Industry Denigrates Women**
WORKING TITLE	**The Benefits of Travel**
REVISED TITLE	**From Katmandu to Kuala Lumpur: A Real Education**

Let your title stand separately from your essay. Do not assume that readers know what your title is when you begin your essay. In the following example, the writer makes the first sentence refer to the title:

```
What "The Red Convertible" Tells Us about War
    This story by Louise Erdrich tells us about a lot
more than simply two brothers and their car.
```

She then revised the first sentence:

```
What "The Red Convertible" Tells Us about War
    We learn about a lot more than the story of two
brothers and their car from Louise Erdrich's atmospheric
short story "The Red Convertible."
```

EXERCISE 4.5 Select a title.
From each of the following pairs of essay titles, choose the title that you think would be more effective. Explain the reasons for your choice.

1. (a) E-mails vs. Letter Writing
   (b) Reviving the Lost Art of Letter Writing in E-mails
2. (a) Chronic Fatigue Syndrome
   (b) Chronic Fatigue Syndrome: Misunderstood and Misdiagnosed?
3. (a) Romance and Lawlessness: America's Fascination with Bonnie and Clyde
   (b) The Romantic Outlaws Named Bonnie and Clyde
4. (a) The Many Practical Uses of Fractions and Percents
   (b) The Benefits of Math
5. (a) Dangerous Music for the Mind
   (b) Rap Music Lyrics: Misogyny in the Name of Art

4g Overcoming writer's block

Most writers, however much they write or even profess to like writing, have at one time or another felt a dreaded block. They sit and stare at the blank screen and then, often, take trips to the refrigerator for comfort. So it is quite likely that on occasion you will feel overwhelmed with the task of organizing your research findings or frustrated because your writing doesn't seem to "sound right." If so, consider these questions and try the strategies.

KEY POINTS

Overcoming Writer's Block

1. Do you have a set of rules that you follow in your writing process, such as "Always begin by writing a good introduction" or "Always have a complete outline before starting to write"? If you do, consider whether your rules are too rigid or even unhelpful. As you gather ideas and do your preparatory drafting, ignore any self-imposed rules that hinder you.

2. Do you edit as soon as you write, and do you edit often? Your desire to write correctly might be preventing you from thinking about ideas and moving forward. Try journal writing, freewriting, brainstorming, or mapping (**3a–3c**).

3. Do you feel anxious about writing, even though you have knowledge of and interest in your topic? Try using some freewriting and brainstorming strategies (**3b, 3c**) or begin writing as if you were talking about your topic with a friend.

4. Do you feel that you do not yet know enough about your topic to start writing, even though you may have done a great deal of research? Try freewriting or try drafting the sections you know most about. Writing will help show you what you know and what you need to know.

If you sit down to a writing task close to the deadline without having done the necessary preliminary work—reading, interpreting, taking notes, and generating ideas—you probably are suffering not from writer's block but from lack of preparation. To be prepared adequately, take time, apply yourself to the task, and use any available print or online tools that can help you write, revise, and edit.

4h Using computer tools (and knowing their limitations)

Your word processor comes with useful tools to help you with editing and proofreading, but they have definite limitations. Electronic checking programs are only as good as their creators, and language is so complex that the programs cannot begin to approximate the power of the human brain.

Thesaurus feature   The thesaurus feature is useful especially when you are writing a second draft and notice too much repetition of a word. In Microsoft Word, go to Tools/Language and then to Thesaurus. When you click on a word or expression, you will be prompted with synonyms and words close in meaning to the one you have highlighted. Before you use a recommended word, however, always check it in a dictionary to discover its nuances of meaning and its patterns of use. One of the options proposed as a substitute for *recommended* in the previous sentence is *suggested,* which would fit. Other suggested words are *optional* and *not compulsory,* which would not fit into the meaning or structure of the sentence. You must always consider the context when you use a thesaurus. See also **39b.**

Spelling-check feature   Spelling-check programs are a boon, helping us catch and correct spelling errors we might otherwise miss. Always run the spelling checker in your word processor to check on spelling throughout your draft. The program will flag any word it does not recognize from its own dictionary. You then have the opportunity to look the word up in the dictionary or try it several ways until the program indicates you have gotten it right. The program may also automatically correct certain typographical or preentered common spelling errors, such as substituting *responsibility* if you happen to type *responsability.*

Be warned, however: the dictionaries of many spelling checkers are incomplete, and therefore you cannot rely on them to find and solve all spelling problems. In addition, a spelling checker will not identify grammatical errors that affect only spelling, such as missing plural or *-ed* endings. Nor will it find any omitted word or a misspelled word that forms another word such as *then* (for *than*), *their* (for *there*), *form* (for *from*), *coarse* (for *course*), or *affect* (for *effect*). Give your drafts a careful proofreading, independent of the spelling checker, and, if possible, have a peer reviewer do so as well.

Grammar-check feature   A grammar-check program, such as MLA Editor or the programs attached to Microsoft Word and Corel WordPerfect, is supposed to analyze your sentences and make suggestions about what might need to be fixed, tightened, or polished. It provides a few helpful observations about simple mechanical matters, such as pointing out that commas and periods need to go inside quotation marks or that quotation marks have not been closed, drawing attention to passive verbs, labeling clichés, or indicating a problem with an easily identifiable error such as "Can the mayor wins?"

It may be worth activating a grammar-check program to catch these basic errors. But be aware that grammar-check programs cannot take content and varied syntax into account, so their capabilities are limited. Some errors they cannot recognize because they do not "understand" the context. For example, if you wrote "The actors were boring" but meant to write "The actors were bored," grammar-check programs would not reveal your mistake.

It pays to exercise extreme caution. A *New York Times* article by John Markoff on 15 April 2002 notes that "Word 2000's grammar checker was unable to identify any of the most common errors." Even more damning is the comment that a writer who once worked on trying to improve Word for writers and editors "could not recall a single instance in which he accepted the advice of Word's grammar checker." The article cites Dr. Bruce Wampler, a computer scientist who programmed Grammatik, as saying that "the grammar checker you get today in Word is not significantly better than the grammar checker you might have used almost ten years ago."

Because of these problems, many writers—including the author of this handbook—deactivate the grammar-check feature while writing because its constant reminders not only interrupt their train of thought but are often wrong.

 ESL NOTE   Caution with a Grammar-Check Program

Never make a suggested change in your draft before verifying that the change is really necessary. A student from Ukraine wrote the grammatically acceptable sentence "What he has is pride." Then, at the suggestion of a grammar-check program, he changed the sentence to "What he has been pride." The program had not recognized the sequence "has is," but had pointed out that *has* needs to be followed by *been*. This, of course, is generally true, but once again, electronic devices can't take context and meaning into account. Don't let computer programs weaken your confidence in your own judgment and grammatical expertise.

Find feature   Often more useful than a grammar-check program is the Edit/Find feature on your computer. Use it to search for problem areas throughout your document, such as the *its/it's* or *then/than* confusion. You can also use this feature to search for quotation marks

—in order to make sure that each quotation has quotation marks at both beginning and end—or to find and delete "filler words" like *really* and *very*.

Word count feature   One tool that you can count on as being both accurate and useful is the Word Count tool (see also **10c**). This feature lets you know how many words your document contains, useful information when you have a length limit. Beware, however, of using it too often in a desperate attempt to reach a prescribed number of words. Your writing will seem padded. Instead, concentrate on the ideas and content that you are conveying, keeping a rough sense of how many pages you have available. (Estimate that a double-spaced page will contain about 250 words.) Then, once you have finished a draft, do the word count and expand or cut as necessary as you prepare your next draft.

For ways to use word processing software and other tools for formatting documents for college, online, or work presentation, see **10, 12, 14,** and **15**.

EXERCISE 4.6   Try out spelling and grammar checkers.
Type these two sentences into your word processor:

> The economists spraedsheets were more simpler then the ones there competitors have prepared. "They was prepared quickly, said the manager.

Now run the spelling and grammar checkers. What do you find, and what conclusions can you draw? In Microsoft Word, go to Tools/Options/Spelling and Grammar and click on Settings to see what Word has been set to find. Do you think you need to change any of those settings? How would *you* correct the sentences?

4i   Editing and proofreading

Even after getting as much electronic input as you can, you still need to edit and proofread your final draft to make sure no errors remain. Examine your draft for grammar, punctuation, and spelling errors not caught by your word processor's checking programs. Often, reading your essay aloud will help you find sentences that are tangled, poorly constructed, or not connected. Looking carefully at every word and its function in a sentence will alert you to grammatical problem areas. Turn to **16–24** for help with standard English, ten common errors, and methods for correcting errors.

As you become aware of the grammatical areas that cause you trouble, keep a list of your errors and corrections and analyze why you make these errors:

- Is your writing influenced by unedited speech?

- Do you speak a dialect and use the dialect forms in place of Standard English forms? In other words, do you use forms that sound familiar from conversations with friends?

- Do you speak a language other than English at home and do you fall back on its linguistic forms when you grapple with new subject matter and complex ideas? For examples, see **41b** ESL.

- Are you trying to take on an "academic" voice that is new to you and makes you feel insecure?

Identify what your three main problems with editing have been in the past, and for each piece of writing that you do, pay particular attention to these areas. Read the relevant sections in the handbook, do the exercises to flex your grammatical muscles, and then turn your attention to a close examination of your draft for each problem area, one at a time. Give your draft a separate reading as you check for each editing problem.

Prepare an edited draft. Familiarize yourself with common proofreading marks (inside back cover), and use them as you check this near-final draft of your document.

KEY POINTS

Proofreading Tips

Try any or all of the following strategies:

1. Do not try to proofread a document on the computer screen. Always print out a hard copy to make it easier to find mistakes.

2. Make an additional copy and ask a friend to read your document aloud while you note places where he or she stumbles over an error.

3. Use proofreading marks to mark typographical and other errors (see the inside back cover).

4. Put a piece of paper under the first line of your text. As you read, move it down line by line to focus your attention on one

(continued)

(continued)

line at a time. Touch each word with the end of a pencil as you either say the word aloud or mouth it silently to yourself.

5. Read the last sentence first, and work backward through your text. This strategy will not help you check for meaning, logic, pronoun reference, fragments, or consistency of verb tenses, but it will focus your attention on the spelling, punctuation, and accuracy of one sentence at a time.

6. Put your manuscript away for a day or two after you have finished it. Proofread it when the content is not so familiar.

EXERCISE 4.7 Mark up a passage with correction marks.
Proofread this paragraph for the writer who drafted it. Use correction marks (inside back cover) to indicate any problems or errors.

Insomnia is a sleep disorder that effects millions of people. Often they turn to over-the-counter pills to relieve their insomnea. Medication, especially self-medication, should not be the first course of action.   Patients should seek the advice of there physician. However, before taking any medication, they should seriously consider other options lifestyle changes can help including cutting back on caffeinated beverages, drinking herbal tea such as chamomile, reading a pleasant book, and writing a "to do" list before they go to bed.

EXERCISE 4.8 Edit your own writing.
Proofread carefully one of your recent first drafts. Look for grammar, punctuation, and spelling errors, as well as poorly constructed sentences (see the advice in **4i**).

4j A student's drafts

Elena Tate was assigned an essay on the topic of "communicating in a multilingual city." The instructor asked for a thesis supported by personal experience. Tate's first draft was an account of her own experiences with learning and using Spanish. She put her draft aside for a while and then, with feedback from classmates, turned her attention to reevaluating it and using her experiences to make a claim and present a thesis. She marked places where editing was needed and wrote comments to guide her revision. Here is her first draft, annotated with her comments after a peer review session.

Multilingual Communication *Find better title.*

Move to end

I always thought that language was one of the most decisive divisions between people. But after learning Spanish and using it in school and at work I see now that studying the gramatical structure of a new language is not nearly as hard as trying to understand someone who leads an entirely different life.

m (insert)

Add new intro and thesis.

I am what one might consider a voluntary bilingual. I could very well have turned out completely monolingual in the dominant language of the United States, like the majority of the United States population; among them, my entire family. Though I did come into contact with speakers of Haitian Creyole and Spanish starting at an early age, I grew up knowing only English in Cambridge, Massachusetts. I was like nearly every other kid who went through the mandatory two-year Spanish instruction program at my public elementary school, I could have forgotten even the little bit that I learned the summer after eighth grade. But I didn't. Now, attending Hunter College in New York City, one of the most multilingual cities in the world, I am proud to consider myself to be bilingual.

fragment

check sp.

Compare to other places.

comma splice

Big jump in time

wordy

I don't pretend to have near native control of two languages, but I can understand, speak, read, and even write well in a language other than my mother tongue and more importantly, I speak both languages for large parts of each day.

Cut? Off topic?

I didn't learn another language during childhood, as it was perfectly acceptable to only speak English. I was taught to value other cultures and to hold them in high esteem as I held my own. I decided to learn another language, because this is the only way you can understand how other people experience life and you can learn from your experiences.

Choppy sentences— make connections

as

Fix pronouns.

A Spanish teacher I had in high school was the first person to really inspire me to do the hard work necessary to really learn Spanish. He made me a promise: "If you can learn Spanish, you will be able to find work easier than if you only know English, and you will form beautiful friendships." At least for me, this worked. I did my homework and tried to absorb his lessons. But something was missing. I had nowhere to really use my Spanish, so it stuck somewhere between the past tense and the subjunctive.

More about him. Connect to class discussions of motivation?

Better word?

Good. Keep this.

The next year, still in high school in Cambridge,
I decided to take a Spanish literature class and a U.S.
history class in the bilingual department. These
courses were taught entirely in Spanish. They were
meant for Hispanic students still learning English.
Anglo students who showed interest and ability were
allowed to enroll as well. It was then that I
understood what the political catchword "immersion"
really meant. Luckily, it was one of the best
experiences I have ever had. I was under no pressure
to replace or reduce my first language, and a language
and a positive self-concept have resulted from my
study of a second language. I can see how it would
have been one of the most traumatic experiences of my
life if I would have been in the opposite situation —
if, instead of embarking on a journey to learn a new
language, I was taking my first steps toward
forgetting my native language.

had (inserted above "would have")

> *Too choppy.*
> *Combine?*

> *Give details.*

> *Delete - this goes beyond the topic of communication.*

Spanish is also linked in my mind to the
real-world work experience. Once I worked at
the Bush terminal industrial complex in Sunset Park,
where thousands of (predominantly) Spanish-speaking
workers produce clothing. I worked there over the
summer to have the experience of a job in
manufacturing. I wanted to know where the products I
buy and use come from and to get a sense of what life
is like for the people who produce them. The garment
industry of Brooklyn employs women and men of all ages.
Many feel that they had those jobs because they have
limited English proficiency. Spanish was definitely the
prevailing language on the job. Even the bosses spoke
or shouted to everyone in their Russian-accented
Spanish. Co-workers of mine listened to English tapes
as they sewed, one attending English classes every
evening after the ten-hour workday. Many felt that
learning English would be their ticket to a more
humane job.

> *Add details.*

> *Make connection with communication, the essay topic*

> *Make smoother & give details.*

> *Verb tenses!*

> *Repetition of word job*

Of course, no one could understand why I was
working there. "You speak English! You're
American! You could be working at a clothing
store! Or a waitress!" they would exclaim. Lots of
my co-workers had never carried on a conversation in

> *Keep direct quotation. It works.*
>
> *Many*

English. One girl who taught me how to use the button-hole machine got the giggles when I spoke to her in English. They all understood that it was the language ~~But?~~ to know if you wanted to advance in the United States. ¶The segregation that takes place, however, is a question that goes much deeper than language. It is a question of class, of ethnicity, of legal status. Even though I could speak to my coworkers in their native language, there was still so much I couldn't understand.

Need better conclusion in separate paragraph.

Tate then took her annotated draft and the notes she had taken during a group peer session in class and during a conference with her instructor and wrote the following revised and expanded draft.

Beyond Language

Thesis

Living in a multilingual city has proven to me that communication can be reached among people who speak different languages. But a multilingual experience also shows that even among people speaking the same language, the ability to communicate may be hindered by deeper rifts, including class and culture. One's native language is simply not the single most important consideration when it comes to relating to people.

The importance of early attitudes to language

I am what one might consider a voluntary bilingual. I could very well have turned out completely monolingual in the dominant language of the United States, like the majority of the U.S. population, among them my entire family. Though I did come into contact with other languages starting at an early age, I never learned a word of anything besides English. It was perfectly acceptable to be monolingual (in English, of course) in Cambridge, Massachusetts, as it is throughout the United States, in contrast to parts of Africa, the Middle East, and Europe, where bilingualism is seen as positive and necessary. Luckily, I did pick up the attitude that to come in contact with other languages and the cultures they reflected would expand my conception of humanity and the world.

I managed to hold on to the little Spanish I gained during the mandatory two-year program at my public elementary school, though I still had no real incentive to know Spanish. Nearly every other student in my class forgot everything the summer after eighth grade. A teacher I had in high school was the first person to inspire me to do the hard work necessary to really learn Spanish. Brent, as we called him, used a lure to focus his unmotivated class. He cleverly incorporated the two pillars of language-learning motivation, the instrumental and integrative, in a single promise: "If you can learn Spanish, you will be able to find work easier than if you know only English, and you will form beautiful friendships."

The importance of language instruction

At least for me, this worked. I did my homework and tried to absorb his lessons. But something was missing. I had nowhere to put my Spanish into practice, and so it stagnated somewhere between the past tense and the subjunctive. The next year, while still in high school in Cambridge, I decided to take a Spanish literature class and a U.S. history class in the bilingual department. These courses, taught entirely in Spanish, were meant for students with nascent English ability, but Anglo students who showed interest and ability were allowed to enroll as well. It was then that I got my first sense of what it means to be the only one in the room who is not fluent in the language being spoken and in the position of having to communicate in an unfamiliar language. It was then that I understood what the political catchword "immersion" really meant. Luckily, it was one of the best experiences I have ever had.

Advantages of having to communicate in a classroom

For one exhausting hour each day I had to pay perfect attention to each word or else quickly become confused and not understand again until the topic was changed and I could start over. I had to decipher a Madrid lisp, a Puerto Rican Spanish devoid of the -*s* sound, and a somersaulting Chilean accent. On top of all that, I actually had to participate and face a grade for my efforts.

However, classrooms are still far from the real world of work. That initial appreciation of language and culture fueled my decision to get a job as a sewing machine operator in Brooklyn's garment industry over the summer. I wanted to get a sense of what it was like to use a language in everyday life, to work in

Language and communication in the real world of work

mnaufacturing, to know who it was who powered the U.S. economy and produced the clothing that I wear every day. I knew that conditions in the plants were bad, and I knew that the work force was composed almost entirely of immigrant workers. I figured that since my Spanish was good, I would be able to get along on the job and get to know some of my coworkers. But it turned out that the language barrier was the least of the barriers between us.

Every morning, I would wake up and board the B35 bus to another world. At the Bush Terminal industrial complex in Sunset Park, thousands of women from Mexico, Ecuador, and other countries produce countless articles of clothing each day. Workers in their teens to their late sixties often work in nonunion shops and are paid "piece rate," which in my factory was three cents a shirt label, far from any legislated "minimum wage." Many feel that their options are restricted because of their low level of English proficiency. Spanish was the prevailing language. Even the bosses spoke or shouted to everyone in their Russian-accented Spanish. However, several of my coworkers listened to English tapes as they sewed. One attended English classes every evening after the ten-hour workday. They all felt that learning English would be their ticket to a more humane job.

Connections between English proficiency and opportunity

Of course, no one could understand why I was working there. "You speak English! You're American! You could be working at a clothing store! Or as a waitress!" they would exclaim. Lots of my coworkers had never carried on a conversation in English. One girl who taught me how to use the buttonhole machine would get the giggles when I spoke to her in English. But they all understood it is the language to know if you want to advance in the United States.

What is more important than language

The segregation that takes place, however, in the workplace and in society at large is a question that goes much deeper than language. It is a question of class, of ethnicity, of legal status. Just by virtue of who I was, of where I had been born, questions that had never even crossed my mind plagued the lives of my coworkers. I didn't know what it was like to leave my native land and not know when I would ever be able to return. I didn't

```
know what it was like to limp for months because I had a
pain in my leg that went untreated. In fact, I had to
quit my first garment job to go back to Boston to see my
doctor, still covered by my mother's health insurance. And
when the boss refused to pay anyone in my area the last
payday before the end of the month, I knew I had
somewhere to turn so that I could pay my rent.
```

```
    I had always thought that language was one of the
most decisive divisions between people. But after
learning a second language, Spanish, and using it in the
different contexts of school and work, it has become
clear to me that studying the grammatical structure of a
new language is not nearly as hard as trying to
understand someone who leads an entirely different life,
whose socioeconomic background differs dramatically from
one's own. There are barriers and bonds beyond language
that separate and connect people much more profoundly. A
truly multicultural society needs to pay attention not
only to language education but also to societal reforms
that begin to break down the barriers of inequality.
```

Conclusion

Recapitulation
of essay and
of thesis

Ends with a
recommendation

 EXERCISE 4.9 Evaluate drafts.
Discuss with classmates the changes Tate made in her second draft.
In what ways has she improved on her first draft? Are there further
changes you would suggest if she were going to write a third draft?

5 Developing and Structuring Paragraphs

It is not hard to signal the beginning of a new paragraph: indent the
beginning of its first sentence five spaces from the left margin or, in
business and online documents, add a blank line. However, a good
paragraph needs more than the mark of indentation or a blank line
above and below it. In the body of an academic essay, a new paragraph should signal a progression in your ideas.

5a Writing a paragraph: the basics

A good paragraph advances your argument, supports your thesis, and
has internal unity. It does not drift in a vague, unfocused way.
Collectively, paragraphs are the building blocks of a piece of writing and

should be shaped and arranged with care. They are, as Stephen King calls them, "maps of intent," letting readers know where you are heading.

Body paragraphs in an essay How do you know when to begin a new paragraph? Use these three points as a guide.

- Begin a new paragraph to introduce a new point in support of your thesis.
- Use a new paragraph to expand on a point already made by offering a further example or evidence.
- Use a paragraph to break up a long discussion or description into manageable chunks that readers can assimilate.

Therefore, both logic and aesthetics dictate when it is time to begin a new paragraph. Think of a paragraph as something that gathers together in one place ideas that connect to each other and to the main purpose announced in the piece of writing.

KEY POINTS

Paragraph Basics

A good paragraph in the body of an academic essay should contain the following:

- one clearly discernible main idea, either explicitly stated (in a topic sentence) or implied clearly in the content of the paragraph, with that idea clearly related to the thesis of the essay
- development and support of its main idea with examples, reasons, definitions, and so on
- unity of content, with no extraneous ideas or asides intruding or interrupting readers' attention to the main idea
- coherence—that is, a logical flow of ideas from one sentence to the next, with the relationships between ideas clearly indicated.

See **5b–5e** for more on these features.

Transitional paragraphs Some paragraphs have more to do with function than with content. They serve to take readers from one point to another, making a connection and offering a smooth transition from one idea to the next. These *transitional paragraphs* are often short.

In her autobiography, *Dust Tracks on a Road*, Zora Neale Hurston tells about meeting the man she fell in love with. One paragraph is devoted to describing how she "made a parachute jump" into love, admiring his intellect, strength, good looks, and manly resolution. The next paragraph provides a transition to the story of how they met:

> To illustrate the point, I got into trouble with him for trying to loan him a quarter. It came about this way.

For introductory and concluding paragraphs, see **5f.**

EXERCISE 5.1   Insert paragraph breaks.
Read the following passages and mark where you think the writers should have inserted a paragraph break. Explain your reasons. For example, does the new paragraph introduce a new point, expand on a point, or break up a long discussion or description into manageable material?

1. (1) Skill in reading is like skill in chess in many respects. (2) Good reading, like good chess, requires rapid deployment of schemata that have already been acquired and do not have to be worked out on the spot. (3) Good readers, like good chess players, quickly recognize typical patterns, and, since they can ignore many small-scale features of the text, they have space in short-term memory to take in an overall structure of meaning. (4) They are able to do all of this because, like expert chess players, they have ready access to a large number of relevant schemata. (5) By contrast, unskilled readers lack this large store of relevant schemata and must therefore work out many small-scale meaning relationships while they are reading. (6) These demanding tasks quickly overload their short-term memories, making their performance slow, arduous, and ineffective. (7) How large is the "large number of schemata" that skilled persons have acquired? (8) It has been estimated that a chess master can recognize about 50,000 positional patterns. (9) Interestingly, that is the approximate number of words and idioms in the vocabulary of a literate person.

—E. D. Hirsch, Jr., *Cultural Literacy*

2. (1) I was twenty-two. (2) I was studying at the School of Fine Arts in Madrid. (3) The desire constantly, systematically and at any cost to do just the opposite of what everybody else did pushed me to extravagances that soon became notorious in artistic circles. (4) In painting class we had the assignment to

paint a Gothic statue of the Virgin directly from a model. (5) Before going out the professor had repeatedly emphasized that we were to paint exactly what we "saw." (6) Immediately, in a dizzy frenzy of mystification, I went to work furtively painting, in the minutest detail, a pair of scales which I copied out of a catalogue. (7) This time they really believed I was mad. (8) At the end of the week the professor came to correct and comment on the progress of our work. (9) He stopped in frozen silence before the picture of my scales, while all the students gathered around us. (10) "Perhaps you see a Virgin like everyone else," I ventured, in a timid voice that was not without firmness. (11) "But I see a pair of scales."

—Salvador Dalí, *The Secret Life of Salvador Dalí*

5b Formulating a topic sentence

When you begin to write or revise a paragraph in an essay, keep in mind what the focus of the paragraph will be and how it will support your thesis. Imagine readers asking you, "What point are you making in this paragraph, and how does it relate to your thesis?" Write a sentence that makes a clear supporting point. You can include such a sentence (known as a *topic sentence*) to guide both the writing and the reading of the paragraph. Here are questions for you to consider:

- What point do you want to make in a paragraph? Make sure the main idea is clear. Readers should be able to discern the point you want to make in a far more specific way than just noting that the paragraph is "about" a topic.

- Are you going to express that point in an actual topic sentence, or do you expect readers to infer the point from the details you provide? In academic writing, it is a common convention to express the point clearly in one sentence within the paragraph. Including such a topic sentence will help you stick to your point and limit a paragraph to discussion of that point. It will also be easy for readers to grasp.

- If you include a topic sentence, where will you position it in the paragraph? In academic writing, a topic sentence frequently begins a paragraph, letting readers know what to expect. Sometimes, though, a writer will prefer to lead up to the statement of the main idea and place it at the end of the paragraph.

KEY POINTS

Placement or Inclusion of a Topic Sentence

1. *Topic sentence at the beginning* If you state the main idea in the opening sentence, readers will then expect the rest of the paragraph to consist of specific details that illustrate and support that topic sentence. This is known as *deductive organization* (for an example, see the first paragraph example in **5d,** item 1).

2. *Topic sentence at the end* You may prefer to begin with details and examples and draw more general conclusions from them in a topic sentence expressed at the end of the paragraph. This strategy is useful for building up to a climax and driving home the point you want to make. This is known as *inductive organization* (for an example, see the paragraph in **5d,** item 3).

3. *Topic sentence implied* It may suit your content and purpose better to not state the main idea explicitly in a topic sentence but to use details vivid enough that readers can easily infer the main point you are making. Do this if your specific details are vivid and lead to an indisputable conclusion.

EXERCISE 5.2 Identify topic sentences in paragraphs using different patterns of organization.
Read the following paragraphs. Then underline the topic sentences and determine the pattern of organization (deductive, inductive, topic sentence implied).

1. Lisa wrote a list of all items they needed. She then went to the store, purchased essentials, and upon returning, packed the overnight bags for the family weekend getaway trip to upstate New York in the Catskills. Her husband Charlie confirmed the reservations at the resort and wrote down the directions. Their son Dave, who had recently received his driver's license, got the car washed and filled the tank with regular unleaded gas. Everyone in the family pitched in. Teamwork is essential in planning a trip.

Pattern of paragraph organization: _____

2. On Wednesday, I ran for a bus and made it. The dentist said I had no cavities. The phone was ringing when I arrived home and even after I dropped my key a couple of times, I answered

it and they were still on the line. The Avon lady refused me service saying I didn't need her as I already looked terrific. My husband asked me what kind of a day I had and didn't leave the room when I started to answer.

—Erma Bombeck, *If Life Is a Bowl of Cherries,*
What Am I Doing in the Pits?

Pattern of paragraph organization: _____

3. There are only three ways to make money. One is to go out and work for it. However, few among us can work forever, and there will likely come a time in our lives when working for a paycheck may not be an option. The second way to make money is to inherit it or to win the lottery. Again, not something we all can count on. The third way, and the only one that is available to all of us for an unlimited amount of time, is to invest what we earn during our working years wisely, so that the money we work so hard for goes to work for us.

—Suze Orman, *The Courage to Be Rich*

Pattern of paragraph organization: _____

5c Writing a unified paragraph

When you write a body paragraph in an essay, you should be able to finish these two following sentences about it without hesitation—and so should your readers:

1. The paragraph is about . . . (What is the topic of the paragraph?)
2. The stated or implied topic sentence of this paragraph is . . . (What is the one main idea the paragraph expresses?)

You should also be able to look at a well-organized expository paragraph and note that the paragraph is unified—that is, that it contains only material that develops and supports the point of the paragraph.

In academic writing, a unified paragraph mirrors the structure of the whole essay: it includes one main idea that the rest of the piece of writing (paragraph or essay) explains, supports, and develops. When you write a paragraph, imagine a reader saying, "Look, I don't have time to read all this. Just tell me in one sentence (or two) what point you are making here." Your reply would express your main point. Each paragraph in an academic essay generally contains a controlling idea expressed in one or two sentences, and all the other sentences in the paragraph relate to and develop and explain that controlling idea. It does not digress or switch topics in midstream. Its content is unified.

The following paragraph is indeed devoted to one topic—tennis—and the first sentence makes a promise to discuss the *trouble* the *backhand* causes *average* players (the key words are italicized). Some of the sentences in the paragraph do discuss that, but in the middle the writer, while still writing about tennis, loses sight of the announced focus in the topic sentence.

> The backhand in tennis causes average weekend players more trouble than other strokes. Even though the swing is natural and free flowing, many players feel intimidated and try to avoid it. Venus Williams, however, has a great backhand and she often wins difficult points with it. Her serve is a powerful weapon, too. When faced by a backhand coming at them across the net, mid-level players can't seem to get their feet and body in the best position. They tend to run around the ball or forget the swing and give the ball a little poke, praying that it will not only reach but also go over the net.

What is Grand Slam winner Venus Williams doing in a paragraph about average players? What relevance does her powerful serve have to the average player's problems with a backhand? The passage can be effectively revised by cutting out the two sentences about Venus Williams.

In academic essays, a paragraph in support of your essay's thesis will usually be unified and focused on one clear topic, whether or not you state it explicitly in one sentence.

EXERCISE 5.3 Consider what to include in a unified paragraph. A student wrote the following topic sentence and brainstorming notes. Which ideas from the brainstorming notes can the student use and develop to write a unified paragraph?

TOPIC SENTENCE

Teenagers who work after school learn valuable lessons: the power and pleasure of earning money, the challenge of budgeting money, and the amount of hard work that goes into earning a dollar.

BRAINSTORMING NOTES

plan	save
budget	not interfere with studies

look ahead	still have social life
think about necessity	be responsible
waste	get to work on time
balance	independence
enjoy self	

5d Developing paragraphs and essays

Whether you are writing a paragraph or an essay, you will do well to keep in mind the image of skeptical readers always inclined to say something challenging, such as "Why on earth do you think that?" or "What could possibly lead you to that conclusion?" You have to show readers that your claim is well founded and supported by experience, knowledge, logical arguments, the work of experts, or reasoned examples. In addition, try to engage readers and provide vital, unique details. This section shows how some writers have used specific details to develop and support the thesis of an essay or the topic sentence (stated or implied) of a paragraph.

The following passages show a range of possibilities. While some writers may choose to use only one method of development in a paragraph (all statistics or all examples, for instance), others may combine methods to make their point in a varied and effective way. In fact, many published nonfiction writers write perfectly clear and acceptable paragraphs containing several methods of development, often with no explicit topic sentence, and sometimes even with more than one main idea.

However, the rule of thumb that has emerged for traditional academic writing is "One main idea per paragraph, with one method of development." Take that for what it is—a helpful guide rather than a straitjacket. Remember, though, that it is your purpose and your content that will determine your approach to your methods of development. Use the following examples to assess how the approach fits each writer's purpose and material and to examine the focus, development, unity, and coherence of the ideas in each passage. Think about which techniques you as a reader find most clear, helpful, and engaging.

1. Giving examples Using examples to develop and support an idea is a common paragraph technique, useful in many types of writing. The following paragraph is from a scientific work. Beginning with a claim in the form of a generalization and supporting it with specific illustrative details (known as *deductive organization*) is a common method of organizing a paragraph. The topic sentence announces the controlling idea: "Ant queens [. . .] enjoy exceptionally long lives." The authors could have stopped there, expecting us to assume that they are right. We might wonder, however, what "exceptionally long" means about the life of an ant. A month? A year? Seven years? The authors anticipate readers' questions by developing and supporting the controlling idea with five examples, which they organize to build to a convincing climax.

> Ant queens, hidden in the fastness of well-built nests and protected by zealous daughters, enjoy exceptionally long lives. Barring accidents, those of most species last 5 years or longer. A few exceed in natural longevity anything known in the millions of species of other insects, including even the legendary 17-year-old cicadas. One mother queen of an Australian carpenter ant kept in a laboratory nest flourished for 23 years, producing thousands of offspring before she faltered in her reproduction and died, apparently of old age. Several queens of *Lasius flavus*, the little yellow mound-building ant of European meadows, have lived 18 to 22 years in captivity. The world record for ants, and hence for insects generally, is held by a queen of *Lasius niger,* the European black sidewalk ant, which also lives in forests. Lovingly attended in a laboratory nest by a Swiss entomologist, she lasted 29 years.
>
> —Bert Hölldobler and Edward O. Wilson, *Journey to the Ants*

The next passage, also from a scientific work, begins with the assertion that chimps and human beings have vast differences, but it then questions that assertion, provides examples of similarities, and leads up to a powerful generalization that sums up all the details. The organizational pattern that begins with specific details and examples and uses them to arrive at a generalization is known as *inductive organization.*

> The differences between me and a chimp are immense. It is hairier, it has a different shaped head, a different shaped body, different limbs, makes different noises. There is nothing about chimpanzees that looks ninety-eight percent like me. Oh, really? Compared with what? If you took two Plasticene models of a mouse and tried to turn one into a chimpanzee, the other into a human being, most of the changes you would

make would be the same. If you took two Plasticene amoebae and turned one into a chimpanzee, the other into a human being, almost all the changes you would make would be the same. Both would need thirty-two teeth, five fingers, two eyes, four limbs and a liver. Both would need hair, dry skin, a spinal column and three little bones in the middle ear. From the perspective of an amoeba, or for that matter a fertilised egg, chimps and human beings are ninety-eight percent the same.

—Matt Ridley, *Genome*

EXERCISE 5.4 Write deductive and inductive paragraphs. Imagine that you and your friends have gone to the library to work on your research papers. Everyone is there except Mary. One of your friends remarks, "Mary needs to start working on her research paper. She can't wait until the night before." Imagine that you are all in accordance with the following statement: Mary needs to begin working on her research paper.

Write a one-paragraph deductive paragraph using supporting details that begins with the topic sentence. Be specific. Add details that indicate why Mary needs to begin working on her research paper. After you write the deductive paragraph, rewrite it as an inductive paragraph. Be sure to start with all the details and then conclude with the topic sentence.

2. Providing reasons When you make a statement of opinion, especially one that may be controversial, letting readers know the reasons for your claim makes the claim seem reasoned, thoughtful, and logical—a good start to establishing trust between you and your readers.

In the following paragraph, Web usability expert Jakob Nielsen predicts that the rate at which Web users upgrade to new versions of a browser (such as Netscape, AOL, or Microsoft Explorer) will slow down from the early years of the Web, when each week 2 percent of users would upgrade to a new browser version, say from version 4.7 to version 5.0. He uses clear markers to signal the sequence of his organizational points: First . . . , Second . . . , Third. . . .

I predict that [browser] version transitions will happen much more slowly in the future. First, the pressure to upgrade is getting weaker because many site designers now understand the need to be backwards-compatible and not require that their visitors use the latest beta releases. Second, the desire to upgrade is weakening because the older browsers are reasonably good and the usability differential between versions is less. In the early years of the Web, there were huge benefits in upgrading to a newer browser, but recent browser upgrades do not seem to have had the same level of innovative benefits. Third, and most important, the user population has changed from a pioneering group of enthusiasts to a more mainstream mass of early adopters. In the early years of the Web, people went online to be online, and collecting new browser releases became a goal in itself and a way to prove to your friends that you were on the cutting edge. Today, people go online for the sake of the content and in order to get their work done. As long as their old browser works perfectly well, they will not go to the trouble of seeking out a new version, downloading it, and installing it.

—Jakob Nielsen, *Designing Web Usability*

3. Telling a story A good way to make a point that will stick in readers' minds is to tell a story. Readers like a good story, and the story will help reinforce the point you want to make. An abstract idea will come alive if you can illustrate it with a story. Organize the events in a story chronologically, from beginning to end, so that readers do not get lost. In the following paragraph, the writer tells a story and draws her point from it. Using *inductive organization,* she begins with background information and the specific details of the story in chronological order and ends with a topic sentence generalization that people with disabilities often experience insensitivity.

Jonathan is an articulate, intelligent, thirty-five-year-old man who has used a wheelchair since he became a paraplegic when he was twenty years old. He recalls taking an ablebodied woman out to dinner at a nice restaurant. When the waitress came to take their order, she patronizingly asked his date, "And what would he like to eat for dinner?" At the end of the meal, the waitress presented Jonathan's date with the check and thanked her for her patronage. Although it may be hard to believe the insensitivity of the waitress, this incident is not an isolated one. Rather, such an experience is a common one for persons with disabilities.

—Dawn O. Braithwaite, "Viewing Persons with Disabilities as a Culture"

4. Including descriptive details If you read the sentence "She grew up in a pretty house," with no more details given, your own imagination would have to fill in the details. You may imagine a small white house in the country. Another reader may imagine an imposing seashore mansion, while yet another will envision a suburban ranch house with a rosebush at the front. Writers who provide details help their readers "see" a place just as they see it by clearly presenting details in an organized way. In the paragraph that follows, we learn about a farm: its location, the appearance of the front of the house, the vegetation at the front, the scent of the flowers, and the surroundings of the house. The author's inclusion of the sounds around the house completes the picture.

> The farm my father grew up on, where Grandpa Welty and Grandma lived, was in southern Ohio in the rolling hills of Hocking County, near the small town of Logan. It was one of the neat, narrow-porched, two-story farmhouses, painted white, of the Pennsylvania-German country. Across its front grew feathery cosmos and barrel-sized peony bushes with stripy heavy-scented blooms pushing out of the leaves. There was a springhouse to one side, down a little walk only one brick in width, and an old apple orchard in front, the barn and the pasture and fields of corn and wheat behind. Periodically there came sounds from the barn, and you could hear the crows, but everything else was still.
>
> —Eudora Welty, *One Writer's Beginnings*

5. Describing by appealing to the senses To help readers see and experience what you see and experience, describe people, places, scenes, and objects by using sensual details that re-create those people, places, scenes, or objects for your readers. In the following paragraph from a memoir about growing up to love food, Ruth Reichl tells how she spent days working at a summer camp in France and thinking about eating. However, she does much more than say "The food was always delicious." Reichl appeals to our senses of sight, smell, touch, and taste. We get a picture of the campers, we smell the baking bread, we see and almost taste the jam, we smell and taste the coffee, and we feel the crustiness of the rolls. We feel as if we are there—and we wish we were.

> When we woke up in the morning the smell of baking bread was wafting through the trees. By the time we had gotten our

campers out of bed, their faces washed and their shirts tucked in, the aroma had become maddeningly seductive. We walked into the dining room to devour hot bread slathered with country butter and topped with homemade plum jam so filled with fruit it made each slice look like a tart. We stuck our faces into the bowls of café au lait, inhaling the sweet, bitter, peculiarly French fragrance, and Georges or Jean or one of the other male counselors would say, for the hundredth time, "*On mange pas comme ça à Paris.*" Two hours later we had a "*gouter,*" a snack of chocolate bars stuffed into fresh, crusty rolls. And two hours later there was lunch. The eating went on all day.

—Ruth Reichl, *Tender at the Bone: Growing Up at the Table*

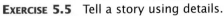

EXERCISE 5.5 Tell a story using details.
Write a paragraph on the distractions that you experience as a college student. In the paragraph, tell a story, use descriptive details, and include sensory details that have a specific appeal to at least one of the senses (sight, hearing, smell, touch, and taste). Be creative.

For review, see "Telling a story" (p. 88), "Including descriptive details" (p. 89), and "Describing by appealing to the senses" (p. 89).

6. Providing one extended illustration You saw in the paragraph on page 86 how a statement about the long life of ant queens is supported by a series of examples and facts. The author of the next paragraph uses one extended illustrative example to explain the point made in the opening sentence.

Paper enables a certain kind of thinking. Picture, for instance, the top of your desk. Chances are that you have a keyboard and a computer screen off to one side, and a clear space roughly eighteen inches square in front of your chair. What covers the rest of the desktop is probably piles—piles of paper, journals, magazines, binders, postcards, videotapes, and all the other artifacts of the knowledge economy. The piles look like a mess, but they aren't. When a group at Apple Computer studied piling behavior several years ago, they found that even the most disorderly piles usually make perfect sense to the piler, and that office workers could hold forth in great detail about the precise history and meaning of their piles. The pile closest to the cleared, eighteen-inch square working area, for example, generally represents the most urgent business, and within that pile the most important document of all is likely to be at the top. Piles are living, breathing archives. Over time they get broken down and resorted, sometimes chronologically and sometimes thematically and sometimes chronologically and thematically; clues about certain documents may be physically embedded in the files by, say, stacking a certain piece of paper at an angle or inserting dividers into the stack.

—Malcolm Gladwell, "The Social Life of Paper"

7. Providing facts and statistics   Facts and statistics provide convincing evidence to help persuade readers of your point. The following paragraph supports with facts and statistics the assertion made in its first sentence (the topic sentence) that the North grew more than the South in the years before the Civil War.

While southerners tended their fields, the North grew. In 1800, half the nation's five million people lived in the South. By 1850, only a third lived there. Of the nine largest cities, only New Orleans was located in the lower South. Meanwhile, a tenth of the goods manufactured in America came from southern mills and factories. There were one hundred piano makers in New York alone in 1852. In 1846, there was not a single book publisher in New Orleans; even the city guidebook was printed in Manhattan.

—Geoffrey C. Ward, *The Civil War: An Illustrated History*

The following paragraph also uses statistics to support a point stated in the first sentence. In a prior paragraph, the writer Lawrence Grossman had described the results of a small-scale media study done by researcher Pete Schulberg; here Grossman broadens the picture.

Schulberg's findings in Portland uncannily match the local picture in the rest of the country. A study of 100 local TV newscasts in 56 cities by the Rocky Mountain Media Watch found that crime occupied 30 percent of what little time was actually devoted to the news (40 percent). Commercials and promos consumed an almost equal amount of time (36 percent). Sports and weather filled 22 percent; anchor chatter, 2 percent.

—Lawrence K. Grossman, "Why Local TV News Is So Awful"

8. Describing or giving instructions for a process Descriptions of the process of doing something usually either list the instructions in chronological order or provide a description of the steps in a sequence.

The following paragraph gives a list of instructions for beginning the process of making a piñata. When you want to tell a reader how to do something, use the active voice and the imperative mood, as this writer does.

Start making a piñata by covering an inflated beach ball with a thin layer of petroleum jelly. Dip newspaper strips into a prepared adhesive and apply them one at a time to the ball. Cover the entire surface of the ball, except for its mouthpiece, with about 10 layers of strips. Then let the paper dry, deflate the ball, and remove it through the mouthpiece opening. Poke two small holes through the surface of the papier-mâché and attach a long, sturdy string. Fill the sphere with candy and prizes. Seal the opening with masking tape.

—Reader's Digest Association, *How to Do Just about Anything*

9. Defining key terms Have you ever read an article and thought "I wonder what the writer means by _____ " (fill in your own word here: *poststructural, elusive, prosthesis, asynchronous instruction, heuristics,* and so on)? Sometimes you will want to clarify and develop a topic by defining a key term, even if it is not an unusual term. Often you will explain what class something fits into and how it differs from others in its class, such as "A duckbilled platypus is a mammal that has webbed feet and lays eggs." Or you will explain and illustrate a term by showing what it is and what it is not, such as "Love is affection and concern for another, not simply sexual desire." In his book on diaries, Thomas Mallon begins by providing an extended definition of his basic terms. He does not want readers to misunderstand him because they wonder about what the differences between a diary and a journal might be. He begins by immediately addressing the terms *diary* and *journal* and examining their use, and then deciding to treat them as having the same meaning.

The first thing we should try to get straight is what to call them. "What's the difference between a diary and a journal?" is one of the questions people interested in these books ask. The two terms are in fact hopelessly muddled. They're both rooted in the idea of dailiness, but perhaps because of *journal*'s links to the newspaper trade and *diary*'s to *dear,* the latter seems more intimate than the former. (The French blur even this discrepancy by using no word recognizable like *diary;* they just say *journal intime,* which is sexy, but a bit of a mouthful.) One can go back as far as Dr. Johnson's *Dictionary* and find him making the two more or less equal. To him a diary was "an account of the transactions, accidents, and observations of every day; a journal." Well, if synonymity was good enough for Johnson, we'll let it be good enough for us.

— Thomas Mallon, *A Book of One's Own: People and Their Diaries*

As necessary, define technical terms for readers, particularly if readers will need to understand the term to understand the rest of your essay. In the following paragraph, the authors establish the meaning of a filmmaking term that they will use in later discussion.

In the original French, *mise-en-scène* (pronounced "meez-ahn-sen") means "staging an action," and it was first applied to the practice of directing plays. Film scholars, extending the term to film direction as well, use the term to signify the director's control over what appears in the film frame. As you would expect from the term's theatrical origins, mise-en-scène includes those aspects that overlap with the art of the theater: setting, lighting, costume, and the behavior of the figures. In controlling the mise-en-scène, the director *stages the event* for the camera.

— David Bordwell and Kristin Thompson, *Film Art: An Introduction,* 3rd ed.

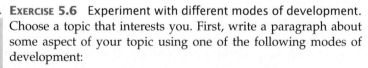

EXERCISE 5.6 Experiment with different modes of development. Choose a topic that interests you. First, write a paragraph about some aspect of your topic using one of the following modes of development:

- Providing one extended illustration (p. 90)
- Providing facts and statistics (p. 91)

- Describing or giving instructions for a process (p. 92)
- Defining key terms (p. 92)

Then write another paragraph on another aspect of your topic using a second mode of development from the preceding list. In groups, discuss how different aspects of your topic worked with the two modes of development that you chose. Did one mode of development work better or less well than the other, and if so, why?

10. Comparing and contrasting When you compare people, objects, or concepts and examine similarities and differences, different types of development achieve different purposes.

Block organization You can deal with each subject one at a time in a block style of organization. This organization works well when each section is short and readers can easily remember the points made. A paragraph or an essay comparing and contrasting writing in college and writing at work could therefore be organized as follows:

Subject A: Writing in college

Point 1: Audience   Instructor or classmates

Point 2: Purpose   To fulfill an assignment

Point 3: Outcomes   Need for revision, evaluation, grade

Subject B: Writing at work

Point 1: Audience   Boss, colleagues, or customers

Point 2: Purpose   To convey information

Point 3: Outcomes   Action, follow-up, filing, evaluation by boss

Point-by-point organization Alternatively, you can consider the important points of similarity or difference in a point-by-point style of organization, referring within each point to both subjects. The preceding material would then be presented as follows:

Point 1: Audience

Writing in college

Writing at work

Point 2: Purpose

Writing in college

Writing at work

Point 3: Outcomes

> Writing in college
>
> Writing at work

The vocabulary of comparing and contrasting Helpful words and terms to use for comparing and contrasting are these:

although	on the contrary
both	on the other hand
however	similarly
in contrast	though
like	where (or whereas)
not . . . but rather	while

Note where these words and terms occur in the sample passages that follow.

The following passage uses a block organization to contrast how Aristotle and Galileo viewed a pendulum—first Aristotle and then Galileo.

> When Aristotle looked at a pendulum, he saw a weight trying to head earthward but swinging violently back and forth because it was constrained by its rope. To the modern ear this sounds foolish. For someone bound by classical concepts of motion, inertia, and gravity, it is hard to appreciate the self-consistent world view that went with Aristotle's understanding of a pendulum. Physical motion, for Aristotle, was not a quantity or a force, but rather a kind of change, just as a person's growth is a kind of change. A falling weight is simply seeking its most natural state, the state it will reach if left to itself. Aristotle's view made sense. When Galileo looked at a pendulum, on the other hand, he saw a regularity that could be measured. To explain it required a revolutionary way of understanding objects in motion. Galileo's advantage over the ancient Greeks was not that he had better data. On the contrary, his idea of timing a pendulum precisely was to get some friends together to count the oscillations over a twenty-four-hour period—a labor-intensive experiment. Galileo saw the regularity because he already had a theory that predicted it. He understood what Aristotle could not: that a moving object

tends to keep moving, that a change in speed or direction could only be explained by some external force, like friction.

—James Gleick, *Chaos*

The following passage compares John Stuart Mill, a British philosopher and economist, and Harriet Taylor, a woman with whom Mill had a close intellectual relationship. The author, Phyllis Rose, organizes the contrast point by point to emphasize the differences in their facial features, physical behavior, ways of thinking and speaking, and intellectual style. (A block organization would have dealt first with all the characteristics of Taylor, followed by all the characteristics of Mill.)

You could see how they complemented each other by the way they looked. What people noticed first about Harriet were her eyes—flashing—and a suggestion in her body of mobility, whereas his features, variously described as chiseled and classical, expressed an inner rigidity. He shook hands from the shoulder. He spoke carefully. Give him facts, and he would sift them, weigh them, articulate possible interpretations, reach a conclusion. Where he was careful, she was daring. Where he was disinterested and balanced, she was intuitive, partial, and sure of herself. She concerned herself with goals and assumptions; he concerned himself with arguments. She was quick to judge and to generalize, and because he was not, he valued her intellectual style as bold and vigorous where another person, more like her, might have found her hasty and simplistic.

—Phyllis Rose, *Parallel Lives: Five Victorian Marriages*

Similarly, Cheryl Mendelson contrasts two grandmothers on the basis of their housekeeping tradition, home decoration, music, ambience, and food tastes and smells, as well as their approaches to knitting.

My maternal grandmother was a fervent housekeeper in her ancestral Italian style, while my paternal grandmother was an equally fervent housekeeper in a style she inherited from England, Scotland, and Ireland. In one home I heard Puccini, slept on linen sheets with finely crocheted edging rolled up with lavender from the garden, and enjoyed airy, light rooms with flowers sprouting in porcelain pots on windowsills and the foreign scents of garlic and dark, strong coffee. The atmosphere was open and warmly hospitable. The other home felt like a fortress—secure against intruders and fitted with stores and tools for all emergencies. There were Gay Nineties tunes on the player piano and English hymns, rooms shaded almost to darkness against real and fancied harmful effects of air and light, hand-braided rag rugs, brightly colored patchwork quilts, and creamed lima beans from the garden. My Anglo-American grandmother taught me to knit American-style, looping the yarn around the needle with a whole-arm motion. My Italian grandmother winced at the sight of this tiring and inefficient method and insisted I do it the way she did, with a barely visible, lightning flick of the last joint on her index finger.

—Cheryl Mendelson, *Home Comforts*

Describing similarities and differences When you want to emphasize similarities as well as differences, you can deal with each in turn, following a point-by-point organization as you do so. This is what the writer of a *New York Times* article on U.S. presidents with sons who also became president chooses to do. He points out first the similarities between John Quincy Adams and George W. Bush and then the differences. Here is the paragraph that details the similarities.

Both Adams and George W. Bush were born to privileged New England families, though Mr. Bush went with his father to Texas and adopted the persona and politics of a down-home Western oil man. Both followed fathers whose presidencies lasted just one term: John Adams, like the elder George Bush, was rejected by the electorate after four years in office. And like the younger Bush, the younger Adams was elected president with a disputed voter mandate and under controversial circumstances.

—Sean Wilentz, "The Father-and-Son Presidencies"

EXERCISE 5.7 Compare or contrast two people.
Write a comparison or contrast essay on two people you know well. You can compare or contrast their work habits, attitudes, styles, appearances, approaches to life, reactions to stresses or crises, clothing, and so on. Use either a block or point-by-point organization. Use the following outline to plan your essay.

BLOCK ORGANIZATION (SUBJECT BY SUBJECT)

Subject A: Subject B:

    Point 1:   Point 1:

    Point 2:   Point 2:

    Point 3:   Point 3:

POINT-BY-POINT ORGANIZATION

Point 1:

    Subject A:

    Subject B:

Point 2:

    Subject A:

    Subject B:

Point 3:

    Subject A:

    Subject B:

11. Dividing or analyzing   As a mode of paragraph development, dividing or analyzing means thoughtfully dividing a subject into its component parts for the purposes of discussion. This approach allows you as a writer to present and analyze a large topic in a manageable way. Similarly, it allows readers to get a better understanding of the whole from a description of the parts. In the following example, the *Columbia Encyclopedia* online helps readers understand the vast concept of *life* itself by breaking it down into six component parts (at <http://www.bartleby.com/65/li/life.html>).

> Although there is no universal agreement as to a definition of life, its biological manifestations are generally considered to be organization, metabolism, growth, irritability, adaptation, and reproduction. . . . Organization is found in the basic living unit, the cell, and in the organized groupings of cells into organs and organisms. Metabolism includes the conversion of nonliving material into cellular components (synthesis) and the decomposition of organic matter (catalysis), producing energy. Growth in living matter is an increase in size of all parts, as distinguished from simple addition of material; it results from a higher rate of synthesis than catalysis. Irritability, or response to stimuli, takes many forms, from the contraction of a unicellu-

lar organism when touched to complex reactions involving all the senses of higher animals; in plants response is usually much different than in animals but is nonetheless present. Adaptation, the accommodation of a living organism to its present or to a new environment, is fundamental to the process of evolution and is determined by the individual's heredity. The division of one cell to form two new cells is reproduction; usually the term is applied to the production of a new individual (either asexually, from a single parent organism, or sexually, from two differing parent organisms), although strictly speaking it also describes the production of new cells in the process of growth.

12. Classifying One way to examine people, objects, or concepts is to classify them, which means to split them up into groups that cover all the options. In the following paragraphs, Matthew Gilbert examines cell phone users by dividing them into three groups, each with a "different psychological need," and devoting one paragraph to each group in the classification. He assumes there are no other possible needs here, an assumption his readers might not agree with. However, he does qualify his classification by saying "As I see it."

> Cell phone use has far exceeded practicality. For many, it's even a bit of an addiction, a prop—like a cigarette or a beer bottle—that you can hold up to your mouth. And each person is meeting a different psychological need by clinging to it.
>
> As I see it, the pack breaks down something like this: Some users can't tolerate being alone and have to register on someone, somewhere, all of the time. That walk down [the street] can be pretty lonely without a loved one shouting sweet nothings in your ear.
>
> Others are efficiency freaks and can't bear to lose 10 minutes standing in line at Starbucks. They have to conduct business while their milk is being steamed, or they will implode. The dividing line between work and home has already become permeable with the growth of telecommuting; cell phones contribute significantly to that boundary breakdown.
>
> Then there are those who like to believe they are so very important to the people in their personal and professional lives

that they must be in constant touch. "Puffed up" is one way to describe them; "insecure" is another.

—Matthew Gilbert, "All Talk, All the Time"

Novelist and short-story writer Tillie Olsen also creates categories or classes in the first paragraph of her poetic essay "Silences" to provide a framework for discussion. Her large subject is writers who produce less over the course of their careers than we would expect or want them to produce.

Literary history and the present are dark with silences: some the silences for years by our acknowledged great; some silences hidden; some the ceasing to publish after one work appears; some the never coming to book form at all.

—Tillie Olsen, "Silences"

In the course of the essay, she then revisits each of these four types, providing examples and commentary.

EXERCISE 5.8 Consider bases for classification.
Write down a number of different ways you could classify each of the following broad topics:

Students in your class

Restaurants in your neighborhood

Current movies showing in the theaters

13. Identifying cause and effect In writing about history, art history, or social movements, an examination of the causes and effects of events and trends can work well. In the following passage, Larry McMurtry begins by identifying a situation and devotes the next two paragraphs to discussing the cause that produced this effect.

The American West has so far produced depressingly little in the way of literature. Out of it may have come a hundred or so good books, a dozen or so very good books; but it has not, as yet, yielded up a great book. In literature it still seems to be waiting its turn. At the beginning of the century the Midwest seemed dominant, in terms of literary gifts and literary energies; then, largely because of Faulkner, the South had a turn, after which the great concentration of American literary energy returned to where it had mainly always been, the East.

Lately, looking through the various collections of photographs by the early photographers of the West—Alexander Gardner, John Hillers, Timothy O'Sullivan, William H. Jackson, and the others—

Karl Bodmer, *View of the Stone Walls on the Upper Missouri*

it occurred to me that one reason the West hasn't quite got a literature was in part because the camera arrived just when it did. The first photographs were taken in the West only about forty years after Lewis and Clark made their memorable trek. By the 1850s there were cameras everywhere, and the romantic landscapes of Catlin, Bodmer, Miller, Moran, and the rest gave way to photography that was almost equally romantic—the photographers, quite naturally, gravitated to the beauty spots, to the grandeur of Yosemite, Grand Canyon, Canyon de Chelly.

Writers weren't needed, in quite the same way, once the camera came. They didn't need to explain and describe the West to Easterners because the Easterners could, very soon, look at those pictures and see it for themselves. And what they saw was a West with the inconveniences—the dust, the heat, the distances—removed.

—Larry McMurtry, *Walter Benjamin at the Dairy Queen*

EXERCISE 5.9 Analyze a cause and effect relationship.
Many writing assignments require an examination of causes and effects. We also examine causes and effects on a daily basis when we ask, for example, "Why is the expressway backed up?" "Why is my printer not working?" or "Why is my money situation what it is?"

By examining causes and effects, we come to better understand our lives and how to improve them. Consider an event or situation that you have experienced recently and examine the causes and effects involved. Write a brief essay on this topic.

14. Providing a solution to a problem   Many articles and many college writing assignments pose a problem and consider possible solutions, sometimes making a strong recommendation for one course of action. An article in the *New York Times* presents the problem of the considerable risks involved for a donor of an organ such as a kidney or part of a liver. After a discussion of the legal and ethical issues, the author devotes the following paragraph to proposing a solution to the problem.

> One way to ensure that the interests of prospective donors are recognized is to create a federal agency that would make certain that hospitals meet minimum standards when employing these new therapies and would monitor how hospital review boards screen potential donors. The boards also need to be able to shield potential donors from coercion. For example, in cases when an individual decides against becoming a donor, a board should simply inform the intended recipient that the potential donor is "not suitable" without further explanation.
>
> —Ronald Munson, "The Donor's Right to Take a Risk"

15. Making an analogy   Making an analogy can be a powerful way to make a complicated topic clear to your readers. The psychiatrist and author David D. Burns, for example, uses an extended analogy in his discussion of how to defeat self-defeating perfectionism.

> Think of it this way—there are two doors to enlightenment. One is marked "Perfection," and the other is marked "Average." The "Perfection" door is ornate, fancy, and seductive. It tempts you. You want very much to go through. The "Average" door seems drab and plain. Ugh! Who wants it?
>
> So you try to go through the "Perfection" door and always discover a brick wall on the other side. As you insist on trying to break through, you only end up with a sore nose and a headache. On the other side of the "Average" door, in contrast, there's a magic garden. But it may never have occurred to you to open up this door and take a look.
>
> —David D. Burns, M.D., *Feeling Good*

In another example, this one on Usenet groups, the authors develop an analogy between Usenet and a river, and they expand and develop this analogy throughout the paragraph, referring even to a "data stream" to preserve the image.

> Usenet is like a river with thousands of tributaries. The main forks in the river lead to the top-level discussion categories (such as "alt"). Follow one of the river's forks and you'll come to smaller branches (such as alt.animals), which lead to tributaries containing messages divided into even more specific topics (such as alt.animals.dogs). Ultimately, your journey will take you to the smallest part of the data stream; the part containing messages from people who are interested in one particular topic (such as alt.animals.dogs.beagles).
>
> —*Basics of Usenet*, <http://groups.google.com/googlegroups/basics.html>

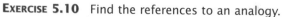

EXERCISE 5.10 Find the references to an analogy.
Working in groups of two or three, examine the preceding paragraph and underline all the words and phrases that extend the analogy made in the first sentence between Usenet newsgroups and a river. Comment on your findings.

16. Providing expert testimony Writers will often provide information from the opinions and research of others to develop a point. Such development strategies are common in college research papers. Here is a paragraph from a *Washington Post* article making the point that the varying prices of goods make shopping complicated, with historical background information provided from a noted historian.

> The historian Daniel Boorstin has written about how the industrial and commercial revolution of the 19th century brought standardized goods—such as clothes pre-made in various sizes rather than made-to-order—at standardized prices. Our current industrial and commercial revolution is reversing these developments. Computers are allowing clothiers from Levi's to Brooks Brothers to offer pants personalized for your personal rear end. On the Internet, you can fine-tune your appetites almost endlessly, and you rarely have to settle for cerise because taupe is out of stock.
>
> —Michael Kinsley, "Consuming Gets Complicated"

5e Strengthening coherence with links, parallel structures, and transitions

However you develop your individual paragraphs, readers expect to move with ease from one sentence to the next and from one paragraph to the next, following a clear flow of argument and logic.

When you construct an essay or paragraph, do not cause readers to grapple with sudden jumps from one idea to another without clear links. Avoid such grasshopper prose. Instead, a piece of writing needs to be coherent, with all the parts connecting clearly to one another—and to the thesis—with links and transitions.

Context links A new paragraph introduces a new topic, but that topic should not be entirely separate from what has gone before. Let readers know the context of the big picture. If you are writing about the expense of exploring Mars and then switch abruptly to the hazards of climbing Everest, readers will be puzzled. You need to state clearly the connection with the thesis: "Exploration on our own planet can be as hazardous and as financially risky as space exploration."

Word links and repetition You can also provide coherence by using repeated words, or connected words, such as pronouns linked to nouns; words with the same, similar, or opposite meaning; or words linked by context. The writer of the following paragraph maintains coherence by repeating words and phrases (italicized) and using pronouns (bold—*she* and *her* to refer to *wife*, and *they* to refer to *Greeks*) to provide a linking chain.

> Entire cultures operate on elaborate systems of *indirectness*. For example, I discovered in a small research project that most Greeks assumed that a wife who asked, "Would you like to go to the party?" was hinting that **she** *wanted to go*. **They** *felt* that **she** wouldn't bring it up if **she** didn't *want to go*. Furthermore, **they** *felt*, **she** would not state **her** *preference* outright because **that** would sound like a demand. *Indirectness* was the appropriate means for communicating **her** *preference*.
> —Deborah Tannen, *You Just Don't Understand*

In the following paragraph, Alice Walker, writing about the writer Zora Neale Hurston, uses the repetition of "without money" to drive her point home.

> Without money, an illness, even a simple one, can undermine the will. Without money, getting into a hospital is problematic, and getting out without money to pay for the treatment is nearly impossible. Without money, one becomes dependent on other people who are likely to be—even in their kindness—erratic in their support and despotic in their expectations of return. Zora was forced to rely, like Tennessee Williams's Blanche, "on the kindness of strangers." Can anything be more

dangerous, if the strangers are forever in control? Zora, who worked so hard, was never able to make a living from her work.

—Foreword to Robert E. Hemenway,
Zora Neale Hurston: A Literary Biography

See also the Worlds of Writing box in **6e** for another example of the effective use of repetition.

Parallel structures as a linking device Parallel structures help readers see the connection between ideas:

United, there is little we cannot do. Divided, there is little we can do.

—John F. Kennedy, Inaugural Presidential Address

The structures can be clauses or phrases, as shown in the following passages, the first four of which are from "Maintenance" by Naomi Shihab Nye. See also **16e** for more on clauses, **16d** for more on phrases, and **19j** for errors arising from faulty parallelism.

Parallel structures: clauses

We saw one house *where walls and windows had been sheathed in various patterns of gloomy brocade.* We visited another *where the kitchen had been removed* because the owners only ate in restaurants.

Parallel structures: verb phrases

Sometimes I'd come home to find her *lounging* in the bamboo chair on the back porch, *eating* melon, or *lying* on the couch with a bowl of half-melted ice cream balanced on her chest.

Parallel structures: absolute phrases

One day she described having grown up in west Texas in a house of twelve children, *the air jammed* with voices, crosscurrents, *the floors piled* with grocery bags, mountains of tossed-off clothes, toys, blankets, the clutter of her sisters' shoes.

Parallel structures: noun phrases

Barbara has the best taste of any person I've ever known—*the best khaki-colored linen clothing, the best books, the name of the best masseuse.*

Parallel structures: prepositional phrases

Adolescence is a tough time for parent and child alike. It is a time between: *between childhood and maturity, between parental protection and personal responsibility, between life stage-managed by grown-ups and life privately held.*

—Anna Quindlen, "Parental Rites," *Thinking Out Loud*

Links signaling a transition Writers use transitional words and expressions to signal relationships between ideas. They can connect clauses within one sentence, one or more sentences in a paragraph, two or more paragraphs, and a paragraph and the thesis. Deborah Tannen, in the passage on page 104, uses "for example" and "furthermore" to indicate meaning connections. The Key Points box that follows identifies the most common uses of transitional expressions and provides examples of each.

KEY POINTS

Transitional Expressions

Adding an idea: also, in addition, further, furthermore, moreover

Contrasting: however, nevertheless, nonetheless, on the other hand, in contrast, still, on the contrary, rather, conversely

Providing an alternative: instead, alternatively, otherwise

Showing similarity: similarly, likewise

Showing order of time or order of ideas: first, second, third (and so on); then; next; later; subsequently; meanwhile; previously; finally

Showing result: as a result, consequently, therefore, thus, hence, accordingly, for this reason

Affirming: of course, in fact, certainly, obviously, to be sure, undoubtedly, indeed

Giving examples: for example, for instance

Explaining: in other words, that is

Adding an aside: incidentally, by the way, besides

Summarizing: in short, generally, overall, all in all, in conclusion

For punctuation with transitional expressions, see **26e**.

 ESL NOTE On Not Overusing Transitional Expressions

Transitional expressions are useful to reinforce meaning connections and connect one sentence to another or one paragraph to another. Make sure, though, that you do not overuse these expressions. Too many of them, used too often, give writing a heavy and mechanical flavor. To add an idea, point out a contrast, or show a result, *and, but,* or *so* may serve the purpose just as well. ▪

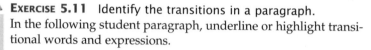

EXERCISE 5.11 Identify the transitions in a paragraph.
In the following student paragraph, underline or highlight transitional words and expressions.

Although Julia is a returning college student, she blends in with the student population. She doesn't let the age difference interfere with her relationships with other students. Before she returned to school, she had concerns about whether or not she would fit in. However, after two semesters of interacting with other students, Julia has gained confidence. The younger students do not treat her differently. In fact, many of her classmates are interested in the reasons why Julia decided to return to school after her ten-year successful career as a nurse. Julia, likewise, shows interest in her classmates and enjoys the dialogue, debate, and controversies that arise during class discussion.

5f Drafting an introduction and a conclusion

Beginnings and endings are important. Try to give readers an idea of what to expect in your essay and make them eager to read more. And once they have read your explanations and arguments, your conclusion should make it clear that you have provided substantive information and covered the important points. Readers should leave your document feeling satisfied, not turning the page and looking for more or shrugging with a "So what?" expression on their faces.

Introduction   Imagine a scene at a party. Someone you have never met before comes up to you and says, "Capital punishment should be abolished immediately." You're surprised. You wonder where this position came from and why you are being challenged with it. You probably think this person rather strange and pushy. Imagine now readers picking up a piece of your writing. Just like people at a party, readers would probably like to know something about the topic and its relevance before you pronounce on it. Think of your introduction as a way to interest readers and give them a taste of what is to come.
Examine the hooks in the following examples.

On the day before Memorial Day, 1983, a poet called me to describe a city he had just visited. He said that one section included mosques, built by the Islamic people who dwelled there. Attending his reading, he said, were large numbers of Hispanic people, forty thousand of whom lived in the same city.

He was not talking about a fabled city located in some mysterious region of the world. The city he'd visited was Detroit.

—Ishmael Reed, "America: The Multinational Society,"
Writin' Is Fightin'

Reed introduces the theme of multinationalism in the United States with the hook of an anecdote that leads readers to expect that the city he describes is in an unfamiliar part of the world. He then grabs readers with a surprise in the last sentence—the city is Detroit—and prepares readers for his discussion of a multinational continent.

As the captain of the Yale swimming team stood beside the pool, still dripping after his laps, and listened to Bob Moses, the team's second-best freestyler, he didn't know what shocked him more—the suggestion or the fact that it was Moses who was making it.

—Robert A. Caro, *The Power Broker:
Robert Moses and the Fall of New York*

This sentence is the first in the introductory chapter of Caro's massive biography of Robert Moses, a powerful force in New York City construction and politics for four decades. He does not begin with where and when Moses was born. Instead, he draws us into the story by making us want to read on to find out what the suggestion was (Moses proposed misleading a donor into giving money to the swim team) and why it was shocking.

Sometimes a writer will jump right in and engage readers with an opinion immediately, especially a provocative one. Here is the introduction to a long essay by B. R. Myers, "A Reader's Manifesto," subtitled "An Attack on the Growing Pretentiousness of American Literary Prose." Here the subtitle and the opening sentence alert us to the topic and to the writer's stance: his dislike for pretentious literary fiction. The rest of the first paragraph establishes a lively tone and an unabashedly individual and somewhat extreme viewpoint. Readers who are interested in what is considered good writing will want to read more to find out what reasons Myers gives for his opinion and what examples he can produce.

Nothing gives me the feeling of having been born several decades too late quite like the modern "literary" best seller. Give me a time-tested masterpiece or what critics patronizingly call a fun read—*Sister Carrie* or just plain *Carrie*. Give me anything, in fact, as long as it doesn't have a recent prize jury's seal of approval on the front and a clutch of precious raves on the back. In the bookstore I'll sometimes sample what all the fuss is about, but one glance at the affected prose—"furious dabs of tulips stuttering," say, or "in the dark before the day yet was"—and I'm hightailing it to the friendly black spines of the Penguin Classics.

—B. R Myers, "A Reader's Manifesto"

If you find it difficult to write an introduction because you are not yet clear about your thesis or how you will support it, wait until you have written the body of your essay. You will find something concrete easier to introduce than something you have not yet written.

When you write an introduction to an essay in the humanities, keep the following points in mind.

 KEY POINTS

How to Write a Good Introduction

Options

1. Make sure your first sentence stands alone and does not depend on readers' being aware of the essay title or an assigned question. For instance, avoid beginning with "This story has a complex plot."

2. Provide context and background information to set up the thesis.

3. Indicate what claim you will make in your essay, or at least indicate the issue on which you will state a claim.

4. Define key terms that are pertinent to the discussion.

5. Establish the tone of the paper: informative, persuasive, serious, humorous, personal, impersonal, formal, informal.

6. Engage readers' interest and provide some kind of hook to make readers want to continue reading.

What to Avoid

7. Avoid being overly general and telling readers the obvious, such as "Crime is a big problem" or "In this fast-paced world, TV is a popular form of entertainment" or "Since the beginning of time, the sexes have been in conflict."

8. Do not refer to your writing intentions, such as "In this essay, I will. . . ." Do not make extravagant claims, such as "This essay will prove that bilingual education works for every student."

9. Do not restate the assigned essay question.

To provide a hook for readers, an introduction might include any of the following:

surprising statistics

a challenging question

a pithy quotation

interesting background details

an unusual fact

an intriguing opinion statement

a relevant anecdote

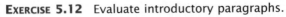

EXERCISE 5.12 Evaluate introductory paragraphs.
Read the following three paragraphs and identify which method the author has chosen to grab readers' attention. Consider whether the author's choice seems effective and why. Methods include, for example, an anecdote, a provocative opinion, a challenging question, interesting background details, an unusual fact, or a pithy quotation.

1. "If I die first and Papi ever gets remarried," Mami used to tease when we were kids, "don't you accept a new woman in my house. Make her life impossible, you hear?" My sisters and I nodded obediently, and a filial shudder would go through us. We were Catholics, so of course, the only kind of marriage we could imagine had to involve our mother's death. We were also Dominicans, recently arrived in Jamaica, Queens, in the early 60s before waves of other Latin Americans began arriving. So, when we imagined who exactly my father might possibly ever think of remarrying, only American women came to mind. It would be bad enough having a *madrastra,* but a "stepmother" . . . .
—Julia Alvarez, "Hold the Mayonnaise"

2. How far can we go in exalting Newton's scientific achievements? Not far enough. Few minds in the intellectual history of humankind have left such an imprint as Newton's. His work represents the culmination of the Scientific Revolution, a grandiose solution to the problem of motion that had haunted philosophers since pre-Socratic times. In doing so, he laid the conceptual foundations that were to dominate not only physics but also our collective worldview until the dawn of the twentieth century.
—Marcelo Gleiser, *The Dancing Universe:*
From Creation Myths to the Big Bang

3. Since 1970, the composition of households and families and the marital status and living arrangements of adults in the United States both experienced marked changes. For example, the proportion of the population made up by married couples with children decreased, and the proportion of single mothers increased, while the median age at first marriage grew over time. Much of this variety has been regularly reported in two separate Census Bureau reports—*Household and Family Characteristics* and *Marital Status and Living Arrangements*. Beginning with the March 2001 Current Population Survey, these two reports are being replaced by this new publication, *America's Families and Living Arrangements.*

> —*America's Families and Living Arrangements*, U.S. Census Bureau,
> <http://www.census.gov/prod/2001pubs/p20-537.pdf>

EXERCISE 5.13 Revise an introduction.
Revise an introduction from one of your most recent papers by using a different hook, such as an anecdote, a provocative opinion, a challenging question, interesting background details, an unusual fact, or a pithy quotation. (See pp. 107–110.)

Conclusion   Think of your conclusion as completing a circle. You have taken readers on a journey from presentation of the topic in your introduction, to your thesis, to supporting evidence and discussion, with specific examples and illustrations. Remind readers of the purpose of the journey. Recall the main idea of the paper and make a strong statement about it that will stick in their minds.

KEY POINTS

How to Write a Good Conclusion

Options

1. Include a summary of the points you have made, but keep it short and use fresh wording.

2. Frame your essay by reminding readers of something you referred to in your introduction and by reminding readers of your thesis.

3. End on a strong note: a quotation, a question, a suggestion, a reference to an anecdote in the introduction, a humorous insightful comment, a call to action, or a look to the future.

(continued)

(continued)
What to Avoid

4. Do not apologize for the inadequacy of your argument ("I do not know much about this problem") or for holding your opinions ("I am sorry if you do not agree with me, but . . .").

5. Do not use the identical wording you used in your introduction.

6. Do not introduce totally new ideas. If you raise a new point at the end, readers might expect more details.

7. Do not contradict what you said previously.

8. Do not be too sweeping in your conclusions. Do not condemn the whole medical profession, for example, because one person you know had a bad time in one hospital.

The paragraph that follows is the concluding paragraph to a chapter on designing a home page on the Web. The chapter includes examples and illustrations, and the concluding paragraph succinctly reinforces the advice:

> In summary, a home page should offer three features: a directory of the site's main content areas (navigation), a summary of the most important news or promotions, and a search feature. If done well, directory and news will help answer the first-time user's need to find out what the site is about in the first place. Even so, always look at the page with an eye to asking, "What can this site do for me?" And remember the name and logo.
> —Jakob Nielsen, *Designing Web Usability*

Exercise 5.14 Improve an unsatisfactory conclusion.
Read the following concluding paragraph from a paper on protecting data from computer viruses. What suggestions would you give to the student writer about how to improve it? Be specific. Then revise the paragraph according to your suggestions.

> This concludes my paper on dangerous computer viruses. Each of the measures mentioned above, if practiced, will help you to avoid having your data destroyed. It's so easy to minimize danger. First, buy an antivirus program. Second, screen unknown data. Third, back up all your files. In doing so, one will, if not eliminate all potential danger, at the very least protect valuable data. Each day more viruses are created, since we can't know what's coming, we can, at the very least use "an ounce of prevention."

Part II
Writing in All Your Courses

We learn about a subject through writing about it. Part II alerts you to strategies for successfully completing a variety of writing tasks that you may meet during your college career. Many of these writing tasks, such as arguments, for example, are frequently called for outside college, too—in letters to the press or to government agencies or business organizations, in business proposals and reports, in Internet discussion groups, and in community service.

6 Writing an Argument

"You shouldn't have told Joe his earring looks terrible. Now he's hurt."

"But I didn't tell him."

"Sarah said you did."

"I didn't."

"You did."

"Get lost."

This exchange about who said what to whom would often be called an argument but is in fact more like a petty disagreement. An argument in the academic or rhetorical sense is a reasoned, logical argument—supported by evidence—designed to persuade an audience to pay attention to significant points you raise. You can write an argument either on a controversial issue or simply on any issue on which you take a position and try to defend that position. For example, you could construct a reasoned, logical written exposition to argue that it is not only a passing fashion fad to pierce body parts but a potentially dangerous practice. Or you could write an argument paper to support your interpretation of a short story. Many writers of arguments will go a step further and try both to convince readers to adopt a certain position and to persuade readers to take some appropriate action or precaution.

Assignments to produce reasoned, logical written exposition occur frequently in courses in the humanities and social sciences, as well as in the work world. One way to become familiar with the techniques of writing arguments is to analyze the arguments you read: What makes a good argument? What types of argument do you find convincing? What types of argument fill you with scorn?

TechNote Useful Web Sites for Writing Arguments

Try the following sites for help with writing arguments.

> *Paradigm Online Writing Assistant,* a site that began at Boise State University at <http://www.powa.org/argufrms.htm>

> The Capital Community College site on writing arguments at <http://ccc.commnet.edu/grammar/composition/argument.htm> with a sample annotated argument paper

 Exercise 6.1 Consider topics for arguments.

Consider and list what occasions you have had in recent months, in either conversation or writing, to argue a point. Think about, for example, your work situation, discussions with friends, opinions offered about movies, family issues, music, food, cars, and academic subjects. On your list, note which topics led to petty disagreements and which sparked fuller arguments in the rhetorical sense, arguments in which you could take a stand and support your view with evidence. Discuss your list with classmates.

6a Evaluate an argument critically.

Arguments are common not only in college essays but also in newspaper articles, letters, courts of law, daily discussions, and Internet newsgroup discussions. Some are responsible, well reasoned, and well constructed. Others lack these qualities. Whether or not you are convinced by the views of the speaker or writer, it is a good habit to step back and evaluate an argument critically, whether it is your own or somebody else's, in order to identify its merits and faults.

When you read an argument, examine the writer's statements with care—and be aware that readers will use the same care when they read an argument that *you* write. Here are questions to ask while reading an argument:

1. What am I reading? A statement of fact, an opinion, an exaggeration, an attack, an emotional belief?

2. How reliable are the writer's statements? Are they measured, accurate, to the point, and fair?

3. What assumptions does the writer make? If a writer argues for a college education for everyone, would I accept the underlying assumption that a college education automatically leads to happiness and success? For more on assumptions, see **6g.**

4. Does the writer present ideas in a convincing way, relying on rational presentation of evidence rather than on emotional language or name-calling?

KEY POINTS

A Good Argument

A good argument

1. deals with an arguable issue (**6b**)
2. takes a position on and makes a clear claim about the topic (**6c**)
3. supports that position with detailed and specific evidence (such as reasons, facts, examples, descriptions, and stories) (**6d**)
4. establishes common ground with listeners or readers and avoids confrontation (**6e**)
5. takes opposing views into account and refutes them or shows why they may be unimportant or irrelevant (**6f**)
6. presents reasons logically (**6g, 6h, 6i**).

6b Select a topic.

If you are not assigned a topic from class discussion or reading, choose one that will be interesting for you to write about and for readers to read about. The topic you choose should be one that is significant and can be debated, such as in what grade standardized testing should begin in schools rather than how many states require standardized tests. The former issue can lead to an arguable claim: "Standardized testing should not begin until the fifth grade" rather than a truism (a statement that is obviously true and is not debatable) such as "Standardized testing is administered in many states."

You probably will want to persuade readers to adopt your point of view. At the very least, you will want them to acknowledge that the claim you make about your topic rests on solid and reliable evidence (**6d**), and that you provide a fair and unbiased approach to this evidence. Let readers discover that you have good reasons for your position.

If the choice of topic for a written argument is up to you, choose one that is fresh. Unless personal involvement and experience drive you to explore topics such as the death penalty, prayer in schools, drug laws, and abortion, it is best to avoid such topics; they have been written about so often that original or interesting arguments are hard to find. In general, avoid issues that are largely knee-jerk reactions to matters of ideology or religion. Your views on these topics will tend to rest on belief rather than logical argument. Beware, also, of saying that you intend to write about "the importance of family," "the church and morality," or "racial prejudice." Such issues might mean a great deal to you personally, but unless you have a clear sense of a logical and debatable claim rather than just strong feelings, you will have difficulty structuring an argument around them and making a valid claim that you can support with evidence.

Brainstorming, reading (books, magazines, and newspapers), and browsing on the Internet in search directories, informational sites, or online discussion groups (see **3f, 11c,** and **48c–48g**) can help you discover novel and timely issues. When you find an interesting topic and your instructor has approved it (if necessary), begin by writing a question about it. Then make lists of the arguments on both (or all) sides.

Because her family had been plagued by a spate of intrusive telephone marketing calls, Jennifer Hopper decided to tackle the topic of telemarketing and its impact on society. She began by thinking that she would claim that telemarketing is more harmful than beneficial. Here are her initial research question and her brainstormed scratch outline (see **3i**) before she began doing research:

TOPIC: The impact of telemarketing on our society

QUESTION: Does telemarketing have more harmful than beneficial effects on our daily lives?

<u>Harmful effects</u>:

Telemarketing intrudes on our privacy.

Some telemarketers prey on the elderly.

Some of their offers are scams.

Telemarketing takes business away from retail stores.

<u>Beneficial effects</u>:

Telemarketing provides jobs, especially for women, students, retirees, and minorities.

It promotes the economy in rural areas.

It provides buying opportunities for people who are elderly, disabled, and homebound.

See **6k** for a draft of Hopper's essay, in which she includes some of the points in this scratch outline and omits or changes others.

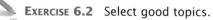

EXERCISE 6.2 Select good topics.

1. Which of the following topics would be good topics on which to base an argument? Explain your reasons for your choices.

TOPICS

genetic engineering of foodstuffs

the meaning of life

your grandmother

controlled hunting of deer in suburban areas

the love life of Tom Cruise (or your favorite celebrity)

abortion

bicycle lanes on all roads

preserving the ecosystem

the afterlife

2. Select one of the topics you earmarked as suitable, identify an interesting and debatable thesis within that topic, and make two lists, one of points that support the thesis and one of points that oppose (argue against) the thesis. Use extra paper as necessary.

Selected topic and thesis: _____
_____
_____

Points in support of thesis: _____
_____
_____

Points that oppose the thesis: _____
_____
_____

6c   Formulate an arguable claim (thesis).

Making a debatable claim   The position you take on a topic constitutes your claim or your thesis. Jennifer Hopper knew that the claim in her argument paper should be debatable, and some claims she considered were "Telemarketing provides jobs and benefits the economy" and "Telemarketers always seek out the elderly and the gullible," both of which would be debatable claims. Avoid the following types of claims, which are not debatable:

- a neutral statement, which gives no hint of the writer's position
- an announcement of the paper's broad subject
- a fact, which is not arguable
- a truism (statement that is obviously true)
- a personal or religious conviction that cannot be logically debated
- an opinion based only on your feelings
- a sweeping generalization

Here are some examples of nondebatable claims, each with a revision.

NEUTRAL STATEMENT	**There are unstated standards of beauty in the workplace.**
REVISED	**The way we look affects the way we are treated at work and the size of our paychecks.**

TOO BROAD	**This paper is about violence on TV.**
REVISED	**TV violence has to take its share of blame for the violence in our society.**

FACT	*Plessy v. Ferguson,* **a Supreme Court case that supported racial segregation, was overturned in 1954 by** *Brown v. Board of Education.*
REVISED	**The overturning of** *Plessy v. Ferguson* **by** *Brown v. Board of Education* **has not led to significant advances in integrated education.**

TRUISM	**Bilingual education has advantages and disadvantages.**
REVISED	**A bilingual program is more effective than an immersion program at helping students grasp the basics of science and mathematics.**

PERSONAL CONVICTION	**Racism is the worst kind of prejudice.**
REVISED	**The best weapon against racism is primary and secondary education.**

OPINION BASED ON FEELING	**I think water-skiing is a dumb sport.**
REVISED	**Water-skiing should be banned from public beaches.**

SWEEPING GENERALIZATION	**Women understand housework.**
REVISED	**The publication of a big new guide to housekeeping and that guide's success among both men and women suggest a renewed interest in the domestic arts.**

Avoiding loaded terms In your claim, avoid sweeping and judgmental words: for instance, *bad, good, right, wrong, stupid, ridiculous, moral, immoral, dumb, smart.*

Changing your claim Sometimes you will have an instant reaction to an issue and immediately decide which position you want to take. At other times, you will need to reflect and do research before you take a stand. Whenever you decide what your position is, formulate a position statement that will serve as your claim or thesis—for example, "Undocumented aliens should [or should not] have to pay higher college tuition fees than citizens or other immigrants." Always keep an open mind. Be prepared to find out more about an issue so that you can make an educated claim with concrete support, and be prepared to change your original opinion as you do your research.

Jennifer Hopper began her argument paper thinking she would make a case on one side of the telemarketing debate ("Telemarketing takes trade away from retail stores, deceives the elderly, and invades everyone's privacy"), only to find that her research produced enough evidence to persuade her to look at the situation from a different angle ("Telemarketing is a valuable source of American dollars and provider of goods and services").

You can read a draft of her essay in **6k**.

Modifying a claim Even if you do not change your position as Jennifer Hopper did, you will often find yourself modifying your claim as you read, think, and write, making it less all-embracing or less extreme. Here is how I myself, the author of this book, modified my claim as I worked on writing an argument about a topic I cared deeply about. I took into account some opposing views, toned down the language, and set limits to my position—not arguing on all the issues raised by the proposed building of a cement factory but focusing specifically on environmental issues of pollution, wildlife, and nature.

Topic: Building a new cement plant

Audience: General audience

Initial question: What will be the effects of a Hudson River valley cement plant on jobs, the local economy, and the environment?

Initial claim (working thesis) after some research: A large new cement plant will irreparably damage the environment of the Hudson River valley.

Modified claim (seeking common ground with readers and acknowledging recognition of opposing views): Although we need to consider the increased demand for building materials and local economic development, a large cement plant on the Hudson River would not only pollute air and water but also threaten wildlife and natural beauty.

WORLDS OF WRITING
Arguments across Cultures: Making a Claim and Staking a Position

The types of arguments described in this chapter are those common in academic and business settings in North America and the Western world. Writers state their views directly, arguing for their viewpoint. The success of their argument lies in the credibility and strength of the evidence they produce in support. But such an approach is not universal. Other languages and cultures may prefer an approach that begins by exploring and evaluating all options rather than by issuing a direct claim. One of the basic principles of writing well—know the audience's expectations—is especially relevant to writing arguments. Bear this in mind when you travel and write in cultures different from your own.

6d Support the claim with reasons and concrete evidence.

Supporting your claim means telling readers what reasons, statistics, facts, examples, and expert testimony bolster and explain your point of view. When readers ask, "Why do you think that?" about your claim, the support you offer answers that question in detail and in a clearly organized way.

Reasons Imagine someone saying to you, "OK. I know your position on this issue, but I disagree with you. What led you to your position?" This is asking you to provide the reasons you have for your conviction. To begin to answer the question, add at least one "because" clause to your claim:

> Claim: Colleges should stop using SAT scores to determine admissions.
>
> Reason: (because) High school grades predict college success with more accuracy.

Once you have formulated a tentative claim, make a scratch outline (see **3i**) listing the claim and your reasons for supporting it. As you work more on your argument, you will need to find specific and concrete evidence to explain and support each reason. Here is an example of the scratch outline I made as I planned what could go into an argument against the building of the cement factory.

A view of the Hudson River

Claim: Although a large cement factory on the Hudson River would satisfy the increased demand for building materials and might help boost the local economy, it would not only pollute air and water but also threaten the wildlife and the natural beauty of the area.

Reasons

1. Drilling, blasting, and mining pose dangers to the local aquifer and to the nearby city's water supply.

2. A 1,800-acre coal-burning plant with a 406-foot stack would emit just under 20 million pounds of pollution a year, including arsenic, lead, and mercury.

3. Smokestack emissions could affect birds; barge traffic and discharge into the river could affect fish.

4. Views portrayed by the Hudson River School of painters would be spoiled.

Concrete evidence You need reasons, but reasons are not enough. You also need to include specific evidence that supports, illustrates, and explains your reasons. Imagine a reader saying after you give one of your reasons, "Tell me even more about why you say that." The details you provide are what will make your argument vivid and persuasive.

Add to the outline any items of concrete evidence you will include to illustrate and explain your reasoning. What counts as evidence? Facts, statistics, stories, examples, and testimony from experts can all be used as evidence in support of your reasons.

 ESL NOTE Evidence Used to Support an Argument

The way arguments are structured, the concept of *expertise,* and the nature of evidence regarded as convincing may vary from one culture to another. In some cultures, for example, the opinions of religious or political leaders may carry more weight than the opinions of a scholar in the field. Looking at newspaper editorials written in your home language and in English will help you discern what differences, if any, exist in the types of evidence used to support an argument. Be sure to consider the readers you will be writing for and the type of evidence they will expect. ■

 EXERCISE 6.3 Generate ideas on an argument for improving your college.
With a group of classmates, decide on an argument for change you would like to present to the administrators of your college. List the specific and concrete details you would provide to show the nature and extent of the problem, the reasons change is necessary, and the ways in which change could be accomplished. List what the opposing views may be and consider how you could answer or counter them.

6e Identify and appeal to the audience, and establish common ground.

Ask who your readers are. Consider the readers you are writing for. Assess what they might know, what assumptions they hold, what they need to know, how they can best be convinced to accept your position, and what strategies will persuade them to respect or accept your views.

When I wanted to argue that a huge new cement plant should not be built alongside a major river and next to a populated area, I needed to consider carefully who my readers would be. Cement company workers, the unemployed, and suppliers of industrial equipment and materials, on the one hand, and doctors, environmentalists, and homeowners, on the other, would bring their own assumptions and biases to the argument. All writers need to consider and address such biases.

If you are writing for readers with no specific prior knowledge, biases, or expertise—known as a *general audience*—remember to include background information: the place, the time, the context, the issues. Do not assume that general readers know a great deal more than you do. For more on audience, see **2c.**

Appeal to readers. Your profile of readers will help you decide what types of appeal to base your arguments on:

- *Rational appeal* This bases an argument's conclusion on logical reasoning from evidence, such as using an Aristotelian syllogism (**6h**) or the Toulmin system of logic (**6g**). Such an appeal is appropriate for academic readers and useful when readers are uninformed or hostile.

- *Ethical appeal* You make an ethical appeal to readers when you represent yourself—as well as any experts and witnesses whom you refer to, paraphrase, or quote—as reliable, reasonable, and even-handed. Such an appeal is appropriate for formal situations in business and academic worlds. In advertising, ethical appeals are often adapted to include testimony from famous people, whether they are experts or not, as when Buick uses Tiger Woods to sell its cars, for example.

- *Emotional appeal* You make an emotional appeal when you try to gain the empathy and sympathy of your readers by assessing their values and using stories and language to appeal to those values. Such an appeal is less common in academic writing than in journalism and the media; it is also appropriate when readers are regarded as either already favorable to the ideas or apathetic.

Here are some examples of brief arguments of the three preceding types:

- *Rational appeal* TV reality shows should include married couples as well as single people. Families watch TV together, and they like to see their way of life represented.

- *Ethical appeal* TV reality shows should include married couples as well as single people. I am a TV producer and family man who has watched many such shows with both single and married people, and I know that viewers agree with me that married couples are underrepresented.

- *Emotional appeal* TV reality shows should include married couples as well as single people. Single people have enough shows devoted to their lifestyle. It surely is time for us married couples to be recognized as a significant part of reality.

Within one extended argument, you probably will find it necessary to use all types of argument to reach the maximum number of readers, each with individual expectations, preferences, and quirks.

Establish common ground.   Remember that readers turned off by exaggerations or extreme language have the ultimate power to stop reading and ignore what you have to say.

KEY POINTS

Ways to Establish Common Ground with Readers

1. Avoid extreme views or language.
2. Write to convince, not to confront.
3. Find ways to point to shared values.
4. Use rational language to refute any arguments that are not valid (**6f**).
5. Acknowledge when your opponents' arguments *are* valid, and work to show why the arguments on your side carry more weight.
6. If possible, propose a solution with long-term benefits for everyone.

In my discussion of the cement plant, for example, I wanted to acknowledge the importance of producing cement locally rather than importing it from other regions and to recognize the need for more local industry and jobs. One solution to the problem of finding common ground is to show how those goals could be achieved by upgrading an existing cement plant rather than building a huge new coal-fired plant.

Use language and rhetorical strategies to include and involve your audience.   When you are presenting an argument and want to inspire your audience to accept your views, you can employ writing strategies that will grab readers' attention.

- Include images and figurative language ("the quicksands of racial injustice," for instance, by Martin Luther King Jr., quoted in the Worlds of Writing box that follows).
- Use clear, everyday words that sound as if you are speaking directly to readers.
- Choose language that establishes common ground, such as the inclusive use of *we* and recognition of shared concerns.

- Avoid insulting or offensive language and name-calling. Labeling someone's views as *ridiculous, ignorant, immoral, fascist,* or *crooked,* for example, is unnecessarily inflammatory.

- Steer clear of sarcastic remarks, such as "They have come up with the amazingly splendid idea of building a gigantic cement factory right in the middle of a natural beauty spot."

- Use repetition and parallel structure to connect ideas and build to a climax (see also **5e** and **19j**).

WORLDS OF WRITING
Rhetorical Approaches to Involve an Audience

Martin Luther King Jr. was a master of rhetorical devices to involve his audience, as you can see in this excerpt from his "I Have a Dream" speech to civil rights protesters in 1963. Note his use of figurative language, his use of *we* to establish commonality with his audience, the use of parallel forms (**5e**) with the repetition of the phrase "Now is the time to . . . ," and the balanced sentences: "to rise from . . . to" and "to lift . . . from . . . to . . . ." Note, too, how well these techniques work in writing as well as in a speech.

We have also come to this hallowed spot to remind America of the fierce urgency of *now.* This is no time to engage in the luxury of cooling off or to take the tranquilizing drug of gradualism. *Now is the time to* make real the promises of democracy. *Now is the time to* rise from the dark and desolate valley of segregation to the sunlit path of racial justice. *Now is the time to* lift our nation from the quicksands of racial injustice to the solid rock of brotherhood. *Now is the time to* make justice a reality for all of God's children.

Getting your listeners or readers to identify with your cause makes them more receptive to the arguments you present and the action you propose.

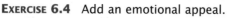

EXERCISE 6.4 Add an emotional appeal.
The following passage presents a logical appeal. What could the writer add to include an emotional appeal, too?

Hunger is not as serious here [in the United States] as in countries where children are so nutrient-deprived that brain growth is impeded. The moderate undernutrition found in the United States affects performance, but recovery is usually possible with adequate diet. Yet if dietary deficiencies persist, learning can suffer. Iron deficiency anemia, which is twice as common in poor as in better-off children, affects cognitive ability. In experiments where people got inexpensive vitamin and mineral supplements, test scores rose from that treatment alone.
—Richard Rothstein, "Lessons: Food for Thought? In Many Cases, No"

6f Refute opposing views.

It is not enough to present your own reasons and evidence for your claim. You also need to take into account any opposing arguments and the reasons and evidence that support those arguments. Examine those arguments, describe the most common or convincing ones, evaluate their validity, applicability, and limitations, and explain what motivates people to take those positions; then discuss the ways in which your reasons and evidence are more pertinent and convincing than theirs.

Be careful to argue logically without insulting your opponents. Take pains to explain rationally why your views differ from theirs. You might choose to do this by following each one of your own points with a discussion of an opposing view. Or you may prefer to devote a section of your essay to dealing with opposing views.

Rather than say, "The fools who want the company to build a cement plant think that it will provide jobs in the area. Get real! The company has publicly stated that there will be only five new jobs created," express a similar sentiment but in a more respectful and effective way:

One of the arguments used by many of those in favor of the proposed cement plant is that it will bring jobs to the area. But that particular argument has little basis in fact. The cement company officials have stated publicly that no more than five new jobs will be added if they build the plant.

> **Exercise 6.5** Write a rebuttal of arguments.
> Read the following passage and write a rebuttal.

The movie business is choking on a smog of nostalgia. Billboards all over town trumpet Universal's big-screen remake of "Leave It to Beaver," in which bad boys steal the Beaver's bike and he gets it back. Though Hollywood has attracted the best and the brightest Ivy Leaguers, they don't seem to understand a very simple fact. We liked *Leave It to Beaver* when we were little. But we're big now. We haven't spent the last few decades educating ourselves and complicating ourselves to prepare for another bout with the Beav. "Hollywood is significantly responsible for the infantilization of America," says Leon Wieseltier, the cultural editor of *The New Republic.*

—Maureen Dowd, "Leave It to Hollywood"

6g Think critically about your argument, and ask Toulmin's four questions.

Thinking critically does not mean criticizing what you read and hear. It means keeping an open mind and asking probing questions. As a reader of arguments, you will want to employ your critical thinking capabilities to examine the reasoning a writer uses and to ferret out the writer's assumptions, biases, and lapses in logic. (See **49** for more on research and critical reading.) Remember, too, that readers will be looking for *your* assumptions, biases, and lapses in logic as they read.

Examine your logic with four questions The four questions in the Key Points box, derived from Stephen Toulmin's *The Uses of Argument,* will provide you with a way to examine your own arguments critically.

Toulmin provides the following illustration of a simple argument, one not complex enough for an essay but clear enough to show the principles:

Claim: Harry is probably a British subject.

Support/data: Harry was born in Bermuda.

Assumption/warrant: A man born in Bermuda will generally be a British subject . . .

Qualifier: . . . unless both his parents were not born in Bermuda or he has become a naturalized American.

KEY POINTS

Four Questions to Ask about Your Argument

1. What is your point? (What are you claiming?)

2. What do you have to go on? (What support do you have for your claim, in the form of reasons, data, and evidence?)

3. How do you get there? (What assumptions—Toulmin calls them "warrants"—do you take for granted and expect the reader to take for granted, too?)

4. What could prevent you from getting there? (What qualifications do you need to include, using *but, unless,* or *if* or adding words like *usually, often, several, mostly,* or *sometimes* to provide exceptions to your assumptions?)

Here is another example, showing how the Toulmin questions can be used to develop the claim and supporting reason introduced in **6d**.

Claim: Colleges should stop using SAT scores in their admissions process.

Support/data: (because) High school grades and recommendations predict college success with more accuracy.

Assumption/warrant: Colleges use SAT scores to predict success in college.

Qualifier: . . . unless colleges use the scores only to indicate the level of knowledge acquired in high school.

Revised claim: Colleges that use SAT scores to predict college success should use instead high school grades and recommendations.

EXERCISE 6.6 Analyze assumptions.

Examine the following arguments. What are the assumptions that connect the claim to the data? Write a short analysis of the warrant (the assumptions). Then write a revised claim, suggesting any necessary qualifiers. Use extra paper as necessary.

1. Claim: Steve is wealthy.

   Support/data: Steve wears designer clothing, drives a Mercedes, and has a summer home.

   Assumption/warrant:_____

   Qualifier: _____

   Revised claim: _____

2. Claim: Rita Fiorella is probably of Italian descent.

   Support/data: She has an Italian last name and long dark hair.

   Assumption/warrant:_____

   Qualifier: _____

   Revised claim: _____

6h Check your logic.

Examine your underlying assumptions. Pay special attention to examining the assumptions that link a claim to the reasons and evidence you provide. Consider whether readers will share those assumptions or whether you need to explain, discuss, and defend them. For example, the claim "Telemarketing should be monitored because it preys on the elderly and the gullible" operates on the assumption that monitoring will catch and reduce abuses. The claim "Telemarketing should be encouraged because it benefits the economy" operates on the assumption that benefit to the economy is an important goal. These different assumptions will appeal to different readers, and some readers may need to be persuaded of the assumptions before they accept your claim or the reasons you give for it.

Note that if you claim that "Telemarketing should be encouraged because it is useful," you are saying little more than, "Telemarketing is good because it is good." Readers are certain to object to and reject such circular reasoning. That is why it is important to ask question 3 on page 129, the question that leads you to examine how you get from your evidence to your claim and what assumptions your claim is based on.

Check the logic of deductive arguments. A deductive argument draws a valid conclusion from true statements. This classical Aristotelian method of constructing an argument is based on a reasoning process known as a *syllogism*. The syllogism presents a major premise, which must be a valid one, and moves to a minor premise and then to a certain conclusion. Here is an example:

Premise 1: Writers for *Vibe* magazine know about hip-hop music.

Premise 2: Dave Bry is a writer for *Vibe* magazine.

Conclusion: Dave Bry knows about hip-hop music.

This argument is both valid (the chain of logical reasoning works) and true (nobody would question the truth of either of the premises). We learn something about all *Vibe* writers; then we learn the identity of one of the writers and make the deduction accordingly.

Always check the logic of your argument by testing for any assumptions or unstated premises that may make your deductive argument untrue or invalid. The following is an invalid argument. The major term in premise 1 (*writers*) does not appear in premise 2 in either its singular or its plural form.

Premise 1: Writers for *Vibe* magazine know about hip-hop music.

Premise 2: Georgia Winston knows about hip-hop music.

Conclusion: Georgia Winston is a writer for *Vibe* magazine.

The problem here is that there could be many explanations for why Georgia Winston knows about hip-hop music: she could collect CDs, go to performances, and read *Vibe* regularly, for example. The conclusion does not follow from the premises. The argument is invalid. (And, in fact, Georgia Winston is a lawyer, not a writer.)

In contrast, in the following syllogism, the conclusion follows logically from the premises. The problem is, though, that the first premise is not true. Many or most of the *Vibe* writers are *not* performers, so the conclusion is not true.

Premise 1: Writers for *Vibe* magazine are professional hip-hop performers.

Premise 2: Dave Bry is a writer for *Vibe* magazine.

Conclusion: Dave Bry is a professional hip-hop performer.

Many statements present an argument, but the argument is abbreviated, with premises left unstated. When you write a sentence using the word *so* or *therefore,* you are arguing by stating a premise and a conclusion. Always be sure that no false assumption or premise makes the argument untrue or invalid, as in the following example:

Mark Greenbaum is an elementary school principal, so he must love teaching.

Here is the syllogism on which that statement is based:

Unstated premise: All elementary school principals love teaching.

Stated premise: Mark Greenbaum is an elementary school principal.

Conclusion: Mark Greenbaum loves teaching.

Notice that the assumption, the unstated premise that all elementary school principals love teaching, is not necessarily true, or at least cannot be proven to be true. The argument needs to be qualified.

Unstated premise: Most elementary school principals love teaching.

Stated premise: Mark Greenbaum is an elementary school principal.

Conclusion: Mark Greenbaum probably loves teaching.

Check the thoroughness of the evidence in inductive arguments. While a deductive argument begins with a generalization and leads to a *certain* conclusion, an inductive argument begins with details that lead to a *probable* conclusion.

Inductive arguments are used often in the sciences and social sciences. Researchers begin with a tentative hypothesis. They conduct studies and perform experiments; they collect and tabulate data; they examine the evidence of other studies. Then they draw a conclusion to support, reject, or modify the hypothesis. The conclusion, however, is not necessarily certain. It is based on the circumstances of the evidence. Different evidence at a different time could lead to a different conclusion. Conclusions drawn in the medical field change with the experiments and the sophistication of the techniques—eggs are good for you one year, bad the next. That is not because researchers are wrong. It is that the nature of the evidence changes.

Avoid flaws in logic. Faulty logic can make readers mistrust you as a writer. Watch out for these flaws as you write and check your drafts.

1. *Sweeping generalization* Generalizations can sometimes be so broad that they fall into stereotyping. Avoid them.

> All British people are stiff and formal.

> The only thing that concerns students is grades.

Readers will be right to wonder what leads to these conclusions. Without any explanation or evidence, these conclusions will simply be dismissed. Beware, then, of the trap of words like *all, every, only, never,* and *always.*

2. *Hasty conclusion with inadequate support* To convince readers of the validity of a generalization, you need to offer enough evidence—usually more than just one personal observation. Thoughtful readers can easily spot a conclusion that is too hastily drawn from flimsy support.

> My friend Arecelis had a terrible time in a bilingual school. It is clear that bilingual education has failed.

> Bilingual education is a success story, as the school in Chinatown has clearly shown.

A conclusion that can be contradicted by any evidence is not a sound conclusion.

3. Non sequitur *Non sequitur* is Latin for "it does not follow." Supporting a claim with evidence that is illogical or irrelevant causes a non sequitur fallacy.

> Maureen Dowd writes so well that she would make a good teacher.

The writer does not establish any connection between good writing and good teaching.

> Studying economics is a waste of time. Money does not make people happy.

Here the writer does not help us see any relationship between happiness and the study of a subject.

4. Causal fallacy You are guilty of a causal fallacy if you assume that one event causes another merely because the second event happens after the first. (The Latin name for this logical flaw is *post hoc, ergo propter hoc:* "after this, therefore because of this.")

> The economy collapsed because a new president was elected.

Was the election the reason? Or did the election happen to occur before the economy collapsed?

> The number of A's given in college courses has increased. This clearly shows that faculty members are inflating grades.

But does it clearly show that? Is it not possible for the cause to be that students are better prepared in high school? Examine carefully any statements you make about cause and effect.

5. Ad hominem attack *Ad hominem* (Latin for "to the person") refers to appeals to personal considerations rather than to logic or reason. Avoid using arguments that seek to discredit an opinion through criticizing a person's character or lifestyle.

> The new curriculum should not be adopted because the administrators who favor it have never even taught a college course.

> The student who is urging the increase in student fees for social events is a partygoer and a big drinker.

Argue a point by drawing attention to the logic of the argument, or lack of it, not to flaws in character. However, personal considerations may be valid if they pertain directly to the issue, as in "The two women who favor the closing of the bar own property on the same block."

6. Circular reasoning In an argument based on circular reasoning, the evidence and the conclusion restate each other, thus proving nothing.

> Credit card companies should be banned on campus because companies should not be allowed to solicit business from students.

> That rich man is smart because wealthy people are intelligent.

Neither of these statements moves the argument forward. They both beg the question; that is, they argue in a circular way.

7. False dichotomy or false dilemma Either/or arguments reduce complex problems to two simplistic alternatives without exploring them in depth or considering other alternatives.

> To improve education, the board can either hire more teachers or build more schools.

Such a statement presents a false dichotomy. Those two options are not the only ways to improve education: science labs could be renovated, computer instruction could be developed, teachers could be assigned to only classroom duties, and so on.

> After September 11, the New York mayor can do one of two things: increase airport security or screen immigrants.

This proposal presents a false dichotomy. These are not the only two options for dealing with potential terrorism. Posing a false dilemma like this will not win you converts to your argument.

EXERCISE 6.7 Examine arguments.
For each of the following statements, determine whether the argument is logical or contains a logical fallacy. If it contains a logical fallacy, identify the logical fallacy and explain why it is a fallacy.

1. The new vice president of sales is untrustworthy because many years ago he was arrested for civil disobedience while in college.
2. Married couples without children often experience societal pressure to have or adopt children.
3. Mary can either matriculate as a full-time student in the fall or wait until the following fall to attend classes.
4. Keeping a diary is cathartic because writing on a daily basis releases bottled-up emotions.
5. All men like sports.

TECHNOTE More about Logical Fallacies on the Web

Go to *Stephen's Guide to the Logical Fallacies* at <http://datanation .com/fallacies> for lists of many more types of logical fallacies, all with explanations and examples. ■

6i Basic argument structures

Your material and your purposes will do a great deal to influence how you organize your argument to achieve the best results. Three common structures used in designing an argument are these: general to specific, specific to general, and problem and solution.

General to specific If you have not had much experience with writing arguments, you may find it useful to work with and adapt the following basic structure for an argument. In use in various forms since classical times, this structure moves from the general to the specific, from thesis to support and evidence. It is used frequently in the humanities and arts.

KEY POINTS
Basic Structure for a General-to-Specific Argument

1. *Introduction* Provide background information on the issue, why it is an issue, and what the controversies are. After you have introduced readers to the nature and importance of the issue, announce your position in a claim or thesis statement, perhaps at the end of the first paragraph or in a prominent position within the second paragraph, depending on the length and complexity of your essay.

2. *Body* Provide evidence in the form of supporting points for your thesis, with concrete and specific details. For each new point, start a new paragraph.

3. *Acknowledgment of opposing views* Use evidence and specific details to describe and logically refute the opposing views. You could also deal with opposing views one by one as you deal with your own points of support.

4. *Conclusion* Return to the issue and your claim. Without repeating whole phrases and sentences, reiterate the point you want to make. End on a strong note.

Specific to general Alternatively, you might choose to begin with data and points of evidence and then draw a conclusion from that evidence. A basic specific-to-general argument looks like this:

Introduction: Background, statement of problem

Data:

    1. Cell phone users admit to being distracted while driving.

    2. Many accidents are attributable to cell phone use.

3. New York State has passed a law against hand-held cell phone use while driving.

4. The AAA and insurance companies report that . . .

Conclusion: Discussion of data and presentation of thesis (generalization formed from analysis of the data): All states should prohibit the use of hand-held cell phones while driving.

In an argument in the sciences or social sciences (see, for example, the APA-style sample paper in section **53f**), writers often begin with a hypothesis that they can test: they list their findings from experimentation, surveys, facts, and statistics, and then from the data they have collected they draw conclusions to support, modify, or reject the hypothesis. Here is an outline of an argument built around a hypothesis:

Introduction: Background, review of the literature

Hypothesis: Statins should be prescribed more widely than they are now to prevent heart attacks.

Data:

1. Decrease in heart failure for patients on statins

2. Need for women to be aware of heart disease and take preventive measures

3. What statins do that exercise and diet cannot do

4. Testimony from three heart-attack patients and six doctors

Conclusion: Analysis of data and confirmation of hypothesis

Problem and solution If your topic offers solutions to a problem, you probably will find it useful to present the details of the problem first and then offer solutions. Consider whether the strongest position for the solution you consider the most desirable is at the beginning of your solutions section or at the end. Do you want to make your strong point early or lead up to it gradually? See **5d,** item 14, for a passage from an argument providing a solution to a problem.

6j Visual arguments

We commonly think of arguments as being spoken or written, and **6a–6i** deal largely with the features of written arguments. However, it is worth noting that another type of argument is widespread—an argument that is presented visually. Think, for example, of arguments made in cartoons, advertisements, drawings, and works of art. The famous

1976 *New Yorker* magazine cover by Saul Steinberg called "View of the World from Ninth Avenue" shows New York City in the foreground, with cars on Ninth Avenue, gradually giving way to New Jersey, Kansas, the Pacific Ocean, and Japan in the background. The argument? That New York City is the center of the world to New Yorkers.

You can supplement your written arguments with visual arguments: maps, superimposed images, photographs, charts and graphs, political cartoons—vivid images that will say more than many words to your readers. An argument essay on animal preservation in the wild, for example, would make a strong emotional impact if its argument included the following picture. This photograph shows a young chimpanzee confiscated from poachers by Kenya Wildlife Service officials in 2003.

© Reuters NewMedia Inc./CORBIS

Visual arguments make their appeals in ways similar to written arguments, appealing to logic, showcasing the character and credentials of the author, or appealing to viewers' emotions. When you write an argument, consider adding to the impact of your thesis by including a visual argument.

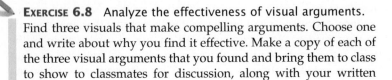

EXERCISE 6.8 Analyze the effectiveness of visual arguments. Find three visuals that make compelling arguments. Choose one and write about why you find it effective. Make a copy of each of the three visual arguments that you found and bring them to class to show to classmates for discussion, along with your written analysis of one image.

6k Sample arguments: A student's essay and a letter in a community newspaper

A student's outline and argument essay   Here is the revised outline and the second draft of Jennifer Hopper's argument paper on telemarketing, written for her first college course in expository writing.

```
Thesis: Telemarketing cannot be written off as a public
nuisance when it is such a valuable source of American
dollars and provider of goods and services.
Introduction:
     Background of problem
     Definition of term
     The two sides of the problem
Supporting points:
     1. Telemarketing targets and promotes business.
     2. Telemarketing provides jobs in rural areas.
     3. Telemarketing supplements earnings and provides
        economic security.
     4. Telemarketing demands verbal and social skills and
        so promotes education.
   Opposition: Actions taken by those who oppose
   telemarketing
     1. Telemarketing is such a nuisance that people
        initiate legislation at national, state, and
        local levels.
     2. People become personally aggressive toward
        callers.
   Refutation of opposing views and tactics
   Solution to problem
```

Jennifer Hopper

Professor Raimes

English 120

26 November 2001

Why Telemarketing Is a Real Job:

The Ongoing War between the Right to

Privacy and Telemarketing

Economic swings bring with them new strategies for success and survival. Before our recent disaster, which precipitated a downturn in our spirits as well as in the economy, we had experienced many years of unprecedented optimism and prosperity. However, before that, about fourteen years ago, our economy was experiencing one of the periodic slumps that have repercussions on people's lives. Many urban dwellers were out of work. Farm owners were being forced to sell their land. Money woes were on all American minds. Some blamed the President. Others pointed to big business owners. But eventually, the United States managed to escape unscathed from the down-spiraling trend. Coincidentally, another phenomenon hit America at about the same time as the economic upswing-- telemarketing.

> Gives background context

Telemarketing is a relatively new way for companies to sell their wares to American shoppers. Rather than having to wait for consumers to choose to shop in their stores and buy from them, businesses have decided to go straight to the customer. This involves millions of telephone calls from company representatives to households across America every day. The demand for workers to make those calls and the billions of dollars' worth of goods and services sold via the calls have created a booming business for telemarketers (Greenwald).

> Defines term

> Refers to a one-page source

Hopper 2

Yet every silver lining has its cloud. There has been
a substantial outcry from the American public about the
irritation of receiving sales calls at home. These
objections have led to legislation by Congress, the
creation of antitelemarketing Web sites on the Internet,
and court battles between private citizens and
telemarketing companies (Raisfield). These developments
center around the issue of Americans' right to privacy
at home and whether telephone solicitations are an
intrusion on that privacy.

Presents one side of issue

Of course, if this is the ugly side of
telemarketing, we must also consider that there is an
important bright side. Telemarketing has proven itself
substantially important to both American workers and
consumers. It increasingly provides millions of jobs to
Americans (growing from 175,000 jobs in 1983 to five
million in 1993) and has sparked the growth and
development of many declining U.S. cities (Greenwald).
Therefore, if some individuals find that telephone
solicitations do them more harm than good, they should
rectify the problem without compromising the rights
of the consumers and workers who benefit from the
industry. In short, telemarketing cannot be written
off as a public nuisance when it is such a valuable
source of American dollars and provider of goods and
services.

Presents other side

Thesis

Although it is difficult to find a person with a
listed phone number who has never received a
telemarketing call, consumers are not the main target
of phone solicitations. Journalist John Greenwald
reports that "pitches to other businesses generate
more than 80% of the revenues of telemarketing and
account for some 90% of its jobs." Just as companies
have found it cheaper to use phone calls rather than
mail to gain customers, they have also found
telemarketing to be a cheaper means of promoting
business than sending sales teams (Greenwald).

Point 1

In some parts of the country, the impact of
telemarketing industries is especially beneficial.
Omaha, Nebraska, is a prime example. In 1995, there were
as few as thirty telemarketing companies located there,
and yet "20,000 or so Omahans--about 5% of the resident
population--work for them dialing out more than one
million quality calls per week" (Singer 66). Omaha
proved to be a profitable site for the industry, from
the viewpoints of both company owners and Omaha
residents. Located right in the middle of the United
States, the town lends itself to "easy access" to all
corners of the country and its four time zones (Singer
69). Not only that, but the majority of Omahan laborers
are reasonably well educated, another advantage in the
telemarketing field. According to New York Times
correspondent James Brooke, a similar situation has
developed in North Dakota, where Native Americans have
been able to take telemarketing jobs near their
reservations. In fact, Native Americans, usually vastly
overlooked by American employers, are catching the
interest of telemarketers. It may not be ascribed to
social consciousness on the part of telemarketing
companies, but it still provides opportunities for a
group of people not known for their earning power.

An important point to note is not just the
number of jobs that telemarketing provides but the
significant economic changes those jobs make in the
lives of the people who hold them. In both Omaha and
North Dakota, farming used to be the way of life
(Brooke). As it became more and more difficult to subsist
on crops and cattle in the United States of the late
20th century, the need arose for another way for locals
to supplement their earnings and gain security.
Telemarketing provides a means for people to keep their
homes and farms by working part-time in a booming
industry. Telemarketing also provides part-time jobs
that are stable and relatively easy. When asked about

Point 2

Point 3

the rigors of her job, Omahan telemarketer Erin Kline responded, "Stressful? More tiring. But to sit here and get paid over 10, 11 bucks an hour to sit on your butt, basically, and make phone calls . . . that's a really good job" (qtd. in Singer 66). Telemarketing jobs are frequently held by housewives, college students, and retired persons.

Telemarketing requires an educated labor force because of the intricate skills involved in closing a sale. Some seem like honest methods of clarifying the telemarketer's pitch by paying attention to language, while others seem more like playing with people's minds. Whatever questions we may raise about the purpose and content of the educational training, we still have to acknowledge that it increases sensitivity to language. In their training, for example, solicitors are taught to be sensitive to what words mean; they are encouraged to use the words "own it" rather than "buy it," "opportunity" as opposed to "deal," and "agreement" instead of "contract" (Fidel 138). The former expressions are said to cause less anxiety than the latter. Stanley Leo Fidel, who makes his living training telemarketers, advises: "Words people should use in their presentations are *you, profit, love, benefit, sale, secure, control, power, easy, simple, guaranteed, new,* and *free*" (148). To convince you to read the rest of this research paper, a skilled telemarketer might say, "Not only will this paper make you more secure in your knowledge of the telemarketing industry, but you'll find it's easy to both read and benefit from. The paper is free, and you're guaranteed to love it, so profit from the information now while the opportunity is within your power." Learning about the power of words is part of the telemarketers' training.

Another useful technique telemarketers learn is that they should try to cultivate common ground by

Point 4
a. Verbal
skills

b. Social
skills

expressing that they are similar to the person at the other end of the line. This includes speaking at the consumer's pace and tone, and asking open-ended questions to discern more personal information (Fidel 159). Even if some of these tactics seem like brainwashing, we must remember they are no different from those employed by salespeople at retail stores. Furthermore, telemarketers are reminded that if a prospective client does not need their product or service, no one will benefit from a forced sale (Allen 101). The customer is stuck with a product he or she cannot use and the company does not project a favorable image.

Yet we can hardly forget the millions of people *receiving* these phone calls. Many Americans express distaste for the entire industry, united in the belief that people's homes should be a safe haven from the rabid commercialism that has permeated all corners of society. Some believe that telemarketing preys on so-called "nice guys" and older people, who are loath to be rude and reject the sale offered, which may even be a scam. Although there has been some legislation regulating the telemarketing industry, it has not been as substantial as the industry's critics had hoped. The Telephone Consumer Protection Act (1992) makes telemarketing calls illegal between the hours of 9 P.M. and 8 A.M. and forces individual telemarketing companies to keep lists of people who have requested no further solicitations (Raisfield). Twenty-three states have initiated a "Do Not Call" list, which informs companies of homes that request no more calls (Murphy 12). However, without national legislation and penalties, consumers often take matters into their own hands.

Two different approaches have been used by aggravated consumers to fight the telemarketing industry. One method was used most notably by a man named Robert Bulmash, whose name is practically

Opposing views

National and state legislation

Hopper 6

synonymous with antitelemarketing. Bulmash took his grievances straight to the American legal system, suing a telemarketing company that had especially plagued him (Sharkey). He has channeled his efforts into heading a group that helps cut down on unwelcome telephone solicitations. Its members' names are given to telemarketing companies who are then informed there is a "service charge" for calling them. If calls continue, Bulmash helps members take legal action against the companies (Raisfield). Bulmash's approach was unique in that he brought his objections to the owners and operators of the company, who would have to deal with the lawsuit.

Other people use less noble tactics. Figure 1 shows that 63% of consumers screen calls or simply hang up. Others are rude or irritating to telemarketers in order to make them hang up or permanently stop calling. One proponent of this technique is Vince Nestico, who has even created a Web site to provide ideas to other exasperated people on how to "torture" telemarketers. He sells tapes that offer such extreme retorts to solicitors as, "Shhh . . . Wait a minute. I'm here robbing the house. Whoa! I think the owners just got home. Can you hold?" (qtd. in Sharkey). Unlike Bulmash, Vince Nestico has decided that the best way to obtain phone lines free of solicitors is to take up his grievances with the employees, not the heads of the telemarketing companies. It is understandable that Nestico is tired of receiving telemarketing calls, but it may be more difficult to comprehend his motivations for trying to capitalize on the sale of goods like the "Telemarketer Torture Tape" he has created.

Are such tapes the mature, responsible way to handle an onslaught of telemarketing calls? Just as the consumer has a right to privacy, the telemarketer has the right to hold a job and not be tormented in the process. If people have a problem with telemarketing

Personal lawsuits

Personal aggressiveness

Refutation of opposing views and tactics

Fig. 1

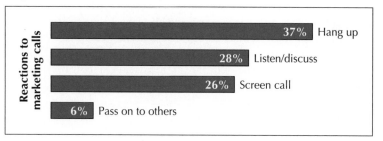

Source: Pitney Bowes. Gerda Gallop-Goodman, "Please Don't Hang Up," <u>American Demographics</u> 23.5 (2001): 28.

as a selling strategy, then they need to take it up with the heads of companies or the government, as many of them already have, or with the Federal Trade Commission, which has a useful Web site on consumer protection at <http://www.ftc.gov/bcp/menu-tmark.htm>. Telemarketers are surely not selling their souls by doing their job, and surely should not be treated as though they were. In the case of Vince Nestico, it seems that if he is eager to make money from a tape to torture telemarketers, he has forgone his right to criticize telemarketing as an unsuitable way to make money.

Solution

It cannot be denied that many American consumers are tired of hearing sales pitches over the phone. We need to find a way to alleviate this backlash without compromising the rights and prosperity of workers at the other end of the line. New and better reforms would certainly be a viable option, particularly a national "Do Not Call" list for all telemarketing companies. This would put no dent in the thriving telemarketing industry, because the people who want to be placed on a "Do Not Call" list are not likely to be interested in buying the telemarketers' wares anyway.

Hopper 8

Conclusion

After learning the industry's employment numbers and sales revenues, we can no longer write off telemarketing as unnecessary and dispensable. It has become important and necessary to places like Omaha and North Dakota, where jobs were and still are badly needed. Telemarketing industries are selling billions of dollars' worth of goods and services to American consumers every year. Not all these sales, or even a majority of them, can be the result of telemarketers supposedly deceiving consumers. Americans who may not agree with telemarketing techniques can fight the industry legally. But telemarketers have as much right to hold down a job without interference as other Americans. Linda Scobee, an Omahan telemarketer, had this in mind when a man attacked her for doing her job. "He said, 'Why don't you get a real job?' and I wanted to say, 'If you'd like to send me a check every month to take care of my kids, I'll stop.' But I didn't. You know, company policy" (qtd. in Singer 69).

Hopper 9

Works Cited

Allen, Margaret. <u>Direct Marketing</u>. London: Kagan Page, 1997.

Brooke, James. "Telemarketing Finds a Ready Labor Market in Hard-Pressed North Dakota." <u>New York Times</u> 3 Feb. 1997: A10. <u>Academic Universe</u>. Lexis-Nexis. City U of New York Lib., New York, NY. 13 Nov. 2001 <http://web.lexis-nexis.com/>.

Fidel, Stanley Leo. <u>Start Up Telemarketing</u>. Washington, DC: Wiley, 1987.

Greenwald, John. "Sorry, Right Number." <u>Time</u> 13 Sept. 1993: 66. <u>Academic Search Premier</u>. EBSCOhost. City U of New York Lib., New York, NY. 10 Nov. 2001 <http://search.epnet.com/direct.asp?an=9309080045&db=aph>.

Murphy, Brian P. "Giving Cold Calls the Cold Shoulder." <u>Business Week</u> 2 July 2001: 12. <u>Academic Search Premier</u>. EBSCOhost. City U of New York Lib., New York, NY. 12 Nov. 2001 <http://search.epnet.com/direct.asp?an=4662397&db=aph>.

Raisfield, Robin. "Telenuisances." <u>New York Magazine</u> 31 Jan. 1994: 31.

Sharkey, Joe. "Answering the Phone as an Act of Revenge." <u>New York Times</u> 22 June 1997: 3. <u>Academic Universe</u>. Lexis-Nexis. City U of New York Lib., New York, NY. 11 Nov. 2001 <http://web.lexis-nexis.com/>.

Singer, Barry. "It's 7 P.M. and 5 Percent of Omaha Is Calling. Want 28 Steaks and a Radio?" <u>New York Times Magazine</u> 3 Dec. 1995: 68- . <u>Academic Universe</u>. Lexis-Nexis. City U of New York Lib., New York, NY. 9 Nov. 2001 <http://web.lexis-nexis.com/>.

A persuasive letter on a community issue Here is an open letter to the governor of New York State, published as a letter to the editor in a local community newspaper. It presents an argument and attempts to persuade the governor to take action.

Calls on Pataki to Intervene in SLC (St. Lawrence Cement)

To the Editor:

I wanted to share with readers this open letter I sent to Governor George Pataki:

I am writing to make you aware of a proposal that has the potential to do great harm to the Hudson Valley and to ask for your help.

This spring, I attended two dinners in New York City hosted by leading environmental organizations where you were rightly honored for your outstanding efforts to improve and preserve the environment of New York State. Listening to the list of accomplishments, even the most cautious judge would have to conclude that your interest is sincere and personal, and that your efforts have been effective.

It is for this reason that I write now in the belief that once you are fully aware of the harm that will result from the proposed project, you will use your political leadership to stop or modify it.

My appeal to you is made particularly urgent by the fact that currently we are experiencing a complete breakdown in political leadership among the local elected officials in Columbia County. For reasons that are not now fully clear, the elected officials who should be protecting the interests of residents of Columbia County are paralyzed, mesmerized, or, in some cases (I fear), compromised by the efforts of a multinational corporation to build a 30-story facility topped by a 40-story smokestack sprawling over 1,800 acres.

This coal-fired cement plant, virtually within the City of Hudson and within view of Claverack, Athens, and Olana, will release 20,000,000 pounds of regulated pollutants each year, according to the DEIS [Draft Environmental Impact Statement]. As proposed, this plant is so large and will produce so much pollution that even the residents of Berkshire County have asked their political leaders and the Massachusetts Department of Environmental Protection to become parties to the permitting process.

Large, dirty, and noisy, this project will destroy southwestern Columbia County, covering a tranquil, economically sound, beautiful rural area of important agricultural lands in fine, gray, dust. The riverfront of Hudson where we are working to build a public park will become a busy industrial dock where millions of tons of coal are off-loaded and millions of tons of cement are on-loaded into barges 800 feet in length in a 24-hour per day operation.

You are familiar with the damage caused by coal-burning power plants operating to the west of New York State. Ozone and acid rain are serious continuing problems for our state, yet this proposal would burn coal at huge rates on the edge of the Hudson River, while the profits are shipped out of the country.

St. Lawrence Cement, a subsidiary of the Swiss bank Holderbank, has attempted to argue that the project should be allowed because of economic benefits to the area. The record of DEC's [Department of Environmental Conservation] hearings held June 20 at Columbia-Greene Community College before Administrative Law Judge Helene Goldberger clearly refutes this notion.

I know you have supported sound economic development for New York State and I support those efforts. I believe, however, that even a quick examination of the record will demonstrate to you that this project will bring economic destruction, not development.

I know there is a legal administrative process for these kinds of projects. I also know the process is not beyond the arena of political action. If this were not the case, St. Lawrence Cement would have not hired an established lobbyist long associated with the state Republican Party to represent its interests in Albany.

Governor Pataki, we desperately need your help and your leadership to save our homes, our health, and our peace of mind. All the people of Columbia, Greene, and northern Dutchess Counties will be deeply in your debt if you look into this proposal.

I am convinced that any fair-minded person examining the consequences of building this plant, as proposed, will have to conclude that the consequences are too grave to be ignored at the highest levels of state government.

Gerald Moore
Hudson

EXERCISE 6.9 Evaluate arguments.
Reread Gerald Moore's argument and respond to the following questions:

1. What strategies does Gerald Moore use to establish common ground with his audience, the readers of the newspaper and the governor?

2. What arguments does he present to try to convince the governor (and the newspaper readers) of his point of view?

3. What comments can you make about the type and logic of the arguments he uses?

7 Writing about Literature

When the poet Ezra Pound describes literature as "news that stays news," he recognizes the enduring power of literature to entertain and instruct. In English and courses in other languages, you probably will be asked to read literature and write about it. Reading literature, with its insights into other worlds, other people, and other cultures, provides not only pleasure but knowledge. And writing about literature helps distill that knowledge and apply it to your own world. A prerequisite to writing well about literature is reading literature thoroughly and analytically.

For examples of students' writing about literature, see **7j** and **8b**.

7a Reading and analyzing literature

What is on a page is read and interpreted differently by different readers, depending on their age, gender, nationality, culture, socioeconomic level, experience, and educational background, as well as their personalities and preferences. Meaning is not fixed in the text and stable across place and time. Rather, it is fluid, depending on what is there on the page, who is doing the reading, and where and when that reader is reading. That is why interpretation and analysis have a large role to play in the appreciation of literature.

Writing about meaning in a literary work, then, involves argument. You argue for your interpretation, for the validity of your response and analysis, for your "take" on the work. The best evidence you can provide to bolster your case is either from the text in question in the form of summary, paraphrase, and quotation, or from other related texts.

When you read literature, it is important to read it thoroughly and critically in order to establish what the important issues are and how you respond to the work and to those issues.

KEY POINTS
Reading Critically

1. Read the work, especially a short work, as many times as you can. The first time, read to enjoy and appreciate the work and to form your first impressions. In later readings, read closely and critically.

2. If the work is short, and particularly if it is a poem, find time to read it aloud.

3. Read with a pencil in your hand. If you own the book or are working with a duplicated copy, underline or highlight significant passages and write your own comments and questions in the margins. Mark only a few places on each page; otherwise, when rereading, you will not know what to pay attention to. If you do not own the book or article, do not mark the actual text; instead, use self-stick notes or make notes on index cards or in a computer file.

4. As you read, note any recurrent patterns, surprises, significant passages, and links to other parts of the text, and make connections to other works, people, or events.

5. Pay attention to the author's use of language, figures of speech, and symbolism.

6. For a long work such as a novel, keep a reading journal. In it, write a summary of each section or chapter and make notes. Add comments on significant passages in the text and record your responses to them. Using the double-entry notebook format (**3a**) is a good idea.

A sample reading journal David Powers, a student in a first-year required writing course, read an excerpt from Keith Gilyard's *Voices of the Self* and wrote this summary and his own comments on it in his reading journal. (See also **10b** for a screenshot of how Powers first used the Comment feature in Microsoft Word to add his own comments to his summary.)

What Gilyard writes

In the excerpt from Keith Gilyard's book Voices of the Self, we learn how a young African American boy, Keith, is uprooted from his home in Harlem and finds himself being stared at and picked on by the white students who make up the rest of his class in a Queens school. To learn about his fellow students without giving too much of himself away was to be Keith's first move and possibly his only means of survival. So while in school, Keith took a back seat and let Raymond (his actual first name) represent his standard English self and do all the talking, all the spying.

My response

I relate to Gilyard's struggle. From kindergarten to my senior year in a Bronx high school, I was either the only one or one of the very few Jewish students. I still remember the yellow "race-percentage" sheet we were given in my homeroom in my junior year. Seventy-seven percent of the school population was Hispanic, 13 percent black, 4 percent white, and 6 percent "other." I remember how many Jewish students there were in John F. Kennedy High School, too—I could count them on one hand!

I am not an African American male. I am an Irish American male whose mother brought him up to believe, follow, and take pride in his Jewish heritage. I, too, needed a mask to hide behind, and it was easier for me than for Gilyard. He could not take refuge behind another color of skin. But when I heard anti-Semitic comments and jokes, I would take refuge behind my Irish appearance and my last name. Even Gilyard shows insensitivity about those different from himself: "I began to wonder [. . .] about what these Jews were learning in those synagogues and those one-afternoon a week Hebrew School classes," he says. <u>These</u> Jews? <u>Those</u> synagogues? Do I detect a derogatory tone? Growing up as a minority makes one ultra-sensitive.

A sample annotated passage   Here is a poem about Rosa Parks, who in 1955 refused to give up her seat on a Montgomery, Alabama, bus to a white man and so inspired the civil rights movement. The poem is shown with a reader's annotations.

Rita Dove

Rosa Parks

Rosa

How she sat there,	Stanzas of three lines: no rhyme
The time right inside a place	Everyday language
So wrong it was ready.	Is the place the bus?
That trim name with	Her name: Parks—park bench
Its dream of a bench	
to rest on. Her sensible coat.	Nice touch of short fragment
Doing nothing was the doing:	Repetition makes the point
the clean flame of her gaze	that she was just *there*.
carved by a camera flash.	Metaphorical language
How she stood up	Almost cinematic description
when they bent down to retrieve	Who are "they"?
Her purse. That courtesy.	

—Rita Dove, "Rosa," in *On the Bus with Rosa Parks*

Exercise 7.1 Read and annotate a passage.
Give the following 1960 poem a critical reading and annotate it accordingly. See the example above.

We Real Cool
Gwendolyn Brooks

The Pool Players.
Seven at the Golden Shovel.

We real cool. We
Left school. We

Lurk late. We
Strike straight. We

Sing sin. We
Thin gin. We

Jazz June. We
Die soon.

7b Types of assignments

Always determine exactly what type of response the assignment calls for. You are not just writing "about" *Hamlet*. That is too general. Consider how you are expected to approach *Hamlet*, what aspects of the play you will address, and what points you want to make. Here are some common types of assignments and suggestions for handling them.

- *Book report/book review.* Include a brief summary of the contents of a book if necessary for the audience, along with an evaluation of the importance of the book and its intended audience (see **8b** for an example).

- *Reaction/response.* Provide a summary of the work if necessary but focus on the connections between the work and your own reading and experience (see **7j** for an example).

- *Interpretation and analysis.* Discuss the meaning of the work from a close reading of the text itself—its theme, structure, universality, moral issues, or significance—addressing questions such as "Who is responsible for the crises in story X?" Give your view of how one or more of the elements of the work (plot, character, relationships, organization, point of view, language, imagery, symbolism, voice, and so on) contribute to the whole (see **7c** for more details).

- *Comparison/contrast.* Compare elements within a work (for example, protagonists, points of view, acts in a play). Or compare several works to examine the treatment of a particular issue, such as "To what extent do the works studied support or refute William Faulkner's view that 'man has a spirit capable of compassion and sacrifice and endurance'?"). Or compare two or more works in terms of content or form (the *Odyssey* and James Joyce's *Ulysses,* for instance), perhaps comparing themes, characterization, or endings (see **7j** for an example).

- *Cultural critique.* Take a specific point of view toward the work, such as examining it as a historical or cultural artifact, as a portrayal of gender roles or gender issues, or as a portrayal of issues of race and class.

- *Formal analysis.* Examine the structure of the text, or take a poststructural view, emphasizing ambiguities and unstated possibilities in the text.

For an explanation of terms often used in essay assignments, see **9b**.

7c Tips for writing about literature

The type of assignment is just one consideration. As you plan to tackle your assignment, keep in mind these seven tips.

1. Identify readers. Are you writing for readers who know the work you are writing about? If your instructor does not specify an audience, and if you know that he or she will be the only person to read the paper, assume a larger audience than this one expert. Think of readers as people who have read the work but not thought of the issues you did.

2. Determine the type of work.   Determine the type of work you are examining (its *genre*). Is it a drama, a novel, a short story, a biography, a sonnet, a polemical article? Ask yourself what you know about its features and what else you have read within that genre.

3. Ask questions about the work.   Narrow your focus from the broad subject of the work to the specific questions you will ask and answer about it. Remember to phrase a question to focus your inquiry for the essay. (See **3f** on finding a topic; see **7e** for questions to ask to analyze a work.)

- What does the work say and mean? This question may lead to a line-by-line explication, usually of a short work such as a poem or of a significant passage from a longer work.

- What elements in the work are significant to understanding it, and what techniques has the writer used to develop those elements? These questions lead to an analysis of important points that relate to the theme of the whole work.

- How does this work compare or contrast to one or more other works? This type of question leads you to fit the work you have selected into a larger context. For this approach you probably will have to do more extensive research than would be necessary for explication or analysis of only one text. See **5d**, item 10, for organizing a comparison and contrast.

4. Formulate a thesis.   A thesis is as necessary when you write about literature as when you do other types of college writing. In your repeated readings and in your notes, interpret what you read in light of other works you have read and of your own experience. Use text annotations, notes, and a double-entry journal, as well as other methods of generating ideas, to help you formulate a claim (see **3a–3g**). Your aim is to persuade readers to consider your interpretation. Here are several sample theses:

W. B. Yeats and James Joyce present radically different perspectives on Ireland.

Nicholson Baker's work has close stylistic links to the author he has written about so admiringly, John Updike.

The green light in *The Great Gatsby* is not necessarily the guiding image of the novel.

5. Avoid summarizing. A brief summary of the work may be necessary to orient readers. However, unless your instructor asks you to begin with a summary, devote your paper to an analysis and interpretation of the work, not simply a description or a summary. If, for instance, the work is *The Great Gatsby,* readers need to see clearly that the paper is not just a retelling of the story but an explanation of your analysis and opinions of *The Great Gatsby,* organized around a thesis. They also need to understand why you advance this thesis. References to the text should help explain your interpretation.

6. Turn to the text for evidence—and do so often. Offer support for your assertions, especially the debatable ones, by giving examples from the text. Text references are the most convincing evidence you can provide. Summarize, paraphrase, and when the exact words or tone are important, quote (**50g–50h**). Any quotation you include should support a point you are making in your essay. Quote only when the word, phrase, or sentence is absolutely necessary. Avoid stringing quotations together (**50h**).

7. Make a distinction between the author and the narrator. As you read a short story, novel, or poem, consider who the narrator is (the narrator is the person represented as telling the story), what the narrator's background is, what happens, and why. Remember that the author is distinct from the narrator—the author has invented the narrator.

7d Common conventions in writing about literature

For drafting and editing, be aware of the conventions that exist for writing about literature.

KEY POINTS

Common Conventions in Writing about Literature

1. *Tense* Use the present tense to discuss works of literature even when the author is no longer alive (**20f**): "Polonius decides to eavesdrop, but the plan misfires tragically." "Edith Wharton presents Ethan Frome as a bitter man."

2. *Authors' names* Use an author's full name the first time you mention it: "Stephen King." Thereafter, and always in parenthetical citations, use only the last name: "King," not "Stephen," and certainly not "Steve."

3. *Titles of works* Underline or italicize the titles of books, plays, journals, films, and other works published as an entity and not as part of a larger work. Use quotation marks to enclose the title of a work forming part of a larger published work: short stories, essays, articles, songs, and short poems.

4. *Quotations* Integrate quotations into your text, and use them for help in making your point (**50h**). Avoid a mere listing and stringing together: "Walker goes on to say. . . . Then Walker states. . . ." When quoting two or three lines of poetry, separate lines by using a slash (/) (**30d**). When using long quotations (more than three lines of poetry or four typed lines of prose), indent one inch; do not add quotation marks; the indented format signals a quotation (**50h**).

5. *Citations* Supply specific references to the literary text under discussion to support your opinions, and cite any references to the work or to secondary sources. (See **50d** for advice on what to cite.) Cite author and page number within your essay for all quotations and references to the work of others; at the end of your paper, attach a list of works cited. Follow the MLA style of documentation (**52**).

 TechNote Electronic Discussion Lists and Web Sites for Literature

Consider joining an electronic discussion list for literature. Consult a directory of lists (such as <http://www.kovacs.com>) to find one that fits your interests. For help with choosing topics and finding and writing about literature, try the following Web sites:

> *Voice of the Shuttle:* <http://vos.ucsb.edu>
>
> *Project Bartleby:* <http://www.bartleby.com> ▪

 Exercise 7.2 Give advice for revising.
Read the following passage written by a student about Colette's "The Hand." What advice would you give the writer on how to improve this piece of writing?

> In the short story *The Hand,* the main character described everything around her with her imagination. It is beautiful. The young girl's initial reaction to her husband is one of admiration and devotion. As she lies next to him in bed, she praises his mouth, full and likable, his skin the color of pink brick, and even

his forehead. The young wife is swept up in the joy of being a newlywed. However, as the young girl perceives his well-mani-cured hands, she begins to perceive something dark and sinister. Her husband's hand takes on an animalistic appearance, "a vile, apelike appearance" (229). She went on to describe it in animalis-tic terms—"its claw, " "a pliant beast" (229). The admiration and joy she experienced previously is replaced with disgust and fear. She stated with emotion and shock, "And I've kissed that hand! . . . How horrible!" She cannot even touch the slice of toast he gives her in the morning. However, at the end she kisses the hand. This gesture, I believe, is demonstrative of the fact that she will settle for a life of submission, not a life of love.

7e Ten approaches to analysis

If your task is to analyze a feature of a work of literature, the ques-tions that follow may be useful in determining which approach you want to take. You could focus on one or more of these features to examine their relationship to and effect on the work as a whole. For more specific details on analyses of prose fiction, poetry, and drama, see **7g, 7h,** and **7i.**

🔑 **KEY POINTS**

Ten Ways to Analyze a Work of Literature

1. *Plot or sequence of events* What happens? In what order? What stands out as important?

2. *Theme* What is the message of the work, the generalization that readers can draw from it? A work may focus, for exam-ple, on making a statement about romantic love, jealousy, sexual repression, ambition, revenge, failure, insanity, para-noia, political corruption, lust, greed, envy, or social inequality.

3. *Characters* Who are the people portrayed? What do you learn about them? What role does gender, ethnicity, or religion play? What effect would changing one of these have on the plot or theme?

4. *Genre* What type of writing does the work fit into—parody, tragedy, love story, epic, sonnet, haiku, melodrama, comedy of manners, mystery novel, for example? How does this work compare to other works in the same genre? What conventions does the author observe, violate, or creatively vary?

5. *Structure* How is the work organized? What are its major parts? How do the parts relate to each other?

6. *Point of view* Whose voice speaks to readers and tells the story? Is the narrator involved in the action or an observer of it? How objective, truthful, and reliable is the narrator? What would be gained or lost if the point of view were changed?

7. *Setting* Where does the action take place? How are the details of the setting portrayed? What role, if any, does the setting play? What would happen if the setting were changed?

8. *Tone* From the way the work is written, what can you learn about the way the author feels about the subject matter and the theme? Can you, for example, detect a serious, informative tone, or is there evidence of humor, sarcasm, or irony?

9. *Language* What effects do the following have on the way you read and interpret the work: word choice, style, imagery, symbols, and figurative language?

10. *The author* What do you know or what can you discover through research about the author and the author's other works—and how do they illuminate this work?

7f Recognizing and analyzing figurative language

The writers of literary works often use figures of speech to create images and intensify effects. When you analyze and interpret works of literature, look for the author's use of figurative language.

Simile A comparison of two basically dissimilar things, using the word *like* or *as* or a similar word; both sides of the comparison are stated

My love is like a red, red rose. —Robert Burns

Like as the waves make towards the pebbled shore,
So do our minutes hasten to their end. —William Shakespeare

The weather is like the government, always in the wrong. —Jerome K. Jerome

Harry picked [the letter] up and stared at it, his heart twanging like a gigantic elastic band. —J. K. Rowling

A pretty girl is like a melody. —Irving Berlin

A woman without a man is like a fish without a bicycle. —Attributed to Gloria Steinem

Metaphor   An implied comparison of two dissimilar things, with no *like* or *as*

The still, sad music of humanity   —William Wordsworth

The quicksands of racial injustice   —Martin Luther King Jr.

All the world's a stage   —William Shakespeare

Alliteration   Repetition of consonant sounds at the beginning of stressed syllables

*P*eter *P*iper *p*icked a *p*eck of *p*ickled *p*eppers.   —Nursery rhyme

He *b*ravely *b*reach'd his *b*oiling *b*loody *b*reast.
                                                —William Shakespeare

Assonance   Repetition or resemblance of vowel sounds

And f*ee*d d*ee*p, d*ee*p upon her p*ee*rless eyes   —John Keats

Bl*a*ckish p*a*ck*a*ge   —Marie Ponsot

Onomatopoeia   Sound of word associated with meaning (as in *growl, hiss*)

M*ur*m*ur*ing of innum*er*able bees   —Alfred, Lord Tennyson

Personification   Description or address of a thing as a person

Rosy-fingered dawn   —Homer

Death, be not proud.   —John Donne

The baby lamb chops demand to be eaten with the hands.

Irony   Saying the opposite of what is meant

Enron, that company of great honesty and integrity, the darling of its stockholders . . .

Zeugma   Use of a word with two or more other words, forming different and often humorous logical connections

The art dealer departed in anger and a Mercedes.

For more on using figurative language in your own writing, see **39e**.

EXERCISE 7.3 Experiment with figurative language.
In groups of two or three, write five sentences about your favorite food, object, activity, sport, or sports figure using at least four of the following stylistic devices: simile, metaphor, alliteration, personification, and irony.

7g Writing about prose fiction

As you read novels, short stories, and plays, remember to ask the journalists' questions (**3e**): Who? What? When? Where? Why? How? For instance, the following questions asked during the first reading will help establish the basic facts about the work: What happened? When and where did it happen? Who did what? How were things done? Why? Then, once you have decided on an approach to your analysis (see **7e**), the list that follows may help draw your attention to issues you can explore in detail.

Plot Sequence of events in the work, causes and effects, conflicts and resolutions

Order of events Chronological, flashbacks, and flashforwards

Character and character development Main characters, who they are, how they interact, if and how they change, and if they reveal themselves through actions or words

Theme The author's main message in the work, a generalization that readers can derive from the work (*theme* is to prose fiction as *thesis* is to essay)

Setting Time and place of the action and cultural/social context

Point of view Position from which the events are described, such as first (*I/we*) or third-person narrator (*he/she/they*)

Stance of the narrator Biased or reliable, trustworthy or untrustworthy, limited or omniscient (this stance might change from chapter to chapter or section to section)

Author Relationship to narrator (can you tell how closely the author identifies with the narrator?) and to plot events; relevant facts of author's life

Structure Shape of the work, chapters, crises, turning points

Tone Attitudes expressed directly or indirectly by the author or narrator

Style Word choice, sentence length and structure, significant features

Language and imagery Word choice, word order, images, sensory language, figures of speech such as similes and metaphors (see **7f** and **39e**)

Symbols Objects or events with special significance or with hidden meanings, such as a rose or a green light

Narrative devices Foreshadowing, leitmotif (a recurring theme), alternating points of view, turning point, deus ex machina ("a god from a machine"—a sudden and unexpected resolution to a problem)—and dénouement (outcome of plot)

See **7j** for sample student essays written about prose fiction.

7h Writing about poetry

In addition to using some of the suggestions in **7g** relating to prose, consider the following factors when you analyze a poem or provide a line-by-line interpretation or explication.

Genre   Epic, pastoral, elegy, love poem, and so on

Form   Sonnet, limerick, or other form, free form or not, rhymed or unrhymed, divided into stanzas or not, line length, meter

Stanza   Lines set off as a unit of a poem (like a paragraph in an essay)

Rhyme scheme   System of end-of-line rhymes that you can identify by assigning letters to similar final sounds. For example, a rhyme scheme for couplets (two-line stanzas) would be *aa bb cc*, and a rhyme scheme for a sestet (a six-line stanza) would be *ababcc*.

Meter   Number and pattern of stressed and unstressed syllables (or *metric feet*) in a line. Common meters are trimeter, tetrameter, and pentameter (three, four, and five metric feet). The following line is written in iambic tetrameter (four metric feet, each with one unstressed and one stressed syllable):

Whŏse woóds / thĕse aŕe / Ĭ thínk / Ĭ knów.   —Robert Frost

Foot   Unit (of meter) made up of a specific number of stressed and unstressed syllables

Punctuation and mechanics   Conventional punctuation or not, conventional capitalization or not

Tone   Approach to the topic, such as humor, anger, cynicism, or affection

Speaker   The person behind the poem, setting tone and attitude to the topic

Sound   Vowel and consonant sounds, harsh or soft effects (test these by reading aloud)

See **7j** for a sample student essay written about poetry.

7i Writing about drama

As you prepare to write about a play, use any of the relevant points listed in **7e**, **7g**, and **7h**. In addition, focus on the following dramatic conventions.

Structure of the play   Acts and scenes

Plot   Episodes, simultaneous events, chronological sequence, causality, climax, turning point

Characters   Analysis of psychology, social status, relationships

Scenes   The point and power of the scenes

Setting   Time, place, and description

Time   Real time depicted (all action takes place in two hours or so of the play) or passage of time

Stage directions   Details about clothing, sets, actors' expressions and voices, information given to actors

Scenery, costumes, music, lighting, props, and special effects   Purpose and effectiveness

Presentation of information   Recognition of whether the characters in the play know things that the audience does not or whether the audience is informed of plot developments that are kept from the characters

See **7j** for a sample student essay written about drama, one that addresses the social status of the characters related to the social structure of the time.

7j   Students' essays on literature

On prose fiction: two assignments

1. *Short response to a short story: analysis of moral position*   This essay was written by Kristi Livingston for an introductory course in critical reasoning at Metropolitan Community College, Omaha, Nebraska. Students were asked to access Richard Brautigan's short story "The Kool-Aid Wino" at <http://www.jough.com> and discuss whether they perceived the boy who made the Kool-Aid as a positive or a negative character.

"The Kool-Aid Wino" Rewrite:

Positive Position

The boy in the story "The Kool-Aid Wino" has received a bad rap. He has been misunderstood and berated for his no-nonsense attitude. His normal need to enjoy life has been mistaken for laziness, and his passion for Kool-Aid has been described as an unnatural and unhealthy obsession.

I found his explanation of why he didn't change for bed to be humorous and refreshing. He said, "Why bother? You're only going to get up anyway. Be prepared for it. You're not fooling anyone by taking your clothes off." This boy has taken his own beliefs, stepped away from what society considers proper, and rejects what he sees as silly tradition. He has a fierce sense of individuality that shines through his no-nonsense attitude.

Also, it has been argued that the boy was lazy. Some people feel that because his physical condition made him unable to do hard, physical labor, he should assume all the household responsibilities. When the boy passed his younger brothers and sisters and didn't change their diapers, people immediately reacted with contempt. However, this was a young boy. Why was it his responsibility to take care of the babies? Isn't that a mother's job? I believe this is a normal child who is simply trying to enjoy his day, as all young children should. Also, the boy never said that he wouldn't do the dishes, he just wouldn't do the dishes before he tended to his favorite part of the day . . . his Kool-Aid making.

Last, and most important, the boy had found a true passion for life through his Kool-Aid. It was during this ceremony that he was able to forget about his handicap and the intense poverty and chaos that surrounded him. It seemed as if he could devote himself fully to his task. This was the one thing that the boy could do without help from others. This was the one thing that the boy could do that gave him a true sense of independence from his family. Now tell me, what's unhealthy in that?

I think the Kool-Aid wino is a positive, rather than a negative, fellow. What was mistaken as a terrible "I-don't-care" attitude is actually a wonderful no-nonsense approach to life. What some people look at as laziness, I take for what it was . . . a boy with a handicap who lived his life in a way that made him happy. And finally, his obsession with his Kool-Aid was not unlike a swimmer's passion for the water. He had practiced and perfected his own art, and found his purpose and place in life through his Kool-Aid reality.

2. Comparing and contrasting works of two authors This essay was written by sophomore Brian Cortijo for a course on multicultural American literature. The assignment was to compare and contrast two collections of stories in the way they present a conception of identity and to focus on analyzing the texts themselves without turning to critical sources. He was writing for his instructor and for classmates, both of whom were familiar with the stories.

Identity and the Individual Self

The collections of stories presented in Sherman Alexie's The Lone Ranger and Tonto Fistfight in Heaven and Edwidge Danticat's Krick? Krack!, while distinct in their subject matter, are strikingly similar in the responses they evoke and their ability, through detached or seemingly detached narratives, to create a sense of collective selfhood for the peoples represented in those narratives. Through connected stories, repetition of themes and events, shifting narrative voice, and honest, unapologetic discussion of the problems and beauty of their personal experiences, Danticat and Alexie provide frank, cohesive portrayals of a Haitian and Native American peoplehood, respectively.

While it may not be the intention of these authors to address such a collective identity, it is clear that each is working from some conception of what that identity is, if not what it should be. Each author has symbols and characters that are used to display the identity in all its glory and shame, all its beauty and horror. For Alexie, both characters and objects are used, each for its own purpose. Most notable among these are Thomas Builds-the-Fire, a symbol of spirituality; Norma, who remains uncorrupted by the life imposed on the Indian peoples; and the seemingly ubiquitous drum, a symbol of religion, presented to Victor by Big Mom. Danticat, by contrast, concentrates more on objects than on characters to embody the ideals and the fears of the identity she is constructing through her narrative. The most prominent among these symbols are the bone soup and the use of braids and, more generally, hair.

Danticat's use of the bone soup in her last story, "Caroline's Wedding," and of the braids in her "Epilogue: Women like Us," is of paramount importance to any claim of

Haitian peoplehood, or Haitian womanhood, that she might try to make. The use of these elements is indicative of the loving imposition and inclusion of past generations into one's own, as well as the attempt to pass down all that has gone before to those who will one day bear the burden of what that past means. Thus, Hermine's soup is her daughter Garcina's soup as well, not because she eats of it, but because those bones—that ancestry—are part of her, and she will one day be responsible for passing them (and it) on. Likewise, Danticat's reader in the epilogue must know her history and her lineage, not only to know how to braid her daughter's hair, but for whom those braids are tied.

[Cortijo includes here a discussion of how each author deals with maintaining identity over time.]

Clearly, no attempt is made by these authors to glorify the identity that they are helping to define. What is vital to the presentation of these collective identities is that they are transcendent of both time and location, and that they are honest, if not visceral, in their telling. As beautifully told as these pieces of fiction are, they represent truth and are unapologetic in presenting the faults and difficulties inherent in that truth. By telling these stories honestly and without pretense, Alexie and Danticat help to reveal what many may not be willing to admit or acknowledge about others or about themselves—the importance, beauty, and complexity of a collective selfhood.

Works Cited

Alexie, Sherman. The Lone Ranger and Tonto Fistfight in Heaven. New York: Harper, 1994.

Danticat, Edwidge. Krick? Krack! New York: Vintage-Random, 1996.

On poetry This essay on a poem by Emily Dickinson was written by sophomore Kate Rudkin for an English course on American literature at Northeastern University. The assignment was to analyze the patterns of imagery in a poem. For reference, a copy of the poem appears after the essay.

An Exploration of Death through
Imperfect Structures

In her Poem #258, Emily Dickinson employs religious and political imagery to discuss personal and universal dilemmas. Words consistently associated with both spirituality and society are used throughout the poem. Through word choice, Dickinson is able to simultaneously discuss her two themes and explore the ways in which they are interrelated. In Poem #258, religious and political figurative language is used to examine the consequences of structure in Dickinson's life and the lives of humans as a whole. Structure is repeatedly associated with the concept of death and its elusive qualities. By intentionally providing multiple structures through which her poem can be interpreted, Dickinson forms a multifaceted view on death and its various degrees of imperceptibility.

In order to comprehend how Poem #258 can be read and how the various religious and political meanings within Poem #258 come together, one must first examine its individual elements. The religious aspects of the poem are more prominent and make a bold appearance in the figurative language of the first stanza. Dickinson's references to "a certain Slant of light" and of "Cathedral Tunes" conjure many church images associated with Christianity. Dickinson continues to use words like "heavenly," "affliction," and "death." She injects her poem with religiously charged words and images in order to establish resounding religious overtones.

While discussion of Poem #258 could be conducted only on its religious figurative language, the closely related political language cannot be ignored. By making political language a necessary part of the religious imagery, Dickinson implies that religion is political. The inevitable connection between the religious and the political shows a greater force at work, feeding the two from the same source. Amazingly, the very same poem that seemed to be discussing Dickinson's personal struggle to find her elusive faith or status of salvation also discusses British colonialism in North America. In a more abstract fashion, the poem also deals with the repercussions of socialization on an individual's freedom and on the freedom of humanity.

The same words or phrases that were used to discuss religion can be used to discuss a political climate when read in a different context.

In Poem #258, Dickinson approaches and explores the meaning of death from as many angles as the poem has interpretations. Death is approached through various "imperfect" structures, such as religious and political structures and ultimately also the structure of the poem itself. Through limitations on form, Dickinson is able to express the limitations of herself and others in attempting to conceive of the notion and meaning of death. Although Dickinson never makes a direct reference to the act of death, everything within Poem #258 is deathlike. The imperceptibility of death is expressed through the failure of the poem's various structures, content and actual, to facilitate an understanding of death. In criticizing religion's and society's inability to illuminate the elusive topic of death, Dickinson is also demonstrating her inability to forge a clear conception.

> There's a certain Slant of light,
> Winter Afternoons—
> That oppresses, like the Heft
> Of Cathedral Tunes—
>
> Heavenly Hurt, it gives us—
> We can find no scar,
> But internal difference,
> Where the Meanings, are—
>
> None may teach it—Any—
> 'Tis the Seal Despair—
> An imperial affliction
> Sent us of the Air—
>
> When it comes, the Landscape listens—
> Shadows—hold their breath—
> When it goes, 'tis like the Distance
> On the look of Death—

Emily Dickinson

On drama Sloan Laurits wrote the following essay in a course, Introduction to Literature, in his second semester in college. The assignment was to follow up on class discussion by writing a two-page essay analyzing *Twelfth Night* in terms of the characters' social roles.

Society in Shakespeare's <u>Twelfth Night</u>

The two houses in Shakespeare's <u>Twelfth Night</u>, Duke Orsino's and Lady Olivia's, are both examples of "the basic Elizabethan social unit" described in Peter Hyland's discussion of "Social Models" (34). All of the characters in the play fit into the social roles Hyland describes. Social class in fact is an essential element of the plot, and without a knowledge of its structure in Elizabethan times we could not make much sense of the complicated plot.

When we first meet the shipwrecked Viola in act 1, scene 2, we understand that she had been a member of the upper class. The Captain refers to her as "Lady," and politely answers all of her questions without asking any of his own. And when he tells her about Duke Orsino, she decides to go to him dressed as a boy and offer her skills as his servant, because she can "sing and speak to him [Orsino] in many sorts of music." As Hyland points out, most commoners were illiterate, and only the children of upper class families were taught etiquette and the arts (35). Viola must be from a noble or very wealthy family.

Most of the characters in the play are actually connected to the house of Lady Olivia, so her house can be appropriately examined as an example of the social hierarchy of the time. Olivia, Sir Toby, and Sir Andrew Aguecheek represent the highest of the three levels; Malvolio, Maria, and Feste the middle class; and the unnamed attendants of the house the lower class. These class distinctions can be seen in the way the characters behave and interact. The relationship of Sir Toby and Sir Andrew reveals their social equality, as throughout the play they always treat each other in the same easy manner, making it obvious that they are comfortable in each other's presence as one would be with one's peers.

When Malvolio discovers the false love letter written by Maria and assumes that it comes from Olivia, he imagines ways to successfully approach her and overcome their class differences. He mentions the "Lady of Strachy [who] married the yeoman of the wardrobe" (2.5.36). Malvolio acknowledges the separation of the two by class status, but remains optimistic concerning their chances of a future together. Later, Malvolio attempts to charm Olivia by following the instructions written in the letter he found but is only seen by Olivia as acting "mad" (3.4.52). She asks Sir Toby to take care of him, and Sir Toby does what was the custom of the time and locks Malvolio in a dark room. The cruel joke played on Malvolio can be seen as a punishment for attempting to break the system of class, for he is the only character in the play who ends up as a victim in the twisting plot.

Malvolio's punishment for his actions can be looked at in two ways: as simply a reflection of the standards of Elizabethan society or as a satiric comment on the absurdity of its class divisions. Either way, the society displayed in Twelfth Night certainly represented the society of Shakespeare's time.

Work Cited

Hyland, Peter. An Introduction to Shakespeare: The Dramatist in His Context. New York: Macmillan, 1996.

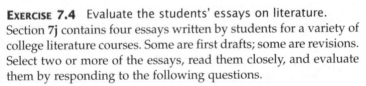

EXERCISE 7.4 Evaluate the students' essays on literature. Section **7j** contains four essays written by students for a variety of college literature courses. Some are first drafts; some are revisions. Select two or more of the essays, read them closely, and evaluate them by responding to the following questions.

1. What assumptions do you think the writers make about their readers?

2. How do you as a reader respond to each piece of writing?

3. How would you assess the language: simple, direct, clear, informal, formal, literary, ornate, technical in terminology? How appropriate is the language for a college essay? Make three lists for each work: slang words, pretentious language, and technical literary terms that you find hard to understand.

4. What point is each writer making? Does the point come across clearly?

5. How do the writers begin? Do they make you want to read on?

6. What comments can you make about the writers' ability to write focused and unified paragraphs?

7. What advice do you have for the writers to improve the piece of writing?

8. Which part of each writer's essay do you like best? Why?

9. Do any of the essays inspire you to want to read the literature under discussion? Which?

8 Writing across the Curriculum

One semester you may be writing about *Hamlet* and the next semester you may move to exploring the census, writing about Chopin's music, discussing geological formations, researching the history of the civil rights movement, or preparing a paper on Sigmund Freud and dreams. You might be expected to write scientific laboratory reports or to manipulate complex statistical data and to use a style of documentation different from one you learned in an English course. As you move from course to course in college, from discipline to discipline, the expectations and conventions of writing will change, along with the recommendations for the documentation styles common in specific disciplines: MLA style in English and the humanities, *Chicago Manual* style in history and art, APA style in the social sciences, and CSE style (formerly CBE) in the sciences and mathematics. See **51e** for more on writing research papers in the disciplines.

8a Different styles for different disciplines

The same topic can be treated in different ways in different disciplines. The style and conventions vary, as do the approaches to content, types of research, methods of documentation, and document design. The three passages that follow, all on the topic of sleep deprivation, illustrate some of the differences.

Science This excerpt is an abstract from a published scientific research article examining brain functions. Note the technical terminology and the use of the passive voice.

> ### Abstract
>
> There are complex and dynamic neural mechanisms affecting cognitive performance following sleep deprivation. These mechanisms are partly different from those used in the

non-sleep deprived state. This research found that the pre-frontal cortex was more responsive following one night of sleep deprivation than after normal sleep. Raised subjective tiredness in sleep-deprived subjects was strongly linked with activation of the prefrontal cortex. It is suggested that the impact of sleep deprivation on cognitive performance and related patterns of cerebral activation may be partly dependent on task-specific demands.

—Sean P. A. Drummond et al., "Altered Brain Response to Verbal Learning Following Sleep Deprivation"

Social sciences The following excerpt is also a published abstract, but this time an abstract of an article describing a sleep deprivation experiment involving groups of people. Note that the language is less technical than in the previous example.

Abstract

In two experiments, 64 male students worked almost continuously for 20 hours without sleep under varying social conditions. In Experiment 1, participants worked either individually or as a group. As hypothesized, performance deteriorated over time, especially in the group condition, which allowed participants to loaf. In Experiment 2, all participants worked in groups, but were instructed that public feedback would be provided either on the group result only or on the individual results of all group members. As expected, when individual results were made public, performance deteriorated less. Overall, the data suggest that fatigue increases social loafing. However, both individualizing the task and providing public individual feedback seem to counteract that effect.

—Claudia Y. D. Hoeksema–van Orden, Anthony W. K. Gaillard, and Bram P. Buunk, "Social Loafing under Fatigue"

Humanities The following passage is an excerpt from a personal essay describing a year of sleepless nights. The essay, written by a student, was published in *Newsweek*. In the personal essay, the first person narrator is naturally acceptable. In other types of writing for the humanities, such as documented essays and analysis of literature or art, use of the first person is sometimes avoided. Check with your instructor for guidelines.

Now a high-school senior, I still remember my freshman year with a shudder; it was the year my friends and I joked about as the Year of Sleepless Nights. It wasn't that I had contracted a rare sleeping disorder or suffered from a bad case of insomnia that particular year; in fact, nothing could have been farther from the truth. I had done what many diligent students do: sacrifice precious sleep for the sake of academic success.

Don't get me wrong; my parents never mandated that I take all the honors classes I could gain admission to. No one told me to take three honors classes. No one, that is, except the little voice in my head that convinced me scholarly success was based upon the number of H's on my high-school transcript. The counselors cautioned me not to do it, students who had fallen into the trap before warned me against it and my parents just left it up to me. Through it all, I just smiled and reassured them, Don't worry; I can handle it. The trouble was, I didn't have the slightest idea what lay ahead.

I soon found myself mired in work. For a person whose friends teased her about being a neat freak, I grew increasingly messy. My room and desk looked like my backpack had exploded. There was no time to talk to friends on the phone, not even on the weekends. Going to bed at midnight was a luxury, 1 a.m. was normal, 3 a.m. meant time to panic and 4 a.m. meant it was time to go to sleep defeated. Most days, I would shuffle clumsily from class to class with sleep-clouded eyes and nod off during classroom lectures. There was even a month in winter when I was so self-conscious of my raccoon eyes that I wore sunglasses to school.

—Jenny Hung, "Surviving a Year of Sleepless Nights"

WORLDS OF WRITING
The Culture of the Academic Disciplines

Each discipline has its own culture and its own expectations of the people who practice in the discipline and write about it. When you take a course in a new discipline, you are joining a new

(continued)

(continued)

"discourse community," with established conventions and ways of thinking and writing. Use the following strategies to get acquainted with the discipline's conventions.

1. Listen carefully to lectures and discussion; note the specialized vocabulary used in the discipline. Make lists of new terms and definitions.

2. Read the assigned textbook, and note the conventions that apply in writing about the field.

3. Use subject-specific dictionaries and encyclopedias to learn about the field. Examples include *Encyclopedia of Religion* and *Encyclopedia of Sociology.*

4. Subscribe to e-mail discussion lists (**11c**) in the field so that you can see what issues people are concerned about.

5. When given a writing assignment, make sure you read samples of similar types of writing in that discipline.

6. Talk with your instructor about the field, its literature, and readers' expectations.

Find out what way of writing and documenting is expected in each of your courses. Although each one may call for some adaptation of the writing process and for awareness of specific conventions, in general you will engage in familiar activities—planning, drafting, revising, and editing. Sections **8b–8d** discuss types of writing conventionally found in major academic disciplines. Section **51e** provides more specific details on writing research papers in the disciplines.

TechNote Useful Sites for Writing across the Curriculum

Try these Web sites for useful advice on writing in all your courses and for more links to other sites:

The Dartmouth University site with advice to nonmajors on writing science: <http://www.dartmouth.edu/~compose/student/sciences/write.html>

The Dartmouth University site with advice to nonmajors on writing in the social sciences: <http://www.dartmouth.edu/~compose/student/soc_sciences/write.html>

The George Mason University Writing Center site on writing in public affairs, management, psychology, biology, and history: <http://writingcenter.gmu.edu/resources/index.html> ■

8b Writing in the humanities and arts

The discipline of the humanities and arts is generally regarded as consisting of art, art history, communications and media, film, theater, history, languages, literature, music, philosophy, religion, and history, though some classify history as a social science. Writing in the humanities and arts is largely expository and interpretive. Only in creative writing courses will you be engaged in creating original works of literature. In many college courses, however, you will be asked to do a close reading or scrutiny of a variety of original works called *primary sources* (such as novels, philosophical works, poems, plays, speeches, performances, diaries, memoirs, photographs, films, and works of art) and also to study critical or evaluative books or articles, called *secondary sources.* See **47e** for more on primary and secondary sources.

 TechNote Web Sites on Primary and Secondary Sources

The following university Web sites provide useful information about, examples of, and links to primary and secondary sources:

> Bowling Green State University: <http://www.bgsu.edu/colleges/library/infosrv/lue/primary.html>
>
> University of California at Berkeley: <http://www.lib.berkeley.edu/TeachingLib/Guides/PrimarySources.html>
>
> Princeton University: <http://www.princeton.edu/~refdesk/primary2.html>

Your instructor will expect you to find your data and evidence in your own reactions, in primary sources, and frequently in secondary sources—what a critic has said about Toni Morrison, Samuel Coleridge, or Jackson Pollock, for example. Here are some points to consider as you write in the humanities and arts.

Guidelines for preparing to do expository writing in the humanities and arts

- Establish what the task entails and tailor your purpose statement accordingly. Some assignments, especially in first-year writing courses, may ask you to write about personal experience and express personal opinions on issues; others will ask you to begin with a text (a work of literature or art, an original document, or a media creation) and respond to, interpret, or analyze that text. A list of terms used in essay assignments is in **9b.**

- Read (or watch or listen to) and analyze primary sources: works of literature, letters, speeches, historical or philosophical documents, newspaper reports, or questionnaires.

- Closely scrutinize and analyze (and maybe compare) primary works of art: architecture, dance, theater, music, opera, or media communication, such as advertisements, films, TV shows, and Web sites.
- Form your own response to works before you consult appropriate secondary sources, such as works of literary criticism, biographies, commentaries, analyses, interpretations, and evaluations of research studies.

Interpretation In the humanities and arts, more than in the sciences and social sciences, your personal response to a work of art or a literary work is important. Every work under discussion needs interpretation; readers and observers play a crucial role in the process of understanding, interpreting, and explaining the meaning of a work of literature, a work of art, or a historical document. Base your interpretations on what you see and hear, referring to the source. Readers will look to the source text to make sure that your interpretations are within the bounds of possibility and good sense.

Appropriate support and expert testimony Whatever your claim, you should always support your conclusions by summarizing, paraphrasing, or quoting from both primary and secondary sources. If your claim is controversial, provide support from recognized expert testimony—for example, from Clement Greenberg if you are making a case for the timely brilliance of abstract expressionism in art or from Susan Sontag if you are arguing for the importance of "camp" in recent popular culture.

The terminology of the discipline For any assignments, become familiar with terms used in the fields of literary analysis (such as *metaphor, persona, dramatic irony, omniscient narrator*), historical analysis (such as *historiography, imperialism, colonialism, carpetbagger, reconstruction, puppet state*), argument (such as *straw man, non sequitur*), and the analysis of works of art (such as *leitmotif, trompe l'oeil, chiaroscuro, tonal value*). Dictionaries in specific fields can be helpful here (**48b**).

The conventions of writing in the discipline Always pay attention to any common conventions in the discipline. For example, two common conventions in writing in the humanities are these:

- Use the present tense to discuss literature and the arts, even for works produced in the past: "Van Gogh's letters show a man in deep distress." "Chaucer reveals his sense of humor in his tales." (See also **7d**.)

- In philosophy papers, use the first person (*I*) less often than in other disciplines in the humanities. Especially avoid "I believe . . ." and "I feel. . . ." What counts more than personal feeling in philosophy and its search for the truth is rational argument and logic.

Types of college writing in the humanities and arts

Analytical/interpretive essay   A type of writing frequently assigned in college courses, the analytical or interpretive essay asks you to write about the meaning and the significance of the component parts of a work of literature, art, or media, or an event in history. Section **7e** details approaches you can take to literary analysis. See **7j** for sample papers about literature.

Analysis/critique of visual texts: art, photographs, advertisements Some of the general principles that apply to writing about literature also apply to writing about works of art: for example, the need for accurate use of specialized terms (*impressionism, abstract expressionism, cubism, encaustic, fresco, mezzotint, foreshortening, chiaroscuro, iconography,* and so on), the need for analysis rather than merely a description, and attention to biographical and cultural influences. Writing about art is similar to writing about works of literature in that writers frequently use the present tense to describe a work, even if the artist is no longer alive: "Berthe Morisot's short strokes of white paint fill the canvas with light and make her *Interior of a Cottage* glow with summer sunshine." They also underline or use italics for the title of a work. In addition to these demands, writing about a work of art involves attention to formal principles of design, such as the characteristics of line, shape, color, light and dark, depth, balance, and proportion.

When you write about a work of art, you probably will find yourself focusing on one of the following:

- technique (print or painting, oil or watercolor, and so on)
- style (the way the artist depicts the world, such as realistic, conceptual, abstract, expressionistic)
- links between the work and social factors
- iconography (how subjects are represented in different times and by different artists)
- analysis of a work or works, concentrating on such aspects as the artist's purpose, audience reactions, sources, historical period of the work, how the work changed in process, or the symbolism of the work

It is a good idea to include an illustration of any artwork you discuss, or to provide a direct link to the work as shown on a Web site.

Consult with your instructor about which style of documentation to use. MLA and *Chicago* are the styles commonly used in writing about art and art history.

The following sample essay was written for Professor Roberta Bernstein's course in modern art (at State University of New York at Albany) in response to the following assignment, one of a series of assignments on a specified artist: "Write an analysis of an individual art work by your artist [this student's artist was Piet Mondrian], discussing craft, visual engagement, and meaning as they apply to that work. Document your sources of information with endnotes as needed." This is Lynn McCarthy's essay, documented in *Chicago* style (**55**) with endnotes.

Piet Mondrian's painting *Trafalgar Square* is dated 1939–43. Normally, an extended date on artwork indicates a continuous period of production until the work is completed. However,

this is not the case with this painting or sixteen others, collectively known as the *transatlantic paintings.*[1]

Essentially these are the works Mondrian began in Paris and London. Some that he considered complete in the years 1935–40 were later finished or reworked in New York City after his October 1940 emigration to the United States.[2] So what viewers can see in *Trafalgar Square* in the bottom right corner, noted on the black grid line, are the numbers 39

Trafalgar Square, 1939–43, by Piet Mondrian (1872–1944). Oil on canvas, 57 1/4″ × 47 3/4″, Gift of Mr. and Mrs. William A. M. Burden (510.1964). © 2002 Mondrian / Holtzman Trust, c/o Beeldrecht / Artists Rights Society, NY. Digital image © The Museum of Modern Art. Licensed by SCALA / Art Resource, NY.

and 43 (not visible in reproduction). The year 1939 is the first date that Mondrian records because at this time he felt it was finished. Later in New York City, he made revisions and adjustments that were completed in 1943, the second number he inscribed.

Trafalgar Square is an oil on canvas that measures 145.2 by 120 cm and today is housed in the Museum of Modern Art in New York City. It is interesting to discover that Mondrian planned out his compositions with colored tape before he applied any paint.[3] Some tape actually still remains on his *Victory Boogie Woogie* (1942–44), which is an unfinished work he was involved in at the time of his death. But what is even more interesting is that although Mondrian preplanned the compositions, we know from x-rays that he reworked the paint on his canvases over and over again.[4] So as methodical and mathematical as we may think Mondrian was, he still felt constant inspiration and intuitive urges to make changes along the way. It is interesting, too, to note that he worked on a flat, horizontal table rather than at an easel.[5] Maybe it was for practical or comfort reasons that he did this, but it also can be seen as a break from the conventional way artists created their works just as their subject matter broke from tradition. I think of how an artist like Jackson Pollock takes this even further by laying his canvas on the floor and walking on and around it, dropping and splattering the paint.

In *Trafalgar Square,* as with all of his work after 1917, Mondrian created a completely nonobjective image. There is no reference to natural forms or representational subject matter. The viewer is presented with just the two-dimensional space of the picture plane, and the forms are arranged on its flat surface. There is no illusion of depth, and the artist has rejected the convention that paintings are often windows to or mirrors of reality. And even though the title refers to a specific place, the painting is not meant to represent Trafalgar Square, but instead it reflects a more general interest Mondrian had in the culture of the metropolis.[6]

Mondrian focuses on pure, simple forms and the balance of the vertical and horizontal. He achieves simplicity by using only the three primary colors—red, blue, and yellow—along with black and white and by using basic rectangular shapes to create a grid layout. There are equal numbers of long vertical and horizontal black bands balancing the composition, which, along with the distribution on blocks of yellow, give the painting solidity and logic. The large red rectangle balanced by the two smaller ones is one element that charges the painting with energy. Otherwise it would seem static since the five large white rectangular areas account for more than half of the canvas space. All of these elements were central to Mondrian's Neo-Plasticism theory. He was intent on "'plastic expression' [which] meant simply the action of forms and colors" and a "new reality" or reality without the illusion or imitation of nature.[7]

This painting is visually engaging because the lines and scattered blocks of color keep one's eye moving around the composition. However, one can follow the elements in an orderly way; it is not at all chaotic. I can see Mondrian's interest in his urban surroundings in this grid work. Personally, I can interpret this composition in two ways. I see it as a type of map view seen from above the street blocks and buildings. But I can also visualize it as the side of a city skyscraper with its façade of rectangular windows and steel beams. So it is both horizontally and vertically balanced even in its interpretation, and offers a pleasing and satisfying image.

Notes

1. Harry Cooper and Ron Spronk, *Mondrian: The Transatlantic Paintings* (New Haven, Conn.: Yale University Press, 2001), 24.

2. Ibid., 24–25.

3. H. Harvard Arnason and Marla F. Prather, *History of Modern Art* (New York: Abrams, 1998), 393.

4. Cooper and Spronk, 237.

5. Arnason and Prather, 383.

6. Cooper and Spronk, 34.

7. Arnason and Prather, 233.

Analysis/critique of film or theatrical performance   An analysis of a theater production is similar to a literary analysis. It looks at plot, character, theme, setting, structure, form, or language in relation to the work as a whole. In addition, theatrical elements of acting, music, lyrics, direction, and staging will come into play.

In an essay titled "1969: How Broadway Reflected the Mood of a Nation," Elizabeth Drew draws on the political context of 1969, audience's expectations, the role of tradition, lyrics, orchestration, and attitudes to sex and religion to analyze, compare, and contrast the Broadway theatrical productions of *Hair* and *1776*. She posits that "*Hair* was revolutionary not only for its electric music qualities, nudity, and untraditional story line but also for its frank language regarding the taboo subjects of race and sex." Here is an excerpt from her essay supporting the first part of that statement:

> As one of the first musicals of the 1969 Tony season, *Hair* served to reinforce the notion that the world of 1968 was remarkably different from previous years. In the opening strains of the very first musical number, we hear an electric guitar. With the exception of one song, *Hair* was orchestrated in an electric rock style, a style new to the Broadway theater. And Act 1 ends with the random nudity of some cast members, symbolizing the characters' vulnerability and protestation of the Vietnam War and demonstrating that the world has changed.
>
>   The play's structure is traditional in the sense that it is written in two acts, discusses the pursuit of love, and finishes with a tremendous musical finale. But it departs from tradition in its storyline. Unlike many musicals that have an underlying plot, *Hair* is written in a style that places the audience in the role of observer. Authors and producers Gerome Ragni and James Rado present their story in an almost "day in the life" way, allowing the characters to communicate both individual emotions and group or "tribal" philosophies to audiences that otherwise relied only on the news media for insight into the younger generation's issues.

When you are writing about a film, it helps to watch it on a VCR or DVD player so that you can repeat the viewing of specific scenes and can freeze a frame to analyze it. In addition to analyzing the features of drama described in **7i**, also consider features of film editing, casting, makeup, camera work, exposure, lighting, framing of shots, and cinematography.

Book review A book review focuses on providing information about the content of the work, perhaps including a summary, along with a critical evaluation of the content, style, language, and organization of the book. See also **7b.** Here is an excerpt from student Jennifer Tang's prize-winning review of Paul Auster's memoir *The Invention of Solitude.*

> Auster shows how complex his father was by bringing in the perspective of the people his father worked with. Ironically, it was in his role as a landlord that his father showed the kind of paternal affection that Auster never received. The tenants who called his father "Mr. Sam" testify to his father's capacity to care about others, and it is a telling detail that his father was most kind to strangers, to those who had no personal association with him.
>
> He was obviously a man who sought to lose himself in his work and seemed to fade once he was forced to come back to his family when he retired. It was his personal life that Auster's father could not face.
>
> In presenting fragments of memory, Auster effectively conveys the fragile nature of his relationship with his father and offers the reader the opportunity to fill in the gaps between them. Unraveling the mystery of his father's remoteness keeps us in suspense, and we are firmly placed in Auster's shoes when the revelation of a murder of his father's father is presented. We can almost see the yellowed newspaper as he reads its lurid headlines. Auster doesn't tell the reader how the event affected his father's behavior; he trusts the reader's intelligence to put all the fragments together to create a full, if not complete picture.
>
> Overall, I found the first part of the memoir to be much more compelling than the second. The second half was filled with literary allusions on the subject of father-and-son relationships that made me feel that Auster was trying to intellectualize what he had earlier approached with such human directness and feeling.

Annotated bibliography Your instructor may ask you to begin work on a research paper by preparing an annotated bibliography—a detailed bibliographical listing of the works you consult, each accompanied by a brief summary of the main points. Jared Whittemore was asked to prepare an annotated bibliography as part of his preparation for his MLA research paper on the community college system (see **52f** for his final draft). The following entry is from his annotated bibliography. Note that full bibliographical details in MLA style are followed by an informative summary.

Significant Historical Events in the Development
of the Public Community College. American Association
of Community Colleges. 13 Feb. 2001 <http://www.aacc.nche
.edu/allaboutcc/historicevents.htm>. This site provides a
timeline charting the significant events in the history
of community colleges, from 1862 to 2001. The timeline
includes historical events, such as the founding of the
first community college in 1901, and tracks important
legislation and publications relating to the development
and improvement of the community college system. It
provides a historical perspective on the implementation
and advancements made in the system in more than a
century.

Research paper See **47–51** for details on writing a research paper, and see examples of humanities research papers in **52f, 55f,** and **56e.**

8c   Writing in the sciences, medicine, and mathematics

Most writing in the natural sciences (astronomy, biology, chemistry, physics, for example), applied sciences (agriculture, engineering, environmental studies, computer science, and nursing, for example), and medicine concerns itself with empirical data—that is, with the explanation and analysis of data gathered from a controlled laboratory experiment or from detailed observation of natural phenomena. Frequently, the study will be a replication of a previous experiment, with the new procedure expected to uphold or refute the hypothesis of that previous experiment. In mathematics, explorations of mathematical models occur, as do analyses of theorems and proofs, but writing is mostly of a specialized nature.

Experimental researchers generally do the following:

- review the literature, identify a problem, and propose a hypothesis about the problem
- review the literature describing relevant experiments and studies

- conduct a carefully controlled study or experiment to test the hypothesis
- collect, chart, analyze, and evaluate the data
- interpret the results
- draw conclusions about whether the results support the hypothesis
- explain the limitations of the study
- discuss the implications of the results and suggest further research

Writers in the sciences are much more likely to generate their own data and evidence from their empirical experiments than they are to base a paper on a logical argument or an analysis of another work in the field. Reviews of the literature relating to a topic are common, but they serve as background material to the writer's own work and to the writer's involvement in the issue at hand.

In science courses, you may be asked to post your papers online for your instructor and classmates. Section **12c** provides detailed instructions.

KEY POINTS

A Model for the Organization of an Experimental Paper in the Sciences

1. Title page
2. Table of contents: necessary for a long paper or for a paper posted online
3. Abstract: a summary of your research and your conclusions
4. Background information: why the study is necessary, your hypothesis, review of other studies
5. Method: with headed subsections on participants, apparatus, procedures
6. Results: backed up by statistics in the form of tables, charts, and graphs
7. Discussion: evaluation of the results from the perspective of your hypothesis
8. Conclusion and recommendations: implications of the results of the study and suggestions for further research
9. References: a list of the works cited in the paper

Guidelines for scientific writing

- Establish a hypothesis and procedures.

- Include an abstract (see examples on pp. 171–172, 187, and in section **54f**).

- Divide your paper into sections, with headings. See the example of the lab report on page 188 and the student paper for an experimental psychology course in **53f**.

- Whenever possible, illustrate your methods with illustrations and your findings with statistical tables, charts, or graphs (see also **10e**). Give each visual a number and refer to it by that number (for example, Figure 1, Table 2). If you are using the CBE/CSE style of documentation, place any figures (charts, tables, photographs, graphs, and so on) in your text close to the point where you first mention them; in APA style, place figures at the end of the paper, after the list of references (see **53f** for an example).

- Introduce a survey of the literature by using the present perfect tense: "Several studies have shown that the mutation may prevent degradation of unknown substrates."

- Give details of specific studies in the past tense: "Cocchi et al. isolated the protein fraction secreted by CD8+ T cells."

- Summarize other research studies rather than directly quoting from researchers.

- Avoid personal reflection and the pronoun *I*.

- Use the passive voice to describe the steps of a procedure: "The muscle was stimulated. . . ."

- Become familiar with technical terms and use them judiciously when writing for an audience who will understand them (that is, readers within the scientific discourse community).

- Follow a recommended style manual.

Types of college writing in the sciences

The table of contents If your paper is long or if you are posting your paper online, provide a table of contents. Jennifer Richards provided one for a paper posted online for the Intelligent Machines Design Lab course in the Department of Electrical and Computer Engineering at the University of Florida. In this course, students have to plan and design a robot. Here is her table of contents for her paper on "Leroy, the 'Go Fishin' Robot." You can find the paper online at <http://mil.ufl.edu/imdl/papers/IMDLFall2000.html>.

Leroy

TABLE OF CONTENTS

The abstract Most scientific papers begin with an abstract that summarizes the study and its results. An abstract is intended to give readers enough information about the sections of the paper, the results of the study, and its significance so that they need to turn to the full article only for the details. Many databases publish abstracts: *Chemical Abstracts* and *Biological Abstracts,* for example.

Here is the abstract Jennifer Richards wrote for her paper on Leroy, the robot she designed. Note that in an online posting, a heading is not centered.

ABSTRACT

This report outlines the complete design of Leroy and describes the desired behaviors and actions necessary for him to complete the set objectives. These objectives include the ability to accept and manage a hand of cards to play a game of "Go Fish" with human counterparts. In order to interact, Leroy and the players must communicate using pushbuttons and LEDs. Figures detailing the construction and arrangement of these critical components are included in this report. Other key parts include the recirculation mechanism where Leroy's cards are kept, the "fishpond" that holds the deck, and the "body" platform that encompasses all moving parts. This report also describes a model test of Leroy's desired behaviors and functions. This test involves a real time investigation into the ability of Leroy to perform a set of critical tasks.

The sample CBE/CSE paper in **54f** includes an abstract. See also pages 171–172 for more examples.

Lab report Students write laboratory reports to describe their controlled experiments in science courses and in experimental psychology courses. Some instructors provide detailed directions on the format they expect for a lab report. If yours does not, follow the guidelines of the *Publication Manual of the American Psychological Association* (APA). This manual describes a report format that generally is acceptable to college instructors in the sciences as well as the social sciences, especially since the APA author/year style closely resembles the author/year style described in the CBE/CSE manual as one of its recommended styles of documentation. (You will find an example of a typical APA-style report of an experimental procedure in **53f**.)

For an APA-style lab report, include a title page, a page header on every page, and an abstract (see **53f**). Divide the report into headed sections.

Include a list of references (**53c** and **53f**) and any notes on separate pages. Finally, attach any tables and figures, such as graphs, drawings, and photographs, on separate pages at the end of your report (see **53f**).

🔑 **KEY POINTS**

Headed Sections of a Lab Report

1. *Introduction* Include the purpose and background of the experiment, your hypothesis, and a review of similar experiments.

2. *Materials and methods* Include subsections with headings such as Apparatus (or Equipment), Participants, and Procedure.

3. *Results* Include observations, statistical data, and mathematical formulae, accompanied when appropriate by tables, charts, and graphs.

4. *Discussion of results* Discuss whether the results bear out the hypothesis and offer explanations for unexpected results.

5. *Conclusion(s)* Fit the results into the larger context of other studies, explain implications, and comment on directions for further study.

The following passage is from Natasha Williams's lab report on microbial genetics conjugation, written for a college cell biology course. This excerpt shows part of the Discussion section, annotated to point out various conventions of science writing.

Discussion	Major section heading is centered.
Conjugation involves transfer by appropriate mating types. F+ and Hfr are donor cells with respectively low and high rates of genetic transfer. F- cells are recipients. Contact between the cell types is made by a conjugation bridge called an F pilus extending from the Hfr cell. The donor chromosome appears to be linearly passed through the connecting bridge. Sometimes this transfer is interrupted. The higher the frequency of recombination, the closer the gene is to the beginning of the circular DNA. In this way one can determine the sequence of genes on the chromosome.	Passive construction, common in lab reports
	Note the use of *one* for general reference
Table 1 shows consistently that histidine is the last amino acid coded with the smallest number of recombinants, and arginine is the second to last coded with the next smallest number of recombinants. However, the results obtained for proline and leucine/threonine vary.	Researcher places Table 1 at end of report and here dicusses its details.

8d Writing in the social sciences

The social sciences include anthropology, business, economics, geography, political science, psychology, and sociology. (Sometimes in the organization of college departments and divisions, history is grouped with the humanities, sometimes with the social sciences.) Social scientists try to understand why people do what they do. They examine how society and social institutions are constructed, how they work (or don't work), and what the ramifications of structures, organizations, and human behavior are. Two types of writing prevail: scholars can lean toward the scientific approach or can adopt an approach more characteristic of the humanities. Some writers in the social sciences, for instance, use empirical scientific methods similar to those used in the natural sciences to gather, analyze, and report their data, with a focus on people, groups, and their behavior. These writers, who stress the "sciences" part of the term, concern themselves largely with data and statistics to draw their conclusions. Writers in the social sciences, especially in psychology, may conduct empirical laboratory research in the way that natural scientists do, but they also frequently rely on data collection by means of surveys and questionnaires, analyzing and reporting their results in tables, charts, and graphs. Numbers, percentages, averages, means, medians—all are important concepts in the social sciences.

Then there are writers in the social sciences who are more social philosophers than scientists. Scholars in fields such as public policy and international relations examine trends and events to draw their conclusions. Ethnographic studies are common too, with researchers taking detailed notes from observing a situation they want to analyze—the behavior of fans at a baseball game, for example, or the verbal reactions of constituents to a politician's tax cut proposals.

When you are given a writing assignment in the social sciences, it will be helpful if you can ascertain (from the approach in class—or just ask) whether your instructor leans toward the humanities or the sciences and whether an empirical study or a philosophical, interpretive essay is more appropriate.

Guidelines for writing in the social sciences

- Understand that the research method you choose will determine what kind of writing is necessary and how you should organize the writing.
- Decide whether your purpose is to describe accurately, measure, inform, analyze, or synthesize information.
- Decide on what kind of data you will use: figures and statistics from experimental research, surveys, the census, or

questionnaires; observational data from case studies, interviews, and on-site observations; or reading.

- For an observational study, take careful field notes that describe accurately everything you see. Concentrate on the facts rather than interpretations. Save the interpretive possibilities for the sections of your paper devoted to discussion and recommendations.

- Back up your own observations and research with a review of the literature in the field.

- Use sections and headings in your paper. For an experimental study, see the APA paper written for a psychology course (**53f**).

- Use specialized terminology when appropriate. Examples in psychology include *affect* and *deviance*.

- Report facts. Add comments and expressions such as "I think" only when this is a specific requirement of the task.

- Use the passive voice when it is not important for readers to know the identity of the person performing the action: "The participants were timed. . . ."

- Present statistical data in the form of tables, charts, and graphs.

- Follow the APA *Publication Manual* or whichever style manual is recommended.

Types of college writing in the social sciences   Writing in the social sciences can follow much the same patterns and procedures as those of either the humanities or the sciences, depending on your purpose, orientation, and training.

Description of empirical research   For a student essay written for an introductory course in experimental psychology and documented in APA style, see **53f**.

Analytical review of the literature available in a field   See **12c** for an example of such a review; the assignment for Rachel Schwartz's essay (posted online for a sociology course) was to review the literature from 1990 to 2000 on the subject of same-sex marriage.

8e Interdisciplinary courses

Sometimes you may take a course that deliberately crosses the boundaries of disciplines to allow a more comprehensive view of a topic. Frequently the courses are taught by two or more instructors from different disciplines, each bringing expertise to the course. The

University of Wisconsin-Madison, for instance, offers interdisciplinary courses in its College of Agricultural and Life Sciences, saying this about the courses:

> These courses reflect the growing need for multidisciplinary interaction in education and research. Interdisciplinary courses expose students to a wide variety of subject material and bridge existing departments.
>
> —University of Wisconsin-Madison
> <http://www.wisc.edu/pubs/ug/04cals/interdis.html>

Examples of interdisciplinary courses offered in several colleges are "Intercultural Communications," "Asians in the United States," "The Holocaust: An Interdisciplinary Inquiry," "Science, Civilization, and Human Creativity," "Scientific Ethos," and "Muslim Diasporas." Some colleges have established interdisciplinary programs too, such as Women's Studies or Asian Studies, in which courses are offered covering or combining, for example, history, politics, literature, art, education, and sociology.

The assignment itself and the recommendations of your instructors will determine how you approach a topic for writing, what kinds of evidence you provide, and which style of documentation is appropriate.

8f   Community service learning courses

Often defined as "experiential learning," service learning projects link college students to their community. For such projects, students volunteer for 20–30 hours of community service in a research laboratory, nursing home, hospice, homeless shelter, AIDS clinic, poor neighborhood school, and so on; they relate their work there to the content of a discipline or a particular course. Courses and coursework are oriented to problems in society that students engage with at a personal level in order to attempt to find some solutions. They also are asked to reflect on their service experiences and demonstrate to the college instructor what they learned. These are the three main types of writing in community service projects:

1. writing done initially with the site supervisor to outline the goals, activities, and desired outcomes of the service project
2. writing done during the service work, such as reports to a supervisor, daily records, and summaries of work completed
3. writing done for the college course—usually reflective reports describing the service objectives and the writer's experiences and assessing the success of the project.

TechNote Samples of Students' Service Course Writing
Projects

Go to the Virginia Tech Service Learning Center site at <http://www
.majbill.vt.edu/SL/> for samples of students' writing in service learning courses. ■

To reflect fully on the work you do, keep an ongoing journal of
your activities, so that you can provide background about the setting
and the work and give specific details about the problems you
encounter and their solutions. Link your comments to the goals of
the project.

The following paragraph is from the reflective journal of a student in a community service course. While enrolled in a microbiol-
ogy course at Kapi'olani Community College in Hawaii, Joanne L.
Soriano worked at an arboretum (a place to study trees) propagating
endangered plant species.

> Through Service Learning, I am able to contribute to the Lyon
> Arboretum's efforts. I made my first visit on February 5th, and
> was taken to their micropropagation lab. In it, my supervisor,
> Greg Koob, showed me racks and racks of test tubes filled with
> plantlets. They were either endangered or native Hawaiian, or
> both. The endangered ones were clones; in some cases they were
> derived from only a few remaining individuals. A major function
> of the lab is to perpetuate these species by growing them in the
> test tubes and then splitting each individual into more test tubes
> as it grows. Thus one specimen can become hundreds, under the
> right conditions. They can be planted on the Arboretum's
> grounds, or sent to various labs to be studied. I am thrilled to be
> given the opportunity to participate in the process.

8g Preparing oral reports

You may be asked to give oral reports or oral presentations in writing courses, in other college courses, and in the business world.
Usually you will do some writing as you prepare your talk, and you
will deliver your oral report either from notes or from a manuscript
text written especially for oral presentation.

Situation, purpose, and audience Consider the background and
expectations of your audience. Jot down what you know about your
listeners and what stance and tone will best convince them of the

validity of your views. For example, what effect do you want to have on the members of your audience? Do you want to inform, persuade, move, or entertain them? What do you know about your listeners' age, gender, background, education, occupation, political affiliation, beliefs, and knowledge of your subject? What do listeners need to know? In a college class, your audience will be your classmates and instructor. It is often desirable to build a sense of community with your audience by asking questions and using the inclusive pronoun *we*.

Preparation   Making an effective oral presentation is largely a matter of having control over your material, deciding what you want to say, and knowing your subject matter well. Preparation and planning are essential.

KEY POINTS

Tips for Preparing an Oral Report

1. Select a topic you are committed to and decide on a clear focus.

2. Make a few strong points. Back them up with specific details. Have a few points that you can expand on and develop with interesting examples, quotations, and stories.

3. Include signposts and signal phrases to help your audience follow your ideas (*first, next, finally; the most important point is . . .*).

4. Structure your report clearly. Present the organizational framework of your talk along with illustrative materials in handouts, overhead transparencies, Microsoft PowerPoint slides (**15c**), posters, charts, or other visuals (**10e**).

5. Use short sentences, accessible words, memorable phrases, and natural language. In writing, you can use long sentences with one clause embedded in another, but these are difficult for listeners to follow.

6. You can effectively use repetition much more in an oral report than in a written report. Your audience will appreciate being reminded of the structure of the talk and points you referred to previously.

7. Meet the requirements set for the presentation in terms of time available for preparation, length of presentation (most people read a page of double-spaced text in just over two minutes), and possible questions from the audience.

8. Prepare a strong ending that will have an impact on the audience. Make sure that you conclude. Do not simply stop or trail off.

You can make your presentation from notes that you memorize or consult as you talk, or you can prepare a special manuscript.

Speaking from notes Speaking from notes is the best way. It allows you to be more spontaneous and to look directly at your audience. Think of your presentation as a conversation. For this method, notes or a key-word outline must be clear and organized, so that you feel secure about which points you will discuss and in what order you will discuss them. Here are a speaker's notes for a presentation of her views on the giving of paternity leave.

1. Children's needs
   Benefits
   Bonding

2. Issue of equity
   Equal treatment for men and women
   Cost

Your notes or outline should make reference to specific illustrations and quotations and contain structural signals so that the audience knows when you begin to address a new point. You can also use slides prepared with your word processor or PowerPoint slides to guide the direction and structure of your presentation (**15c**). For a short presentation on a topic that you know well, use notes with or without the visual aid of slides. Do not read aloud, especially in front of a small audience.

Speaking from a manuscript Writing out a complete speech may be necessary for a long formal presentation, but even if you do this, you should practice and prepare so that you do not have to labor over every word. Remember, too, to build in places to pause and make spontaneous comments. The advantages of speaking from a prepared manuscript are that you can time the presentation exactly and that you will never dry up and wonder what to say next. The disadvantages are that you have to read the text and that reading aloud is not easy, especially if you want to maintain eye contact with your audience. If you prefer to speak from a complete manuscript text, prepare the text for oral presentation as follows:

- Triple-space your text and use a large font.
- When you reach the bottom of a page, begin a new sentence on the next page. Do not start a sentence on one page and finish it on the next.
- Highlight key words in each paragraph so that your eye can pick them out easily.

- Underline words and phrases that you want to stress.

- Use slash marks (/ or //) to remind yourself to pause. Read in sense groups (parts of a sentence that are read as a unit—a phrase or clause, for example—often indicated by a pause when spoken and by punctuation when read). Mark your text at the end of a sense group.

- Number your pages so that you can keep them in the proper sequence.

The following excerpt from a student's text prepared for an oral report shows some distinctive features.

1

Short and direct

Should men get and take paternity leave? Of

Signpost to structure

course they should. Here's why. / First, everyone

benefits if fathers have a chance to bond with

their children--the father, the mother, and most

of all, the infant. The literature we have read in

this class tells us that <u>crucial bonding</u> takes

place between mother and child in the early days

after birth. // But the issue is not only one of

personal need for bonding. It's an issue of

<u>social and gender equity</u>. If women are granted

time off from work and often take it, men should

Direct quotation

take time off, too. "But business and industry

can't afford it," I hear you say. Let's look at

what it would cost. . . .

Question used to draw the audience in

Pause mark

Informal language

Practice, practice, practice Whether you speak from notes or a manuscript, practice is essential.

- Practice not just once but many times. Try tape-recording yourself, listening to the tape, and asking a friend for comments.

- Speak at a normal speed and at a good volume. Speaking too quickly and too softly is a common mistake.

- Imagine a full audience; use gestures and practice looking up to make eye contact with people in the audience.
- Beware of filler words and phrases like *OK, well, you know,* and *like.* Such repeated verbal tics annoy and distract an audience.
- Do not punctuate pauses with *er* or *uhm.*

ESL NOTE Dealing with Nerves

If you have only recently moved to speaking and writing in English, having to speak in front of others may seem intimidating. Make sure you know your material thoroughly. Practice and make sure you know when to pause and how to pronounce all the words. Ask someone to listen to you practice and give you helpful hints. Then relax. You'll be surprised at how sympathetic and understanding an audience can be— a "foreign" accent can often charm away the perception of errors. ▪

Audiovisual aids If you use visual aids to outline your talk and provide essential information, check your equipment and practice with it. If you use an overhead projector or PowerPoint slides (see **15c**), the font size must be large enough for people at the back of the room to read, and the colors you choose should be clear—black on white is best. Use headings and bulleted lists (**10d**) to make your material clear. When you speak, remember to face the audience, not the projector or screen. Do not provide lengthy or complicated visual aids; otherwise, your audience will be reading them instead of listening to you.

Presentation and performance It is natural to feel some anxiety before the actual presentation, but most people find that their jitters disappear as soon as they begin talking, especially when they are well prepared.

Look frequently at your listeners. Work the room so that you gaze directly at people in all sections of the audience. In *Secrets of Successful Speakers,* Lilly Walters points out that when you look at one person, all the people in a V behind that person will think you are looking at them. Bear in mind that no matter how well prepared a report is, listeners will not respond well if the presenter reads it too rapidly or in a monotone or without looking up and engaging the audience. Remember to smile.

8h Preparing a portfolio

Selecting work to include in a portfolio gives you an opportunity to review your progress over time and to assess which pieces of writing best reflect your abilities and interests. Choose pieces that indicate both the range of topics covered in the course (or in your course of study) and the types of writing you have done. To show readers that you are able to produce more than one type of writing, include pieces on different topics, written for different purposes. If your instructor does not issue specific guidelines for presenting your portfolio, use those in the Key Points box.

KEY POINTS

Presenting a Portfolio

1. Number and date drafts; clip or staple all drafts and final copy together.

2. To each separate package in your portfolio add a cover sheet describing the contents of the package (for example, "In-class essay" or "Documented paper with three prior drafts").

3. Include a brief cover letter to introduce the material and yourself.

4. Pay special attention to accuracy and mechanics. Your semester grade may depend on the few pieces of writing that you select to be evaluated, so make sure that the ones you include are carefully edited and well presented.

Sample cover letter This cover letter introduces readers to the writer and to the material in the portfolio they are about to read.

Dear Reader:

In this portfolio you will find the results of my hard work in my Expository Writing class during the last semester. Throughout this time, under the guidance of my professor, I learned to write essays, do research, critique others' papers by working in groups, and edit my work "with great care," as my professor kept reminding me.

When I first came to Hunter College, I was not sure I would make it through, since this was the first time I had had to learn in English. But after taking this course in my second semester, I feel more confident about my writing and better prepared for future courses.

Reading this portfolio, you will find out about my identity as a newly married woman, children's dreams, and the moral dilemmas in shooting an elephant (not my experience but a George Orwell work). I tried to choose a variety of topics and types of writing to include here so that you get a sense of what I can do. In addition, my research paper on the role of women in Virginia Woolf's time, which I began with fear but ended with pride, makes the point that the glass ceiling has not broken in the last sixty or seventy years, though it may show a few cracks.

I hope you will enjoy reading my work because that would mean that Professor Raimes succeeded in getting this Polish student to write well in English.

Sincerely,

Magdalena Wisniewska

EXERCISE 8.1 Evaluate portfolio letters.

Which of the two following portfolio cover letters effectively introduces the body of work produced by the student during the semester? Discuss why you chose one over the other.

1.

Dear Reader:

Your eyes are probably tired from reading so many portfolios. I'll make my letter brief. In this portfolio you will find examples of all the hard work my teacher made me do this semester. There is an essay on names (about my name, Jonah) which I revised twice; an essay on multiculturalism, about the multiculturalism debate that is going on right now; and an essay on gender roles in the workplace, which has support, like quotations, facts, and statistics. In this short research paper I did not use any long quotations because my teacher told us that they are not appropriate for this type of writing, the short research paper. They can be appropriate for other, longer types of research papers, but don't look for them in this paper, because they purposefully aren't there.

These three types of writing show how I write in different situations: at home, in school, and with research. The topics are interesting and diverse. These examples pretty much speak for themselves and sum things up in terms of the semester and all that it held and all I learned.

I hope you like my work.

Enjoy,

Jonah Lore

2.

Dear Reader,

This portfolio represents the best of the writing I produced this semester in English 120, Expository Writing. As you will see, the overarching theme or thread is identity, which is based on our text <u>Identities: Readings from Contemporary Culture</u>.

The first piece is a take-home essay entitled "Self-Esteem: Loving the Self." In this essay, I compare Alice Walker's experience in "Beauty: When the Other Dancer Is the Self" to my own experience. Like Walker, I experienced a childhood injury that resulted in a temporary loss of self-esteem.

For my research paper, I chose to write about the effectiveness of bilingual programs. As a product of the bilingual education system, I felt an affinity with the topic. The most challenging aspect of writing this essay was not conducting research, but rather keeping the personal pronoun "I" out of the paper. The last piece is an in-class essay on the topic of what it means to be American.

Exploring the issue of identity has made me look seriously at the different facets of my experience. I want to invite you to a glimpse of who I am and who I was during the fall of 2002.

Sincerely yours,
Mia Banton

9 Writing under Pressure

Pressure is a fact of life in college. Papers are due, exams are looming, you are working, and you have a family crisis. You stay up late night after night trying to get it all done. Unfortunately, this book can't produce a magic formula to make the pressure go away. Remember, though, that most instructors are sympathetic about genuine emergencies (even though they won't accept the "fact" that a grandmother dies three times in one semester). This section offers advice that you might find useful in pressured moments.

9a Essay exams

Essay exams are an important part of your life as a student. In an examination setting, you have to write quickly on an assigned topic. Learn how to cope with these tests so that you don't dread them. The advantage of an essay over a multiple-choice test is that you can include in your answer more of the information you have learned. Knowing the material of the course thoroughly will give you a distinct advantage, allowing you to choose the facts and ideas you need and to present them clearly.

KEY POINTS

How to Approach an Essay Exam

1. For a content-based essay test, review assigned materials and notes; assemble facts; underline, annotate, and summarize significant information; predict questions on the basis of the material your instructor has covered in detail in class; and draft some answers. Go into the exam knowing that you are well prepared with necessary information.

2. Highlight or underline key terms in the assigned questions (see **9b** and the sample essay exam that follows). Ask for clarification if necessary.

3. Decide what information is relevant and how the information connects to the assigned question.

4. Think positively about what you know. Work out a way to highlight the details you know most about. Stretch and relax.

5. Plan your time. Jot down a rough schedule; allow the most time for the questions that are worth the most points. To increase your confidence, answer the easiest question first.

6. Make sure you formulate a thesis if it is called for in the essay question. Include key words from the question in formulating your thesis.

7. Make a scratch outline (see **3i**) to organize your thoughts. Jot down specific details as evidence for your thesis.

8. Focus on providing detailed support for your thesis. In an exam essay, this is more important than an elaborate introduction or conclusion.

9. Write your essay, using a new paragraph for each new point of support and making connections and transitions between the ideas in the paragraphs.

10. Read your essay, checking for content, logic, and clarity. Make sure you answered the question.

A sample essay exam   Here are Professor Barbara Apstein's essay exam question (Bridgewater State College, Massachusetts), and student Alexander Thompson's highlighting of key words, scratch outline, and finished essay.

In her book *A Distant Mirror: The Calamitous Fourteenth Century,* historian Barbara Tuchman makes the following observation: "The conflict between the reach for the divine and the lure of earthly things was to be the central problem of the Middle Ages" (New York: Knopf, 1978: 6).

To what extent does this statement apply to the *Canterbury Tales*? In other words, does the conflict between the "reach for the divine" and the "lure of earthly things" seem to you to be very important in Chaucer's poem, somewhat important, or not important at all? Explain your point of view, using specific details and examples from at least three of the prologues and/or tales. (2 typed pages: 20 points)

Alexander Thompson's scratch outline:

Issue: Earthly (pleasures of the world, material riches) vs. divine (religious life, spiritual leadership of church, serving God)

Thesis: Conflict is very important.

Support:

Prioress

coy smile

eating

anti-Semitism

Monk

likes hunting

not humble—hypocritical

Friar

enjoys life

earns profit from penances—also hypocritical

Exam Essay #2

The conflict between the "reach for the divine" and "the lure of earthly things" is an idea that Chaucer displays in several characters in The Canterbury Tales, but particularly the members of the church. This is shown in the General Prologue with his descriptions of the Prioress, the Monk, and the Friar. These are figures who would have been well respected for their standing in the church and the community, and yet all three are described as not completely dedicated to the church because of their inability to give up the everyday pleasures in life.

Not even two full lines into the Prioress's description in the General Prologue we see a hint that this nun may have other concerns in her life besides her devotion to God. The line describing her smile as "ful simple and coy" (C. 7) would not be what we would expect for a nun, especially an older nun who should be a role model for the younger ones. It suggests that she may be flirtatious and enjoys or craves attention. "In curteisie was set ful muchel hir lest" (C. 7), which describes the elegance of her eating, again is not how we would expect her to be described. Instead we would expect a nun to be humble in the way she looked at people and the way she ate. To go one step further, the tale, which deals with themes of anti-Semitism, would not be something we would expect from a nun. Chaucer is not necessarily criticizing nuns or even this nun in particular but is reminding us that members of the church are still people who are not perfect. Even though they are held to a higher standard than the rest of us, they still share many of the habits that are common to everyone.

The very next description in the General Prologue is that of the Monk, and he shares in this conflict as well. We think of monks as being close spiritually to God, people who should be held to a higher standard than the rest of the common people. However, like the Prioress he has much in common with the common people. Again the opening lines of his description tell us something about him that we would not necessarily associate with a monk. The line "An outridere, that lovede venerie" (C. 8) describes him as a hunter, someone who enjoys the outdoors and sport. Hunting seems to go against the Christian belief of loving all God's creatures, and we would expect a monk to spend nearly all of his time studying or teaching scriptures, but again we are shown a member of the church who does not give up the everyday things that regular people enjoy. Also he is described as "ful fat" (C. 8) indicating that he is not humble and is not really concerned with how a clergy member should present himself, but rather lives his life to please himself rather than others. Ironically his tale is almost an instruction manual in how a person should behave in the eyes of God. Chaucer is either making fun of a clergy member to point to hypocrisy in the church or he is simply showing that these people are no different from us.

The Friar has much in common with the Monk in that he has pledged to live a humble life and yet he lives life to the fullest, enjoying every minute. He is described as being "wantowne and merry" (C. 8), telling us from the opening lines that he is also far from humble and more of an everyday person who enjoys life. This character is said to earn a profit from hearing penances, which suggests again that Chaucer is pointing out hypocrisy in the church by giving him characteristics of the common man such as a love of fun and having a good time.

All of these members of the church are on a higher pedestal than the rest of us, but they never give up the everyday pleasures of life such as good food, social gatherings, and sport. They are clearly conflicted in the "reach for the divine" and "the lure of earthly things."

EXERCISE 9.1 Evaluate essay exam questions.
Describe what makes a fair and successful essay exam question and what makes a poor and frustrating one. Then, using the reading material you have done for this class, construct a good essay exam question. Bring it to class and discuss with classmates.

9b Terms used in essay assignments and short-answer tests

For essay exams, short-answer tests, and any assigned writing tasks, always read the question carefully and make sure you understand what you are being asked to do. Essay questions often contain the following verbs:

analyze   Divide into parts and discuss each part

argue   Make a claim and point out your reasons

classify   Organize people, objects, or concepts into groups

compare   Point out similarities

contrast   Point out differences

define   Give the meaning of

discuss   State important characteristics and main points

evaluate   Define criteria for judgment and examine good and bad points, strengths and weaknesses

explain   Give reasons or make clear by analyzing, defining, contrasting, illustrating, and so on

illustrate   Give examples from experience and reading

relate   Point out and discuss connections

9c   Short-answer tests

In short-answer tests, use your time wisely. So that you know how long you should spend on each question, count the number of questions and divide the number of minutes you have for taking the test by the number of questions (add 1 or 2 to the number you divide by, to give yourself time for editing and proofreading). Then for each answer decide which points are the most important ones to cover in the time you have available. You cannot afford to ramble or waffle in short-answer tests. Get to the point fast and show what you know.

Make sure you do not miss a class before the test; instructors will often review material that will appear on the test, and if you pay careful attention, you will pick up hints as to the type of questions that will be asked and the material that will be covered. For both essay exams and short-answer tests, always read the questions carefully, underline the key terms used, and make sure you understand what each question asks you to do. Before a test, familiarize yourself with the terms in essay exams and short-answer tests (**9b**).

Short answers to an exam question in a sociology course   The following questions and short answers are posted on a Web site for a philosophy course at California State University, Dominguez Hills, at <http://www.csudh.edu/sociology/mdtrm.htm>. They are accompanied by the commentaries of the instructor, Professor Jeanne Curran. The letters and words within square brackets are her corrections of the student's text.

Question: How does the tension of which Habermas speaks fit into the individual versus the structural control of society?

[Student 1:] Structural control of society is use[d] to protect the individual right[s] of a society or people who must live together. Each citizen has a right in the U.S. to freedom of choice, according to Habermas; the tension occurs due to society limiting the freedom of choice of the individual.

[Instructor:] *This is a good example of someone struggling with the concept. The answer is short, leaving out much of the elaboration I would like, but it is on point, considers both structural and individual, as requested, and links the idea to Habermas's system of law.*

[Student 2:] The tension [comes from] an individual's right to make free choices within the limits or norms that have been set by society, as a whole. The limits were set to maintain moral freedom for all of us who are a part of it. Though our constitution dictates that all within our society are free, there are limits that have been set. These limits are there to protect the whole society, so that others have the right to choose within those same limits. Obedience to self-imposed law is true freedom, our willingness to accept and adhere.

[Instructor:] *Well stated. Follows the text answer closely, but gives a clear sense that you have grasped the concept. Good last sentence links the idea to Habermas's requirements for social integration, "self-imposed," and "willingness to adhere."*

[Student 3:] The tension is that of the individual and the limits they place on their own freedom for the good of the rest of society. The society ensures the freedom of individuals by limiting the rights of the individual freedom. The individual and society then have a collective agreement, which in turn brings legitimacy to the system.

[Instructor:] *Good statement of tension between individual freedom and good of social community. Good link to Habermas in emphasis on "collective agreement" and "legitimacy." More concise than I would have liked. I would have liked you to spell out how important the collective nature of agreement is to Habermas, and more precisely how he defines legitimacy. But that was our fault for leaving too little space.*

EXERCISE 9.2 Identify key terms in essay exam questions.

In the following questions, underline key terms that writers should address when they respond to the following essay exam questions from various courses.

1. In Chapter 10, we explored the controversial issues surrounding the death penalty. Write a 350-word essay arguing for or against the death penalty, making reference to some or all of these issues. You have the entire class period.

2. Define "coup d'état."

3. Compare and/or contrast the major characteristics of the Romantic period in Britain with the Augustan period in Britain. Be sure to refer to at least two writers who you believe are representative of each period.

4. What are the various ways rocks can be classified?

5. Discuss the key issues presented by both candidates during the last mayoral election.

6. Evaluate the significance of Maslow's "Hierarchy of Needs."

7. Explain the effects of current immigration policies on families and children.

9d Assignment deadlines

When instructors assign papers, they usually assign a due date. Note the date and make yourself a schedule of work to be done and steps to be accomplished, working backwards from the due date to the date the paper is first assigned. Section **47c** shows a sample schedule for writing a research paper. Adapt this schedule for shorter, less demanding papers.

If you don't even start a major paper until the evening before it is due, you are bound to feel helpless, desperate, and depressed about your dwindling GPA. In short, *get started early*. There is no better way to avoid panic. Then you will be able to say with a degree of confidence as you near the deadline, "The paper doesn't have to be perfect. It just has to be done." Work on finishing a draft to hand in—however rough or "drafty" it is. If you feel you still need additional time to revise, an instructor is likely to be more sympathetic to a request for an extension of the deadline if you show that you have made a genuine effort and have produced a solid draft.

Part III
Writing with Technology and Writing for Work

Not too long ago, people who wrote for work, school, or pleasure used to argue about their preferences: yellow legal pads or notebook, pen or pencil, two or three drafts. In 1957, the writer Truman Capote announced proudly that he did all his writing, even his typing, in bed: "I write my first version in longhand (pencil). Then I do a complete revision, also in longhand. [. . .] Then I type a third draft on yellow paper, a very special kind of yellow paper. No, I don't get out of bed to do this. I balance the machine on my knees."

Now, whenever or wherever we write, we deal increasingly with technology. We use computers to produce, revise, edit, and store a piece of writing. Design operations that used to be time-consuming with a typewriter, such as inserting headers and footers, inserting tables and graphs, and including illustrations, we now do swiftly and accurately with a word processing program. We can easily add color and visuals and produce professional-looking documents right at our desks. In our personal lives, in educational settings, and at work, we also use computers to write online, communicating with others and collaborating over the Web. In fact, we are fully immersed in a technological context in which we now plan, write, revise, store, design, and transmit our documents.

10 Designing Documents and Using Word

Word processing programs provide help in both writing and designing a document, and this section outlines the many features they provide.

A word of caution: If you do not own a computer and instead use one at a computer lab at your college, consider handwriting or typing a first draft at home or in the library and deciding at least in a preliminary way what you need to do to revise. Then at the lab, where time is rationed and long waits are the norm, work from your marked-up draft and type it. Remember to also take a disk or CD-RW with you to save your draft.

10a Word processing programs, software, and Web sites

Word processing programs Word processing programs include features to ease the process of writing, revising, editing, collaborating with others, and formatting your finished document. They allow you to perform the following operations:

- check the spelling of the document
- delete text and save it as a separate file
- copy a section of text and paste it into another draft or into a totally different document
- number pages automatically
- insert a header or footer without having to type it over and over again on each individual page
- automatically count the number of words
- access an online thesaurus to avoid overusing the same words
- search for words and punctuation that you often use incorrectly, evaluate them, and replace them if warranted
- design the format of your finished document (font, spacing, margins, text features, color, visuals, and the like)
- insert comments and revisions in your own document or someone else's

For details on using Microsoft Word for writing and formatting documents, see **10c.** For details on the specifics of formatting for college essays, see **10g.**

Computer software programs to help with writing and editing As you look for a topic to write about or as you generate ideas about an assigned topic, you may wish to use software programs or Web sites for help. These tools can supplement brainstorming, freewriting, mapping, journal writing, and other approaches (see **3a–3e**). Software such as Inspiration can help with developing ideas and organizing thinking. Software such as Writer's Helper can also help with responding to writing and with revising and editing. And software such as Writer's Workbench and MLA Editor can help with analyzing a document, pointing out possible trouble spots, and suggesting revisions. For editing, too, grammar-checking software and online advice sites are available, though see **4i** on the limitations of grammar-checking programs. Your college computer lab may offer some of the software on its network. Always check to see what tools are available for you to use.

EXERCISE 10.1 Use a style- or grammar-checking program.
A. The passage that follows is also available on the *Universal Keys* Web site. Copy and paste the passage into a document on your own computer and run it through any style- or grammar-checking program your college computer lab offers. What suggestions does the program make? Discuss with classmates how useful (or not useful) those suggestions are.

If I had a boat, I'd sleep on it every once in a while, moored out on the open ocean, but not too terribly far out, because though I hate the city I'd like the comfort of house lights twinkling on the shore as the waves would rock me to sleep. If a storm would come I would jump up and immediately bustle about the ship. Battening hatches that wouldn't need battening, tying down things already nailed, and basically making a great wet fool out of myself. All the while I would be shouting challenges at the whether to try it's worst, because by God, me and the ship weren't giving up without a fight! And I'd probably get tremendously wet and catch a whale of a cold. But it would still be wonderful, because it would be the boat and me, just the boat and me, alive against the Sea.

B. Now take a passage from a paper you have written for one of your classes and run it through the same program. How helpful are the suggestions it makes? Does it catch every mistake? Does it suggest any incorrect "corrections"?

Web sites to help with writing For generating and organizing ideas and getting help with grammar, go to these sites:

Capital Community College Guide to Grammar and Writing: <http://ccc.commnet.edu/grammar/>

Purdue University Online Writing Lab: <http://owl.english .purdue.edu>

The Elements of Style by William Strunk Jr.: <http://www.bartleby.com/141>

The following sites provide exercises on grammar, punctuation, and mechanics:

Digital Keys Online: <http://college.hmco.com/keys.html>

Houghton Mifflin *eLibrary of Exercises:* <http://college.hmco.com>

ESL NOTE Useful Web Sites for ESL Students

Dave's ESL Café: <http://www.eslcafe.com>

Activities for ESL Students: <http://a4ESL.org>

10b Tools for revising and collaborating

Revising on the computer means using the basic word processing features of Delete, Cut, Copy, and Paste. It also means becoming adept at saving as a new file any material you delete that might be useful to you later or even in another document. (See **4b** for more on managing files.) Other useful features are AutoCorrect, Find, Replace, Comment, and Track Changes.

AutoCorrect   The AutoCorrect feature in Word allows you to take shortcuts and to save time. If, for example, you are writing about "housing preservation," you can simply write "hp" whenever you want to write "housing preservation." To set this feature, go to the Tools menu, select AutoCorrect, and then select the AutoCorrect tab. In the Replace text box, type your shortcut (the text you wish to replace) and then in the With text box, type the text you want to take the place of the shortcut.

Find and Replace   The Find feature helps you find phrases that you tend to overuse. Use it to look for instances of "there is" or "there are," for example, and you will see if you are using either phrase too often. If you suspect you may have overused a key word or phrase in your essay ("pedagogy" or "addictive personality," for instance), you can find and check each instance of its use, substituting new words or eliminating any repetition.

Insert a Comment   The Comment feature on the Insert menu allows you, your classmates, or your instructor to ask questions or write a note in the middle of a draft. The place where a comment is inserted will be highlighted on your screen and you can see the comment appear at the end of your document. You can then choose to print your document with or without the comments showing. This feature allows you to interact with your text as you write and helps remind you of leads to follow and points to check.

Here is a screenshot of student David Powers's summary (see **7a**) and his own interpolated comments:

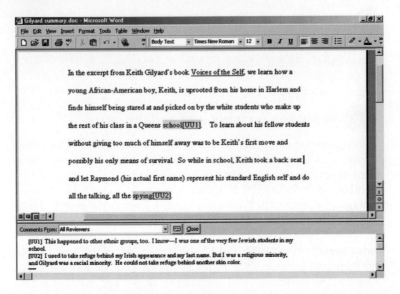

In the excerpt from Keith Gilyard's book _Voices of the Self_, we learn how a young African-American boy, Keith, is uprooted from his home in Harlem and finds himself being stared at and picked on by the white students who make up the rest of his class in a Queens school[UU1]. To learn about his fellow students without giving too much of himself away was to be Keith's first move and possibly his only means of survival. So while in school, Keith took a back seat and let Raymond (his actual first name) represent his standard English self and do all the talking, all the spying[UU2].

[UU1] This happened to other ethnic groups, too. I know—I was one of the very few Jewish students in my school.
[UU2] I used to take refuge behind my Irish appearance and my last name. But I was a religious minority, and Gilyard was a racial minority. He could not take refuge behind another skin color.

Track Changes The Track Changes feature on the Tools menu allows you to mark and highlight additions and changes to your own document or one you receive via e-mail that you have copied into your word processing program. This feature lets you see clearly on the screen and on the printed page the changes you have made (see an example in **10c**). The Accept or Reject Changes option allows you to accept or reject all the changes or each change separately, and it will make the changes to your document automatically. You can also compare two drafts by using the Track Changes/Compare Documents feature. Simply load in a file containing a draft that you want to compare to the current draft, and the program will highlight the differences in the two drafts.

EXERCISE 10.2 Search and add comments to a document. Imagine a long document beginning with the following passage. Which words might you search the whole document for? Where might you add a comment, and what would the comment be?

One of the most predominant battle cries of civilization, as we toddle into the twenty-first century, is "Look it up on the Internet!" Indeed, it is almost a cliché nowadays to say that the Internet has vastly affected the way the world works. Business transactions, market research, the distribution of music, pictures, and postcards; all these things can now be done in the unfathomable reaches of cyberspace. Of course, distribution and publication of literature is no exception, and cannot escape the all-encompassing embrace of the fiber-optic octopus. As if television hadn't done enough damage to books and booksellers, the Internet now gives people one less reason to leave the house, and one less reason to find a bookstore that has anything resembling character.

—Benjamin Gould (student), "The Role of the Internet in Publishing: A Chilling Look at the Apocalypse"

EXERCISE 10.3 Use Track Changes feature to work collaboratively. Copy the following passage from the *Universal Keys* Web site, and paste it into your word processing program. Use the Track Changes feature to make changes to the text. Then work with another student. E-mail him or her the passage with your suggestions. Your partner will open the document in Word and decide whether to accept or reject each change. Print out the final version after you have accepted or rejected changes and show it to your partner.

Pablo Neruda, like so many great poets, had an immense reverence for things. From socks to cats to artichokes, from the sea to the word, Neruda was able to see a beauty not usually revealed to the common eye. His eyes took on a childlike quality, examining the world around him with intense curiosity and innocence, allowing him to see attributes overlooked, and at times not even imagined, by others. Not only in Neruda's subject matter, but also in his choice of wording in the descriptions of such things, do we see his gift for noticing beauty and connections. He often strikes those without his gift as odd or surreal. For Neruda, however, his vision was just that: his vision, his slant on reality. This perception of his gave him the insight that allowed him to find beauty all around, whereas others might search for it the world over.

—Benjamin Gould (student), "Pablo Neruda"

10c Features of Microsoft Word for college writing

Writing college essays or business documents is very different from writing e-mail messages. Editing and formatting are important. Fortunately word processors make most of the basic operations available at a click of the mouse.

The examples that follow are for Microsoft Word 2000, but earlier and later versions of Word and other word processing programs offer similar features and commands. The online Help menu also provides detailed instructions on all features of the program. Instructions for basic features are also available online at <http://www.baycongroup.com/wlesson0.htm>, and for advanced features at <http://www.utexas.edu/cc/training/handouts/adword.html/>.

Word Processing Commands: Mouse or Keyboard	Microsoft Word 2000 for Windows
Make a command apply to the whole document	Edit/Select All (Ctrl+A)
Set margins for the whole document (usually 1"–1$\frac{1}{2}$")	File/Page Setup/Margins
Do not right justify (that is, do not align on right)	Formatting toolbar/select Align Left button *or* Format/Paragraph/Alignment text box
Insert headers and footers, including page numbers	View/Header and Footer
Insert a footnote	Insert/Footnote
Check spelling and grammar	Standard toolbar/ ✓ button *or* press F7
Find a word	Edit/Find or Ctrl+F
Replace a word	Edit/Replace or Ctrl+H
Add page numbers on all or selected pages	Insert/Page Numbers
Change font (typeface)	Format/Font *or* Formatting toolbar/Font text box
Count the number of words	Tools/Word Count
Change case (lower or upper, that is, capital)	Format/Change Case
Center text (for a title or heading)	Formatting toolbar/Center button
Make a numbered or bulleted list	Formatting toolbar/Numbered List or Bullets button *or* Format/Bullets and Numbering
Change line spacing	Format/Paragraph/Line Spacing
Add a superscript number	Format/Font/Superscript
Insert a table	Table/Insert
Add comments to a document	Insert/Comment

The screen captures of Word 2000 that follow provide illustrations of how to use its editing and formatting functions, though be aware that the appearance of the toolbars may vary according to the installation. Different versions of Word and other word processing programs may vary in features and the commands to access them.

File/Page Setup   Set page size, paper orientation, margins, and layout (page selection for headers and footers, line numbering, and so on). Do this before you start your document, or from the Edit menu select Select All or highlight a portion of your document to set. (You may want to change the margins after you have written part or all of your document.) Print Preview shows what your pages will look like before you actually print.

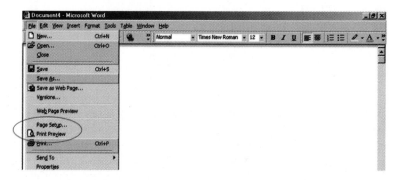

Edit   The Edit menu lets you cut, copy, and paste a selected part of your document (select by clicking and dragging the mouse). You can also use the Select All feature from the Edit menu to select the whole document and then copy it and paste it in another file or program. The Find and Replace functions are useful if you decide you want to make changes in words you have used—to avoid repetition, for example.

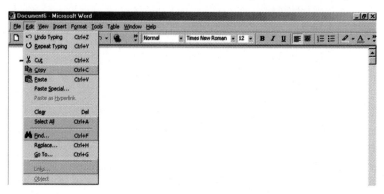

View/Header and Footer By opening the View menu, you will be able to select the Header and Footer option. The Header and Footer toolbar allows you to (a) include a page number along with any text, (b) include the date and time, and (c) toggle between the choice of headers or footers. Headers and footers will adjust automatically to any changes in the pagination of your document. You type the information once only, and it appears in the place you specify on every page.

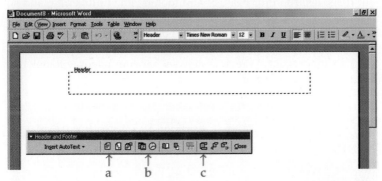

Insert/Page Numbers, Comment, Footnote, Picture, and Hyperlink Use the Page Numbers command if you want only page numbers and no additional text in your header or footer. Select whether you want the page number to appear on the first page.

From the Insert menu, you can also insert date and time, comments, symbols such as ✓, footnotes, captions, cross-references, clip art, charts, pictures, and automatic hyperlinks to URLs.

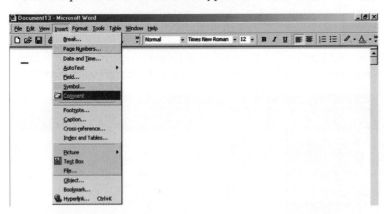

Format The Format menu takes you to the following features:

- Font: changing typeface, style, and size as well as using superscripts (useful for *Chicago*-style citations)

- Paragraph: options for line spacing and indenting (see the screen captures that follow for how to set the special command for the hanging indents used in an MLA list of works cited)
- Bullets and Numbering for lists, Borders and Shading, Columns, Tabs, Drop Cap
- Change Case: changing your text from capital letters to lower-case or vice versa
- Style: changing font, line spacing, lists, and header formats

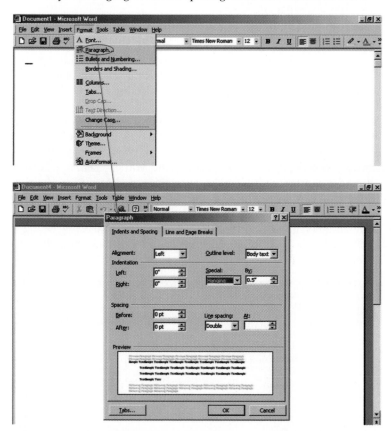

You can also use the Formatting toolbar to select various formatting features. This toolbar is shown in the example that follows. (Turn toolbars on and off using View/Toolbars.)

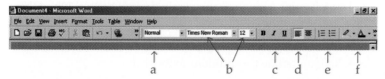

a. Text styles: Choose among Normal text, several list formats, various levels of heading styles (Heading 1, Heading 2, Heading 3, and so on), or Envelope style.

b. Font and font size: You can select a font (typeface) and size here.

c. Font style: You can select text and make it bold, italic, or underlined here.

d. Text alignment: This is useful for centering a title or heading. Otherwise use left alignment. Do not use the Align Right or Justify button for college essays.

e. Lists and indenting: These buttons provide shortcuts for making a numbered or bulleted list and changing indentations.

f. Borders, highlighting, font color: These buttons provide options for borders of paragraphs, tables, table cells, and graphics; highlighting text in a choice of colors; and selecting a font color.

Tools   From the Tools menu, you can set how you want the spelling and grammar checkers to function, you can get an immediate count of the number of words in your document, you can access the thesaurus (Tools/Language/Thesaurus), and you can set AutoCorrect to replace shortcut words, make corrections, and format mechanics. Here, too, is where you find the Track Changes feature, which allows you to highlight changes, deletions, and additions in a document and then gives you the option of accepting or rejecting changes and comparing an original document with one including changes (**10b,** p. 212).

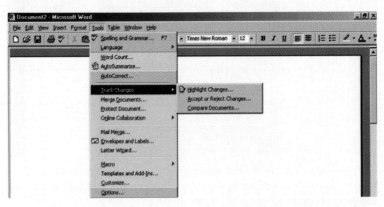

The following sample is of an early draft of section **12b** with an editor's contributions:

- Blue = deletions of the original electronically transmitted text
- Red, underlined = additions to the text

- Red, underlined, and enclosed in square brackets [ ] = comments on the text

The lines in the margin mark places where comments, additions, or deletions have been made.

> The language commonly used for Web site design is HTML (Hypertext Markup Language). Other languages are available for more advanced Web pages. In HTML files, the visible text is supplemented by specific instructions, known as "tags" which are enclosed in brackets (<...>). However, those of you who shudder at the sight of ~~codes~~ such tags and the often rather messy looking "source code" can begin by using a program ~~with~~ which creates the underlying HTML tags automatically, like driving a car without knowing or caring what the carburetor does. Recent versions of word processing programs automatically can convert a document and save it as an HTML file. [Note, however, that the code created by Microsoft Word 2000 is really XML rather than basic HTML.]

Table Design and insert your own table with this feature. When you select Insert/Table from the Table menu, you can then select the numbers of columns and rows you want. Be sure to leave an extra line above where you will insert a table, or you will not be able to add text there.

EXERCISE 10.4 Make formatting changes.

The passage that follows appears on the *Universal Keys* Web site. Find the passage, copy and paste it into your word processing program, and do the following. Remember to select or highlight text to which you want to apply formatting changes.

- Change the line spacing from single to double.
- Make the list of items after "Here are the most common tools you will need" into a numbered list.
- Change the list from a numbered to a bulleted list.
- Change the font to Times Roman and the font size to 12 throughout the document.

- Do a word count.
- Add a header with your last name and the page number on the top right of the page.
- Change the text to Justify and then change it back to Align Left. Watch to see what happens.
- Center the heading.
- Find the places where the word "people" occurs. Revise any of these that you think need revising.
- Use the Comment feature to add your own comment or question at one point in the text.

Then print your final copy and compare your results with a classmate's results. How similar do your documents look?

BICYCLE MAINTENANCE

Many people who own bicycles feel that the only way to have them properly cared for is to take them to a bike shop. However, even the most mechanically uninclined people can learn the skills necessary to perform the simple bicycle maintenance that can keep them on the road.

The first step is to make sure you have the right tools for the job. Here are the most common tools people will need: adjustable wrenches, metric Allen wrenches, flat-head screwdriver, Phillips-head screwdriver, bicycle pump, and tire levers.

The most common problem for the bike rider is the flat tire. Luckily, it is also one of the easiest to fix. First, you remove the wheel from the bicycle, so that you can work with it more easily. To do this, you may need to use two adjustable wrenches, unless you have a quick-release system. Once the wheel is off the bike, use the tire levers to remove the tire from the wheel's rim. This can be hard at first, but once the lever is under the tire, you should be able to slide it all the way around, prying the tire off as you go.

After removing the tire, you can now access the tube, which is the part that contains the air. Depending on what type of flat you have, there are two things you can do at this point. The first is to patch the tube. To do this, pump the tube full of air so that you'll be able to tell where the hole is. There will probably be a hissing sound, and you can feel the air escaping. You may need to fill a sink or bucket with water and submerge the tube so you can see the bubbles where the leak is. Once you've isolated the hole, you can apply a patch and put your wheel back together.

If the hole is too big, you may need to replace your tube.

EXERCISE 10.5 Redesign a document.

Copy and paste the passage for this exercise from the *Universal Keys* Web site. Imagine the text as part of a proposal for a new marketing strategy, to be read by your boss and workplace colleagues. Redesign the document to improve its clarity and attractiveness. Compare your finished document to your classmates' versions.

International Marketing Systems
To: Board of Directors
From: Ed Visor, Assistant Marketing Manager
Re: New Strategies
As we enter the new fiscal year, it is imperative that our company adapt to changes in the marketplace, in order to remain on equal or better footing with our competition. The problem we face is twofold: First, we must adjust our current strategies regarding the younger demographic. We have, in the past, ignored the presence of a younger marketplace, yet statistics show that more and more people are entering the economy at an early age. Rather than ignore this trend, we should capitalize on it by directing more of our merchandising and advertising budgets toward the teen age group.

Second, and perhaps more importantly, we must diversify and expand our product line. While our competition has widely increased the variety of products they offer over the last year, our own line has remained completely unchanged. With the marketplace showing the growth that it has over the last six months, we simply cannot afford to allow our product line to stagnate. We must explore the options available to us in reshaping our product, not only to catch up to our competitors, but also to cover the areas that they have ignored, and thereby attract new business.

10d Typefaces, color, headings, lists, and columns

Typefaces (fonts)   Select your fonts (typefaces) with care. Do not overdo the varieties. Best are

- Times Roman, 12-point size, for the body of the text. This is a *serif* font, with little strokes—serifs—at the top and bottom of individual characters: Times Roman.

- **Arial** or some other *sans serif* font for captions and headings. The word *sans* is French for "without"; a sans serif font does not have the little strokes at the top and bottom of the characters.

Courier is an alternative if you want a typewriter look, with all characters the same width. Avoid using ornamental fonts such as *Caflish Script* and 𝕺𝖑𝖉𝖊 𝕰𝖓𝖌𝖑𝖎𝖘𝖍 𝕿𝖊𝖝𝖙.

Note that if you are designing a Web page or an online communication, readers' settings of their browser configurations determine which fonts can be displayed. Netscape, for instance, lets users choose whether to use the fonts specified in the original document or to override the specified fonts for a selected default font. The simpler the font you choose, the more likely readers are to see the font of your choice.

For the body of your text in a college essay or business communication, stick to 10- to 12-point type. Use larger type only for headings and subheadings in business, technical, or Web documents. Never increase font size to achieve a required page length. You will convey desperation, and you certainly will not fool your instructor.

Note: MLA and APA guidelines do not recommend typeface changes or bold type for titles and headings. See the sample papers in **52f** and **53f**.

Color Color printers and online publication have made the production of documents a much more jazzy enterprise than was possible until just recently. You can include graphs and illustrations in color, and you can highlight headings or parts of your text by using a different color typeface. However, simplicity and readability should prevail. Use color only when its use will enhance your message. Certainly, in the design of business reports, newsletters, brochures, and Web pages, color can play an important and eye-catching role (see **10e, 10f, 13,** and **15c**). But for college essays, the leading style manuals ignore the use of color.

Headings Headings divide text into helpful chunks and give readers a sense of your document's structure. Main divisions are marked by first-level headings, subdivisions by second-level and third-level headings.

In the heading structure of this section (**10d**), for example, the first-level heading is "Typefaces, color, headings, lists, and columns." Second-level subheadings are "Typefaces," "Color," "Headings," and so on.

For headings, bear in mind the following recommendations:

- If you use subheadings, you should use at least two—not just one.

- Whenever possible, use the Style feature from the Format menu (or use the Style text box on the Formatting toolbar) to determine the level of heading you need: Heading 1, 2, 3, and so on.

- Style manuals, such as the one for APA style, recommend specific formats for headings. Follow these recommended formats. See **53f** for an APA paper with headings.

- If necessary, adjust the format of each level of heading: centered, flush left (aligned at the left with the margin edge of your text), or indented five spaces.

- Decide on typeface features for each level of heading: bold, capital, underlined, italic, different size, or different font color. If you adjust one heading, you can apply the changes to all headings of the same level.

- Keep headings clear, brief, and parallel in grammatical form (for instance, all commands: "Set Up Sales Strategies"; all beginning with *-ing* words: "Setting Up Sales Strategies"; or all noun-plus-modifier phrases: "Sales Strategies"). See **5e** and **19j** for more on parallelism.

Lists   Lists are particularly useful in business reports, proposals, and memos. They direct readers' attention to the outlined points or steps. Decide whether to use numbers, dashes, or bullets to set off the items in a list (see **10c**, p. 217). Introduce the list with a sentence ending in a colon; for an example, see the sentence introducing the bulleted list in the previous section on "Headings." Items in the list should be parallel in grammatical form (all commands, all *-ing* phrases, all noun phrases, for example) and should not end with a period unless the listed items are complete sentences. See **5e** and **19j**.

Columns   Columns are useful for preparing newsletters and brochures. In Word, go to Format/Columns to choose the number of columns and the width. Your text will be automatically formatted. See **10f** for an example of a brochure using columns.

10e Visuals

The technology of scanners, photocopiers, digital cameras, and downloaded Web images provides the means to make documents more functional and more attractive by allowing the inclusion of visual material. Frequently, when you are dealing with complicated data, the best way to get information across to readers is to display it visually.

All up-to-date word processing programs make it easy for you to download a Web graphic into your own document (in Word, right-click on the image and click on Save Image As). However, be aware of copyright restrictions on your using a downloaded graphic in any public communication. (See *Finding Images on the Web* at <http://www.bu.edu/library/training/webimages.htm> for instructions on downloading and inserting images and interpretations of copyright law.) Resizing an image may lead to a loss of quality, but you can easily crop the image to fit your needs if you download a Web image into Netscape Composer or into Microsoft Photo Editor. Remember, though, that you must cite the source of any material that you download and include in your own work, listing the URL and the date of access. See **52–56** for various systems of documenting online sources.

In a college essay read only by your classmates and instructor, it is enough to cite the source of any borrowed visuals you include. If you intend to publish your work in print or online in any forum, however, you must also get written permission from the originator of the visual material before you use it and cite it.

You can also easily create your own tables and graphs to accompany your written text by using the capabilities offered by computer software and word processing programs.

KEY POINTS
Using Visuals

1. Decide which type of visual presentation best fits your data and where you should place your visuals—within your text or in an appendix. See "Types of Visuals," which follows.

2. When you choose to include a visual from the Web in your own Web document, make sure it is not so large and complex that it will take a long time for readers to download.

3. Whenever you place a visual in your text, introduce it and discuss it fully before readers come across it. Do not just make a perfunctory comment like "The results are significant, as seen in Table 2." In your discussion, indicate where the visual appears ("In the graph below" or "In the pie chart on page 8"), and carefully interpret or analyze the visual for readers, using it as an aid that supports your points, not as something that can stand alone.

4. Give each visual a title, number each visual if you use more than one of the same type, and credit the source.

5. Do not include visuals simply to fill space or make your document look colorful. Every visual addition should enhance your content and provide an interesting and relevant illustration.

Types of visuals Here is a table summarizing which types of data lend themselves to specific types of visualization. More information about and examples of each type of visual material follow.

Type of information	Example	Type of visualization
Statistical or descriptive data	Total population for each of the 50 U.S. states	Table
Numerical values over time for one characteristic (variable)	Annual number of BA degrees in mathematics	Line graph or bar chart

Type of information	Example	Type of visualization
Numerical values over time for several characteristics	Annual number of BA degrees for several disciplines	Multiple-line graph
Breakdown of one characteristic (variable)	Ethnicity: non-Hispanic white, non-Hispanic African American, Hispanic, Asian, other	Pie chart or bar chart
Breakdown of one characteristic for different subgroups (correlation)	Ethnicity (as above) but separate for men and women	Parallel pie charts or stacked/clustered bar charts
Individual numerical values for each case	Total population for the 50 U.S. states	Bar chart

Tables Tables are useful for presenting descriptive data (as in Table 1 below) or for showing a large amount of numerical information in columns and rows. They can be created easily with word processing programs (see **10c,** p. 219). Use the same number of decimals for data in tables, and align the decimal points.

TABLE 1   Percent of U.S. Households with Internet Access by Education of Householder, 1998 and 2000*

	December 1998	August 2000	Point Change	Expansion Rate
Less than high school	5.0	11.7	6.7	**134.0**
High school graduate	16.3	29.9	13.6	**83.4**
Some college	30.2	49.0	**18.8**	62.3
College graduate	46.8	64.0	**17.2**	36.8
Postgraduate	53.0	69.9	**16.9**	31.9

*Note: **Bold** indicates above the average 15.3-point change and 58.4 percent expansion rate. Data from U.S. Department of Commerce, using U.S. Bureau of the Census Current Population Survey supplements.

Source: *Falling through the Net: Toward Digital Inclusion, A Report on Americans' Access to Technology Tools,* Oct. 2000, National Telecommunications and Information Administration, Table 1–2 <http://www.ntia.doc.gov/ntiahome/fttn00/ Falling.htm#t31> (22 July 2002).

Graphs and charts Graphs and charts come in many forms and are useful for presenting data and comparisons of data. Many software products allow you to produce graphs and charts easily, and even standard word processing software gives you several ways to present your numbers in visual form. In Word 2000, for example, go to Insert/Picture/Chart and in the Chart screen go to Chart/Chart Type. You will be able to select a type of chart and enter your own details, such as title, labels for axes, numbers, and data labels.

Simple line graph Use a line graph to show changes over time. Figure 1 has a clear caption, states the source of the data, and clearly makes the point that "the political engagement of entering college students reached an all-time low" in the election year of 2000.

FIGURE 1 Freshman Interest in Politics, 1966–2000*

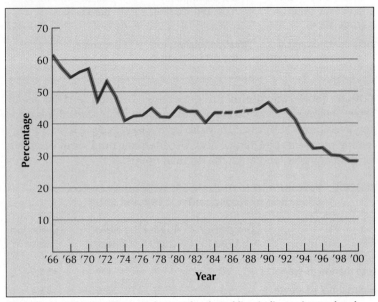

*Data from 269,413 college students. (The dotted line indicates interpolated and estimated statistics.)

Source: L. J. Sax et al., *An Overview of the 2000 Freshman Norms,* Los Angeles, Higher Education Research Institute, UCLA, January 2001 <http://www.gseis.ucla.edu/heri/heri.html> (22 July 2002).

KEY POINTS

Using Graphs and Charts

1. Use a graph or chart only to help make a point.
2. Set up a graph or chart so that it is self-contained and self-explanatory.
3. Make sure that the items on the axis of a graph are proportionately spaced.
4. Always provide a clear caption.

5. Use precise wording and place labels directly on a graph.

6. Provide necessary details about any sample population studied or time frames used. You may need to give this information in a footnote below the graph or chart.

7. Always give details about the source of the information if the data are not your own.

Multiple-line graph Line graphs such as Figure 2 are especially useful for showing comparisons of sets of data over time.

FIGURE 2   Declining Interest in Medical and Health Careers: 1971–2000, Men and Women*

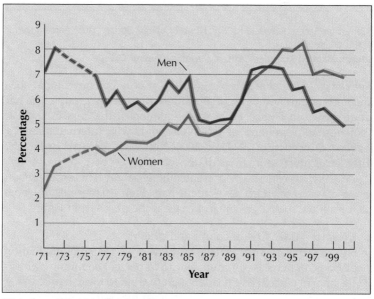

*Data from 269,413 college students.

Source: L. J. Sax et al., *An Overview of the 2000 Freshman Norms,* Los Angeles, Higher Education Research Institute, UCLA, January 2001 <http://www.gseis.ucla.edu/heri/00_exec_summary.htm> (22 July 2002).

Pie chart Use a pie chart (or pie graph) to show how fractions and percentages relate to one another and make up a whole. The pie chart shown in Figure 3 displays the results of a survey in a sociology course in Spring 2001. The pie chart was produced with Word 2000 (Insert/Picture/Chart). Note that it is important to provide information about the number of respondents (N =), especially with a small local survey, so that percentage figures can be put into perspective.

FIGURE 3 Internet/Web Experience*

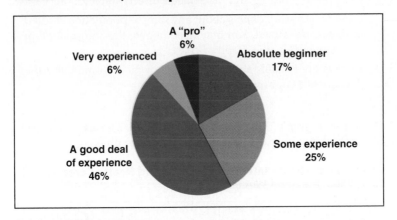

*Computer Access Survey, Soc. 241, Hunter College, Spring 2001 (Percentages based on N=48)

Source: Manfred Kuechler, Dept. of Sociology, Hunter College.

Bar chart A bar chart (or bar graph) is useful to show comparisons and correlations and to highlight differences among groups. The bar chart shown in Figure 4 is a representation of the data in Table 1, showing the percentage of U.S. households with Internet access by levels of education in 1998 and 2000. Note how the chart makes the differences much more immediately obvious.

A bar chart can also be presented horizontally. This arrangement makes it easier to attach labels to the bars. Figure 5 presents the same data from the sociology course survey as the pie chart in Figure 3.

> **EXERCISE 10.6** Create charts and graphs.
> Suppose that at your college 43 percent of the students live on campus, 29 percent commute by car, 18 percent commute by bicycle, and 10 percent live near enough to walk to the campus. Using your word processing program, create a pie chart to display these data. Then create a bar graph.

Illustrations, clip art, and Web graphics Your computer software provides many standard images (clip art) and photographs that you can use freely in your documents, without any copyright or cost concerns. In Word, for instance, find the clip art at Insert/Picture. Some Web sites offer free images to download: try <http://www .clipart.com> for free graphics and links to other clip art sites. Other useful sites are as follows:

<http://www.screamdesign.com>

<http://www.angelfire.com/wv/hmfic/free.html>

FIGURE 4   Percent of U.S. Households with Internet Access by Education of Householder, 1998 and 2000

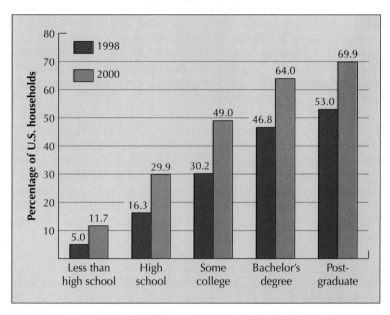

Source: *Falling through the Net: Toward Digital Inclusion, A Report on Americans' Access to Technology Tools,* Oct. 2000, National Telecommunications and Information Administration, Figure 1–8 <http://www.ntia.doc.gov/ntiahome/fttn00/Falling.htm#f11> (22 July 2002).

FIGURE 5   Internet/Web Experience*

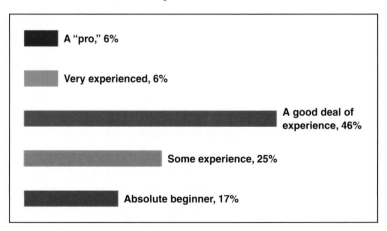

*Computer Access Survey, Soc. 241, Hunter College, Spring 2001 (Percentages based on N=48)

Source: Manfred Kuechler, Dept. of Sociology, Hunter College.

<http://dir.yahoo.com/computers_and_internet/graphics>

<http://www.barrysclipart.com>

Google at <http://images.google.com> and AltaVista at <http://www.altavista.com/cgi-bin/query?pg=q&stype=simage> also let you search for specific images. Clip art images are often simplistic and clichéd—crudely drawn balloons, a pen, or a wine glass, for example—so before downloading an image, always ask what it adds to the ideas you want to convey.

Sophisticated and original graphics are usually copyrighted, so if you intend to use an image in a document that you post on the Web or make available in print, you need not only to download the image and cite the source, but also to get permission from the creator to use and disseminate it. For a college paper, you may want to include an illustration you find on the Web, such as a map, a photograph of an author, a work of art, or an illustration from an online encyclopedia. You can do so without getting permission, but you must cite the source.

Exercise the same caution with photographs and other graphics as you do with clip art. Do not include illustrations just because you find them and like them. An illustration should add to and supplement your text, not merely provide a decorative touch. If your document is to be posted on the Web, readers who have slow Internet connections or videocards may find it time-consuming or even impossible to download elaborate images, so keep images small and simple.

EXERCISE 10.7 Use clip art.
Your word processing program probably has many clip art files. Browse through the categories (Insert/Picture/Clip Art) and practice inserting them into a word document. How effective are the pictures? Are there some you would or would not use in your papers for other classes? Give reasons.

10f Design principles: brochures, newsletters, and flyers

When you are producing material that will be printed or photocopied and then distributed to many people, you will want to take extra care to create a document that is attractive and effective. Attention to design increases the chance that your brochure, newsletter, or flyer will be read and have the effect that you intend. While there is never a single "right" way to arrange information and images on a page, some basic principles can help you design a successful print communication.

1. *Plan.* Consider the audience and the purpose of your document: Who will read the document? How and when will people see the document? What is the most important message you are communicating? Does the document need to relate to any other documents in a series from your school or organization?

2. *Experiment.* Leave time to try out variations in the document format: to experiment with type sizes and fonts, to add more or less white space at different places, to test various colors or arrangements—in short, to play with the design and get feedback from sample audience members. This way you can see what surprises and delights people and what puzzles or bores them.

3. *Value readability and clarity.* Consider the proportion of one element to another within your piece, so that important information is highlighted or given priority and nothing appears overly crowded or illegibly small.

4. *Keep consistency and coherence* from page to page in matters of margins, typefaces, headings, captions, borders, column widths, and so forth. While you do not want the document to be dull, you also do not want it to be a distracting, shifting jumble of formats and type styles. *Note:* If you are using a desktop publishing program, set up a grid or template to block out the consistent placement of headings, columns, margins, and boxed features for each document you are designing. The lines of a grid appear on your computer but will not appear when the document is printed; they become like an empty vessel into which you "pour" your content.

5. *Give careful consideration to the following design variables:*

   • *Type size and font*   For the main text of your document, choose a readable type size, not one that is uncomfortably small or that has letters that are hard to decipher. Serif fonts (the ones with little protruding edges on all the letters) are more readable and thus the best choice for the main body of a print document. For headlines and headings, use a limited number of other larger type sizes. Headings should help to organize material for the reader and establish a hierarchy of importance among different sections of the document.

   • *Use of white space*   Cut and condense your text as necessary to allow for a generous amount of white space in your margins and borders and above and below headings.

- *Leading (the amount of space between lines of type)*   When lines of type are set too close together, one on top of the other, they are hard to read, so adequate line spacing is important. Extra line spacing can also be used to indicate paragraph breaks.

- *End-of-line alignment*   Lines of type can be justified—spaced out uniformly to be all the same length—or set with a "ragged right" margin. Justified lines appear more formal, have a greater type density, and can create a lot of hyphenated words; lines that are ragged right create a less formal and more open look.

- *Column width and line length*   In general, the wider the column or line of type, the easier it is for a reader to lose his or her place. Shorter columns and shorter lines of type are easier to read.

- *Rules (printed lines)*   Horizontal and vertical rules of various thicknesses can be effective in setting off columns, headings, pull-out quotations, photos, and captions.

- *Boxes and sidebars*   These elements separate smaller segments of material from the larger flow of text. Boxing a part of your document can give it extra emphasis or attention.

- *Reversed type*   With this technique, type appears white against a black or other colored background. *Note:* Reversed type becomes hard to read when the type is very small.

- *Screened backgrounds or images*   If your document is to be printed with black ink and you want a certain section of your document to have a gray background, printers can create that effect by "screening" the section at a certain percentage, which you specify. They apply the print at a graded density, from 100% (solid color) to 10% (very light gray). Ink of any color can be screened. Red ink will become pink if screened, blue ink will become light blue if screened, and so on.

- *Bleed images or bleed type*   This effect makes an image or word appear as if it is running off the side of the page. It can be used to create drama, excitement, and a sense of an expanded design space.

In college and community life, much information is shared through brochures, newsletters, and flyers. The following sample documents demonstrate some principles of effective design.

MODEL DOCUMENT 1   Community Brochure Offering Services (Front)

Photo of prop with background cut away creates illusion of depth.

What is MassHealth?

Use of two colors creates fields within whole and highlights main heading.

MassHealth is a state program that pays for health care for qualified people living in Massachusetts with low and medium incomes.

Even some people who have private health insurance can get MassHealth. If you qualify, MassHealth can give you health-care benefits directly or by paying part or all of your health-insurance premiums.

Blank space left throughout so information is not crowded.

What does MassHealth offer?

MassHealth offers a broad range of health-care services by paying for part or all of a MassHealth member's health insurance, or paying medical providers for services given to MassHealth members. MassHealth covers doctor visits, prescription drugs, hospital stays, and many other important services.

Who can get MassHealth?

MassHealth offers benefits to a wide range of people who meet eligibility rules. We look at your family size and income to decide if you or your family can get MassHealth. If you are aged 65 or older, we also count some of your assets. Income levels are shown on the back page. All uninsured children who cannot get MassHealth are eligible for preventive health-care coverage from another state program called the Children's Medical Security Plan (CMSP).

See the next page for the reverse side of this brochure.

MODEL DOCUMENT 2 Community Brochure Offering Services (Back)

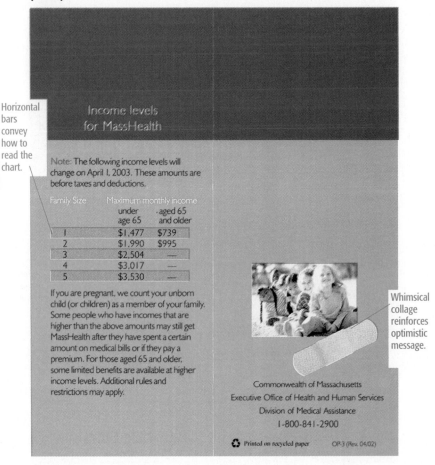

Horizontal bars convey how to read the chart.

Income levels for MassHealth

Note: The following income levels will change on April 1, 2003. These amounts are before taxes and deductions.

Family Size	Maximum monthly income under age 65	aged 65 and older
1	$1,477	$739
2	$1,990	$995
3	$2,504	—
4	$3,017	—
5	$3,530	—

If you are pregnant, we count your unborn child (or children) as a member of your family. Some people who have incomes that are higher than the above amounts may still get MassHealth after they have spent a certain amount on medical bills or if they pay a premium. For those aged 65 and older, some limited benefits are available at higher income levels. Additional rules and restrictions may apply.

Whimsical collage reinforces optimistic message.

Commonwealth of Massachusetts
Executive Office of Health and Human Services
Division of Medical Assistance
1-800-841-2900

♻ Printed on recycled paper   OP-3 (Rev. 04/02)

Illustration reproduced courtesy of the Massachusetts Division of Medical Assistance.

Overall, this brochure creates a friendly, welcoming, problem-solving mood. It sends its reassuring message visually as well as through its words and numbers.

MODEL DOCUMENT 3   Community Brochure Offering Volunteer Opportunities (Front)

See the next page for the reverse side of this brochure.

MODEL DOCUMENT 4 **Community Brochure Offering Volunteer Opportunities (Back)**

Tan background sets off introduction.

EVERY CHILD DESERVES A CHILDHOOD.

Research shows that the first years in a child's life are critical for health, self-esteem and intellectual development. For homeless children, those needs are often overlooked.

There are more than 1.5 million homeless children in the U.S. In Boston, there are 500 homeless families and 1,500 homeless children each year. Over half of the homeless children in Massachusetts are under 5 years old.

WHAT IS OUR MISSION?

The Horizons Initiative is a non-profit organization in Boston that is exclusively dedicated to serving homeless children and their families.

Extra space between lines enhances readability of message.

Our mission is to provide homeless children in our community with the nurturing, stimulation and opportunities for educational play that all children need to learn and grow in healthy ways; and to improve these children's lives over the long-term by providing their parents with the tools they need to achieve social and economic self-sufficiency.

HOW YOU CAN HELP AS A VOLUNTEER.

We are in need of patient, dependable individuals to volunteer as Playspace Activity Leaders with children living in area homeless shelters.

Specifically, you would be responsible for preparing and leading activities, games and projects with a group of 1-5 children.

A commitment of 2 hours per week, for a minimum of 6 months, and attendance at our 6-hour training session is required. Shelters are located in more than 16 communities in the Greater Boston area. Day and evening times are available.

TAKE THE FIRST STEP.

For more information on volunteering, or for a Playspace Activity Leader application, please call 1.800.560.7702 or visit The Horizons Initiative website at www.horizonsinitiative.org today.

The second color, dark green, highlights important information, making it stand out from the rest of the text.

Logo repeated for coherence.

VOLUNTEER FOR

The Horizons Initiative
Helping Hands For Homeless Children
Call 1.800.560.7702 to volunteer

Courtesy of The Horizons Initiative, Dorchester, Massachusetts.

Overall, this brochure makes a clear, direct appeal, with no excess clutter.

MODEL DOCUMENT 5 Literary Newsletter (Front)

CYNTHIA CROSSEN'S

BOOKED

JULY 2002

VOLUME I / NUMBER 2

Bold use of type catches the eye, with the white letters reversed out of the background gray.

DEAR READER,

If you've ever been to a car or boat show, as I have (with pleasure!), you can picture Book Expo, the publishing trade's annual convention, which was held at the Jacob Javits convention center in New York this year. As usual, the place was packed, and some intersections—where Random House met Simon & Schuster, for example—turned into the literary equivalent of Times Square. Book Expo is ostensibly for the trade, and some buyers and sellers do business, but for the most part it's more circus than trade convention, with hundreds of eager authors trying to make eye contact with the people strolling by.

You couldn't look at Book Expo and think, "The publishing business is in trouble."In 2001, an estimated 114,000 new book titles were published in the U.S., more than 15,000 of those adult fiction. And despite the oft-heard lamentation about big publishers eating up little publishers, there were hundreds of independent presses represented. Reading capsule descriptions of upcoming books, it seemed miraculous to me that people could still come up with original ideas—"a social history of the tea room craze"; "Zen baby pairs age-old wisdom with bright-eyed babies"; "Gaydar—the ultimate insider guide to the gay sixth sense"; and "race, sex and the 1898 Wilmington massacre."

By publishing so many titles, the publishing industry tacitly ackn...

It's ironic that Charles Dickens's nickname was

"The Inimitable," considering how many books have been described by critics or publishers as "Dickensian." The label is supposed to be complimentary, despite Anthony Trollope's assessment of Dickens's style: "Jerky, ungrammatical and created by himself in defiance of the rules...No young novelist should ever dare to imitate the style of Dickens." Nevertheless, these have been accused of trying:

FINGERSMITH by Sarah Waters
JACK MAGGS by Peter Carey
MR. IVES' CHRISTMAS by Oscar Hijuelos
A SON OF THE CIRCUS by John Irving
THE CIDER HOUSE RULES by John Irving
THE HOUSE OF SLEEP by Jonathan Coe
WICKED by Gregory Maguire
UNDERWORLD by Don DeLillo
A MAN IN FULL by Tom Wolfe
LONDON FIELDS by Martin Amis
THE TIN DRUM by Gunther Grass
ANGELA'S ASHES by Frank McCourt
A TREE GROWS IN BROOKLYN by Betty Smith
A SUITABLE BOY by Vikram Seth
FELICIA'S JOURNEY by William Trevor

I have read nine of these books, a few in my youth, and the common denominators seem to be length and depiction of poverty. Of course, Jack Maggs is literally Dickensian—the author, Peter Carey, borrows a character from Great Expectations and spins out the rest of his life. Fingersmith is also Dickensian in time, place and mood. But many others take place in contemporary America, and then there's Das Kapital—1,000 pages of stubbornly difficult prose.

I doubt Dickens would take exception to most of these comparisons, but I would understand if he objected to the following snippet from the Texas Business Weekly.

"It was the best of times; it was the worst of times."
Charles Dickens, A Tale of Two Cities
"This quote may be overused, a little 'played' even for my taste, but it definitely captures the spirit and realities that face the Class of 2002. Some may even feel that our MBA careers are ending with the same flare as this depressing, overwrites Dickensian novel as the Class of 2002 moseys back through the guillotine that is the 'real world.'"

I bought "Breaking Clean," Judy Blunt's memoir of her girlhood and marriage on Montana ranches, because a friend had read a review and thought it sounded like an interesting, and bracing, antidote to self-pity. We think we have it bad? What if we had to go eye to eye with the elements—grassfires, blizzards, drought, ornery animals? Few

Americans struggle this way anymore, natural forces so casually and regularly obliterating their backbreaking work.

I generally liked Breaking Clean, so I couldn't have been more appalled to read, in the New York Times, that an incident Blunt described in the first chapter didn't happen. The anecdote concerned her former father-in-law, whom Blunt portrayed as a brutish pig. Blunt recalled a day when lunch for the hay crew was late because she was writing, and "Frank" was so angry he took her typewriter to the shop and crushed it with a sledgehammer.

The pseudonymous Frank is a real living person (named John), who responded to the story by writing a letter to his local newspaper, the Phillips County [Montana] News, such an event had not happened. Blunt, to her credit, conceded that Frank didn't use a sledgehammer or even a typewriter. "There is truth in every scene [in the first pages of the book]," Blunt explained to the New York reporter, "but the facts are less reliable."

Suddenly I liked the book a lot less.

Maybe Blunt was naïve, led astray by an editor. At the Street Journal, we called great anecdotes we had to leave out because of dubious veracity, "too good to check." But could even the graduate of a one-room schoolhouse see the difference between fact and fiction? Did Blunt lie in memoirs, the author is allowed to make things up.

Probably, and where's the evidence to the contrary? Today, memoirs are sold with a wink, if events didn't unfold exactly this way, they could have. Close enough. Who's hurt by a little embellishment here and there? Of course, as Blunt learned, people can be hurt. But I think there's more at stake than individual's feelings, especially since so many of the people depicted in memoirs are conveniently dead. The coulda-been memoir is a redefinition of the genre to the literary equivalent of a docudrama.

For those authors who must hew to the facts—biographers, for example—it's surely galling to see how flagrant memoirists ignore the distinctions between "there's probably a scene where this happened" and "I bet this is what happened." I remember what I felt at the time: I recall being uneasy reading Mary Carr's chilling memoir. The knowing that while she may have captured the essence of her early years, she just certainly invented details to establish a dialogue with which to ornament the actual facts.

Why, if they're inventing things, don't they just call Breaking Clean a novel? Because even as this cynical fact is still more powerful than fiction.

I hope this is the second issue of Booked you're reading. If you did not receive the first issue and would like to, please e-mail me at booked@cynthiacrossen.com or write to me at Long and Winding Rd., Garrison, NY 10524. Also, I welcome names and addresses of other readers who might enjoy Booked.

Three-column format limits the length of each line, making the type easier to read.

Central box calls out one topic being discussed—the number of books described these days as "Dickensian."

Distinct areas of the newsletter are created by the use of different screened backgrounds.

INSIDE

Readers Question
My Judgment

Hangovers in
Fiction and Fact

Plus: Recommendations
And a Few Paragraphs About Dogs

See the next page for the final panel of this newsletter.

MODEL DOCUMENT 6 Literary Newsletter (Back)

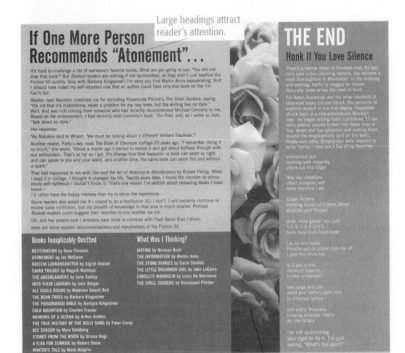

Design by Laura Tolkow, text by Cynthia Crossen. Reproduced with permission.

Overall, this newsletter's design is contemporary and open, establishing a pleasing forum for the exchange of ideas and opinions.

MODEL DOCUMENT 7   Nonprofit Organization's Newsletter

Top banner uses summery colors and a seasonal graphic image.

The white letters of the newsletter's title stand out well. They are "dropped out" or "reversed out" of the background color.

The photos bring to life this article on summer interns.

Stylish, compact logo conveys the group's identity in a memorable way.

Large initial capital letters emphasize or announce the beginning of each article.

A three-column arrangement organizes material well.

Courtesy Bookbuilders of Boston.

This newsletter's function is to link members of an organization. Its design effectively accommodates the needs for photos, a preview panel, a masthead, and news articles.

MODEL DOCUMENT 8 Flyer Announcing Classes

Black bars anchor the design, framing the images and message.

The photo images are placed off-center, creating a dynamic and interesting effect.

The pale ("screened back") type adds depth and interest to the page without cluttering it.

Creative placing of the captions here makes the information clear, but not in the way.

Design by Marlies Gielissen. Courtesy Impulse Dance, Boston, Massachusetts.

This poster's design captures the vibrant and energetic spirit of the place being presented.

MODEL DOCUMENT 9   Flyer Announcing a Production

Title is large and visible, set
against an appropriate
graphic pattern of snow.

Same distinctive
font is used for
both title and
playwright's
name.

Use of the blue
color scheme
continues the idea
of cool, frosty
weather.

Information about the play
is large and readable.

Poster designed by Anna C. McDonald. Courtesy Harvard University.

Everything about the poster is clear, concise, simple, and easy
to read.

10g Formats for college papers (hard copy)

Perhaps you are wondering why this section refers to *formats* and not just to *a format* for college essays. The plural is necessary because the various organizations that offer guidelines for manuscript preparation (as found in the MLA, APA, and CBE/CSE manuals, and the *Chicago Manual of Style*) provide different sets of recommendations and because various disciplines and individual instructors have their own preferences. Whichever format you choose, use your word processor's functions to help with your design.

A major format consideration is the destination of your document. Will you be presenting your essay on paper (hard copy), e-mailing it (to your instructor, your classmates, or both), or posting it on the Web? You will need to think of a hard-copy document in a linear way because readers will progress methodically from beginning to end and information must fit logically within the whole. For a Web posting, in contrast, hotlinks (electronic links to other Web sites or other sections of your essay) in your essay can do the work of descriptive and substantive footnotes, references to sources, and examples of external evidence. An essay prepared for Web posting also needs internal divisions, each with an internal link so readers can go directly to a specific section. For details on posting a college essay online, see **12c**.

Formatting guidelines Here are basic guidelines for preparing your essay on paper, whichever style guide you follow. See **10a** and **10c** for more on the formatting tools on your word processor.

KEY POINTS

Guidelines for College Essay Format

1. *Paper* White bond, unlined, $8\frac{1}{2}$" × 11"; not erasable or onionskin paper. Clip or staple the pages.

2. *Print* Always use dark black printing ink.

3. *Margins* 1" all around for MLA style. For other styles, $1\frac{1}{2}$" may be acceptable. Lines should not be justified (should not align on right).

4. *Space between lines* Uniformly double-spaced.

5. *Spaces after a period, question mark, or exclamation point* Most style manuals suggest one space. Your instructor may prefer two in the text of your essay.

6. *Type font and size* Use a standard type font (such as Times New Roman or Courier), not a font that looks like handwriting. Select a regular size of 10 to 12 points.

7. *Page numbers* Put in the top right margin (in MLA style, put your last name before the page number). Use arabic numerals with no period (see below).

8. *Paragraphing* Indent ½" (5 spaces) from the left.

9. *Title and identification* On the first page or on a separate title page. See the examples that follow.

10. *Parentheses for sources cited* In MLA and APA styles, for any written source you refer to or quote, including the textbook for your course (for an electronic source, give author only); then add at the end a list of works cited (see **52** and **53**).

Title and identification of essay Your instructor may prefer a separate title page or ask you to include the identification material on the first page of the essay.

Title and identification on the first page The following sample shows one format for identifying a paper and giving its title. The MLA recommends this format for papers in the humanities.

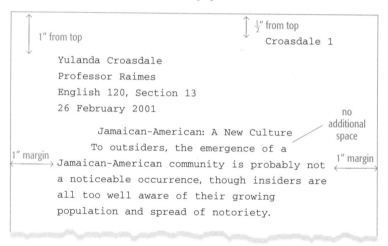

At the top of subsequent pages, write the page number in the upper right corner, preceded by your last name. No period or parentheses accompany the page number. See **10c,** page 216, on creating the page header with word processing program commands.

Title and identification on a separate title page In the humanities, include a title page only if your instructor requires one or if you include an outline. On the title page include the following, all double-spaced:

- *Title:* Centered, about one-third of the way down the page. Do not enclose the title in quotation marks, do not underline it, and do not put a period at the end.

- *Name:* Centered, after the word *by,* centered on a separate line.

- *Course information:* Course and section, instructor, and date, each centered on a new line, either directly below your name or at the bottom of the title page.

If you include a title page, you do not need to also include the title and identification on your first page.

Title centered, about 1/3 of way down page
No quotation marks, no underlining, no period

          Jamaican-American: A New Culture

Name, centered   By Yulanda Croasdale

Course information, centered

          English 120, Section 13
          Professor Ann Raimes

Date, centered   26 February 2001

11 Communicating Online

The arrival of the printing press in the tenth and eleventh centuries in China and Korea and then at the beginning of the fifteenth century in Europe dramatically changed the culture of the written word and in Europe heralded a cultural era known as the Renaissance ("rebirth"). A manuscript was no longer one document written by hand (from the Latin *scriptus:* written; *manu:* by hand), but something reproducible for distribution to many readers. Equally revolutionary has been the arrival of Internet access and online communications. We can send e-mail messages around the world in an instant, to be read by people we do not know and have never met and probably will never meet. We can read their documents immediately without having to search for them in a library or bookstore.

WORLDS OF WRITING
Going Online: A Revolution in Reading and Writing

- By the end of 2002, estimates are for 135 million e-mail users in the United States—59 percent of the U.S. population of adults and teens (source: *Emarketer* at <http://www.emarketer.com>, from <http://www.sims.berkeley.edu/how-much-info>).

- Around 36.5 billion messages are sent in a year in discussion mailing lists.

- Online texts generally feature documents divided into sections and subsections, headings, short paragraphs, and easily accessible information. Readers do not like to keep scrolling through a long document. They want pointers to what the document contains (a table of contents and hyperlinks to major points and keywords), and they expect to be able to navigate their way with ease into, through, out of, and back again into a document.

- Online readers do not read a document as they would read a printed page. Online reading presents distractions in the form of hyperlinks to other parts of the text or to totally different sites on the Web. Readers will jump in and out of a document you post—and you have to be prepared for the fact that when they jump out, you need to provide them with a motive and clear directions as to how to get back in again.

- Online readers tend to be purposeful, not leisurely. They want a quick answer to a question, or they want to find information about one subject of interest. This is not like curling up in an armchair with a good novel.

11a Writing for online readers

Writing for a computer screen differs from writing for the printed page. Particularly when you post messages on e-mail discussion lists and bulletin boards, pay careful attention to the following.

Length Be brief. State your main points clearly at the start. One screen holds about 250 words, and online readers do not want to scroll repeatedly to find out what you are saying.

Links Insert links to other documents to provide information about and support for points that you make. Every link should serve a purpose within your document. Make it clear where links go and what readers are likely to find if they click on the link.

Attachments and graphics Writing online entails not just a linear progression of text but attachments to e-mail in the form of text or audio files, Web pages, graphics, even greeting cards. On the Web we are constantly exposed to color, flashing and moving images, and many elements that may appear distracting. Always consider how attachments and graphics will add to your message and help you make a point (see **10e**). Consider your audience, too. An academic audience may not expect or welcome flashing and moving images, while other audiences welcome them and may even discount a site that does not use them.

11b E-mail netiquette and style

Communicating online is so different from reading and writing via print that conventions and accepted ways of operating (net etiquette, known as "netiquette") have developed. Familiarize yourself with the conventions of the accepted use policy set up by your Internet service provider (ISP) or your college. Then follow accepted norms.

E-mail conventions For a Web page of links to useful sites on netiquette, go to <http://www.pbs.org/uti/guide/netiquette.html>.

Subject heading Help your e-mail readers know at a glance what your message is about. Always include a subject heading and make it clear and concise.

Name Always include your full real name. Do not expect your message recipients to recognize you from your e-mail identity, especially if it is something like *greatguy@aol.com*. It is a good idea to construct a "signature file" that will appear automatically at the end of every message you send. To do this, go to the Help menu of your e-mail program.

Lines, paragraphs, and length   Keep posts short (one screen) and paragraphs brief so readers can take in the information at a glance. Use numbered or bulleted lists to present a sequence of points as brief items that are readily seen and absorbed.

Format   Most e-mail programs can handle all kinds of formatting, giving you choices of fonts, colors, columns, and graphics. Some readers may deliberately restrict the capabilities of their e-mail program as a protection against viruses, so use only basic automatic HTML (hypertext markup language) formatting features, such as bold and italic fonts. Be careful about including graphics in your message; they will not necessarily work for all readers. However, when you reply to a message, most e-mail programs will automatically determine the format used by the original sender and will adjust accordingly.

Quoting a whole message or part of a message   Do not include an entire message with your reply unless you find it necessary for clarity or if you refer to it point by point. Include only parts of a message that you respond to directly.

Forwarding messages   Never forward a message indiscriminately. Consider first whether the recipient will need or appreciate the forwarded message. In addition, make sure that forwarding does not violate rules established by your college or business organization. If necessary, ask the original sender for permission to forward the message. He or she can then veto the idea if anyone is likely to be offended or harmed.

Spelling   Many e-mail programs include a spelling checker. Use this tool, especially for postings that go out to many readers.

Capital letters   Do not write a whole message or section of a message all in capital letters. Capitals are difficult to read and for readers they represent SHOUTING.

Mechanics   E-mail programs usually support most of the text features of word processors, such as varying font and type size or boldface or italic type. However, sometimes these features may not carry over from one system to another if your recipient opts for plain text messages. Make sure that your words themselves carry the meaning you intend. See section **34** for more on punctuation to use when writing online.

Caution and tact   Be careful about what you say and how you say it. Sarcasm and attempts at humor can misfire. Criticism can hurt. A reader can easily forward your message to another person or to an entire list—even though that reader is not supposed to do so without your permission first. Remember, too, that an e-mail message cannot communicate body language. Your reader cannot see a twinkle in your eye or a warm smile. Try to make your message reader-friendly. Often, including a salutation helps: "Hi, Ann," for example.

Flames   Sometimes a writer fires off a message full of anger and name-calling. Such a message is called a *flame*. Avoid flaming. If someone flames you, do not get drawn into battle.

Citations   If you quote or use ideas or graphics from another source, give credit to the original writer and provide documentation (see **52–56**) so that your readers can track down the original. If you are writing in a public forum, ask the original writer for permission to use his or her work.

E-mail style and register   Considering your audience and your readers' expectations is as important in writing online as in writing on paper. Because of the spread of e-mail into business and other organizations, e-mail is no longer considered only an informal means of communication. It may have begun as an informal, quick means of communication, but now it is so widespread that it has as many levels of formality (known as *registers*) as printed documents do. E-mail messages can be businesslike and serious, even when writers use contracted forms (*isn't, can't*) and a conversational tone. They can be formal and academic. Or they can be unedited and speechlike, as with casual messages to friends.

Use slang, abbreviations such as *BTW* ("by the way"), *GTG* ("gotta go"), and *BCNU* ("be seeing you"), and sideways "smileys" such as :-) and :-(only when you are absolutely certain that readers expect and understand them. Also avoid using nonstandard spelling and verbal shortcuts, such as "RU going 2 the theater w/o her?"

E-mail offers a quick and efficient means of transporting a document. Edit your e-mail before sending if you are writing to people whom you do not know well and whom you want to take your ideas seriously—for example, your boss, business associates, or the anonymous subscribers to a discussion list. If you own your own computer with an e-mail program that includes a spelling checker and word processing capability, then your e-mails can always be edited. If you use an e-mail program such as Pine, or if you use a Web interface and not an e-mail client such as Eudora or Outlook Express, consider writing your e-mail document on a word processor, where you can revise and edit it for clarity. Then copy and paste it into an e-mail system to send it. Such a strategy is also useful if your college restricts the amount of time you can spend online.

KEY POINTS

A Checklist for E-Mail Style and Register

1. What will your reader expect?
   - formal language
   - standard but informal English
   - colloquialisms, slang, and abbreviations

   How does your document measure up to those expectations?

2. What is a reader likely to think or say after reading your e-mail communication?
   - This e-mail was written quickly and was not checked.
   - This makes just the right assumptions about me as a reader.
   - I hate all these abbreviations and slang words.
   - I could send this to my boss.

   Is that what you want a reader to think?

3. Have you checked your grammar and spelling? Should you do so for this reader? Will this reader judge your abilities according to what he or she reads?

4. Which of the following can you find? How appropriate are they for readers?
   - smileys
   - abbreviations, such as *LOL* ("laughing out loud") or *IMHO* ("in my humble opinion")
   - contractions
   - technical words (jargon)
   - pretentious language (trying to sound important and academic)
   - typographical, spelling, or punctuation errors
   - familiar and colloquial phrases (*OK*; *cool dude*; *yeah*; *ugh*)

ESL NOTE Being Informal in a Language Not Your Own

If you learned English in a formal classroom setting, you know that it is difficult to strike the right note with informality, colloquial expressions, slang, and humor. When the stakes are high—if you are writing to a prospective employer or to your college professor, for example—it is often better to aim for clarity and accuracy and to use everyday words and expressions rather than attempt to be trendy. ▪

Online addresses In online addresses, pay attention to accuracy of punctuation and capital letters. Both matter; one slip can invalidate an address and cause you great frustration—or send your message to a real but wrong address.

E-mail addresses An e-mail address consists of the user's name, the @ sign, then the name of the domain (the host computer). The last element of the domain name identifies the type of site or the country of origin. There are never any spaces between any of the parts. Many user names are case-sensitive, so use capital and lowercase letters accurately.

name of organization

user name Houghton Mifflin Company

▶ **Tom_Cutler@hmco.com**

type of site (commercial)

WHAT THE ENDINGS OF SOME ONLINE ADDRESSES MEAN

.edu	educational site	.org	noncommercial organization
.com	commercial site	.mil	military site
.biz	business	.info	informational site
.gov	government site	.uk	United Kingdom
.cn	China	.ca	Canada

When you include an e-mail address in your own text, italicize it or, if writing online, enclose it in angle brackets:

▶ **Please send mail to *Tom_Cutler@hmco.com* after May 1.**

▶ **Please send mail to <Tom_Cutler@hmco.com>.**

You can also include an HTML *mailto:* link in a document so that clicking on a person's name will immediately generate a new e-mail message.

Internet site addresses Each Web or other Internet address (known as a URL—uniform resource locator) begins with what is called a protocol tag (such as <http://> or <ftp://>). Web addresses frequently contain www (for World Wide Web) followed by the name of the server and type of organization, each separated by a dot (.), with no spaces anywhere in the address. The domain name ends with a suffix that indicates the type of site, such as .com, .gov, and .edu.

protocol   ┌──── domain ────┐
▶ **http://college.hmco.com**
Houghton Mifflin Company   commercial site

protocol   ┌──── domain ────┐
▶ **http://euclid.math.fsu.edu**
educational site
a Florida State University Department of Mathematics site

Often a reference to a more specific linked site is added in a directory path after a single forward slash in the address:

protocol   ┌──── domain ────┐ ┌─── path ───┐
▶ **http://college.hmco.com/products.html**

A tilde (~) in a Web address signals that the page is maintained by an individual in a larger institution, often a university. Such a page will be a personal page, not part of the official Web page of the organization.

protocol   ┌───── domain ─────┐ ┌─ path ─┐
▶ **http://www.polsci.uiowa.edu/~liu.html**

Note, also, that individuals can have their own domain names, as in <http://www.stephenking.com>.

Web addresses are often very long. Copy them exactly, or, better still, select them and use the Copy and Paste functions from the Edit menu to avoid a slip. When you include a URL in a piece of writing, italicize it or enclose it in angle brackets. In an MLA-style works-cited list, use angle brackets to enclose all electronic addresses. If you need to spread an address over two lines, break it after a slash (MLA style) or before a period. Whichever style you follow, be consistent.

▶ **Recent press releases are available at <http://www.whitehouse.gov>.** [Shows break after the protocol slashes]

▶ **The *Internet TESL Journal* provides grammar quizzes for ESL students at <http://www.aitech.ac.jp/~iteslj/quizzes/grammar.html>.** [Shows break after a slash]

▶ **The ESL Help Center is at <http://www.eslcafe.com/help/>.** [Shows break before a period]

If you want to copy, paste, and link to a URL that is split into two lines as these are, you will need to splice the URL together again into one line before you use the Copy and Paste functions. If you copy only one line or if you copy the URL with a space at the end of the first line, the link will not work.

Attachments to e-mail documents Most e-mail programs allow you to send your own text files and Web pages as attachments to your e-mail so that readers can open them, view them, and easily file them if necessary. Use the attachment option in your e-mail program and simply attach the name and location of the file you want to send. First, however, you have to ensure that your word processing program is compatible with your recipient's. If it is not, you may subject a reader to a page of incomprehensible symbols. Try saving and attaching your own document in RTF (rich text format) or in HTML to avoid issues of incompatible programs and alarming gobbledygook on the screen (though RTF files saved on a Mac may not open in Microsoft Windows).

Note: Attachments can harbor computer viruses, so always be cautious about opening any attachments to an e-mail message. Open attachments only from known senders and keep your antivirus software up-to-date.

EXERCISE 11.1 Critically assess an e-mail message.
Read the e-mail message that follows. Discuss with classmates which features you would find effective or not effective.

To: Joe-mail@company.com

From: Jane-mail@company.com

Subject: stuff we need

hey how's it going? :-) listen, I was wondering if you could help me with something regarding a few of our clients. we need to get some information about them, and i think you have the files in your office. the most important one is this guy, larry smith. you should have a sheet with his info on it, if you could fax that over, that'd be great. BTW, we need it yesterday, so please send it ASAP. oh, FYI, and this is **VERY IMPORTANT,** we need the sales figures for March by, get this, 8am Friday, so make sure you have someone fax or mail those over pronto. sorry to dump all this stuff on you :-(FWIW, I think we all need a vacation.

EXERCISE 11.2 Examine e-mail messages.
Analyze the last five e-mail messages you have received. Which one does the best job of using appropriate style, mechanics, and netiquette, and why? Suggest ways in which the others could be improved.

11c E-mail discussion lists, newsgroups, Web forums, and bulletin boards

Are you interested in Peter Gabriel, the St. Louis Cardinals, bonsai, beagle puppies, orchids, the Argentine tango, the Battle of Antietam? The Web provides thousands of forums for you to not only find information but also enter discussions with others and make your own contributions. Since many of the groups and forums are not moderated or refereed in any way, you must always be careful about evaluating the reliability of a source of information, but any discussion group can be valuable not only for the information it provides but also for the ideas that emerge as participants discuss an issue and tease out its complexities.

You can subscribe to a discussion list (not with money, but just by applying to be a participant in the discussion) and become a regular participant, learning the names of other participants and their interests. Or you can simply find newsgroups, or forums and bulletin boards attached to Web sites, to which anyone can post messages for anyone else to read at any time, with no registration or login.

E-mail subscription discussion lists Discussion lists may be public or private. The administrators of even a public list may screen potential subscribers carefully even though generally there is no fee for subscribing. Private lists and professionally moderated lists, especially those with a technical or educational focus, can be reliable sources of factual information and informed opinion. Use *Topica* at <http://www.topica.com> or *CataList* at <http://www.lsoft.com/lists/listref.html> to find public lists that cover a topic you are interested in. To participate in an e-mail list, you need only an e-mail address and a mail program.

When you join an e-mail discussion list, all the messages posted are sent automatically to the e-mail accounts of all those who have registered as subscribers. Lists are managed by specific software programs, such as Listserv, Listproc, and Majordomo, which have similar but not identical procedures. See <http://www.hkbu.edu.hk/~mkt2330/listserv.html> for information on the commands for lists. And see <http://maxweber.hunter.cuny.edu/eres/docs/eres/SOC325.22_KUECHLER/ho-lists.htm> for a step-by-step demonstration, with screen-shots, of how to subscribe to a list. For general guidelines, use the tips in the Key Points box.

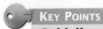

Guidelines for Participating in Mailing Lists

1. A list has two addresses: the *posting* address (to send messages to all subscribers) and the *subscription* address (to send commands about managing your subscription). To differentiate between them, think of the difference between sending a letter to the editor of a printed newspaper for possible publication and sending a note to the circulation manager about a vacation suspension of your subscription.

2. Use the subscription address (not the posting address) to subscribe, suspend, or unsubscribe to a list (or make any changes in your subscription details). Leave the subject line blank, and include no signature or signature file in the message section—just the command to the list software. Follow the list's directions for the commands. The wording must be exact. Here are examples of how Mike Myers would (a) subscribe to and (b) post messages to two discussion lists:

An Emily Dickinson discussion	A discussion between researchers and the Central European Archive for Empirical Social Research

a. To: listserv@listserv.uta.edu
   Sub Dicknson Mike Myers
	a. To: majordomo@icpsr.umich.edu
	   Subscribe eurobarometer

b. To: dicknson@listserv.uta.edu	b. To: eurobarometer@icpsr.umich.edu

3. When you send commands or post messages to a list, always use exactly the same e-mail address, even if you have several. The list server will recognize your commands and your messages only under the original address from which you subscribe. If you change your e-mail address, unsubscribe and then subscribe again with the new address.

4. Make a folder in your e-mail program for the list's instructions and messages you want to save. It is especially important to keep a copy of the list instructions, sent to you automatically after you subscribe, so that you know, for instance, if you can suspend mail during vacations and, if so, how.

5. Whatever you do, lurk before you post! Spend time reading and browsing in the list or the list archives (Web archives are easier to use—look for a list that provides them) before you start sending messages to everyone on the list.

6. Manage the volume of mail. A mailing list may generate 30, 100, or more messages a day, so after a few days away, you may feel overwhelmed. Use the options the list provides to select—for example, Nomail, Digest, or Index. Nomail temporarily suspends the sending of messages to your mailbox; Digest allows you to get only one bundle of mail every day; Index simply lists the messages once a day, and you retrieve the ones you want to read. However, not all options are available for all lists.

7. If you want to reply only to the sender of a message, do not send your message to the whole list (choose "Reply," not "Reply All"). Make sure you know who will actually receive your message. Do not complain to Manuel about Al's views and then by mistake send your reply to the whole list, including Al.

8. Avoid sending a message like "I agree" to the many subscribers to the list. Make your postings substantive and considerate, so subscribers find them worth reading.

9. Do not forward a posting from one list to another unless you ask the sender for permission.

In addition to joining e-mail lists that require registering for a subscription, you can contribute spontaneously to online discussion group forums where anyone can read and post messages. Such forums are known by several different names—newsgroup, Web forum, bulletin board—and differences exist in the software managing them, as discussed in the following paragraphs.

Usenet newsgroups   The oldest system of bulletin boards started in 1979—long before the Internet and the Web became popular—and is known as Usenet ("user network"). Today tens of thousands of newsgroups cover every imaginable topic.

Newsgroup names   Newsgroup names begin with identifiers such as *rec.* (recreation), *sci.* (science), *comp.* (computing), *biz.* (business), and *alt.* (alternatives—a wide variety of topics). These tags give a rough indication of the subject matter: *alt.alien.visitors; alt.English.usage; biz.com.accounting; comp.ai.nat-lang; rec.arts.movies.production.*

Newsreader access   Usenet newsgroups can be accessed via a newsreader (now often bundled with a Web browser or a mail program), which connects to a special news server at your ISP or your college. In AOL, for instance, go to Internet/Newsgroups/Add to find newsgroups you can access.

Web access to newsgroups Some special Web sites offer access to newsgroups via a user-friendly Web interface. One of the best of these sites is at <http://groups.google.com>. There you can use a search engine to search for subjects and keywords that interest you, and you can read recent postings. Postings are organized by "threads" consisting of the first introduction of a new topic and responses pertinent to that topic.

Note: However you access newsgroups, keep in mind that postings stay posted for only a limited time, no control whatsoever exists over the postings, and you are likely to come across postings that offend your political, religious, or humanitarian beliefs. Be aware of some Internet dangers, too, especially for young children and teenagers. (See <http://www.safekids.com/safeteens/safeteens.htm> for more details.) In short, Usenet is anarchy. Nobody is in charge.

Web forums, chat pages, and bulletin boards Some restricted, some open to anyone, Web forums (also called chat pages) and bulletin boards are attached to Web pages and provide the opportunity for interaction and debate on topics pertinent to the page. Bulletin boards are often attached to course Web pages or to writing center sites (such as at Colorado State University or at Hunter College), so that students can send questions and instructors or tutors can respond. Here is an example of a discussion board assignment for a first-year writing course in the course management system Blackboard. Students respond to the assigned prompt and to each other's postings:

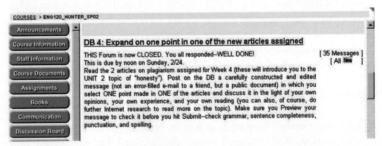

Be sure to consider purpose and audience when you post messages to a class discussion board for a college course. This is not a private e-mail message to a friend but a public document, posted on your course site for all your classmates and your instructor to read. These readers will form judgments about you from what they read. So consider carefully the ideas you express, the language you use, and the level of formality and accuracy that is appropriate.

Public discussion boards provide a venue where you can remain not known to any of the readers. Still, the forum is a public one, so don't ignore the principles of netiquette. Carlsbad Caverns National Park (at <http://www.carlsbad.caverns.national-park.com/wwwboard/carlchat.htm>) and many other national parks provide such forums.

Carlsbad Caverns National Park Chat Page

Hall of Giants - NPS Photo

Press "Reload or Refresh" when you post a message to ensure that it was posted

[Post Message] [FAQ]

- visiting carlsbad caverns - jsauseda *14:56:52 01/30/02* (1)
  - ○ Contact the park by phone - Sagebrush *17:25:06 01/31/02* (0)
- Bat Phobics - manny oteyza *13:01:56 01/25/02* (0)
- Slaughter Canyon Cave - S. G. Slaughter *16:18:31 01/21/02* (0)
- tours? - k.c. *19:42:30 01/16/02* (0)
- memories - Martha Johanna Robison *13:43:45 01/09/02* (0)
- Wedding - Mary Crutchfield *02:13:20 12/08/01* (0)
- ranger mr. pat ramsey - georgecasey ahl *05:33:45 12/06/01* (0)
- which tour? - pat addison *17:20:35 11/16/01* (0)
- Transp from Carlsbad to Guadalupe HQ? - Michael Meares *10:08:30 10/06/01* (0)
- Flash photography - Henry Thorsen *12:49:17 09/25/01* (0)
- fishing licence requirements - sasquatch *04:19:55 08/27/01* (0)
- WEDDING UNDER GROUND????? - Mac *17:16:06 6/30/101* (1)
  - ○ Re: WEDDING UNDER GROUND????? - Nick Hellmer *06:54:13 11/27/01* (0)

EXERCISE 11.3   Examine a chat page.

For a lively chat page, frequently on serious and current topics (with handy ideas for research papers), go to the online magazine *Slate*, where readers respond to daily articles in a forum called The Fray. Reach *Slate* at <http://www.slate.msn.com> and click the Discuss button. What is the issue, and what interesting points do the participants make? Report to your classmates.

EXERCISE 11.4 Examine a chat page or a newsgroup.
Go to a Usenet group or to a chat page attached to a Web site that interests you. Read the last five messages posted. What do the messages tell you about the interests and concerns of those participating in the discussion?

11d Chat rooms, MOOs, and MUDs

The discussions in the forums described in **11c** do not take place in real time. For all of them, you post a message, and then later, when someone logs on and takes the time to write, you may get a response.

Chat rooms and buddy lists, in contrast, operate in real time. Cable News Network, for instance, offers chat rooms to discuss CNN programs. A college writing center may offer to set up a chat room where a tutor can discuss an essay online with a student (see Colorado State University's site at <http://writing.colostate.edu/sndpaper/discuss.htm>). Course management systems such as Blackboard and WebCT also provide the opportunity for using a virtual classroom.

MUDs (multiuser domains) and MOOs (multiuser domains, object-oriented) are often accessed through a telnet protocol at <telnet://>, but more and more are now accessible via the Web. They provide and describe real-time settings and spaces for interaction and role-playing. Conversations get going when a MOO or MUD is set up for a specific time on a topic, so that it can be a virtual community for a specific purpose. You can find a partial listing of MOOs at <http://www.csun.edu/~hceng028/#moo-list>. A catalog of MUDs is available at <http://www.mudconnect.com>. Visit and learn the basic commands and conventions before you enter an ongoing conversation, such as always typing &join to ask if you may join in. See <http://www.hunter.cuny.edu/ieli/moo-cmd.html> for more on MOO commands. Abbreviations such as *ttyl* ("talk to you later") and *irl* ("in real life") are commonly used in MOOs.

11e Web-enhanced courses, distance learning, and virtual classrooms*

Increasingly, colleges offer courses in which the instructor makes use of Web technology either to supplement traditional classroom teaching (called Web-enhanced or hybrid courses) or to replace physical classroom meetings altogether by meeting in cyberspace (a version of

---

* The information in **11e** has been provided by Manfred Kuechler, Department of Sociology, Hunter College.

distance learning). First, mainly graduate courses were taught online, but now more and more undergraduate courses make use of this technology. For more on this, consult *Interactive Education: Impact of the Internet on Learning & Teaching* at <http://ubmail.ubalt.edu/~harsham/interactive.htm>.

Many course Web sites are not open to the general public, partly in order not to violate the "fair use" limitation on using material copyrighted by third parties, and partly because faculty want to protect what they perceive as their own intellectual property. And, especially with respect to distance learning, colleges want to protect their economic interest by restricting access to students who have paid tuition fees. One of the nation's leading universities, however, Massachusetts Institute of Technology, is setting an example by making the contents of all its courses available on the Internet. For details, see <http://web.mit.edu/ocw/>.

Colleges frequently use special course management software (CMS) to make it easier for instructors and students to utilize the tools of online courses. Two of the most widely used CMS are Blackboard and WebCT. Such systems provide course Web sites with generally accessible areas (though access is often restricted to students officially enrolled in the course), where the instructor can post the syllabus, course materials, announcements, quizzes and exams, as well as areas requiring logins by individual students to personally check grades and exam results. These systems also offer a "drop box" where a student can submit files to the instructor and receive files with comments back from the instructor. Increasingly, therefore, if you take Web-enhanced courses, you may be required to produce papers in a Web-suitable format (like HTML) to allow posting and easy access on a course Web site. See **12c** for tips on posting academic writing online.

In addition, course management software provides course-specific discussion boards, personal home pages where students can introduce themselves to the rest of the class, and real-time chat areas (also referred to as *synchronous chat* or *virtual classrooms*), where students and instructor or just groups of students can "meet" at a prearranged time to discuss reading assignments, group projects, or posted papers. Some more elaborate virtual classrooms also allow communication via one-way (just instructor to students) or two-way audio.

In distance learning and in online courses, you may never meet the students enrolled with you in the course, but you may be asked to work collaboratively on some assignments, using a discussion board or virtual classroom to conduct discussions and sharing drafts of assignments via e-mail. For more on peer review, see **4d;** for more on collaborative writing, see **4e.**

12 Writing Online for Academic Purposes

A document written for presentation on paper has very different requirements from a document designed to be posted online. You need to recognize the online culture of hypertext in order to make your online postings appropriate for the medium, useful, and attractive.

12a The nature of hypertext

When we read a printed document, we read mainly from beginning to end, though we may do some skimming and scanning and peek at the end of a murder mystery to see whether the butler actually did it. Basically, though, reading print is a linear process, as one word follows another, one idea follows another, one paragraph follows another. In contrast, when we read HTML-created documents in e-mail or on the Web, we can follow the links. Even in an e-mail message from a friend, we may read only a line or two and then come across an underlined or highlighted hyperlink that takes us to another document, with its own hotlinks, anywhere on the Internet. This kind of online reading is not linear; rather, it is associative and digressive. Often we start reading a Web page and then half an hour later, after following interesting links, we find ourselves pages and pages away and wonder how we got there.

12b HTML

Text posted on the Web will usually be in HTML (hypertext markup language) format, which any browser can display (though other languages are available for advanced Web pages). In HTML files, the visible text is supplemented by specific instructions, known as "tags," that are enclosed in angle brackets (< . . . >). However, if the sight of such tags and the often rather messy-looking source code makes you shudder, you can begin by using a program that creates the underlying HTML tags automatically (this is like driving a car without knowing or caring what the carburetor does).

Recent versions of word processing programs (Microsoft Word and Corel WordPerfect) can automatically convert a document and save it as an HTML file. In Word, for example, you simply produce your document in the usual way; then when you save it, go to Edit/Save As, and change Save As Type from Word Document to Web Page. The HTML commands are done for you, automatically.

The HTML code used by Word is not fully compatible with all browsers. Those that are compatible are WYSIWYG ("what you see is what you get") HTML editors (such as Netscape Composer) and—if you go high end—Adobe GoLive or Macromedia Dreamweaver. All of them have the ability to insert links and graphics very easily without your inserting special codes—the programmers did the work for you, sparing you the immediate need to learn HTML.

Many universities offer students home pages with their e-mail accounts and run workshops on Web page design. Once you are no longer a beginner and want to do complex operations, then you will need to know how to fine-tune commands to get the look exactly right. The learning curve for HTML is steep initially, but people get the hang of it quite quickly. One good HTML tutorial is at <http://www.cwru.edu/help/introHTML/toc.html>.

Another way to become familiar with HTML is to look at a document on the screen and then see how it gets that way and what codes have been used. You can get a start on this by finding a page of text and links and then going to View/Page Source or View/Source to find out its HTML structure. The illustration that follows shows an announcement posted on an online writing course in the course management system Blackboard. The text seen on the screen is this:

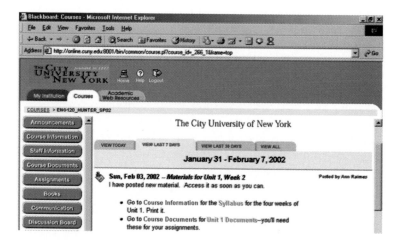

Here is the same announcement text in HTML, as it was produced with Netscape Composer:

```
</head>
<body>
I have posted new material.  Access it as soon as you can.

<ul>
<li>
Go to <b><font color="#3366FF">Course Information></font>
   </b> for the <b><font color="#FF0000">Syllabus</font>
   </b><font color="#000000">for the four weeks of Unit 1.
   Print it.</font></li>

<li>
<font color="#000000">Go to </font><b><font color="#3366FF">
   Course Documents</font></b><font color="#000000">
   for </font><b><font color="#FF0000">Unit 1 Documents
   </font></b><font color="#000000">—you'll need these for
   your assignments.</font></li>
```

12c Posting academic writing online

You may be required to submit an essay for a course online rather than in hard copy. Your instructor may ask you to e-mail him or her an attachment, or, in a hybrid or asynchronous distance-learning course, you may be required to submit your essays in a drop box or post them on a class bulletin board for the instructor and other students to read and comment on. In either case, keep in mind the following general guidelines and ask your instructor for instructions specific to the course, format, and type of posting.

KEY POINTS

Posting an Essay or Research Paper Online

1. *Structure* Set up a structure with sections and subsections (called "fragments"), all with headings.

2. *Links to sections from a table of contents* Provide a table of contents, with an internal link anchored to each fragment, marked with a "bookmark" or "target," and give each bookmark or target a name. Readers can then click on and go directly to any section they are interested in.

3. *Internal hyperlinks* Use internal hyperlinks (Insert/Hyperlink) to connect readers directly to relevant sections of your text, content notes, and visuals. Also provide a link from a hard-copy source cited in the body of your paper to the entry in your list of works cited.

4. *External hyperlinks* Use external hyperlinks to connect to Web documents from references in the body of your paper and from your list of works cited. Word has a function that will automatically convert any string starting with <http://> into a hyperlink (Tools/AutoCorrect/AutoFormat, and then check Replace Internet And Network Paths With Hyperlinks).

5. *No paragraph indentation* Do not indent for a new paragraph. Instead, leave a line of space between paragraphs.

6. *Attribution of sources* Make sure that the link you give to an online article in a database is a persistent link and not one that works only for a few hours or days. For more information on finding persistent links and on evaluating and citing online sources and authors, see <http://www.lehigh.edu/~inref/guides/persistentlinks2.htm>.

7. *List of works cited or list of references* Give a complete list, with URLs, even if you provide external links to the sources from the body of your paper. If a reader prints your paper, the exact references will then still be available.

Here is an excerpt from the beginning of Rachel Schwartz's sociology course report titled "The Debate over Same-Sex Marriage in the United States: 1990 to the Present." Her instructor limited the assignment to an informational review of the literature available in a specific field (not an argument with a thesis arguing for or against same-sex marriage) and gave specific directions on how to prepare the review for online publication on the course Web site. Note the features specific to online publication, such as the table of contents with hyperlinks (all underlined) to each section, and the hyperlinks in her text to external URLs. See the *Universal Keys* Web site for this online report.

TABLE OF CONTENTS

Overview

Introduction: Marriage and Domestic Partnership

Detailed Chronology

- Hawaii 1990–1996

- Federal Response to Hawaii: Defense of Marriage Act

OVERVIEW

In the United States, same-sex couples may not marry, which prevents them from obtaining the rights and privileges associated with marriage (Price-Livingston, 2000).

This has become an issue of national debate in the past ten years because of a court case in Hawaii (New York State Senate: Protection of Human Rights, 1999). In 1993, the Supreme Court of the State of Hawaii said that the state's criteria for issuing marriage licenses might violate anti-sex-discrimination portions of the Hawaii State Constitution (*Baehr v. Lewin*, 1993) because it did not allow couples of the same sex to obtain a marriage license.

Since then, almost all other states have taken up debate of the issue. In California, a public vote on the issue resulted in a hotly contested and expensive campaign. Vermont's court rendered a unique decision, and the ensuing legalization of a civil union for same-sex couples has opened up new areas of debate and activity.

Public opinion data show that Americans do not support same-sex marriage but may be willing to consider alternatives that offer same-sex couples some rights. Data also suggest that support for same-sex marriage may be growing.

The primary actors in the controversy over same-sex marriage are the national organizations on both sides of the issue. Gay and lesbian advocacy organizations including Lambda Legal Defense and Education Fund (2001) and the National Gay and Lesbian Task Force (2001) are active in the "Freedom to Marry" movement by acting as co-counsel in court cases and by organizing grassroots supporters. Conservative religious organizations, such as Focus on the Family (2001), Family Research

Council (2000), and Concerned Women for America (2001) highlight a "pro-family" agenda, and are active in promoting Defense of Marriage bills at the state level.

INTRODUCTION: MARRIAGE AND DOMESTIC PARTNERSHIP

Although many people tend to think of marriage as primarily a personal issue involving community, family, and religion, it is also a legal issue. Once married, a couple is subject to "1,049 laws in 13 categories including social security, housing, employment benefits, and immigration and naturalization" (United States General Accounting Office, 1997).

The institution of marriage is chiefly regulated at the state level. States issue marriage licenses, certificates, and divorce papers. They set their own laws about who may or may not be legally married (Cornell Law School Legal Information Institute, 2001).

[end of excerpt]

References

Baehr v. Lewin. (1993, May 27). Supreme Court of Hawaii. (Full text in Appendix).

Concerned Women for America. (2001). *Our core issues.* Retrieved from http://www.cwfa.org/library/

Cornell Law School. (2001). *Marriage: An overview.* Legal Information Institute. Retrieved from http://www.law.cornell.edu/topics/marriage.html

Family Research Council. (2000). *Mission statement.* Retrieved from http://www.frc.org/site/index.cfm?get=about

Focus on the Family. (2001). *Our guiding principles.* Retrieved from http://www.family.org/welcome/aboutfof/a0000078.html

Lambda Legal Defense and Education Fund. (2001). *About Lambda.* Retrieved from http://www.lambdalegal.org/cgi-bin/pages/about

National Gay and Lesbian Task Force. (2001). *About NGLTF.* Retrieved from http://www.ngltf.org/about/index.cfm

New York State Senate. (1999, May 27). *Protection of Human Rights,* Narrative N92101. Retrieved from http://www.senate.state.ny.us/Docs/sofl/HUR/HUR001.html

Price-Livingston, S. (2000, January 20). *Research Report on Same-Sex Marriage.* Connecticut Office of Legislative Research. Retrieved from http://www.cga.state.ct.us/olr/

United States General Accounting Office. (1997, January 31). *Defense of Marriage Act* (Letter Report Number OGC-97-16). Retrieved from http://frwebgate.access.gpo.gov/cgi-bin/useftp.cgi?IPaddress=162.140.64.21&filename=og97016.txt&directory=/diskb/wais/data/gao

The list of references (selected to match the excerpt from the paper) follows the general guidelines of APA style (**53**), adapted for the online environment. The list is double-spaced only between entries, and the entries are not indented as they would be in hard copy. The URLs and references in the text of the essay appear as hyperlinks.

In addition, because this was an assigned college paper to be completed within a short period of time, and the other students and the instructor were the only readers, the instructor told students it was not necessary to include the date when they accessed the material.

The references reveal some of the problems inherent in posting papers online. Because some of the cited sources were available only in subscription databases with nonpermanent URLs, the student downloaded the complete documents and included them in an Appendix on the course Web site with password-restricted access, so that the readers in her course could access the material at any time. If she had not restricted access to the documents retrieved from subscription databases, she would have run into problems of copyright.

13 Designing a Personal Web Site

The intricacies of designing a professional Web site are many—and beyond the scope of this writing handbook. However, many students and community organizations find that even a simple Web site is a good way to make contacts and provide information. This section contains advice on setting up a clear and useful site.

13a Planning and organizing

Though the terms are often used interchangeably, a "Web page" can be viewed in a single window (though some scrolling may be necessary), and a "Web site" consists of a number of interrelated (linked) Web pages. Strictly speaking, Allison Marsh's Web site at <http://www.student.richmond.edu/2001/amarsh/public_html/index.html> (illustrated in **13d**) consists of one start page, three second-level pages (university and professional information, personal information, and e-mail), and many third-level pages. In addition, many pages are subdivided into frames, and a decorative "side frame" is used on more than one page. You will generate one page at a time, but you should start by considering the following:

- What is your purpose? What content do you want to provide? What message do you want to get across?
- Who do you think will visit your site? What will your visitors expect?
- How do you want to structure the site? How will visitors navigate around the site?
- How much maintenance will the site need (updating links and content, for example)?

Then draw a site map—that is, a flow chart that shows the logic of how the different parts of the site relate to each other.

Decide if you want to use single pages or pages divided into frames. Keep in mind that the way Web pages are displayed on a visitor's screen depends on the size and setup of the visitor's monitor and the type, version, and setup of the browser he or she uses. What may look terrific on your own station may look messy on the station of a visitor, or—worse yet—parts of your page may not display at all. Basic HTML gives you only limited control of how your pages display on other stations. Therefore, keep your start (home) page simple, think twice before using nonstandard features (Javascripts, Java applets, and so on), and make sure that all links to the other pages within your own site and to external sites are easily recognizable and clearly indicate what content they lead to.

Allison Marsh's home page (p. 269) clearly links to three other pages within her site, which in turn link to other pages, internally and externally. Here is the site map for the first levels of her site.

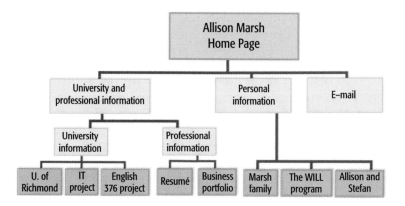

13b Tips for Web site design

Tips for Web site design

KEY POINTS
Web Site Design Guidelines

1. Keep pages short—as a general rule, no more than two to three screens.
2. Set your own monitor to a resolution not higher than 800 X 600 and make sure all the text is visible on your screen without horizontal scrolling.
3. Keep sentences short and direct.
4. Break text into short passages.
5. Use headings and provide internal links to the headings.
6. Use visuals—such as pictures, diagrams, photographs, graphs, clip art, or animations—to enhance and illustrate ideas. Graphics should offer more than a distraction. Pay attention to the file size of such add-ons. It is often possible to reduce the file size significantly with only a minimal loss of image quality.
7. Choose descriptive text or images as "anchors" for links. Check on their reliability and keep them up-to-date.
8. Use color and background patterns judiciously. Blue type on a black swirling background may look interesting, but it can be difficult to read.
9. Be sensitive to issues of accessibility for people with disabilities, such as using descriptive text as well as images, offering alternatives to visual and auditory material, and providing a zoom function. The site at <http://www.webaim.org/howto> offers tutorials and useful simulations. Also refer to the *Bobby* site developed by the Center for Applied Special Technology at <http://bobby.watchfire.com>.
10. Keep the site uncluttered for ease of navigation.
11. Include relevant navigational links from each page of your site to other pages, such as the home page. Consider the use of a navigation bar that appears on each page of your site. Update your site regularly to maintain the links to external URLs.
12. Include your own e-mail address for comments and questions about your site. State the date of the last page update.
13. Do not include personal information, such as your home address and telephone number.

If you download and use text and graphics in your site, ask for permission and acknowledge that you received permission to use the material. Also, provide full documentation for your sources.

13c Useful resources for site design

For more on Web site preparation, consult the following:

- Johndan Johnson-Eilola, *Designing Effective Web Sites: A Concise Guide* (Boston: Houghton, 2001)
- Elizabeth Castro, *HTML 4 for the World Wide Web* (Berkeley: Peachpit, 2000)
- Jakob Nielsen, *Designing Web Usability* (Indianapolis: New Riders, 1999)
- Jennifer Niederst, *Web Design in a Nutshell* (Cambridge: O'Reilly, 1999)
- *Builder.com,* offering help for site builders and useful Web page design tips at <http://builder. com.com>
- Web design instructions by Tim Berners-Lee at <http://www.w3 .org/Provider/Style/Introduction.html>
- Library of Congress Resource Page for HTML: at <http://www. loc.gov/iug/html40>

13d Sample student Web sites

Allison Marsh, who is now working for a consulting firm, graduated from the University of Richmond, Virginia. This is her undergraduate Web site, available at <http://www.student.richmond.edu/2001/ amarsh/public_html/>.

Home Page

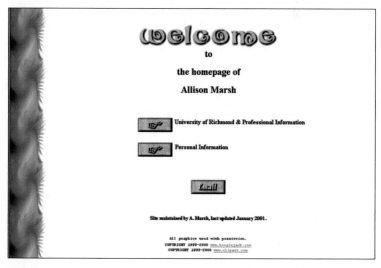

Link from "University of Richmond & Professional Information"

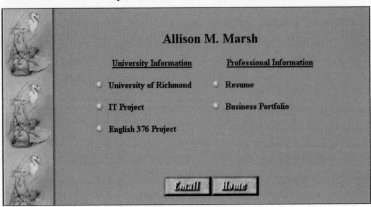

Link from "Business Portfolio"

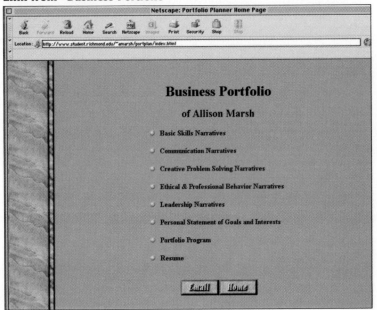

Here are pages from the Web site of Sebastian F. G. White, a student at Alfred University, Alfred, New York. His home page offers links to his résumé, a personal photo site, an architectural project on buildings in upstate New York, and his e-mail. Navigational links back to the home page appear on each page of the site. The site is at <http://students.alfred.edu/~whitesf>.

Home Page

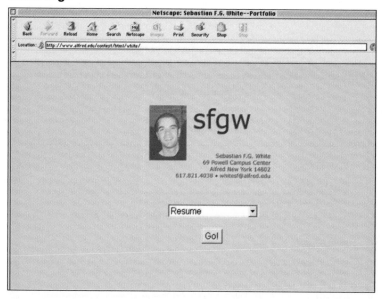

Link to Architecture Project Page

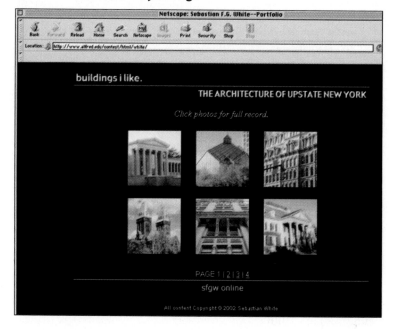

Link to Résumé Page

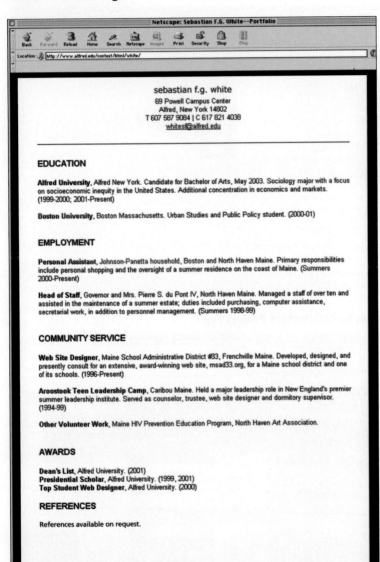

Netscape: Sebastian F.G. White--Portfolio

Location: http://www.alfred.edu/contest/html/white/

sebastian f.g. white
69 Powell Campus Center
Alfred, New York 14802
T 607 587 9084 | C 617 821 4038
whitesf@alfred.edu

EDUCATION

Alfred University, Alfred New York. Candidate for Bachelor of Arts, May 2003. Sociology major with a focus on socioeconomic inequity in the United States. Additional concentration in economics and markets. (1999-2000; 2001-Present)

Boston University, Boston Massachusetts. Urban Studies and Public Policy student. (2000-01)

EMPLOYMENT

Personal Assistant, Johnson-Panetta household, Boston and North Haven Maine. Primary responsibilities include personal shopping and the oversight of a summer residence on the coast of Maine. (Summers 2000-Present)

Head of Staff, Governor and Mrs. Pierre S. du Pont IV, North Haven Maine. Managed a staff of over ten and assisted in the maintenance of a summer estate; duties included purchasing, computer assistance, secretarial work, in addition to personnel management. (Summers 1998-99)

COMMUNITY SERVICE

Web Site Designer, Maine School Administrative District #33, Frenchville Maine. Developed, designed, and presently consult for an extensive, award-winning web site, msad33.org, for a Maine school district and one of its schools. (1996-Present)

Aroostook Teen Leadership Camp, Caribou Maine. Held a major leadership role in New England's premier summer leadership institute. Served as counselor, trustee, web site designer and dormitory supervisor. (1994-99)

Other Volunteer Work, Maine HIV Prevention Education Program, North Haven Art Association.

AWARDS

Dean's List, Alfred University. (2001)
Presidential Scholar, Alfred University. (1999, 2001)
Top Student Web Designer, Alfred University. (2000)

REFERENCES

References available on request.

sfgw online

> **EXERCISE 13.1** Explore a student's Web site.
> Access Sebastian White's site at <http://students.alfred.edu/ ~whitesf > and make a site map similar to the one on page 267.

> **EXERCISE 13.2** Search for students' Web sites.
> Use a search engine to find students' Web sites. Select one that is particularly clear and attractive and report on it to your classmates.

14 Writing for Employment*

14a Preparing your résumé: length and format

Although recruiters sometimes refer to the résumé as a *wilawid* ("What I've learned and what I've done"), the emphasis in the résumé should be on the future rather than on the past: you must show how your education and work experience have prepared you for future jobs—specifically, the job for which you are applying. The résumé and accompanying application letter (cover letter) are crucial in advancing you beyond the mass of initial applicants and into the much smaller group of potential candidates invited to an interview.

Résumé length How much is too much? Surveys of employment and human resources executives consistently show that most managers prefer a one-page résumé for the entry-level positions typically sought by recent college graduates; a two-page résumé may be appropriate for unusual circumstances or for higher-level positions.

A one-page résumé is *not* the same as a two-page résumé crammed onto one page by means of small type and narrow margins. Your résumé must be attractive and easy to read. Shorten your résumé by making judicious decisions about what to include and then by using concise language to communicate what is important. Do not, on the other hand, make your résumé *too* short. A résumé that does not fill one page may tell the prospective employer that you have little to offer.

Résumé format Choose a simple, easy-to-read typeface, and avoid the temptation to use a lot of "special effects" just because they're available on your computer. One or two typefaces in one or two different sizes should be enough. Use a simple format, with lots of white space, short paragraphs, and a logical organization. Through the use

---

* This section has been adapted from Scot Ober's *Contemporary Business Communication*, 5th ed. (Boston: Houghton, 2003). Used with permission.

of type size and style, indentation, bullets, and the like, make clear which parts are subordinate to main features. One of your word processor's built-in résumé templates is a good place to start.

Format your résumé on standard-size paper ($8\frac{1}{2}'' \times 11''$) so that it can be filed easily. Also, avoid brightly colored papers: they will get attention but perhaps the wrong kind. Dark colors do not photocopy well, and you want photocopies of your résumé (whether made by you or by the potential employer) to look professional. Choose white or an off-white (cream or ivory) paper of good quality—at least 20-pound bond.

Finally, your résumé and application letter must be 100 percent free of error—in content, spelling, grammar, and format. Ninety-nine percent accuracy is not good enough when you are seeking a job. One survey of large-company executives showed that fully 80 percent of them had decided against interviewing a job seeker because of poor grammar, spelling, or punctuation in his or her résumé. Don't write, as one job applicant did, "Education: Advanced Curses in Accounting," or as another did, "I have an obsession for detail; I make sure that I cross my i's and dot my t's." Show right from the start that you are the type of person who takes pride in your work.

14b Preparing your résumé's content

Fortunately, perhaps, there is no such thing as a standard résumé; each is as individual as the person it represents. There are, however, standard parts of the résumé—those parts recruiters expect and need to see to make valid judgments.

Identifying information It doesn't do any good to impress a recruiter if he or she cannot locate you easily to schedule an interview; therefore, your name and complete address (including phone number and e-mail address) are crucial.

Your name should be the very first item on the résumé, arranged attractively at the top. Use whatever form you typically use for signing your name (for example, with or without initials). Give your complete name, avoiding nicknames, and do not use a personal title such as *Mr.* or *Ms.*

If you will soon be changing your address (as from a college address to a home address), include both, along with the relevant dates for each. If you are away from your telephone most of the day and no one is at home to answer it and take a message, you would be wise to secure phone company voice mail, invest in an answering machine, or get permission to use the telephone number where you

KEY POINTS

Résumé Content

Include on your résumé

1. Name, address, phone number, and e-mail address
2. Job objective
3. College major, degree, name of college, and graduation date
4. Jobs held, employers, dates, and duties
5. Special aptitudes and skills

Do not include on your résumé

1. Bases for discrimination
   - Religion
   - Ethnicity
   - Age
   - Gender
   - Photograph
   - Marital status
2. High school activities

work as an alternate phone listing. The important point is to be available for contact.

Increasingly, employers are also expecting an e-mail address to be listed. An e-mail address not only provides another means of contact but also sends a nonverbal message that you are computer savvy. And, of course, if you have your own personal Web page (**13d**) that highlights your accomplishments in a positive and professional manner, include that address as well.

Job objective   The job objective is a short summary of your area of expertise and career interest. Most recruiters want the objective stated so that they will know where you might fit into their organization. Don't force the employer to guess about your career goals. Furthermore, don't waste the objective's prominent spot at the top of your résumé by giving a weak, overly general goal:

WEAK   **Challenging position in a progressive organization.**

For your objective to help you, it must be personalized—both for you and for the position you are seeking. Also, it must be specific enough to be useful to the prospective employer but not so specific as to exclude you from many types of similar positions. The following job objective meets these criteria:

STRONG   **Position in personal sales in a medium-size manufacturing firm.**

If your goals are so broad that you have difficulty specifying a job objective, either eliminate this section of your résumé or develop several résumés, each with a different job objective and emphasis.

Be aware that an increasing number of large corporations have begun scanning the résumés they receive into their computer systems and then searching this computerized database by keyword. Be certain, therefore, that the title of the actual position you desire and other relevant terms are included somewhere in your résumé.

Education   Unless your work experience has been extensive, fairly high level, and directly related to your job objective, your education is probably a stronger job qualification than your work experience and should therefore come first on the résumé.

List the title of your degree, the name of your college and its location if needed, your major and (if applicable) minor, and your expected date of graduation (month and year).

List your grade-point average if it will set you apart from the competition (generally, at least a 3.0 on a 4.0 scale). If you have made the dean's list or have financed a substantial portion of your college expenses through part-time work, savings, or scholarships, mention that. Unless your course of study provided distinctive experiences that uniquely qualify you for the job, avoid listing college courses.

Work experience   Work experience—*any* work experience—is a definite plus. It shows the employer that you have had experience in satisfying a superior, following directions, accomplishing objectives through team effort, and being rewarded for your labors. If your work experience has been directly related to your job objectives, consider putting it ahead of the education section, for emphasis.

In relating your work experience, use either a chronological or functional organizational pattern.

In a *chronological* arrangement, you organize your experience by date, describing your most recent job first and working backward. This format is most appropriate when you have had a strong continuing work history and much of your work has been related to your job objective (see p. 277). About 95 percent of all résumés are chronological, beginning with the most recent information and working backward.

Résumé in Chronological Format

This résumé presents the most recent job experience and education first and works backward.

225 West 70th Street
New York, NY 10023
Phone: 212-555-3821
E-mail: agomez@nyu.edu

Aurelia Gomez

Objective	Entry-level staff accounting position with a public accounting firm	Provides specific enough objective to be useful
Experience	Summer 2002 — **Accounting Intern:** Coopers & Lybrand, NYC • Assisted in preparing corporate tax returns • Attended meetings with clients • Conducted research in corporate tax library and wrote research reports	Places work experience before education because applicant considers it to be her stronger qualification
	Nov. 1998– Aug. 2000 — **Payroll Specialist:** City of New York • Worked in a full-time civil service position in the Department of Administration • Used payroll and other accounting software on both DEC 1034 minicomputer and Pentium III • Represented 28-person work unit on the department's management-labor committee • Left job to pursue college degree full-time	Uses action words such as *assisted* and *conducted;* uses incomplete sentences to emphasize the action words and to conserve space
Education	Jan. 1996– Present — Pursuing a 5-year bachelor of business administration degree (major in accounting) from NYU • Expected graduation date: June 2003 • Attended part-time from 1996 until 2001 while holding down a full-time job • Have financed 100% of all college expenses through savings, work, and student loans • Plan to sit for the CPA exam in May 2004	Provides degree, institution, major, and graduation date Makes the major section headings parallel in format and in wording Formats the side headings for the dates in a column for ease of reading
Personal Data	• Helped start the Minority Business Student Association at NYU and served as program director for two years; secured the publisher of *Black Enterprise* magazine as a banquet speaker • Have traveled extensively throughout South America • Am a member of the Accounting Society • Am willing to relocate	Provides additional data to enhance her credentials
References	Available on request	Omits actual names and addresses of references

Résumé in Functional Format

RAYMOND J. ARNOLD

OBJECTIVE

Labor relations position in a large multinational firm that requires well-developed labor relations, management, and communication skills

SKILLS

LABOR RELATIONS
- Majored in labor relations; minored in psychology
- Belong to Local 463 of International Office Workers Union
- Was crew chief for the second-shift work team at Wainwright Bank

MANAGEMENT
- Learned time-management skills by working 30 hours per week while attending school full-time
- Was promoted twice in three years at Wainwright Bank
- Practiced discretion while dealing with the financial affairs of others; treated all transactions confidentially

COMMUNICATION
- Developed a Web page for Alpha Kappa Psi business fraternity
- Ran for senior class vice president, making frequent campaign speeches and impromptu remarks
- Took elective classes in report writing and business research
- Am competent in Microsoft Office XP and Internet Research

EDUCATION

B.S. Degree from Boston University to be awarded June 2003
Major: Labor Relations; Minor: Psychology

EXPERIENCE

Bank teller, Wainwright Bank, Boston Massachusetts: 2000-Present
Salesperson, JC Penney, Norfolk, Nebraska: Summer 1998

REFERENCES

Available from the Career Information Center
Boston University, Boston, MA 02215, phone: 617-555-2000

15 TURNER HALL, BOSTON UNIVERSITY, BOSTON, MA 02215 PHONE: 617-555-9833 • E-MAIL: RJARNOLD@BU.EDU

Introduces three skill areas and expands on each with bulleted examples

Relates each listed item directly to the desired job

Provides specific evidence to support each skill

Uses bullets to highlight the individual skills (asterisks would have worked just as well)

Leaves more space *between* the different sections than *within* sections (to clearly separate each section)

Weaves work experiences, education, and extracurricular activities into the skill statements

Avoids repeating the duties given earlier

In a *functional* arrangement, you organize your experience by type of function performed (such as supervision or budgeting) or by type of skill developed (such as human relations or communication skills). Then, under each, are specific examples (evidence) as illustrated on page 278. Functional résumés are most appropriate when you are changing industries, moving into an entirely different line of work, or reentering the work force after a long period of unemployment, because they emphasize your skills rather than your employment history and let you show how these skills have broad applicability to other jobs.

In actual practice, the two patterns are not mutually exclusive; you can use a combination. Remember that the purpose of describing your work history is to show the prospective employer what you have learned *that will benefit the organization.* No matter what your previous work, you have developed certain traits or had certain experiences that can be transferred to the new position. On the basis of your research into the duties of the job you are seeking, highlight those transferable skills.

If you can honestly do so, show in your résumé that you have developed as many of the following characteristics as possible:

- ability to work well with others
- communication skills
- competence and good judgment
- innovation
- high-level computer proficiency
- reliability and trustworthiness
- enthusiasm
- honest and moral character
- increasing responsibility

Complete sentences are not necessary. Instead, start your descriptions with action verbs, using present tense for current duties and past tense for previous job duties or accomplishments. Active verbs such as the following make your work experience come alive: *accomplished, controlled, designed, developed, evaluated, increased, managed, supervised,* and *trained.* Avoid weak verbs such as *attempted, endeavored, hoped,* and *tried,* and avoid sexist language such as *manpower* and *chairman.* When possible, ensure credibility by listing specific accomplishments, giving numbers or dollar amounts. Highlight especially those accomplishments that have direct relevance to the desired job.

VAGUE   I worked as a clerk in the cashier's office.

REVISED   Balanced the cash register every day; was the only part-time employee entrusted to make nightly cash deposits.

VAGUE   Worked as a bouncer at a local bar.

REVISED   Maintained order at Nick's Side-Door Saloon; learned firsthand the importance of compromise and negotiation in solving problems.

VAGUE   Worked as a volunteer for Art Reach.

REVISED   Personally sold more than $1,000 worth of tickets to annual benefit dance; introduced an "Each one, reach one" membership drive that increased membership every year during my three-year term as membership chairperson.

As illustrated in the last example, if you have little or no actual work experience, show how your involvement with professional, social, or civic organizations has helped you develop skills that are transferable to the workplace. Volunteer work, for example, can help develop valuable skills in time management, working with groups, handling money, speaking, accepting responsibility, and the like. In addition, most schools offer internships in which a student receives course credit and supervision while holding down a temporary job.

It has been said that the closest any of us comes to perfection is when we develop our résumé, which has also been called "a balance sheet without any liabilities." Employers recognize your right to highlight your strengths and minimize your weaknesses. However, you must never lie about anything and must never take credit for anything you did not do. A simple telephone call can verify any statement on your résumé. Don't risk destroying your credibility before being hired, and don't risk the possibility of being dismissed later for misrepresenting your qualifications.

Other relevant information   If you have special skills that might give you an edge over the competition (such as knowledge of a foreign language or Web page creation competence), list them on your résumé. Although employers assume that college graduates today have competence in word processing, you should specify any other particular software skills you possess.

Include any honors or recognitions that have relevance to the job you are seeking. Memberships in business-related organizations demonstrate your commitment to your profession, and you should list them if space permits. Likewise, involvement in volunteer, civic, and other extracurricular activities gives evidence of a well-rounded individual and reflects your values and commitment.

Avoid including any data that can become grounds for a discrimination suit—such as information about age, gender, race, religion, disabilities, and marital status. Do not include a photograph. Some employers like to have the applicant's Social Security number included as an aid in verifying college or military information. If you have military experience, include it.

Other optional information includes hobbies and special interests, travel experiences, and willingness to travel. Such information may be included if it has direct relevance to your desired job and if you have room for it, but it may be safely omitted if you need space for more important information.

References   A reference is a person who has agreed to provide information to a prospective employer regarding a job applicant's fitness for a job. As a general rule, the names and addresses of references need not be included on the résumé. Instead, give a general statement that references are available. This policy ensures that you will be contacted before your references are called. The exception to this practice arises if your references are likely to be known by the person reading the résumé; in this case, list their names.

Your references should be professional references rather than character references. The best ones are employers, especially your present employer. University professors with whom you have had a close and successful relationship are also valuable references.

14c Preparing an electronic résumé

An electronic résumé is a résumé that is stored in a computer database designed to help manage and initially screen job applicants. These résumés come from a variety of sources. Applicants may simply mail or fax a paper copy of their standard résumé, which is then scanned into a database. They may fill out (type in) an online résumé form and submit it. They may send the résumé as an e-mail message; or they may post their résumé on the Internet, using a bulletin board system, a newsgroup, or a personal home page. See **13d**, page 272 for a student's résumé posted on his Web site. Note, too, the directions provided by Eli Lilly and Company for copying and pasting a résumé directly into an online form, shown on page 282.

Electronic résumés provide many benefits—both to the recruiter and to the job seeker:

- The job seeker's résumé is potentially available to a large number of employers.
- The job seeker may be considered for positions of which he or she wasn't even aware.
- The initial screening is done by a bias-free computer.
- Employers are relieved of the drudgery of having to manually screen and acknowledge résumés.
- A focused search can be conducted quickly.
- Information is always available until the individual résumé is purged from the system (usually in six months).

Building appropriate keywords into your résumé is essential to successfully using automated résumé systems. Keywords are the descriptive terms that employers search for when trying to fill a position. They are the words and phrases employers believe best sum-

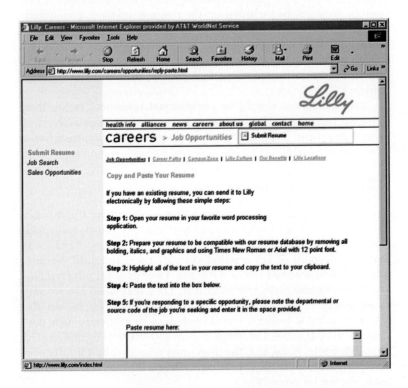

marize the characteristics that they are seeking in candidates for particular jobs, such as college degree, foreign language skills, job titles, specific job skills, software packages, or the names of competitors for whom applicants may have worked. Examples of key terms include *human resources manager, Hughes Aircraft, Windows XP,* or *ISO 9000.*

Optical character recognition (OCR) software creates an ASCII (text) file of your résumé, and artificial intelligence software then "reads" the text and extracts important information about you. Thus, your first hurdle is *to be selected by the computer.*

Because you can never be sure how your résumé will be treated, you should prepare two résumés—one for the computer to read and one for people to read. When mailing a résumé, you may wish to include both versions, making note of that fact in your cover letter. Differences between the two versions concern both content and format.

Content guidelines for electronic résumés Using your standard résumé as a starting point, make these modifications to ensure that your résumé is "computer-friendly" and to maximize the chance that your résumé will be picked by the computer for further review by humans:

- Think "nouns" instead of "verbs" (users rarely search for verbs). Use concrete words rather than vague descriptions. Include industry-specific descriptive nouns that characterize your skills accurately and that people in your field use and commonly look for. (Browse other online résumés, newspaper ads, and industry publications to see what terms are currently being used.)

- Put keywords in proper context, weaving them throughout your résumé. (This strategy is considered a more polished and sophisticated approach than listing them in a block at the beginning of the résumé.)

- Use a variety of different words to describe your skills and don't overuse important words. In most searches, each word counts once, no matter how many times it is used.

- Because your résumé is going to look very bland in plain ASCII text, stripped of all formatting, consider adding a sentence such as this one to the end of your posted résumé: "An attractive and fully formatted hard-copy version of this résumé is available on request."

See page 284 for an example of an electronic résumé.

Electronic Résumé

Runs longer than one page (acceptable for electronic résumés)

Includes notice of availability of a fully formatted version

Begins with name at the top, followed immediately by addresses (both an e-mail address and a home page address)

Emphasizes, where possible, nouns as keywords

Uses only ASCII characters; all text is one size with no special formatting; no rules, graphics, columns, tables, and the like are used

Uses vertical line spaces (Enter key) and horizontal spacing (space bar) to show relationship of parts

Formats lists with asterisks instead of bullets

```
PERSONAL DATA
     * Helped start the Minority Business Student
       Association at New York University and served as
       program director for two years; secured the
       publisher of BLACK ENTERPRISE magazine as a banquet
       speaker
     * Have traveled extensively throughout South America
     * Am a member of the Accounting Society
     * Am willing to relocate

REFERENCES
     Available upon request

NOTE
     An attractive and fully formatted hard-copy version
     of this resume is available upon request.
```

```
AURELIA GOMEZ
     225 West 70 Street
     New York, NY 10023
     Phone: 212-555-3821
     Email: agomez@nyu.edu

OBJECTIVE
     Entry-level staff accounting position with a public
     accounting firm

EXPERIENCE
     Summer 2002
     Accounting Intern: Coopers & Lybrand, NYC
     * Assisted in preparing corporate tax returns
     * Attended meetings with clients
     * Conducted research in corporate tax library and
       wrote research reports

     Nov. 1998-Aug. 2001
     Payroll Specialist: City of New York
     * Full-time civil service position in the Department of
       Administration
     * Proficiency in payroll and other accounting
       software on DEC 1034 minicomputer and Pentium III
     * Representative for a 28-person work unit on the
       department's management-labor committee
     * Reason for leaving job: To pursue college degree
       full-time

EDUCATION
     Jan. 1996-Present
     Pursuing a 5-year bachelor of business
     administration degree (major in accounting) from NYU
     * Expected graduation date: June 2003
     * Attended part-time from 1996 until 2001 while
       holding down a full-time job
     * Have financed 100% of all college expenses through
       savings, work, and student loans
     * Plan to sit for the CPA exam in May 2004
```

An Electronic Résumé in an E-mail Message

When formatted in plain ASCII text, an electronic résumé can be sent as an e-mail message with the assurance that it will arrive in readable format.

KEY POINTS

Creating an Electronic Résumé

1. Create a traditionally formatted résumé, and save it as you normally would (so that you will always have the formatted version available).

2. Save the résumé a second time as a text-only file; most word processors allow you to save a file as an ASCII or DOS file, which has a file name with a *.txt* extension. Special formatting, fonts, tabs, margin changes, and the like are lost in a text file.

(continued)

(continued)

By saving your scannable résumé as a text file, you can view a printout of your résumé as it will look after it has been scanned by the prospective employer.

3. Reopen the text file and make any needed changes to your résumé (see the remaining guidelines). Make sure you always save the document as a text file—not as a word processing document.

4. To ensure accurate reading by computer software, make the format as plain as possible. Do not change typefaces, justification, margins, tabs, font sizes, and the like; do not insert underlines, bold, or italic; and do not use horizontal or vertical rules, graphics, boxes, tables, or columns. None of these will show up in a printout or scan of a text file. (If necessary for clarity, you can insert a row of hyphens to simulate a horizontal rule.)

5. Use a line length of no more than 70 characters per line. Because you can't change margins in a text file, press Enter at the ends of lines if necessary.

6. Do not divide (hyphenate) words at the end of a line.

7. Change bullets to * or + signs at the beginning of the line; then insert spaces at the beginning of runover lines to make all lines of a bulleted paragraph begin at the same point.

8. Press the space bar (instead of the tab) to show any needed indentions.

9. Type your name on the first line by itself, use a standard address format below your name, and type each phone number on its own line. Include an e-mail address if possible.

10. Make the résumé as long as necessary (most database résumés average two to three pages).

11. After making all needed changes, as a test, mail your text file in the body of an e-mail message to yourself or to a friend to see how it looks after being mailed. This step will help you identify any more formatting problems before you send it out to possible employers.

12. Use white $8\frac{1}{2}'' \times 11''$ paper, printed on one side only. Do not use textured paper.

13. Submit a clean, laser-printed original copy; do not fold or staple.

14. If responding via e-mail, use the job title or noted reference number as the subject of your message. Always send the

résumé in the body of the e-mail message. Don't assume that you can attach a word-processed document to an e-mail message; it may or may not be readable.

15. Whenever you update your résumé, remember to update both versions.

14d Writing a job application (cover) letter

An application letter communicates to the prospective employer your interest in and qualifications for a position within the organization. The letter is also called a cover letter because it introduces (or "covers") the major points in your résumé, which you should include with the application letter. A solicited application letter is written in response to an advertised vacancy, whereas an unsolicited application letter (also called a prospecting letter) is written to an organization that has not advertised a vacancy.

Most job applicants use the same résumé when applying for numerous positions and then use their application letter to personalize their qualification for the specific job for which they are applying.

Because the application letter is the first thing the employer will read about you, it is of crucial importance. Make sure the letter is formatted appropriately, looks attractive, and is free of typographical, spelling, and grammatical errors. Don't forget to sign the letter and enclose a copy of your résumé (or perhaps both versions—formatted and plain-text). An application letter should be no longer than one page.

Address and salutation Your letter should be addressed to an individual rather than to an organization or department. Remember, the more hands your letter must go through before it reaches the right person, the more chances for something to go wrong. Ideally, your letter should be addressed to the person who will actually interview you and who will likely be your supervisor if you get the job.

If you do not know enough about the prospective employer to know the name of the appropriate person (the decision maker), you probably have not gathered enough data. If necessary, call the organization to make sure you have the right name—including the correct spelling—and position title. In your salutation, use a courtesy title (such as *Mr.* or *Ms.*) along with the person's last name.

Some job-vacancy ads are blind ads; they do not identify the hiring company by name and provide only a box number address, often in care of the newspaper or magazine that contains the ad. In such a

Job Application Letter

This is an example of a solicited application letter; it accompanies the résumé on page 284.

March 13, 2003

Mr. David Norman, Partner
Ross, Russell & Weston
452 Fifth Avenue
New York, NY 10018

Dear Mr. Norman:

Subject: EDP Specialist Position (Reference No. 103-G)

Identifies the job position and source of advertising

My varied work experience in accounting and payroll services, coupled with my accounting degree, has prepared me for the position of EDP specialist that you advertised in the March 9 *New York Times*.

Emphasizes a qualification that might distinguish her from other applicants

In addition to taking required courses in accounting and management information systems as part of my accounting major at New York University, I took an elective course in EDP auditing and control. The training I received in this course in applications, software, systems, and service-center records would enable me to immediately become a productive member of your EDP consulting staff.

Relates her work experience to the specific needs of the employer

My college training has been supplemented by an internship in a large accounting firm. In addition, my two and one-half years of experience as a payroll specialist for the city of New York have given me firsthand knowledge of the operation and needs of nonprofit agencies. This experience should help me to contribute to your large consulting practice with governmental agencies.

After you have reviewed my enclosed résumé, I would appreciate having the opportunity to discuss with you why I believe I have the right qualifications and personality to serve you and your clients. I can be reached by phone after 3 p.m. daily.

Sincerely,

Aurelia Gomez

Provides a telephone number (may be done either in the body of the letter or in the last line of the address block)

Aurelia Gomez
225 West 70 Street
New York, NY 10023
Phone: 212-555-3821
Email: agomez@nyu.edu

Enclosure

situation, you (and all others responding to that ad) have no choice but to address your letter to the newspaper and to use a generic salutation, such as "Dear Human Resources Manager." Insert a subject line to identify immediately the purpose of this important message.

Opening and body   The opening paragraph of a solicited application letter is fairly straightforward. Because the organization has advertised an opening, it is eager to receive quality applications, so use a direct organization: state (or imply) the reason for your letter, identify the particular position for which you are applying, and indicate how you learned about the opening.

Your opening should be short, interesting, and reader-oriented. Avoid tired openings such as "This is to apply for . . ." or "Please consider this letter my application for. . . ." Maintain an air of formality. Don't address the reader by a first name and don't try to be cute. Avoid such attention-grabbing (but unsuccessful) stunts as sending a worn, once-white running shoe with the note "Now that I have one foot in the door, I hope you'll let me get the other one in" or writing the application letter beginning at the bottom of the page and working upward (to indicate a willingness to start at the bottom and work one's way up). Such gimmicks send a nonverbal message to the reader that the applicant may be trying to deflect attention from a weak résumé.

Then, in a paragraph or two, highlight your strongest qualifications and show how they can benefit the employer. Show—don't tell; that is, provide specific, credible evidence to support your statements, using wording different from that used in the résumé. Tell an anecdote about yourself ("For example, recently I . . ."). Your discussion should reflect modest confidence rather than a hard-sell approach. Avoid starting too many sentences with *I*.

VAGUE: **I am an effective supervisor.**

REVISED: **Supervising a staff of five counter clerks taught me . . .**

Closing   You are not likely to get what you do not ask for, so close by asking for a personal interview. Indicate flexibility regarding scheduling and location. Provide your phone number and e-mail address, either in the last paragraph or immediately below your name and address in the closing lines.

After you have reviewed my qualifications, I would appreciate your letting me know when we can meet to discuss further my employment with Connecticut Power and Light. I will be in the Hartford area from December 16 through January 4 and could come to your office at any time that is convenient for you.

Or:

> I will call your office next week to see if we can arrange a meeting at your convenience to discuss my qualifications for working as a financial analyst with your organization.

Use a standard complimentary closing (such as "Sincerely"), leave enough space to sign the letter, and then type your name, address, phone number, and e-mail address. Even though you may be sending out many application letters at the same time, take care with each individual letter. You never know which one will be the one that actually gets you an interview. Sign your name neatly in blue or black ink, fold each letter and accompanying résumé neatly, and mail.

KEY POINTS
Checklist for Job Application Letters

1. Use your job application letter to show how the qualifications listed in your résumé have prepared you for the specific job for which you're applying.

2. If possible, address your letter to the individual in the organization who will interview you if you're successful.

3. When applying for an advertised opening, begin by stating the reason for the letter, identify the position for which you're applying, and tell how you learned about the opening.

4. When writing an unsolicited application letter, first gain the reader's attention by showing that you are familiar with the company and can make a unique contribution to its efforts.

5. In one or two paragraphs, highlight your strongest qualifications and relate them directly to the needs of the specific position for which you're applying. Refer the reader to the enclosed résumé.

6. Treat your letter as a persuasive sales letter: provide specific evidence, stress reader benefits, avoid exaggeration, and show confidence in the quality of your product.

7. Close by tactfully asking for an interview.

8. Maintain an air of formality throughout the letter. Avoid cuteness.

9. Make sure the finished document presents a professional, attractive, and conservative appearance and that it is 100 percent error-free.

14e Writing after the interview

After you have had an interview with a prospective employer, follow up with an immediate thank you note. (For a sample, see p. 292.) Send or fax a prompt, brief business letter to the interviewer (and anyone else you spoke to). Thank the person for his or her time, review your qualifications, and express your interest in the position and in further communication. Richard Nelson Bolles, author of the famous job-search manual *What Color Is Your Parachute?,* stresses the importance of writing a postinterview thank you note, citing seven reasons:

1. It indicates that you have good people skills.
2. It reminds the busy employer that you were there and who you are.
3. It can be circulated to other people in the organization who were not at the interview.
4. It allows you to say that you would be interested in talking further.
5. It gives you a chance to relay any point you may have forgotten to mention or to correct any miscommunication.
6. It can give you an advantage over other applicants for the same position who have not followed up with a thank you note.
7. It makes it easier, later, to ask the person who interviewed you for additional job leads, even if you do not get the job.

Taking the time to write a brief thank you note conveys that you are an organized, personable, and efficient person with good communication skills—often the very qualities that a potential employer is looking for.

15 Writing in the Work World

15a Writing business letters

Basic features of a business letter   A good business letter usu-ally has the following six qualities:

1. It is brief.
2. It clearly conveys to the reader information and expectations for action or response.
3. It lets the reader know how he or she will benefit from or be affected by the proposal or suggestion.
4. It is polite.
5. It is written in relatively formal language.
6. It contains no errors.

Interview Follow-up Letter
The interview follow-up letter should be written within a day or two of the job interview.

April 15, 2003

Mr. David Norman, Partner
Ross, Russell & Weston
452 Fifth Avenue
New York, NY 10018

Dear Mr. Norman:

Thank you for the opportunity to interview for the position of EDP specialist yesterday. I very much enjoyed meeting you and Arlene Worthington and learning more about the position and about Ross, Russell & Weston.

I especially appreciated the opportunity to observe the long-range planning meeting yesterday afternoon and to learn of your firm's plans for increasing your consulting practice with nonprofit agencies. My experience working in city government leads me to believe that nonprofit agencies can benefit greatly from your expertise.

Again, thank you for taking the time to visit with me yesterday. I look forward to hearing from you.

Sincerely

Aurelia Gomez

Aurelia Gomez
225 West 70 Street
New York, NY 10023
Phone: 212-555-3821
Email: agomez@nyu.edu

Annotations (left margin):

Addresses the person in the salutation as he or she was addressed during the interview

Begins directly, with an expression of appreciation

Mentions an incident that occurred and relates it to the writer's background

Closes on a confident, forward-looking note

WORLDS OF WRITING
Business Letters across Cultures

Basic features of business letters vary from culture to culture. Business letters in English avoid both flowery language and references to religion, elements that are viewed favorably in some other cultures. Do not assume that there are universal conventions. When writing cross-cultural business letters, follow these four suggestions:

1. Use a formal style; address correspondents by title and family name.

2. If possible, learn about the writing conventions of your correspondent's culture.

3. Use clear language and summary to get your point across.

4. Avoid humor; it may fall flat and could offend.

Technical requirements of a business letter

Paper and page numbering Use $8\frac{1}{2}" \times 11"$ white unlined paper. If your letter is longer than one page, number the pages beginning with page 2 in the top right margin.

Spacing Type single-spaced, on one side of the page only, and double-space between paragraphs. Double-space below the date, the inside address, and the salutation. Double-space between the last line of the letter and the closing. Quadruple-space between the closing and the typed name of the writer, and then double-space to *Enc.* (enclosing materials) or *cc:* (when sending a copy to another person).

Left and right margins The sample letter on p. 295 uses a block format: the return address, inside address, salutation, paragraphs, closing, and signature begin at the left margin. The right margin should not be justified; it should be ragged (with lines of unequal length) to avoid awkward gaps in the spacing between words. The modified block format places the return address and date, closing, and signature on the right.

Return address If you are not using business letterhead, give your address as the return address, followed by the date. Do not include your name with the address. If you are using business stationery on which an address is printed, you do not have to write a return address.

Inside address   The inside address gives the name, title, and complete address of the person you are writing to. With a word processing program and certain printers, you can use this part of the letter for addressing the envelope.

Salutation   In the salutation, mention the recipient's name if you know it, with the appropriate title (*Dr., Professor, Mr., Ms.*), or just the recipient's title (*Dear Sales Manager*). If you are writing to a company or institution, use a more general term of address (*Dear Sir or Madam*) or the name of the company or institution (*Dear Gateway 2000*). Use a colon after the salutation in a business letter.

Closing phrase and signature   Capitalize only the first word of a closing phrase, such as *Yours truly* or *Sincerely yours*. Type your name four lines below the closing phrase (omitting *Mr.* or *Ms.*). If you have a title (*Supervisor, Manager*), type it underneath your name. Between the closing phrase and your typed name, sign your name in ink.

Other information   Indicate whether you have enclosed materials with the letter (*Enc.*) and to whom you have sent copies (*cc: Ms. Amy Ray*). The abbreviation *cc:* used to refer to *carbon copy* but now refers to *courtesy copy* or *computer copy.* You may, however, use a single *c:* followed by a name or names, to indicate who besides your addressee is receiving the letter.

Envelope   Choose an envelope that fits your letter folded from bottom to top in thirds. Use your computer's addressing capability to place the name, title, and full address of the recipient in the middle of the envelope, and your own name and address in the top left-hand corner. Include ZIP codes. Word processing programs include a function (Tools) that allows you to create labels for envelopes.

   Businesses frequently use e-mail to conduct correspondence. In a business letter sent by e-mail, be just as careful about style, editing, and proofreading as you would be in a hard-copy version. You do not want to be seen as someone who litters correspondence with grammatical errors. Your mistakes may only be typographical errors. But how will the recipient know that?

Sample business letter   The sample letter on page 295 uses a block format, with all parts aligned at the left. This format is commonly used with business stationery.

Standard Business Letter

This letter is shown in block style with standard punctuation.

November 1, 20— ↓ 4

The arrows indicate how many lines to space down before typing the next part. For example, ↓ 4 after the date means to press Enter four times before typing the recipient's name.

Ms. Ella Shore, Professor
Department of Journalism
Burlington College
North Canyon Drive
South Burlington, VT 05403 ↓ 2

Dear Ms. Shore: ↓ 2

Subject: Newspaper Advertising

Thank you for thinking of Ben & Jerry's when you were planning the advertising for the back-to-school edition of your campus newspaper at Mountainside College. We appreciate the wide acceptance your students and faculty give our products, and we are proud to be represented in the *Mountain Lark*. We are happy to purchase a quarter-page ad, as follows.

• The ad should include our standard logo and the words "Welcome to Ben & Jerry's." Please note the use of the ampersand instead of the word "and" in our name. Note also that "Jerry's" contains an apostrophe.

• We would prefer that our ad appear in the top right corner of a right-facing page, if possible.

Our logo is enclosed for you to duplicate. I am also enclosing a check for $375 to cover the cost of the ad. Best wishes as you publish this special edition of your newspaper. ↓ 2

Sincerely, ↓ 4

Joseph W. Dye

Joseph W. Dye
Sales Manager ↓ 2

rmt
Enclosures
c: Advertising Supervisor

Reference initials: initials of the person who typed the letter (if other than the signer)
Notations: indications of items being enclosed with the letter, copies of the letter being sent to another person, special-delivery instructions, and the like

30 Community Drive • South Burlington, Vermont • 05403-6828 • Tel: 802/846-1500 • www.benjerry.com

15b Writing business memos

Basic features of a memo A memo (from the Latin *memorandum,* meaning "to be remembered") is a message from one person to someone else within an organization. It can be sent on paper or by e-mail. A memo usually reports briefly on an action, raises a question, or asks permission to follow a course of action. It addresses a specific question or issue in a quick, focused way, conveying information in clear paragraphs or numbered points.

Standard Memorandum
A memorandum is sent to someone within the same organization.

Barnes & Noble Inc.
Booksellers Since 1873
122 Fifth Avenue New York, NY 10011
(212) 633-3300

→ TAB

MEMO TO: Max Dillon, Sales Manager ↓ 2

FROM: Andrea J. Hayes ↓ 2 *ajh*

DATE: February 25, 20— ↓ 2

SUBJECT: New-Venture Proposal ↓ 3

Heading

The arrows indicate how many lines to space down before typing the next part. For example, ↓ 2 after the date means to press Enter twice before typing the recipient's name.

Body

I propose the purchase or lease of a van to be used as a mobile bookstore. We could then use this van to generate sales in the outlying towns and villages throughout the state.

We have been aware for quite some time that many small towns around the state do not have adequate bookstore facilities, but the economics of the situation are such that we would not be able to open a comprehensive branch and operate it profitably. However, we could afford to stock a van with books and operate it for a few days at a time in various small towns throughout the state. As you are probably aware, the laws of this state would permit us to acquire a statewide business license fairly easily and inexpensively.

With the proper advance advertising (see attached sample), we should be able to generate much interest in this endeavor. It seems to me that this idea has much merit because of the flexibility it offers us. For example, we could tailor the length of our stay to the size of the town and the amount of business generated. Also, we could customize our inventory to the needs and interests of the particular locales.

The driver of the van would act as the salesperson, and we would, of course, have copies of our complete catalog so that mail orders could be taken as well. Please let me have your reactions to this proposal. If you wish, I can explore the matter further and generate cost and sales estimates in time for your next manager's meeting. ↓ 2

Reference initials
Attachment notation

jmc
Attachments

Begin a memo with headings such as *To, From, Date,* and *Subject;* such headings are frequently capitalized and in boldface type. In the first sentence, tell readers what your point is. Then briefly explain, giving reasons or details. Single-space the memo. If your message is long, divide it into short paragraphs or include numbered or bulleted lists and headings (see **10d**) to organize and draw attention to essential points. Many computer programs provide a standard program for memo format. The design and headings are provided; all you do is fill in what you want to say.

15c Preparing business presentations: PowerPoint and other tools

When you have to give an oral presentation, a useful tool is presentation software such as Microsoft PowerPoint, in its Office suite of programs, or Corel Presentations. These programs allow you to create and save slides to accompany your oral presentation. For general guidelines for oral presentations, see **8g.**

The value of a multimedia (PowerPoint) presentation Using a tool like PowerPoint to prepare a presentation gives you access to organizing tools. As the name suggests, PowerPoint forces you to think of your main points and organize them. Preparing slides that illustrate the logic of your talk helps you separate the main points from the supporting details, and the slides keep you focused as you give your presentation. Your audience follows your ideas not only because you have established a clear principle of organization, but also because the slide on the presentation screen reminds them of where you are in your talk, what point you are addressing, and how that point fits into your total scheme. Presentation software also allows you to include sound, music, and movie clips to illustrate and drive home the points you want to make.

Preparation The illustration on page 298 shows a PowerPoint screen (Office 2000, 9.0), with its choices of format for a slide: you can select anything from a title slide, a bulleted list, a table, a graph, text and graph, an organization chart, clip art and text, to a blank screen. Toolbars provide you with the means to insert your content into the slide you choose: text, line drawing, line types, shapes, and color. Additional toolbars make it possible to insert a graph, clip art, and animation effects, such as a text line dropping in from the side or top, flying in, appearing one letter at a time, or flashing.

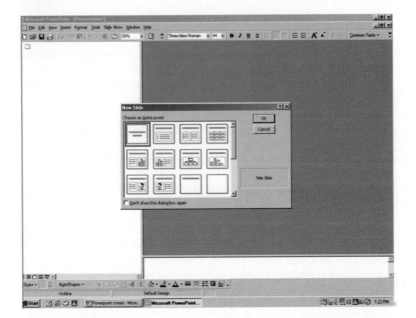

The slides you prepare can be used as a basis for overhead transparencies or 35 mm slides, as handouts, or as outlines for the audience or yourself. But the best use of the slides is direct projection from the computer onto a large screen.

You can import material from Microsoft Word and Microsoft Excel into a PowerPoint slide. PowerPoint comes with a self-paced tutorial, too.

Presentation A computer with your PowerPoint slides can be connected to a screen for your presentation. Once you have prepared, sorted, and saved your slides, you can access them with a click. A slide can diagram the structure of your talk or provide material to support the points you make.

A PowerPoint specialist has advised, "If you have something to show, use PowerPoint." *Show* is the important word. Do not expect your audience to read a lot of text. PowerPoint is not for writing paragraphs and essays. It's for getting the audience's attention with the main points and illustrative details. Outlines, bulleted points, tables, pie charts, and graphs are what PowerPoint does well.

Sample slides The two PowerPoint slides shown on page 299 were prepared by New York City agencies. The first, designed by a member of the Municipal Water Finance Authority, outlines three

New York City

- Vast system of waterways
- Water quality monitored daily
- Sewage treatment plants throughout system

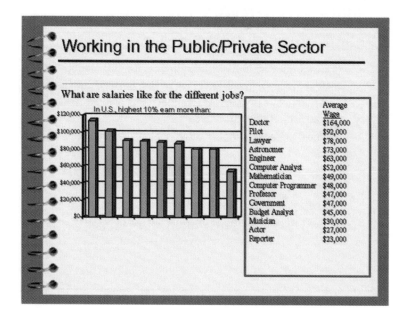

Working in the Public/Private Sector

What are salaries like for the different jobs?

In U.S., highest 10% earn more than:

	Average Wage
Doctor	$164,000
Pilot	$92,000
Lawyer	$78,000
Astronomer	$73,000
Engineer	$63,000
Computer Analyst	$52,000
Mathematician	$49,000
Computer Programmer	$48,000
Professor	$47,000
Government	$47,000
Budget Analyst	$45,000
Musician	$30,000
Actor	$27,000
Reporter	$23,000

major points to be covered by a presentation and discussion, along with an illustrative map to accompany the presentation. The second, part of a presentation on employment in the public sector given by the chief economist at the New York City Office of Management and Budget, shows complex data illustrating how government employees and budget analysts fare in an earnings comparison.

The following material was prepared by Mary Rose Quinn, a librarian at the Saugus Public Library. In her own words, here is her account of developing a presentation that she gave at a conference.

My presentation was part of a panel discussion that I gave, with three colleagues, on wireless technology for the Massachusetts Library Association Annual Conference. We each had about 20 minutes. The audience was librarians who were investigating wireless networks for their own libraries.

- In planning and preparing this presentation, I first opened PowerPoint, selected Design Template, clicked on Presentations, and looked among the generic business-oriented templates that are available there. I was looking for the PowerPoint outlines that I thought would best fit or match with the content and aims of my presentation and that I could use as a guide.

Wireless Project Overview

- Wireless access is available at SPL for the public
  - Allows patrons to use their own equipment with wireless LAN adapters or standard Ethernet cards and our "bridge" to access library resources
  - Allows patrons to borrow library laptops to conduct research
  - Provides additional access to online resources at peak library use times
  - Provides access in additional places/spaces in the library where hard-wired systems are not possible or practical

Features & Benefits - Education

- A student may borrow a wireless laptop after school in the Homework Center to complete a history project using the databases provided by the state, region, or library
  - He/she may print out the project on the network printer available to both wireless and wired users or copy it to disk, or e-mail the information
  - The assignment outline is available to the student on the library's Homework Zone Site

- I soon decided to choose PowerPoint's outline entitled "Product and Services Overview" because that was what I was going to do—give an overview of a product and a service, namely our wireless networking program. This outline provided the background and borders for the slides and the overall framework for my presentation. Into that, I cut and pasted several slides from two other templates: the "Recommending a Strategy" and the "Project Overview" files.

- I then filled in local details of my topic, the Saugus wireless network project, over the sample information provided in the PowerPoint template.

- After developing the basic outline of my talk, I photographed areas in the library with the library's digital camera, available for loan. The pictures were then stored on a floppy disk.

- I copied the pictures from the floppy disk into the My Documents folder so I could later "Insert" the pictures into the appropriate slide. (To include pictures, from the Insert drop-down menu, choose Image, then Select File, and from File, find the picture you wish to insert.)

- Some pictures I overlapped for a collage effect. The beauty of PowerPoint is that you can resize the pictures to fit your slide. I also used a few clip art items that I downloaded from an images site on the Internet, using .gif or .jpeg files. Usually, right-clicking on the picture and using Save As downloads and saves the graphic.

- Next, I prepared my handouts for the presentation, both detailed copies of the points I was going to cover (so people would not have to take notes), and copies of other instructional material and promotional flyers that we developed at our library.

- Finally, I practiced the presentation until I felt comfortable and could deliver it smoothly. I think in the end I was successful in giving the audience a quick look at real-life wireless applications in a new building.

Sentences

Accuracy and Style

Science fiction writer and editor Teresa Neilson Hayden, in *Making Book,* characterizes English as "a generous, expansive, and flexible language," but adds, "a less charitable description would characterize it as drunk and disorderly." The task of editing, she claims, is to try to impose "a degree of regularity on something that is inherently irregular." What exists to help you move away from irregularities that appear in your writing is a set of conventions that go under the label of Standard English.

The American Heritage Dictionary defines Standard English as "the variety of English that is generally acknowledged as the model for the speech and writing of educated speakers." This variety of English, with all its quirks, irregularities, rules, and exceptions, may be politically and sociologically branded as the language of those in power in society; nevertheless, its practices are what readers expect in the academic and business worlds. Writing instructors often hear students complain that making changes in their writing to conform to Standard English hinders their creativity. But in fact, being creative and meeting readers' expectations are not mutually exclusive aims.

Whether you write in a college course, a business setting, or in your local community, and whether you present your ideas on paper or on the screen, paying close attention to the clarity, style, and accuracy of your work always pays off. Readers who expect Standard English will get distracted and aggravated by awkward turns of phrase, grammatical errors, inappropriate word choice, convoluted sentences, misleading punctuation, and spelling errors; they may even lose interest and give up. However insightful and original your ideas may be, readers will soon become impatient if those ideas are not expressed in sentences that follow conventions determined by the history of the language and the prescriptive power of its educated users.

In sections 16–46, you will find answers to common questions about correct grammar, punctuation, style, and usage. You will also find passages labeled "Variation" that recognize language change and writers' flexibility in the face of so-called *rules* of language.

16 How a Sentence Works

When you write, you use words to form sentences, sentences to form paragraphs, and paragraphs to give shape and logic to a document. The structure of a sentence is governed by conventions of English that readers expect to see followed.

16a Parts of speech

The words that make up sentences are traditionally classified into eight types, called **parts of speech.** Note that the part of speech is attached not to a word but to its function in a sentence. Some words can function as several different parts of speech:

▶ They *respect* their boss. [*Respect* is here a verb.]

▶ *Respect* is a large part of a business relationship.

[*Respect* is here a noun.]

Nouns Words that name a person, place, thing, or concept are called **nouns.**

TYPES OF NOUNS

Type of noun	Function	Examples
COMMON		
Countable (**42a**)	Names people, places, objects, concepts; can be counted; has a plural form, usually with -s or -es, though some are irregular	teacher/teachers, party/parties, leaf/leaves, proposal/proposals, dish/dishes, man/men, goose/geese

(continued)

TYPES OF NOUNS (continued)

Type of noun	Function	Examples
COMMON		
Uncountable (**42b**)	Names a mass or an abstraction; cannot be counted; has no plural form	furniture, money, rice, advice, information, happiness
Collective (**21g**)	Names a group	family, society, clergy
Compound (**21h**)	Names a person or thing by using several parts of speech in combination	toothbrush, mother-in-law, passerby, cover-up
Noun derived from verb, with -ing (**21e**)	Names an action; used as subject or object of a verb or preposition	*Swimming* is healthy. She likes *swimming.* She bought flippers for *swimming. But not:* He is swimming across the lake. [Here *swimming* is part of the verb.]
PROPER		
Name (**42f**)	Names a specific person, place, or thing; needs capital letters for main words	Harry Potter, the Empire State Building, Hinduism, Shakespeare, Italy, Italians

A noun is often used with other words to form a noun phrase. These other words include an article (*a, an, the*), a possessive pronoun (*my, your, his, her, its, our, their*), a demonstrative (*this, that, these, those*), numbers, quantity words, adjectives, and adjective phrases. The following are noun phrases: *a difficult problem, his aged parents, six broken computers, these impossibly dilapidated barns, complex information.*

Pronouns A **pronoun** is a word that stands in for and refers to a noun, a noun phrase, or another pronoun. Examples include *it, she, his, those, themselves, whom, whoever, anyone.*

In writing, a pronoun usually refers to a noun phrase stated just before it in the text (its antecedent—**22d**).

noun phrase antecedent
                                        pronoun
▶ My sister loves shoes. She bought three pairs last week.

Pronouns are of several types. Illustrations follow.

PERSONAL PRONOUNS

Type of personal pronoun	Function	Examples
Subject form (**22a**) *I, you, he, she, it, we, they*	Refers to a specific person, place, or thing known to the reader; forms the subject of the verb	The director is leaving. *She* promises to return.
Object form (**22a**) *me, you, him, her, it, us, them*	Refers to a specific person, place, or thing known to the reader; forms the object of the verb or preposition	Maria knows Michalis well. She likes *him.*
Possessive form (**22b**) Adjective (used with a noun): *my, your, his, her, its, our, their*	Answers the question "Whose?" and tells whom something belongs to or is attached to	The accident is *their* fault.
Stand-alone pronoun: *mine, yours, his, hers, ours, theirs*		The twins paid for the skateboard. It is clearly *theirs.*
Intensive (**22h**) *myself, yourself, himself, herself, oneself, itself, ourselves, yourselves, themselves*	Emphasizes stated noun or pronoun	The mayor *himself* was at the scene immediately.
Reflexive (**22h**) *myself, yourself, himself, herself, oneself, itself, ourselves, yourselves, themselves*	Refers to person or thing receiving the action, the same person or thing who does the action	The president incriminated *himself* in his testimony. Cells reproduce *themselves.*

See the Key Points box on page 443 for the forms of personal pronouns.

OTHER PRONOUNS

Type of pronoun	Function	Examples
Demonstrative (**21j**) Singular: *this, that* Plural: *these, those*	Identifies and refers to a noun phrase or a clause nearby in the text	The firm offers free computer training. We advise you to sign up for *this.*

(continued)

OTHER PRONOUNS *(continued)*

Type of pronoun	Function	Examples
Relative (**24a**) *who, whom, whose, which, that*	Introduces a dependent relative clause by making reference to a stated noun or pronoun	People *who* live in the city can walk their dogs in the park.
Pronoun beginning a noun clause (**16e**) *whoever, whomever, whichever, what, whatever*	Makes a reference to something or someone	*Whoever* guesses accurately wins the prize. She praises *whatever* her students write.
Interrogative (**22i**) *who, whom, what, whose, which, whoever, whomever*	Introduces a question	*Who* wrote that article? *What* can we deduce?
Indefinite *anyone, somebody, everyone, nobody, anything, none, some* (for a full list, see **21i**)	Makes a nonspecific reference; some indefinite pronouns are singular and some are plural	*Something* is about to happen. Most students know the rules; *some* do not. *Everyone* is celebrating.
Reciprocal *each other, one another*	Refers to one part of a plural antecedent	The sisters look after *each other*.

Verbs   A **verb** is a word that tells about actions or states of being, often with the help of auxiliary verbs (forms of *do, be,* and *have;* and *will, would, can, could, shall, should, may, might,* and *must*):

- An **active verb** tells what a subject (a person, place, thing, or concept) does. It tells about an action: The puppy *is barking.* The proposal *created* unusual possibilities.

- A **passive verb** tells what is done to a subject: The proposal *was contested.* The cake *has been eaten.*

- A **linking verb** tells what a subject is, seems, becomes, looks, or appears. It tells about a state of being. It links the subject to a word or idea that describes or renames it: They *are* happy. He *seems* efficient. Julia *became* captain of the team.

A verb is a necessary part of a sentence. A **complete verb** is made up of a **main verb** along with any auxiliaries necessary to indicate person, number, tense, mood, and voice. Forms such as *to see, seeing,* and *seen* are not complete (or *finite*) forms; they cannot function as the complete verb of a clause.

The complete verb and the main verb

- Every complete verb phrase ends with the main verb:

		PREDICATE	
	COMPLETE VERB PHRASE		
SUBJECT		MAIN VERB	REST OF PREDICATE
The athletes		practiced	every day last week.
They	have been	practicing	all day today.
He	should	practice	this week.
She	is	practicing	in the gym.

- Auxiliary verbs often are needed with a main verb to form a complete verb phrase:

	PREDICATE		
	COMPLETE VERB PHRASE		
SUBJECT	AUXILIARY VERB	MAIN VERB	REST OF PREDICATE
They	have been	recognized.	
She	did	recognize	him.
He	was	wearing	a disguise.

- Modal auxiliary verbs provide nuances of meaning, such as intention, ability, permission, advisability, necessity, and expectation (see **43b**). The modal auxiliaries, which can be used with other auxiliaries, are *will, would, can, could, shall, should, may, might,* and *must.* Note that a modal is always immediately followed by a base form (*have, be,* and *take* in the following examples):

	PREDICATE			
	COMPLETE VERB PHRASE			
SUBJECT	MODAL AUXILIARY	AUXILIARY VERB	MAIN VERB	REST OF PREDICATE
They	might	have been	driving	too fast.
The car	should	be	repaired	right away.
You	must		take	driving lessons.

Features of verbs

1. The base form (the form found in the dictionary) of a verb fills the slot in sentences like this: They will _____. It might _____.

2. A verb has five forms (**20b**):
   - a base (no -*s*) form (*sing*)
   - an -*s* form (*sings*)
   - an -*ing* form (*singing*)
   - a past tense form (*sang*)
   - a past participle form (*sung*)

3. Both the past tense and the past participle forms of regular verbs, such as *decide, watch, talk,* and *play,* end in -*d* or -*ed:* decid*ed,* watch*ed,* talk*ed,* play*ed.* The past tense and past participle of irregular verbs, such as *bring, ride, write,* and *quit,* are formed in different ways: *brought, brought; rode, ridden; wrote, written; quit, quit.*

4. A complete verb—a main verb with any necessary auxiliaries—indicates tense (present, past, and future) and aspect (progressive or perfect):
   - Present, past, and future: *walk, walked, will walk; sing, sang, will sing*
   - Progressive aspect: *was running, will be traveling, are working*
   - Perfect aspect: *has watched, should have examined*
   - Perfect progressive aspect: *has been considering, will have been writing, might have been complaining*

5. In the present tense, a main or auxiliary verb generally changes form to reflect person (*I, you, he/she/it, we, they*) and number (singular and plural) (**21a**): I *am,* you *are,* he *is;* the children *walk,* the child *walks.*

6. A verb that can be followed by a direct object can show active or passive voice (**20l**):
   - Active: The dog bit the intruder. [The dog does the action—biting.]
   - Passive: The intruder *was bitten* by the dog. [The subject of the sentence, *the intruder,* had something done to him—he did not do the biting.]

7. A verb indicates mood:
   - Indicative mood in a statement or question: He *goes* to church every week. *Do* they *go* to church every week?
   - Imperative mood in a command: *Go* away!
   - Subjunctive mood expressing a speculation about a hypothetical condition, a wish, a request, a demand, a recommendation (**20k**): If they *went* on vacation, they would feel better.

8. A verb is either transitive (it is followed by a direct object) or intransitive (with no direct object):

direct object
▶ **Their generosity** *surprises* **us every day.** [Transitive verb]

▶ **Accidents** *happen.* [Intransitive verb]

9. A verb has forms that cannot function as a complete main verb. These forms, known as **verbals,** are the infinitive form (*to go, to see,* and so on), the *-ing* form used as a noun or an adjective, and the *-ed* form used as an adjective. For more on these forms, see **43c–43f.**

Adjectives   **Adjectives** are words that provide information about nouns and pronouns. They do not take a plural *-s* ending, though some have a different plural form—for example, *this* car; *these* cars.

Features of adjectives

1. Adjectives describe (*purple* boots), point to (*those* boots), or tell the quantity of (*some* boots) nouns and pronouns.

2. Adjectives precede nouns or follow linking verbs: He is wearing *purple* boots. His boots are *purple.*

3. Descriptive adjectives have comparative and superlative forms: *big, bigger, biggest; helpful, less helpful, least helpful.*

4. Some adjectives function as limiting adjectives or determiners:

   • Articles: *a, an,* and *the: a* scarred old elm tree

   • Demonstratives: *this, that, these,* and *those: this* tickly red feather boa

   • Numerical determiners: *one, two, first, second,* and so on: the *Fifth* Amendment

   • Interrogative: *who, which, what, whose: Which* chapter did you read?

   • Possessive: *my, your, his, her, its, our, their: His* day will come.

   • Quantity: *each, few, other, some, many, much: Much* time has elapsed.

Some words can function as adjectives in one context and as pronouns in other contexts.

adjective
▶ **Many cars have been sold.**

pronoun (no following noun)
▶ **The cars are on sale. Many were sold last week.**

For more on adjectives, see **23.**

Adverbs   **Adverbs** provide information about verbs, adjectives, other adverbs, and some kinds of clauses. They answer one of the following questions: *When? Where? Why? How? Under what conditions?* and *To what extent?*

Features of adverbs

1. Many adverbs end in *-ly: quickly, immediately, intelligently.*
2. Some common adverbs do not end in *-ly: not, very, well,* and "time" adverbs such as *always, soon, often, sometimes, first,* and *never.*
3. Adverbs modify verbs, adjectives, adverbs, and clauses.

modifies verb

▶ Allen Iverson dunked *brilliantly.*

modifies adjective

▶ Iverson is an *extremely* energetic player.

modifies adverb

▶ Iverson played *spectacularly* well.

modifies whole clause

▶ *Undoubtedly,* Iverson is a player with promise.

4. Adverbs usually use *more* and *most* and *less* and *least* to form comparisons: *more efficiently, less eagerly, most aggressively, least confidently.*
5. Adverbs that modify a whole clause and signify its relationship to the previous clause are known as **conjunctive adverbs.** (See the accompanying chart.) They are used as transitional expressions to connect ideas within a sentence or among sentences. For the punctuation to use with conjunctive adverbs, see **26e.**

CONJUNCTIVE ADVERBS

Conjunctive adverbs	Function
also, besides, furthermore, incidentally, moreover	To add an idea
however, nevertheless, nonetheless, conversely, rather	To point out a contrast
alternatively, instead, otherwise	To provide an alternative
similarly, likewise	To show similarity
first, second (and so on), *next, then, subsequently, meanwhile, previously, finally*	To show time, order, and sequence
therefore, consequently, accordingly, thus, hence	To show result
certainly, indeed	To affirm with emphasis

See also **5e** for a Key Points box showing transitional expressions, including conjunctive adverbs.

Conjunctions   Conjunctions are words that "join together." They connect two or more similar parts of a sentence—that is, words, phrases, or clauses.

What conjunctions do

1. **Coordinating conjunctions** connect two sentence elements of similar type and equal weight:

   Two words: ham *and* eggs

   Two phrases: She cannot decide whether to fly to Florida *or* to take the train.

   Two clauses: He tore a ligament, *so* he dropped out of the race.

   The coordinating conjunctions are *and, but, or, nor, so, for,* and *yet.*

2. **Subordinating conjunctions** connect two clauses of unequal weight—that is, one is an independent clause, and the other is dependent on and subordinate to that clause. The conjunction specifies the logical relationship between the two clauses, answering questions such as the following:

   WHEN? *Before* they left, they changed dollars to Euros.

   After they arrived, they went straight to bed.

   When they saw their hotel, they were ecstatic.

   Until they saw Venice, they had been car fanatics.

   WHY? *Because* they had enough money, they had one meal at the best restaurant in town.

   UNDER WHAT CONDITIONS? *If* they can, they will return next year.
   See **16e** for a list of subordinating conjunctions.

3. **Correlative conjunctions** work in pairs to connect equivalent grammatical elements: *either/or, neither/nor, both/and, not only/but also:*

   Neither whales *nor* dolphins are fish.

   His firm has moved, so *either* he will have to change jobs *or* commuting will become a big part of his life.

Prepositions   Prepositions—often little words—convey details about relationships. A preposition connects a noun, pronoun, or other noun equivalent to another noun, pronoun, or noun equivalent, such as a noun clause or an *-ing* form. Every preposition is part of a prepositional phrase that serves as an adjective or adverb.

> preposition   preposition   preposition
> ▶ **At dawn, a bird with a red crest flew into the open doorway.**

Some common prepositions are

about	before	from	regarding
above	behind	in	through
across	below	into	to
after	beneath	like	toward
against	between	off	under
among	by	on	until
around	during	outside	without
as	except	over	
at	for	past	

Prepositional phrases are often idiomatic: *on occasion, in love.* To understand their use and meaning, consult a good dictionary. See also **45** ESL.

Interjections   Words that express emotion and can stand alone—*Ha! Wow! Ugh! Ouch! Say!*—are called **interjections.** Interjections are not used frequently in academic writing. The more formal ones (such as *alas, oh*) are sometimes used in poetry:

> But she is in her grave, and, oh,
> The difference to me!
>
> —William Wordsworth

EXERCISE 16.1 Identify parts of speech.
On the lines after each sentence, identify the two parts of speech that are underlined in the sentence.

EXAMPLE:

Nelson <u>Mandela</u>, the former president of South Africa, spent nearly thirty years in prison <u>for</u> his work to end apartheid.

    Mandela   <u> noun </u>

    for   <u> preposition </u>

1. <u>He</u> <u>wrote</u> an autobiography called *Long Walk to Freedom.*

    He   <u>   </u>

    wrote   <u>   </u>

2. In his book, Mandela says, "I am not <u>truly</u> free if I am taking away someone else's freedom, just as surely as I am not free when my freedom is taken away from <u>me</u>."

   truly _____

   me _____

3. <u>Many</u> additional writers have also used their talents to fight for <u>freedom</u> for themselves and others.

   many _____

   freedom _____

4. Writers such as Frederick Douglass, Aleksandr Solzhenitsyn, <u>and</u> Mary Wollstonecraft called attention <u>to</u> injustices that they saw around them.

   and _____

   to _____

5. The Lithuanian poet Czeslaw Milosz <u>once</u> asked, "What <u>is</u> poetry which does not save nations and peoples?"

   once _____

   is _____

Segregated beach

Nelson Mandela

16b What a sentence is, needs, and does

What a sentence is   You have probably heard various definitions of a sentence, the common one being that a "a sentence is a complete thought." Sometimes it is. Sometimes it is not, depending on what one expects by "complete." In fact, that definition is not particularly helpful. How complete is this thought?

▶ **He did not.**

You probably do not regard it as complete because it relies on text around it, on other sentences, to tell what it was he did not do.

▶ **She always made an effort to be punctual. He did not.**

Still, it is a grammatically correct sentence.

What a sentence needs

KEY POINTS

The Necessary Features of a Written English Sentence

1. It begins with a capital letter.
2. It ends with a period (a "full stop" in British English), question mark, or exclamation point. A semicolon can provide a partial ending, taking readers on to the next idea without a full stop.
3. It must contain at the very least a subject (noun, pronoun, noun clause, infinitive, or -*ing* form, or an implied *you* subject as in "Run!") and a predicate in an independent clause telling *who* or what *does* (or *is*) [what]. The predicate must contain a complete verb, as indicated in the chart in italics:

SUBJECT	VERB + REST OF PREDICATE
Birds	*sing.*
Max	*was* tired.
Everyone	*wants* security.
The driver	*had forgotten* to signal.
His three sisters	*sent* him a hammock.
Bills and mortgage payments	*must have consumed* most of his salary.
Skating	*can be* wonderful exercise.
What you wrote	*should have been edited.*

Sentences like these, with no attachments to the basic subject + predicate framework are called *simple sentences*. See **16c** for patterns of simple sentences and see **16f** for other sentence types.

4. Modifying words, phrases, and clauses can be attached to the subject + predicate framework of the simple sentence.

──── independent clause ────
──── subject ────   ┌─ predicate ─┐
▶ The birds on the branch outside my window sing loudly
──── dependent clause ────
subject ┌──── predicate ────┐
whenever I fill the feeder with seeds.

──── phrase ────
▶ After playing with his brother for three hours and
──── ind. clause ────
subject ┌─ predicate ─┐   │ subject ┌──
running all over the beach, Max was so tired that he fell
dependent
──── clause ────
──── predicate ────
asleep instantly.

Read more about writing complete sentences and avoiding sentence fragments in **18**. For more on adding words, phrases, and clauses to a simple sentence, turn to **16d, 16e,** and **16g**.

What a sentence does   A sentence can function as a statement, question, command, or exclamation.

SENTENCE FUNCTIONS

Sentence function	What it does	Example
Declarative	Makes a statement	Lower interest rates help home buyers.
Interrogative	Asks a question	Who can afford to buy a house on the beach?
Imperative	Gives a command	Watch this space.
Exclamatory	Expresses surprise or emotion	This expensive restaurant has had no fewer than fifteen violations!

Most of the sentences in expository and academic writing are declarative statements, though an occasional question is useful to draw readers into thinking about a topic. An occasional exclamatory sentence can be powerful, too, but bear in mind that, according to *The New York Times Manual of Style and Usage,* "When overused, the exclamation point loses impact, as advertising demonstrates continually."

ESL NOTE Language and Sentence Structure

The shape of a sentence varies from language to language—in German, for instance, the verb does not necessarily follow the subject (*Gestern habe ich ihm einen Brief geschrieben* is literally translated as *Yesterday have I him a letter written*). In other words, the structure of a sentence is not fixed across languages. If English is not your native language, keep its basic structures in mind as you write and revise. Use your first language to help you with ideas, but avoid transferring sentences from one language to another without first reminding yourself of the features of words and sentences in English. ■

16c The basis of a sentence: subject and predicate

A sentence in English minimally consists of a **subject** (person, place, thing, or concept) that is doing an action, is being something, or is being acted upon in the **predicate.** The predicate makes a comment or assertion about the subject.

▶ **A huge storm rattled the windows.**

[A thing doing the action]

▶ **Physics is a challenging subject.**

[A concept being something]

▶ **The president was impeached.**

[A person being acted upon; somebody else did the impeaching]

A simple subject is one word (*storm, physics, president*); a complete subject includes the simple subject and all its modifiers (*a huge storm, the president*). A predicate must always include a main verb or auxiliaries with a main verb, such as *sit, sat, will sit, persuades, persuaded, might persuade, should be working, must have been built,* along with any modifiers and any objects or complements.

Finding the subject To test what the subject of a sentence is, ask a question about the verb. This questioning is easy with a short simple sentence:

verb
▶ **Henry smiled.**

[Who smiled? Henry. *Henry* is the subject of the sentence.]

verb
▶ **Laura is pregnant.**

[Who is pregnant? Laura. *Laura* is the subject of the sentence.]

▶ The ball was thrown. *(verb over "was thrown")*

[What was thrown? The ball. *The ball* is the complete subject.]

These sentences have simple subjects, just one or two words. Often, though, a subject consists of more than just the simple subject of one word. Again, to determine what the simple subject is, ask a question about the verb and shrink the answer down to one word.

▶ **His new boss left.**

Who left? His new *boss.* [The complete subject is *His new boss.*]
   When you ask the same question about the much longer simple sentence that follows, the answer is still the same simple subject:

▶ The *boss* of the successful new computer company *left* the

elegantly furnished conference room.

(annotations: simple subject — complete subject — verb; predicate)

Compound subjects and compound predicates   A subject may consist of two or more nouns, pronouns, or other noun substitutes (infinitives, *-ing* forms, noun clauses) usually joined by *and.*

▶ *Juan and Rafael* **fell asleep.** *(compound subject)*

▶ *Li Chen and I* **waded in the ocean.** *(compound subject)*

Similarly, a predicate may consist of two or more verbs, known as a **compound predicate**:

▶ Li Chen and I *waded in the ocean and collected shells.* *(compound predicate)*

EXERCISE 16.2   Identify the subject and predicate in a simple sentence.
In each of the following sentences, underline the complete subject once and underline the predicate twice. Then write *S* over the simple subject and *V* over the verb. Remember that the verb may consist of more than one word and that sentences can have more than one subject or verb.

EXAMPLE:

                S   V
Many people in the United States carry too much credit-card debt.

1. Most experts consider some types of debt, such as a mortgage, financially necessary.

2. However, credit-card debt never benefits an individual's long-term financial goals.

3. Today even college students without jobs or credit records can usually acquire credit cards easily.

4. Unfortunately, many students charge expensive purchases and pay only the minimum balance on their cards every month.

5. Graduating from college with a large credit-card debt can severely limit a person's opportunities.

Seven basic predicate patterns Here are seven common predicate patterns (the components of the predicate appear in brackets).

1. Subject + Predicate [Verb] The basic pattern for a simple statement in English is a simple subject followed by a predicate consisting only of a verb.

    S   V
▶ **Babies cry.**

    S   ┌────V────┐
▶ **The book was published.**

Even when elements are added to the simple sentence, the subject and verb maintain their key positions.

    simple subject
┌──────────────── S ────────────────┐ ┌── V ──┐
▶ **All the *babies* in the hospital nursery *are crying*.**

┌──────────── complete subject ────────────┐
│   simple subject   │
▶ **The sensational book about Hollywood in its heyday**
┌── verb ──┐
was published by the company that also runs a major studio.

 ESL NOTE Subject and Verb across Languages

Not all languages require a subject and a verb. English requires both, except in a command. See **44a** ESL. ▪

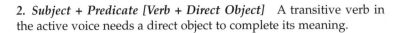

2. Subject + Predicate [Verb + Direct Object] A transitive verb in the active voice needs a direct object to complete its meaning.

> ┌── S ──┐ V DO
> ► **Many people wear glasses.**

In this sentence, the direct object (DO) completes the meaning of the verb by telling what many people wear. Verbs that take a direct object are known as transitive verbs. To identify a direct object, ask *Who[m]?* or *What?* about the verb:

> ┌────────────────── S ──────────────────┐
> ► **The *artist* who lives in the large apartment on the sixth floor**
>
> V ┌──────── DO ────────┐
> *owns* **five cute Weimaraner *puppies*.**

[What does he own? *Five cute Weimaraner puppies* is the direct object.]

Intransitive verbs, such as *lie* (meaning "recline"), *sit*, and *rise*, do not take a direct object.

3. Subject + Predicate [Verb + Subject Complement] Some verbs, such as *be, seem, become, look,* and *appear,* are linking verbs. They are followed by a noun or an adjective phrase that refers to and renames or describes the subject. This noun or adjective phrase is known as a subject complement (SC).

> S V SC
> ► **George is the president of the club.**

> S V SC
> ► **The president of the club is George.**

> ┌──────── S ────────┐ V SC
> ► **The *players* on the visiting team look fit.**

4. Subject + Predicate [Verb + Indirect Object + Direct Object] Some transitive verbs, such as *give, send,* and *offer,* can be followed by an indirect object (IO), naming the person or thing to whom or for whom the action of the verb takes place, and by a direct object (DO). You can test for an indirect object by asking *To whom?* or *For whom?*

> ┌──────── S ────────┐ V ┌── IO ──┐ ┌── DO ──┐
> ► **The *director* of the play *gave* his leading *lady* one exquisite *rose*.**

See ESL Note on page 324.

5. Subject + Predicate [Verb + Direct Object + Object Complement] The object complement (OC) refers to and renames or describes the direct object.

> S V ┌── DO ──┐ ┌── OC ──┐
> ► **They named the football *star* Rookie of the Year.**

ESL NOTE   No *to* before an Indirect Object

Do not add the word *to* in front of an indirect object that precedes the direct object.

No   **I gave to the driver a tip.**

            I gave to her a tip.

YES   **I gave the driver a tip.**

            I gave her a tip.

Use the word *to* or *for* only when the verb is followed directly by the direct object. Then use a prepositional phrase with *to* or *for* in place of an indirect object.

▶ **I gave a tip to the driver.**

See also **44c** ESL.   ▨

6. *(Subject implied) + Predicate [Verb +]*   A command is the only type of sentence that has only a predicate and an implied rather than a stated subject. The unstated, implied subject of a command is always *you.*

           V

▶ **[You] Leave me alone!**

7. *Verb + Subject + Rest of Predicate*   In Standard English sentences, the verb precedes the subject in inverted order in specific contexts—such as in questions and after adverbs such as *here, there, never, seldom,* and *rarely,* and after phrases used for emphasis at the beginning of a sentence. Here are some of the patterns that you are likely to read or use in your writing:

              V
            S

▶ **Did the committee finish its work?**

             V   S

▶ **Next to the river runs a superhighway.**

          V S V

▶ **Never have I been so tired.**

          V   S   V

▶ **Not only does the novel entertain, but it also raises our awareness of poverty.**

          V S

▶ **So eager was I to win that I set off before the starter's gun.**

        V   S   V

▶ **Rarely has a poem achieved such a grasp on the times.**

Modifiers added to subjects or predicates Descriptive words (adjectives, adverbs, and phrases) included in the subject or predicate to expand the meaning are known as **modifiers.** In the examples that follow, the simple subject + predicate structures are *computer + whirred* and *It + was.* The words in italics expand the meaning of the subject and predicate.

▶ *The powerful new* **computer whirred** *disconcertingly.* **It was** *decidedly distracting.*

EXERCISE 16.3 Identify direct and indirect objects.
In each of the following sentences, first circle the active verb or verbs. Remember that a verb can consist of more than one word. Then underline the complete direct object. If there is an indirect object, underline the complete indirect object twice.

EXAMPLE:

A government sponsored breeding program(is giving) endangered California condors a chance to survive.

1. The federal California condor reintroduction program encountered some obstacles in 2001.

2. In June, a captive condor had laid an egg.

3. Biologists then gave a now-wild female condor the unhatched egg.

4. She subsequently hatched it and was raising the chick.

5. Unfortunately, the surrogate mother briefly left the chick alone in the nest.

6. Another condor entered the nest, attacked the chick, and killed it.

7. This chick's death brought the condor reintroduction program its first setback.

8. Then a few days later a year-old condor in flight hit a power line and died.

9. Nevertheless, the reintroduction program still offers the condors their best hope for survival.

10. Wildlife conservationists still regard surrogate-mother condors as potentially good mothers.

EXERCISE 16.4 Find subjects and verbs in your own writing. Take a piece of your own writing. Underline the complete verbs. Circle the subject of each verb.

16d Phrases

A **phrase** is a group of related words that lacks a subject, a verb, or both. A phrase cannot function as a sentence; it must be part of the subject or predicate of an independent or a dependent clause. Phrases perform a number of grammatical functions.

Noun phrase A noun phrase can function as a subject, an object, or an appositive phrase defining or renaming a preceding noun or pronoun.

┌───── noun phrase as subject ─────┐
▶ **An elegant sequined evening gown was on sale.**

┌───── noun phrase as object ─────┐
▶ **She bought an elegant sequined evening gown.**

┌───── appositive noun phrase (26d) ─────┐
▶ **Her latest purchase, an elegant sequined evening gown, now hangs in her closet.**

Verb phrase A verb phrase consists of all the words that together make up the complete verb of a clause. (A *complete* verb indicates time—when the action mentioned in the clause takes place; see **16a** and **20e**.)

┌── verb phrase (complete verb) ──┐
▶ **That embarrassing letter should have been destroyed years ago.**

Verbal phrase Some phrases begin with parts of verbs. These parts of verbs (called *verbals* or *nonfinite verbs*) can never function alone as a complete verb; they do not tell about person, number, tense, mood, or voice.

No
┌───── S ─────┐ V
The children on the beach building sandcastles.
[Fragment: *building* is a verbal, not a complete verb]

Yes
┌───── S ─────┐ ┌── V ──┐
The children on the beach were building sandcastles.

Yes
┌───── S ─────┐
The children on the beach building sandcastles
V
are all in the same family.

Verbals are the present participle (*-ing*) form used as an adjective, the past participle (*-ed*) form used as an adjective, the *-ing* form used as a noun (a *gerund*), and the infinitive form (*to* + base form) used as a noun, adjective, or adverb. A verbal phrase consists of one of these verbals and any words that modify it. Examples follow.

Participle phrase A participle phrase can never stand alone as a sentence.

```
            ┌─────────── past participle phrase ───────────┐   S      V
▶ Frightened by her own loud heartbeat, she tried to stay calm.
```

```
            ┌── past participle phrase ──┐
      S                                   V
▶ Noises heard from afar seem louder at night.
```

```
  ┌── -ing participle phrase ──┐   S      V
▶ Hurrying across the grass, she heard a loud crash.
```

A participle phrase at the beginning of a sentence must always describe the subject; otherwise, it is a misplaced or dangling modifier (**19b, 19c**), as in *Hurrying across the grass, a loud crash startled her.* (The *crash* was not hurrying; *she* was.)

-*ing* phrase used as a noun (gerund) An -*ing* verbal can function as a noun. When it does, it is known as a *gerund*.

```
  ┌── -ing noun phrase (subject) ──┐
▶ The blaring of a car horn made her angry.
```

```
              -ing noun phrase
          ┌──── (object) ────┐
▶ He enjoys singing in the rain.
```

Infinitive phrase An infinitive phrase (*to* + base form of verb) can function as a noun, adverb, or adjective.

```
  ┌── (noun subject) ──┐
▶ To return to Beijing was her dream.
```

```
              ┌── (noun direct object) ──┐
▶ She planned to return to Beijing.
```

```
  ┌────── (adverb) ──────┐
▶ To return to Beijing, she took a job as an English teacher.
```

```
              ┌────── (adjective) ──────┐
▶ She had a plan to return to Beijing.
```

Prepositional phrase A prepositional phrase consists of a preposition and a noun or pronoun called the *object* of the preposition. A prepositional phrase functions as an adjective or adverb.

```
prepositional phrase          prepositional phrase          prepositional phrase
  ┌── (adverb) ──┐               ┌── (adjective) ──┐             ┌── (adverb) ──┐
▶ Without fail, the eerie music from the park began at midnight.
```

Absolute phrase An absolute phrase begins with a noun phrase followed by a verbal or a prepositional phrase. It contains no verb form that indicates tense. An absolute phrase modifies a whole sentence and is set off from the rest of the sentence by a comma.

⌐absolute phrase, modifying the whole sentence ¬
▶ **She stood in suspense, the clanging noises growing louder.**

absolute phrase,
⌐modifying the whole sentence ¬
▶ **Her thoughts in turmoil, she decided to consult a lawyer.**

Adjective phrase An adjective phrase contains an adjective and may contain other words and phrases. It modifies a noun or pronoun.

phrase used as an adjective after a noun, not before
⌐   ¬
▶ **The person responsible for the profits refused to take credit.**

adjective phrase
⌐   ¬
▶ **Sad to leave, Mohamed stalled and brushed some lint from his hat.**

For more on word order with adjective phrases, see **44b,** ESL.

EXERCISE 16.5 Identify phrases.
In the following sentences, identify the underlined phrases as one of the following types: noun phrase, verb phrase, participle phrase, gerund phrase, infinitive phrase, prepositional phrase, absolute phrase, or adjective phrase. Then identify its function in the sentence.

EXAMPLE:

In the Middle Ages, most advances in science occurred <u>in the Arab world</u>.

type of phrase: _prepositional phrase_

function in sentence: _adverb modifying the verb occurred_

1. <u>The astronomer and philosopher Nasir al-Din al-Tusi</u> spent many years in the Persian city of Alamut.

    type of phrase: _____

    function in sentence: _____

2. <u>Using Alamut's well-known library</u>, al-Tusi researched and wrote about scientific topics.

    type of phrase: _____

    function in sentence: _____

3. According to al-Tusi's later claims, he <u>had been kept</u> in Alamut against his will.

type of phrase: _____

function in sentence: _____

4. Nevertheless, <u>to work in the library there</u> must have been the fulfillment of a dream for a brilliant scholar such as al-Tusi.

type of phrase: _____

function in sentence: _____

5. Among the works <u>completed by al-Tusi in Alamut</u> were treatises on mathematics, ethics, and astronomy.

type of phrase: _____

function in sentence: _____

6. In the mid-thirteenth century, Alamut was surrounded by the armies of the warrior Hulagu, <u>the grandson of Genghis Khan</u>.

type of phrase: _____

function in sentence: _____

7. <u>His reputation as a scholar ensuring his safety</u>, al-Tusi was transported to Baghdad in 1256 by the conqueror Hulagu.

type of phrase: _____

function in sentence: _____

8. <u>Knowing of al-Tusi's reputation as a genius</u>, Hulagu appointed the astronomer to serve as one of his ministers.

type of phrase: _____

function in sentence: _____

9. Hulagu built an observatory <u>for al-Tusi's use</u> in what is now Iran.

type of phrase: _____

function in sentence: _____

10. Al-Tusi and his followers' work at the observatory is now credited with <u>establishing the basis of modern astronomy</u>.

type of phrase: _____

function in sentence: _____

16e Independent and dependent clauses

A clause contains a subject and a predicate. A clause can either stand alone (*independent*) or be attached to and dependent on another clause. A *dependent clause* must be attached to an independent clause to form a complete sentence.

Independent clause An independent clause is a group of related words that contains at least a subject and a verb and does not begin with a subordinating word. It can be punctuated as a sentence when standing alone. In each sentence you write, the predicate should include a complete verb and make a comment or assertion about the subject (except in commands, p. 324).

SUBJECT	VERB/PREDICATE
Eyesight	*deteriorates.*
Many people	*wear* glasses.
Audre Lorde	*is* a poet.
Lorde's poems and essays	*make* one think.

A subject can also be a noun formed from a verb (an -*ing* participle [gerund] or an infinitive) or a noun clause, as in the following examples.

SUBJECT	VERB/PREDICATE
-*ing* form (gerund)	
Winning	*is* not everything.
infinitive phrase	
To do one's best	*is* more important.
noun clause	
How the players train	*makes* all the difference.

Connecting Independent Clauses: Coordination Use a coordinating conjunction—*and, but, or, nor, so, for, yet*—usually preceded by a comma, to connect two independent clauses in one sentence. For more on the stylistic options of choosing coordination or subordination, see **37c**.

▶ **Thomas Wolfe's manuscript was eleven hundred pages, but his editor cut it substantially.**

Dependent clause A dependent clause contains a subject and a predicate but cannot stand alone. A clause beginning with a subordinating conjunction, such as *if, when, because, although,* or *since,* or with a relative pronoun, such as *who, which,* or *that,* needs to be attached to an independent clause. The idea in a dependent clause is subordinate to the idea in the independent clause.

A sentence can contain any number of independent and dependent clauses, but it must always contain at least one independent clause. Never punctuate a dependent clause alone as a sentence (see **18**).

Dependent clauses fall into three types, according to their role in a sentence, functioning as adverbs, adjectives, or nouns.

Adverb Clauses Adverb clauses provide information about the verbs, adjectives, or adverbs in an independent clause. They answer questions such as *when, how, where, why, for what purpose or reason, under what conditions,* and *to what extent,* and they express logical relationships between the ideas of the independent and dependent clauses. Adverb clauses begin with subordinating conjunctions.

RELATIONSHIPS THAT SUBORDINATING CONJUNCTIONS EXPRESS

time: when, whenever, until, till, before, after, while, once, since, as soon as, as long as

place: where, wherever

reason/cause: because, as, since

condition: if, even if, unless, provided that

contrast: although, though, even though, whereas, while

comparison: than, as, as if, as though

purpose: so that, in order that

result: so . . . that, such . . . that

By attaching a dependent clause to an independent clause—using *subordination*—you provide information about the relationship between clauses.

INDEPENDENT CLAUSES	**The two-way radio had rechargeable batteries and no usage fees. She decided to buy it.**

———————— dependent clause, showing reason ————————

COMBINED BY SUBORDINATION	**Because the two-way radio had rechargeable batteries**

———————————— ┌— independent clause —┐
and no usage fees, she decided to buy it.

INDEPENDENT CLAUSES	**The pitcher hurled the broken bat at the running batter. The crowd jeered.**

———————— dependent clause, showing time ————————

COMBINED BY SUBORDINATION	**When the pitcher hurled the broken bat at the**

┌— independent clause —┐
running batter, the crowd jeered.

INDEPENDENT CLAUSES
The quiz show host immediately moved on to the next question. He could see one of the contestants trying to shout out an answer.

COMBINED BY SUBORDINATION

———————— independent clause ————————
The quiz show host immediately moved on to

——————————————┐ ┌— dependent clause, showing contrast —
the next question although he could see one of

————————————————————————————
the contestants trying to shout out an answer.

Adverb clause before independent clause As a general rule, if an adverb clause precedes the independent clause, use a comma to separate the two clauses. See also **26c**.

┌——— dependent clause ———┐ ┌— comma independent clause ———┐
▶ **If you send that memo, the columnist will be angry.**

Some writers do omit the comma, but if you adopt the general rule of always choosing to use a comma, you will avoid errors and ambiguities that can occur if you inadvertently leave out a necessary comma, as in the following example.

No
When the anthropologists were eating bears were circling their tent.

[Leaving out the comma could make a reader read the sentence as "When the anthropologists were eating bears"—not what the writer intended.]

YES
When the anthropologists were eating, bears were circling their tent.

Adverb clause after independent clause Ordinarily, no comma is needed when the dependent clause follows the independent clause.

▶ **The columnist will be angry if you send that memo.**

However, when the adverb clause is nonrestrictive (that is, adds information that contrasts rather than modifies and limits), set it off with a comma (**26d**).

▶ **My boss prefers phone calls, whereas I like e-mail.**

Adjective clauses Adjective clauses (also called *relative clauses*) provide information about nouns or pronouns.

INDEPENDENT CLAUSES
The contestant quickly claimed the prize. The contestant knew the correct answer.

COMBINED BY
ADJECTIVE
(RELATIVE)
CLAUSE
The contestant who knew the correct answer quickly claimed the prize.

The subordinating words that introduce adjective clauses are relative pronouns, such as *who, whom, whose, which,* and *that.* For more on relative pronouns and relative clauses, see **24.**

────── adjective (relative) clause ──────
▶ **The kick that brought the crowd to its feet broke the impasse.**

┌ adjective (relative) clause ┐
▶ **The soccer player whose head is bowed missed a kick.**

Noun clauses A noun clause functions like a noun in a sentence. Noun clauses are introduced by subordinating words such as *what, that* (or omitted *that*), *when, why, how, whatever, who, whom, whoever,* and *whomever.* (A clause that you can replace with the pronoun *something* or *someone* is a noun clause.)

noun clause
┌── = *something* ──┐
▶ **He wants to know what he should do.**

┌── noun clause = *something* ──┐
▶ **The fans wish that the match could be replayed.**

┌ noun clause = *someone* ┐
▶ **Whoever scores a goal will be a hero.**

EXERCISE 16.6 Identify dependent clauses.
In the following sentences underline any dependent clauses. Note that some sentences may contain only independent clauses.

EXAMPLE:

Scientists <u>who study the brain</u> disagree about the nature of dreams. <u>Because dreams cannot be examined by direct observation</u>, scientists have to rely on the dreamers' description of their dreams.

1. In 1900, Sigmund Freud, a former neurologist, published a book called *The Interpretation of Dreams,* which discussed the purpose of dreams.

2. Freud believed that dreams reveal the sleeper's unconscious desires in a disguised form.

3. Today modern psychoanalysts are less interested in dream interpretation, and some disagree with Freud's theories.

4. One of these is Dr. J. Allan Hobson, a psychiatrist at Harvard Medical School, who considers dreams simply a byproduct of the sleeping brain.

5. The activity of the brain stem produces dream images, but according to Dr. Hobson this activity is random.

6. However, Mark Solms of the Royal London School of Medicine, a neuropsychologist, holds a different view and maintains that dreams help to motivate people to pursue goals.

7. Dr. Solms's opinion is more in line with Freud's century-old theory because Freud saw providing motivation as one purpose of dreams.

8. Although everyone without brain damage appears to dream, dreams may serve different functions for people in different societies.

9. For example, according to a Finnish researcher, when people in hunter-gatherer societies dream about threatening events, they apparently unconsciously use these dreams to prepare responses to the threats.

10. Freud abandoned the physical study of the brain, neurology, to study the workings of the mind, but neurologists today use dreams to understand how the brain and the mind work together.

EXERCISE 16.7 Identify independent clauses.
Underline the independent clauses in the passage by Ruth Reichl on pages 89–90.

EXAMPLE:

When we woke up in the morning, <u>the smell of baking bread was wafting through the trees.</u>

Note: The subordinating word *that* can sometimes be omitted from an adjective clause or a noun clause (p. 333).

EXERCISE 16.8 Identify clauses.
In the following passage by Calvin Trillin, which type of clause dominates: independent or dependent? How many clauses make

up the second sentence? Find an example in the passage of coordinate independent clauses.

> In fact, most people find us rather traditional. My wife and I have a marriage certificate, although I can't say I know exactly where to put my hands on it right at the moment. We have two children. We have a big meal on Christmas. We put on costumes at Halloween. (What about the fact that I always wear an ax-murderer's mask on Halloween? This happens to be one of the peculiarities.) We make family decisions in the traditional American family way, which is to say that the father is manipulated by the wife and the children. We lose a lot of socks in the wash. At our house, the dishes are done and the garbage is taken out regularly—after the glass, cans and other recyclable materials have been separated out. We're not talking about a commune here.
>
> —Calvin Trillin, "A Traditional Family"

EXERCISE 16.9 Find clauses in your own writing.
Take a recent piece of your own writing. Underline in pencil all the independent clauses. Underline subordinate dependent clauses in another color pen or pencil.

16f Sentence types

You saw several examples of simple sentences in **16c**, sentences with a subject and a predicate in only one independent clause. But as you know, writing is much more varied. When you review a draft of your writing, check to see whether your sentences connect well to each other and flow gracefully. A string of simple sentences may seem to readers like a grade school primer—*See Spot run; Jane saw Spot*—sentences not exactly guaranteed to excite your readers. If you examine and revise how the sentence before and the sentence after are related to the sentence under consideration, then you should be able to vary your sentences and include a mix of the four sentence types: simple, compound, complex, and compound-complex sentences.

1. A *simple sentence* contains one independent clause.

   ▶ **Kara raised her hand.**

2. A *compound sentence* contains two or more independent clauses connected with one or more coordinating conjunctions (*and, but, or, nor, so, for, yet*), or with a semicolon alone, or with a semicolon and a transitional expression (**5e**).

   ┌─ independent clause ─┐   ┌────── independent clause ──────┐
   ▶ **She raised her hand, and the whole class was surprised.**

r— independent clause —┐   r— independent clause —┐
▶ **She raised her hand, but nobody else responded.**

r— independent clause —┐ r———— independent clause ————┐
▶ **She raised her hand; the whole class was surprised.**

r— independent clause —┐   r— independent clause —
▶ **She raised her hand; as a result, the whole class was**

————┐
surprised.

3. A *complex sentence* contains an independent clause and one or more dependent clauses (**16e**).

                                                    independent
r———————— dependent clause ————————┐ r— clause ———
▶ **Because she had never volunteered before, the whole class**

————————┐ r— dependent clause —┐
was surprised when she raised her hand.

                                            r— independent
                                            clause
r——————— dependent clause ———————┐ r—————
▶ **The student who had never volunteered before decided to**

————————┐
raise her hand.

independent
r— clause —┐ r———— dependent clause ————┐
▶ **Kara wondered what the response would be.**

4. A *compound-complex sentence* contains at least two independent clauses and at least one dependent clause.

r——— dependent clause ———┐ r———— independent clause ————┐
▶ **When she raised her hand, the whole class was surprised,**

r——— independent clause ———┐ r— dependent clause —┐
and the professor waited eagerly as she began to speak.

EXERCISE 16.10 Identify sentence functions and sentence types. In each of the following sentences, first underline any dependent clause once and any independent clause twice. Then identify each sentence by function (declarative, interrogative, imperative, or exclamatory) and by type (simple, compound, complex, or compound-complex) on the line following each sentence.

EXAMPLE:

Oscar Wilde may be best known as a playwright, but he was

also a poet, novelist, journalist, essayist, and writer of children's

stories.   *declarative, compound*

1. As Oscar Wilde predicted in his youth, his writings have become his "great monument." _____

2. Wilde was famous in his twenties for his quick wit and clever retorts, and he was celebrated for his plays, particularly *The Importance of Being Earnest,* which has been called "one of the greatest English comedies of all time." _____

3. Has anyone ever seen the play without laughing out loud? _____

4. At the end of the twentieth century, Wilde's plays were again being performed on Broadway, and movie versions of them were being filmed. _____

5. See the original film of *The Importance of Being Earnest* if you possibly can, since it is a perfect comedy of manners. _____

6. Another successful play in New York at the end of the millennium was based on the transcripts of Wilde's sensational trial. _____

7. Wilde, married and the father of two children, became notorious later in life when he was arrested and jailed for having a homosexual relationship. _____

8. When the father of Wilde's young lover accused him of sodomy, Wilde retaliated by suing for libel, but he lost his case. _____

9. Was Wilde out of his mind to sue for libel, or did he expect his great popularity to protect him? _____

10. Wilde died a pauper in Paris at the age of forty-six, but his works continue to be read and performed, so his lost reputation has been restored. _____

> **EXERCISE 16.11** Identify types of sentences.
> In the passage by Jakob Nielsen on pages 87–88, identify and label (1) a simple sentence, (2) a compound sentence, (3) a complex sentence, and (4) a compound-complex sentence. Compare your findings with those of your classmates, and discuss why you think Nielsen used those sentence types. Discuss what you think the effect would be if all the sentences were simple sentences.

16g Building up sentences

A sentence can be made up of many parts and still be a correctly structured sentence. The following examples show some of the many types of possible additions to a simple sentence. A note of caution, though: Although complicated structures can be technically correct, they may not be effective, as some of the following sentences illustrate.

┌ independent clause ┐
► The lawyer roared.

modifier (adjective)
► The brilliant lawyer roared.

modifier (adverb)
► The brilliant lawyer roared loudly.

prepositional
┌─ phrase ─┐
► The brilliant lawyer roared loudly with laughter.

┌─────── compound subject ───────┐
► The brilliant lawyer and his client roared loudly with laughter.

modifier (adverb)
► Finally, the brilliant lawyer and his client roared loudly with laughter.

┌─────────── adverb clause (time) ───────────┐
► Finally, while they listened to the tapes on the bugging device, the brilliant lawyer and his client roared loudly with laughter.

► Finally, while they listened to the tapes on the bugging device,
┌─────── compound predicate ───────┐
the brilliant lawyer and his client roared loudly with laughter
and gave each other high-fives.

► Finally, while they listened to the tapes on the bugging device, the brilliant lawyer and his client roared loudly with laughter
┌─── adverb clause (reason) ───┐
and gave each other high-fives because they knew they had
found a way to win the case.

┌─── absolute phrase ───┐
► Finally, their hearts beating fast while they listened to the tapes on the bugging device, the brilliant lawyer and his client roared loudly with laughter and gave each other high-fives because they knew they had found a way to win the case.

▶ Finally, their hearts beating fast while they listened to the
tapes on the bugging device, the brilliant lawyer and his client
roared loudly with laughter and gave each other high-fives

because they knew they had found a way to win the case that
—— adjective clause (relative) ——⌐
had once seemed unwinnable.

▶ Finally, their hearts beating fast while they listened to the
tapes on the bugging device, the brilliant lawyer and his client
roared loudly with laughter and gave each other high-fives
because they knew they had found a way to win the case that
⌐— coordinate independent clause —
had once seemed unwinnable, but each of them was smart

enough to realize the opposition's strength.

▶ Finally, their hearts beating fast while they listened to the
tapes on the bugging device, the brilliant lawyer and his client
roared loudly with laughter and gave each other high-fives
because they knew they had found a way to win the case that
had once seemed unwinnable, but each of them was smart

enough to realize the opposition's strength and what pitfalls

noun clause as direct object ⌐
lay ahead.

By the end, the sentence is getting unwieldy. But it is still structured
accurately as a compound-complex sentence.

EXERCISE 16.12 Build up sentences from a simple sentence.
Build up two of the following simple sentences by adding modifiers, phrases, and clauses correctly connected to the basic subject
+ predicate.

The girl sang.   The novel is romantic.
The instructor gave a lesson.   My computer froze.
The dog ate my homework.   The architects decided.
The reviewer panned the restaurant.   People sweat.

REVIEW EXERCISE FOR SECTION 16 Identify sentence elements.
In the following passage, identify and list each of the numbered
sentence elements. Choices include dependent clause, independent
clause, simple subject, complete subject, active verb, passive verb,

linking verb, subject complement, direct object, indirect object, object complement, adjective, adverb, prepositional phrase, participle phrase, gerund phrase, infinitive phrase, or conjunction.

EXAMPLE:

Toussaint L'Ouverture's successes gave <u>Haitian revolutionaries</u> a reason to continue their struggle.
  <u>indirect object</u>

    (1) <u>After the American Revolution had ended,</u> other countries responded to the idea that a tyrannical government (2) <u>could be overthrown</u>. A revolution began in France in 1789, and soon French colonial rulers also faced trouble. (3) <u>A group of slaves and former slaves on the island of Saint-Domingue, now called *Haiti,*</u> rebelled against the French government there in 1791. A former slave named François Dominique Toussaint became an able leader of the slave rebellion and insisted that every human had a (4) <u>universal</u> right to freedom and citizenship. When a French (5) <u>governor</u> of the island noted that Toussaint's soldiers could (6) <u>always</u> find an opening through enemy lines, Toussaint adopted the surname *L'Ouverture,* (7) <u>which means</u> "the opening." The slave rebellion was successful, and the French rulers abolished (8) <u>slavery</u> on Saint-Domingue in 1793. Toussaint L'Ouverture's continuing calls for independence for his homeland (9) <u>met</u> with sympathy from President John Adams, who had also been a (10) <u>revolutionary</u>. Adams appointed a consul to the island in 1799 and hinted that the United States would not be opposed to (11) <u>recognizing an independent Saint-Domingue</u>. However, in 1800 the United States had elected (12) <u>Thomas Jefferson</u> the new (13) <u>president</u>. Jefferson was less (14) <u>enthusiastic</u> about supporting the new country. Since he (15) <u>had been</u> a firm believer in the necessity of both the American Revolution (16) <u>and</u> the French Revolution, Jefferson did not approve of a nation (17) <u>made up of Afro-Caribbean slaves</u> who had won their own freedom. (18) <u>Although</u> the nation did become independent, acquiring the name *Haiti* in 1804, Toussaint L'Ouverture did not live to see that event. (19) <u>He was betrayed and captured by Napoleon's troops in 1802,</u> and he died the following year (20) <u>in a French prison</u>. He is still honored as a freedom fighter and the father of Haitian independence.

17 Top Ten Sentence Problems: A Checklist

This section introduces you to ten of the most common problems facing all writers of Standard English sentences, drawn from classrooms over more than thirty years.

COMMON PROBLEMS

1. Phrase fragments
2. Clause fragments
3. Run-on sentences and comma splices
4. Mixed constructions
5. Wrong verb forms
6. Inappropriate tense shifts
7. Lack of subject-verb agreement
8. Wrong pronoun case and reference
9. Adjective/adverb confusion
10. Double negatives

Read through this section to explore problems that instructors have pointed out in your writing and that you are likely to face again. The purpose of this list is to make you aware of common errors. To learn more about any of the sentence problems—for more definitions, details, and examples—turn to the sections mentioned in the cross-references.

1. Phrase fragments   To be complete, a sentence must have both a subject and a complete verb. A phrase fragment lacks a subject, a complete verb, or both. Identify phrase fragments and edit to attach them to a sentence that contains a subject and a complete verb (**18b**).

No   **Whoever wrote, "Not a creature was stirring, not even a mouse," never had mice in the wall.** *Creating a terrible racket at night.*

[Lacks a subject and a complete verb]

Yes   **Whoever wrote, "Not a creature was stirring, not even a mouse," never had mice in the wall. They create a terrible racket at night.**

Whoever wrote, "Not a creature was stirring, not even a mouse," never had mice in the wall creating a terrible racket at night.

No   **She never talks about her inner feelings.** *Her feelings of fear or joy.* [Lacks a verb]

Yes   **She never talks about her inner feelings of fear or joy.**

No   **She is looking for new acting parts.** *The more varied, the better.* [Lacks a subject and a verb]

Yes   **She is looking for new acting parts, the more varied, the better.**

2. Clause fragments A dependent clause must always be connected to an independent clause. If you begin a sentence with *when, because, if, although, whereas,* or some other subordinating conjunction, or with a relative pronoun such as *who, which,* or *that,* connect that clause to an independent clause (**18c**).

▶ The play failed, ~~Because~~ it received three bad reviews.
because

▶ Fog can interfere with film projection at a drive-in movie

theater, ~~Whereas~~ power outages sometimes interrupt the show
, whereas

at a mall cinema.

▶ The manager reprimanded all the slackers, ~~Who~~ had been
spending too much time at the water cooler.
who

3. Run-on sentences and comma splices A sentence should not run on into another sentence without appropriate end punctuation. Separate or revise independent clauses that are connected incorrectly (see **18g** and **18h**).

▶ He trained hard he never considered the strain.
He

▶ The city is lively, the restaurants and clubs are open late.

▶ The film has been released, however, it has not come to
our theater.

4. Mixed constructions Look for sentences that might make readers say "Huh?"—sentences that begin in one way but end in another, resulting in fuzzy syntax (**19a**). Readers should be able to tell clearly who (or what) is doing what (**36a**).

▶ In ~~the~~ essay "Notes of a Native Son" ~~by~~ James Baldwin
his

discusses growing up in Harlem with his strict father.

▶ ~~Scientists cloned a cat~~ has some resemblance to its
biological mother.
The cat the scientists cloned

▶ Because movies don't show history accurately ~~makes us~~ all
wonder about the truth.
we

5. Wrong verb forms   Be sure to use standard verb forms. Avoid nonstandard forms, such as *brung, has went, should of, have being noticed, have drank* (**20a, 20b, 20c**).

▶ The cloned kitten could have ~~came~~ out to be dangerous.
   _{come}

▶ The parents should ~~of~~ supported the teacher in her decision to fail the students.
   _{have}

6. Inappropriate tense shifts   Avoid flip-flopping between past and present time without reason (**20i**).

▶ Foote ~~wrote~~ about Shiloh and describes its aftermath.
   _{writes}

▶ We lived without furniture for six weeks this fall while the movers ~~are~~ all busy, the bank ~~is~~ processing a loan, and
   _{were}   _{was}

school began.

7. Lack of subject-verb agreement   In the present tense, use the same form of the verb for each person except third person singular. For the verb *be*, see **20d**.

I, you, we, they	walk
he, she, it	walks

▶ the owner ~~have~~   ▶ the author suggest
   _{has}   _s

▶ she ~~don't~~   ▶ It pose a problem.
   _{doesn't}   _s

▶ The students in the class likes peer response.

However, determining what is a singular subject can be difficult: see **21** for detailed explanations and examples.

8. Wrong pronoun case and reference   Check that subject and object pronouns are correct (**22a**), and avoid ambiguous or unclear pronoun references (**22c**).

▶ ~~Me and my sister~~ went to Florida.
   _{My sister and I}

▶ The incident in the story reminds him of my mother and ~~I~~. *me*

▶ When Dean and George crossed the border with two
friends, ~~they~~ searched all the luggage. *customs officers*

9. Adjective/adverb confusion Use the appropriate forms of
adjectives and adverbs in the right places (**23a–23c**).

▶ They did ~~good~~ in the playoffs. *well*

▶ They managed to compete ~~real~~ well in the playoffs. *really*

Well is an adverb and needs an adverb as a modifier, not an adjective.

10. Double negatives Double negatives can be vibrant in speech and
are customary in some dialects, but avoid them in formal writing (**23g**).

▶ They don't have ~~no~~ problems with the proposal. *any*

▶ He ~~can't~~ hardly wait. *can*

EXERCISE 17.1 Identify
problems.
Each of the following
items contains one of the
top ten sentence prob-
lems. Find and correct the
problem in each sentence.
Then write the type of
problem on the line fol-
lowing the sentence.

EXAMPLE:

When an ecosystem
becomes less diverse. ~~A~~ *a*
disease that strikes one

Diadema sea urchin

kind of plant or animal can affect every creature in the food
chain. _clause fragment_

   1. In 1983, a mysterious disease attacks sea urchins in the
Caribbean and killed most of the species known as
Diadema. _____

2. According to the Smithsonian Tropical Research Institute. The sea urchin plague caused the biggest die-off ever reported for a marine animal. _____

3. In a 3.5-million-square-kilometer area of the Caribbean had once been home to millions of *Diadema* sea urchins.

_____

4. Algae began to spread quickly in this vast ocean area. After 97 percent of the *Diadema* urchins that had once controlled the algae's growth by eating them died. _____

5. Soon, the algae had grew over many of the coral reefs, preventing young coral from attaching and building on top of older coral. _____

6. Consequently, the coral reefs of the Caribbean have been dying off since 1983 scientists now know that their survival depends on the algae-eating services of the *Diadema* sea urchins. _____

7. *Diadema* sea urchins had not always been the only algae-controlling species in this part of the Caribbean; several species of fish and them had once competed to eat the aquatic plants.

_____

8. Then overfishing removed most of the other algae eaters of the coral reefs so that for a time the sea urchins could dine real well on the algae until they, too, began to disappear. _____

9. Scientists from a Florida laboratory has a plan to reintroduce *Diadema* sea urchins to the algae-choked waters. _____

10. Marine biologists do not have no illusions that simply bring-ing sea urchins back to the Caribbean can save the reefs, but the experiment is a hopeful start. _____

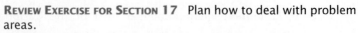

REVIEW EXERCISE FOR SECTION 17   Plan how to deal with problem areas.

Keep a written record of any of the top ten problems you, your classmates, tutor, or instructor identify in your writing. Write down each problem sentence and one way to revise it. Identify the nature of each problem. Write down which sections may help you deal with those problems and how you intend to work on identifying and correcting those types of errors. As time goes on, you should find yourself adding fewer and fewer examples to the list.

18 Sentence Fragments, Run-Ons, and Comma Splices

The boundaries of a sentence are important in Standard English. Readers expect the beginnings and endings of sentences to occur at anticipated points and with appropriate signals in the form of punctuation marks. Misleading signals mislead readers. Do not use a comma to mark the end of a sentence, and never use a period if a group of words is not a complete sentence. Indicate the end of a sentence with a period, question mark, or exclamation point (**25**).

18a   What is a fragment?

Speech is filled with fragments, and nobody expects otherwise.

> Done your essay?
> 'Fraid not.
> Again?
> Not my fault this time.
>
> Where were you yesterday?
> At the beach.
> Who with?
> Joe and Tom.
> Cool.

But writing is different from speech. Writers do not have intonation, face-to-face contact, gestures, and facial expressions at their disposal to help them communicate. They have to rely on structure and punctuation—the look of words and sentences on the page or screen. Readers of formal, academic writing will expect only a complete sentence to be punctuated as a complete sentence. They always expect complete sentences, not fragments.

KEY POINTS

What Is a Sentence Fragment?

A sentence fragment is a string of words punctuated as a sentence but missing one or more crucial elements. See **16b** for the necessary features of a sentence. Identify your own sentence fragments by asking these three questions about a series of words you punctuate as a sentence:

1. Does the "sentence" have a complete verb?

      were
   ▶ **We watched the rehearsal. The jugglers practicing for four hours.**

   [The verb is not complete. "The jugglers practicing for four hours" is a fragment.]

2. Does the verb have a subject?

      They argued
   ▶ **They drove for six days. Argued all the way.**

3. Is there an independent clause—a subject + predicate not introduced with a subordinating word (a subordinating conjunction, a relative pronoun, or a word introducing a noun clause)?

      because
   ▶ **The spectators shrieked. Because the race was so close.**

   ["Because the race was so close" is an adverb clause not attached to an independent clause. It is a fragment.]

A phrase not attached to an independent clause, a dependent clause not attached to an independent clause, and an independent clause with no subject or complete verb are all sentence fragments.

You need to watch out for them and edit them. Often you can fix a fragment by connecting it to a closely related sentence in your text.

18b Identifying and correcting a phrase fragment

A phrase is a group of words that lacks a subject, a verb, or both (**16d**). A phrase fragment is a phrase incorrectly punctuated as if it were a complete sentence.

┌── fragment: infinitive phrase ──┐
▶ He wanted to make a point. **To prove his competence.**

┌── fragment: *-ing* participle phrase ──┐
▶ Althea works every evening. **Just trying to keep up with her**

boss's demands.

┌── fragment: past participle phrase ──┐
▶ Ralph talked for hours. **Elated by the company's success.**

fragment: prepositional phrase
▶ They kept dialing the boss's phone number. **With no luck.**

┌── fragment: noun phrase (appositive) ──┐
▶ A prize was awarded to Ed. **The best worker in the company.**

fragment: noun phrase
┌── (appositive) ──┐
▶ The family set out for the new country. **A country with**

freedom of religion.

fragment: noun phrase
▶ Nature held many attractions for Thoreau. **First, the solitude.**

Methods of correcting a phrase fragment

1. Attach the phrase to a nearby independent clause.

              to
▶ He wanted to make a point, ~~To~~ prove his competence.
[Simply remove the period and capital letter.]

              the
▶ A prize was awarded to Ed, ~~The~~ best worker in the

company. [Use a comma before an appositive phrase, and remove the capital letter.]

▶ The family set out for a new country, ~~A country~~ with freedom of religion.

Or, for emphasis:

▶ **The family set out for a new country—a country with freedom of religion.**

2. Change the phrase to an independent clause.

She is just

▶ **Althea works every evening, ~~Just~~ trying to keep up with her boss's demands.** [Add a subject and a complete verb.]

he valued

▶ **Nature held many attractions for Thoreau. First, the solitude.** [Add a subject and a verb.]

3. Rewrite the whole passage.

was so   *elated*   *that he talked for hours.*

▶ **Ralph ~~talked for hours. Elated~~ by the company's success.**

[Make the fragment into a clause, and connect it to another clause with a subordinating word—in this case, one showing a result.]

EXERCISE 18.1   Identify and correct phrase fragments.

In each of the following items, identify any phrase fragment and correct it either by attaching it to a nearby independent clause or by changing it to an independent clause. Some sentences may be correct.

EXAMPLE:

American popular music has had an enthusiastic following

since

around the world, ~~Since~~ the early days of rock and roll.

1. Every country has its own musical styles. Based on the traditional music of its people.

2. Having its own tradition as the birthplace of jazz, blues, and rock music. The United States has long been one of the world's leading exporters of popular music.

3. In spite of enjoying enormous popularity in their own countries. Many performers from Europe, South America, Africa, and Asia have had a hard time attracting American fans.

4. Some American musicians have championed their favorite artists from abroad. Examples include Neneh Cherry's duet with the Senegalese performer Youssou N'Dour and Beck's tribute to the late French singer-songwriter Serge Gainsbourg.

5. Although some U.S. music fans pay attention to foreign musical styles, most Americans buy the music they know from American top-40 radio and MTV. Songs also loved by fans around the world for sounding typically American.

6. However, not all Americans are native English speakers. Listening exclusively to English-language music.

7. Latin music has had some crossover success in the United States. Propelled, at least at first, by the high percentage of Spanish-speaking people in this country.

8. On American radio and television today, some of the most popular male acts are Latin pop stars. Singing sensations such as Marc Anthony, Ricky Martin, and Enrique Iglesias.

9. These singers are considered crossover artists because they have achieved mainstream success by singing in English. After making earlier recordings in Spanish.

10. Perhaps there will be a time when artists can have big hits with songs sung in a foreign language. At present, however, singing in English is almost always required for being successful in America.

18c Identifying and correcting a dependent clause fragment

A dependent clause cannot stand alone. The subordinating words that introduce dependent adverb clauses include, for example, *because, if, unless, when, whenever, while, although,* and *after* (see p. 331 in **16e** for a list); *that, which, who, whom,* or *whose* introduce adjective clauses; and words such as *what, when, why,* or *whatever* introduce noun clauses (p. 333). A clause introduced with any subordinating word must be attached to an independent clause.

▶ The family set out for a new country. A country in which they could practice their culture and religion.
   ┌──────── fragment ────────┐

▶ Lars had always wanted to be a stand-up comic. Because he liked to make people laugh.
   ┌──── fragment ────┐

▶ Rosa often talks about her relationship with her parents. How she grew up following her family's values.
   ┌──────── fragment ────────┐

Note: Some "time" words (such as *after, before, since,* and *until*) can function as prepositions, adverbs, or subordinating conjunctions:

adverb
▶ We ate dinner. After, I left.

subordinating conjunction
▶ After we ate dinner, I left.

Methods of correcting a dependent clause fragment

1. Connect the dependent clause to an independent clause.

   ▶ The family set out for a new country in which they could practice their culture and religion.

   ▶ Rosa often talks about her relationship with her parents,
     and how
     ~~How~~ she grew up following her family's values.

2. Delete the subordinating conjunction (see the list on p. 331). The dependent clause then becomes an independent clause, which can stand alone.

> Lars had always wanted to be a stand-up comic. ~~Because he~~ liked to make people laugh.

He

Beginning a sentence with a dependent clause A subordinating conjunction (such as *because, when,* or *although*) at the beginning of a sentence does not automatically signal a fragment. A correctly punctuated sentence may begin with a subordinating conjunction introducing a dependent clause, as long as the sentence also contains an independent clause.

As you edit your own work, if you begin your sentence with an adverb clause, always make sure you put a comma rather than a period at the end of that clause. A period at the end of an adverb clause at the beginning of a sentence creates a sentence fragment—as in *Because he liked to make people laugh.*

Look for the following pattern whenever you begin a sentence with a capitalized subordinating conjunction:

Because (When, Although, Since, etc.)..., subject + predicate.

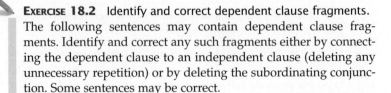

> **Because Lars had always wanted to make people laugh, he decided to be a stand-up comedian.**

> **When the circus arrives in town, the elephants parade along the main street.**

EXERCISE 18.2 Identify and correct dependent clause fragments. The following sentences may contain dependent clause fragments. Identify and correct any such fragments either by connecting the dependent clause to an independent clause (deleting any unnecessary repetition) or by deleting the subordinating conjunction. Some sentences may be correct.

EXAMPLE:

A study by psychologists at the University of Kentucky in
Lexington offers interesting results, ~~That~~ that support a relationship
between thinking positively and living a long life.

1. A group of nuns wrote autobiographies sixty years ago. When they were young women.

2. Because the nuns all had similar lifestyles and social status. Psychologists have looked closely at the autobiographies and compared the lives of the writers.

3. Not surprisingly, few nuns reported negative emotions. Since they knew that their Mother Superior would read the autobiographies.

4. However, some reported having "very happy" experiences and a positive attitude about the future. Others were more neutral.

5. Psychologists discovered that the nuns who had expressed positive views lived an average of seven years longer than the other nuns. A conclusion that indicates that looking on the bright side may be good for a person's health.

6. The nuns' autobiographies have also been studied by experts in Alzheimer's disease. Who were hoping to discover clues about the illness.

7. Researchers examined the autobiographies to find out. If the nuns who later developed the disorder had provided hints in their writing.

8. After they had analyzed the autobiographies. The researchers found an interesting difference between the nuns who had developed Alzheimer's disease and the nuns who had not.

9. The nuns whose memories had remained intact throughout their lives had used more complicated syntax. When they had written about their experiences.

10. Although the research findings are fascinating, no one knows how syntax and Alzheimer's are linked. Using complicated syntax may not cause any changes in a person's brain.

18d Identifying and correcting a fragment resulting from a missing subject, verb, or verb part

Every sentence must contain a subject and a complete verb in an independent clause. A word group that is punctuated like a sentence but lacks a subject or a verb or has an incomplete verb that does not show tense (**20a** and **20d**) is a fragment.

▶ The commuters were staring hopefully down the track. Just

——— fragment: missing subject ———
wanted to get to work on time.

——— fragment: incomplete verb ———
▶ Overcrowding is a problem. Too many people living in one area.

— fragment: missing verb —
▶ The candidate explained his proposal. A plan for off-street

parking.

Methods of correcting Add a subject to the fragment, add a complete verb, or recast the passage.

They just
▶ The commuters were staring hopefully down the track. ~~Just~~
wanted to get to work on time.

▶ The commuters were staring hopefully down the

just wanting
track. ~~Just wanted~~ to get to work on time.

▶ Overcrowding is a problem. Too many people~~are~~living in one area.

▶ Overcrowding is a problem~~with too~~Too many people living in one area.

▶ The candidate explained his ~~proposal.~~ A plan for off-street parking.

▶ The candidate explained his proposal. ~~He emphasized a~~ A plan for off-street parking.

 ESL NOTE Subject *it* Required

Never omit an *it* subject even in a dependent clause. Remember that every clause needs both a subject and a predicate.

▶ The essay won a prize because~~it~~was so well researched. ■

 EXERCISE 18.3 Identify and correct fragments resulting from missing subjects, verbs, or verb parts.
In each of the following items, identify and correct any fragment resulting from a missing subject, verb, or verb part either by adding the necessary subject, verb, or verb part or by rewriting. Some items may be correct.

EXAMPLE:

Many parts of the United States now face a shortage of teachers.
~~People~~ Few people are willing to put up with evening and weekend work,

unruly classes, and a smaller paycheck than other professions

offer.

1. Teachers were once regarded as committed, admirable professionals. People earning more respect than money.

2. Today, many teachers feel that they do not even command respect. Just seem to get blamed when students do not do well in class.

3. Most people enter teaching with high ideals. Young graduates hoping to make a difference in a child's life.

4. To many young people today, however, teaching seems less attractive than ever. Trying to remain idealistic is difficult in the face of low pay, large classes, and disrespect from politicians and parents who accuse teachers of performing their jobs badly.

5. Better training, higher pay, and more respect from political figures might help attract bright, motivated young people to the teaching profession. Might make them choose the classroom over a business or legal career.

18e Identifying and correcting a fragment consisting of one part of a compound predicate

A predicate with two parts joined by *and, but, or,* or *nor* (known as a **compound predicate**) should not be split into two sentences. Both parts of the predicate must appear in the same sentence.

⌐———— fragment ————
▶ After an hour, the dancers changed partners. **And adapted to a**

different type of music. [The compound predicate is "*changed* partners and *adapted* to a different type of music."]

Method of correcting Correct the fragment by removing the period and capital letter.

　　　　　　　　　　　　　　　　　　and
▶ After an hour, the dancers changed partners, ̶A̶n̶d̶ adapted to a different type of music.

EXERCISE 18.4 Identify and correct fragments consisting of part of a compound predicate.
In each of the following items, identify and correct any fragment containing part of a compound predicate by joining it to the independent clause containing the rest of the predicate. Some items may be correct.

EXAMPLE:

Carl Linnaeus, an eighteenth-century Swedish botanist, placed

all living things into carefully defined categories/ ~~And~~ created a

and

system for naming every creature and plant.

1. Entomologists, scientists who study insects, often discover new species. And get the opportunity to name the creatures that they find.

2. Most people who name a new species either choose a name in honor of someone who assisted with the discovery. Or describe the species—often in Latin—with the new name.

3. However, the discoverer of a new wasp in the genus *Heerz* wanted to add humor to the new discovery. And called the wasp *Heerz tooya*.

4. One entomologist wanted to compliment Far Side cartoonist Gary Larson. And named a newly discovered owl louse *Strigiphilus garylarsoni* in 1989.

5. Entomologists do serious work with insects, but many of them also appear to have a sense of humor about their discoveries.

18f Using fragments intentionally

Advertisers and writers occasionally use fragments deliberately for a crisp, immediate effect: "What a luxury should be." "Sleek lines." "Efficient in rain, sleet, and snow." "A magnificent film." Novelists and short story writers use fragments in dialogue to simulate the immediacy and fragmentary nature of colloquial speech. Journalists and nonfiction writers often use a fragment for a stylistic effect, to make an emphatic point:

> Maybe we are looking backward because we are unable to live in the future anymore, because the future comes so fast that we can't look forward to it. Or because one can feel happier in the past by being selective about it.
>
> —Roger Rosenblatt, "The Downside of Talking to the Dead"

> I've sat in the spider-haunted remains of the living room where Evelyn wrote her letter, and looked out at the view she described, which doesn't look in the least like Argyllshire, or Kent, or Sussex. Not even little bits of it. Not even *slightly*.
>
> —Jonathan Raban, *Bad Land: An American Romance*

In academic writing, too, writers sometimes use a fragment intentionally to make an emphatic point.

> He [Dylan Thomas] lived twenty-four years after he began to be a poet. Twenty-four years of poetry, dwindling rapidly in the last decade.
>
> —Donald Hall, *Remembering Poets*

You will also find fragments used intentionally in question form. This use is quite common in academic writing.

> The point of the expedition is to bring them back alive. But what then?
>
> —Carl Sagan, *Cosmos*

By all means, use fragments when you are writing dialogue or when you need to achieve a specific emphatic effect. However, when you are writing expository papers in college or business reports, use intentional fragments sparingly.

18g Identifying run-on (or fused) sentences and comma splices

If you run two independent clauses together without any punctuation or any coordinating conjunction between them, readers may not know where one idea ends and the next one begins.

RUN-ON ERROR **The lion cubs were fighting the elephants were snoozing.**

This error is called a *run-on* (or *fused*) *sentence.* If you use only a comma to connect independent clauses, the meaning may be clear, but the sentence is a *comma splice*—a sentence in which the clauses are improperly joined together (spliced) only with a comma.

COMMA SPLICE ERROR **The lion cubs were fighting, the elephants were snoozing.**

Here a reader seeing the comma would anticipate a series: *The lion cubs were fighting, the elephants were snoozing, and the seals were splashing.*

REVISED **The lion cubs were fighting, and the elephants were snoozing.**

Here are more examples (for ways to correct these, see **18h**):

RUN-ON (FUSED) SENTENCES

┌──── independent clause ────┐ ┌──── independent clause ────┐
▶ **My mother's name is Marta my father's name is George.**

┌── independent clause ──┐ ┌──── independent clause ────┐
▶ **Success is their goal happiness comes a close second.**

COMMA SPLICES

┌──── independent clause ────┐ ┌── independent clause ──┐
▶ **The train picked up speed, the scenery flashed by.**

┌──── independent clause ──┐ ┌──── independent clause ────┐
▶ **Salmon swim upstream, they leap over huge dams to reach**

┌────────────────┐
their destination.

┌──────── independent clause ────────┐ ┌──
▶ **Some parents support bilingual education, however, many**

                                    transitional expression
┌── independent clause ──┐
oppose it vociferously.

VARIATION Comma splices and run-ons are used in advertising, journalism, and other writing for stylistic effect.

▶ **W. [George W. Bush] and Hillary [Clinton] took radically**
                              comma splice emphasizing contrast
different paths. She clutched her husband's coattails, he

clutched his father's.   —Maureen Dowd, *From A to Y at Yale*

                    comma splice emphasizing contrast
▶ **It's not that I'm afraid to die, I just don't want to be there when it happens.**   —Woody Allen, *Without Feathers*

Readers of academic expository writing may prefer a period or semicolon or a recasting of the sentence. Take the stylistic risk of an intentional comma splice only if you are sure what effect you want to achieve and you are sure readers will realize your intentions. See also **26b**, Variations. ∎

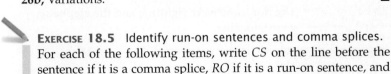

EXERCISE 18.5 Identify run-on sentences and comma splices. For each of the following items, write *CS* on the line before the sentence if it is a comma splice, *RO* if it is a run-on sentence, and *OK* if the sentence is correctly written.

EXAMPLE:

_____CS_____ Many consumers want to buy American cars, unfortunately, choosing an American car is not as easy as it sounds.

1. _____ Often a car's parts are made in one country and assembled in another, can the car be considered American if the whole thing is not manufactured in this country?

2. _____ Sometimes car companies manufacture parts in the United States and also put cars together here however, these companies may have their headquarters in Japan.

3. _____ People who buy cars sold by Ford, an automaker whose name implies "made in the United States" to many Americans, may not know that the vehicles may have been assembled in Mexico.

4. _____ On the other hand, most Honda Accords are made in Ohio in fact, the Honda Corporation now manufactures more cars in the United States than in Japan.

5. _____ As several American auto manufacturers have become part of multinational corporations, globalization has made "buying American" increasingly difficult, consumers can no longer simply rely on the make of a car to determine its country of origin.

18h Correcting run-on sentences and comma splices

You can correct run-on sentences and comma splices in the following five ways. Select the one that works best for the sentence you are editing.

Method 1 Separate the independent clauses into individual sentences with a period (or question mark or exclamation point, if required).

▶ Success is their goal ~~happiness~~ Happiness comes a close second.

▶ Beavers cut down trees with their teeth, ~~they~~ They use the trees for food and shelter.

Method 2 Separate the independent clauses with a semicolon if the clauses are joined by a transitional expression (which is followed by a comma) or if their ideas are closely related.

▶ Some parents support bilingual education; however, many oppose it vociferously.

▶ The hummingbird is amazing; its wings beat fifty to seventy-five times per second.

Method 3 Separate the independent clauses with a comma and a coordinating conjunction (*and, but, or, nor, so, for, yet*).

▶ My mother's name is Marta, and my father's name is George.

▶ Woodpeckers look for insects in trees, but they do not intentionally destroy live trees.

Method 4 Make one clause dependent by adding a subordinating conjunction (see the list on p. 331).

▶ Whenever the ~~The~~ beavers dammed up the river, the rise in the water level destroyed the trees.

▶ The scenery flashed by when the train picked up speed.

Method 5 Make one clause a phrase beginning with an *-ing* participle and attach the phrase to the remaining independent clause.

▶ Salmon swim upstream, ~~they leap~~ leaping over huge dams to reach their destination.

EXERCISE 18.6 Correct run-on sentences and comma splices.
For each of the following items, write *CS* on the line if it is a
comma splice or write *RO* if it is a run-on sentence. Then correct
the error by using one of the five methods described in **18h**.

EXAMPLE:

_____CS_____ Pierre de Fermat, who was a brilliant mathematician,
                                          but
left a puzzle in the margin of a book,ₙhe died without providing

its solution.

1. _____ Pierre de Fermat was a lawyer by trade his passion

    was mathematics.

2. _____ Fermat discussed his ideas in correspondence with

    other mathematicians nevertheless, as a modest man, he

    refused to have his name attached to any published work on

    mathematics.

3. _____ Fermat regarded prime numbers with a special fas-

    cination, he formulated a theory about prime numbers in 1640

    that later became famous as Fermat's Last Theorem.

4. _____ In his notes, Fermat said that the theorem had a

    "marvelous" proof however, he claimed that he did not have

    enough room in the margin to write it down.

5. _____ Some mathematicians believed that a short, elegant

    answer existed, they struggled to find the proof of Fermat's

    Last Theorem.

6. _____ No one has ever found a short proof of the theorem

    most mathematicians now think that Fermat did not have one,

    either.

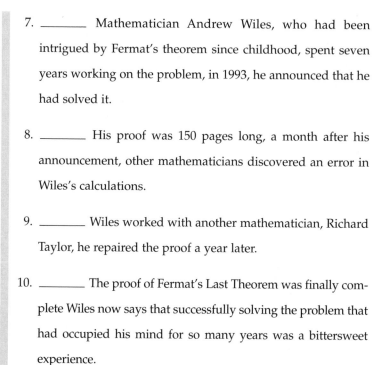

7. _____ Mathematician Andrew Wiles, who had been intrigued by Fermat's theorem since childhood, spent seven years working on the problem, in 1993, he announced that he had solved it.

8. _____ His proof was 150 pages long, a month after his announcement, other mathematicians discovered an error in Wiles's calculations.

9. _____ Wiles worked with another mathematician, Richard Taylor, he repaired the proof a year later.

10. _____ The proof of Fermat's Last Theorem was finally complete Wiles now says that successfully solving the problem that had occupied his mind for so many years was a bittersweet experience.

REVIEW EXERCISE FOR SECTION 18 Revise a passage.
Rewrite the following passage, revising any fragments, run-on sentences, and comma splices. Identify each type of error in the margin. Some sentences may be correct.

Millions of Americans express a belief in extrasensory perception, or ESP, they believe that certain people have psychic abilities. Movies like *The Sixth Sense* and commercials for telephone psychics add to the common perception. That psychic abilities are real. Newspapers and television news shows are frequently too ready to provide a forum for self-proclaimed psychics. And too quick to dismiss the skeptical viewpoint—if the writers even bother to find out what skeptics believe. People who believe in ESP claim that skeptics are curmudgeons. Who automatically reject any claim about paranormal abilities, no matter how compelling the evidence. The truth is that no psychic has ever been able to demonstrate his or her abilities under controlled laboratory conditions, even though a skeptical organization, the James Randi Educational Foundation, has offered a million-dollar prize as an incentive for genuine psychics to step forward. People trained as magicians scoff at the performances of television psychics. Insisting that the techniques used are nothing more than "cold reading" tactics long favored by fortunetellers. Which any competent actor can learn. Although skeptics are often accused of belittling the feelings of grieving people, many would respond that the bereaved do not need to be cheated into thinking that their lost loved ones are in contact with television psychics. If there are "psychic" frauds preying on human grief. They should be exposed before any more innocent sufferers become pawns in their con games.

19 Sentence Snarls

Snarls, tangles, and knots are as difficult to deal with on a bad writing day as on a bad hair day, though they may not be as painful. Sentences with structural inconsistencies give readers trouble. They make readers do the work of untangling. This section points out how to avoid or edit common snarls.

19a Avoid fuzzy syntax.

Revise sentences that begin in one way and then veer off the track, departing from the original structure. When you mix constructions, make faulty comparisons, or tangle your syntax (the structure of a sentence), you confuse readers.

Some
▶ ~~With some~~ professors who never give grades like to write
comments.   [Who are the people who "like to write comments"? The prepositional phrase *with some professors* cannot serve as the subject of the sentence.]

Pay special attention to sentences beginning with *with, by -ing,* or *when -ing.*

MIXED
CONSTRUCTION
When wanting to take on a greater role in business might lead a woman to adopt new personality traits. [Readers get to the verb *might lead* without knowing what the subject is.]

POSSIBLE
REVISIONS
When wanting to take on a greater role in business, a woman might adopt new personality traits. [This version provides a grammatical subject—*woman*—for the independent clause.]

Wanting to take on a greater role in business might lead a woman to adopt new personality traits. [This version deletes the preposition *By* and eliminates the prepositional phrase; now the *-ing* phrase functions as the subject of *might lead.*]

When you make comparisons, be sure to tell readers clearly what you are comparing to what. (See also **22a, 22b,** and **23i.**)

FAULTY
COMPARISON
Like Wallace Stevens, her job strikes readers as unexpected for a poet. [It is not her job that is like the poet Wallace Stevens; her job is like his job.]

REVISED
Like Wallace Stevens, she holds a job that strikes readers as unexpected for a poet.

Revise sentences that ramble on to such an extent that they become tangled. Make sure your sentences have clear subjects and verbs, and use coordination or subordination effectively. For a concise style, cut and check for action (**35, 36**).

TANGLED
The way I feel about getting what you want is that when there is a particular position or item that you want to try to get to do your best and not give up because if you give up you have probably missed your chance of succeeding.

POSSIBLE
REVISION
To get what you want, keep trying.

Note, though, that a sentence can be long and filled with phrases and clauses but still be grammatically accurate and stylistically acceptable, as in the examples in **16g.** Tailor the length and complexity of your sentences to what you want to express and to readers' preferences.

EXERCISE 19.1 Correct fuzzy syntax: mixed constructions and faulty comparisons.

In each of the following items, suggest corrections for any mixed constructions or faulty comparisons.

EXAMPLE:

Adopting
~~By adopting~~ the poetic techniques popular in colonial America enabled Phillis Wheatley to find an audience for her writings.

1. Phillis Wheatley's education, which was remarkable mainly because she received one, a rare luxury for a slave girl in the American colonies.

2. Wheatley, kidnapped from her homeland and sold into slavery when she was about seven, an experience that must have been traumatic.

3. By learning to read and write gave Phillis an opportunity to demonstrate her aptitude for poetry.

4. Like Alexander Pope, iambic pentameter couplets were Phillis Wheatley's preferred poetic form.

5. Publishing a book of poems, Phillis Wheatley, becoming famous partly because she was an African slave who could compete as a poet with well-educated white men.

6. Her work, poems in a very formal eighteenth-century style that found aristocratic admirers in America and England.

7. With the deaths of Mr. and Mrs. Wheatley, when Phillis was in her twenties, left her free but also penniless.

8. Like Zora Neale Hurston in the twentieth century, an impoverished, lonely death followed a loss of public interest in

Wheatley's writings, but scholars discovered her work posthumously and realized her contribution to American literature.

19b Position modifiers appropriately.

A modifier is a word or phrase that describes or limits another word or phrase. Put modifiers in the right place. Keep single words, phrases, and clauses next to or close to the sentence elements that they modify.

Place a phrase or clause close to the word or words it modifies.

MISPLACED **Sidel argues that young women's dreams will not always come true in her essay.** [Will the dreams come true in Sidel's essay or does Sidel argue in her essay?]

REVISED **In her essay, Sidel argues that young women's dreams will not always come true.**

Keep subject, verb, and object in close connection. Sentences are clearer for a reader when all the parts are clearly connected. Once you have announced the subject, do not make readers wait too long for a verb.

NO **The main *character* in the play, because the director in a rash moment had given the part to his inexperienced brother, *turned out* to be the weakest portrayal.**

YES **Because the director in a rash moment had given the part to his inexperienced brother, the main *character* in the play *turned out* to be the weakest portrayal.** [Putting the adverb clause first creates expectation and keeps the subject and verb of the independent clause together.]

Similarly, do not delay a direct object to the end of a sentence.

NO **The actors *had to rehearse* over a period of two days without a break *all the dramatic scenes*.**

YES **The actors *had to rehearse all the dramatic scenes* over a period of two days without a break.**

Place modifiers (*only, even,* and so on) carefully. Place a modifier such as *only, even, just, nearly, merely,* or *simply* immediately before the word it modifies. Consider the differences in meaning in the following sentences:

▶ She *only* likes Tom. [Does she love him?]

▶ She likes *only* Tom. [Does she like Juan?]

▶ *Only* she likes Tom. [Does anyone else like Tom?]

The meaning of a sentence changes significantly as the position of *only* changes, so careful placement is important.

▶ *Only* the journalist began to investigate the forgery.
[and nobody else]

▶ The journalist *only* began to investigate the forgery.
[but did not finish]

▶ The journalist began to investigate *only* the forgery.
[and nothing else]

Make sure the modifier's position does not produce ambiguity. Do not make readers guess which part of a sentence a modifier refers to. A modifier that is ambiguous is often called a **squinting modifier** because it looks two ways at once.

No **The writer who was being interviewed**

aggressively **defended the violent scenes in**

his novel. [Who was being aggressive here—the interviewer in his approach to the interview or the writer in his own defense?]

Yes **The writer who was being *aggressively* interviewed defended the violent scenes in his novel.**

The writer who was being interviewed defended

the violent scenes in his novel *aggressively*.

Consider the case for splitting an infinitive. You split an infinitive when you place a word or phrase between *to* and the verb: *He tried to immediately answer the question.* At one time, a split infinitive was regarded as an error—if not in grammar, at least in grace—and the general advice was always to avoid splitting an infinitive.

VARIATION   Now, however, *The New Oxford Dictionary of English* finds the use of split infinitives "both normal and useful," as in "To boldly go where no man has gone before" (*Star Trek*). However, such splitting may still irritate some readers, especially when a clumsy sentence is the result, as in the following:

clumsy split infinitive (*to inform*)

▶ We want to sincerely, honestly, and in confidence inform you of our plans for expansion.

Use common sense. Read a sentence aloud. If you think your readers may fret over a split infinitive and if the sentence works just as well without splitting the infinitive, then revise the sentence. If the sentence is clear and effective with the split and the split helps to avoid ambiguity or clumsy syntax (*She saw it as a necessity to always achieve perfection in her work*), then keep it—but get ready *to boldly face* any criticism.   ■

EXERCISE 19.2   Correct misplaced modifiers.
Revise any of the following sentences in which the placement of modifiers could be improved. Some sentences may not need revision.

EXAMPLE:

only
By July 2002, two sisters had ~~only~~ competed against each other four times in the finals of a Grand Slam tennis tournament.

1. In 1884, the sisters Maud and Lilian Watson, years before women's tennis was a professional sport, played against each other in the first Wimbledon ladies' championship final.

2. More than a century later, two young California sisters who played tennis seriously began to hope that they would someday rule the tennis world.

3. In September 2001, those sisters, Venus and Serena Williams, faced each other after demolishing their semifinals opponents in the final match of the U.S. Open.

4. Millions of viewers watched as the first Grand Slam tennis championship was shown on prime-time television to feature two African American players.

5. With a serve that has been measured at 127 miles per hour, most fans anticipated that the winner would be Venus.

6. Venus Williams won in two sets, who had won four of the five professional matches against her younger sister before the U.S. Open.

7. However, in 2002, Serena was able to powerfully and skillfully win against her older sister in the French Open, Wimbledon, and U.S. Open finals.

8. Richard Williams, the father of Venus and Serena, who has only been their coach and manager, refuses to watch the matches.

9. Richard Williams taught all five of his daughters to play tennis when they were preschoolers on the public courts in South Central Los Angeles.

10. Venus and Serena Williams prefer to play against other opponents, but as both of them continue to excel in tennis, they are likely to face each other again across the net.

EXERCISE 19.3 Change meaning by changing the position of a modifier.
How many meanings can you get from the following sentence about a bus accident by placing the word *only* in a variety of positions? What are the positions, and what are the meanings that result from each position?

The passenger hurt his arm.

19c **Avoid dangling modifiers.**

A modifier that is not grammatically linked to the noun or phrase it is intended to describe is said to be dangling. A sentence must contain a word or phrase that the modifier is intended to modify, as the following examples illustrate.

DANGLING **Walking into the house, the telephone rang.**

[The sentence says the telephone was walking.]

DANGLING **Delighted with the team's victory, the parade route was decorated by the fans.**

[The sentence says the parade route was delighted.]

Fix a dangling modifier in one of the following ways.

Method 1 Retain the modifier, but make the subject of the independent clause the person or thing modified.

REVISED **Walking into the house, we heard the telephone ring.**

REVISED **Delighted with the team's victory, the fans decorated the parade route.**

Method 2 Change the modifier phrase into a clause with its own subject and verb.

REVISED **While we were walking into the house, the telephone rang.**

REVISED **Because the fans were delighted with the team's victory, they decorated the parade route.**

VARIATION Not all dangling modifiers are equal. Some are awkward and may make readers laugh (*After boiling for five hours, Granny May turned off the cabbage*), while others, particularly those with *it* used as a filler subject, are barely noticeable. The latter can be overlooked by professional writers, editors, and readers, as for example in the passage by Larry McMurtrey on pages 100–101: [. . .] *looking through the various collections of photographs by the early photographers of the West* [. . .] *it occurred to me that I* [. . .]. Some filler *it* subject was not doing the looking; Larry McMurtrey was. But readers can easily adjust to that usage and will not always feel confused. Still, it ultimately may please readers more (especially English instructors) if you are consistent and do not let your modifiers dangle. ■

EXERCISE 19.4 Identify dangling modifiers.
Classify each of the following sentences as *A* (if the sentence contains no dangling modifier), *B* (if the sentence contains a dangling modifier that is a clear error), or *C* (if the sentence contains a dangling modifier that might not offend the average reader). Then revise any sentences classified as *B* or *C*.

EXAMPLE:

                                              I spotted
____B____ Browsing at the bookstore, a copy of the new
translation of the *Iliad* caught my eye.

1. _____ Translating literature from one language into another,
   it is important to strive for both literal accuracy and a similar
   effect to that of the original work.

2. _____ Turning the Greek of the *Iliad* into English in 1997,
   Robert Fagles managed to translate the words accurately while
   keeping the poetry lyrical and muscular.

3. _____ Awarded several prizes for his translation of the *Iliad*,
   many educators delighted in using Fagles's book to show their
   students the difference that a good translation can make.

4. _____ Turning a lively, intelligent book from another culture
   into a dry, dull, or inaccurate English-language text, a reader's
   perspective can be distorted by a bad translation.

5. _____ Helping people everywhere appreciate the beauty
   and power of literature from around the world, cultural awareness improves with every great translation.

19d **Avoid shifts in mood, pronoun person and number, and direct/indirect quotation.**

Unwarranted shifts in your sentences can disconcert readers. (See also **20i** on avoiding unnecessary shifts in verb tense.)

Do not make an abrupt shift in mood, especially between statement and command or between subjunctive and indicative. If you are writing declarative statements, use the indicative mood (see **16a**) consistently.

▶ The students in this university should do more to keep the

    They should pick
place clean. ~~Pick~~ up the litter and treat the dorms like home.

Keep the mood consistent. Do not begin in the indicative mood and then switch to the imperative. Choose one mood or the other, not both.

No   College administrators have issued several directions: Students should use only the south parking lots and do not park on the grass.

Yes   College administrators have issued several directions: Students should use only the south parking lots and should not park on the grass.

Yes   College administrators have issued several directions: Use only the south parking lots and do not park on the grass.

Be careful with conditional sentences (*if* or *unless*) and avoid a shift in mood (**20k**).

                                                          were
▶ He would be able to make significant changes if only he ~~is~~ more organized.

Do not shift person, number, and point of view. To make generalizations about people, use *they, we, you,* or *one* and use them consistently. Be consistent in using first, second, or third person pronouns. For example, if you begin by referring to *one,* do not switch to *you* or *we.* Also avoid shifting unnecessarily between third person singular and plural forms. Note, though, that long passages devoted to discussing what "one" does become vague and pretentious for readers.

SHIFT   *One* needs a high salary to live in a city because *you* have to spend so much on rent and transportation.

POSSIBLE REVISIONS   *One* needs a high salary to live in a city because *one* has to spend so much on rent and transportation.

People need a high salary to live in a city because *they* have to spend so much on rent and transportation.

A high salary is necessary in a city because rent and transportation cost so much.

See also **22g** on when to use and when to avoid using *you*.

Do not shift between direct and indirect quotation, with or without quotation marks. See **20j** and **44d** ESL for more on quotations.

SHIFT   The client told us that he wanted to sign the lease and would we prepare the papers.

REVISED   The client told us that he wanted to sign the lease and asked us to prepare the papers.

SHIFT   She wanted to find out whether any interest had accumulated on her account and was she receiving any money.

REVISED   She wanted to find out whether any interest had accumulated on her account and whether she was receiving any money.

EXERCISE 19.5 Correct inappropriate shifts: mood, pronoun person and number, direct and indirect quotations.
On the line after each of the following sentences, identify inappropriate shifts in mood by writing *M*, inappropriate shifts in pronoun person by writing *PP*, inappropriate shifts in pronoun number by writing *PN*, and inappropriate shifts in direct and indirect quotations by writing *Q*. Then revise each inappropriate shift.

EXAMPLE:

people
Sharks do occasionally attack swimmers, but ~~you~~ are more likely to be killed by a falling television than by a shark bite.
  PP

1. When a tourist in Florida wants an underwater adventure, you can swim in the ocean with sharks. _____

2. In 2001, a series of shark attacks on the east coast of the United States made Florida Fish and Wildlife Conservation commissioners ask whether swimmers were being too careless or were tourist attractions that feature swimming with sharks the cause of the problem? _____

3. When a tour operator puts bait in the water before a shark swim, they may be teaching sharks to associate people with food. _____

4. If sharks were fed too frequently by human beings, the commissioners wondered, will the big fish be more likely to endanger swimmers? _____

5. The curator of the International Shark Attack File told commissioners that the feeding probably didn't contribute to the attacks and would they tell people more about the good behavior of sharks. _____

6. The shark attacks shocked people around the country, and you heard about the attacks constantly in the late summer of 2001. _____

7. A shark can seem ferocious, but they are often in more danger from humans than humans are from the sharks. _____

8. People should not be frightened by the shark's torpedolike body, scaly skin, and sharp teeth. Try to learn about the shark's habits instead. _____

9. Some scientists believe that if a person studies sharks, they will understand ocean ecosystems better. _____

10. Some species of sharks have become endangered because so many people like the taste of it. _____

19e Make subject and predicate a logical match: avoid faulty predication.

To avoid confusing readers, never use a subject and predicate that do not make logical sense together (see **16c**).

 Building
▶ ~~The decision to build~~ an elaborate extension onto the train station made all the trains arrive late.
[It was not the decision that delayed the trains, but the building of the extension.]

 Finding the
▶ ~~The~~ solution to the problem is a hard task.
[A solution is not a task.]

EXERCISE 19.6 Avoid faulty predication.
In each of the following items, revise any sentence containing a subject and predicate that do not make logical sense together. Some sentences may be correct.

EXAMPLE:

 The
~~The coverage of the~~ Watergate scandal destroyed many Americans' faith in government.

1. The home of the Democratic National Committee was occupying a suite at the Watergate Hotel in Washington, D.C., in 1972.

2. A call to the police from a Watergate employee caught five men with eavesdropping equipment breaking into the suite.

3. The Nixon White House's attempts to cover up the involvement of senior officials led to the downfall of the Nixon presidency.

4. The reason the public became aware of crimes by high officials in the Nixon White House was because of reporting done by *Washington Post* journalists in the early 1970s.

Bob Woodward and Carl Bernstein

5. The determination of Bob Woodward and Carl Bernstein, two young *Post* reporters, traced a cover-up all the way to President Nixon.

6. Courageous action by the *Post*'s publisher, Katharine Graham, made the decision to continue running Woodward and Bernstein's Watergate reports when other papers feared to print the information.

7. At that time, the position of Katharine Graham was the only woman heading a major news organization.

8. The scorn of one official targeted by Woodward and Bernstein's investigation treated Graham with contempt; he apparently believed that she could be intimidated.

Katharine Graham

9. Katharine Graham instead personally telling Woodward and Bernstein and their editor, Ben Bradlee, not only to stick with the story but also to forge ahead with the investigation.

10. Creating the *Post*'s reputation as one of the country's top news sources began with its coverage of Watergate.

19f Avoid faulty predication with definitions and reasons.

When you write a definition of a term, use parallel structures on either side of the verb *be*. In formal writing, avoid defining a term by using *is when* or *is where* (or *was when, was where*).

No   **A tiebreaker in tennis *is where* they play one final game to decide the set.**

Yes   **A tiebreaker in tennis is the final deciding game of a tied set.**

Writing about reasons, like writing definitions, has pitfalls. Avoid *the reason is because* in Standard English. Grammatically, an adverb clause beginning with *because* cannot follow the verb *be*. Instead, use *the reason is that,* or recast the sentence.

No   *The reason* **Tiger Woods lost *is because* he could not handle the weather in Scotland.**

Yes   *The reason* **Tiger Woods lost *is that* he could not handle the weather in Scotland.**

Yes   **Tiger Woods lost *because* he could not handle the weather in Scotland.**

VARIATION   In speech, *the reason is because* is common and would probably hardly be noticed or tagged as an error. In writing, though, consider the audience and your writing situation. If formality and correctness are important to readers, avoid using *the reason is because*. Similarly, you may hear and see in print *the reason why*. Use *the reason that* in its place.

                                                that

▶ The TV commentator explained the reason ~~why~~ Tiger Woods lost.

Another possibility is to omit *that* if the meaning is clear without it.

▶ **The TV commentator explained the reason Tiger Woods lost.** ■

EXERCISE 19.7 Avoid faulty predication with definitions and reasons.

In each of the following sentences, identify and revise any faulty predication. Some sentences may be correct.

EXAMPLE:

cash grants

Farm subsidies are ~~where~~ the government gives farmers ~~money~~ to help them grow certain crops.

1. One reason for farmers to receive subsidies is because they set aside part of their land for wildlife conservation.

2. Conservation, which is where the land is preserved in the most natural state possible, accounts for about 9 percent of farm subsidies in the United States.

3. Wetland preservation is when farmers stop draining swampy land and allow it to remain as a habitat for ducks and other waterfowl.

4. The main reason why the duck population is rebounding after ten years of decline is that a large percentage of farmers in North Dakota accepted subsidies to preserve wetlands on their property.

5. Federal subsidies for conservation were originally proposed by environmental groups, but the programs are now supported enthusiastically by organizations such as the National Rifle Association because the subsidies also benefit hunters.

19g Avoid using an adverb clause as the subject of a sentence.

An adverb clause cannot function as the subject of a sentence. (See **16e** on adverb clauses.)

Swimming
▶ ~~Because she swims~~ every day does not guarantee she is healthy.

[The subject is now a noun (gerund) phrase, *Swimming every day,* instead of a clause, *Because she swims every day.*]

, they
▶ When beavers eat trees destroys the woods.

[The dependent clause *When beavers eat trees* is now attached to an independent clause with its own subject, *they.*]

19h Include all necessary words and apostrophes.

Include necessary words in compound structures.   If you omit a verb form from a compound verb, the main verb form must fit into each part of the compound; otherwise, you must use the complete verb form (see **19j** and **37e** on parallel structures).

tried
▶ He has always and will always try to preserve his father's good name in the community.   [*Try* fits only with *will,* not with *has.*]

Include necessary words in comparisons.   See also **23i**.

as
▶ The volleyball captain is as competitive or even more competitive than her teammates.

Sometimes you create ambiguity if you omit the verb in the second part of a comparison.

did
▶ He liked baseball more than his son   [Omitting *did* implies that he liked baseball more than he liked his son.]

Include apostrophes with words that need them.   Include an apostrophe to indicate possession or a contraction.

's
▶ My mother's expectations differed from Jing-Mei's mother.

▶ He cant' understand her reasoning.
        ^

See also **23i** and **28c**.

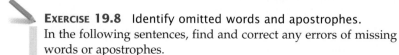

EXERCISE **19.8** Identify omitted words and apostrophes.
In the following sentences, find and correct any errors of missing words or apostrophes.

EXAMPLE:

                                                    at
Quantum mechanics inspires new ways of looking and thinking
                                                    ^
about the universe.

1. One physicist seriously claims that there are as many universes or even more universes than the human mind can
   imagine.

2. This theory, known as the Many Worlds Interpretation, has
   always and may always be considered by many other physi-
   cists to be nothing more than a poetic way of thinking about
   quantum mechanics.

3. However, their basically metaphorical view of the Many
   Worlds Interpretation differs from David Deutsch.

4. Deutsch, an Oxford physicist, regards the Many Worlds
   Interpretation as more realistic than, for example, Stephen
   Hawking.

5. Deutsch's book *The Fabric of Reality* argues for the existence of
   infinite parallel universes populated by people who are similar
   but not quite the same as the individuals existing in our own
   universe.

19i State the grammatical subject only once.

Even when a phrase or clause separates the subject and verb of a clause, do not restate the subject, either with the same word or in pronoun form. (See also **44f** ESL.)

restated subject

▶ The nurse who took care of my father for many years ~~she~~ gave him comfort and advice.

When the subject is a whole clause, do not add an *it* subject.

▶ What may seem moral to some ~~it~~ is immoral to others.

EXERCISE 19.9 Avoid restating subjects.

In the following passage, cross out any restated subjects.

EXAMPLE:

Mother Ann Lee, who was an extremely unusual eighteenth-century woman, ~~she~~ founded the United Society of Believers in Christ's Second Appearing, a group that was also called the Shakers.

The Shakers, a religious sect that was founded in England in 1747 by Mother Ann Lee, were an offshoot of the Quakers. The Shaker belief in gender equality and the surprising fact that the Shaker leader was female they were viewed with suspicion in eighteenth-century England, and the Shakers faced persecution there. The group emigrated to the United States in search of religious freedom in 1774. Mother Lee's followers, who lived celibate lives in gender-segregated houses, they worked and prayed communally and replenished their numbers by recruiting. The Shakers were never a large group, but their numbers grew steadily until the twentieth century. The idea of choosing celibacy it now seems peculiar to many Americans, and the Shakers, indeed, have nearly died out since the group stopped accepting new members decades ago. However, some of the Shakers' beliefs have found modern admirers: their view that "beauty rests on utility" and the exquisitely crafted furniture designs they created to embody that view they are more popular than ever.

 EXERCISE 19.10 Write sentence completions.
Make the following items into complete sentences, making sure you name only one grammatical subject in each independent clause.

EXAMPLE:

The book I read on my summer vacation _told a story of_
World War II .

1. The student who is the head of student government
2. Whatever you can do to help
3. Why a writer would want to avoid using the letter *e*
4. The big oak trunk sitting in the corner of the little girl's room
5. Computer programs aiming to identify grammar errors

19j Use parallel structures.

Structures are parallel when they have the same form. Use parallel structures to help readers see connections between the ideas in a sentence and to bring stylistic cohesion and emphasis to your writing. Section 5e gives examples of parallel structures used to help produce cohesion in a text. Be consistent and keep connected structures, however long and complicated, parallel in form. The following sentence contains parallel -*ing* phrases as direct objects:

▶ When on vacation, they enjoy *playing* volleyball,
      bicycling on country roads, and
      snorkeling in the Gulf waters.

Use similar grammatical structures in parts of the sentence with a similar function.

NOT PARALLEL **He wants a new girlfriend, to buy a house, and find a good job.**

PARALLEL **He wants a new girlfriend, a house, and a good job.**

PARALLEL **He wants to have a new girlfriend, to buy a house, and to find a good job.**

Parallel structures with paired (correlative) conjunctions When your sentence contains correlative conjunctions, pairs such as *either . . . or, neither . . . nor, not only . . . but also, both . . . and, whether . . . or,* and *as . . . as,* the structure after the second part of the pair should be exactly parallel in form to the structure after the first part.

▶ He made up his mind *either* to paint the van *or* ^to^ sell it to another buyer.   [*To paint* follows *either*; therefore, *to sell* should follow *or*.]

▶ She loves *both* swimming competitively *and* ~~to play~~ ^playing^ golf.

[An -*ing* form follows *both*; therefore, an -*ing* form should also follow *and*.]

▶ The drive to Cuernavaca was *not only* too expensive *but also* ~~was~~ too tiring to do alone.   [*Too expensive* follows *not only*; therefore, *too tiring* should follow *but also*.]

Parallel structures in comparisons When making comparisons with *as* or *than,* use parallel structures. In the following examples, the revisions could have used either the infinitive form (*to drive, to take*) in both parts of the sentence, or the -*ing* form.

▶ ~~Driving~~ ^To drive^ to Cuernavaca is *as* expensive *as* to take the bus.

▶ ~~To take~~ ^Taking^ the bus is less comfortable *than* driving.

EXERCISE 19.11   Avoid lack of parallelism.
In the following sentences, revise any errors in parallelism. Some sentences may be correct.

EXAMPLE:

Evangelist Aimee Semple McPherson made news in 1926 for

running a successful radio ministry, preaching in a Los Angeles

temple, and ~~her disappearance~~ ^disappearing^ during an ocean swim.

1. Aimee Semple McPherson was not only the founder of a phenomenally successful ministry but became the first female evangelist to preach on the radio.

2. McPherson's thousands of followers reacted with shock and horror in May 1926 when the evangelist either staged her own disappearance or kidnappers captured her.

3. Resurfacing in Mexico, McPherson claimed to have escaped from kidnappers by walking through the desert for seventeen hours, but she showed no signs of dehydration, heavy sweating, or that she had been sunburned.

4. Was McPherson having an affair with her married radio engineer, telling the truth about the kidnapping, or did she simply need a break from the pressures of celebrity?

5. Not knowing the truth about her disappearance is perhaps more fascinating than to be sure of what happened to Aimee Semple McPherson.

> **REVIEW EXERCISE FOR SECTION 19** Identify and revise sentence snarls.
> Identify and revise any sentence snarls in the following passage. Some sentences may not contain any errors.

Many people think that electroshock therapy was only used to treat mental illness until the middle of the twentieth century. You may be surprised to learn that this radical therapy is still used as a treatment of last resort for certain diseases. The reason is because electroshock therapy, which triggers a grand mal epileptic seizure in the patient, somehow alleviates symptoms of such mental illnesses as depression. No one knows why the convulsions are effective, but they do seem to help many patients.

Because the treatment works is no excuse for torturing people who are already suffering, however, and electroshock in the 1930s was undoubtedly a hideous procedure. Placed on a gurney with electrodes applied to the temples, doctors simply sent a strong electric current into the patient's brain. The resulting convulsions sometimes caused patients either to dislocate a joint or bones were broken. Eventually, advances in medical research made the decision to provide patients with anesthetics and muscle relaxants before electroshock therapy was administered. By changing the procedure dramatically reduced injuries to patients.

Electroshock therapy continues to strike many people as barbaric. Many doctors who have and continue to claim success from electroshock therapy believe, however, that it can be a better treatment for major depression than drugs. Nevertheless, sending electric current into a patient's brain it still seems extreme, and no one today would suggest that a patient undergo the procedure if any other treatment seems likely to work.

20 Verbs

A verb tells what a person, thing, or concept does or is.

▶ **The community college in my county** *provides* **opportunities for disadvantaged students.**

Ask the following question about a clause to determine the verb:

Who (or what) does (or is) (what)?

[Answer: The community college *provides* opportunities.]

The base form of a verb (the form with no endings or vowel changes) will fit into one or both of the following slots:

▶ **They will** _____

[They will provide.]

▶ **It might** _____

[It might provide.]

See also **20d** for modal auxiliary verbs, such as *can* and *should*, which do not fit this pattern. For more on what a verb is and how it functions, see **16a.**

20a Verb basics

The verb phrase of a clause provides the following information:

Tense: present, past, future	They *decide.* They *decided.* They *will decide.*
Aspect: simple, progressive, perfect, perfect progressive	The following examples show aspects of present tense: He *works.* He *is working.* He *has worked.* He *has been working.*
Person: the person speaking, being spoken to, being spoken about	We *try.* You *try.* She *tries.*
Number: singular, plural	The room *is* gloomy. The rooms *are* gloomy.
Voice: active, passive	The city *has demolished* the building. The building *has been demolished* by the city.
Mood: indicative (makes a statement or asks a question), imperative (gives a command), subjunctive (expresses a hypothetical condition, recommendation, and so on)	She *cleaned* her room. *Clean* your room right now. The boss suggested that she *clean* her office.

KEY POINTS
Verb Types

1. **Complete verb** All the words of a verb phrase make up the complete verb of a clause: She *might have been promoted.* An *-ing* verb form by itself cannot be a complete verb.

   is
   ▶ She preparing a report.
      ^

   (continued)

(continued)

2. **Main verb** The main verb is the part of a complete verb phrase that occurs after any auxiliaries: She might have been *promoted*.

3. **Auxiliary verb** An auxiliary verb is a helping verb (see **20d**). It helps provide information to complete the meaning of the main verb of a clause. It provides information about the following:

   - tense and aspect (They *have* left. She *did* not leave. We *are* leaving.)
   - voice (The suspects *are being* questioned. The police *are* questioning them now.)
   - mood (*Do* not make a mistake. If she *were* mayor, she would build more housing.)

   The auxiliary verbs are *am, is, are, was, were, has, have, had, do, does, did*. The forms *be, being,* and *been* also occur in auxiliary verb phrases, after another auxiliary or modal auxiliary: has *been* trying; might *be* performing; were *being* written.

4. **Modal auxiliary verb** A modal auxiliary verb provides information about future time (*will*), intention, possibility, ability, advisability, and necessity (see also **20d** and **43b** ESL). The modal auxiliaries are *will, would, can, could, shall, should, may, might,* and *must*.

5. **Transitive verb** A transitive verb is followed by a noun phrase, pronoun, *-ing* noun form, or noun clause as its direct object:

   - My friends *painted the cabinet*.
   - He *invited her* to the party.
   - They *enjoy skiing*.
   - We *do* not *know what he intended*.

   A transitive verb can be used in the passive voice: The cabinet *was painted* by my friends. The dictionary indicates whether a verb is transitive (*tr.* or *vt*) or intransitive (*intr.* or *vi*). See **20c** and **20l**.

6. **Intransitive verb** An intransitive verb is not followed by a direct object: The tornado *occurred* at night. It cannot be used in the passive voice. See **20c** and **20l**.

7. **Linking verb** A linking verb provides information about the subject: They *are* actors. He *looks* happy. The steak *smells* good. He *became* the leader.

20b Forms of regular and irregular verbs

Although you might use a variety of verb forms when you speak, readers generally expect formal writing to conform to Standard English usage. All verbs except *be* have five forms.

Regular verbs The five forms of regular verbs follow a predictable pattern. Once you know the base form, you can construct all the others:

1. base form (no -*s*): the form listed in a dictionary
2. -*s* form: the third person singular form of the present tense
3. -*ing* form (the *present participle*): needs auxiliary verbs to function as a complete verb
4. past tense form: functions as a complete verb, without auxiliary verbs
5. past participle: also called the -*ed* form; needs auxiliary verbs to function as a complete verb (*has selected, was selected*).

REGULAR VERBS

BASE	-*s*	*-ing* PRESENT PARTICIPLE	PAST TENSE	PAST PARTICIPLE
paint	paints	painting	painted	painted
smile	smiles	smiling	smiled	smiled
watch	watches	watching	watched	watched

Irregular verbs In contrast, irregular verbs do not use -*ed* to form the past tense and the past participle. (See **20d** for the forms of irregular verbs *be, do,* and *have.*)

IRREGULAR VERBS

BASE	-*s*	*-ing* PRESENT PARTICIPLE	PAST TENSE	PAST PARTICIPLE
take	takes	taking	took	taken
go	goes	going	went	gone
swim	swims	swimming	swam	swum

The following list shows common irregular verbs. Notice the past tense form and past participle of each one.

BASE FORM	PAST TENSE	PAST PARTICIPLE
arise	arose	arisen
bear	bore	born

BASE FORM	PAST TENSE	PAST PARTICIPLE
beat	beat	beaten
become	became	become
begin	began	begun
bend	bent	bent
bet	bet	bet, betted
bind	bound	bound
bite	bit	bitten
bleed	bled	bled
blow	blew	blown
break	broke	broken
bring	brought	brought
build	built	built
burst	burst	burst
buy	bought	bought
catch	caught	caught
choose	chose	chosen
cling	clung	clung
come	came	come
cost	cost	cost
creep	crept	crept
cut	cut	cut
deal	dealt	dealt
dig	dug	dug
do	did	done
draw	drew	drawn
drink	drank	drunk
drive	drove	driven
eat	ate	eaten
fall	fell	fallen
feed	fed	fed
feel	felt	felt
fight	fought	fought
find	found	found
flee	fled	fled

BASE FORM	PAST TENSE	PAST PARTICIPLE
fly	flew	flown
forbid	forbad(e)	forbidden
forget	forgot	forgotten
forgive	forgave	forgiven
freeze	froze	frozen
get	got	gotten, got
give	gave	given
go	went	gone
grind	ground	ground
grow	grew	grown
hang*	hung	hung
have	had	had
hear	heard	heard
hide	hid	hidden
hit	hit	hit
hold	held	held
hurt	hurt	hurt
keep	kept	kept
know	knew	known
lay	laid	laid (see also **20c**)
lead	led	led
leave	left	left
lend	lent	lent
let	let	let
lie	lay	lain (see also **20c**)
light	lit, lighted	lit, lighted
lose	lost	lost
make	made	made
mean	meant	meant
meet	met	met
put	put	put
quit	quit	quit
read	read	read

Hang meaning "put to death" is regular: *hang, hanged, hanged.*

BASE FORM	PAST TENSE	PAST PARTICIPLE
ride	rode	ridden
ring	rang	rung
rise	rose	risen (see also **20c**)
run	ran	run
say	said	said
see	saw	seen
seek	sought	sought
sell	sold	sold
send	sent	sent
set	set	set (see also **20c**)
shake	shook	shaken
shine (intr.)	shone	shone
shoot	shot	shot
shrink	shrank	shrunk
shut	shut	shut
sing	sang	sung
sink	sank	sunk
sit	sat	sat (see also **20c**)
sleep	slept	slept
slide	slid	slid
slit	slit	slit
speak	spoke	spoken
spend	spent	spent
spin	spun	spun
spit	spit, spat	spit
split	split	split
spread	spread	spread
spring	sprang	sprung
stand	stood	stood
steal	stole	stolen
stick	stuck	stuck
sting	stung	stung
stink	stank, stunk	stunk
strike	struck	struck, stricken

BASE FORM	PAST TENSE	PAST PARTICIPLE
swear	swore	sworn
sweep	swept	swept
swim	swam	swum
swing	swung	swung
take	took	taken
teach	taught	taught
tear	tore	torn
tell	told	told
think	thought	thought
throw	threw	thrown
tread	trod	trodden, trod
understand	understood	understood
upset	upset	upset
wake	woke	waked, woken
wear	wore	worn
weave	wove	woven
weep	wept	wept
win	won	won
wind	wound	wound
wring	wrung	wrung
write	wrote	written

20c Verbs commonly confused

You may need to give special attention to certain verbs that are similar in form but differ in meaning. Some of them can take a direct object; these are called *transitive verbs*. Others never take a direct object; these are called *intransitive verbs*. (See also **16c,** p. 323, and **44c** ESL.)

1. *rise, arise:* to get up, to ascend (intransitive)

   raise: to lift, to cause to rise (transitive)

BASE	-s	-ing	PAST TENSE	PAST PARTICIPLE
rise	rises	rising	rose	risen
raise	raises	raising	raised	raised

▶ Sarah *rose* early to fix breakfast for the family.

▶ The bread *rose* as soon as she put it in the oven.

▶ She *raised* her daughter by herself.

2. *sit:* to occupy a seat (intransitive)

   set: to put or place (transitive)

BASE	-s	-ing	PAST TENSE	PAST PARTICIPLE
sit	sits	sitting	sat	sat
set	sets	setting	set	set

   sitting
▶ He has been ~~setting~~ on the bench and staring for half an hour.

   set
▶ She ~~sat~~ the vase on the middle shelf.

3. *lie:* to recline (intransitive; not followed by a direct object)

   lay: to put or place (transitive; followed by a direct object)

BASE	-s	-ing	PAST TENSE	PAST PARTICIPLE
lie	lies	lying	lay	lain
lay	lays	laying	laid	laid

Note the possibility for confusion especially with the form *lay* being both the base form of the transitive verb and the past tense form of the intransitive verb. (But, then, whoever said language was logical?)

   lay
▶ I ~~laid~~ down for half an hour.

   lying
▶ I was ~~laying~~ down when you called.

   Lay
▶ ~~Lie~~ the map on the floor.

VARIATION You are likely to come across many variations of the *lie/lay* distinction. Confusion is commonplace. You will certainly hear people say things like "Grandma laid down for a nap" or "She lay the dress out on the bed." You will also come across confusion of the forms in (presumably) edited writing: "Do you want a comfortable mattress to lay down on?" and "He just laid there, asking for help." Yes, people will understand you, but they may also notice that you do not seem to be aware of the difference between the two forms and regard that negatively. So avoid falling into the common trap. Make a point of showing you *are* aware of the distinction between *lie* and *lay*. ∎

In addition, note the verb *lie* ("to say something untrue"), which is intransitive.

BASE	-s	-*ing*	PAST TENSE	PAST PARTICIPLE
lie	lies	lying	lied	lied

▶ He *lied* when he said he had won three trophies.

EXERCISE 20.1 Use commonly confused verbs correctly.
In each of the following sentences, choose the verb needed in the sentence from the choices in parentheses and underline it. Then write the correct form of the verb in the blank.

EXAMPLE:

Most children who are __raised__ (<u>raise</u> / rise) in the United States learn the Pledge of Allegiance in elementary school.

1. Francis Bellamy, the author of the Pledge of Allegiance, wanted to add the word *equality* when he _____ (set / sit) down the line *with liberty and justice for all* in 1892.

2. He knew, however, that many Americans at that time would _____ (raise / rise) objections, because equality for women and African Americans was not a widely accepted idea a hundred years ago.

3. Although Bellamy was a Baptist minister, he did not _____ (set / sit) down to write a prayer; the original version of the Pledge of Allegiance does not contain the phrase *under God*.

4. Responsibility for adding *under God* to the Pledge must _____ (lay / lie) with Congress, which voted to include those words in 1954.

5. Bellamy _____ (lay / lie) plans to incorporate the Pledge into a flag-raising ceremony in honor of the 400th anniversary of the discovery of America, and since then, his pledge has been a popular addition to American ceremonies of all kinds.

20d *Do, have, be,* and the modal auxiliaries

The verb and auxiliary *do* *Do* can serve as a main verb, with or without auxiliaries. Forms of *do* can serve as either main verbs or auxiliaries:

Present: (I, you, we they) *do*
(he, she, it) *does*

Past: *did*

-*ing* form: *doing*

Past participle: *done*

Use a *do* auxiliary to form a negative, a question, or an emphatic statement.

DO AS A MAIN VERB	**She *did* the job quickly. They have *done* well. He is *doing* his best.**
DO AS AN AUXILIARY	**She *did* not *quit*. He *does* not *approve*. *Do* you *agree*? He *does*, indeed, *trust* their promises.**

The verb and auxiliary *have*   *Have* can serve as a main verb, with its own auxiliaries if necessary; or you can use *have, has,* or *had* as an auxiliary verb with another main verb.

> Present: (I, you, we, they) *have*
> (he, she, it) *has*

> Past: *had*

> *-ing: having*

> Past participle: *had*

▶ They *have* a huge apartment. They should *have* a house-warming party soon.

*[labels: main verb — *have*; main verb (base form) — *have*]*

▶ They *have* furnished the room beautifully. The table *has* been painted maroon.

*[labels: auxiliary — *have*; auxiliary — *has*]*

▶ He *has* never *had* a raise.

*[labels: auxiliary — *has*; main verb — *had*]*

Use *have* and *has* as an auxiliary to form the present perfect tense (see **20f**). Use *had* as an auxiliary to form the past perfect tense (see **20g**). The forms of *have* can be used as auxiliaries in both the active and the passive voices:

▶ The sun *has* set. [Active]

▶ The paintings *have* been stolen. [Passive]

The verb and auxiliary *be*   The verb *be* has eight forms, including three present tense forms (*am, is, are*) and two past tense forms (*was, were*).

BASE	PRESENT TENSE FORMS	*-ing*	PAST	PAST PARTICIPLE
be	am, is, are	being	was, were	been

You can use the appropriate forms of *be* as main verbs or as auxiliaries. The auxiliary *be* is used in both the active and the passive voices:

▶ **My uncle *was winning.*** [Active]

▶ **However, he *was overtaken* at the finish line.** [Passive]

For more on the use of *be, being* and *been,* see page 400.

        main verb   main verb
▶ **The tigers *are* hungry. The antelope *is* afraid.**

        main verb
▶ **The jungle *was* quiet.**

   auxiliary   auxiliary   auxiliary
▶ **She *is* jogging. I have *been* dreaming. They *were* arrested.**

     auxiliary
▶ **He will *be* rewarded.**

> ### WORLDS OF WRITING
> ### Language and Dialect Variation with *Be*
>
> In some languages (Chinese and Russian, for example), forms of *be* used as auxiliaries ("She *is* singing") or as linking verbs ("He *is* happy") can be omitted. In some spoken dialects of English (African American Vernacular, for example), subtle linguistic distinctions not possible in Standard English can be achieved; for instance, the omission of a form of *be* and the use of the base form in place of an inflected form (a form that shows number, person, mood, or tense) signal entirely different meanings.
>
> | VERNACULAR | STANDARD |
> | --- | --- |
> | He busy. | [temporarily] He is busy [now]. |
> | She be busy. [habitually] | She is busy [all the time]. |
>
> Standard English always requires the inclusion of an inflected form of *be.*
>
>   are
> ▶ **Latecomers always at a disadvantage.**

Auxiliaries and modal auxiliaries Both an independent clause and a dependent clause need a complete verb. The *-ing* form and the past participle are not complete verbs because they do not show tense. They need auxiliary or modal auxiliary verbs to complete their meaning in a clause. (See **43b** ESL for the meanings of modal auxiliary verbs.)

AUXILIARY VERBS	MODAL AUXILIARY VERBS	
do: do, does, did	will, would	shall, should
be: be, am, is, are, was, were, being, been	can, could	may, might, must
have: have, has, had		

Auxiliary verbs and modal auxiliary verbs can be used in combination. Whatever the combination, the form of the main verb is determined by the auxiliary that precedes it.

AUXILIARY VERB	FOLLOWED BY	EXAMPLE
do, does, did	Base form	Does she *travel* much?
will, would, can, could, shall, should, may, might, must	Base form	She will *send* him an angry letter.
have, has had	Past participle	The song has *ended*.
am, is, are, was, were, be, been	*-ing* (for active voice only)	They are still *applauding*.
am, is, are, was, were, be, been, being	Past participle (for passive voice only)	The singer was *applauded* loudly.

WHICH FORM SHOULD I USE?

1. Immediately after *do, does, did,* and the nine modal auxiliaries—*will, would, can, could, shall, should, may, might,* and *must*—use the base form.

   ▶ The singer *didn't smile* once.

   ▶ *Did* the audience *leave*?

   ▶ He *should have* stayed longer.

   ▶ Time *will pass.*

   ▶ They *must be* trying to find a parking space.

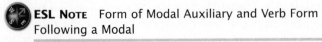

ESL NOTE   Form of Modal Auxiliary and Verb Form Following a Modal

A modal auxiliary never changes form or takes an *-s* ending. The form of the verb after a modal auxiliary is always the base form, never a verb with an *-s* or *-ed* ending.

▶ They should~~s~~ offer to help.

▶ Everyone can enjoy~~s~~ the view.

> have
▶ The band might ~~has~~ finished playing.

2. Immediately after *has, have,* and *had,* use the past participle.

▶ It *has snowed.*

▶ They *had eaten* when I arrived.

▶ It *has been* snowing for five hours.

▶ They should *have gone.*

[Not: They should *have went.*]

In informal speech, we run sounds together, and the pronunciation may be mistakenly carried over into writing.

> have
▶ She should ~~of~~ left that job last year.

The pronunciation of the contraction *should've* is probably responsible for the nonstandard form *should of.* Edit carefully for the appearance of the word *of* in place of *have* in verb phrases.

3. Immediately after *am, is, are, was, were, be* and *been,* use the *-ing* form for active voice verbs.

▶ She *is taking* her driving test.

▶ You *were watching.*

▶ He might have *been driving.*

▶ They could *be jogging.*

ESL NOTE The *-ing* Form

To form a complete verb, always use a *be* auxiliary before the *-ing* form. The *-ing* form alone can never be a complete verb in a clause.

> are
▶ The poets and the novelists on the faculty planning to give a public reading.

See **43a** ESL.

4. Immediately after *am, is, are, was, were, be, been,* and *being,* use the past participle for the passive voice (see **20l**).

▶ They *were taken* **to a tropical island for their anniversary.**

▶ **The faucet should** *be fixed.*

▶ **The pie might have** *been eaten.*

▶ **The suspects are** *being watched.*

ESL NOTE What Comes before *Be, Been,* and *Being*

1. Modal auxiliary + *be*

▶ *might be* **late,** *could be* **jogging** (active), *will be* **presented** (passive)

2. *have, has, had* + *been*

▶ *have been* **driving** (active), *has been* **eaten** (passive)

3. *am, is, are, was, were* + *being*

▶ **You** *are being* **silly.** (active)

▶ **He** *was being* **followed.** (passive)

EXERCISE 20.2 Use verb forms correctly.
In the following passage, correct any errors in the use of verbs and auxiliaries.

EXAMPLE:

        is
Cladistics ~~be~~ the science of determining evolutionary
relationships by examining the shared physical characteristics
of organisms.

Scientists have always try to analyze which organisms are related to each other and to place them into family trees. Paleontologists interested in determining the descendants of an ancient creature must to rely on the fossil record. By comparing the creature's body structure and bones with those of living organisms, these scientists can making educated guesses about the relationship between a fossilized animal and a modern-day one.

Today, the science of DNA analysis is offering new clues into how creatures be related to one another; many of the answers so far surprising. One recent DNA discovery convinced many scientists that the grebe—a small, stocky, diving bird—should of been classified as a cousin of the flamingo rather than as a relative of the loon and other diving birds. Flamingo fossils more than fifty million years old have been discover, but nothing in the flamingo ancestors' body type suggested this relationship with the grebe. Fossils have no DNA, so using this valuable new technique will not solves many questions about classifications of ancient organisms. However, many scientists already wondering what other surprises DNA testing might bring.

20e Time and verb tenses

Tenses indicate time as perceived by the speaker or writer. Verbs change form to indicate present or past time: *We play. We played.* To indicate future time, English uses the modal auxiliary *will* (*We will play*) as well as expressions such as *be + going to* (*We are going to play when our work is finished*). For each time (present, past, and future), we can use auxiliary verbs with the main verb to convey completed actions (perfect forms), actions in progress (progressive forms), and actions that are completed by some specified time or event and also emphasize the length of time in progress (perfect progressive forms).

The following examples illustrate aspects of active voice verbs referring to past, present, and future time. For passive voice verbs, see **20l.**

PAST TIME

Simple past	They *arrived* yesterday. They *did* not *arrive* today.
Past progressive	They *were leaving* when the phone rang.
Past perfect	Everyone *had left* when I called.
Past perfect progressive	We *had been sleeping* for an hour before you arrived.

PRESENT TIME

Simple present	He *eats* Wheaties every morning.
	He *does* not *eat* eggs.
Present progressive	They *are working* today.
Present perfect	She *has* never *read* Melville.
Present perfect progressive	He *has been living* here for five years.

FUTURE TIME (USING WILL)

Simple future	She *will arrive* soon.
	She *will* not (won't) *be* late.
Future progressive	They *will be playing* baseball at noon tomorrow.
Future perfect	He *will have finished* the project by Friday.
Future perfect progressive	By the year 2007, they *will have been running* the company for twenty-five years.

Other modal auxiliaries can substitute for *will* and thus change the meaning: *must arrive, might be playing, may have finished, should have been running* (see 43b ESL).

 ESL Note Verbs Not Used in Progressive Form

Use simple tenses but not progressive forms with verbs expressing ideas related to the senses, preference, emotion, or thought (for example, *smell, taste, prefer, want, need, appreciate, know, understand*), as well as with verbs of possession, appearance, and inclusion (for example, *own, possess, seem, resemble, contain*).

▶ The fish in that showcase ~~is smelling~~ bad.
　　　　　　　　　　　　　smells

▶ They ~~are possessing~~ different behavior patterns.
　　　possess

20f Present tenses

Simple present Use the simple present tense for the following purposes:

1. To make a generalization

　▶ Babies *sleep* a lot.

　▶ A baseball player *dreads* the words "blown save."

2. To indicate an activity that happens habitually or repeatedly

 ▶ We *turn* the clocks ahead every April.

 ▶ He *works* for Sony.

 ▶ They *take* vacations in Puerto Rico.

3. To discuss literature and the arts even if the work was written in the past or the author is no longer alive

 ▶ In *Zami,* Audre Lorde *describes* how a librarian *introduces* her to the joys of reading.

 When used in this way, the present tense is called the *literary present.* However, when you write a narrative of your own, use past tenses to tell about past actions.

 ▶ Then the candidate ~~walks~~ up to the crowd and ~~kisses~~ all the
 _{walked}   _{kissed}
 babies.

4. To express future time in a dependent clause beginning with a conjunction such as *if, when, before, after, until,* or *as soon as*

 ▶ When they ~~will~~ arrive, the meeting will begin.

 [Use *will* only in the independent clause. Use the simple present in the subordinate clause.]

Present progressive   Use the present progressive to indicate an action in progress at the moment of speaking or writing.

 ▶ It's spring and the grass *is growing.*

 ▶ Publishers *are getting* nervous about plagiarism.

Present perfect and present perfect progressive   Use the present perfect in the following instances:

1. To indicate that an action that occurred at some unstated time in the past is related to present time

 ▶ They *have worked* in New Mexico, so they know its laws.

2. To indicate that an action that began in the past continues to the present

 ▶ They *have worked* for the same company ever since I have known them.

 If you state a time in the past when something occurred and ended, use the simple past tense, not the present perfect.

 ▶ They ~~have worked~~ in Arizona three years ago.
 _{worked}

Use the present perfect progressive when you indicate the length of time an action has been in progress up to the present time.

▶ They *have been dancing* for three hours.

  [This implies that they are still dancing.]

20g Past tenses

Use the past tenses consistently. Do not switch to present or future for no reason (see **20i**).

Simple past Use the simple past tense when you specify exactly when an event occurred or when you write about a past time.

▶ She *married* him last month.

▶ World War I soldiers *suffered* in the trenches.

When the sequence of past events is indicated with words such as *before* or *after,* use the simple past for both events.

▶ She *knew* how to write her name before she *went* to school.

Past progressive Use the past progressive for an activity in progress over time or at a specified point in the past.

▶ They *were working* all day yesterday.

▶ He *was lifting* weights when I called.

Past perfect Use the past perfect or the past perfect progressive only when one past event was completed before another past event or stated past time.

▶ Ben *had cooked* the whole meal by the time Sam arrived.

  [Two events occurred: Ben cooked the meal; then Sam arrived.]

▶ He *had been cooking* for three hours when his sister finally offered to help.

  [An event in progress—cooking—was interrupted in the past.]

  Make sure that the past tense form you choose expresses your exact meaning.

▶ When the student protesters marched into the building at noon, the administrators *were leaving.*

  [The administrators were in the process of leaving. They began to leave at, say, 11:57 a.m.]

▶ **When the student protesters marched into the building at
noon, the administrators** *had left.*

[There was no sign of the administrators. They had left at 11 a.m.]

▶ **When the student protesters marched into the building at
noon, the administrators** *left.*

[The administrators saw the protesters and then left at 12:01 p.m.]

EXERCISE 20.3 Identify verb tenses.
In each of the following sentences, identify the tense of the underlined verb.

EXAMPLE:

A monument in Fort Greene Park in Brooklyn, New York, <u>honors</u>
the memory of the prisoners of war during the American
Revolution who died on prison ships anchored in New York
Harbor. ___*simple present*___

1. Between 1776 and 1783, the British <u>sent</u> most captured American soldiers to New York City, which was occupied by the British throughout the Revolutionary War.

   _____

2. More than eleven thousand American prisoners <u>had died</u> on
   New York's British prison ships before the war ended.

   _____

3. On the most notorious ship, the *Jersey,* work parties of prisoners <u>were</u> routinely <u>removing</u> six or eight corpses each day during the war. _____

4. Most Americans <u>have</u> never <u>heard</u> about the prison ships, so
   they are unaware that nearly twice as many people died there
   as died in combat during the entire Revolutionary War.

   _____

5. Public funding paid for a monument to the prisoners, which
   <u>has been standing</u> in Fort Greene Park since 1907.

   _____

EXERCISE 20.4 Use present tenses correctly.
In each of the following sentences, correct any errors in the use of
present tense verb forms. Some sentences may be correct.

EXAMPLE:

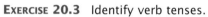

What ~~did~~ babies ~~observed~~ when they look at faces?

1. Within a few hours of birth, newborn babies are showing a preference for looking at human faces.

2. Cognitive psychologists determine what has interested babies by measuring how long they look at certain patterns or objects.

3. Recent studies have shown that babies' brains have been forming the ability to differentiate faces by the time the babies are a few months old.

4. Scientists have not yet come to an agreement on whether babies are born with the ability to recognize faces or whether they are simply born with a preference for certain shapes and contours.

5. Scientific debate on the subject is raging, but as further studies will be completed, our understanding of how humans learn face recognition will continue to grow.

EXERCISE 20.5 Use past tenses correctly.
In the following passage, correct any errors in the use of past tense forms. Some sentences may be correct.

EXAMPLE:

                    have been
Since the late 1970s, teenagers ~~were~~ buying every hip-hop
                              ^
record they can find.

In 1973, Clive Campbell, a Jamaican immigrant who lived in the Bronx, New York, since 1967, christened himself "DJ Kool Herc" and began to work as a neighborhood disc jockey. During his childhood in Jamaica, Campbell saw performers known as *toasters* talking rhythmically over reggae music. At dance parties in the Bronx, DJ Kool Herc had chanted rhymes while he played popular records. His favorite parts of the records, the parts that had made the crowds dance, were the instrumental breaks, some of which were lasting only fifteen seconds. Kool Herc began buying two copies of the records with the best breaks and performing with two turntables, which he manipulated by hand so that the fifteen-second break could last as long as the crowd enjoyed it. DJ Kool Herc's innovation had been creating the music now known as hip-hop.

20h · *-ed* endings: past tense and past participle forms

Both the past tense form and the past participle of regular verbs end in *-ed*. This ending causes writers trouble because in speech the ending is often dropped—particularly when it blends into the next sound.

> ▸ They wash*ed* two baskets of laundry last night.

Standard English requires the *-ed* ending in the following instances:

1. To form the past tense of a regular verb

> ▸ He ask*ed* to leave early.

2. To form the expression *used to,* indicating past habit

> ▸ They use*d* to smoke.

3. To form the past participle of a regular verb after the auxiliary *has, have,* or *had* in the active voice or after a form of *be* (*am, is, are, was, were, be, being, been*) in the passive voice (see **20l**)

> ▸ She has work*ed* there for a long time. [Active]
> ▸ The work will be finish*ed* tomorrow. [Passive]

4. To form a past participle for use as an adjective

> ▸ Put in some chop*ped* meat. ▸ The frighten*ed* boy ran away.

Note: The following *-ed* forms are used with verbs such as *be* and *get.* Some can also be used with *seem, appear,* and *look.*

concerned	embarrassed	scared
confused	married	surprised
depressed	prejudiced	used (to)
divorced	satisfied	worried

Do not omit the -*d* ending. In addition, note also the form *supposed to* (not *suppose to*).

> ►I was surprise^d to see how many awards they won.

> ►Parents get worr^{ied} when their children are depress^{ed}.

> ►The general was suppose^d to be in charge.

Do not confuse the past tense form and the past participle of an irregular verb. A past tense form stands alone as a complete verb, but a past participle does not.

> ►They ~~done~~ well.
>   ^{did}

EXERCISE 20.6 Use -*ed* endings correctly.
In each of the following sentences, edit errors in -*ed* forms of verbs. Some sentences may be correct.

EXAMPLE:

Technology has ~~change~~ the classroom experience for many students.
^{changed}

1. College classrooms use to be seen as places where professors lectured to passive students, with only the most verbal students participating in discussions of the material.

2. Today, however, many professors have noticed the difference computers can make in their students' ability to join in class discussions.

3. For some courses, students are expose to Web sites filled with multimedia materials as well as to more typical readings on a given subject.

4. Before attending class, students are often ask to participate in e-mail discussions on a topic related to what they are studying; the discussions usually continue in the classroom.

5. Professors who once notice the same students doing all the talking in every class maintain that starting discussions in writing on a listserv is more likely to enable all students to participate.

20i Avoiding unnecessary tense shifts

If you use tenses consistently throughout a piece of writing, you help readers understand what is happening and when. Check that your verbs consistently express present or past time, both within a sentence and from one sentence to the next.

TENSE SHIFTS **Selecting a jury *was* difficult. The lawyers *ask* many questions to discover bias and prejudice; sometimes the prospective jurors *had* the idea they *are acting* in a play.**

REVISED **Selecting a jury *was* difficult. The lawyers *asked* many questions to discover bias and prejudice; sometimes the prospective jurors *had* the idea they *were acting* in a play.**

When you write about events or ideas presented by another writer, use the literary present (see **20f**).

▶ **The author illustrated the images of women in two ways, using advertisements and dramas on TV. One way shows women who advanced their careers by themselves, and the other shows those who used beauty to gain recognition.**

Tense shifts are appropriate in the following instances:

1. When you signal a time change with a time word or phrase

signal for switch from past to present

▶ **Harold *was* my late grandfather's name, and *now* it *is* mine.**

2. When you follow a generalization (present tense) with a specific example of a past incident

—————— generalization ——————
▶ **Some bilingual schools *offer* intensive instruction in**

—————— specific example ——————
English. My sister, for example, *went* to a bilingual school where she *studied* English for two hours every day.

EXERCISE 20.7 Correct tense shifts.

In the following passage, correct any unnecessary tense shifts.

EXAMPLE:

Anthropologist Cai Hua's book *A Society without Fathers*

describes
or *Husbands: The Na of China* ~~described~~ a tribe in Yunnan
                               ^

                               marry
province whose members rarely ~~married~~.
                              ^

The Na tribe of southern China are an isolated people with an unusual social system. A typical Na household did not consist of a nuclear or extended family made up of a husband and wife and their relatives; Na households are made up of mothers, children, sisters, and brothers, but no fathers. The Na did not marry, and women conceived children when the men make secret midnight visits to their homes. Such visits happened frequently. Cai Hua explained that either a man or a woman can propose such a visit, and the person who receives the proposition is free to accept or reject it. Women and men appeared to have equal power in Na society. Unlike most other social groups known to anthropologists, the Na had no words for infidelity or promiscuity, and there was apparently no stigma attached to men or women who have many lovers.

20j Tenses in indirect quotations

An indirect quotation reports what someone said. It does not use quotation marks. When the verb introducing an indirect quotation is in a present tense, the indirect quotation should preserve the tense of the original direct quotation. See also **19d** and **44d** ESL.

DIRECT   "The client *has signed* the contract."

                    present ┌──────── indirect quotation ────────
INDIRECT   The lawyer *tells* us that the client *has signed* the
                                                  └──────────┐
            contract.

When the introductory verb is in a past tense, use forms that express past time in the indirect quotation.

DIRECT   "The meetings are over and the buyer has signed the contract."

INDIRECT   Our lawyer *told* us that the meetings *were* over and the buyer *had signed* the contract.

In longer passages, preserve the sequence of tenses showing past time throughout the whole indirect quotation.

▶ Our lawyer, Larraine, told us that the meetings *were* over and the buyer *had signed* the contract. Larraine's firm *had reassigned* her to another case, so she *was leaving* the next day.

Note: Use a present tense after a past tense introductory verb only if the statement is a general statement that holds true in present time.

▶ Our lawyer *told* us she *is* happy with the progress of the case.

EXERCISE 20.8   Use the correct tense in indirect quotations. In each of the following sentences, correct any errors in verb tense. Some sentences may be correct.

EXAMPLE:

In 1996, two sportsmen reported that they ~~have~~ found a human skeleton in a riverbank in Kennewick, Washington.

had

1. James Chatters, the forensic anthropologist who examined the bones, at first believed that the skeleton is a modern murder victim.

2. He then told authorities that he had noticed a prehistoric arrowhead embedded in the skeleton's pelvic bone.

3. After the skeleton had been determined to be over 9,000 years old, Native American groups announced that they want to rebury the bones.

4. Tribal leaders claim that the bones were those of an ancient tribal ancestor.

5. Many scientists argue that the skull's features did not resemble a Native American's face and that researchers needed to study the bones to find out all they could about the history of ancient peoples in this country.

20k Verbs in conditional sentences, wishes, requests, demands, and recommendations

Conditions When *if* or *unless* is used to introduce a dependent clause, the sentence expresses a condition. Four types of conditional sentences are used in English: two refer to actual or possible situations, and two refer to speculative or hypothetical situations. The Key Points box summarizes the four types. Each one is also explained and illustrated in more detail.

1. Conditions of fact Sentences expressing conditions of fact refer to actual situations or make generalizations. They state what may be real and true. (The word *when* can also introduce clauses in sentences expressing conditions of fact.) Use the same tense, usually the present simple, in both the dependent and the independent clauses. (See **16e** on clauses.)

▶ If the sun's rays *are* strong, our skin *burns*.

▶ House sales *increase* if mortgage rates *go* down.

▶ Prices *fluctuate* unless the government *intervenes*.

2. Conditions of prediction/possibility Sentences expressing conditions of prediction look to the future and predict what will happen if certain circumstances prevail. Use the present tense in the dependent clause and *will* (or another modal auxiliary) plus the base form of the verb in the independent clause to express future time.

▶ If it *rains* this afternoon, I *will stay* home.

▶ If I *get* married, I *might wait* a few years before I have children.

▶ They *will* not *drive* to Kansas unless their car *has* a new muffler.

▶ Housing sales *will decline* unless mortgage rates *decrease*.

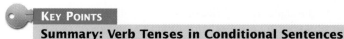
🔑 **KEY POINTS**

Summary: Verb Tenses in Conditional Sentences

MEANING EXPRESSED	*IF* CLAUSE	INDEPENDENT CLAUSE
1. Fact	Simple present	Simple present

▶ **If people *earn* more, they *spend* more.**

MEANING EXPRESSED	*IF* CLAUSE	INDEPENDENT CLAUSE
2. Prediction/ possibility	Simple present	*will, can, should, might* + base form

▶ **If you *turn* left here, you *will end up* in Mississippi.**

MEANING EXPRESSED	*IF* CLAUSE	INDEPENDENT CLAUSE
3. Speculation about present or future	Simple past *or* subjunctive *were*	*would, could, should, might* + base form

▶ **If he *had* a cell phone, he *would use* it.**
[But he does not have one.]

▶ **If she *were* my lawyer, I *might* win the case.**
[But she is not.]

MEANING EXPRESSED	*IF* CLAUSE	INDEPENDENT CLAUSE
4. Speculation about past	Past perfect (*had* + past participle)	*would have could have should have might have* ⎫⎬⎭ + past participle

▶ **If they *had saved* the diaries, they *could have sold* them.**
[But they did not save them.]

3. Conditions of speculation about present or future time
Sentences expressing conditions of speculation consider hypothetical situations in the present or the future. Use the simple past tense in the dependent clause and *would* (or another modal auxiliary verb) plus the base form of the verb in the independent clause.

▶ **If they *worked* harder on the job, they *might* get a promotion.**
[They may or may not work harder.]

▶ **If we *had* a million dollars, we *would make* a donation to the museum.** [We don't have a million dollars.]

The Use of Subjunctive **Were** *in Place of* **Was**   With speculative conditions about the present and future using the verb *be, were* is used in place of *was* in the dependent *if* clause. This use of *were* to indicate hypothetical situations involves what is called the *subjunctive mood.*

▶ **If I *were* an Alaskan, I *would* probably *choose* to live in Anchorage.** [I am not an Alaskan.]

▶ **If my aunt *were* sixty-five, she *could get* a discount air fare.** [My aunt is sixty.]

4. Conditions of speculation about the past Sentences that look back to past events and speculate about an entirely different outcome also express hypothetical conditions. Use the past perfect tense in the dependent clause and *would have* (or another modal auxiliary verb) plus the past participle in the independent clause to speculate about past time.

▶ **If they *had saved* more money, they *would have moved* to a bigger apartment.**

[The opposite is true: they didn't save, so they didn't move.]

Blending Some blending of conditional meaning and tenses can occur, as in the case of a condition that speculates about the past in relation to the effect on the present.

▶ **If I *had bought* a new car instead of this old wreck, I *would feel* a lot safer today.**

The Use of **Would** When writing Standard English, use *would* only in the independent clause, not in the conditional clause. However, *would* occurs frequently in the conditional clause in speech and in informal writing.

▶ **If the fish fry committee** ~~would show~~ ^{showed} **more initiative, people might attend their events more ^ regularly.**

▶ **If I** ~~would have~~ ^{had} **heard him say that, I would have been angry.**

Would, Could, *and* Might *with Conditional Clause Understood* Would, could, and *might* are used in independent clauses when no conditional clause is present. These are situations that are contrary to fact, and the conditional clause is understood.

▶ **I *would* never *advise* her to leave college without a degree. She *might come back* later and blame me for her lack of direction.**

Wishes Like some conditions, wishes deal with speculation. For a present wish—about something that has not happened and is therefore hypothetical and imaginary—use the past tense or subjunctive *were* in the dependent clause. For a wish about the past, use the past perfect: *had* + past participle.

A WISH ABOUT THE PRESENT

▶ I wish I *had* your attitude.

▶ I wish that Shakespeare *were* still alive.

A WISH ABOUT THE PAST

▶ Some union members wish that the strike *had* never *occurred*.

▶ He wishes that he *had bought* a lottery ticket.

Requests, demands, and recommendations The subjunctive also appears after certain verbs, such as *request, command, insist, demand, move* (meaning "propose"), *propose,* and *urge.* In these cases, the verb in the dependent clause is the base form, regardless of the person and number of the subject.

▶ The dean suggested that students *be* allowed to vote.

▶ He insisted that she *submit* the report.

▶ I move that the treasurer *revise* the budget.

Some idiomatic expressions preserve the subjunctive in Standard English—for example, *far* be *it from me, if need* be, *as it* were.

EXERCISE 20.9 Use correct verb tenses in conditional sentences. In each of the following sentences, correct any errors in the use of verb tenses. Then identify which of the four types of conditional sentences the item represents.

EXAMPLE:

              ate
If domestic dogs ~~would eat~~ the same diet that their wild ancestors ate, they might not have tooth and gum problems.
#3 Speculation about the present (hypothetical situation)

1. If prehistoric canines would have eaten crunchy, bite-sized food, they would probably have lost most of their teeth at an early age.

2. If dogs eat commercial dog food, plaque will tend to collect on their teeth.

3. If people would allow their pet dogs to forage for their own food, the canines might develop stronger teeth.

4. Unless pet owners managed to brush their dogs' teeth daily—which is difficult to do, even with a cooperative dog—their pets will develop gum diseases and lose their teeth, just as humans do.

5. Veterinarians believe that if commercial kibble was made with larger pieces and a chewier texture, it could clean dogs' teeth effectively.

20/ Passive voice

In the active voice, the grammatical subject is the doer of the action, and the sentence tells "who's doing what." The passive voice, on the other hand, tells what "is done to" the subject of the sentence. The person or thing doing the action may or may not be mentioned but is always implied: "My car has been repaired [by somebody at the garage]."

ACTIVE

┌─ subject ─┐ ┌─ active voice verb ─┐ ┌─ direct object ─┐
▶ **Alice Walker** **wrote** *The Color Purple.*

PASSIVE

┌─────────── passive voice ───────────┐
┌─ subject ─┐ ┌─ verb ─┐ ┌─ doer or agent ─┐
▶ *The Color Purple* **was written** **by Alice Walker.**

When to use the passive voice   Use the passive voice sparingly. However, do use it specifically in two cases.

1. Use the passive voice when the doer or agent in your sentence (the person or thing acting) is unknown or is unimportant.

   ▶ **The pandas are rare. Two of them will be returned to the wild.**
   [It is not important to mention who will return the pandas to the wild.]

2. Use the passive voice to establish a topic chain from one clause or sentence to another.

> ▶ He had a lot of people working for him, maybe sixty, and most of them liked him most of the time. Three of them *will be* seriously *considered* for his job.
>
> —Ellen Goodman, "The Company Man"
>
> [The idea of *people* in the first sentence sets up the need for *three of them*, which necessitates the passive voice verb.]

> ▶ I remember to start with that day in Sacramento [. . .] when I first entered a classroom, able to understand some fifty stray English words. The third of four children, I *had been preceded* to a Roman Catholic school by an older brother and sister.
>
> —Richard Rodriguez, *Hunger of Memory*
>
> [The passive voice preserves the chain of *I* subjects.]

For more on using the passive voice to make old and new information connect well, see **37b**.

Verbs to use with the passive voice   Use the passive voice only with verbs that are transitive in English. Intransitive verbs such as *happen, occur,* and *try (to)* are not used in the passive voice.

▶ The ceremony ~~was~~ happened yesterday.

have
▶ Morality is an issue that ~~was~~ tried to explain ~~by~~ many philosophers.

How to form the passive voice   The complete verb of a passive voice sentence consists of a form of the verb *be* followed by a past participle.

verb: *be* +
receiver   past participle   doer omitted or named after *by*
┌─ as subject ─┐ ┌─────────┐
▶ The windows   are cleaned   (by someone) every month.

With different tenses, note the forms of the verb in the passive transformations:

TENSE AND ASPECT	ACTIVE VOICE	PASSIVE VOICE
Simple present	Someone *cleans* the windows every month.	The windows *are cleaned* every month.
Present progressive	Someone *is cleaning* the windows right now.	The windows *are being cleaned* right now.

TENSE AND ASPECT	ACTIVE VOICE	PASSIVE VOICE
Present perfect	Someone *has* just *cleaned* the windows.	The windows *have* just *been cleaned.*
Present perfect progressive	Someone *has been cleaning* the windows for hours now.	[rare]
Simple past	Someone *cleaned* the windows yesterday.	The windows *were cleaned* yesterday.
Past progressive	Someone *was cleaning* the windows all yesterday afternoon.	The windows *were being cleaned* all yesterday afternoon.
Past perfect	Someone *had cleaned* the windows before the family moved in.	The windows *had been cleaned* before the family moved in.
Past perfect progressive	Someone *had been cleaning* the windows for several hours when the wedding began.	[rare]
Simple future	Someone *will clean* the windows tomorrow.	The windows *will be cleaned* tomorrow.
Future progressive	Someone *will be cleaning* the windows during the meeting this afternoon.	[rare]
Future perfect	Someone *will have cleaned* the windows by the end of the workday.	The windows *will have been cleaned* by the end of the workday.
Future perfect progressive	Someone *will have been cleaning* the windows for eight hours by the time the caterers arrive.	[rare]

Auxiliaries such as *would, can, could, should, may, might,* and *must* can also replace *will* when the meaning demands it.

▶ **The windows** *might be cleaned* **next month.**

▶ **The windows** *should have been cleaned* **already.**

The passive voice in scientific writing   In scientific writing, the passive voice is often preferred to indicate objective procedures. Scientists and engineers are interested in analyzing data and in performing studies that other researchers can replicate. The individual doing the experiment is therefore relatively unimportant and usually is not the subject of the sentence.

▶ The experiment *was conducted* in a classroom. Participants *were instructed* to remove their watches prior to the experiment.

Caution with the passive voice   Generally your writing will be clearer and stronger if you name the subject and use verbs in the active voice to tell "who's doing what." If you overuse the passive voice, the effect will be heavy and impersonal (see also **36c**).

UNNECESSARY PASSIVE	He *was alerted* to the danger of drugs by his doctor and *was persuaded* by her to enroll in a treatment program.
REVISED	His doctor *alerted* him to the danger of drugs and *persuaded* him to enroll in a treatment program.

EXERCISE 20.10   Identify active and passive voices.
In each of the following sentences, write *P* on the line before each sentence that is in the passive voice and *A* before each sentence that is in the active voice. Then rewrite each passive voice sentence as active whenever it is possible or advisable to do so and underline the verb that you changed.

EXAMPLE:

Each acre of the fertile rice fields of southern China yields more
__P__ ~~More~~ than a thousand pounds of rice ~~is yielded by each~~ ~~acre of fertile rice fields of southern China.~~

1. _____ The sticky rice that brings the highest prices in China is often attacked by rice blast, a fungus that destroys the rice crop.

2. _____ A farmer in Yunnan province discovered that he could nearly eliminate rice blast by planting alternating rows of sticky rice and long-grain rice.

3. _____ The technique of alternating rows of rice was then adopted widely.

4. _____ The application of expensive and toxic fungicides that had been used to fight the rice blast was discontinued by most farmers.

5. _____ Healthier fields, bigger rice yields, and more money for the farmers were subsequently produced by this low-tech, environmentally sound agricultural method.

REVIEW EXERCISE FOR SECTION 20 Correct verb errors.
Edit the following passage by correcting any verb errors, including the use of unnecessary passive voice. Underline any verbs that you change.

The legend of Prester John was a fable that had circulated throughout most Christian countries of Europe for several centuries during the Middle Ages. The legend first appears in the twelfth century, and it continued to reappear until at least the sixteenth century. Stories about an immensely wealthy Christian ruler of a vast land somewhere in Asia were brought back to Europe by people who had claimed to have traveled to the then-mysterious East, and a large audience was entertained by these stories.

Some stories attach to Prester John are typical medieval marvel tales—travelers' tall tales about unusual people and creatures in exotic foreign lands. Through a popular letter supposedly written by Prester John himself, credulous Europeans learned that John's country has a province full of horned men with one eye in the front of their heads and three or four in the back. The letter also describes "wild bulls of seven horns, white bears, and the strangest lions of red, green, black, and blue color."

In many other stories, the life of Prester John resembled the life of Alexander the Great, which also circulated regularly in legends during the Middle Ages. Like Alexander, Prester John was suppose to have acquire his massive kingdom by defeating armies in Asia. Christian crusaders in medieval Europe, who feared the growing power of Islam, must of found the idea of a Christian conqueror in Asia comforting, even if it never proved to be true. Then, after Europeans became aware of the Christian kingdom of Abyssinia (now Ethiopia), many stories stated that the kingdom of Prester John laid in Africa.

Although scholars are now knowing that many of the travelogues disseminated in medieval Europe were pure fiction, many people of the time had believed the story of Prester John, perhaps simply because they wanted it to be true. In the media-saturated world of the twenty-first century, sophisticated readers may find it easy to laugh at those who were believing in the existence of Prester John. However, the tall tales, urban legends, and Internet hoaxes that have been circulating today demonstrate that modern life produced its own unstoppable legends.

21 Subject-Verb Agreement

21a What is agreement?

A subject can be first, second, or third person. A third person subject, in some tenses, will need to agree with a specific third-person form of the verb.

Person and Number

Person	Singular	Plural
First	I like ice cream.	We like yogurt, too.
Second	You like spinach.	You like cake.
Third	My brother likes clams.	My cousins like shrimp.
	He likes clams.	They like shrimp.
	My sister likes garlic.	My parents hate garlic.
	She likes garlic.	They hate garlic.

You need to be concerned about agreement when using the simple present tense (*like/likes*) and when using *am, is, are, do, does, have, has, was,* or *were* as an auxiliary verb.

21b The -*s* ending

In the simple present tense in standard English, a third person singular subject always takes a singular verb (with -*s*), and a plural subject always takes a plural verb (with no -*s*).

SINGULAR SUBJECT	PLURAL SUBJECT
A baby *cries*.	Babies *cry*.
He *loses*.	They *lose*.
His brother *plays* baseball.	Her brothers *play* soccer.

Difficulties arise because the ending -*s* serves two functions. It is added to both nouns and verbs, but for different reasons.

1. An -*s* ending on a noun is a plural signal: *Her brothers always wear black.* [She has more than one brother.]

2. An -*s* ending on a verb is a singular signal; -*s* is added to a third person singular verb in the present tense: *Her plumber wears gold jewelry.*

Most simple present verbs show agreement with an -*s* ending. Note the irregular forms of the auxiliary verbs in the following table: *has, is,* and *does*. Note, too, that the verb *be* has three instead of two present tense forms, so the person of the subject determines whether you use *am, are,* or *is*. In addition, *be* is the only verb to show agreement in the past tense, where it has two forms: *were* for second and third person plural, and *was* for the first and third person singular.

SUBJECT-VERB AGREEMENT

BASE FORM	like	have	be	do
SIMPLE PRESENT: SINGULAR				
First person: I	like	have	am	do
Second person: you	like	have	are	do
Third person: he, she, it	likes	has	is	does
SIMPLE PRESENT: PLURAL				
First person: we	like	have	are	do
Second person: you	like	have	are	do
Third person: they	like	have	are	do

 KEY POINTS

Two Key Points about Agreement

1. Follow the "one -s rule." Generally, you can put an -s on a noun to make it plural, or you can put an -s on a verb to make it singular. (But see the irregular forms *is* and *has,* above.) An -s on both subject (as plural ending) and verb (as singular ending) is not Standard English.

   No   **My friends comes over every Saturday.**

   [Violates the "one -s rule"]

   Yes   **My friend comes over every Saturday.**

   My friends come over every Saturday.

2. Do not omit a necessary -s.

   His supervisor wantʂ him to work the night shift.

   The bookʂ on my desk describe life in Tahiti.

   She *uses* her experience, *speaks* to the crowds, and *winʂ* their confidence.

 ESL NOTE   Modal Auxiliaries and Agreement

Modal auxiliaries never add an -s ending, and the verb form following them is always the base form of the verb, even with a third person singular subject: I *can sing;* she *should go;* he *might be* leaving; she *must have* been promoted (**20d** and **43b** ESL). ▪

WORLDS OF WRITING
Issues of Subject-Verb Agreement

Many languages make no change in the verb form to indicate number and person, and several spoken versions of English, such as London Cockney, Caribbean Creole, and African American Vernacular (AAV), do not observe the standard rules of agreement.

▶ **Cockney: He *don't* never wear that brown whistle.**

[The standard form is *doesn't;* other nonstandard forms in this sentence are *don't never* (a double negative) and *whistle*—short for *whistle and flute,* rhyming slang for *suit.*]

▶ **AAV: She *have* a lot of work experience.**

Use authentic forms like these when quoting direct speech; for your formal academic writing, though, follow the subject-verb agreement conventions of Standard English.

EXERCISE 21.1 Correct basic subject-verb agreement.

In each of the following sentences, correct any errors in subject-verb agreement. Some sentences may contain more than one error, and some sentences may be correct.

EXAMPLE:

       divide
Psychologists ~~divides~~ risks into categories: risk may be known or unknown, controllable or uncontrollable.

1. Every day, a person have to evaluate risks and make choices based on those evaluations, such as whether to get a flu shot, whether to eat meat, and whether to stop smoking.

2. People sometimes makes irrational choices in attempts to avoid uncontrollable risks.

3. Even experts in risk assessment are not immune to making a riskier choice that seems more controllable, like driving to a distant destination instead of flying.

4. The average person fear unknown dangers—nuclear attack, for instance—more than known ones, even if the evidence show that everyday risks cause more harm.

5. After a disaster, when people's nerves is on edge, unknown and uncontrollable risks seem more frightening than they does in normal, everyday life.

21c Words between the subject and the verb

When words separate the subject and verb, find the verb and ask "Who?" or "What?" about it to determine the simple subject. Ignore the intervening words. See **16c,** page 321.

▶ **The child picking flowers looks tired.**

[Who looks tired? The subject, *child*, is singular.]

▶ **Her collection of baseball cards is valuable.**

[What is valuable? The subject, *collection*, is singular.]

▶ **The government's proposals about preserving the environment**

cause controversy.

[What things cause controversy? The subject, *proposals*, is plural.]

Do not be confused by intervening words ending in -*s*, such as *always* and *sometimes.* The -*s* ending still must appear on a present tense verb if the subject is singular.

▶ **His assistant always make mistakes.**

s

Phrases introduced by *as well as, along with,* and *in addition to* that come between the subject and the verb do not change the number of the verb.

▶ **His daughter, as well as his two sons, want him to move nearby.**

s

EXERCISE 21.2 Ignore words between the subject and verb. In each of the following sentences, underline the simple subject. Then correct any errors in subject-verb agreement.

EXAMPLE:

Environmentalists in the United States and Canada finally

have
~~has~~ some good news about the pollution in the Great Lakes.

1. An international agency monitoring the air and water quality around the Great Lakes have discovered a previously unknown ecological process.

2. Toxic chemicals banned for at least a quarter of a century is dispersing from the lakes into the air.

3. Since 1992, Lake Ontario, along with the other lakes, have released tons of PCBs and other dangerous chemicals in a self-cleaning process.

4. Massive pollution in the enormous lakes were first brought to public attention thirty years ago, and pollution remains a serious problem there.

5. The lakes' "exhaling," according to researchers, help to clean the water without posing any danger to human beings.

21d Agreement after a linking verb

Linking verbs such as *be, seem, look,* and *appear* are followed by a complement, and a subject complement should not be confused with a subject (see **16c**). Make the verb agree with the subject stated before the linking verb, not with the noun complement that follows the verb.

plural	singular		singular	plural
┌─ subject ─┐	┌ complement ┐		┌─ subject ─┐	┌ complement ┐

▶ **Rare books are her passion.**   ▶ **Her passion is rare books.**
plural verb   singular verb

▶ **My favorite part of city life *is* the parties.**

▶ **Parties *are* my favorite part of city life.**

> **EXERCISE 21.3** Make subjects and verbs agree and identify linking verbs.
> In the following passage, underline the subject in each independent clause. Then correct any errors in subject-verb agreement. Write *LV* over any linking verbs.

EXAMPLE:

> LV
>
> are
> There ~~is~~ many security <u>questions</u> involved in cryptography.
> ^

Do the government have the right to keep certain kinds of information out of the hands of the public? There is no easy answers to this question. When the science of cryptography was being developed, the National Security Agency wanted to restrict access to powerful, unbreakable codes. After all, using codes are one way that a government keeps information from its enemies, and breaking codes allows a government to find out what its enemies are planning. N.S.A. agents worried that unbreakable codes would allow enemies of the United States to conceal their activities from U.S. intelligence. Cryptographers won the right to develop and distribute their new codes to the general public, and unbreakable codes have certainly been a boon to the computer science and communications industries. Does these codes also hamper efforts to discover what terrorists are doing? Probably, say cryptographers. However, technologies that scientists decide not to develop out of fear of the results is a potential danger: if someone else develops these technologies, they can be used against anyone who has not considered their potential. There is dangers in cryptography, but perhaps there is even more problems in avoiding the issue. Somewhere in the future is the answers to these and other urgent security questions.

21e   When the subject follows the verb

When the subject follows the verb in the sentence, make the subject and verb agree.

1. Questions In a question, the auxiliary verb agrees with the subject.

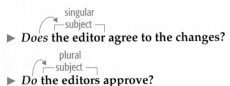

singular
┌─ subject ─┐
▶ *Does* **the editor agree to the changes?**

plural
┌─ subject ─┐
▶ *Do* **the editors approve?**

┌─────────── plural subject ───────────┐
▶ *Do* **the editor and the production manager agree to them?**

2. Initial *here* or *there* When a sentence begins with *here* or *there*, the verb agrees with the subject.

singular
┌ subject ┐
▶ **There** *is* **a reason to rejoice.**

┌ plural subject ┐
▶ **There** *are* **many reasons to rejoice.**

However, avoid excessive use of initial *there* (see **36b**): *We have a reason to rejoice.*

 ESL Note Agreement with Subject *It*

It does not follow the same pattern as *here* and *there*. The verb in a sentence beginning with *it* is always singular.

▶ **It** *looks* **like a good match.**

▶ **It** *is* **hundreds of miles away.** ▪

3. Inverted word order When a sentence begins not with the subject but with a phrase preceding the verb, the verb still agrees with the subject (see also **16c**).

plural
┌─ prepositional phrase ─┐ verb ┌─ plural subject ─┐
▶ **In front of the library sit two stone lions.** [Who or what performs the action of the verb? Two stone lions do.]

21f Tricky subjects

1. *Each* and *every* *Each* and *every* may seem to indicate more than one, but grammatically they are singular words. Use them with a singular verb.

▶ Each of the cakes *has* a different frosting.

▶ Every change in procedures *causes* problems.

2. -*ing* verb form as subject With a subject beginning with the -*ing* verb form used as a noun (called a *gerund*, see **16d**), always use a singular verb form.

singular
⌐ subject ⌐
▶ Playing the piano in front of a crowd *causes* anxiety.

3. Singular nouns ending in -*s* Some nouns that end in -s (*news, economics, physics, politics, mathematics, statistics*) are not plural. Use them with a singular verb.

▶ The news *has* been bad lately.   ▶ Politics *is* dirty business.

4. Phrases of time, money, and weight When the subject is regarded as one unit, use a singular verb.

▶ Five hundred dollars *seems* too much to pay.

▶ Seven years *was* a long time to spend at college.

But

▶ Seven years have passed.

5. Uncountable nouns An uncountable noun (*furniture, jewelry, equipment, advice, happiness, honesty, information, knowledge*) encompasses all the items in its class. An uncountable noun does not have a plural form and is always followed by a singular verb (**42b** ESL).

▶ That advice *makes* me nervous.

▶ The information found in the press *is* not always accurate.

6. One of *One of* is followed by a plural noun (the object of the preposition *of*) and a singular verb form. The verb agrees with the subject *one*, not with the object of the preposition.

▶ *One* of her friends *loves* to tango.

▶ *One* of the reasons for his difficulties *is* that he spends too much money.

For agreement with *one of* and *the only one of* followed by a relative clause, see **24c**.

7. The number of/a number of The phrase *the number of* is followed by a plural noun (the object of the preposition *of*) and a singular verb form.

▶ The number of reasons *is* growing.

With the phrase *a number of,* meaning "several," use a plural verb.

▶ A number of reasons *are* listed in the letter.

8. Percent Use a singular or plural verb, according to how the quantity is perceived.

▶ Forty percent of available housing *is* owned by the city.

▶ Polls report that 10 percent of the voters *are* undecided.

9. The title of a work or a word referred to as the word itself Use a singular verb with the title of a work or a word referred to as the word itself. Use a singular verb even if the title or word is plural in form. See also **31a** and **31d**.

▶ *Cats has* finally ended its long run on Broadway.

▶ In her story, the word *dudes appears* five times.

21g Collective nouns

Generally, use a singular verb with a collective noun (*class, government, family, jury, committee, group, couple, team*) if you are referring to the group as a whole.

▶ My family *goes* on vacation every year.

Use a plural verb if you wish to emphasize differences among individuals or if members of the group are thought of as individuals.

▶ His family *are* mostly artists and musicians.

▶ The jury *are* from every walk of life.

If that usage seems awkward, revise the sentence.

▶ His close relatives *are* mostly artists and musicians.

▶ The members of the jury *are* from every walk of life.

Some collective nouns, such as *police, poor, elderly,* and *young,* always take plural verbs.

▶ **The elderly** *deserve* **our respect.**

EXERCISE 21.4 Make verbs agree with tricky subjects and collective nouns.

In each of the following sentences, underline the simple subject of each independent clause and correct any errors in subject-verb agreement.

EXAMPLE:

Every possible <u>complaint</u> about the violence of soccer players

and their fans ~~have~~ been made at one time or another since the

sport began around 1100 C.E.

has

1. To play soccer, a team need few things other than a ball, a field, and a group of opponents.

2. When medieval British warriors defeated a Danish chieftain on the battlefield a millennium ago, their kicking the loser's head around the bloody fields were the origin of soccer, according to a hard-to-prove legend.

Soccer

Fans

3. There was still violent aspects of the game in the 1100s when whole towns, each with hundreds of players, competed against each other on fields several miles long.

4. One of the signs that soccer would eventually be the world's most popular sport were that soccer was banned repeatedly in fourteenth- and fifteenth-century England; a number of kings was worried that soldiers who played soccer would not spend enough time at archery practice.

5. Modern soccer follows rules drawn up at Cambridge University in 1863, but the sport's following among some devoted but aggressive fans have ensured that soccer's bloody reputation does not disappear entirely.

21h Compound subjects with *and*, *or*, and *nor*

With *and* When a subject consists of two or more parts joined by *and*, treat the subject as plural and use a plural verb.

plural subject ——— plural verb
▶ **His instructor and his advisor** *want* **him to change his major.**

However, if the parts of the compound subject refer to a single person or thing, use a singular verb.

singular subject (one person) ——— singular verb
▶ **The restaurant's chef and owner** *makes* **good fajitas.**

singular subject — singular verb
▶ **Fish and chips** *is* **a popular dish in England, but it is no longer served wrapped in newspaper.**

With *each* or *every* When *each* or *every* is part of a compound subject, the verb is singular.

▶ **Every toy and game** *has* **to be put away.**

▶ **Each plate and glass** *looks* **new.**

With *or* or *nor* When the parts of a compound subject are joined by *or* or *nor*, the verb agrees with the part nearer to it.

▶ Her sister or her parents *plan* to visit her next week.

▶ Neither her parents nor her sister *drives* a station wagon.

EXERCISE 21.5 Use correct subject-verb agreement with compound subjects.
In each of the following sentences, underline the subject or subjects of each independent clause and correct any errors in subject-verb agreement. Some sentences may be correct.

EXAMPLE:

is
Every statue, painting, and photograph of human beings ~~are~~ forbidden by fundamentalist factions of Islam.
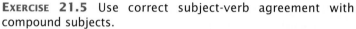

1. In the Bamiyan valley of eastern Afghanistan, a 150-foot Buddha, believed to have been the largest standing Buddha in the world, and a 120-foot Buddha was carved out of sandstone cliffs in the fourth or fifth century.

2. During that period, when the Silk Route wound through the mountains of Afghanistan, wandering Buddhist monks or a caravan of silk or ivory merchants was a common sight in the Bamiyan valley, which was home to Buddhist monasteries until the arrival of Islam in the ninth century.

3. The Buddhas of Bamiyan and other art from Afghanistan's non-Islamic past was destroyed by order of Taliban leaders in March 2001.

4. A Taliban commander and leader of the operation to destroy the statues were reported to have said that the statues represented a woman and her husband.

5. Neither the protests before the destruction of the Buddhas nor the global outrage expressed afterward were enough to convince Taliban leaders that the Buddhas had been an important part of Afghan history.

21i Agreement with indefinite pronouns and quantity words

Words that refer to nonspecific people or things are known as indefinite pronouns. These indefinite pronouns, as well as words and phrases that refer to quantity, pose interesting questions of agreement. Some take a singular verb (even the word *everyone*, which may seem to be plural); some take a plural verb; and some take a singular or a plural verb, depending on what they refer to. Some are used alone as a pronoun; others are used with a countable or uncountable noun in a noun phrase (for more on this, see **42a** and **42b** ESL). In addition, usage may differ in speech and writing. What is the best way to deal with these questions of agreement? Look at the following examples, learn the lists, try out your own sentences, and make a note of sentences you read that use the words.

INDEFINITE PRONOUNS USED WITH A SINGULAR VERB

anybody	everyone	nothing
anyone	everything	somebody
anything	nobody	someone
everybody	no one	something

▶ **Nobody** *knows* **the answer.**

▶ **Someone** *has* **been sitting on my chair.**

▶ **Everyone** *agrees* **on the author's intention**

▶ **Everything about the results** *was* **questioned in the review.**

QUANTITY WORDS REFERRING TO A COUNTABLE NOUN
AND USED WITH A SINGULAR VERB

another	every
each	neither (see p. 436)
either	none (see p. 436)

▶ **Another company** *has* **bought the land.**

▶ **Each of the chairs** *costs* **more than $300.**

▶ Of the two options, neither *was* acceptable.

▶ Every poem *contains* a stark image.

QUANTITY WORDS REFERRING TO AN UNCOUNTABLE NOUN
AND USED WITH A SINGULAR VERB

a great deal (of)	much (of)
(a) little	less (see p. 436)
a(n) _____ amount (of)	

▶ Less *has* been accomplished than we expected.

▶ A great deal of information *is* being released.

▶ Much of the machinery *needs* to be repaired.

▶ An enormous amount of equipment *was* needed to clean up the spilled oil.

QUANTITY WORDS REFERRING TO A PLURAL COUNTABLE NOUN
AND USED WITH A PLURAL VERB

both	many
a couple/number of	other/others
(a) few (see **46c** ESL)	several
fewer (see p. 436)	

▶ She has written two novels. Both *receive* praise.

▶ Many *have* gained from the recent stock market fluctuations.

▶ Few of his fans *are* buying his recent book.

▶ A number of articles *refer* to the same statistics.

QUANTITY WORDS USED WITH A PLURAL VERB TO REFER TO A PLURAL COUNTABLE
NOUN OR WITH A SINGULAR VERB TO REFER TO AN UNCOUNTABLE NOUN

all	half	most	some
any	more	no	

▶ All the students *look* healthy.
   [The plural countable noun *students* takes a plural verb.]

▶ All the furniture *looks* old.
   [The uncountable noun *furniture* takes a singular verb.]

▶ You gave me some information. More *is* necessary.
   [*More* refers to the uncountable noun *information*.]

▶ **You gave me some facts. More *are* needed.**

[*More* refers to the countable noun *facts*.]

▶ **Some of the jewelry *was* recovered.**

[The uncountable noun *jewelry* takes a singular verb.]

▶ **Some of the windows *were* open.**

[The plural countable noun *windows* takes a plural verb.]

A note on *none, neither, less,* and *fewer*

None Some writers prefer to use a singular verb after *none* (*of*), because *none* means "not one": *None of the contestants has smiled.* However, as *The American Heritage Dictionary* (4th ed.) points out about *none,* "The word has been used as both a singular and a plural noun from old English onward." In formal academic writing, a singular or a plural verb is therefore technically acceptable: *None of the authorities has* (or *have*) *greater tolerance on this point than H. W. Fowler.* As with many issues of usage, however, readers form preferences. Check to see if your instructor prefers the literal singular usage.

Neither The pronoun *neither* is, like *none,* technically singular: *The partners have made a decision; neither wants to change the product.* In informal writing, however, you will see it used with a plural verb, especially when it is followed by an *of* phrase: *Neither of the novels reveal a polished style.* Ask your instructor about his or her preferences.

Less and fewer Technically, *less* refers to a singular uncountable noun (*less spinach*), *fewer* to a plural countable noun (*fewer beans*). In journalism and advertising, and especially on supermarket signs (*12 items or less*), *less* is often used in place of *fewer.* In formal writing, however, use *fewer* to refer to a plural word: *In the last decade, fewer Olympic medalists have been using steroids.*

For agreement with *one of,* see page 429. For agreement with *one of* and *the only one of* followed by a relative clause, see **24c**.

EXERCISE 21.6 Use correct subject-verb agreement with indefinite pronouns and quantity words.

In each of the following sentences, choose the verb that agrees with the subject, and underline the subject.

EXAMPLE:

<u>Nothing</u> (was / ~~were~~) dearer to Edward Gorey than the New York City Ballet, except perhaps his six cats.

1. Many of the small, hand-lettered, meticulously illustrated books by Edward Gorey (concerns / concern) macabre events, yet most of Gorey's stories (is / are) hilarious.

2. In the story "The Wuggly Ump," for example, every human character (ends up / end up) being eaten by the title monster, yet the tale itself looks and sounds like a Victorian nursery rhyme.

3. Anyone who saw Gorey in person (is / are) sure to remember the tall, bearded man in a floor-length fur coat and sneakers, dressed like one of the odd characters that he drew.

4. A number of interviewers and critics (was / were) able to talk to the eccentric writer, illustrator, and designer before his death in 2000, and a great deal (has been / have been) written about the intersections of his life and his art.

It would carry off objects of which it grew fond,
And protect them by dropping them into the pond.

Illustration from *The Doubtful Guest* © 1957 Edward Gorey. Used with permission of the Estate of Edward Gorey.

5. Gorey admitted that some of his eccentricity (was / were) genuine although some of his behaviors (was / were) deliberately cultivated for shock value.

21j Demonstrative pronouns and adjectives (*this, that, these, those*) as subject

A demonstrative adjective must agree in number with the noun it modifies. Ask "Is the noun singular or plural?"

SINGULAR	PLURAL
this	these
that	those
this solution	these solutions
that problem	those problems

A demonstrative pronoun must agree in number with its antecedent (see **22d**).

▶ **The mayor is planning changes. These will be controversial.**

EXERCISE 21.7 Use correct subject-verb agreement with demonstrative pronouns and adjectives.
In each of the following sentences, correct any errors in the use of demonstrative pronouns and adjectives and the verbs that follow them. Some sentences may be correct.
EXAMPLE:

                                                                This
Australia's Antarctic base has begun a cleanup. ~~These~~ will
remove more than three thousand tons of garbage.

1. Since the exploration and experimentation began in Antarctica, people from more than forty nations have come to the icy continent to establish research bases. This is home to researchers year-round.

2. Unfortunately, humans create waste, and these are beginning to contaminate Antarctica's environment.

3. Experts believe that Antarctic explorers and scientists have abandoned more than 330,000 tons of waste. These waste include building materials, chemicals, batteries, and other residue of human presence.

4. Australia has contracted with a French environmental services company for 240 cargo containers. These giant bins will be filled with garbage from the Australian base camp in Antarctica, known as Casey, and shipped back to Australia for disposal.

5. Once the cleanup at Casey has been completed, Australia plans to share the containers. This could be used by other nations' research bases to remove additional garbage before Antarctica's pristine ecosystem is harmed.

21k Possessive pronouns as subject

To determine whether the verb after a one-word subject such as *mine* or *hers* should be singular or plural, find the word or phrase the possessive pronoun refers to. That antecedent determines whether the verb is singular or plural. Possessive pronouns such as *mine, his, hers, ours, yours,* and *theirs* can refer to both singular and plural antecedents (see **22d**).

singular
— subject — singular verb
▶ **Her average is good, but *mine is* better.**

plural
— subject — plural verb
▶ **His grades are good, but *mine are* better.**

21*l* Agreement with a *what* clause as the subject

When a clause introduced by *what* functions as the subject of an independent clause, use a third person singular verb in the independent clause.

——— subject ———
▶ **What they are proposing *concerns* us all.**

When the verb is followed by the linking verb *be* and a plural complement, some writers use a plural verb. However, some readers may object.

▶ **What I need *are* black pants and an orange shirt.**

You can avoid the issue by revising the sentence to eliminate the *what* clause.

▶ **I need black pants and an orange shirt.**

EXERCISE 21.8 Use the correct verb with possessive pronouns as subject and with subject clauses beginning with *what*.
In the following sentences, correct any problems with agreement between possessive pronoun subjects and their verbs or with agreement between subject clauses beginning with *what* and their verbs. Some sentences may be correct.

EXAMPLE:

Eighteenth-century society did not even have a word for the

state of boredom, but ours do. *(does)*

1. What boredom means in modern American culture is the subject of a new book by Patricia Meyer Spacks.

2. Like Robert Burton's book, *The Anatomy of Melancholy,* hers are a study of a common mental state.

3. According to Spacks, what people really feel when they say they are bored are often dislike or confusion.

4. Medieval people's lives did not allow for boredom because they spent so much time simply trying to survive; ours permits us to be bored because we have the luxury of free time.

5. What is ironic about modern boredom are the enormous number of diversions people have invented to avoid it at all costs.

REVIEW EXERCISE FOR SECTION 21 Use correct subject-verb agreement.

In the following passage, correct any errors in subject-verb agreement.

There is more people of African descent living in Brazil than in any other country outside of Africa. Although only about ten million of Brazil's 170 million people identifies themselves as black, according to a recent survey, an additional 40 percent of the population call themselves *pardo,* meaning "dark," or *mulato* or *mestiço,* indicating mixed European and African ancestry. There are more than three hundred Brazilian words for skin color, so racial categories in the country is difficult to define. Brazil is a multiracial society that prides itself on avoiding racial divisions like that found in the United States. However, what is clear are that economic and social problems trouble many black Brazilians. Some argue that poor self-image and discrimination based on skin color has contributed to keeping Brazilians from claiming their African ancestry.

The problems of black Brazilians are hard to ignore. Brazil was the last country in the western hemisphere to outlaw slavery. The average income of white-skinned Brazilians are twice the average earnings of blacks. Only 2% of Brazilian college students are black. Brazilian newspaper advertisements for jobs in the private sector often requires applicants to have a "good appearance," a phrase most Brazilians agree is a code for "whites only." Even on television, soap operas and commercials rarely offers roles for black actors. As a solution, the Brazilian Congress have suggested a system of quotas that would require 30% of political candidates, 25% of actors on every television show, 20% of civil service employees, and 20% of college students to be black or of mixed race. Some Brazilians insist that quotas will fail in Brazil, but many hopes that such a quota system will increase opportunity for blacks in the country. Politics do not always provide good solutions for difficult social problems. However, the future of a great number of Brazilians looks bleak unless the country find a way to reduce the problem of racial discrimination.

22 Pronouns

A pronoun is a word that substitutes for a noun, a noun phrase, or another pronoun (see **37b**).

▶ Jack's hair is so long that *it* hangs over *his* collar.

▶ Philip Larkin, *who* worked as a librarian,

did not directly refer to *his* work in *his* poems.

22a Use the correct forms of personal pronouns.

Personal pronouns change form to indicate person (first, second, or third), number (singular or plural), and function in a clause.

After a linking verb In formal academic writing, use the subject form of a personal pronoun after a linking verb. (See **16c** on linking verbs.)

▶ Was that Minnie Driver? It was *she*. [Informal: "It was her."]

▶ It was *she* who sent the flowers.

[Many writers would revise this sentence to sound less formal: "She was the one who sent the flowers."]

After a verb and before an infinitive Use the object form of a personal pronoun after a verb and before an infinitive. When a sentence has only one object, this principle is easy to apply.

▶ The dean wanted *him* to lead the procession.

KEY POINTS

Summary of Forms of Personal Pronouns

PERSON	SUBJECT	OBJECT	POSSESSIVE (+ NOUN)	POSSESSIVE (STANDS ALONE)	INTENSIVE AND REFLEXIVE
First person singular	I	me	my	mine	myself
Second person singular and plural	you	you	your	yours	yourself/ yourselves
Third person singular	he she it	him her it	his her its	his hers its [rare]	himself herself itself
First person plural	we	us	our	ours	ourselves
Third person plural	they	them	their	theirs	themselves

Difficulties occur with compound objects.

                  him and me
▶ The dean wanted ~~he and I~~ to lead the procession.

In a compound subject or compound object with *and* (I *or* me? he *or* him?) To decide which pronoun form to use with a compound subject or compound object, mentally recast the sentence with only the pronoun in the subject or object position.

    ┌─── subject ───┐   ┌─── object ───┐
▶ He and his sister invited my cousin and me to their party.

  [He invited me.]

        I
▶ Jenny and ~~me~~ went to the movies.

  [If *Jenny* is dropped, you would say *I went to the movies,* not *me went to the movies.* Here you need the subject form, *I.*]

me
▶ They told my brother and ~~I~~ to wait in line.

[If *my brother* is dropped from the sentence, you would say *They told me to wait in line*. Here you need the object form, *me*.]

After a preposition   After a preposition, you need an object form.

▶ I started off rapping for people just like myself, people who were in awe of wealth and flash. It was a conversation *between me* and *them*.

—Ice-T, *Observer*, 27 Oct. 1991

He   *me*
▶ ~~Him~~ and his brother waved to my colleague and ~~I~~.

[*He* waved to my colleague. They waved to *me*.]

me
▶ Between you and ~~I~~, the company is in serious trouble.

In appositive phrases and with *we* or *us* before a noun   When using a personal pronoun in an appositive phrase (a phrase that gives additional information about a preceding noun), determine whether the noun that the pronoun refers to functions as subject or as object in its own clause.

— direct object ──►   appositive phrase
▶ The supervisor praised only two employees, Ramon and me.

— subject ──►   appositive phrase
▶ Only two employees, Ramon and I, received a bonus.

Similarly, when you consider whether to use *we* or *us* before a noun, use *us* when the pronoun is the direct object of a verb or preposition, *we* when it is the subject.

object of preposition
▶ LL Cool J waved to us fans.

subject
▶ We fans have decided to form a club.

In comparisons   When writing comparisons with *than* and *as*, decide on the subject or object form of the personal pronoun by mentally completing the meaning of the comparison. (See also **23i**.)

▶ She is certainly not more intelligent than I. [. . . than I am.]

▶ Jack and Sally work in the same office; Jack criticizes his boss more than she. [. . . more than Sally does.]

▶ **Jack and Sally work in the same office; Jack criticizes his boss more than her.** [. . . more than he criticizes Sally.]

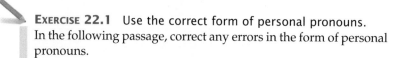

EXERCISE 22.1   Use the correct form of personal pronouns. In the following passage, correct any errors in the form of personal pronouns.

EXAMPLE:

Although Marie and Pierre Curie made important scientific

discoveries, both ~~her~~ *she* and ~~him~~ *he* spent years being unable to

afford a decent laboratory to work in.

Marie Curie, born Maria Sklodowska in Poland in 1867, devoted her life to pure science in the hope that humans would benefit from what she discovered. Her parents, poor teachers, wanted she and her siblings to get an education. Marie went to Paris to study at the Sorbonne when she was twenty-four; her work as a governess had earned her enough money to educate she and her older sister. Marie struggled to learn French and overcome her deficient early education in physics and mathematics—subjects that girls in Poland such as her and her sister had not been allowed to study. When she completed her master's degree in physics in 1894, she placed first in her class. Pierre Curie, who was doing research on magnetism, and her met when Marie was searching for a laboratory she could use. Although Pierre did not have space for Marie in his lab, him and her fell in love and married.

The Curies did much of their innovative research in a small lab set up in an abandoned shed because both she and him believed that scientists should not waste valuable research time trying to make money. Marie did work on uranium and thorium, and it was her who invented the term *radioactivity*. In 1903, three scientists, Pierre and her, along with Henri Becquerel, shared the Nobel Prize in Physics. At around the same time, Pierre and Marie discovered the elements polonium (named after Marie's homeland)

Marie and Pierre Curie

and radium. In 1911, after her husband's death, an unprecedented second Nobel Prize, this time in chemistry, was awarded to she alone. Marie Curie died in 1934 as a result of years of exposure to radiation, but her legacy continued. The Curies' daughter Irene, who had learned physics and chemistry from Marie and was nearly as skilled in scientific research as her, shared a Nobel Prize in Chemistry with her husband, Frederic Joliot-Curie, in 1935.

22b Use appropriate possessive forms of pronouns.

Distinguish between the adjective form of the possessive personal pronoun and the pronoun itself, standing alone.

▶ The large room with three windows is *her* office.

[*Her* is an adjective.]

▶ The office is *hers*.

[*Hers*, the possessive pronoun, can stand alone.]

Note: The word *mine* does not follow the pattern of *hers, theirs, yours,* and *ours.* The form *mines* is not Standard English.

mine
▶ The little room on the left is ~~mines~~.
  ^

When a possessive pronoun functions as a subject, its antecedent determines singular or plural agreement for the verb. (See **21k.**)

▶ My shirt is cotton; hers *is* silk.   [Singular antecedent and singular verb]

▶ My gloves are black; hers *are* yellow.   [Plural antecedent and plural verb]

Possessive pronoun before an *-ing* form   Generally, use a possessive personal pronoun before an *-ing* verb form used as a noun (a *gerund*).

▶ We would appreciate *your* participating in the auction.

▶ We were surprised at *their* winning the marathon.

VARIATION Sometimes the *-ing* form is a participle functioning as an adjective. In that case, the pronoun preceding the *-ing* form should be the object form.

▶ We saw *them* giving the runners foil wraps.   ■

No apostrophe with possessive personal pronouns   Even though possessive in meaning, the pronouns *yours, ours, theirs, his,* and *hers* should never be spelled with an apostrophe. Use an apostrophe only with the possessive form of a noun.

▶ That coat is *Maria's.*

▶ That is *her* coat.

▶ That coat is *hers.*

▶ These books are the *twins'.* (28c)

▶ These are *their* books.

▶ These books are *theirs.*

No apostrophe with *its* as a possessive pronoun   The word *it's* is not a pronoun; it is the contraction of *it is* or *it has.* An apostrophe is never used with *its,* the possessive form of the pronoun *it* (28f).

▶ **The paint has lost *its* gloss.**

▶ *It's* **not as glossy as it used to be.** [It is not as glossy . . .]

Comparisons using possessive forms Note how using *them* in place of *theirs* in the following sentence would change the meaning by comparing suitcases to roommates, not suitcases to suitcases.

▶ **It's really hard to be roommates with people if your suitcases are much better than *theirs*.** —J. D. Salinger, *The Catcher in the Rye*

Forgetting to use the appropriate possessive form in the next example, too, could create a misunderstanding: are you comparing a house to a person, or his house to her house?

▶ **I like his house better than I like her.** ^s^

EXERCISE 22.2 Use the correct possessive pronoun form.
In each of the following sentences, correct any errors in the use of possessive forms of pronouns. Some sentences may be correct.

EXAMPLE:

Bonhoeffer tried to convince other Germans to oppose Nazi
views of racial purity, and ~~him~~ ^his^ playing gospel records in
Nazi Germany required courage.

1. When Dietrich Bonhoeffer was a visiting pastor at Harlem's Abyssinian Baptist Church in 1931, the congregation was pleased with him learning to love gospel music.

2. As a white German Protestant among African American worshippers, Bonhoeffer at first worried that his life was too different from them.

3. When Bonhoeffer returned to Germany, something of their's went with him: members of the church gave him several gospel records.

4. Dietrich Bonhoeffer's opposition to the Nazi regime led to him putting his life on the line by participating in the plot to assassinate Hitler in 1944; it's failure resulted in his imprisonment and execution.

5. Bonhoeffer's influence still appears in today's Germany, where the popularity of gospel music is still growing as a result of his championing of it decades ago.

22c Make a pronoun refer to a clear antecedent.

A pronoun substitutes for a noun, a noun phrase, or a pronoun already mentioned. The word or phrase that a pronoun refers to is known as the pronoun's *antecedent*. Antecedents should always be clear and explicit.

▶ **Although the Canadian skater practiced daily with *her* trainers, *she* didn't win the championship.**

State a specific antecedent. Be sure to give a pronoun such as *they* or *it* an explicit antecedent.

▶ **When Mr. Rivera applied for a loan, they outlined the procedures for him.** [The pronoun *they* lacks an explicit antecedent.]

▶ **When Mr. Rivera applied to bank officials for a loan, *they* outlined the procedures for him.**

When you use a pronoun, make sure it does not refer to a possessive modifier. You may need to revise to make your reference clear.

George Orwell
▶ **In ~~George Orwell's~~ "Shooting an Elephant," ~~he~~ reports an incident that shows the evil effects of imperialism.**

[The pronoun *he* cannot refer to the possessive noun *Orwell's*.]

Make sure, too, that you revise a sentence in which *it* is left hanging, making a vague reference to a word in a phrase, such as "in the essay" or "in the article":

Lance Morrow's essay

▶ ~~In the essay by Lance Morrow, it~~ points out the problems of
 ^
choosing a name.

Or In his article, Lance Morrow points out the problems of choosing a name.

Avoid ambiguous pronoun reference. Readers should never
wonder what your pronouns refer to.

AMBIGUOUS   My husband told my father that he should choose
the baby's name.   [Does *he* refer to *husband* or *father*?]

REVISED   My husband told my father to choose the baby's name.

REVISED   My husband wanted to choose the baby's name and
told my father so.

AMBIGUOUS   He had to decide whether to move to

California. This was not what he wanted to do.

[Does *This* refer to making the decision or to moving to
California?]

REVISED   He had to decide whether to move to California. The
decision was not one he wanted to make.

REVISED   He had to decide whether to move to California.
Moving there was not something he wanted to do.

AMBIGUOUS   Briggs noticed Mellersh as he passed by the fountain
and ducked behind a hedge, and, thinking himself
unobserved, took out binoculars.

REVISED   Briggs noticed Mellersh passing by the fountain and
ducking behind a hedge. Briggs, thinking himself
unobserved, took out binoculars.

EXERCISE 22.3 Use clear antecedents with pronouns.
In each of the following sentences, rewrite any sentence in which
a pronoun lacks a clear antecedent.

EXAMPLE:

officials
At the U.S. Patent and Trademark Office, ~~they~~ do not
                                              ^
endorse health claims made by any product.

1. Any food supplement or vitamin can obtain a patent, but it may not be effective.

2. The U.S. Patent Office's purpose is to help inventors lay claim to their unique creations, but it does not investigate whether a creation actually does what its inventor claims.

3. Consumers want products to perform miracles, but they are frequently disappointing.

4. If a food supplement or vitamin has questionable value, they may try to sell the product by advertising the fact that it is patented.

5. When a product label implies that its being patented proves a health claim, consumer advocates advise buyers to beware.

22d Make a pronoun agree in number with its antecedent.

A plural antecedent needs a plural pronoun; a singular antecedent needs a singular pronoun.

plural antecedent   plural pronoun
▶ The *investigators* intercepted a phone call. *They* found the proof they needed.

singular antecedent   singular pronoun
▶ The *detective* questioned several witnesses, but *she* was not able to determine who the accomplices were.

Make a demonstrative pronoun agree with its antecedent. The demonstrative pronouns *this* and *that* refer to singular nouns; *these* and *those* refer to plural nouns: *this house/that house, these houses/those houses* (**21j**).

singular antecedent
▶ He published his autobiography two years ago. This was his first book.

———— plural antecedent ————

▶ **One reviewer praised his honesty and directness. Those were qualities he had worked hard to develop.**

Make a pronoun agree with a generalized (generic) antecedent. Generic nouns name a class or type of person or object, such as *a student* meaning "all students" or a *company* meaning "any company" or "all companies." Do not use *they* to refer to a singular generic noun.

singular antecedent ⌐¬ plural pronoun

FAULTY
AGREEMENT
When a student is educated, they can go far in the world.

singular antecedent ⌐¬ singular pronoun

REVISED
When a student is educated, he or she can go far in the world.

plural antecedent ⌐¬ plural pronoun

REVISED
When students are educated, they can go far in the world.

Increasingly, you see in advertising, journalism, and informal writing a plural pronoun referring to a singular antecedent, as in the following car advertisement:

faulty agreement

▶ **One day *your child* turns sixteen and you let *them* borrow the keys to the wagon.**

However, many readers still expect a pronoun to agree with its antecedent in formal academic writing. Often the best solution is to make the antecedent plural.

people

▶ **We should judge a~~ person~~ by who they are, not by the color of their skin.**

Make a pronoun agree with an indefinite pronoun or quantity word. Indefinite pronouns, such as *everyone, somebody,* and *nothing* (p. 434), are singular in form, so they occur with a singular verb. Some quantity words, such as *each, either, every,* and *neither,* are also singular in form (p. 434). A singular antecedent needs a singular pronoun to refer to it. But which singular pronoun should you use—*he, she,* or both? To avoid gender bias (**22e** and **39f**) and possible clumsiness, writers often use the plural *they* to refer to a singular indefinite pronoun. Some readers, however, may object to this usage, so revising the sentence is a good idea.

SINGULAR PRONOUN WITH GENDER BIAS	**Everyone picked up *his* marbles and ran home to do his homework.**
REVISED BUT CLUMSY	**Everyone picked up *his or her* marbles and ran home to do *his or her* homework.**
REVISED BUT INFORMAL	**Everyone picked up *their* marbles and ran home to do *their* homework.** [The plural pronoun *their* refers to a singular antecedent.]
	VARIATION: You will probably often hear and read sentences like this one, but readers of informal academic prose may object to the fact that grammatically the plural pronoun *their* refers to a singular antecedent. Unless you know your audience well, play it safe and revise. ∎
PROBABLY BEST	**The *children* all picked up their marbles and ran home to do *their* homework.**

Make a pronoun agree with the nearer antecedent when the parts of a compound antecedent are joined by *or* or *nor*. When the elements of a compound antecedent are connected by *or* or *nor*, a pronoun agrees with the element that is nearer to it. If one part of the compound is singular and the other part is plural, put the plural antecedent closer to the pronoun and have the pronoun agree with it.

▶ **Either my friend or my brother has left *his* bag in the hall.**

▶ **Neither Bill nor the campers could find *their* soap.**

Make a pronoun agree with a collective noun. Use a singular pronoun to refer to a collective noun (*class, family, jury, committee, couple, team*) if you are referring to the group as a whole.

▶ **The class revised *its* examination schedule.**

▶ **The committee has not yet completed *its* report.**

Use a plural pronoun if members of the group named by the collective noun are considered to be acting individually.

▶ **The committee began to cast *their* ballots in a formal vote.**

EXERCISE 22.4 Use correct pronoun-antecedent agreement.
In each of the following sentences, correct any errors in pronoun-antecedent agreement, revising sentences as necessary. Some sentences may be correct.

EXAMPLE:

> the work of
> In wartime, a country's intelligence community ~~finds that~~ ~~their work~~ has tremendous importance and urgency.

1. If a historian studies World War II, they will learn how important intelligence was for the Allied victory.

2. At first, however, U.S. intelligence was unable to identify the risk of a Japanese attack, and their failure brought the country into the war.

3. Neither the head of the F.B.I. nor his counterparts at the State Department, Army, and Navy allowed other government officials access to secrets their agents had discovered, and the result was American unpreparedness for the attack on Pearl Harbor.

4. In December 1941, an American could easily have felt that his country might lose the war against the Japanese military and the still-undefeated German army.

5. Everyone involved in decoding German and Japanese messages deserves their share of the credit for the ultimate defeat of the Axis powers in 1945.

22e Avoid gender bias in pronouns.

Personal pronouns For many years, the pronoun *he* was used routinely in generic references to unspecified individuals in certain roles or professions, such as student, doctor, lawyer, and banker; and *she* was used routinely in generic references to individuals in roles such as nurse, teacher, secretary, or typist. This usage is now considered biased language.

NOT	**When an accountant learns a foreign language,** *he*
APPROPRIATE	**gains access to an expanded job market.**

To revise such sentences that make general statements about people, roles, and professions, use one of the following methods:

1. Use a plural antecedent plus *they* (see also **22d** and **39f**).

▶ **When accountants learn a foreign language,** *they* **gain access to an expanded job market.**

2. Rewrite the sentence to eliminate the pronoun.

▶ **An accountant who learns a foreign language gains access to an expanded job market.**

3. Use a singular antecedent plus *he or she.*

▶ **When an accountant learns a foreign language,** *he or she* **gains access to an expanded job market.**

The problem with option 3 is that awkward and repetitive structures can result when such a sentence is continued.

▶ **When an accountant learns a foreign language,** *he or she* **gains access to an expanded job market once** *he or she* **has decided on** *his or her* **specialty.**

Use the *he or she* option only when a sentence is relatively short and does not repeat the pronouns. See also agreement with indefinite pronouns (**21h** and **22d**).

EXERCISE 22.5 Avoid gender bias.
Rewrite the following sentences as necessary to remove any gender-biased pronouns. Some sentences may not need revision.

EXAMPLE:

~~Every~~ concerned ~~parent wants her~~ children to have the best possible education.
All concerned parents want their children to have the best possible education.

1. In the past, a first grade teacher might teach her students to read by asking them to sound out letters.

2. In the last two decades of the twentieth century, many a principal asked his school to teach reading using new theories.

3. Advocates of whole language theory hoped that a student who
might otherwise have fallen behind his peers in reading would
be encouraged by a method that eliminated lesson-based
primers and spelling tests.

4. However, many parents were concerned to discover that their
children were not reading or spelling well by the third grade.

5. By the end of the century, any lawmaker who advocated whole
language theory in schools in his constituency was likely to face
angry parents who wanted a return to spelling and reading
basics.

22f Be consistent in your perspective.

It is important to be consistent with the perspective from which you
are writing. Pronouns can help maintain consistency. Consider the
person and number of the pronouns you use:

- Are you emphasizing the perspective of the first person (*I* or
  we)?
- Are you primarily addressing the reader as the second person
  (*you*)?
- Are you, as is more common in formal academic writing, writing about the third person (*he, she, it, one,* or *they*)?

Avoid confusing readers by switching from one perspective to
another.

INCONSISTENT   **We** are all born with some of *our* **personality already
established in** *us*. **However,** *I* **believe that experiences
also help shape who** *you* **are.**

REVISED   **We** are all born with some of *our* **personality already
established in** *us*. **However, experiences also help
shape who** *we* **are.**

INCONSISTENT | *The company* decided to promote only three mid-level managers. *You* had to have worked there for ten years to qualify.

REVISED | *The company* decided to promote only three mid-level managers. *The employees* had to have worked there for ten years to qualify.

EXERCISE 22.6 Maintain a consistent point of view.
Revise the following passage as needed so that it maintains a consistent point of view.

EXAMPLE:

Residents
~~People~~ do not always see eye to eye with others in their

communities; talking about a novel might be a way to bring

people
~~us~~ together.

    Several municipalities around the United States—from small towns to the city of Chicago—are trying a new method to establish a sense of community: all residents are being encouraged to read the same book at the same time. When we read a book that we can discuss with our neighbors, we have a common ground for discussion. In the summer of 2001, ten thousand or more Chicagoans were reading Harper Lee's classic novel, *To Kill a Mockingbird.* You did not have to be a promoter of the reading program to hope that the novel's powerful portrayal of racism in the rural South could inspire discussions among all facets of the city's diverse population. Can reading books help us unite? Many around the country hope that book discussion groups held on a large scale can prove to people that they really are part of a community. Even if you don't agree with other readers about a book, the fact that you have read it means that you have something in common.

22g Use the pronoun *you* appropriately.

In formal writing, do not use the pronoun *you* when you mean "people generally." Use *you* only to address readers directly and to give instructions.

No **Credit card companies should educate students about how to handle credit. *You* should not have to find out the problems the hard way.**

[This usage assumes readers are all students and addresses them directly. Some readers will not feel included in the group addressed as "you." A reader addressed directly in this way might think, "Who, me? I don't need to be educated about credit and I have no problems."]

Yes **Turn to the next page, where *you* will find an excerpt from Edith Wharton's novel that will help *you* appreciate the accuracy of the details in this film.**

Edit uses of *you* if you are making a generalization about a group or if using *you* entails a switch from the third person.

▶ While growing up, ~~you~~ teenagers face arguments with ~~your~~ their parents.

▶ It doesn't matter if young professionals are avid music admirers or comedy fans; ~~you~~ they can find anything ~~you~~ they want in the city.

EXERCISE 22.7 Use the pronoun *you* appropriately.
In each of the following sentences, decide if the pronoun *you* is used appropriately. If the use is inappropriate, revise the sentence. Some sentences may be correct.

EXAMPLE:

Nutritionists know how valuable deep-green vegetables are
in ~~your~~ a person's diet.

1. If you are like most Americans, you do not eat enough green, red, orange, and yellow fruits and vegetables.

2. Scientists have discovered that deeply colored vegetables and fruits provide you with important phytochemicals that inhibit cancer, regulate cholesterol, and offer other health benefits.

3. The average American eats more white potatoes than any other vegetable, but you get fewer healthy antioxidants from such white or pale-colored vegetables.

4. Studies have shown that eating more colorful fruits and vegetables can help you lose weight more effectively than concentrating on a low-fat diet.

5. To improve your chances of living a long and healthy life, you should choose two servings of fruit or vegetables a day from each of the four color groups.

22h Use standard forms of intensive and reflexive pronouns.

Intensive pronouns emphasize a previously mentioned noun or pronoun. Reflexive pronouns identify a previously mentioned noun or pronoun as the person or thing receiving the action.

INTENSIVE **The president *himself* appeared at the gates.**

REFLEXIVE **He introduced *himself*.**

INTENSIVE AND REFLEXIVE PRONOUNS

	SINGULAR	PLURAL
First person	myself	ourselves
Second person	yourself	yourselves
Third person	himself	themselves
	herself	
	itself	

Note: Do not use an intensive pronoun in place of a personal pronoun in a compound subject.

> Joe and ~~myself~~ will take care of the design of the newsletter.

I (caret above "myself")

Forms such as *hisself, theirself,* and *theirselves* occur in spoken dialects but are not Standard English.

EXERCISE 22.8 Correct intensive and reflexive pronouns.
In the following sentences, correct any errors in intensive and reflexive pronouns. Some sentences may be correct.

EXAMPLE:

Scientists who have successfully cloned animals such as sheep
themselves
have not cloned ~~theirselves~~—or at least not yet.

1. The process of cloning is not complicated: a cloned cell gets a nucleus from the animal to be cloned, and a jolt of electricity convinces the cell to begin replicating it as if it had been fertilized.

2. The famous cloned sheep, Dolly, is a thriving adult and mother of healthy lambs, but her cloner hisself has expressed concerns about potential problems with cloning humans.

3. After the death of a second cloned sheep whose lungs had not developed properly, Ian Wilmut, director of the group that cloned Dolly, convinced himself that human cloning could result in children with terrible medical problems.

4. Of course, since cloning began to appear possible, both scientists and nonscientists have debated among theirselves about the ethics of cloning a human being.

5. Some argue that any people who cloned themselves would believe they owned their cloned human, but others point out that a clone himself is simply a genetic copy, just as identical twins are.

22i Use *who* and *whom* and *whoever* and *whomever* correctly.

In all formal writing situations, distinguish between the subject and object forms of the pronouns used to pose questions (interrogative pronouns) or to introduce a dependent noun clause (**16e**).

SUBJECT	OBJECT
who	whom (or, informally, *who*)
whoever	whomever

In questions In a question, ask yourself whether the pronoun is the subject of its clause or the object of the verb. Test the pronoun's function by rephrasing the question as a statement, substituting a personal pronoun for *who* or *whom*.

▶ **Who wrote that enthusiastic letter?**

[*He* wrote that enthusiastic letter. Subject: use *who*.]

▶ **Whoever could have written it?**

[*She* could have written it. Subject: use *whoever*.]

▶ **Whom were they describing?**

[They were describing *him*. Object: use *whom*.]

VARIATION In speech and informal writing, *who* frequently replaces *whom* as a question word for the direct object, probably because to some people *whom* tends to sound overly correct and formal, verging on the pompous. *The Columbia Quiz Book* goes with *who* when it labels its first set of questions "Who Did Romeo Love?" The humorist Calvin Trillin sums up the views of many writers: "As far as I'm concerned, *whom* is a word that was invented to make everyone sound like a butler" (in "Whom Says So?"). Assess which form your readers are likely to expect. ■

In dependent noun clauses When introducing a dependent clause with a pronoun, determine whether to use the subject or object form by examining the pronoun's function in the clause. Ignore expressions such as *I think* or *I know* when they follow the pronoun; they have no effect on the form of the pronoun.

subject of clause
▶ **They want to know who runs the business.**

subject of clause (who runs the business)
▶ **They want to know who I think runs the business.**

object of *to* [the manager reports to him or her]

▶ **They want to know whom the manager reports to.**

subject of clause

▶ **I will hire whoever is qualified.**

object of *recommends*

▶ **I will hire whomever my boss recommends.**

For uses of *who* and *whom* in relative clauses, see **24a**.

EXERCISE 22.9 Use *who*, *whom*, *whoever*, and *whomever* correctly.

In each of the following sentences, cross out the incorrect pronoun contained within the parentheses.

EXAMPLE:

V. S. Naipaul

The writer V. S. Naipaul, (who / ~~whom~~) claims that he does not "stand for any country," won the Nobel Prize for Literature in 2001.

1. V. S. Naipaul, (who / whom) was raised in Trinidad by Indian parents, now lives in England.

2. Naipaul, (who / whom) one of the Nobel jury members called "the first global Nobelist," has written frequently about the problems of people in former colonies of England.

3. The author has targeted (whoever / whomever) expresses religious intolerance, and he has been denounced by fundamentalists in the Islamic world, (who / whom) he has written about recently.

4. Naipaul, (who / whom) is married to a Pakistani Muslim, has never shied away from criticizing, irritating, or infuriating readers of any religious or ethnic background.

5. His keen eye sees through (whoever / whomever) he describes in his books.

REVIEW EXERCISE FOR SECTION 22 Correct errors in pronoun use. In the following passage, revise any errors in pronoun use. Remember to make all necessary changes to the sentence if you change a pronoun.

By some estimates, 70 percent of all of the antibiotics produced in the United States are used to promote growth in healthy
livestock. In 1998, in a report by the National Research Council
and the Institute of Medicine, they said that feeding antibiotics to
farm animals contributed to the rise of some antibiotic-resistant
bacteria and that this could make human beings sick. Papers published in a 2001 issue of the *New England Journal of Medicine* also
concluded that you should be concerned about the use of antibiotics to make livestock grow more quickly and about the bacteria
that are becoming harder to kill as a result.

When David G. White and a team of researchers from the
Food and Drug Administration tested two hundred packages of
supermarket chicken for salmonella, his researchers and himself
discovered thirty-five samples of bacteria that were resistant to at
least one antibiotic. L. Clifford McDonald and other scientists
from the Centers for Disease Control and Prevention also tested
supermarket chicken for an even more frightening study; their's
found that 350 of 407 samples contained *Enterococcus faecium,* 250
samples of which were resistant to a potent new antibiotic cocktail
called Synercid. You carry *E. faecium* in your intestines naturally,
but it can cause illness if you get sick from something else. Today,
a doctor usually prescribes Synercid if his patient's illness is
caused by *E. faecium* because the bacteria have grown resistant to
the antibiotic that was previously used. McDonald believes that
the use of an antibiotic related to Synercid as a growth promoter
in farm animals has led to bacteria's increasing resistance to
Synercid.

Everyone should be concerned about the rise in antibiotic-resistant bacteria; whether or not they eat meat, they could some-day be infected with a bug that is difficult to defeat. If antibiotics continue to be used simply to make livestock bigger, humans will have a harder time protecting theirselves against bacteria that were once easy to kill. Antibiotics have contributed greatly to improved human health in the past century, and no one whom understands the power of these miracle drugs should support its misuse.

23   Adjectives and Adverbs

Adjectives describe, or modify, nouns or pronouns. They do not add -*s* or change form to reflect number or gender.

▶ Analysts acknowledge the *beneficial* effects of TV.

▶ He tried a *different* approach.

▶ The depiction of rural life is *accurate*.

▶ She keeps her desk *tidy*.

▶ The policy serves to keep the taxpayers *happy*.

 **ESL NOTE**   No Plural Form of an Adjective

Never add a plural -*s* ending to an adjective that modifies a plural noun.

▶ He tried three *differents* approaches. ▪

Adverbs modify verbs, adjectives, and other adverbs, as well as whole clauses.

▶ She settled down *comfortably*.

▶ The patient is demanding a *theoretically* impossible treatment.

▶ *Apparently*, the experiment was a success.

23a **Use correct forms of adjectives and adverbs.**

No single rule indicates the correct form of all adjectives and adverbs.

Adverb: adjective + -ly Many adverbs are formed by adding *-ly* to an adjective: *soft/softly; intelligent/intelligently.* Sometimes when *-ly* is added, a spelling change occurs: *easy/easily; terrible/terribly.*

Adjectives ending in -ic To form an adverb from an adjective ending in *-ic*, add *-ally* (*basic/basically; artistic/artistically*), except for *public*, whose adverb form is *publicly*.

Adjectives ending in -ly Some adjectives, such as *friendly, lovely, timely,* and *masterly,* already end in *-ly* and have no distinctive adverb form.

adjective
▶ She is a **friendly** person.

┌─ adverbial phrase ─┐
▶ She spoke to me in a **friendly way**.
adjective

Irregular adverb forms Certain adjectives do not add *-ly* to form an adverb.

ADJECTIVE	ADVERB
good	well
fast	fast
hard	hard

adjective
▶ He is a **good** cook.

adverb
▶ He cooks **well**.

adjective
▶ She is a **hard** worker.

adverb
▶ She works **hard**.

[*Hardly* is not the adverb form of *hard*. Rather, it means "barely," "scarcely," or "almost not at all": *I could* hardly *breathe in that stuffy room.*]

Note: Well can also function as an adjective, meaning "healthy" or "satisfactory": *A well baby smiles often. She feels well.*

EXERCISE 23.1 Use correct forms of adjectives and adverbs. In each of the following sentences, correct any errors in adjective or adverb forms. Some sentences may be correct.

EXAMPLE:

Amish adolescents face issues of independence and

basically
conformity that are ~~basicly~~ the same as those confronting

other young Americans.

1. People in Amish communities live without electricity or cars, in isolation from the modern world, where technology makes activities such as work and travel go swift.

2. Members of the church live strict by its rules, but a young person in an Amish household does not join the church until adulthood.

3. Amish teenagers are allowed to break church rules and experiment with the outside world; many non-Amish are shocked to learn how widely accepted such behavior is in the Amish community.

4. The great majority of young Amish do eventually join the church, and those who feel that they are not suited good to a highly regulated life may decide to join a more tolerant Amish group in another area.

5. A church member who breaks the rules faces excommunication and shunning by others in the community, so Amish groups try hardly to encourage young people to get over their interest in experimentation before they join the church.

23b Know when to use adjectives and adverbs.

In speech, adjectives (particularly *good, bad,* and *real*) are often used to modify verbs, adjectives, or adverbs. This is nonstandard usage. Use an adverb to modify a verb or an adverb.

▶ They fixed the latch ~~good~~. *well*

▶ I sing ~~real good~~. *really well*

▶ She speaks very ~~clear~~. *clearly*

▶ They sing ~~bad~~. *badly*

EXERCISE 23.2 Use adjectives and adverbs appropriately.
In the following passage, correct any errors in adjective or adverb use.

EXAMPLE:

>   *really*
> High school sports are ~~real~~ important to many communities.

    Participating in a team sport can teach many good lessons to high school students. They can learn sportsmanship, the value of practicing to improve skills, and the strength that comes from working good together. However, many administrators, teachers, alumni, and students take high school athletics too serious. When students are forced to practice football in full uniforms in real hot weather at the beginning of the school year, the coaches' priorities are misplaced. When communities rally around champion high school athletes who have behaved extremely bad or even committed crimes, the communities are sending a terrible message to both athletes and nonathletes about the importance of a winning team. Sports should be fun, and although winning is important, playing good and honorable should be the most important goal of a high school team.

23c   Use adjectives after linking verbs.

After linking verbs (*be, seem, appear, become*), use an adjective to modify the subject. (See **16c** on subject complements.)

▶ That steak is good.

▶ Her new coat seems tight.

▶ She feels bad because she sings so badly.

Some verbs (*appear, look, feel, smell, taste*) are sometimes used as linking verbs, sometimes as action verbs. If the modifier tells about the subject, use an adjective. If the modifier tells about the action of the verb, use an adverb.

ADJECTIVE   She looks *confident* in her new job.

ADVERB   She looks *confidently* at all the assembled partners.

ADJECTIVE   The waiter feels *bad*.

The steak smells *bad*.

ADVERB   The chef smelled the lobster *appreciatively*.

Note: Use a hyphen to connect two words used as an adjective when they appear before a noun. Do not use a hyphen when the words follow a linking verb with no noun complement.

► **Sonny Rollins is a well-known saxophonist.**

► **Sonny Rollins is well known.**

EXERCISE 23.3 Use adjectives and adverbs correctly after linking verbs.
In each of the following sentences, correct any errors in adjective and adverb use. Some sentences may be correct.

EXAMPLE:

suddenly
The aurora borealis appeared ~~sudden~~ in the sky.

1. The Norwegian scientist Kristian Birkeland felt certainly about the cause of the aurora borealis (or northern lights).

2. The lights, which hang like a brightly colored curtain in the night sky, look spookily to most observers.

3. Birkeland looked careful at the lights from a Norwegian mountaintop in midwinter during his 1899 expedition to study the phenomenon.

4. His two expeditions to observe the northern lights appeared successful, but some members of his scientific teams were badly injured or killed in the severe winter conditions.

Northern Lights

5. He appeared madly to some colleagues, but Birkeland finally determined that sunspots caused the aurora borealis.

23d Use correct forms of compound adjectives.

A compound adjective consists of two or more words used as a unit to describe a noun. Many compound adjectives contain the past participle -ed verb form: *flat-footed, barrel-chested, broad-shouldered, old-fashioned, well-dressed, left-handed.* Note the forms when a compound adjective is used before a noun: hyphens, past participle (-ed) forms where necessary, and no noun plural (-s) endings.

▶ **They have a** *five-year-old* **daughter.**
[Their daughter is five years old.]

▶ **She gave me a** *five-dollar* **bill.** [She gave me five dollars.]

▶ **He is a** *left-handed* **pitcher.** [He pitches with his left hand.]

For more on hyphenation with compound adjectives, see **33j.**

EXERCISE 23.4   Use compound adjectives correctly.
In each of the following sentences, correct any errors in the use of compound adjectives.

Example:

Augusta Persse was twenty-eight years old when she

married her ~~sixty three years old~~ neighbor, Sir William

sixty-three-year-old

Gregory, owner of Coole Park in Galway, Ireland.

1. Lady Gregory's twelve years marriage ended with her husband's death, and afterward she began to finish her husband's incomplete autobiography.

2. Her friendship with the well known poet W. B. Yeats was profitable for both of them: they inspired each other and collaborated on one act plays.

3. One play, *Cathleen ni Houlihan,* was an enormous success; although Yeats took credit for it, the manuscript contains pencil written notes that prove how much Lady Gregory had contributed.

4. Lady Gregory became the director of Dublin's famous Abbey Theatre; she won several hard fought battles over the theater's right to present plays such as John Millington Synge's *The Playboy of the Western World* and Sean O'Casey's *The Plough and the Stars.*

5. Many of the hand-pick plays that Lady Gregory championed are still considered masterpieces of Irish literature.

23e Know where to position adverbs.

An adverb can be placed in various positions in a sentence.

▶ *Enthusiastically,* she ate the sushi.

▶ She *enthusiastically* ate the sushi.

▶ She ate the sushi *enthusiastically.*

Do not place an adverb between a verb and a short direct object (**44b** ESL).

▶ She ate ⌐*enthusiastically*⌐ the sushi.

Put adverbs that show frequency (*always, usually, frequently, often, sometimes, seldom, rarely, never*) in one of four positions:

1. At the beginning of a sentence

   ▶ *Sometimes* **I just sit and daydream instead of writing.**

When *never, seldom,* or *rarely* occurs at the beginning of the sentence, word order is inverted (see also **16c**).

   ▶ *Never will* **I let that happen.**

2. Between the subject and the main verb

   ▶ **They** *always* **arrive half an hour late.**

3. After a form of *be* or any auxiliary verb (such as *do, have, can, will, must*)

   ▶ **They are** *always* **unpunctual.**

   ▶ **She is** *seldom* **depressed.**

   ▶ **He has** *never* **lost a game.**

4. In the final position

   ▶ **He goes to the movies** *frequently.*

Note: Never place the adverb *never* in the final position.

EXERCISE 23.5   Position adverbs correctly.
In the following passage, revise any sentence containing a misplaced adverb.

EXAMPLE:

> *often*
> He has read ~~often~~ the century-old diaries of Antarctic explorers.
> ⌃

In the nineteenth and twentieth centuries, polar exploration attracted usually courageous and foolhardy explorers. Many of these explorers kept journals or wrote books, and even today their writings are popular. Why would modern people want to read them? Perhaps the charm of these tales for modern readers lies in the strangeness of the quests. Seldom the early polar explorers gave satisfying reasons for their journeys: on one British expedition to the South Pole, biologists endured weeks of the coldest weather ever recorded in order to collect specimens that scientists at home did not want. Another fascinating feature of polar exploration adventures is that they frequently were fatal: the most celebrated heroes of polar exploration have been those often who failed. Captain Robert Scott, who lost the race to the South Pole and then died in the attempt to return home, is always almost portrayed sympathetically. Rarely Roald Amundsen, the man who beat Scott to the Pole, is mentioned unless his name comes up in discussions of Scott's doomed journey. The romance of failure and of fool's errands entices readers today; modern writers about polar exploration try to find frequently explanations of why these people took such risks. Never the answers can be known with certainty. However, generations of readers will be grateful always that the explorers preserved records of their astonishing journeys to the Poles.

23f Know the usual order of adjectives.

When two or more adjectives modify a noun, they usually occur in the order listed in the Key Points box. Commas separate coordinate adjectives that offer subjective evaluation; their order can be reversed, and the word *and* can be inserted between them (26g). No commas separate adjectives in the other categories listed in the box.

KEY POINTS

Guide to the Order of Adjectives

1. Determiner: articles (*a, an, the*), demonstrative adjectives (*this, that, these, those*), possessives (*its, our*), quantity words (*many, some*), numerals (*five, nineteen*)

2. Coordinate adjective (subjective evaluation): *interesting, delicious, comfortable, inexpensive, heavy, tedious*

3. Adjective describing size: *little, big, huge, tiny*

4. Adjective describing shape: *round, square, rectangular*

5. Adjective describing age: *new, young, old*

6. Adjective describing color: *white, red, blue*

7. Adjective describing national origin: *Italian, American*

8. Adjective describing architectural style or religious faith: *Gothic, Romanesque, Catholic, Buddhist*

9. Adjective describing material: *oak, ivory, wood(en)*

10. Noun used as an adjective: *kitchen* cabinet, *writing* desk

     1   2   5   9   10
▶ **the lovely old oak writing desk**

     1   3   6   9
▶ **many little white ivory buttons**

     1   2   4   10
▶ **that beautiful square kitchen table**

     1   2   7   9
▶ **his efficient European wood stove**

     1   2   2
▶ **her efficient, hardworking assistant**

    [Commas occur only between coordinate adjectives of subjective evaluation.]

As a general rule, avoid long strings of adjectives. Two or three adjectives of evaluation, size, shape, age, color, national origin, faith, or material should be the limit.

EXERCISE 23.6 Use adjectives in the correct order.
In each of the following sentences, make any necessary changes in the order of adjectives and use of commas.

EXAMPLE:

> ~~Dark, winter, short~~ days can cause some people to become
> depressed.
>
> *Short, dark winter* (above struck-out text) ^

1. In northern states in wintertime, many office workers spend most of the daylight hours indoors.

2. Architects are beginning to design some new big buildings to admit as much natural light as possible.

3. A building with features such as skylights, large windows, or an atrium reduces the need for artificial light, but the most money-saving one benefit of outside light is its effect on many workers.

4. A recent architectural study demonstrated that workers in buildings with natural light were happier, more productive employees than workers in dark or artificially lighted offices.

5. Concerned employers can help their office workers maintain a positive outlook through winter dreary months by ensuring that workplaces are brightly lit, preferably with natural light.

23g Avoid double negatives.

Adverbs like *hardly, scarcely,* and *barely* are considered negatives, and the contraction *-n't* stands for the adverb *not.* Some languages and dialects allow the use of more than one negative to emphasize an idea, but Standard English allows only one negative in a clause. Avoid double negatives.

No **We do*n't* have *no* excuses.**

Yes **We do*n't* have *any* excuses. [Or] We have *no* excuses.**

No **She did*n't* say *nothing.***

YES   She did*n't* say *anything.* [Or] She said *nothing.*

No   They ca*n't hardly* pay the rent.

YES   They can *hardly* pay the rent.

EXERCISE 23.7 Avoid double negatives.
Rewrite the following sentences as necessary to correct any double negatives.

EXAMPLE:

People with age-related deafness ~~don't~~ rarely hear high-pitched sounds as well as low-pitched ones.

1. People speaking to a hearing-impaired elderly person often pitch their voices higher to make themselves heard, but studies have shown that using a higher pitch doesn't help the person's perception none.

2. In an elderly person, perception of higher-frequency sounds, such as high-pitched voices, isn't no better than perception of lower-frequency sounds; in fact, perception of higher-frequency sounds is often much worse.

3. Usually, a person with age-related hearing loss doesn't hear no distortion in low-frequency sounds—these may actually sound louder to older people than they do to younger ones.

4. In one study, elderly people exposed to rock music, with its low-frequency bass and drum sounds, consistently rated it as louder than young people did; however, the study didn't necessarily demonstrate nothing about whether elderly or youthful people hear better.

5. Psychologists point out that people exposed to music that they can't hardly bear always think it is louder than fans of the music think it is.

23h Know the comparative and superlative forms of adjectives and adverbs.

The *comparative* and *superlative* forms of adjectives and adverbs are used for comparisons. Use the comparative form to compare two people, places, things, or ideas; use the superlative to compare more than two.

Regular forms Add the ending *-er* to form the comparative and *-est* to form the superlative of both short adjectives (those that have one syllable or those that have two syllables and end in *-y* or *-le*) and one-syllable adverbs. (Change *-y* to *-i* if *-y* is preceded by a consonant: *icy, icier, iciest.*) Generally, a superlative form is preceded by *the* (*the shortest distance*).

	COMPARATIVE (COMPARING TWO)	SUPERLATIVE (COMPARING MORE THAN TWO)
short	shorter	shortest
pretty	prettier	prettiest
simple	simpler	simplest
fast	faster	fastest

With longer adjectives and with adverbs ending in *-ly,* use *more* (for the comparative) and *most* (for the superlative). Note that *less* (comparative) and *least* (superlative) are used with adjectives of any length (*less bright, least bright; less effective, least effective*).

	COMPARATIVE	SUPERLATIVE
intelligent	more intelligent	most intelligent
carefully	more carefully	most carefully
dangerous	less dangerous	least dangerous

If you cannot decide whether to use *-er/-est* or *more/most*, consult a dictionary. If there is an *-er/-est* form, the dictionary will say so.

Note: Do not use the *-er* form with *more* or the *-est* form with *most.*

▶ The first poem was ~~more~~ better than the second.

▶ Boris is the ~~most~~ fittest person I know.

Irregular forms The following common adjectives and adverbs have irregular comparative and superlative forms:

	COMPARATIVE	SUPERLATIVE
good	better	best
bad	worse	worst

much/many	more	most
little	less	least
well	better	best
badly	worse	worst

Than *with comparative forms* To compare two people, places, things, or ideas, use the comparative form and the word *than*. If you use a comparative form in your sentence, you need *than* to let readers know what you are comparing with what.

than the previous one
▶ This course of action is more efficient.
                                        ^

Comparative forms are also used without *than* in an idiomatic way.

▶ The *harder* he tries, the *more satisfied* he feels.

▶ The *more,* the *merrier.*

Absolute adjectives Do not use comparative and superlative forms of adjectives that imply absolutes: *complete, empty, full, equal, perfect, priceless,* or *unique.* In addition, do not add intensifying adverbs such as *very, totally, completely,* or *absolutely* to these adjectives. To say that something is "perfect" implies an absolute, rather than something measured in degrees.

a
▶ He has ~~the most~~ perfect view of the ocean.
         ^

▶ They bought a ~~totally~~ unique quilt at an auction.

EXERCISE 23.8 Use comparative and superlative forms correctly. In the following passage, correct any errors in comparative and superlative forms of adjectives and adverbs.

EXAMPLE:

Before farmers and fishermen in India had access to cell
                    worse
phones, they fared ~~worst~~ when marketing their goods than
                   ^
they do today.

In the United States, the first people to have cellular telephones were the most rich members of the population. In India, in contrast, many poor and working-class people have been among the people who have adopted cell phone technology the quickest. Many of these people live and work in areas that are not served by traditional land telephones, and they are finding that cell phones are one of the usefullest inventions for improving a small business. Fishermen in western India, for example, have no other access to telephones from their boats, and calling the markets before heading to shore with the day's catch allows them to find the most high prices. Growers of produce in rural areas are also beginning to rely on cell phones to find the most high prices for their wares.

Indian cellular companies are responding to a real need in the country—there are far more few telephones per household in India than in the industrialized world—but they are also creating more greater demand. The cell phone marketers have made a tremendous effort to increase the numbers of cellular telephones in the country, offering new customers efficienter service than land lines provide while also making cell phone calls widelier available and most affordable. For the time being, at least, the introduction of cell phone technology has created totally unique opportunities for both cell phone marketers and consumers in India.

23i   Avoid faulty or incomplete comparisons.

Make sure that you state clearly what items you are comparing. Some faulty comparisons can give readers the wrong idea. See **19h, 22a, 22b**.

INCOMPLETE   **He likes the parrot better than his wife.**

To avoid suggesting that he prefers the parrot to his wife, clarify the comparison by completing the second clause.

REVISED   **He likes the parrot better *than his wife does.***

Edit sentences like the following:

▶ My essay got a higher grade than Maria^{'s}.
[Compare the two essays, not your essay and Maria.]

▶ Williams's poem gives a more objective depiction of the

painting than Auden^{'s}. [To compare Williams's poem with
Auden's poem, you need to include an apostrophe; otherwise,
you compare a poem to the poet W. H. Auden.]

Comparisons must also be complete. If you say that something is
"more efficient," your reader wonders, "More efficient than what?"

▶ Didion shows us a home that makes her feel more tied to her

than her home in Los Angeles does
roots.   [Include the other part of the comparison.]

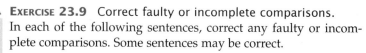

EXERCISE 23.9   Correct faulty or incomplete comparisons.
In each of the following sentences, correct any faulty or incomplete comparisons. Some sentences may be correct.

EXAMPLE:

Two Stanford University linguists think that the click

think they are
languages are older than some linguists.

1. Khoisan, or click, languages, whose vocabularies include clicking sounds, are more prevalent in southwestern Africa.

2. The members of the Hadzabe tribe in the East African country
   of Tanzania speak a Khoisan language similar to the San and
   !Kung tribes of West Africa.

3. Genetic comparisons between the San people and the Hadzabe
   people prove that their genes differ more than any other two
   populations in the world.

4. To some linguists, including Alec Knight and Joanna Mountain
   of Stanford University, these genetic differences prove that the

San and Hadzabe populations diverged very early in the development of human beings; Knight and Mountain believe this clue means that Khoisan languages are older.

5. Was the original human language a click language? Knight and Mountain are more convinced of that possibility than they were before learning of the genetic comparisons, but they admit that there are other possible explanations for the fact that two geographically distant tribes both speak Khoisan languages.

REVIEW EXERCISE FOR SECTION 23 Correct errors in adjective and adverb use.
In the following passage, correct any errors in adjective and adverb use.

Recently, paleontologists have discovered the complete fossils of five 110 million years old ancestors of modern crocodiles. The fossils of *Sarcosuchus imperator,* which means "emperor of the flesh eating crocodiles," were found in an African ancient riverbed. The skull of one adult animal measures four and a half feet long, and scientists estimate that the creature's length would have been more than thirty-five feet; modern crocodiles don't rarely reach half that size. In a photograph released by scientists at the University of Chicago, the skull of the *Sarcosuchus* looks enormously next to the skull of a modern crocodile.

The skeletons of juvenile *Sarcosuchus* found in Africa provide fortunately clues to the lives and habits of the giant prehistoric crocodiles. They did not grow especially quick: at forty years of age, the creatures were not yet adults, and they may not have reached maturity until they were fifty or sixty. They were covered with stiff bony plates that were similarly to armor, so they did not move lively. The

Sarcosuchus had smooth, stout teeth that worked good for grabbing and crushing its prey. Like its present day descendants, *Sarcosuchus* had eyes and nostrils on top of its skull, so it was built totally perfect for lurking underwater and grabbing prey on the riverbank. Other ancient reptiles may have been more larger, but the prehistoric crocodile's great similarity to its modern descendants allows humans today to imagine the fearsome ancient creatures vividly. Most people who see the *Sarcosuchus* skull are certain to feel relievedly that this prehistoric creature no longer roams the rivers of the earth.

24 Relative Clauses and Relative Pronouns

Relative clauses are introduced by relative pronouns: *who, whom, whose, which,* and *that.* Relative clauses are also called *adjective clauses* because they modify nouns and noun phrases in the same way as adjectives do. Relative clauses follow the nouns to which they refer. A dependent relative clause refers to a word or words (its *antecedent*) in an independent clause. See **16e** for more on clauses.

> ┌─ relative clause ─┐
> ▶ **The girl *who* can't dance says the band can't play.**
> —Yiddish proverb

24a Use an appropriate relative pronoun: *who, whom, whose, which,* or *that.*

The forms of relative pronouns vary in speech and writing and in informal and formal usage. In academic writing, use the relative pronouns designated *formal* in the discussion that follows.

Human antecedents   In formal writing, use *who, whom,* and *whose* to refer to people.

RELATIVE PRONOUNS: HUMAN ANTECEDENTS

SUBJECT	OBJECT	POSSESSIVE
who	whom (sometimes omitted) that (informal)	whose

For *who* and *whom* as question words, see **22i.**

The form of the relative pronoun depends on the pronoun's grammatical function in its own clause. To identify the correct form, restate the clause, using a personal pronoun.

subject of clause

▶ **The teachers who challenge us are the ones we remember.**

[*They* challenge us.]

object of clause

▶ **The teachers whom the students honored felt proud.**

[The students honored *them.* (*Whom* may be omitted.)]

possessive

▶ **The teachers whose student evaluations were high won an award.** [*Their* student evaluations were high.]

VARIATION *Whom* is the grammatically correct form of the relative pronoun in the direct object position in its own clause. However, in speech and informal writing, it often tends to be replaced by *who.* When in doubt as to whether to use *who* or *whom,* and if you cannot work out which is grammatically appropriate, opt for *who.* Readers are far less likely to accept *whom* in place of *who* than the other way around. See also **22i.** ■

Phrases such as *I know, he thinks,* and *they realize* inserted into a relative clause do not affect the form of the pronoun.

subject of clause

▶ **We should help children who we realize cannot defend**

themselves. [*They* cannot defend themselves.]

Nonhuman antecedents: animals, things, and concepts Standard English, unlike languages such as Spanish, Arabic, and Thai, uses different relative pronouns for human and for nonhuman antecedents. Use *that* or *which* to refer to only nonhuman antecedents.

who

▶ **The teacher ~~which~~ taught me math in high school was strict.**

RELATIVE PRONOUNS: NONHUMAN ANTECEDENTS		
SUBJECT	OBJECT	POSSESSIVE
that	that (sometimes	of which (formal)
which	omitted)	whose (informal)
(see	which (sometimes	
24d)	omitted)	

Use the relative pronoun *that* to refer to an antecedent naming an animal, a thing, or a concept (such as *success* or *information*). When the relative pronoun *that* functions as the direct object in its clause, it can be omitted.

▶ **They stayed at a hotel *that* had two pools and a sauna.**

[*That* is the subject of the relative clause.]

▶ **They stayed at a hotel *that* their friends had recommended.**

[*That* is the direct object in the relative clause.]

▶ **They stayed at a hotel their friends had recommended.**

[*That* as direct object in the relative clause can be omitted.]

▶ **They stayed at a hotel the name *of which* I can't remember.**
[Formal]

▶ **They stayed at a hotel *whose* name I can't remember.**
[Informal]

See **24d** and **24g** for the use of *that* and *which* in restrictive and nonrestrictive clauses.

EXERCISE 24.1 Use relative pronouns correctly.
In the following passage, revise any incorrect or informal use of relative pronouns.

EXAMPLE:

No one could dispute the fact that George Lucas, ~~which~~ who created the *Star Wars* films, is a marketing genius.

When George Lucas made the movie *Star Wars* in 1977, he told people whom asked about the film's box-office prospects that it would make sixteen million dollars. In fact, the original *Star Wars,* whose story was based on old movie serials and comic book adventures, went on to become the second-highest-grossing film of all time. However, the real money-making potential of the *Star Wars* films lies in the merchandise accompanies them. Lucas, that owns the licenses for all of the merchandise, was said to have earned about four billion dollars from sales of those products even before the release of *Star Wars: Episode I—The Phantom Menace* in 1999. Before that film appeared, reporters who newspapers assigned to write *Phantom Menace* stories were typically business journalists rather than film reviewers. Many of the stories they wrote estimated that *The Phantom Menace* would make a profit even if no tickets to the film were ever sold. Not surprisingly, some film reviewers and moviegoers that saw *The Phantom Menace* were disappointed; even less surprisingly, the film was a hit, and fans continue to buy the merchandise.

24b Make the verb agree with the antecedent of a subject relative pronoun.

Determine subject-verb agreement within a relative clause by asking whether the antecedent of a subject relative pronoun is singular or plural.

▶ **The book that *is* at the top of the bestseller list gives advice about health.** [The singular noun *book* is the antecedent of *that*, the subject of the singular verb *is* in the relative clause.]

────── relative clause ──────

▶ **The books that *are* at the top of the bestseller list give advice about health, success, and making money.**

[The plural noun *books* is the antecedent of *that*, the subject of the plural verb *are* in the relative clause.]

24c Check agreement in relative clauses after *one of* and *the only one of.*

The phrase *one of* is followed by a plural noun phrase. However, the verb can be singular or plural, depending on the meaning.

▶ **Juan is one of the employees who *work* long hours.**

[Several employees work long hours. Juan is one of them. The plural word *employees* is the antecedent of *who,* the subject of the plural verb *work* in the relative clause.]

┌─ antecedent ─┐   singular verb
▶ **Juan is the only one of the employees who** *works* **long hours.**

[Only Juan works long hours.]

EXERCISE 24.2 Make verb and antecedent of subject relative pronoun agree.

In each of the following sentences, correct any subject-verb agreement errors within the relative clauses. Then draw an arrow from any subject relative pronoun to its antecedent. Some sentences may be correct.

EXAMPLE:

make
Keeping costs down is one of the reasons that ~~makes~~ most health maintenance organizations require approval for certain treatments.

1. Most people who participate in group insurance plans now use some form of managed care.

2. Many insurance companies require any patients who participates in managed care plans to get a referral from their primary care physician before seeing an expensive specialist.

3. This practice, which are known as "gatekeeping," often infuriates both patients and physicians.

4. In some cases, patients may believe that a particular specialist is the only one of the doctors in the group who know how to treat a particular condition.

5. Everyone in the plan who need to see a specialist must first make an appointment with a primary care physician to get his or her referral; many patients resent having to make this extra visit.

6. In addition, many insurance companies pay lower fees to any doctor in a managed care plan who refer patients to a specialist for treatment, so doctors are often reluctant to make referrals.

7. Any patients in managed care who sees a specialist without a referral usually have to pay for the full cost of the visit.

8. According to some analysts, feeling angry about being forced to get a primary care physician's permission to see a specialist is one of the situations that causes patients to sue their doctors.

9. One of the surprises that has come from a recent study of health maintenance organizations is the finding that few patients made unnecessary visits to specialists when referrals were not required.

10. In spite of this finding, many experts still support some version of gatekeeping because they think that patients who get a specialist's care should nevertheless let the primary care physicians who knows them best participate in decisions about treatment.

24d Distinguish between restrictive and nonrestrictive relative clauses.

The two types of relative clauses, restrictive and nonrestrictive, fulfill different functions and need different punctuation (**26d**).

RESTRICTIVE **The people** *who live in the apartment above mine* **make a lot of noise at night.**

The writers *who lived in Harlem in the 1940s* **started a great tradition.**

NONRESTRICTIVE **The Sullivans,** *who live in the apartment above mine,* **make a lot of noise at night.**

Zora Neale Hurston, *who was a leading writer of the Harlem Renaissance,* **was greatly influenced by her mother.**

Restrictive relative clause A restrictive relative clause provides information essential for identifying the antecedent and restricting its scope.

FEATURES

1. The clause is not set off with commas.
2. An object relative pronoun can be omitted.

3. *That* (not *which*) is preferred for reference to nonhuman antecedents.

▶ **The teachers *who challenge us* are the ones we remember.**

[The independent clause—"The teachers are the ones"—leads us to ask, "Which teachers?" The relative clause provides information that is essential to completing the meaning of the subject; it restricts the meaning from "all teachers" to "the teachers who challenge us."]

▶ **The book [*that*] *you gave me* was fascinating.**

[The relative pronoun *that* is the direct object in its clause ("You gave me the book") and can be omitted.]

Nonrestrictive relative clause A nonrestrictive relative clause provides information that is not essential for understanding the antecedent. It refers to and describes a proper noun (which names a specific person, place, or thing and begins with a capital letter) or a noun that is identified and unique.

FEATURES

1. The antecedent is a unique, designated person or thing.
2. The clause is set off by commas.
3. *Which* (not *that*) is used to refer to a nonhuman antecedent.
4. An object relative pronoun cannot be omitted.

▶ *War and Peace,* **which you gave me, is a fascinating novel.**

[The independent clause—"*War and Peace* is a fascinating novel"—does not promote further questions, such as "Which *War and Peace* do you mean?" The information in the relative clause ("which you gave me") is almost an aside and not essential for understanding the independent clause.]

EXERCISE 24.3 Identify restrictive and nonrestrictive clauses. In each of the following sentences, underline each relative clause and write *R* or *NR* on the line before the sentence. There may be more than one relative clause in a sentence. Then make sure that each clause is punctuated correctly and that the correct form of the relative pronoun is used.

EXAMPLE:

___R___ People/who speak a pidgin language/are finding a way to bridge the communication gap.

1. _____ When a person who speaks only English and a person, who speaks only Spanish, must communicate, they will

find common ground by using the simple grammar and vocabulary of pidgin.

2. _____ Pidgin which is not spoken as a native tongue by anyone is different from creolized language.

3. _____ When a language, that started out as pidgin, becomes the common speech of a community, that language has been creolized.

4. _____ For example, Haitian Creole that is a language with its own complex grammar and vocabulary came from the pidgin speech created by slaves from many cultures, who were forced to live and work together.

5. _____ Creolized languages which often develop when pidgin speakers raise children in a multicultural community demonstrate both the creativity of human beings—even in terrible hardship—and the depth of the human need to communicate with other people.

24e Check relative clauses beginning with quantity words (*most of, some of, one of*).

Relative clauses beginning with a quantity word such as *some, none, many, much, most,* or *one* followed by *of which* or *of whom* are always nonrestrictive. Use a comma to set off such a clause.

▶ They selected five candidates, one of whom would get the job.

▶ The report mentioned five names, none of which I recognized.

You need only the relative pronoun, not a personal pronoun in addition.

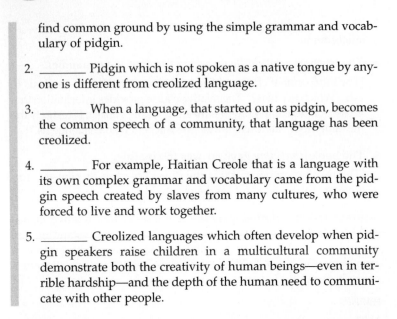

most of whom
▶ I tutored some students, ~~which most of them~~ were my
classmates.
                              ^

EXERCISE 24.4 Use relative clauses with quantity words correctly. In each of the following sentences, correct any errors in relative pronouns or punctuation. Some sentences may be correct.

EXAMPLE:

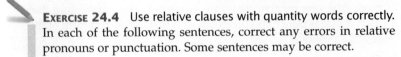

whom
Previous Nobel Prize winners in economics, ~~who~~ many of ~~them~~
have advocated free-market capitalization, were not surprised
                                                              ^
when Amartya Sen won in 1998.

1. As early as the beginning of the 1960s, the economist Amartya Sen was writing arguments, most of which were ignored by other social scientists, that women suffered terrible inequalities in the developing world and that these inequalities harmed local economies.

Amartya Sen

2. Sen continues to advocate gender-specific aid programs to help poor women in developing countries, who many of them lack even basic education.

3. Economists around the world have begun to acknowledge the accuracy of Sen's economic theories some of which focus on the advantages of treating women as full members of a society.

4. New groups of social scientists many of whom have been inspired by Sen's groundbreaking work are investigating the ways that improving women's status in developing countries can also lead to improvements in family income, education, nutrition, and life expectancy.

5. Sen has now set up two foundations, which both of them aim to reduce illiteracy and gender inequality in India and Bangladesh, to put his theoretical views into practice in the developing world.

24f Take care when a relative clause contains a preposition.

When a relative clause contains a relative pronoun within a prepositional phrase, do not omit the preposition. Keep in mind these three points:

1. Directly after the preposition, use *whom* or *which*, never *that*.

———— relative clause ————
▶ **The man *for whom* we worked last year has just retired.**

2. If you place the preposition after the verb, use *that* (or you can omit *that*), but do not use *whom* or *which*.

      [that]
▶ The man ~~whom~~ we worked for was efficient.

      [that]
▶ The security measures ~~which~~ the mayor had insisted on made him unpopular.

3. Do not add an extra personal pronoun object after the preposition at the end of the relative clause.

▶ The company [that] I worked for ~~it~~ last summer has gone bankrupt.

▶ The theater company [that] they are devoted to ~~it~~ has produced six new plays this season.

EXERCISE 24.5 Use relative clauses with prepositions correctly. In the following passage, correct any errors in relative clauses containing prepositions.

EXAMPLE:

       which
A terrible day on ~~that~~ few airplanes were in U.S. airspace proved to have some benefits for climatologists.

    Jet airplanes leave trails in the sky called *contrails,* which are made of frozen exhaust fumes. Eventually, the contrails become cirrus clouds. Scientists which weather is part of a research question for have often wondered how these contrails affect climate. Is some warming of which people call it the *greenhouse effect* caused by these clouds? Climatologists had long known that the best way to measure the effect of contrails would be to conduct a controlled study: data should be collected, some of that should be from periods of heavy air traffic and some from periods when no planes were flying. The problem was that planes were always flying. However, when nearly all flights over the United States were suspended after the terrorist attacks on New York and Washington, D.C., on September 11, 2001, climatologists had a brief opportunity to collect data from skies which no airplanes were flying in. These scientists hope to use the data that was gathered on September 12 to learn whether contrails affect global warming.

24g **Know when to use *that* as a relative pronoun.**

When to use *that* In Standard English, for a nonhuman antecedent, use *that* rather than *which* in the subject position and use *that* (or omit *that*) as an object in a restrictive relative clause. Never use *what* as if it were a relative pronoun.

that
▶ The book ~~which~~ won the prize is a love story.

[that]
▶ The deal ~~what~~ she was trying to make fell through.

[that]
▶ Everything ~~which~~ she does for United Way is appreciated.

Use *that* rather than *who* when referring to groups of people.

that
▶ The class ~~who~~ meets here is late.

When not to use *that* In the following instances, use *which* or *whom* instead of *that*.

1. In nonrestrictive clauses supplying extra information (see **24d**)

   ▶ Ellsvere Shopping Center, *which* was sold last month, has changed the whole area.

2. Directly following a preposition

   ▶ The woman to *whom* they gave the award is a famous physicist.

   In informal contexts, however, the preposition is likely to occur at the end of the clause; in this case, *that* can be used or omitted.

   ▶ The woman [that] I was talking to is a famous physicist.

EXERCISE 24.6 Use *that* correctly as a relative pronoun. In each of the following sentences, correct any errors in the use of relative pronouns. Some sentences may be correct.

EXAMPLE:

that
Methamphetamine is a drug ~~what~~ is becoming a serious problem in some rural states.

1. Methamphetamine laboratories, that are illegal and consequently unregulated by the government, produce large amounts of toxic waste.

2. For every pound of methamphetamine which is made in these drug labs, six pounds of poisonous chemicals are created.

3. The use of a drug what was once rare in this country has increased dramatically in the last ten years, and waste from the illegal methamphetamine labs is becoming a serious environmental problem.

4. The toxic byproducts, which can include acids, benzene, and other lethal chemicals, are often dumped on the ground by the drug manufacturers, and from there the toxins can seep into water supplies.

5. In many cases, even when the labs are discovered and closed down, no one cleans up the sites; agencies who deal with criminal activities rarely notify environmental agencies or any other groups that might take responsibility for removing the toxic waste.

24h Position a relative clause close to its antecedent.

To avoid ambiguity, place a relative clause as close as possible to its antecedent. (See also **19b** on misplaced modifiers.)

AMBIGUOUS **He searched for the notebook all over the house that his friend had forgotten.**

[Had his friend forgotten the house?]

REVISED **He searched all over the house for the notebook that his friend had forgotten.**

24i Avoid using a pronoun after a relative clause to rename the antecedent.

Although this kind of usage occurs in informal speech and in many other languages, avoid it in formal writing. (See also **44f** ESL.)

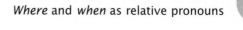

► My colleague who moved to Italy three years ago and has his own apartment in Milan ~~he~~ has a good life.

EXERCISE 24.7 Position relative clauses correctly and delete unnecessary pronouns.
In the following sentences, correct any ambiguity caused by the position of the relative clause and remove any repetitive pronouns.

EXAMPLE:

that is being decoded
The fish genome will reveal information useful to genetic researchers ~~that is being decoded.~~

1. Fugu is considered a delicacy in Japan, but only the most adventurous eaters are willing to order a meal when dining at a restaurant that might contain a deadly poison.

2. A chef must train for many months before being legally allowed to serve the potentially deadly puffer fish who wants a license to prepare fugu.

3. Although many people who have heard about daredevil restaurant-goers ordering fugu they wonder why anyone would be interested in the ugly and possibly toxic fish, geneticists have long been fascinated by the puffer fish known as *Fugu rubripes*.

4. The fugu's genome, which is shorter than that of any other vertebrate on earth, it has now been almost completely deciphered by an international team of scientists.

5. Geneticists hope that their analysis of the puffer fish genome will speed scientists' identification of human gene functions, which is like a condensed version of the complex human genome.

24j Use *where* and *when* as relative pronouns when appropriate.

When you refer to actual or metaphoric places and times, you can use *where* to replace *in which, at which,* or *to which,* and you can use *when* to replace *at which*, *in which*, or *on which*. Do not use a preposition with *where* or *when*.

▶ The morning on which she graduated was warm and sunny.

▶ The morning *when* she graduated was warm and sunny.

▶ The village in which he was born honored him last year.

▶ The village *where* he was born honored him last year.

However, use *where* or *when* only if actual time or physical location is involved.

▶ The influence of the Sapir-Whorf hypothesis, ~~where~~ behavior is regarded as influenced by language, has declined.

EXERCISE 24.8 Use *where* and *when* appropriately.
In each of the following sentences, revise any inappropriate uses of *where* and *when* as relative pronouns. Some sentences may be correct.

EXAMPLE:

                                                      in which
Spelunking is one name for the profession or hobby ~~where~~
people explore caves, but most cave explorers prefer the
term *caving*.

1. In 1838, Stephen Bishop, a seventeen-year-old slave, arrived at Kentucky's Mammoth Cave, to where he had been sent to work as a guide.

2. Bishop was a popular guide, but he was also a great and fearless explorer, squeezing through tight passages in which no humans had been for centuries.

3. In a single year where Bishop explored previously unknown parts of the cave, he doubled the explored portion of Mammoth Cave, earning fame—but not freedom—and attracting hundreds of tourists to the site.

4. Bishop discovered the underground river in Mammoth Cave, which blind fish and crustaceans live, and in 1842 he drew a careful map of the cave that was used by explorers for the next forty years.

5. In 1972, cave explorers found a passage called Hanson's Lost River that led from another Kentucky cave system into Mammoth Cave; the explorers later discovered that the passage through where they had crawled to make the connection was marked on Bishop's 130-year-old map.

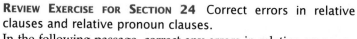

REVIEW EXERCISE FOR SECTION 24 Correct errors in relative clauses and relative pronoun clauses.
In the following passage, correct any errors in relative pronouns and relative clauses.

The QWERTY typewriter and computer keyboard, that is named for the first six letters on the left-hand side, was invented in the late nineteenth century. That keyboard came into common use precisely because it prevented typists which used it from typing fast. The typewriter keys which were used in those days became tangled if they moved too quickly, so slow typing was actually beneficial. However, the situation soon changed. The typewriters which were more mechanically sophisticated and faster that were in use by the 1920s, so the QWERTY system was holding typists back instead of allowing them to type their fastest. At that time Dr. August Dvorak, whom taught at the University of Washington, began to research keyboard layouts.

Dr. Dvorak, of which his original plan was to create a keyboard that could be used by a one-handed typist, studied both the most common letters used in several languages and the physiology of the human hand. He applied this research to create a new layout for the keyboard. The Dvorak keyboard, which it has all of the most frequently used letters in the home row, increased typing speeds for experienced typists and was easy for beginners to learn. The time at when Dr. Dvorak completed his design was shortly before World War II, and a planned change from the QWERTY system to the Dvorak was put aside during the war. In the meantime, the QWERTY keyboard had become a tradition. However, users who the QWERTY system is troublesome for today have an option if they use modern computers, most of that allow users to shift to the Dvorak system if they prefer it. Some Dvorak keyboard advocates believe that beginning typists should learn the Dvorak system, where common words are learned quickly, instead of the QWERTY system. Perhaps Dr. Dvorak's keyboard may yet become the standard of the future.

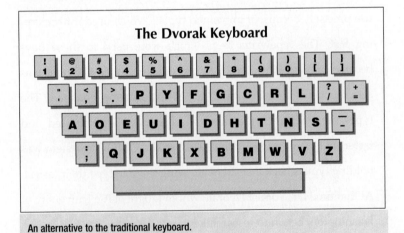

The Dvorak Keyboard

An alternative to the traditional keyboard.

Adapted from *The Dvorak Keyboard* by Randy Cassingham (1986), <www.Dvorak-keyboard.com>. Used with permission of the author.

Part V
Punctuation, Mechanics, and Spelling

498

When you think about how many ways you can say "That's great" to convey different meanings, you will realize the importance of intonation to speech. In writing, punctuation replaces intonation. It is much more than a set of obscure rules, much more than a few marks to split up sentences. Punctuation serves to regulate the flow of information through a sentence, showing readers how to read your ideas: how to separate, anticipate, and emphasize individual words, phrases, clauses, and sentences. The following headline from the *New York Times,* "Stock Fraud Is Easier, and Easier to Spot," says that stock fraud is not only easy to engage in but also easy to detect. Without the comma, however, the sentence would send a different message: it would say that detecting stock fraud is becoming increasingly easy.

Keep in mind that there is no ideal model of punctuation, no prescribed length for a sentence. Where a sentence ends and divides depends on your style and what you want to say. The writer Ernest Hemingway advised writers to keep punctuation conventional: "The game of golf would lose a good deal if croquet mallets and billiard cues were allowed on the putting green. You ought to be able to show that you can do it a good deal better than anyone else with the regular tools before you have a license to bring in your own improvements."

25 Periods, Question Marks, and Exclamation Points

Periods, question marks, and exclamation points often function to signal the end of a sentence.

▶ **I have lost my pencil.**

▶ **Have you taken it?**

▶ **It's behind your ear!**

By convention, one or two spaces then follow the end punctuation and another sentence begins. The Modern Language Association (MLA), in its list of Frequently Asked Questions at <http://www.mla.org>, recommends leaving one space after a punctuation mark at the end of a sentence but sees "nothing wrong with using two spaces after concluding punctuation marks." Ask your instructor for her or his preference.

25a Period (.)

A period in British English is descriptively called a "full stop." The stop at the end of a sentence is indeed full—much more of a stop than a comma provides. Periods are also used, though, with abbreviations, decimals, and amounts of money, as in the following examples.

1. Use a period to end a declarative sentence—a sentence that makes a statement.

▶ **The interviewer asked the CEO about the company's finances.**

2. Use a period to end a sentence concluding with an indirect question.

No   The interviewer asked the CEO how much did the company make last year?

No   The interviewer asked the CEO how much the company made last year?

Yes   The interviewer asked the CEO how much the company made last year. [For more on verbs and word order in indirect questions, see also **19d, 20j,** and **44d** ESL.]

3. Use a period to end an imperative sentence—a command—that does not express strong emotion.

▶ Note the use of metaphor in the last paragraph.

▶ Turn left at the iron sculpture.

4. Use a period to signal an abbreviation. In these instances, use only one space after the period:

▶ **Mr. Mrs. Dr. Rev. Tues. etc.**

[*etc.* is short for *et cetera,* Latin for "and so on," "and the others"]

Some abbreviations contain internal periods. Do not include a space after these internal periods:

▶ **a.m. p.m.** *or* **A.M. P.M. i.e. e.g.**

[*i.e.* is short for *id est,* Latin for "that is"; *e.g.* is short for *exempla gratia,* Latin for "for example"]

See also **32b.**

5. For some abbreviations with capital letters, use or omit periods. Just be consistent.

▶ **A.M.** or **AM**

▶ **P.M.** or **PM**

▶ **U.S.A.** or **USA**

When ending a sentence with an abbreviation, do not use two periods:

▶ The plane left at 7 A.M. [not 7 A.M..]

Note: In MLA style, do not use periods in uppercase initials of names of government agencies or other organizations, acronyms (abbrevia-

tions pronounced as words), Internet abbreviations, or common time
indicators. See **32b**.

ACLU	BC	HUD	NAACP	NPR
AD	FAQ	IBM	NASA	URL
AIDS	HTML	IRS	NOW	USC

**6. Use a period followed by one space at the end of each entry
in a list of works cited.** Note, though, that an APA entry ending
with a URL does not conclude with a period. See page 852.

**7. Use a period in writing figures with decimals and amounts
of money greater than a dollar.**

▶ **3.7 $7.50**

25b Question mark (?)

Questions are useful devices to engage readers' attention. A question
will draw readers into thinking about an issue, to which you can then
provide the answer. Such questions are known as *rhetorical questions.*

▶ **Many cooks nowadays are making healthier dishes. How do
they do this? For the most part, they use unsaturated oil.**

Use the following guidelines with questions.

**1. Use a question mark at the end of a sentence to signal a direct
question. Do not use a period in addition to a question mark.**

No   **What is he writing?.**

Yes   **What is he writing?**

**2. Use a question mark at the end of each question in a series
of questions.**

▶ **In "A Rose for Emily," how does Emily relate to the town? How
does the town relate to her?**

If the questions in a series are not complete sentences, you still need
question marks. A question fragment may begin with a capital letter
or not. Just make your usage consistent.

▶ **Are the characters in the play involved in the disaster?
Indifferent to it? Unaware of it?**

▶ **Are the characters in the play involved in the disaster?
indifferent to it? unaware of it?**

3. Use a question mark at the end of a direct question but not at the end of an indirect question (19d, 20j, and **44d** ESL).**

DIRECT   The interviewer asked, "When is the recession going to end?"

INDIRECT   The interviewer asked when the recession was going to end.

4. In MLA style, do not use a comma with a question mark.

▶ "What is the meaning of life?" the writer asks.

VARIATION   Many writers do use both a comma and a question mark. The following example is from a book review by Elizabeth Spires in the *New York Times Book Review*.

▶ In answer to "Who is the most important one?," Sonja declares it is "those who are closest to heaven. . . ."

Such usage may help make it clear to readers that the sentence continues after the question mark.   ■

5. Do not use a question mark or an exclamation point enclosed in parentheses to convey irony or sarcasm.

No   The principal, that great historian (?), proposed a new plan for the history curriculum.

YES   The principal, who does not seem to know much about history, proposed a new plan for the history curriculum.

Note: You may occasionally come across a question mark used to express uncertainty in a statement or used within parentheses to express uncertainty about the information offered.

▶ "She jumped in?" he wondered.

▶ Plato (427?–347 BC) founded the Academy at Athens.

Use the question mark with a date only if the date is generally not established, and even then it is often better to rephrase the sentence using *about* or *approximately*. In addition, if the uncertainty is a result of your not knowing an exact date, find it out. Don't announce that you do not know by using a question mark.

REVISED   He wondered if she had jumped in.

REVISED   Plato, who lived from approximately 427 to 347 BC, founded the Academy at Athens.

See **32b,** page 560, for more on the use of BC and its alternative, BCE.

25c Exclamation point (!)

An exclamation point at the end of a sentence indicates that the writer considers the statement amazing, surprising, or extraordinary. In general, follow the advice given by two writers. First, the novelist F. Scott Fitzgerald urged in 1958: "Cut out all these exclamation points. An exclamation point is like laughing at your own joke." And in 1974, science writer Lewis Thomas said it even more strongly:

> Exclamation points are the most irritating of all. Look! They say, look at what I just said! How amazing is my thought! It is like being forced to watch someone else's small child jumping up and down crazily in the center of the living room shouting to attract attention. If a sentence really has something of importance to say, something quite remarkable, it doesn't need a mark to point it out.
>
> —"Notes on Punctuation"

So avoid exclamation points. Let your words and ideas carry the force of any emphasis you want to communicate.

No   **The last act of her play is really impressive!**

Yes   **The last act resolves the crisis in an unexpected and dramatic way.**

If you feel you absolutely have to include an exclamation point to get your point across in dialogue or with an emphatic command or statement, do not use it along with a comma, a question mark, or a period indicating the end of a sentence.

▶ **"Just watch the ball!" the coach yelled.**

▶ **How is it possible that the New York Yankees came back to tie and then win a World Series game in the bottom of the ninth inning and not just once, but twice?**

Note, however, that an exclamation point or a question mark can be used with a period that signals an abbreviation:

▶ **Where were you at 11 p.m.?**

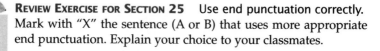

REVIEW EXERCISE FOR SECTION 25 Use end punctuation correctly. Mark with "X" the sentence (A or B) that uses more appropriate end punctuation. Explain your choice to your classmates.

EXAMPLE:

_____ A. The Web site asks users whether they are so afraid of flying that they avoid airplanes in all circumstances?

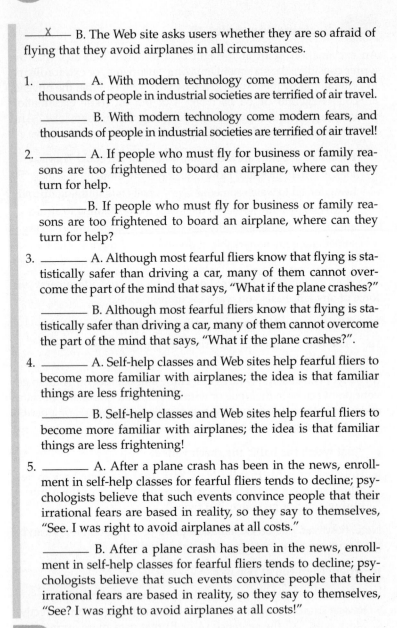

_____X_____ B. The Web site asks users whether they are so afraid of flying that they avoid airplanes in all circumstances.

1. _____ A. With modern technology come modern fears, and thousands of people in industrial societies are terrified of air travel.

_____ B. With modern technology come modern fears, and thousands of people in industrial societies are terrified of air travel!

2. _____ A. If people who must fly for business or family reasons are too frightened to board an airplane, where can they turn for help.

_____B. If people who must fly for business or family reasons are too frightened to board an airplane, where can they turn for help?

3. _____ A. Although most fearful fliers know that flying is statistically safer than driving a car, many of them cannot overcome the part of the mind that says, "What if the plane crashes?"

_____ B. Although most fearful fliers know that flying is statistically safer than driving a car, many of them cannot overcome the part of the mind that says, "What if the plane crashes?".

4. _____ A. Self-help classes and Web sites help fearful fliers to become more familiar with airplanes; the idea is that familiar things are less frightening.

_____ B. Self-help classes and Web sites help fearful fliers to become more familiar with airplanes; the idea is that familiar things are less frightening!

5. _____ A. After a plane crash has been in the news, enrollment in self-help classes for fearful fliers tends to decline; psychologists believe that such events convince people that their irrational fears are based in reality, so they say to themselves, "See. I was right to avoid airplanes at all costs."

_____ B. After a plane crash has been in the news, enrollment in self-help classes for fearful fliers tends to decline; psychologists believe that such events convince people that their irrational fears are based in reality, so they say to themselves, "See? I was right to avoid airplanes at all costs!"

26 Commas

A comma separates parts of a sentence; a comma alone does not separate one sentence from another. When readers see a comma, they think, "These parts of the sentence are being separated for a reason."

Readers have expectations as to how a sentence will progress, and a misplaced or missing comma can throw off their understanding. Look at the following sentence, which misuses the comma:

▶ The rain fell, the roof fell in.

Here the comma is an error, forming a comma splice (see **18g**). Readers reading this and seeing the comma would then expect a third item in a series, something like the following:

▶ The rain fell, the roof fell in, **and Jake fell into a depression.**

But when the sentence does not continue in the expected way because a comma is misused, readers feel thwarted and have to backtrack to make sense of the writer's intention. Readers would have no difficulties with any of the following revisions:

▶ The rain fell. The roof fell in.

▶ The rain fell; the roof fell in.

▶ The rain fell, and the roof fell in.

Use the guidelines in this section to determine when to use a comma. If you absolutely cannot decide whether commas are appropriate, follow this general principle: *When in doubt, leave them out.* Readers find excessive use of commas more distracting than a few missing ones.

26a Two checklists—comma: yes, comma: no

The two checklists provide general rules of thumb. Details and more examples of each rule follow in the rest of section **26**.

KEY POINTS

Comma: Yes

1. Before a coordinating conjunction (*and, but, or, nor, so, for, yet*) to connect independent clauses, including commands, but optional if the clauses are short (*Wharton entertained and James visited*) and optional in British English usage (**26b**).

   ▶ The producer of the drama wanted to change the ending, but the author refused.

   ▶ Accept your fate, and learn to accept it cheerfully.

2. After most introductory words, phrases, or clauses (**26c**)

   ▶ During the noisy party, the neighbors complained.

(continued)

(continued)

3. To set off any extra (nonrestrictive) information included in a sentence ("extra commas with extra information") (**26d**)

   ▶ My father, a computer programmer, works late at night.

   ▶ The Federalists sought help from their leader, the diminutive James Madison.

4. To set off transitional expressions and explanatory inserts (**26e**)

   ▶ The ending, however, is disappointing.

   ▶ On the other hand, little girls talk to maintain community and contact.

   ▶ And girls, I hasten to add, will often emulate their mothers.

5. To separate three or more items in a series (**26f**)

   ▶ They ordered eggs, bacon, and potatoes.

   ▶ Kazan used music ingeniously, let his actors interpret crucial scenes, and constantly choreographed scenes with geometric precision.

   See also **27c** for the use of semicolons in a series.

6. Between coordinate evaluative adjectives (**23f** and **26g**)

   ▶ We ate a delicious, well-prepared, and inexpensive meal.

7. After a verb that introduces a quotation (**26h**)

   ▶ She gasped, "We haven't a moment to lose!"

KEY POINTS

Comma: No

See **26j** for additional details and examples.

1. Not between subject and verb

   ▶ The actor we saw in *Get Shorty* plays Tony in *The Sopranos.*

   However, use two commas to set off any extra information inserted between subject and verb (see **26d**):

   ▶ The actor we saw in *Get Shorty,* directed by Barry Sonnenfeld, plays Tony in *The Sopranos.*

2. Not before part of a compound structure that is not an independent clause

   ▶ She won the trophy and accepted it graciously.

   ▶ Poet Marie Ponsot has published only five books of poetry but has discarded many poems in her eighty-one years.

3. Not *after* a coordinating conjunction connecting two independent clauses, but *before* it

   ▶ The movie tried to be engaging, but it failed miserably.

4. Not between two independent clauses without a coordinating conjunction (use either a period and a capital letter or a semicolon instead)

   ▶ He won; she was delighted.

5. Not between an independent clause and a following dependent clause introduced by *after, before, because, if, since, unless, until,* or *when* (neither before nor after the subordinating conjunction)

   ▶ She will continue working for the city until she has saved enough for graduate school.

   ▶ His prose comes alive when he describes the battle scenes.

6. Not before a clause beginning with *that*

   ▶ They warned us that the meeting would be difficult.

7. Not before and after essential, restrictive information (see also 26d)

   ▶ The player who scored the goal became a hero.

8. Not between a verb and its object or complement

   ▶ The best gifts are food and clothes.

   ▶ The task was to feed and clothe all the survivors.

9. Not after *such as*

   ▶ Popular fast-food items, such as hamburgers and hot dogs, tend to be high in fat.

EXERCISE 26.1 Identify commas: yes or no.

In the passage, identify commas that are used correctly with a check mark and commas that are used incorrectly with an X. For those marked as correct, give the number of the item in the

Comma: Yes Key Points box that explains why the comma is correct.

EXAMPLE:

√(2)

Since the first computers were invented, people have tried to find

×

out if computers, can actually learn to think.

The notion of artificial intelligence, is one of the most intriguing, controversial ideas in computer programming today. Anyone, who studies computers, has probably wondered whether modern computers are learning to think. Alan Turing, who helped to develop computers during and after World War II, believed that the only way to tell if a computer could think was to ask it questions. According to him, if the computer gave answers that were indistinguishable from those of a human, the computer could be considered intelligent. John Searle, a philosopher at the University of California at Berkeley, argued that a computer that was able to create intelligent-sounding answers to questions need not actually understand anything, it might simply be popping out replies based on the rules it had absorbed. Does a machine such as, the chess-playing computer Big Blue qualify as a thinking mechanism, or, has it simply learned the rules of chess well enough to simulate thought? One reason, that this question is difficult to answer is that human thought is difficult to define and quantify. No one, apparently, has yet figured out exactly what causes consciousness, and no one understands exactly how human brains think. As Searle points out, "I think we could

> build a thinking machine; it's just that we don't have the
>
> faintest idea how to go about it, because we don't know how
>
> the brain goes about it."

26b Comma before a coordinating conjunction, connecting independent clauses

To connect independent clauses with a coordinating conjunction (*and, but, or, nor, so, for,* or *yet*), place a comma before the conjunction. Your sentence should look like this:

COMMA WITH COORDINATING CONJUNCTION

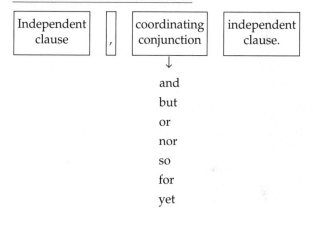

- ▶ The managers are efficient, but personnel turnover is high.
- ▶ The juggler juggled seven plates, and we all cheered.
- ▶ Teachers can ask for a specific assignment, or their supervisors can make plans for the whole school.
- ▶ The novel did not sell well, nor was it favorably reviewed.
- ▶ The soldiers had been well trained, so they knew exactly what to do.
- ▶ The Monarch butterflies are heading south, for winter is clearly on the way.
- ▶ Drugs are available for heart disease, yet many have unpleasant side effects.

VARIATIONS

1. If the two independent clauses are short, some writers omit the comma before the conjunction.

   ▶ **He offered to help and he meant it.**

   But if you always include it, you will never be wrong.

   ▶ **He offered to help, and he meant it.**

2. If the second clause presents a contrast, particularly after a negative, some writers use just a comma without a coordinating conjunction. See **18g**.

   ▶ **Chicano Spanish is not correct, it is a living language.**
   —Gloria Anzaldúa, "How to Tame a Wild Tongue"

   ▶ **His dog doesn't just bark, it bites.**

   Readers of academic prose, however, may regard this as a comma splice error and may prefer a semicolon, a period, or a dash in place of the comma.

   ▶ **His dog doesn't just bark—it bites.**

3. If the two independent clauses contain internal commas, you can use a semicolon in place of a comma between the two clauses.

   ▶ **When he was awarded the prize, the actor praised his director, who had first offered him the part; but he refused to acknowledge the author.**

■

EXERCISE 26.2 Use commas before coordinating conjunctions connecting independent clauses.
Combine each of the sentence pairs into a single sentence, using a coordinating conjunction and a comma.

EXAMPLE:

Patrick O'Brian wrote twenty novels about the voyages of a sea
captain and a naval doctor during the Napoleonic ~~Wars.~~ *Wars, but O'Brian*
~~O'Brian~~ died after beginning to write their twenty-first

adventure.

1. Patrick O'Brian once said that he was a derivative writer. All of his information came from "log books, dispatches, letters, memoirs, and contemporary reports" from two centuries ago.

The Battle of Trafalgar

2. O'Brian wrote about adventure on the high seas and naval battles. He also brought the manners and customs of naval society to life.

3. O'Brian's books are filled with obscure naval terminology. Many readers who have little interest in sailing ships have become devoted fans of Jack Aubrey and Stephen Maturin, the main characters in his twenty-volume series.

4. A *New York Times* book review once called O'Brian's books "the best historical novels ever written." Readers recognize that the characters are every bit as realistic as the descriptions of life on a British naval ship.

5. O'Brian's fans can simply keep rereading the twenty novels about Aubrey and Maturin. They can help support the cookbooks, glossaries, and Web sites devoted to exploring every detail of O'Brian's texts.

26c Comma after an introductory word, phrase, or dependent clause

1. Use a comma to signal to readers that the introductory part of the sentence has ended. It says, in effect, "Now wait for the independent clause."

The sentence pattern looks like this:

COMMA AFTER INTRODUCTORY ELEMENT

| Introductory word, phrase, or dependent clause | , | independent clause. |

introductory word ⌐——— independent clause ———⌐
► However, many researchers disagree.

⌐ introductory phrase ⌐ ⌐——— independent clause ———⌐
► Fifteen years ago, Burma was renamed Myanmar.

⌐——— dependent clause ———⌐ ⌐——— independent clause ———⌐
► If you blow out all the candles, your wishes will come true.

VARIATION If the introductory element is only one word or a short phrase establishing the time frame, many writers omit the comma.

► Soon the climate will change.

► In a few months children learn to crawl, walk, and talk.

However, if you want to apply a rule consistently, it will never be wrong to include a comma:

► Soon, the climate will change.

► In a few months, children learn to crawl, walk, and talk.   ■

2. Never omit the comma after an introductory phrase or clause if a misreading could result.

MISREADING POSSIBLE   When active viruses can spread easily.

REVISED   When active, viruses can spread easily.

MISREADING POSSIBLE   While she was cooking her cat ran off with a lamb chop.

REVISED   While she was cooking, her cat ran off with a lamb chop.

MISREADING POSSIBLE   **Until this spring fever was the most serious symptom treated at the health center.**

REVISED   **Until this spring, fever was the most serious symptom treated at the health center.**

3. Take special care with an -*ing* phrase at the beginning of a sentence. An -*ing* word can begin an introductory phrase (and the phrase will end with a comma), or it can be the subject of the sentence, in which case use no comma between the subject and the verb.

INTRODUCTORY PHRASE   **Investigating the DNA evidence, the**

subject verb

detectives found the attacker.

SUBJECT

— subject — verb

Investigating the DNA evidence led detectives to the attacker.

26d Commas to set off an extra (nonrestrictive) phrase or clause

The sentence pattern for the use of commas with nonrestrictive elements looks like this:

COMMAS WITH NONRESTRICTIVE ELEMENTS

| Beginning of independent clause | , | nonrestrictive element | , | rest of clause. |

| Independent clause | , | nonrestrictive element. |

| Nonrestrictive element | , | independent clause. |

Commas signal that the extra, nonessential information they set off (useful and interesting as it may be) can be removed without radically altering or limiting the meaning of the independent clause (**16e**). Think of paired commas as handles that can lift the enclosed information out of the sentence without making the sentence's meaning confusing.

— nonrestrictive element —

▶ **The Colosseum, Rome's most famous landmark, once held crowds of more than fifty thousand people.**

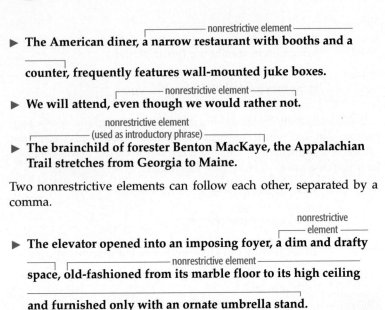

┌─────────── nonrestrictive element ───────────┐
▶ The American diner, a narrow restaurant with booths and a

┌───────┐
counter, frequently features wall-mounted juke boxes.

┌─────── nonrestrictive element ───────┐
▶ We will attend, even though we would rather not.

nonrestrictive element
┌────────── (used as introductory phrase) ──────────┐
▶ The brainchild of forester Benton MacKaye, the Appalachian
Trail stretches from Georgia to Maine.

Two nonrestrictive elements can follow each other, separated by a comma.

nonrestrictive
┌──── element ────┐
▶ The elevator opened into an imposing foyer, a dim and drafty

────┐ ┌─────── nonrestrictive element ─────────────┐
space, old-fashioned from its marble floor to its high ceiling

┌──────────────────────────────────────┐
and furnished only with an ornate umbrella stand.

Note: A phrase or clause that limits or restricts the meaning of the independent clause is said to be restrictive (essential). A restrictive phrase or clause cannot be removed without changing the meaning of the sentence. Do not use commas to set off restrictive information.

┌ restrictive element ┐
▶ We will attend if we have time.

[The phrase "if we have time" is essential to the meaning of this sentence. If it were removed, the sentence would convey a different message, "We will attend" instead of "We might attend."]

┌─────── restrictive element ───────┐
▶ The players who practice often and keep fit are usually the
ones who succeed.

The restrictive element is essential. If it were removed, the sentence would be "The players are usually the ones who succeed." A reader would wonder, "Which players?" The clause "who practice often and keep fit" restricts the meaning of "the players" to a subgroup.

   In the following example, the same clause "who practice often and keep fit" does not restrict the subject to a subgroup of teammates. Readers can grasp fully the meaning of "His daughter's Little League teammates win every game." Rather, the clause adds additional, nonessential information, which is nonrestrictive and therefore set off with commas.

┌─nonrestrictive element─┐
► His daughter's Little League teammates, who practice often

┌──────────┐
and keep fit, win every game.

See **24d** for more on restrictive and nonrestrictive relative clauses.
Use commas to set off the following nonrestrictive elements:

1. An appositive phrase An appositive phrase renames or gives additional information about a noun or pronoun. If the phrase were omitted, readers might lose some interesting details but would still be able to understand the message.

┌────── appositive phrase ──────┐
► A collector since childhood, the gallery owner decided to leave his sculptures to a museum.

appositive
┌── phrase ──┐
► She loves her car, a red Toyota.

┌────── appositive phrase ──────┐
► His dog, a big Labrador retriever, is afraid of mice.

[If you read "His dog is afraid of mice," you would not necessarily need to know what type of dog he owns.]

► Salinger's first novel, *The Catcher in the Rye*, captures the language and thoughts of teenagers.

[The commas are used because Salinger obviously wrote only one *first* novel, and the title provides supplementary information, not information that identifies which novel the writer means.]

2. A participle or prepositional phrase Nonrestrictive participle and prepositional phrases add extra descriptive, but not essential, information.

► My boss, wearing a red tie and a green shirt, radiated the holiday spirit.

► The poet's study, in which she spent her final months, is now a shrine.

3. Extra information in a relative clause When you give nonessential information in a relative clause introduced by *who, whom,* or *which* (never *that*), set off the clause with commas.

► My boss, who wears bright colors, is a cheerful person.

[The independent clause "My boss is a cheerful person" does not lead readers to ask "Which boss?" The relative clause does not restrict the meaning of *boss*.]

▶ **His recent paintings, which are hanging in our local restaurant, show dogs in various disguises.** [The relative clause, introduced by *which*, merely provides the additional fact that his recent paintings are on display in the restaurant.]

Do not use commas with relative clauses providing essential, restrictive information (**24d** and **26j**).

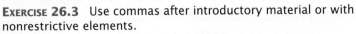

⌈restricts *people* to a subgroup⌉

▶ **People who wear bright colors send an optimistic message.**

[The relative clause, beginning with *who*, restricts "people" to a subgroup: not all people send an optimistic message; those who wear bright colors do.]

EXERCISE 26.3 Use commas after introductory material or with nonrestrictive elements.

Add any necessary commas. Some sentences may be correct.

EXAMPLE:

Working for a major chemical manufacturer Charles Baldwin

an engineer helped to develop the symbol that identifies

biohazards.

1. Realizing that laboratories and medical facilities around the world all needed to dispose of biohazards researchers wanted a symbol that would indicate to everyone which material was infectious.

2. Designers who create symbols want them to be memorable.

3. However the biohazard symbol needed to be unlike any other symbol.

4. In 1966 the symbol which is three-sided so that it looks the same if seen upside-down or sideways was chosen.

5. With its vivid orange color, a shade determined to be the most visible of all colors under most conditions the symbol was soon accepted by the Centers for Disease Control, the Occupational Safety and Health Administration, and the National Institutes of Health.

26e Commas with transitional expressions and explanatory insertions

1. Transitional expressions Transitional expressions such as *on the other hand* and words such as *therefore* and *however* (conjunctive adverbs) connect or weave together the ideas in your writing and act as signposts for readers. (See **5e** for a list of these expressions.) Use commas to set off a transitional expression from the rest of the sentence. If the transitional expression is at the end of a sentence, introduce it with a comma and follow it with a period. Note the following patterns:

COMMAS TO SET OFF TRANSITIONAL EXPRESSIONS

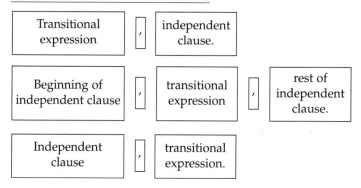

▶ **My dog is afraid of mice. However, most Labrador retrievers are courageous.**

▶ **Most Labrador retrievers, however, are courageous.**

▶ **Most Labrador retrievers are courageous, however.**

Note: When you use a transitional word or expression such as *however, therefore, nevertheless, above all, of course,* or *in fact* at the beginning of an independent clause, end the previous clause with a period or a semicolon. Then place a comma after the transitional expression.

▶ **My dog is afraid of mice; however, most Labrador retrievers are courageous.**

▶ **The party was a success. In fact, it was still going on at 2 a.m.**

See also **26c**.

2. Explanatory insertions Sometimes writers insert a phrase or a clause to make a comment, to offer an example, or to point out a contrast. Insertions used for these purposes are set off by commas.

▶ The consequences will be dire, I think.

▶ Seasonal allergies, such as those caused by ragweed, are a common affliction.

▶ The best, if not the only, solution is to apologize and start over.

▶ His assets, not his earnings, are being scrutinized.

26f Commas separating three or more items in a series

Readers see commas between items in a series and think, "This is a list." If you said a series aloud, you would probably pause between items; in writing, you use commas to separate them. Here is a common sentence pattern:

COMMAS WITH ITEMS IN A SERIES

| item 1 | , | item 2 | , and | item 3 |

The item can be a word, phrase, or clause.

WORDS **The performance was tasteful, emotional, and dramatic.**

However, do not insert a comma between the last adjective of a series and the noun the adjectives modify (**26g**):

▶ The long, thorough, tireless/investigation yielded the expected results.

PHRASES **Searching through the drawer, the detective found a key, a stamp, three coins, and a photograph.**

VARIATIONS For stylistic effect, a writer may not include the word *and* before the last item in the series of words or phrases.

▶ Etiquette books provide guidance on celebrations, travel customs, polite communications, weddings, funerals.

In a series of words or phrases, some writers, particularly journalists or those using British English, will omit the comma separating the last item from the one before it—*snow, sleet and freezing rain.* Though you will see this usage, it is better to use a comma between each item in a list so that your meaning is always clear.

▶ The director achieved a romantic atmosphere with soft music, soothing dialogue about love ̰and happy couples.

[Without the comma after *love,* readers could think that the dialogue was about happy couples.] ∎

CLAUSES **The report questioned why the collapse occurred, what could have been done to prevent it, and who was responsible.**

Note: Use commas only between each of the items in a series. Do not insert a comma to signify the beginning or end of the series.

▶ **Some basic terms in economics are/ supply, demand, and consumption.**

▶ **France, Dorset, and the Lake District/ exerted a significant influence on Wordsworth's poems.**

26g Commas between coordinate evaluative adjectives

Adjectives are *coordinate* when their order can be reversed and the word *and* can be inserted between them without any change in meaning. Coordinate adjectives (such as *beautiful, delicious, exciting, noisy*) make subjective and evaluative judgments. Separate coordinate adjectives with commas. See **23f.**

▶ **Energetic, efficient people are the ones he likes to hire.**

▶ **Efficient, energetic people are the ones he likes to hire.**

Do not, however, put a comma between the final adjective of a series and the noun it modifies.

▶ **Energetic, efficient, and polite salespeople are in demand.**

When each adjective in a series modifies all the adjectives that follow it and gives objectively verifiable information about, for instance, number, size, shape, color, or nationality, the adjectives are said to be *cumulative,* not coordinate.

▶ **Entering the little old stone house brought back memories of her childhood.**

[The house is made of stone. The stone house is old. The old stone house is little.]

Do not separate cumulative adjectives with commas.

26h Comma with a direct quotation

Use a comma to separate the verb from the direct quotation. The verb may come either before or after the quotation.

▶ **When asked what she wanted to be later in life, she replied,**
  "An Olympic swimmer."

▶ **"I want to be an Olympic swimmer," she announced confidently.**

  [The comma is inside the quotation marks.]

However, do not add a comma to a quotation that ends with a question mark or an exclamation point (but see p. 502 for a variation).

No   **"What do you want to be?," she asked.**

Yes   **"What do you want to be?" she asked.**

In addition, do not insert a comma before a quotation that is integrated into your sentence:

No   **The advertisers are promoting, "a healthier lifestyle."**

Yes   **The advertisers are promoting "a healthier lifestyle."**

EXERCISE 26.4 Use commas with transitional expressions, items in a series, coordinate adjectives, and direct quotations. Add any necessary commas; delete any that are unnecessary.

EXAMPLE:

A surprising perplexing proposal from the U.S. Department
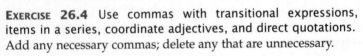

of Energy would allow the recycling of steel that is slightly

radioactive.

    The Department of Energy proposed in October 2001 to recycle

scrap metal from weapons and research plants that are going to be

demolished in Tennessee, Kentucky, Ohio, South Carolina and

Colorado. Radiation has, unfortunately contaminated the surface of

the metals that the DOE plans to recycle. Over a million tons of the

contaminated metal will be available for recycling in the next fifteen

years if the proposal is accepted.

First however, the DOE is, funding an environmental study of the plan analyzing the feasibility of recycling and reusing only those metals that meet lower radiation standards, and scheduling public hearings around the country. On one side scrap metal dealers have expressed preliminary support for the proposal. Citizens who live near steel-recycling plants on the other hand have asked the DOE to reject the proposal as an irresponsible environmentally unsound, idea. In Minnesota, which has steel-recycling plants, a public hearing drew many concerned, outspoken, citizens who testified that they did not want radioactive material trucked through their neighborhoods. In addition many noted that they would not want the government to allow scrap metal plants to add radioactive steel to the items that the plants manufacture, such as, snow shovels eyeglasses forks, and, cars. One woman announced "I propose that our federal government have a zero tolerance for any release of radioactive materials because I'm scared." Minnesota's largest steel-recycling plant has in fact already announced that it has rejected the DOE plan. The manager of the DOE environmental study said that the department would abide by the study's results.

26i Special uses of commas

1. To make the meaning clear and prevent misreading   Use a comma to separate elements in a sentence that may otherwise be confusing.

▶ **He who can, does. He who cannot, teaches.**

—George Bernard Shaw, Man and Superman

[Usually a comma is not used to separate a subject from the verb. Here the comma is necessary to prevent confusing the readers.]

2. With an absolute phrase Use a comma to set off a phrase that modifies the whole sentence (an absolute phrase).

absolute phrase
▶ The audience looking on in amusement, the valedictorian blew kisses to all her favorite instructors.

3. With a date Use a comma to separate the date from the year and the day from the date:

▶ On May 14, 1998, the legendary singer Frank Sinatra died.

▶ The poet laureate is reading in San Francisco on Wednesday, May 1.

Do not use a comma when you mention only the month and date (May 14) or month and year (May 1998).

4. With numbers Use a comma (never a period) to divide numbers into thousands.

▶ 1,200   ▶ 515,000   ▶ 34,000,000

No commas are necessary in years (*2004*), numbers in addresses (*3501 East 10th Street*), or page numbers (*page 1008*).

5. With scene or line references In the body of your text (not in a parenthetical reference) use a comma between act and scene and between page and line: act 3, scene 4; page 14, line 9.

6. With titles Use commas to set off a person's title or degree.

▶ Stephen L. Carter, PhD, gave the commencement speech.

7. With an inverted name Use a comma between the last name and the first:

▶ Dillard, Annie

8. With the parts of an address

▶ Alice Walker was born in Eatonton, Georgia, in 1944.

However, do not use a comma before a ZIP code: Newton, MA 02459.

9. With a conversational tag or tag question

▶ Yes, Salinger's daughter, like others before her, has produced a memoir.

▶ She has not won a Pulitzer Prize, has she?

10. With a direct address or salutation

▶ Whatever you build next, Mr. Trump, will cause controversy.

26j When not to use commas: nine rules of thumb

1. Do not use a comma to separate a verb from its subject.

▶ The gifts she received from her colleagues made her realize her value to the company.

▶ Interviewing so many women in the United States helped the researcher understand the "American dream."

Between a subject and verb, you may need to put two commas around inserted material, but never use just one comma.

```
          subject
```
▶ The engraved plaque, given to her by her colleagues on her

```
              verb
```
last day of work, made her feel respected.

2. Do not use a comma within a compound structure when the second part of the compound is not an independent clause.

▶ Amy Tan has written novels and adapted them for the screen.

▶ Tan has written about her mother and the rest of her family.

3. Do not use a comma after a coordinating conjunction that connects two sentences. The comma goes before the conjunction, not after it.

▶ *The Joy Luck Club* is supposed to be good, but I missed it when it came to my local movie theater.

4. Do not use a comma to join two independent clauses when no coordinating conjunction is present. Instead, end the first clause with a period and make the second clause a new sentence, or insert a semicolon between the clauses. Use a comma only if you connect the clauses with a coordinating conjunction. (See **18h** for ways to correct a comma splice, the error that results when two independent clauses are incorrectly joined with a comma.)

▶ **Amy Tan has written novels; they have been adapted for the screen.**

VARIATION Some writers, however, do use a comma between two independent clauses when the clauses use parallel structures to point out a contrast (see also **18g** and **26b,** variation 2).

▶ **She never insults, she just criticizes.**

If you do not know readers' expectations on this point, play it safe and separate the clauses with a period or a semicolon. ■

5. Do not use a comma to separate an independent clause from a following dependent clause introduced by *after,* *before, because, if, since, unless, until,* **or** *when.*

▶ **The test results were good because all the students had studied in groups.**

▶ **The audience broke into a wild applause when the young poet finished his reading.**

6. Do not use a comma to separate a clause beginning with *that* **from the rest of the sentence.**

▶ **The girl in Tan's story tried to convey to her mother that she did not have to be a child prodigy.**

Note: A comma can appear before a *that* clause when it is the second comma of a pair before and after extra information inserted as a nonrestrictive phrase.

▶ **He skates so fast, despite his size, that he will probably break the world record.**

7. Do not use commas around a phrase or clause that provides essential, restrictive information.

▶ **Alice Walker's essay "Beauty: When the Other Dancer Is the Self" discusses coping with a physical disfigurement.**

[Walker has written more than one essay. The title restricts the noun *essay* to one specific essay.]

Similarly, a restrictive relative clause introduced by *who, whom, whose, which,* or *that* is never set off by commas. The clause provides essential, identifying information (see also **24d** and **26d**).

▶ **The teachers praised the children who finished on time.**

[The teachers didn't praise all the children; they praised only the ones who finished on time.]

8. Do not use a comma to separate a verb from its object or complement.

▶ **The qualities required for the job are punctuality, efficiency, and the ability to work long hours.**

9. Do not use a comma after *such as*.

▶ **They bought kitchen supplies such as detergent, paper towels, and garbage bags.**

REVIEW EXERCISE FOR SECTION 26 Use commas correctly.
Add any necessary commas, delete any that are unnecessary, and replace commas with periods or semicolons as needed.

"All men are created equal" wrote Thomas Jefferson but his deeds did not always match his eloquent words. Like most of the other aristocratic landowners in Virginia, Jefferson the author of the Declaration of Independence founder of the University of Virginia and third president of the United States, owned slaves. One of them was a woman named, Sally Hemings who was one-quarter African, and was probably the daughter of Jefferson's father-in-law and a half-African slave, if this genealogy is correct Hemings was the half-sister of Jefferson's late wife, Martha. Indeed observers at the time noted that, Hemings looked remarkably like Martha Jefferson, who had died on September 6 1782, when Jefferson was thirty-nine.

In 1802 a disgruntled former employee reported that President Jefferson, was the father of Hemings's three children.

Jefferson never responded publicly to the charge but, many people noticed the resemblance between him and the Hemings children. The believable scandalous rumors continued to circulate for years after Jefferson's death in 1826. A few historians speculated, that Jefferson's nephews might have fathered the Hemings children but, most ignored the story altogether. Yes it was true that slaveholders had often been known to impregnate slave women, yet such an act was difficult for many white Americans to reconcile with their views of one of the country's founders.

In the 1990s DNA tests were used to determine whether Jefferson could have been the father of Sally Hemings's children. The tests showed a match between the DNA of Jefferson's closest male relative's descendants, and the descendants of Hemings's youngest son, Eston. Clearly either Jefferson or a close relative was Eston's father. Most historians are now convinced that, Jefferson did father at least one of the Hemings children. A recent biography of Jefferson was called *American Sphinx* and the third president does, indeed seem to have hidden many secrets. Whether the revelations about his relationship with Hemings will change the way Americans feel about this Founding Father, remains to be seen.

27 Semicolons and Colons

A colon (:) may look like a semicolon (;)—one is two dots, the other a dot above a comma—but they are used in different ways, and they are not interchangeable. Note the use of the semicolon and colon in the following passage discussing the musical number "Cheek to Cheek" in the Astaire and Rogers film *Top Hat:*

[Ginger] Rogers is perhaps never more beautiful than when she's just listening; she never takes her eyes off him and throughout this scene I don't think she changes her expression once. The modesty of the effect makes her look like an angel: such a compliant, unasking attitude, handsome beyond expectation in such a fierce woman.

—Arlene Croce, *The Fred Astaire and Ginger Rogers Book*

Ginger Rogers and Fred Astaire

27a When to use a semicolon (;)

A period separates independent clauses with finality; a semicolon (such as the one you have just seen in this sentence) provides a less distinct separation and indicates that an additional related thought or item will follow immediately. As essayist Lewis Thomas comments in "Notes on Punctuation": "The period tells you that that is that; if you didn't get all the meaning you wanted or expected, anyway you got all the writer intended to parcel out and now you have to move along. But with a semicolon there you get a pleasant little feeling of expectancy; there is more to come." Use a semicolon instead of a period when the ideas in two independent clauses are closely connected and you want readers to expect more.

Here are the patterns for semicolons used between independent clauses:

SEMICOLONS

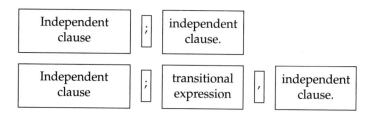

27b Semicolon between independent clauses

Use a semicolon to separate—and connect—two closely related independent clauses that are not joined by a coordinating conjunction (**16f**).

▶ **Biography tells us about the subject; biographers also tell us about themselves.**

A comma between the two independent clauses would produce a comma splice, and no punctuation at all would produce a run-on sentence (see **18g**). Do not use a capital letter to begin a clause after a semicolon. Semicolons are often used when the second independent clause contains a transitional expression, such as a conjunctive adverb—*however, therefore, nevertheless, moreover*—or a phrase—*in fact, as a result, above all, on the other hand*. (See **5e** and **37c** for more on transitional expressions.)

▶ **The results of the study support the hypothesis; however, further research with a variety of tasks is necessary.**

27c Semicolons between clauses or items in a series containing internal commas

Generally, you will use a comma to separate two independent clauses connected by a coordinating conjunction:

▶ **Our dependence on foreign oil supplies is economically problematic, yet SUVs are dominating our roads.**

However, use a semicolon in place of a comma if the independent clauses themselves contain commas.

▶ **Our dependence on foreign oil supplies, constantly discussed in the press, is economically problematic; yet SUVs, those gas-guzzling monsters, are dominating our roads.**

Items in a series are usually separated by commas (see **26f**). However, to avoid ambiguity, use semicolons to separate long listed items when internal commas are present.

▶ **When I cleaned out the refrigerator, I found a chocolate cake, half-eaten; some canned tomato paste, which had a blue fungus growing on the top; and some possibly edible meat loaf.**

In addition, use semicolons to separate a series of long independent clauses that contain internal commas, even if a coordinating conjunction is present before the last item in the series.

▶ Some students planned to do library research; those who were working on controversial, debatable issues turned to databases; and several, among them the best writer in the class, decided to use interviews and a questionnaire.

27d When not to use a semicolon

1. Do not use semicolons interchangeably with colons.   Do not use a semicolon to introduce a list or explanation. Use a colon instead (**27e**).

▶ They contributed a great deal of food; salad, chili, and dessert.

2. Do not use a semicolon after an introductory phrase or dependent clause, even if the phrase or clause is long.   Using a semicolon will produce a fragment. Use a comma instead.

▶ With the advent of sound in the world of Hollywood movies; the whole nature of stardom changed.

▶ Because the training period was so long and arduous for all the players; the manager allowed one visit by family and friends.

3. Do not overuse semicolons.   Use a semicolon in place of a period only when the link between two independent clauses is strong. If you are in doubt as to whether a semicolon is appropriate, using a period will probably be a safe course.

EXERCISE 27.1   Know when to use and when not to use a semicolon.
Add semicolons and change commas to semicolons as needed. Remove unnecessary semicolons or replace them with colons or commas as needed.

EXAMPLE:

Jan Harold Brunvald is the man who coined the term *urban*

legend; he once said that the truth never stands in the way of a

good story.

Many urban legends are the kinds of stories that people use to

frighten one another around a campfire. Some of the best-known ones are about escaped lunatics and murderers such as the man with a hook for a hand who terrorizes a young couple who, while parked on a deserted road, hear a radio broadcast about him, the man who telephones a babysitter with dire warnings, finally revealing that he is calling from another extension in the same house, and the killer who hides in the back seat of a woman's car or under the bed in her dorm room. These stories are chilling but faintly unbelievable, we all realize, eventually, that they are not true.

27e When to use a colon (:)

A colon (:) signals anticipation. It follows an independent clause and introduces information that readers will need. A colon tells readers, "What comes next will define, illustrate, or rename what you have just read." Use one space after a colon.

Here are the colon patterns:

COLONS

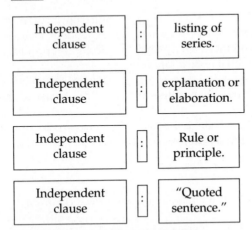

Use a colon in the following situations.

1. Use a colon after an independent clause to illustrate a concept by providing a listing of a series of examples.

▶ The students included three pieces of writing in their portfolios: a narrative, an argument, and a documented paper.

2. Use a colon after an independent clause to introduce an explanation, expansion, or elaboration.

▶ [Galileo] understood what Aristotle could not: that a moving object tends to keep moving.

—James Gleick, *Chaos*

▶ After an alarming cancer diagnosis and years of treatment, Lance Armstrong was victorious: he won the Tour de France and had a son.

▶ The author has performed a remarkable feat: she has maintained suspense to the last page.

VARIATION Some writers prefer to use a capital letter after a colon introducing an independent clause. Be consistent in your usage. ∎

3. Use a colon followed by a capital letter to introduce a rule or principle.

▶ The main principle of public speaking is simple: Look at the audience.

4. Use a colon in salutations, precise time notations, titles, and biblical citations.

Letters and memos	**Dear Chancellor Witkin:**
	To: The Chancellor
Hours and minutes	**7:20 p.m.**
Titles and subtitles	*Backlash: The Undeclared War against American Women*
Biblical citations	**Genesis 37:31–35.** [Here, a period could be used in place of the colon.]

5. Use a colon to introduce a quotation that is not integrated into the structure of your sentence and is not introduced by a verb like *say*.

▶ Emily Post has provided an acceptable alternative to our always trying to outdo others: "To do *exactly as your neighbors do* is the only sensible rule."

6. Use a colon to introduce a long quotation that you set off from your own text. See **50h** for an example.

27f When not to use a colon

1. Do not use a colon directly after a verb (such as a form of *be*, *consist of*, or *include*).

▶ The two main effects were the improvement of registration and an increase in the numbers of advisers.

▶ The book includes a preface, an introduction, an appendix, and an index.

2. Do not use a colon after a preposition (such as *except* and *regarding*) or *such as*.

▶ The novel will please all readers except academics, linguists, and lawyers.

▶ They packed many different items for the picnic, such as taco chips, salsa, bean salad, pita bread, and egg rolls.

3. Do not use a colon after *for example*, *especially*, or *including*.

▶ His taste is so varied that his living room includes, for example, antiques, modern art, and art deco lighting fixtures.

EXERCISE 27.2 Know when to use and when not to use a colon. Make any changes so that colons are used correctly.

EXAMPLE:

Turtles are a unique life form, no other creature has a rigid shell made up of vertebrae and ribs.

1. The professor required each student to have a copy of *Herpetology An Introductory Biology of Amphibians and Reptiles.*

2. Turtles are divided into two main branches according to the way they retract their necks into their bodies, the cryptodire branch, which means *hidden neck,* can pull their heads completely into their shells, but the pleurodire branch, which means *side neck,* can only partially retract their heads.

3. Turtles are different from other reptiles because: their chest cavities cannot expand when they inhale.

4. Turtles can survive without air much longer than other reptiles, some turtles have lived for as long as thirty-three hours without oxygen.

5. Many species of turtles can take in oxygen through sacs which emerge from the turtle's digestive and urogenital cavity; turtles share this unusual method of breathing with life forms such as: dragonfly nymphs and sea cucumbers.

REVIEW EXERCISE FOR SECTION 27 Use semicolons and colons correctly.
Correct any errors in the use of semicolons and colons.

Japan has long been one of the most homogeneous of the modern industrial nations, many Japanese protect their cultural identity so strongly that foreigners are rarely allowed to feel a part of Japan, no matter how long they and their families remain in the country. Foreign nationals who make Japan their home are not required to send their children to school as Japanese parents must, in addition, non-Japanese are not covered by Japan's national health insurance. Many foreign nationals, consequently; consider Japan only a temporary home. However, the Japanese population is: getting older, with more retirees than new babies throughout the country, currently, the Japanese birthrate is one of the lowest in the world. To keep the economy alive and pay for pensions for retired workers and their families; Japan must find more workers. The

United Nations now recommends that Japan begin to encourage immigration.

Many Japanese emigrants in the early nineteenth century went to Brazil to work. In the 1990s, Japan began to allow Brazilians of Japanese descent to return to Japan on temporary work visas today, there are a quarter of a million Brazilians in Japan, and many of them now hold permanent visas. Japan has: two Brazilian television channels, four Brazilian newspapers, and forty-one Brazilian schools. Although many of these Brazilians have Japanese ancestors; they are culturally Brazilian, and the Brazilian and Japanese cultures occasionally clash. Some Japanese in cities with large Brazilian populations complain that Brazilians do not comply with Japanese regulations, some Brazilians say that the Japanese make them feel unwelcome. Accepting cultural diversity is rarely easy; and it may be more difficult in Japan, where a single culture has been dominant for centuries. One thing, however, is certain; Japan must accommodate foreign workers if the nation's economy is to survive the population slump.

28 Apostrophes

Apostrophes indicate ownership or possession (*Fred's books, the government's plans*). They can also signal omitted letters (*who's, can't*).

28a Two checklists—apostrophe: yes, apostrophe: no

The two checklists provide general rules of thumb. Details and more examples of each rule follow in the rest of section **28**.

KEY POINTS

Apostrophe: Yes

1. Use *-'s* for the possessive form of all nouns except plural nouns that end with *-s: the hero's misfortune, the actress's Academy Award.*
2. Use an apostrophe alone for the possessive form of plural nouns that end with *-s: actresses' lives, the heroes' misfortunes.*
3. Use an apostrophe to indicate the omission of letters in contracted forms such as *didn't* and *they're.*
4. Use *it's* only for "it is" or "it has": *It's a good idea; it's been a long time.* (The possessive form of the pronoun *it* is spelled with no apostrophe: *The house lost its roof.*)

KEY POINTS

Apostrophe: No

1. Generally, do not use an apostrophe to form the plurals of nouns. (See **28e** for rare exceptions.)

   ▶ Flock's of sheep dot the hillsides in Scotland.

   ▶ Scholarship students' need to maintain a high grade point average.

2. Never use an apostrophe before an *-s* ending on a verb. (Note that *let's* is short for *let us;* the *-s* is not a third person singular present tense ending.)

   ▶ The author let's his characters take over.

   ▶ The word ~~imply's~~ ^{implies} that the mood is somber.

   ▶ He ~~try's~~ ^{tries} hard to correct his spelling.

3. Do not write possessive pronouns (*hers, its, ours, yours, theirs*) with an apostrophe.

4. Do not use an apostrophe to form the plural of names: *the Browns.*

5. Do not use an apostrophe to indicate possession by inanimate objects such as buildings and items of furniture; instead, use *of: the roof of the hotel, the back of the desk.*

28b *-'s* to signal possession

As a general rule, to signal possession, use *-'s* with singular nouns, with indefinite pronouns, and with plural nouns that do not form the plural with *-s.*

the child's books	anybody's opinion
the children's toys	today's world
this month's budget	Mr. Jackson's voice
someone else's idea	their money's worth
the author's voice	this year's curriculum

1. Individual and joint ownership To indicate individual ownership, use the possessive form with each person you mention.

▶ **Updike's and Roth's recent works received glowing reviews.**

▶ **Teachers' and students' ideas about good teaching often differ.**

To show joint ownership, use the possessive form only with the last person you mention.

▶ **Sam, Sue, and Pat's house has just been sold to a single buyer.**
 [Sam, Sue, and Pat own the house jointly.]

2. Compound nouns Add *-'s* to the last word in a compound noun.

▶ **my brother-in-law's car**

3. Singular nouns ending in *-s* When a singular noun ends in *-s,* add *-'s* as usual for the possessive.

▶ **Thomas's toys**   ▶ **his boss's instructions**

However, when a singular noun ending in *-s* is a long word or ends with a *z* or *eez* sound, an apostrophe alone is sometimes used: *Erasmus' rhetoric, Euripides' dramas.*

28c Apostrophe with a plural noun ending in *-s*

When a plural noun already ends in *-s,* add only an apostrophe.

▶ **the students' suggestions**   ▶ **my friends' ambitions**
 [more than one student]   [more than one friend]

Remember to include an apostrophe in comparisons with a noun understood (**19h** and **23i**):

▶ **His views are different from other professors'.**

 [... from other professors' views]

> **EXERCISE 28.1** Use apostrophes to signal possession. Correct any errors in the use of apostrophes.

EXAMPLE:

In parts of Africa that have been devastated by AIDS, doctors

who practice Western-style medicine are looking at traditional

~~healer's~~ healers' roles in treating the sick.

1. Doctors and healers' ideas about useful treatments for people infected with the AIDS virus sometimes conflict with each other.

2. For example, traditional healers often prescribe emetics to cause vomiting, and if a patients' treatment also includes retroviral drugs, the patient may expel the drugs before they take effect.

3. Because many doctors in Africa understand their patients faith in traditional healing, some doctors are trying to work with healers rather than fighting them.

4. Some healers have agreed to attend conferences' at hospitals, where they learn to wear latex gloves when treating patients and to use alcohol to clean razor blades' edges and porcupine quills that have contacted any patients' body fluids.

5. Many patients trust healer's more than they trust doctor's, so hospitals in some areas have deputized traditional healers to monitor their patients intake of AIDS drugs and their mental well-being.

28d Apostrophe with contractions

1. Use contractions to represent informal speech.

▶ Let's roll!

In a contraction (*shouldn't, don't, let's, we're, I'm, they've, should've*), the apostrophe appears where letters have been omitted. To test whether an apostrophe is in the correct place, mentally replace the missing letters. The replacement test, however, will not help with *won't*, which is the contraction for *will not*.

Note: Some readers object to contractions in formal academic writing because they view them as colloquial and informal. It is safer not to use contractions unless you know readers' preferences.

can't	cannot	they'd	they had *or* they would
didn't	did not	they're	they are
he's	he is *or* he has	it's	it is *or* it has
's	is, has, *or* does (How's it taste?)	let's	let us (Let's go.)

2. Use an apostrophe to take the place of the first part of a year or decade.

▶ **the greed of the '80s**   ▶ **the Spirit of '76**

  [the 1980s]   [the year 1776]

Note: Fixed forms spelled with an apostrophe, such as *o'clock* and the poetic *o'er*, are contractions ("of the clock," "over").

28e -'s for plurals only in special instances

The general rule is that -'s is not used to form a plural. However, there are a few exceptions. Use the following four guidelines.

1. Use -'s for the plural form of letters of the alphabet. Italicize or underline only the letter, not the plural ending (**31d**).

▶ **Maria picked all the *M*'s out of her alphabet soup.**

▶ **Georges Perec's novel called *A Void* has no *e*'s in it at all.**

2. Use -'s for the plural form of a word referred to as the word itself. Italicize or underline the word named as a word, but do not italicize or underline the -'s ending (see **31d**).

▶ **You have too many *but*'s in that sentence.**

3. Be consistent with the plural forms of numbers, acronyms, and abbreviations (see 32b). MLA and APA styles prefer no apostrophe in the plural form of numbers, acronyms, and abbreviations.

▶ **the 1900s**   ▶ **CDs**   ▶ **FAQs**   ▶ **VCRs**

VARIATION   You will frequently see such plurals spelled with -'s: the 1900's, CD's. Just be consistent in your usage. ∎

4. Never use an apostrophe to signal the plural of common nouns or personal names.

No   **big bargain's, the Jackson's**

Yes   **big bargains, the Jacksons**

28f **The difference between *it's* and *its***

When deciding whether to use *its* or *it's,* think about meaning. *It's* is a contraction meaning "it is" or "it has." *Its* is the possessive form of the pronoun *it* and means "belonging to it." See also **22b.**

It is
▶ **It's a good idea.**   ▶ **The committee took its time.**

EXERCISE 28.2 Use apostrophes correctly with contractions in special instances and with *it's.*
Correct any errors in the use of apostrophes.

EXAMPLE:

     its
Trainspotting has ~~it's~~ fans in Great Britain, and airplane spotters
aren't
~~are'nt~~ unusual either.

1. Although theyre often regarded as geek's by people who do'nt share their passion, trainspotters are devoted to their hobby of watching trains and noting engine numbers.

2. Planespotting, a variation of trainspotting, resulted in legal difficulties in 2001 for a group of vacationing Briton's who were arrested and accused of spying on airfields in Greece.

3. The arrests led to a diplomatic rift between Great Britain and Greece, with the Britons claiming that theyd merely been enjoying the Greek Air Force celebrations and the Greeks claiming

that the spotters were illegally monitoring pilots conversations and observing high-security military installations.

4. Its not surprising that the Greek police were unfamiliar with planespotting, since the hobby attracts few people outside of it's British birthplace.

5. "Its an embarrassment," said one Greek official; the detained Britons may have been accustomed to seeing their passions ridiculed at home, but they probably were'nt expecting to meet such a reception abroad.

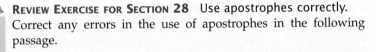

REVIEW EXERCISE FOR SECTION 28 Use apostrophes correctly. Correct any errors in the use of apostrophes in the following passage.

Vermonts legislature passed a law in 2000 that recognizes gay and lesbian civil unions in its state as the equivalent of marriage. Since it's passage, the law has attracted gay tourists to Vermont, which is currently the only one of the fifty states that grant's gay and lesbian couples the right to all of the benefits of marriage. In the first year of the new laws' existence, two thousand gay and lesbian couples got civil-union licenses (in the same period, about five thousand heterosexual couples got traditional marriage licenses). Eighty percent of the gay and lesbian couples werent Vermont residents; the great majority of them celebrated civil unions' and then went home to states that didn't recognize their new status under the law. Most took vows for symbolic reasons, aware that they probably would'nt gain any legal rights' from the civil union.

Aside from slightly increasing the number of tourist visits to Vermont, has the law changed anything? Theres been a political backlash in more conservative parts of the state: five legislators who voted for the law werent reelected, and opponents of the law still argue that its going to make Vermont "a gay state." More than thirty other state's legislatures hurriedly passed "defense-of-marriage" laws that explicitly say that same-sex unions are not valid in those states. However, many of the gay and lesbian couple's trips to Vermont seem to them, at least, to be rewarding. Most feel that its important to have official recognition, even if only in one small state, of the two partners commitment to each other.

29 Quotation Marks

Quotation marks indicate where a quotation begins and ends. The text between the quotation marks repeats the exact words that someone said, thought, or wrote. For omitting words, see **30e**.

29a Guidelines for using quotation marks

KEY POINTS

Quotation Marks: Basic Guidelines

1. Quote exactly the words used by the original speaker or writer.
2. Pair opening quotation marks with closing quotation marks to indicate where the quotation ends and your ideas begin.
3. Use correct punctuation to introduce and end a quotation, and place other marks of punctuation carefully in relation to the quotation marks.
4. Enclose the titles of short works such as short stories and poems in quotation marks.
5. Enclose short definitions and translations in quotation marks.

Details and more examples of each guideline follow.

29b Introducing and ending a quotation

1. After an introductory verb such as *said*, *stated*, or *wrote*, use a comma followed by quotation marks and a capital letter to introduce a direct quotation.

▶ It was Erma Bombeck who said, "Families aren't dying. They're merging into conglomerates."

—"Empty Fridge, Empty Nest"

For British English variations on double quotation marks and the punctuation used with quotation marks, see the Variation note in item 4.

2. Use a colon after a complete sentence introducing a quotation that is not integrated into your text, and begin the quotation with a capital letter.

▶ Woody Allen always tries to make us laugh even about serious issues like wealth and poverty: "Money is better than poverty, if only for financial reasons."

—*Without Feathers*

3. When a quotation is integrated into the structure of your own sentence, use no special introductory punctuation other than the quotation marks.

▶ Phyllis Grosskurth comments that "anxiety over money was driving him over the brink."

—*Byron: The Flawed Angel*

4. Put periods and commas inside quotation marks, even if these punctuation marks do not appear in the original quotation.

▶ When Henry Rosovsky characterizes Bloom's ideas as "mind-boggling," he is not offering praise.

—*The University: An Owner's Manual*

VARIATION In British English, and noticeably in older texts, usage varies and can be significantly different from American English usage. In some British English publications, you will find single quotation marks used for quotations (and double quotation marks for a quotation inside a quotation), and commas and periods placed outside the closing quotation mark.

BRITISH   His reaction was one of stupefied amazement: 'Our father never called you a "genius", and I'm certain he never even thought it'.

AMERICAN   His reaction was one of stupefied amazement: "Our father never called you a 'genius,' and I'm certain he never even thought it." ■

Note that in a documented paper, when you use a parenthetical citation after a short quotation at the end of a sentence, you put the period at the end of the citation, not within the quotation. (But see **29f** for long quotations.)

▶ **Geoffrey Wolff observes that when his father died, there was nothing to indicate "that he had ever known another human being" (11).**   *—The Duke of Deception*

5. Put question marks and exclamation points inside the quotation marks if they are part of the original source, with no additional period. When your sentence is a statement, do not use a comma or period in addition to a question mark or exclamation point.

▶ **She asked, "Where's my mama?"**

6. Put an added question mark, exclamation point, semicolon, or colon outside the closing quotation marks. If your sentence contains punctuation that is your own, not part of the original quotation, do not include it within the quotation marks.

▶ **The chapter focuses on this question: Who are "the new American dreamers"?**

29c Quotation marks in dialogue

Do not add closing quotation marks until the speaker changes or you interrupt the quotation. Begin each new speaker's words with a new paragraph.

interruption
┌ of quotation ┐
▶   **"I'm not going to work today," he announced. "Why should I? I worked all weekend. My boss is away on vacation. And I have a headache."**

┌─────── change of speaker ───────┐
    "Honey, your boss is on the phone," his wife called from the bedroom.

If a quotation from one speaker continues for more than one paragraph, place *closing* quotation marks at the end of only the final paragraph of the quotation. However, place *opening* quotation marks at the beginning of every paragraph, so readers realize that the quotation is continuing.

29d   Double and single quotation marks

Enclose quotations in double quotation marks. Enclose a quotation that occurs within another quotation in single quotation marks.

▶ Margaret announced, "I have read 'The Lottery' already."

VARIATION   British usage can be different: *Margaret announced, 'I have read "The Lottery" already'.* See the Variation note in **29b** for more on the differences between British and American usage in quotations. Always use the conventions your readers will expect. ■

29e   Quotation marks around titles of short works, definitions, and translations

In your writing, enclose in quotation marks the title of any short works you mention, such as a short story, a poem published with other poems, an article, a song, or a chapter.

▶ Ishmael Reed's essay "America: The Multinational Society" begins with an illuminating quotation.

▶ "Everything That Rises Must Converge"   [short story]

▶ "Kubla Khan"   [poem]

For long poems published independently, use italics or underlining.

▶ <u>The Wasteland</u>

▶ *Leaves of Grass*

Use quotation marks to enclose a translation or a definition.

▶ The abbreviation *p.m.* means "post meridiem."

29f   When not to use quotation marks

1. Do not put quotation marks around indirect quotations.

▶ One woman I interviewed said that her husband argued like a lawyer.

2. Do not put quotation marks around clichés, slang, or trite or ironic expressions.   Instead, revise to eliminate the cliché, slang, or trite expression. See also **39d** and **39g**.

                                                  involvement.
▶ All they want is ~~"a piece of the action."~~

3. Do not put quotation marks at the beginning and end of long indented quotations. When you use MLA style to quote more than three lines of poetry or four typed lines of prose, indent the whole passage one inch (or ten spaces) from the left margin. Do not enclose the quoted passage in quotation marks, but retain any internal quotation marks. See **50h** for an illustration.

4. Do not put quotation marks around the names of parts of long works or unpublished works.

▶ Peter Conrad's introduction to *Pride and Prejudice* discusses Austen as ironist.

5. On the title page of your own essay, do not put quotation marks around your essay title. Use quotation marks in your title only when it contains a quotation or the title of a short work.

▶ The Advantages of Bilingual Education

▶ Charles Baxter's "Gryphon" as an Educational Warning

EXERCISE 29.1   Use quotation marks correctly.
Correct any errors in the use of quotation marks and related punctuation.

EXAMPLE:

W. H. Auden did not like the line that reads, "We must love

one another or ~~die".~~
　　　　　　　　　　die."
　　　　　　　　　　　^

1. Auden's poem *September 1, 1939,* in which the poet prays to: "Show an affirming flame", was widely circulated on the Internet and reprinted in newspapers and magazines after the events of September 11, 2001.

2. Auden did not want the poem included in his collected works because he felt that it was, "infected with an incurable dishonesty.

3. Peter Steinfels wondered if a 2001 version of Auden's poem would "be found guilty of what has come to be labeled "moral equivalence"."

4. "There is a new demand," Steinfels wrote in the *"New York Times"* that ideas and language, especially about war and peace but also about religion and moral obligation, be precise and explicit."

5. The poem, which was written after the Nazi invasion of Poland in 1939, says that history 'has driven a culture mad.'

REVIEW EXERCISE FOR SECTION 29 Use quotation marks correctly. Correct any errors in the use of quotation marks and related punctuation.

Child psychologist Bruno Bettelheim wrote that fairy tales, with their archetypal evil characters, terrifying situations, and improbable happy endings, could tell children a great deal, "about the inner problems of human beings and of the right solutions to their predicaments in any society". In a newspaper article called Old Theory Could Explain Love of Harry Potter, Richard Bernstein argues that Bettelheim's analysis of fairy tales reveals the reasons for the staggering popularity of J. K. Rowling's books. Although Bernstein sees the book *Harry Potter and the Sorcerer's Stone* as "a fairly conventional supernatural adventure story", he admits that children find the books "as powerful as the witch of "Hansel and Gretel." Bernstein analyzes the narrative and concludes that, "Harry's story, [. . .] with its early images of alienation, rejection, loneliness and powerlessness leading to its classically fairy tale ending, contains the same basic message that Bettelheim described."

Bernstein is not alone in writing for adults about the Harry Potter "phenomenon." Academic conferences call for papers on Rowling's books; one asked graduate students and professors to ponder the ways that the books "embody, extend, exploit, or enfeeble the fantasy genre". On the Internet, fan fiction sites are filled with Harry Potter stories written for adults. Lori Summers, the author of a fan fiction story called Harry Potter and the Paradigm of Uncertainty, which features Harry and his friend Hermione as young adults, notes that "she intended the story for adult fans of the Harry Potter series." Although children helped the Rowling books to reach "number one" on the bestseller lists, it is clear—in spite of the reservations of adults like Bernstein—that many adults are equally captivated by Harry Potter.

30 Other Punctuation Marks

30a Dashes

Dashes (—) suggest a change of pace. They alert readers to something unexpected or to an interruption. Form a dash by typing two hyphens, putting no extra space before, between, or after them. Recent software will transform the two hyphens into one continuous dash.

▶ **Armed with one weapon—his wit—he faced the crowd.**

▶ **The accused gasped, "But I never—" and fainted.**

▶ **In America there are two classes of travel—first class and with children.**   —Robert Benchley, in Robert E. Drennan, *The Algonquin Wits*

Commas can be used to set off appositive phrases, but dashes are preferable when the phrase itself contains commas.

▶ **The contents of his closet—torn jeans, frayed jackets, and suits shiny on the seat and elbows—made him reassess his priorities.**

30b Parentheses

Use parentheses to mark an aside or provide additional information.

▶ **Chuck Yeager's feat (breaking the sound barrier) led to increased competition in the space industry.**

Also use parentheses to enclose citations in a documented paper and to enclose numbers or letters preceding items in a list.

▶ **(3) A journalist reports that in the course of many interviews, he met very few people who were cynical about the future of the country (Lamb 5).**

30c Brackets

1. Square brackets ([ ]) When you insert words or make changes to words within a quotation, enclose the inserted or changed material in square brackets. Be careful to insert only words that help the quotation fit into your sentence grammatically or that offer necessary explanation. Do not insert words that substantially change the meaning.

▶ **Maxine Hong Kingston agrees with reviewer Diane Johnson that the memoir form "can neither [be] dismiss[ed] as fiction nor quarrel[ed] with as fact."**

On occasion, you may need to use brackets to insert the Latin word *sic* (meaning "thus") into a quoted passage in which an error occurs. Using *sic* tells readers that the word or words that it follows were present in the original source and are not your own.

▶ **Richard Lederer tells of a man who did "exercises to strengthen his abominable [sic] muscles."**

Square brackets can also be used in MLA style around ellipsis dots that you add to signal an omission (**30e**).

2. Angle brackets (<>) Use angle brackets to enclose e-mail addresses and URLs (Web addresses), particularly in an MLA style works-cited list. See **34a** and **52c**.

30d Slashes

Use slashes (/) to separate two or three lines of poetry quoted within your own text. For quoting more than three lines of poetry, see **50h**.

▶ **Philip Larkin asks a question that many of us relate to: "Why should I let the toad *work* / Squat on my life?"**

Slashes are also used in expressions such as *and/or* and *he/she* to indicate options. However, be careful not to overuse these expressions.

30e Ellipsis dots

When you omit material from a quotation, indicate the omission—the ellipsis—by using spaced dots (. . .). The following passage by Ruth Sidel, on page 27 of *On Her Own: Growing Up in the Shadow of the American Dream,* is used in the examples that follow.

> These women have a commitment to career, to material well-being, to success, and to independence. To many of them, an affluent life-style is central to their dreams; they often describe their goals in terms of cars, homes, travel to Europe. In short, they want their piece of the American Dream.

1. Words omitted from the middle of a quotation In MLA and APA styles, use three ellipsis dots when you omit material from the middle of a quotation. MLA style also allows for square brackets around the dots so that readers will know that the dots are not part of the original text (**50h**).

MLA **Ruth Sidel reports that the women in her interviews "have a commitment to career . . . and to independence" (27). OR [. . .]**

APA **Ruth Sidel reports that the women in her interviews "have a commitment to career . . . and to independence" (1990, p. 27).**

2. Words omitted at the end of your sentence When you omit part of a quotation and the omission occurs at the end of your own sentence, insert ellipsis dots after the sentence period, followed by the closing quotation marks, making four dots in all.

▶ **Ruth Sidel presents interesting findings about jobs and money: "These women have a commitment to career, to material well-being. . . ."**

When a parenthetical reference follows the quoted passage, put the final sentence period after the parenthetical reference:

▶ **Ruth Sidel presents interesting findings about jobs and money: "These women have a commitment to career, to material well-being . . ." (27).**

3. Complete sentence omitted When you omit a complete sentence or more, insert three ellipsis dots.

▶ **Sidel tells us how "an affluent life-style is central to their dreams; . . . they want their piece of the American dream" (27).**

4. Line of poetry omitted When you omit one or more lines of poetry from a long, indented quotation, indicate the omission with a line of dots that is approximately as long as a complete line of poetry in the original—enclosed in square brackets if you are using MLA style.

▶ This poem is for the hunger of my mother
. . . .
who read the Blackwell's catalogue
like a menu of delights
and when we moved from Puerto Rico to the States
we packed 100 boxes of books and 40 of everything else.
—Aurora Levins Morales, *Class Poem*

5. When not to use ellipsis dots Do not use ellipsis dots when you quote only a word or a phrase because it will be obvious that material has been omitted:

▶ The women Sidel interviewed see an "affluent life-style" in their future.

Note: Also use three dots to indicate uncertainty, a pause, or an interruption.

▶ After watching the mystery for two hours, I braced myself for those annoying words, "To be continued . . .".

REVIEW EXERCISE FOR SECTION 30 Use other punctuation marks correctly.
Correct any errors in the use of dashes, parentheses, brackets, slashes, and ellipsis dots. (Citations should conform to MLA style.)

1. George Harrison—the most reclusive member of the Beatles, and the one who urged most strongly that the band stop playing live shows, died on November 29, 2001.

2. Beatles fans from all over the world mourned the death of the second member of the most famous rock band in history [John Lennon had been murdered more than twenty years before Harrison died of cancer].

3. Harrison (known to fans everywhere simply as "George," whose songwriting took a back seat to that of Lennon and

McCartney, still wrote some of the Beatles' biggest hits, including "Something," "While My Guitar Gently Weeps," and "Here Comes the Sun."

4. Obituaries noted Harrison's interest in Eastern music and religion (at the time of his death, he remained a follower of a form of Hinduism he called Krishna Consciousness

5. In many of the films in which Harrison either had a starring role or made a cameo appearance, *A Hard Day's Night, Help!*, a Beatles parody called *All You Need Is Cash* starring members of Monty Python (and produced by Harrison), *Monty Python's Life of Brian*, his sly sense of humor was apparent.

6. In *The Beatles Anthology*, Harrison noted, "As a band, we were tight . . . We could argue a lot among ourselves, but we were very, very close". . . . [83]

7. For most music lovers, Harrison will be forever associated with a band that broke up in 1970, but his 1987 album, *Cloud Nine*, "[won] over a new generation of fans (. . .) born after the Beatles' demise." (Rees and Crampton 256)

8. Expressing sorrow at Harrison's death, Paul McCartney said, "He (was) really just my baby brother" (Kozinn A1).

31 Italics and Underlining

Use italic type or underlining to highlight a word, phrase, or title in your own writing. Most word processing programs offer italic type. Usually, though, in manuscript form, underlining is more distinctive and therefore often preferred, particularly in MLA bibliographical lists and in material to be typeset. Ask your instructor which to use. For underlining when writing online, see **34b**.

▶ Woolf's novel *Orlando* was written for Vita Sackville-West. OR
Woolf's novel <u>Orlando</u> was written for Vita Sackville-West.

▶ In <u>The Psychology of Time</u>, we learn about perceptions of
filled and empty time. OR In *The Psychology of Time*, we learn
about perceptions of filled and empty time.

31a Italics or underlining for titles of long, whole works

In the body of an essay, italicize or underline the titles of books, magazines, newspapers, plays, films, TV series, long poems, musical
compositions, Web sites, online databases, and works of art.

▶ <u>The Sun Also Rises</u>	▶ *Survivor*	▶ <u>Newsweek</u>
▶ *The English Patient*	▶ <u>Mona Lisa</u>	▶ *InfoTrac*

For exceptions, see **31f.**

EXERCISE 31.1 Use italics correctly for titles of long, whole works.
In each of the following sentences, correct any errors in the italicization of titles. Indicate where to add or eliminate italics or
underlining as needed. Some sentences may be correct.

EXAMPLE:

> New Yorker
> A notice in the ~~New Yorker~~ attracted some art lovers to the
> New York University
> symposium at ~~New York University.~~

1. In his book Vermeer's Camera, Philip Steadman argues that
Vermeer used a mechanical device to project images onto his
canvas that he could trace before painting them.

2. The device, a box containing an optical lens, is known as a camera obscura, and Steadman and others believe that Vermeer
could not have created paintings like "Kitchen Maid" with such
photographic precision without mechanical help.

3. In 2001, the painter David Hockney, believing that
Caravaggio, Ingres, van Eyck, and other Old Masters used

optical devices to enhance the realism of their paintings, assembled a panel of art historians and scientists in New York to debate the issue.

4. In an article called *Paintings Too Perfect? The Great Optics Debate,* the *New York Times* reported on the spirited disagreements that followed.

5. Even panelists discussing van Eyck's Arnolfini Wedding, a painting that depicts an optical device, were unable to concur on whether the artist had used technological assistance to create the painting; still, after the symposium, Hockney reported, "I learned some things."

31b Italics or underlining for main entries in a list of works cited

If you use the MLA style of documentation, underline main entries (for example, title of book or long work; name of journal, newspaper, or magazine; work of art; name of database; or title of Web site) in your list of works cited. In APA, *Chicago,* and CGOS styles, use italics for the main entries. See sections **52, 53, 55,** and **56** for details and examples.

31c Italics or underlining for names of ships, trains, airplanes, and spacecraft

▶ <u>Mayflower</u>   ▶ *Silver Meteor*   ▶ *Mir*

Do not underline or italicize the abbreviations sometimes preceding them: USS *Constitution.*

31d Italics or underlining for letters, numerals, and words referring to the words themselves, not to what they represent

▶ The sign had a large <u>P</u> in black marker and a <u>3</u> in red.

▶ *Zarf* is a useful word for some board games.

31e Italics or underlining for words from other languages

Expressions not commonly used in English should be italicized or underlined. However, do not overuse such expressions because they tend to sound pretentious.

▶ **The headmaster frequently talked to baffled parents about his Weltanschauung.**

▶ **The picture shows the model in a state of *deshabille*.**

Do not italicize common expressions such as these: et al., croissant, nom de plume, and film noir.

31f When not to use italics or underlining

Do not italicize or underline the following:

- the names of sacred works such as the Bible, books of the Bible (Genesis, Psalms), and the Koran (Qur'an)
- the titles of documents and laws, such as the Declaration of Independence, the Constitution, and the Americans with Disabilities Act
- the titles of short works, such as poems, short stories, essays, and articles (use quotation marks for these)
- the title of your own essay on your title page (**29f**)
- statements that you want to emphasize

▶ **The climb was ~~so scary~~.**
                    hair-raising.

Instead, select a word that conveys the emphasis you want to express.

REVIEW EXERCISE FOR SECTION 31 Use italics and underlining correctly.
Underline any words that need italicization or underlining and remove any unnecessary underlining or quotation marks.

In the nineteenth century, phrenology—the study of bumps on the skull and their relation to the personality—was a popular pseudoscientific practice, and one of the best-known phrenologists was Lorenzo Fowler. Along with his brother Orson, Lorenzo

Fowler headed the <u>Phrenological Institute</u> in New York City, where the two trained other phrenologists, and Lorenzo gave readings to celebrities such as Julia Ward Howe, author of <u>The Battle Hymn of the Republic</u>. The Fowler brothers saw themselves as leaders of a progressive movement; they ran the publishing company that put out the first edition of Walt Whitman's "Leaves of Grass." They also published the Phrenological Journal, hoping

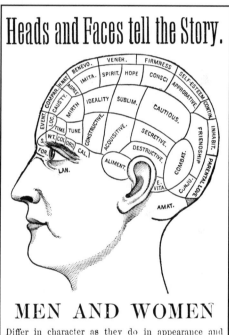

Nineteenth-century phrenology:
A map of head

that phrenological analysis could lead people to correct defects of character that had been revealed by their cranial protrusions.

In 1872, Samuel Clemens, who had written Huckleberry Finn and many other works under the <u>nom de plume</u> Mark Twain, visited Fowler under an assumed name and obtained a reading and a phrenological chart. Clemens, who was an early champion both of scientific innovations like fingerprinting (which is featured in his novel "Pudd'nhead Wilson") and of inventions that proved to be dismal failures, wanted to put phrenology to the test. The results amused him: in "The Autobiography of Mark Twain," Clemens notes that Fowler found a spot on his skull that "represented the total absence of the sense of humor." Months later, Clemens returned for a second reading, identifying himself both as Clemens <u>and</u> as Mark Twain, and was given a reading and a chart that "contained several sharply defined details of my character, but [. . .] bore no recognizable resemblance to the earlier chart."

Clemens remained convinced that phrenology was quackery, and others soon agreed. By 1900, phrenology had fallen out of favor. Even in the twenty-first century, however, the use of terms such as highbrow and lowbrow, which came from phrenology, demonstrates the influence that this idea once had.

32 Capital Letters, Abbreviations, and Numbers

32a Capital letters

Always consult a dictionary if you are not sure whether to capitalize a word. A dictionary will indicate if a noun is a proper noun demanding a capital letter:

▶ King James Bible

▶ King Charles spaniel

Use the following eight guidelines for capitalization.

1. Always capitalize _I_, even in e-mail communications.

▶ They announced that I had won the prize.

2. Capitalize the first word of a sentence, after a period, question mark, or exclamation point.

▶ Why do the wealthy send their children to residential colleges? They want the benefits of a liberal-arts education.

3. Capitalize the first word of a sentence quotation—if it is capitalized in the original passage.

▶ Quindlen says, "This is a story about a name," and thus tells us the topic of her article.

However, when you quote part of a sentence, do not begin the quotation with a capital letter.

▶ When Quindlen says that she is writing "a story about a name," she is telling us the topic of her article.

4. Capitalize proper nouns and proper adjectives. Begin the names of specific people, places, and things with a capital letter.

TYPES OF PROPER NOUNS AND ADJECTIVES	EXAMPLES
Names of people	Albert Einstein, Madonna, T. S. Eliot, Bill Gates
Names of nations, continents, planets, stars, and galaxies	Hungary, Asia, Mercury, the North Star, the Milky Way
Names of mountains, rivers, and oceans	Mount Everest, the Thames, the Pacific Ocean
Names of public places and regions	Golden Gate Park, the Great Plains, the Midwest
Names of streets, buildings, and monuments	Rodeo Drive, the Empire State Building, the Roosevelt Memorial
Names of cities, states, and provinces	Toledo, Kansas, Nova Scotia

TYPES OF PROPER NOUNS AND ADJECTIVES	EXAMPLES
Days of the week and months	Wednesday, March
Holidays	Labor Day, the Fourth of July
Organizations and companies	the Red Cross, Microsoft Corporation
Institutions (including colleges, departments, schools, government offices, and courts of law)	University of Texas, Department of English, School of Business, Defense Department, Florida Supreme Court
Historical events, named periods, and documents	the Civil War, the Renaissance, the Roaring Twenties, the Declaration of Independence
Religions, deities, revered persons, and sacred texts	Buddhism, Islam, Muslim, Baptist, Jehovah, Mohammed, the Torah, the Koran (Qur'an)
Races, tribes, nations, nationalities, and languages	the Navajo, Greece, Spain, Spanish
Registered trademarks	Kleenex, Apple, Bic, Nike, Xerox
Names of ships, planes, and spacecraft	the USS *Kearsage,* the *Spirit of St. Louis,* the *Challenger*

Note: Do not capitalize nouns naming general classes or types of people, places, things, or ideas: *government, jury, mall, prairie, utopia, traffic court, the twentieth century, goodness, reason.* For the use of capital letters in online writing, see **34c**.

5. Capitalize a title before a person's name.

▶ The reporter interviewed Senator Thompson.

▶ The residents cheered Grandma Jones.

However, do not use a capital letter when a title is not attached to a person's name.

▶ Each state elects two senators.

▶ My grandmother is ninety years old.

When a title substitutes for the name of a known person, a capital letter is often used.

▶ Have you spoken with the Senator [senator] yet?

6. Capitalize major words in a title. In titles of published books, journals, magazines, essays, articles, films, poems, and songs, use a capital letter at the beginning of all words except articles *(the, a, an)*, coordinating conjunctions *(and, but, or, nor, so, for, yet)*, *to* in an infinitive *(to stay)*, and prepositions unless they begin or end a title or subtitle.

"A Matter of Identity"

"Wrestling with the Angel: A Memoir"

7. Capitalize the first word of a subtitle, even if it is an article, a coordinating conjunction, *to*, or a preposition.

▶ *Reflections from the Keyboard: The World of the Concert Pianist*

8. Be consistent with using a capital or lowercase letter after a colon. Usage varies. Usually a capital letter is used if the clause states a rule or principle (**27e**). Make your usage consistent.

EXERCISE 32.1 Use capital letters correctly.
Capitalize any letters that are incorrectly lowercase and change any incorrect capital letters to lowercase letters.

EXAMPLE:

During the ~~civil war~~, a ~~Doctor~~ from Kentucky tried to spread
      Civil War   doctor
a ~~Virus~~ to cities in the ~~north~~.
 virus   North

1. Biological warfare may strike modern Americans as Barbaric, but during the French and Indian war, smallpox-infected blankets given to Native Americans helped to decimate their numbers.

2. in the 1860s, Dr. Luke blackburn tried the same tactic, giving or selling clothing from patients with Yellow fever to Soldiers in the Union Army.

3. According to some historians, the Doctor hoped to spread Yellow Fever in washington and new York; president Jefferson Davis of the confederate States of America probably knew about and approved of the plan.

4. Fortunately for citizens of the north, yellow fever cannot be passed from one person to another by skin contact. although Dr. Blackburn's plot was discovered on the day of Lincoln's Assassination, he was never prosecuted in a Court of Law.

5. Blackburn eventually became the Governor of Kentucky, where he worked for penal and educational reform. A statue of the good samaritan marks his grave in frankfort cemetery.

32b Abbreviations and acronyms

For abbreviations commonly used in online writing, see **34e**. The list below shows you when and how to use abbreviations.

1. Abbreviate titles used with people's names. Use an abbreviation, followed by a period, for titles before or after names. The following abbreviated titles precede names: *Mr., Mrs., Ms., Prof., Dr., Gen.,* and *Sen.* The following abbreviated titles follow names: *Sr., Jr., PhD, MD, BA,* and *DDS.* Do not use a title both before and after a name: *Dr. Benjamin Spock* or *Benjamin Spock, MD.* Do not abbreviate a title if it is not attached to a specific name.

> ► Pat Murphy Sr. went to the ~~dr.~~ twice last week.

doctor

2. Abbreviate the names of familiar institutions, countries, tests, diplomas, individuals, and objects. Use abbreviations of the names of well-known institutions (*UCLA, YWCA, FBI, IBM*), countries (*USA* or *U.S.A.*), tests and diplomas (*SAT, GED*), individuals (*FDR*), and objects (*DVD*). If you use a specialized abbreviation, first use the term in full followed by the abbreviation in parentheses; then use the abbreviation.

> ► **The Graduate Record Examination (GRE) is required by many graduate schools. GRE preparation is therefore big business.**

3. Abbreviate terms used with numbers. Use the abbreviations such as *BC, AD, a.m., p.m., $, mph, wpm, mg, kg,* and other units of measure only when they occur with specific numbers.

> ► **35 BC**
>
> [meaning "before Christ," now often replaced with *BCE,* "before the common era" to avoid reference to one religion: **35 BCE**]

▶ **AD 1776**

[*anno domini,* "in the year of the Lord," now often replaced with *CE,* "common era," used after the date: **1776 CE**]

▶ **2:00 a.m./p.m.**

[*ante* or *post meridiem,* Latin for "before" or "after midday"]

Alternatives are A.M./P.M. or AM/PM. Be consistent. But do not use these abbreviations and other units of measure when no number is attached to them.

money
▶ **His family gave him a wallet full of $ to spend on vacation.**
              ^

afternoon.
▶ **They arrived late in the ~~p.m.~~**
                           ^

4. Abbreviate common Latin terms.   In notes, parentheses, and source citations, use abbreviations for common Latin terms. In the body of your text, use the English meaning.

ABBREVIATION	LATIN	ENGLISH MEANING
etc.	et cetera	and so on
i.e.	id est	that is
e.g.	exempli gratia	for example
cf.	confer	compare
N.B.	nota bene	note well
et al.	et alii	and others

5. With the plural form of an abbreviation, use -s (not -'s).   Do not use an apostrophe to make an abbreviation plural (see **28e**).

▶ **She has over a thousand CDs.**

▶ **Both his VCRs are broken.**

6. Do not abbreviate familiar words to save time and space.   In formal writing, write in full expressions such as the following:

&	and
bros.	brothers [Use "Bros." only if it is part of the official name of the business.]
chap.	chapter
Mon.	Monday
nite	night

NJ	New Jersey [Abbreviate the name of the state only in an address, a note, or a reference.]
no.	number [Use the abbreviation only with a specific number: "No. 17 on the list was deleted."]
Oct.	October [Write names of days and months in full, except in some works-cited lists.]
soc.	sociology [Write names of academic subjects in full.]
thru	through
w/	with

EXERCISE 32.2 Use abbreviations and acronyms correctly. Correct any errors in the use of abbreviations or acronyms.

EXAMPLE:

According to ~~Mister~~ Mr. Sid Green, who teaches ~~H.S.~~ high school ~~hist.~~ history in ~~CA~~ California,

some U.S. colleges and universities no longer require students to

take the SAT.

1. An early adopter—someone who buys new devices and gadgets as soon as they are available—probably owned CD's when most people still bought records, rents DVD's while others still watch videos on their VCR's, and picks out CD-ROM's as holiday gifts.

2. The acupuncturist's receptionist referred to him as Doctor Loren Selwyn, but I later discovered that he was Loren Selwyn, doctor of philosophy, not Loren Selwyn, medical doctor.

3. Ms Krebs could type so many w.p.m. that the computer printer was spewing out pp. long after she had stopped working for the eve.

4. Sen Hammond helpfully told us that the New Year's Eve party would be held on Dec. 31, but he neglected to say what time we should arrive.

5. Akhenaton, orig. known as Amenhotep, ruled ancient Egypt until his death in about 1358 before the Common Era.

32c Numbers

Conventions for using numerals (actual figures) or words vary across the disciplines.

1. Numbers in the humanities and in business letters

Use words for numbers expressible in one or two words and for fractions (*nineteen, fifty-six, two hundred, one-half*).

Use numerals for longer numbers (*326; 5,625; 7,642,000*).

Use a combination of words and numerals for whole millions, billions, and so on (*45 million, 1 billion*).

2. Numbers in scientific and technical writing

Use numerals for all numbers above nine.

Use numerals for numbers below ten only when they show precise measurement, as when they are grouped and compared with other larger numbers (*5 of the 39 participants*), or when they precede a unit of measurement (*6 cm*), indicate a mathematical function (*8%; 0.4*), or represent a specific time, date, age, score, or number in a series.

Use words for fractions: *two-thirds*.

3. Numbers beginning a sentence

In both the humanities and the sciences, spell out numbers that begin a sentence.

▸ **One hundred twenty-five members voted for the new bylaws.**

▸ **Six thousand fans have already bought tickets.**

 ESL Note Singular and Plural Forms of *Hundred*, *Thousand*, and *Million*

Even after plural numbers, use the singular form of *hundred, thousand,* and *million.* Add *-s* only when there is no preceding number.

▸ **Five *hundred* books were damaged in the flood.**
[not five hundreds]

▸ ***Hundreds* of books were damaged in the flood.** ▪

4. Special uses of figures (numerals) In nonscientific writing, use numerals for the following:

Time and dates	6 p.m. on 31 May 2003
Decimals	20.89
Statistics	median score 35
Addresses	16 East 93rd Street
Chapter, page, scene, and line numbers	chapter 5; page 97; scene 2, line 44
Quantities appearing with abbreviations or symbols	6°C (for temperature Celsius), $21, 6'7"
Scores	The Knicks won 89–85.

For percentages and money, numerals and the symbol *(75%, $24.67)* are usually acceptable, or you can spell out the expression if it is fewer than four words (*seventy-five percent, twenty-four dollars*).

5. Plural forms of figures Be consistent in your usage. MLA style prefers no apostrophe to form the plural of a numeral.

▶ **in the 1980s**   ▶ **They scored in the 700s in the SATs.**

33 Spelling and Hyphenation

In a famous book for children by A. A. Milne, Winnie-the-Pooh, a bear, complains about having "wobbly" spelling: "It's good spelling but it Wobbles, and the letters get in the wrong places." Many of us can sympathize. This section provides you with some of the basic hyphenation and spelling rules, which are worth learning, along with some lists of troublesome words for you to refer to, learn, and add to.

33a Checking spelling

With a spelling checker, Winnie-the-Pooh would not have produced such wobbly spelling, but a spelling checker is still of limited use. Even if you check your spelling with computer software, you still need to proofread. A program will not alert you to a word used in place of a similar word (a homonym, such as *cite* used in place of *sight* or *site*). Nor will it alert you to a typographical slip if the word you mistakenly type is actually a word, such as if you write *form* in place of *from*. It also will not alert you to variant spellings across dialects of English. So a spelling checker is only a beginning (**4h, 4i**).

One of the best tools at your disposal is a dictionary, for here you can check spelling, find the various word forms associated with a word (*benefit/benefited*, for example), or discover when a silent *-e* is retained or dropped before a suffix (as in *likable* or *likeness*). See **39b** for an example of the amount of information available at your fingertips in a dictionary. If you feel insecure about your spelling, be sure to keep your own list of "My Spelling Words" and add to it whenever you make an error, are surprised by the spelling of a word, or look up a word for confirmation. See **33g** and **33h** for spelling.

VARIATION Differences exist in spelling and meaning among the world's Englishes: British English, American English, African American English, Australian English, Singaporean English, Hong Kong English, Indian English, Caribbean English, and so on. For example, a *cell phone* in the United States is a *mobile phone* in England and a *handphone* in Singapore. The Worlds of Writing box provides examples of differences in spelling and meaning between British English (the original dialect of the author of this book) and American English. ■

WORLDS OF WRITING
British and American English:
Differences in Spelling

BRITISH	AMERICAN	BRITISH	AMERICAN
colour	color	theatre	theater
humour	humor	centre	center
learnt	learned	criticise	criticize
travelled	traveled	judgement	judgment
cheque	check	defence	defense
neighbour	neighbor	programme	program
towards	toward	jeweller	jeweler

Differences in Meaning

Note the potential for confusion.

BRITISH	AMERICAN
bonnet (of car)	hood
windscreen	windshield
boot	trunk

BRITISH	AMERICAN
car park	parking lot
dual carriageway	divided highway
roundabout	traffic circle, rotary
lift	elevator
nappy	diaper
dummy	pacifier
pudding	dessert
eiderdown	comforter
braces	suspenders
vest	undershirt
waistcoat	vest
trousers	pants
pants	underwear
chips	french fries
crisps	potato chips
over the road	across the street
mind (verb)	object (I don't mind. Do you mind?)
mind (verb)	watch out for (as in "Mind the gap!")

EXERCISE 33.1 Check the spelling of words.
In the following pairs of words, check (✓) which you think is correctly spelled. If you think both spellings are acceptable in different contexts, check both. Then turn to a dictionary to look up the words. If you make any errors, start your own spelling list with those words.

EXAMPLE:

a. ___✓___ responsible

b. _____ responsable

1. a. _____ principle   4. a. _____ suprise
   b. _____ principal   b. _____ surprise

2. a. _____ independance   5. a. _____ Febuary
   b. _____ independence   b. _____ February

3. a. _____ address   6. a. _____ truly
   b. _____ adress   b. _____ truely

7. a. _____ affect   9. a. _____ succeed

   b. _____ effect   b. _____ suceed

8. a. _____ harrass   10. a. _____ loose

   b. _____ harass   b. _____ lose

33b Plurals of nouns

1. Regular plural forms   The regular plural of nouns is formed by adding *-s* or *-es* to the singular word.

    essay, essays   match, matches

To form the plural of a compound noun, attach the *-s* to the main noun in the phrase.

    mothers-in-law   passersby

Proofread carefully for plural forms that form the plural with *-s* but make other changes, too, such as the following:

  -f OR *-fe* → *-ves*

  thief, thieves   (*Exceptions:* beliefs, roofs, chiefs)

  wife, wives

  -o → *-oes*   *-o* → *-os*

  potato, potatoes   hero (sandwich), heros

  tomato, tomatoes   photo, photos

  hero (man), heroes   piano, pianos

  CONSONANT + *-y* → *-ies*   VOWEL + *-y* → *-ys*

  family, families   toy, toys

  party, parties   monkey, monkeys

2. Irregular plural forms (no *-s* ending)

    man, men   foot, feet

    woman, women   tooth, teeth

    child, children   mouse, mice

3. Plural forms borrowed from other languages   Words borrowed from other languages, particularly Greek and Latin words, frequently borrow the plural form of the language, too.

    basis, bases   nucleus, nuclei

    thesis, theses   vertebra, vertebrae

hypothesis, hypotheses   alumnus (m.), alumni
criterion, criteria   alumna (f.), alumnae

4. Plural forms with no change Some words have the same form in singular and plural: moose, deer, sheep, species.

33c Doubling consonants

Doubled consonants form a link between spelling and pronunciation because the doubling of a consonant signals a short vowel sound.

1. Double the consonant when the verb stem contains one vowel plus one consonant in one syllable.

slip, slipping, slipped   hop, hopping, hopped

The doubled consonant preserves the short vowel sound. Compare the pronunciation of *hop, hopping, hopped* with *hope, hoping, hoped.* Say the words aloud and compare the vowel sounds in *write, writing,* and *written.*

2. Double the consonant when the verb stem contains two or more syllables with one vowel plus one consonant in the final stressed syllable.

refer, referring, referred   control, controlling, controlled

Compare *travel, traveling, traveled* and *cancel, canceling, canceled,* which have the stress on the first syllable. (Note that British English prefers the spellings *travelling, travelled; cancelling, cancelled.*)

3. Double the consonant when the suffix -*er* or -*est* is added to one-syllable adjectives ending in one vowel plus one consonant.

big, bigger, biggest   hot, hotter, hottest

4. Double the *l* when adding -*ly* to an adjective that ends in one -*l*.

careful, carefully   successful, successfully

33d Spelling with -*y* or -*i*

VERB ENDS IN CONSONANT + -*y*	-*ies*	-*ying*	-*ied*
cry	cries	crying	cried
study	studies	studying	studied

VERB ENDS IN

VOWEL + -*y*	-*ys*	-*ying*	-*yed*
play	plays	playing	played

Exceptions: pay/paid, say/said, lay/laid

VERB ENDS IN

VOWEL + -*e*	-*ies*	-*ying*	-*ied*
die	dies	dying	died

TWO-SYLLABLE ADJECTIVE

ENDS IN -*y*	-*i* WITH A SUFFIX
happy	happier, happily, happiness

TWO-SYLLABLE ADJECTIVE

ENDS IN -*ly*	-*lier*	-*liest*
friendly	friendlier	friendliest

33e Internal *ie* or *ei*

This traditional rhyme helps with the decision about whether to use *ie* or *ei*:

I before *e*
Except after *c*
Or when sounded like *ay*
As in *neighbor* and *weigh*.

The following examples illustrate those guidelines:

i BEFORE *e*	*e* BEFORE *i* AFTER *c*	*e* BEFORE *i* WHEN SOUNDED LIKE *ay*
believe	receive	vein
relief	ceiling	reign
niece	deceive	sleigh

Exceptions:

i BEFORE *e* EVEN AFTER *c*	*e* BEFORE *i*, NOT AFTER *c*	
conscience	height	seize
science	either/neither	foreign
species	leisure	weird

33f Adding a suffix

1. Keep a silent -*e* before an -*ly* suffix.

immediate, immediately   sure, surely

Exceptions: true, truly; whole, wholly; due, duly

2. Keep a silent -*e* before a suffix beginning with a consonant.

state, statement   force, forceful   rude, rudeness

Exceptions: acknowledge, acknowledgment; judge, judgment; argue, argument

3. Drop a silent -*e* before a suffix beginning with a vowel.

hope, hoping   observe, observant

write, writing   remove, removable

Exceptions: enforce, enforceable; change, changeable. Retaining the -*e* preserves the soft sound of the preceding consonant.

4. With adjectives ending in -*le*, drop the -*le* when adding -*ly*.

sensible, sensibly

5. With adjectives ending in -*ic*, add -*ally* to form the adverb.

basic, basically   characteristic, characteristically

Exception: public, publicly

6. Pay attention to the suffixes -*able*, -*ible*, -*ant*, -*ent*, -*ify*, and -*efy*. More words end in -*able* than in -*ible*. Learn the most common -*ible* words:

eligible   incredible   irresistible   legible

permissible   responsible   terrible   visible

Unfortunately there are no rules of thumb to help you decide whether to use the suffix -*ant* or -*ent*. Learn common words with these suffixes and have your dictionary handy for others.

-ANT	-ENT
defiant	confident
observant	convenient
relevant	existent
reluctant	imminent
resistant	independent

The suffix *-ify* is more common than *-efy.* Learn the four *-efy* words:

liquefy   putrefy   rarefy   stupefy

EXERCISE 33.2 Correct misspelled words.
In each of the following sentences, correct any misspelled words. Some sentences may not contain any errors.

EXAMPLE:

In the wake of high school ~~violance~~ *violence*, drug use, and other

problems in the last ten years, many schools have adopted a

"zero ~~tolerence~~ *tolerance*" policy.

1. After school shootings in Jonesboro, Paducah, and elswhere, some school administraters decided not to take any chances with students carring weapons.

2. A "zero tolerance" policy that called for students to face suspention if they were caught with guns, knifes, or any potencial weapon took effect in many schools.

3. In one school, a seven-year-old boy who had a two-inch-long toy gun on his key chain was suspended when the chain fell out of his pocket and was noticed by other childs.

4. His mother protestted that suspending students for carrying toies was ridiculous and that schools had an obligation to use common sense.

5. In other areas, many schools have also been declareing "zero tolerance" policys toward posession of drugs and other infractions of the rules.

6. Unbelieveably, a first grader was suspended in Colorado for shareing his candy with freinds because teachers did not

recognize the brand (which was sold in the town's major supermarket).

7. A declareation of "zero tolerance" means that schools decide that they will automaticly punish any student who even appears to have broken the rules.

8. The policy allows school personnel no leeway to decide for themselves whether the student's behavior warrants punishment.

9. "Zero tolerance" rules were in place in many school districts even before the horrefying shootings at Columbine High School in Littleton, Colorado, and since then these policys have become even more popular.

10. Although a "zero tolerance" policy probably would have prevented the Littleton killers from showing videeos in class featuring violent attacks, would it realy have alerted anyone in the boys' familys, nieghborhood, or school to the real danger?

33g Words frequently misspelled

This list of words that students in writing classes frequently misspell cannot be complete because so many spelling errors can be common to one but not to another writer. Some may always hesitate before writing the word *address* (one *-d* or two?), while others may have no problem with that word but worry about the spelling of *responsible* (with an *-i* or with an *-a*?). Keep a list of your own troublesome words and add them to the list that follows. See also the Worlds of Writing box on British and American spelling in **33a**.

accidentally	appearance	career
accommodation	beginning	careful
admission	beneficial	cemetery
adolescent	benefited	choice
aggressive	business	cigarette

conscience	harass	relevant
conscious	height	responsible
convenient	hypocrisy	rhyme
decision	independence	rhythm
definitely	intention	secretary
develop	necessary	separate
disappear	neighbor	sincerely
discipline	occur	speech
drawer	omitted	studying
embarrass	parliament	success
environment	personnel	successful
exercise	preferred	surprise
existence	professor	thorough
foreign	pronunciation	truly
forty	psychology	until
government	pursue	vegetable
grammar	receive	Wednesday

EXERCISE 33.3 Correct words frequently misspelled.
Correct any misspellings. Some sentences may be correct.

EXAMPLE:

A prominent psychiatrist has been ~~studing~~ *studying* the problems of
celebrity and its effect on people who suddenly find
themselves famous.

1. Dr. Robert B. Millman, a proffesor at Cornell Medical School,
   was the first person to identify a physchological disorder that
   he calls *acquired situational narcissism.*

2. Classical narcissism, which begins to develope at around age
   four, causes people to have grandiose ideas about themselves
   and prevents them from empathizing with others, but classical
   narcissists may not recieve the attention they expect.

3. People who suddenly become stars in a sport or in an entertainment field, however, can expect to attract fawning attention
   with every public appearence.

4. According to Dr. Millman, all of the people who surround a celebrity and pay attention to his or her carreer and extra-curricular activities bear some responsability for creating the celebrity's acquired situational narcissism.

5. Most narcissists do not seek help for their narcissism; rather, they become disturbed by the sympthoms, such as depression, and persue treatment for those.

33h Words commonly confused

A homonym is a word that is pronounced the same as another word but has a different meaning. The following list brings together some homonyms and other commonly confused words so you can review them easily. Add to this list as you come across more examples in your own reading and writing. *Note:* Entries printed in blue are explained further in 57, the Glossary of Usage.

accept   to receive (v.)
except   not including (prep.)
expect   to anticipate (v.)

access   a means of entering (n.)
excess   an amount beyond what is sufficient (n.)

acclamation   a shout of approval (n.)
acclimation   the process of adapting to a situation (n.)

adapt   to adjust (to something) (v.)
adopt   to take up or to take into a family (v.)

adverse   hostile (adj.)
averse   opposed to (adj.)

advice   an opinion (n.)
advise   to offer advice (v.)

affect   to influence (v.)
effect   result (n.) *or* to bring about (v.)

aid   to help (v.) *or* a person *or* device that helps (n.)
aide   an assistant (n.)

air   the atmosphere (n.)
err   to make a mistake (v.)
heir   one who inherits (n.)

aisle   space between rows of seats (n.)
isle   island (n.)

all ready   totally prepared (adj.)
already   by this time (adv.)

all together   simultaneously (adv.) *or* all in one place (adj.)
altogether   totally (adv.)

allowed   past tense form of "to allow" (v.)
aloud   by voice, orally (adv.)

allude   to refer to (v.)
elude   to avoid (v.)

allusion   reference (n.)
illusion   false idea (n.)

altar   a religious or ceremonial table (n.)
alter   to change (v.)

amend   to improve a text (v.)
emend   to improve a text by
   editing (v.)

ante   poker stake or a price to be
   paid (n.) *or* to make payment (v.)
anti-   prefix meaning against or
   opposite (pref.)

anyone   anybody (pron.)
any one   one from a group (n.)

amoral   neither moral nor immoral
   (adj.)
immoral   morally wrong (adj.)

arc   curve (n.) *or* to travel along a
   curved path (v.)
ark   large boat (n.) *or* refuge or
   shelter (n.) *or* a chest (n.)

are   plural form of "to be" (v.)
our   possessive form of "we"
   (pron.)
hour   unit of time (n.)

area   a region or surface (n.)
aria   a melody or vocal piece (n.)

ascent   the act of going up (n.)
assent   to agree (v.) *or* agreement
   (n.)

assay   to analyze (v.) *or* an analysis
   (n.)
essay   a short composition (n.) *or* to
   try (v.)

assistance   help (n.)
assistants   plural of "assistant" (n.)

assure   to promise (v.)
ensure   to make certain (v.)
insure   to make financially secure
   (v.)

awhile   for some time (adv.)
a while   a period of time (n.); needs
   to be preceded by "for"

axes   plural of "ax," a cutting tool
   (n.) *or* plural of "axis" (n.) *see next
   word*
axis   a straight line used for
   reference (n.)

bare   naked (adj.)
bear   to carry (v.) *or* a type of large,
   furry animal (n.)

basal   basic (adj.)
basil   an herb used for seasoning
   (n.)

beach   the shore (n.) *or* to haul
   ashore (v.)
beech   a type of tree

be   to exist *or* occur (v.)
bee   stinging insect (n.) *or* a
   competitive social gathering (n.)
   or the letter *b*

belief   an idea or thought (n.)
believe   to think or suppose (v.)

berry   a small fruit (n.)
bury   to cover with dirt (v.)

berth   a place for sleeping or for a
   ship to dock (n.)
birth   the act of being born (n.)

bite   to cut, grip, or tear with the
   teeth (v.)
byte   a sequence of computer
   information (n.)

board   a plank of wood (n.)
bored   not interested (adj.)

bough   a branch (n.)
bow   to bend respectfully (v.) *or* the
   front of a boat (n.) *or* a weapon
   (n.) *or* a type of knot (n.)

brake   a device that reduces speed
   (n.) *or* to reduce speed (v.)
break   to divide into pieces (v.)

bread   food (n.)
bred   part tense form of "to breed"
   (v.)

buy   to purchase (v.)
by   near (prep.)

canvas   heavy, coarse fabric (n.)
canvass   to examine thoroughly
   (v.) *or* to solicit votes (v.) *or* a poll
   (n.)

capitol a building in which a legislature meets (n.)

capital a seat of government *or* available wealth (n.) *or* foremost (adj.)

cell small compartment (n.)
sell to offer for sale (v.)

censor to suppress what is considered objectionable (v.)
censure to criticize (v.)

cent coin indicating one one-hundredth (n.)
scent odor (n.)
sent part tense form of "to send" (v.)

cereal food (n.)
serial pertaining to a series (adj.)

cite to quote (v.)
site a location (n.)
sight view or vision (n.)

coarse rough (adj.)
course a route or path (n.) *or* to run or to flow (v.)

complement to complete or add something (v.)
compliment to praise (v.)

conscience awareness of right and wrong (n.)
conscious awake or aware (adj.)

council group formed to make decisions (n.)
counsel advice (n.) *or* to give advice (v.)

decent respectable (adj.)
descent movement downward (n.)
dissent to disagree (v.) *or* disagreement (n.)

desert a dry environment (n.) *or* abandon (v.)
dessert sweet final course of a meal (n.)

device an object used for a particular purpose (n.)
devise to design (v.)

dew water condensation (n.)
do to perform or make happen (v.)
due owed or appropriate (adj.) *or* something owed (n.)

die to cease living (v.) *or* plural of dice (n.)
dye to color (v.) *or* chemical used to color something (n.)

discreet tactful (adj.)
discrete separate (adj.)

disease illness (n.)
decease to die (v.)

dual double (adj.)
duel combat between two people (n.)

eave the overhang of a roof (n.)
eve the evening (n.)

elicit to draw out (v.)
illicit illegal (adj.)

emigrate to leave a country (v.)
immigrate to come to a country (v.)

eminent well known (adj.)
imminent about to happen (adj.)

everyday usual (adj.)
every day frequently (adv.)

fair good (adj.) *or* equitable (adj.)
fare a fee (n.) *or* to get along (with a task) (v.)

farther more distant (adj.)
further more distant (adj.) *or* additional or additionally (adj. or adv.)

fir a type of evergreen tree (n.)
fur the hair of an animal (n.)

florescence   period of flowering (n.)
fluorescence   emission of radiation (n.)

flour   cooking ingredient (n.)
flower   a plant (n.)

flu   an illness (n.)
flew   part tense form of "to fly" (v.)
flue   a channel for conveying air or smoke (n.)

forth   forward (adv.)
fourth   number four in a series (n.) *or* one of four equal parts (n.)

foreword   introductory note (n.)
forward   toward the front (adv.) *or* located near the front (adj.)

fort   fortified shelter (n.)
forte   strength (n.) *or* loudly (adv.)

gaff   large metal hook (n.)
gaffe   social mistake (n.)

gild   to cover with a thin layer of gold (v.)
guild   association of tradespeople (n.)

gorilla   a large ape (n.)
guerrilla (*or* guerilla)   a member of a small military group (n.)

grate   to shred (v.) *or* a framework of parallel bars (n.)
great   large (adj.) *or* very good (adj.)

hangar   a storage place for aircraft (n.)
hanger   an object on which to hang things (n.)

hare   a rabbit (n.)
hair   filaments or cylindrical strands growing from the skin of mammals (n.)

hardy   healthy or courageous (adj.)
hearty   warm and exuberant (adj.) *or* robust (adj.)

hear   to listen (v.)
here   at/to this location (adv.)

heard   part tense form of "to hear" (v.)
herd   group of animals (n.)

heroin   a drug (n.)
heroine   a female hero (n.)

hoar   frosty coating (n.)
whore   a prostitute (n.)

idle   not busy (adj.) *or* to pass time without working (v.)
idol   object of worship (n.)

install   to set in position (v.)
instill   to implant (v.)

knead   to mix by pressing with the hands (v.)
need   to lack or require something (v.) *or* a necessity (n.)

knew   part tense form of "to know" (v.)
new   not old (adj.)

knows   form of "to know" (v.)
nose   part of face containing sense of smell (n.)

knot   an interlacing bond or hard lump (n.) *or* to fasten or entangle (v.)
not   expresses denial or refusal (adv.)

know   to grasp or understand (v.)
no   negative expression (adv., adj., or interj.)

lacks   plural of "lack," a deficiency (n.) *or* form of "to lack" (v.)
lax   loose, not strict (adj.)

laps   plural of "lap" (n.) *or* form of "to lap" (v.)
lapse   to fall from a standard (v.) *or* a minor failure (n.) *or* a pause (n.)

later   after a specific time (adj.)
latter   the second of two named things (adj.)

leach   to empty or drain (v.)
leech   blood-sucking parasite (n.)

lead   heavy metal (n.) or (*pronounced "leed"*) to guide (v.)
led   part tense form of "to lead" (v.)

lessen   to reduce (v.)
lesson   something to be learned (n.)

liar   one who does not tell the truth (n.)
lyre   harp (n.)

links   associations, loops forming a chain, *or* golf course (n.)
lynx   type of cat (n.)

loan   something given temporarily (n.)
lone   alone, solitary (adj.)

loose   not tight (adj.)
lose   to misplace (v.) *or* to be defeated (v.)

made   part tense form of "to make" (v.)
maid   an unmarried woman or a woman servant (n.)

magnate   a powerful person (n.)
magnet   an object that attracts (n.)

male   pertaining to the masculine sex (adj.) *or* one who is masculine (n.)
mail   material sent by the postal system (n.) *or* to send by post (v.)

main   most important (adj.)
mane   hair on the neck of some animals (n.)

maybe   perhaps (adv.)
may be   could be (v.)

meat   flesh (n.)
meet   to join with or become introduced to (v.)

medal   an award of recognition (n.)
meddle   to interfere (v.)
metal   material made from minerals (n.)
mettle   courage, strength of character (n.)

miner   one who mines (n.)
minor   of little importance (adj.) *or* one who is underage (n.)

naval   relating to ships (adj.)
navel   the mark where the umbilical cord was attached (n.) *or* a central point (n.)

oar   paddle (n.)
or   used to indicate an alternative (conj.)
ore   a mineral (n.)

one   individual (n.) *or* first number (n.)
won   part tense form of "to win" (v.)

overdo   to do more than necessary (v.)
overdue   late (adj.)

pain   suffering (n.) *or* to injure or be the cause of injury (v.)
pane   segment of glass (n.)

palate   the roof of the mouth (n.) *or* the sense of taste (n.)
palette   a small board for mixing paints (n.) *or* a range of colors or qualities
pallet   a platform for cargo (n.) *or* a small or straw-filled bed (n.)

parlay   to manipulate an asset to greater advantage (v.)
parley   to have a discussion (v.) *or* a discussion (n.)

passed   part tense form of "to
   pass" (v.)
past   the time before the present (n.)
   or previous (adj.) or beyond (prep.)

peace   tranquillity (n.)
piece   a portion (n.)

peak   pointed top of a roof or
   mountain (n.) *or* to reach the
   maximum (v.)
peek   to look quickly (v.) *or* a brief
   look (n.)
pique   to provoke (v.) *or*
   indignation (n.)

pear   a type of fruit (n.)
pair   two of something (n.)

personal   private (adj.)
personnel   employees (n.)

peer   an equal (n.) *or* to look
   intently (v.)
pier   a dock (n.)

plain   clear or simple (adj.) *or* a
   field (n.)
plane   a vehicle for air travel (n.)

poor   lacking in wealth or quality
   (adj.)
pore   opening in skin or leaf (n.)
pore (over)   to study carefully (v.)
pour   to make liquid flow (v.)

precede   to come before (v.)
proceed   to go forward (v.)

principal   important (adj.) *or* the
   head of a school (n.)
principle   a standard or rule (n.)

profit   monetary gain (n.) *or* to gain
   from (v.)
prophet   someone who predicts (n.)

rain   precipitation (n.) *or* to fall
   from above (v.)
reign   to rule (v.) *or* a period of
   ruling (n.)
rein   part of a horse's harness (n.)
   or to control (v.)

raise   to elevate (v.)
raze   to level to the ground,
   demolish (v.)
rise   to get up (v.)

respectfully   showing respect
   (adv.)
respectively   in the order
   mentioned (adv.)

right   correct (adj.) *or* to make
   correct (v.)
write   to form words on paper (v.)

role   a function or position (n.)
roll   to move on wheels or by
   tumbling (v.) *or* register (n.), as
   in "to call the roll"

sail   to travel by boat (v.)
sale   the act of selling (n.)

seam   a line formed by sewing (n.)
seem   to appear (as) (v.)

set   to place (v.)
sit   to rest (v.)

shear   to shave or trim (v.)
sheer   thin and transparent (adj.) *or*
   pure (adj.) *or* steep (adj.) *or* to
   swerve (v.)

shone   part tense form of "to
   shine" (v.)
shown   part tense form of "to
   show" (v.)

sleight   clever trick (n.) *or* dexterity
   (n.)
slight   small in size (adj.)

sole   solitary (adj.) *or* the bottom of
   a shoe (n.) *or* a type of fish (n.)
soul   spirit (n.)

son   a male offspring (n.)
sun   the star nearest Earth (n.)

stake   pointed piece of wood or
   metal (n.) *or* risk (n.) *or* to claim
   possession (v.)
steak   a slice of beef (n.)

stationary   not moving (adj.)
stationery   paper (n.)

steal   to take unlawfully (v.)
steel   strong metal (n.)

straight   not bent (adj.)
strait   narrow channel of water (n.)

tartar   a hard deposit on teeth (n.)
   or a type of sauce served with
   fish (n.)
tarter   more sharp-tasting (adj.)

taught   part tense form of "to
   teach" (v.)
taut   pulled tight (adj.)

team   two or more people or
   animals working together (n.)
teem   to be full of things (v.)

than   used to make unequal
   comparisons (conj.)
then   at that time (adv.)

threw   part tense form of "to
   throw" (v.)
through   in one side and out the
   other (prep.)

their   belonging to them (pron.)
there   in that place (adv.)
they're   contraction of "they are" (v.)

tic   a muscle spasm (n.)
tick   a blood-sucking arachnid (n.)

tide   movement of the ocean (n.)
tied   part tense form of "to tie" (v.)

to   toward (prep.)
too   also (adv.)
two   a number between one and
   three (n.)

vain   conceited (adj.)
vane   device for determining wind
   direction (n.)
vein   a blood vessel (n.)

vale   a valley (n.)
veil   something that conceals (n.) or
   to conceal (v.)

veracious   honest (adj.)
voracious   very eager to eat (adj.)
   or greedy (adj.)

waist   mid-section (n.)
waste   trash (n.) or to spend
   uselessly (v.)

waive   to give up voluntarily (v.)
wave   to move freely in the air (v.)
   or a movement of water or a
   hand (n.)

way   passage or route (n.) or
   method (n.)
weigh   to determine weight (v.)

weak   not strong (adj.)
week   seven days (n.)

wear   to have on (v.)
were   past tense form of "to be" (v.)
we're   contraction of "we are" (v.)
where   in what place (adv.)

weather   climate (n.) or to endure
   (v.)
whether   used in direct questions
   to introduce one alternative or
   used to introduce alternative
   possibilities (conj.)

which   what particular one (pron.)
witch   female sorcerer (n.)

whirl   to spin (v.)
whorl   a spiral shape (n.)

wood   material made from trees
   (n.)
would   form of "will" used to
   make requests or indicate
   uncertainty (v.)

whose   possessive form of "who"
   (pron.)
who's   contraction of "who is" or
   "who has" (v.)

your   possessive form of "you"
   (pron.)
you're   contraction of "you are" (v.)

EXERCISE 33.4 Choose correct spelling.

Correct misspellings that are caused by confusing one word with another.

EXAMPLE:

Every year or so, another new trend develops in the ~~exorcise~~ *exercise* world, and each one is supposed to be easier and better ^than the last.

1. People are usually encouraged to exercise regularly and vigorously in order to achieve the desired affect.

2. However, a recently popular kind of exercise demands that participants lift weights extremely slowly, and experts in the technique advice three days of rest between bouts of exercising.

3. The slow-lifting technique is not new, as allot of people who have discovered it believe; it was actually developed in 1982.

4. At that time, the technique gave impressive results to women who were suffering from severe osteoporosis; before they're slow workouts, most were not strong enough too follow a typical weight-training regimen.

5. A recent study by the *Journal of Sports Medicine and Physical Fitness* showed that slow lifting was effective in building strength, but of the 147 subjects who participated in the study, only two wanted to continue the training; the rest felt that the workouts were all together too grueling.

EXERCISE 33.5 Use confusing words correctly.

Write a short paragraph on any topic using as many words as possible from the preceding list of words commonly confused. In your paragraph, underline the words that you have used from the list.

33i Multinational characters: accents, umlauts, tildes, and cedillas

Words and names in languages other than English may be spelled with special marks above or under a letter, such as an accent (è or é), an umlaut or dieresis (ö), a tilde (ñ), or a cedilla (ç). Microsoft Word provides ways of producing multinational characters. The basic principle is that you press CTRL and the punctuation key most similar to the mark you need, release the keys, and press the letter. The letter then appears with its mark. Alternatively, you can go to the Windows Control panel, click on Keyboard, and then go to Language and Add Language. There you can switch to a specific language or to the U.S.-International English keyboard definition.

TechNote A Useful Web Site for Writing in Other Languages

Go to <http://www.starr.net/is/type/kbh.html> for a site titled *International Accents and Diacriticals: Theory, Charts, and Tips*. This site, prepared by Irene Starr of the Foreign Language Resource Center at the University of Massachusetts, provides charts of how to use Word, Wordperfect, or a Macintosh computer to produce the multinational characters, instructions on accessing and using the International English keyboard, and links to sites useful for those writing non-Roman alphabets.

33j Hyphens

Use hyphens to divide a word or to form a compound. For the use of hyphens online, see **34d**.

1. Hyphens with prefixes Many words with prefixes are spelled without hyphens: *cooperate, nonrestrictive, unnatural*. Others are hyphenated: *all-inclusive, anti-intellectual*. Always use a hyphen when the main word is a number or a proper noun: *all-American, post-1990*. If you are unsure about whether to insert a hyphen before a prefix, check a dictionary.

2. Hyphens in compound nouns and adjectives Some compound nouns are written as one word (*toothbrush*), others as two words (*coffee shop*), and still others with one or more hyphens (*role-playing, father-in-law*). Always check an up-to-date dictionary.

Hyphenate compound adjectives preceding a noun: *a ten-page essay, a well-organized party, a law-abiding citizen.* When the modifier follows the noun, no hyphen is necessary: *The essay was ten pages long. The party was well organized. Most citizens try to be law abiding.*

Do not insert a hyphen between an *-ly* adverb and an adjective or after an adjective in its comparative (*-er*) or superlative (*-est*) form: *a tightly fitting suit, a sweeter sounding melody.*

3. Hyphens in spelled-out numbers Use hyphens when spelling out two-word numbers from twenty-one to ninety-nine. (See **32c** for more on spelling out numbers.)

▶ **Twenty-two applicants arrived early in the morning.**

Also use a hyphen in spelled-out fractions: *two-thirds of a cup.*

4. End-of-line hyphens Most word processors either automatically hyphenate words or automatically wrap words around to the next line. Choose the latter option to avoid the strange and unacceptable word division that sometimes appears with automatic hyphenation.

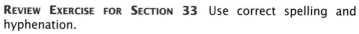

REVIEW EXERCISE FOR SECTION 33 Use correct spelling and hyphenation.
Correct any misspellings and hyphenation errors.

Recently, researchers who study chimpanzees have come to the suprising conclusion that groups of chimpanzees have their own traditions that can be past on to new generations of chimps. The chimps do not aquire these traditions by instinct; instead, they learn them from other chimps. When a scientific journal published analysises of chimpanzee behavior, the author revealed that the every day actions of chimpanzees in seperate areas differ in significant ways, even when the groups belong to the same subspecies. For instance, in one West African group, the chimps are often seen puting a nut on a stone and using another peice of stone to crack the nut open, a kind of behavior never observed in other groups of chimpanzees. Sceintists have also observed the chimps teaching there young the nut opening method, and chimps in other places that crack nuts differently teach their young they're own way. Researchers have therefor concluded that chimpanzees have local traditions.

Frans de Waal, who has been studing primates, wrote a book makeing the arguement that these learned behaviors should be considered kinds of culture. The word culture has traditionly been used to describe human behavier, but may be, he says, a new definition is needed. Considering this startlingly-new theory of chimpanzee "culture," some researchers think that humans now have an un-deniable obligation to protect the lives of all remaining wild chimpanzees rather than zeroeing in on just a few of the threatenned animals. The lost of a single group of wild chimpanzees would, they say, destroy something irreplacable, a unique culture with its own traditions and way of life.

34 Online Guidelines for Punctuation and Mechanics

34a Punctuation in URLs

Punctuation marks communicate essential information in Web site addresses—Uniform Resource Locators—and in e-mail addresses. Be sure to include all marks when you write an address, and if you need to spread a URL over more than one line, split it after a slash (MLA style) or before a punctuation mark. Do not split the protocol <http://>. Use angle brackets to enclose e-mail and Web addresses. Do not include any additional punctuation within the angle brackets.

▶ The Modern Language Association, whose Web site is at <http://www.mla.org>, provides examples of documenting Web sources.

34b Underscoring, underlining, and italics online

In World Wide Web pages and in HTML (hypertext markup language), underlining indicates a link to another site, so underlining is not available for other uses. When you write for publication on the Web, use italics to indicate titles and other usually underlined expressions. In e-mail, use underscore marks instead of italics and underlining, as in this sentence:

▶ **Just read Joyce's _Ulysses_to get a flavor of Dublin.**

[The underscore marks precede and follow the word that would have been italicized or underlined.]

34c Capital letters online

Lowercase and capital (uppercase) letters are significant (the technical term is *case-sensitive*) in e-mail addresses and URLs, so keep careful records of which are used. If you make a mistake, you will be unable to make a connection. Similarly, the names of many systems and search engines have specialized capitalization (WebCrawler, AltaVista).

Avoid using capitalized text (the whole text, not just initial letters) in e-mail communications and electronic discussion groups. In both places, the prolonged use of capital letters is regarded as "shouting" and may offend readers. See also **11b**.

34d Hyphens online

Some e-mail addressess include hyphens, so never add a hyphen to indicate that you have split an address between lines. When an e-mail address includes a hyphen, do not break the line at a hyphen because readers will not know whether the hyphen is part of the address.

Technological vocabulary changes quickly. We already have new combined words such as *online* and *download*. You will find both *e-mail* and *email*. The MLA prefers the hyphenated spelling, *e-mail*, but the tendency is for common words like this to move toward closing up. Whichever form you use, use it consistently.

34e Asterisks and abbreviations online

Asterisks (*) Some older e-mail providers do not support text features such as italics or underlining. In such cases, use asterisks before and after a word or phrase for emphasis.

▶ They were *decidedly* antagonistic.

Abbreviations Many abbreviations in the electronics world have become standard fare: *CD-ROM, RAM, HTML, PIN,* and more. In addition, the informal world of online communication leads to informal abbreviations, at least in personal e-mail messages. Abbreviations such as *BTW* ("by the way") and *TTYTT* ("to tell you the truth") are used in e-mail but should not appear in more formal written communications.

What is style? William Strunk Jr. and E. B. White in their classic book *The Elements of Style,* 4th edition, define it as the sound "words make on paper." That sound is important to readers and affects their response to a piece of writing and their willingness to continue reading. Sometimes, even when ideas are well organized, readers can suffer from the so-called MEGO reaction to a piece of writing—"My Eyes Glaze Over." Readers are bored by wordiness, flatness, inappropriate word choice, clichés, and sentences constructed without interesting variations. Working on sentence structure and style can help prevent that glazing over.

With acknowledgment to Joseph Williams's *Style: Ten Lessons in Clarity and Grace,* 6th edition, sections **35–39** examine five anti-MEGO strategies, called here the "Five C's of Style."

WORLDS OF WRITING
Style across Cultures

It is impossible to identify one style as the best. What is considered good (or appropriate) style varies according to the writer's purpose and the expectations of the anticipated readers. Country, culture, region, ethnic heritage, language, gender, class—all can play a role in writing and in influencing what readers define as style. What may please readers in one language and culture in one setting in one part of the world may seem too flat or too adorned in another. The Japanese novelist Junichuro Tanizaki, for example, gives writers this advice, "Do not try to be too clear; leave some gaps in the meaning." He illustrates this approach by comparing it to keeping "a thin sheet of paper between the fact or the object and the words that give expression to it" (in Edward G. Seidensticker's introduction to *Some Prefer Nettles*). Strunk and White give different advice: "The approach to style is by way of plainness, simplicity, orderliness, sincerity." Good style is relative.

Follow these guidelines for determining an appropriate style for each document you write.

1. Consider context and readers' expectations. Assess where you are writing, what your purpose is, and what readers will expect in the part of the world you reside in and in the context you inhabit (such as an academic, business, or community setting).

> What are readers' stylistic preferences in terms of organization and format of the document?
>
> What elements should be included and excluded?
>
> How direct or indirect do readers expect you to be in stating opinions and making recommendations?
>
> What formulaic expressions are commonly in use (such as "Sincerely yours" or "In conclusion")?
>
> What language will readers be comfortable with: short or long sentences, plain or ornate language and sentence structure, everyday words or technical vocabulary?

2. Address the underlying structure of your piece of writing. Work first on generating ideas and organizing them clearly and logically. Once you have organized your content and found a clear structure for expressing your ideas, then you can turn your attention to conscious presentation of the ideas, fine-tuning your style so that it appeals to specific readers.

3. Be adaptable.   Choose a style as you choose your clothes: the right outfit for the occasion. One style will not fit all. If you develop an effective figurative style for short stories, do not continue to use it in business communications or e-mail.

4. Favor a plain style rather than writing to impress readers. Focusing on style does not mean focusing on ornate or stuffy language. For many writing situations in North America, the best style is often what is known as a "plain style"—something that is clear and easy for readers to follow. The following sentences, part of an e-mail message, are not in the plain style. They are overdressed and stuffed with bureaucratic nothings: "It has been a pleasure assisting you. It is my hope that the information provided would be of great help with regards to your concern." The same message can be conveyed more directly: "I hope I have helped you solve your problem."

5. Less is often more.   In most types of college and business writing, a good style is writing that does not draw attention to itself with flourishes and flowery language. Avoid trying to dazzle readers with big words and obscure turns of phrase or overloading your writing with adjectives and adverbs: *The perky little red-haired twin sat languidly in the comfortable, overstuffed green-striped armchair and bit enthusiastically into a red and yellow, fleshy, overripe peach.* Such prose is as overripe as the peach.

6. Keep the presence of a "self." Think of formal, academic style as something that makes readers realize that a real person has written the document—a person with a strong sense of self and a conviction that the ideas in the piece of writing are interesting, credible, and well presented. Do not fade into insignificance behind bland overgeneralities.

KEY POINTS
Style in College Essays: A Checklist for Revision

1. Do any parts seem wordy or repetitive? Make your writing concise. Cut what you can. (See **35.**)

2. Are any sentences flat because of an unnecessary *there is* or *there are*, too many prepositional phrases (**16d**), or passive voice verbs? If so, ask "Who's doing what?" and revise. (See **36.**)

3. Do any passages seem jumpy, disconnected, and not easy to follow? Have you used coordination and subordination effectively? Aim for coherence and make clear connections. (See **37.**)

4. Do any passages seem weak and apologetic? Commit to critical thinking, to a point of view, to an appropriate tone, and to confident language. (See **38.**)

5. Could any of your words baffle, bore, or offend a reader? Choose exact, concrete words, and eliminate clichés and language that is biased, inappropriate, or stuffy. (See **39.**)

6. Have you used a style-check/grammar-check program and exercised caution in taking its suggestions (see **4h**)? Computer style-check programs alert you to such problems as possibly wordy phrases, repetition, clichés, sexist language, and colloquial usage. However, often they are not attuned to the subtleties of language and grammar. Never simply accept a suggestion as accurate.

35 The First C: Cut

You can improve most of your writing if you focus on stating your ideas succinctly. Examine your writing for unnecessary ideas, sentences, phrases, and individual words. Sometimes you may be tempted to pad your work to fill an assigned number of pages. However, work on filling pages with substantive information and commentary, not with empty words.

35a Cut repetition and wordiness.

Say something only once and in the best place.

▶ The Lilly Library ~~contains many rare books. The books in~~

~~the library are~~ carefully preserved**s**, ~~The library also houses~~
                                         ^
many rare books and manuscripts.
~~a manuscript collection.~~
                         ^

director of
▶ Steven Spielberg, ~~who has directed~~ the movie ~~that has~~
                                    ^
~~been~~ described as the best war movie ever made, ~~is~~
~~someone who~~ knows many politicians.

▶ California residents voted to abolish bilingual education**/**
~~The main reason for their voting to abolish bilingual~~

because
~~education was that~~ many children were being placed
                     ^

indiscriminately into programs and kept there too long.

If your draft says something like "As the first paragraph states" or "As previously stated," beware. Such phrases probably indicate that you have repeated yourself.

35b Cut formulaic phrases.

Writers sometimes use formulaic phrases in a first draft to keep the writing process going. In revision, these wordy phrases should come out or be replaced with shorter or more concise expressions.

FORMULAIC	CONCISE
at the present time	now
at this point in time	
in this day and age	
in today's society	
are of the opinion that	believe
have the ability to	can
is dependent upon	depends on
last but not least	finally
prior to	before
concerning the matter of	about

FORMULAIC	CONCISE
because of the fact that	because
due to the fact that	
in spite of the fact that	although

In *The Elements of Style,* William Strunk Jr. and E. B. White rail against any use of the phrase "the fact that," seeing it as "especially debilitating." Their advice? Cut it out.

▶ Few people realize ~~the fact~~ that the computer controlling the *Eagle* lunar module in 1969 had less memory than a cheap wristwatch does today.

▶ A 1999 Gallup poll revealed ~~the fact~~ that almost six percent of Americans believe the moon landing in 1969 was a hoax.

The *Eagle* lunar module

EXERCISE 35.1 Cut wordiness and formulaic phrases.
Edit the following sentences to eliminate wordiness and formulaic phrases.

EXAMPLE:

<u>Although</u>
~~In spite of the fact that~~ Michael Jordan has decided to play basketball again, fans are not likely to see incredible ~~and unbelievable~~ athletic feats from their hero ~~again.~~

1. Michael Jordan first retired from basketball in 1993 and tried to begin a career in the game of baseball, but he returned to the

Chicago Bulls in the spring of 1995 because of the fact that he had not been successful enough in baseball to reach the major leagues.

2. When Jordan retired again in 1999, he told reporters that he was "99.9 percent" sure that he would never return to basketball, but basketball fans who loved the game were of the opinion that he had meant to leave himself a loophole.

3. At the point in time when Jordan began working out on a basketball court again, many people thought he was planning a comeback, but Jordan insisted that he was simply and solely trying to lose weight.

4. Finally, in the fall of 2001, Jordan, who at the time was then thirty-eight years old, revealed that he would play with the Washington Wizards and donate his first year's salary to victims of the September 11 attacks.

5. Jordan had owned a part of the Washington Wizards, a team with a poor record in the 2000–2001 season, prior to making the decision to sell his stake in the team and come in as a player.

35c As appropriate, cut references to your intentions.

In writing for the social sciences or sciences, the main goal is usually to provide information. In those disciplines, therefore, you may acceptably state how you intend to structure your argument (for example, *This paper describes three approaches to classifying germs*) and then summarize that structure again at the end of the essay—thus presenting a plan of your organization at both the beginning and the end of the essay.

In the humanities, readers usually are not interested in explanations of your thinking process and plan of organization. Eliminate references to the organization of your text and your own planning, such as *In this essay, I intend to prove . . .* or *In the next few paragraphs, I hope to show . . .* or *In conclusion, I have demonstrated . . .* or *What I want to say here is . . .*

35d Cut redundant words and phrases.

Trim words that simply repeat an idea expressed by another word in the same phrase: *basic* essentials, *true* facts, circle *around*, cooperate *together*, *final* completion, return *again*, refer *back*, *advance* planning, consensus *of opinion*, *free* gift. Also edit redundant pairs: *various and sundry, hopes and desires, each and every,* and any redundant phrases.

▶ The task took ~~diligence and~~ perseverance.

has
▶ His surgeon ~~is a doctor with~~ a great deal of clinical experience.

> **EXERCISE 35.2** Cut redundant words and phrases.
> Edit to eliminate redundant words and phrases.
>
> **EXAMPLE:**
>
> The Strangler cases ~~terrified and~~ unnerved Bostonians until 1965, when Albert DeSalvo confessed to the eleven murders.

1. The nephew of one of the Boston Strangler's murder victims began to investigate his aunt's case in 1999 to prove to his own mother that the Strangler had been caught, but he eventually became mentally certain that Albert DeSalvo, the confessed killer of the victims, was not guilty.

2. In the 1960s, the public was told that DeSalvo had admitted details in his confession that only the murderer or killer would have known.

3. DeSalvo was never convicted of the Strangler murders, but he went to prison where he was jailed for another crime and was fatally stabbed there in 1973.

4. DeSalvo seemed to have exclusive and inside knowledge of the murders, but others have since noted that he had heard many

details from lawyers and police officials, and DeSalvo was known for his complete and total recall of each and every thing he had been told.

5. Since the victim's nephew got involved, lawyers and forensic specialists have been cooperating together to investigate new leads and DNA evidence that could either exonerate DeSalvo or finally prove him guilty at last.

35e Cut material quoted unnecessarily.

Quote only as much material from a source as is needed to support your point. Often a phrase or clause will be enough; quoting a whole sentence or more than one sentence is usually unnecessary.

No **Film critic Elvis Mitchell says of *Harry Potter and the Sorcerer's Stone:* "The most awaited movie of the year has a dreary, literal-minded competence, following the letter of the law as laid down by the author" in its close portrayal of the book.**

Yes **Film critic Elvis Mitchell says that the long-anticipated *Harry Potter and the Sorcerer's Stone* suffers from "a dreary, literal-minded competence" in its close portrayal of the book.**

REVIEW EXERCISE FOR SECTION 35 Make appropriate cuts.
Edit the following passage to eliminate any unnecessary material.

With computer graphics imaging becoming more lifelike and realistic in today's society, filmmakers in the motion picture industry are now able to create animated characters who could conceivably take the place of human beings or people in leading roles onscreen. Nonliving stars are not a completely and totally unknown quantity, of course. Mickey Mouse and Bugs Bunny are cartoon characters who earned millions of fans in spite of the fact that they did not exist in the real world outside of an animation studio. King Kong, who was the first stop-motion animation star, thrilled and delighted audiences beginning in the decade of the 1930s because of the fact that he was believably realistic at that point in time. However, modern innovations in computer graphics make cartoons and stop-motion characters look quaint and dated. At the present time, filmmakers are resolved and determined to create "synthespians" who will look, move, speak, and talk in such a realistic manner that audiences will be awed, and studios are enlisting animators with expertise and experience in computer graphics rather than traditional old-fashioned cartoonists to model the new breed of cyber-actors. Some film and movie critics are of the opinion that filmmakers are failing to grasp something vital and important, which is that audiences want genuine and honest emotion and creative storytelling rather than whizbang special effects and computer graphics. They argue that no computer-generated synthespian will ever really matter or be important to filmgoers unless his or her films are well written and well directed.

36 The Second C: Check for Action

"Check for action" means to convey to readers a clear sense of who (or what) is doing what. As a general rule, use vigorous sentences with vivid, expressive verbs. Avoid bland forms of the verb *be* (*be, am, is, are, was, were, being, been*) or verbs in the passive voice (see **201**).

36a Ask "Who's doing what?" about subject and verb.

Wherever possible, let the subject of your sentence perform the action, and use expressive verbs. Ask these questions:

Who or what is doing the action?
Is it the subject of the clause?
If not, could it be and should it be?

                                subject   verb
WORDY   **The mayor's approval of the new law was due to the
         voters' suspicion of concealment of campaign funds
         by his deputy.**

This dull thud of a sentence uses the verb *was*, which conveys no sense of action. The subject of the verb is an abstract noun, *approval*—not exactly informative or interest-grabbing. The use of the weak verb *to be* leads to an excess of abstract nominalizations (nouns formed from verbs) and of prepositional phrases. The sentence contains three abstract nouns formed from verbs (*approval/approve, suspicion/suspect,* and *concealment/conceal*), as well as five prepositional phrases: *of the new law, due to voters' suspicion, of the concealment, of campaign funds,* and *by his deputy.* Asking "Who's doing what?" helps unpack the dense mass:

WHO'S DOING WHAT?	
SUBJECT	VERB
the mayor	approved
the voters	suspected
his deputy	had concealed

REVISED   **The mayor approved the new law because voters
           suspected that his deputy had concealed campaign funds.**

Always put verbs to work to make a sentence strong.

                                                        celebrates
▶ **In Nicholson Baker's *The Mezzanine*, a long footnote is about
  the concept of perforation.**
                                                        ^

EXERCISE 36.1   Ask "Who's doing what?"
Rewrite each of the following sentences using vivid, expressive verbs.

EXAMPLE:

Can   *solve*
Are genetically engineered pigs a solution to pressing
  ^   ^
environmental problems?

1. Factory hog farms are problematic due to the small quarters
   and their housing of thousands of pigs, with the resulting
   excretion of many tons of manure.

2. Contents of the manure include phosphorus and other chemicals that are pollutants of water supplies and cause harm to
   humans, fish, and wildlife.

3. Canadian researchers are the developers of a new strain of genetically engineered pig with lower phosphorus content in its manure.

4. The "Enviropig" is a delight to industrial pork producers but not to environmental groups, which are against genetic modification of foods.

5. The reduction of industrial hog-farming pollution is necessary, but the Enviropig is a technical solution while environmental groups are hoping for the end of the raising of hogs in small, enclosed areas by farmers.

36b Use caution in beginning a sentence with *there* or *it*.

For a lean, direct style, rewrite sentences in which *there* or *it* occupies the subject position (as in *there is, there were, it is, it was*). Revise by using verbs that describe an action and subjects that perform the action. Asking "Who's doing what?" helps here, too.

WORDY   **There was a discussion of the health care system by the politicians.** [Who's doing what?]

REVISED   **The politicians discussed the health care system.**

WORDY   **There is a big gate guarding the entrance to the park.**

REVISED   **A big gate guards the entrance to the park.**

WORDY   **It is a fact that Arnold is proudly displaying a new tattoo.**

REVISED   **Arnold is proudly displaying a new tattoo.**

TechNote Searching for Uses of *It* and *There*

Use the Find function of your word processing program to find all instances in your draft of *it is/was, there is/are,* and *there was/were*. If you find a filler subject with little purpose, revise.

EXERCISE 36.2 Revise sentences beginning with *there* or *it*. Rewrite each sentence to eliminate *there* or *it* wherever possible.

EXAMPLE:

        Families
~~There are families~~ known as "travelers" ~~who~~ live in mobile homes in Ireland and lead nomadic lives.

1. It is traditional for some families in Ireland to travel from place to place instead of settling permanently in one location.

2. There are deep-seated prejudices among many Irish people against the traveler families.

3. Although most travelers share the Catholic faith and the Celtic background of the majority of Irish people, it is not unusual for travelers to face discrimination and accusations of thievery.

4. There have been instances in which parents have removed children from local schools after traveler children arrived.

5. There is a law in Ireland requiring communities to begin providing water and other basic services to traveler populations by 2004, but few districts have made plans to comply.

36c Avoid unnecessary passive voice constructions.

The *passive voice* tells what is done to the grammatical subject of a clause ("The turkey *was cooked* too long"). Extensive use of the passive voice makes your style dull and wordy. When you can, replace it with active voice verbs.

PASSIVE   **The problem will be discussed thoroughly by the committee.**

ACTIVE   **The committee will discuss the problem thoroughly.**

If you are studying in the social sciences or sciences, disciplines in which readers are primarily interested in procedures and results rather than who developed or produced them, you will find passive voice constructions are more common and more acceptable than in the humanities. For example, in lab reports and experiments, you will read *The rats were fed* instead of *The researchers fed the rats*. For acceptable uses of the passive voice, see **20l** and **37a**.

TECHNOTE Using Grammar-Check Software

Grammar checkers will point out passive voice constructions. If you have a tendency to overuse the passive voice, use a grammar checker to alert yourself to the places that you can check. However, use the grammar checker as only a guide; programs sometimes identify structures wrongly. Use the grammar checker simply to send you back to your sentence to reread and check it. ▪

EXERCISE 36.3 Avoid unnecessary passive voice constructions. Rewrite any passive voice constructions in the active voice.

EXAMPLE:

~~Wild animals~~ have ~~been~~ hunted ~~by poachers~~ in national parks all over the world.
Poachers ... *wild animals*

1. In some wildlife preserves abroad, a radical new strategy has been adopted by conservationists.

2. Even in preserves that are supposed to be safe, many threatened wild species are either captured by poachers for the thriving black market in exotic pets or killed for their valuable body parts.

3. Poachers have been asked by wildlife organizations to use their knowledge of animals and animal habitats to contribute to wildlife preservation.

4. Many poachers have agreed to stop hunting endangered animals in exchange for a living wage and health benefits for themselves and their families; instead, information about the animals in the preserves is now collected by former poachers.

5. Local economies in poor areas near the preserves have long been supported by poaching, but with this new approach, local

young people can see that working to support wildlife conservation is a better and safer way to earn a living than illegal poaching.

REVIEW EXERCISE FOR SECTION 36 Check for action.
Revise any sentences that could be made more vigorous.

Alzheimer's disease is a terrible affliction of the elderly in the United States and around the world. People are robbed by the disease of a lifetime of memories, and family members often care for patients who no longer recognize them. There can be years of round-the-clock care required to help an Alzheimer's patient, and such care is expensive. A heavy toll is taken on any stricken family by this disease.

However, there is hope offered by new research to those who fear that they may develop this illness. The rate of people affected by Alzheimer's in India is the lowest in the world, and scientists have been investigating possible reasons. The Indian diet is considered by some scientists to be an answer. There is a spice called curcumin that is common in Indian curries, and it is being tested by researchers as a possible preventive medicine. In one intriguing study, a diet rich in curcumin was fed to laboratory mice bred to develop brain defects similar to those produced by Alzheimer's, and the result was the development of fewer brain defects in the mice during the aging process. It is not yet known whether curcumin or other spices will help reduce the number of people developing Alzheimer's; if curcumin does prove to be effective, it will take some time for scientists to discover the reasons. Someday, perhaps, there will be a currently unknown property of curcumin found by researchers that will reveal a solution to the puzzle of Alzheimer's.

37 The Third C: Connect

In coherent pieces of writing, information that has been mentioned before is linked to new information in a smooth flow, not in a series of grasshopper-like jumps. Connect ideas clearly for maximum coherence.

37a Use consistent subjects and topic chains for coherence.

Readers expect to be able to connect the ideas beginning a sentence with what they have already read. From one sentence to the next, avoid jarring and unnecessary shifts from one subject to another. Let your subjects form a topic chain.

JARRING SHIFT *Memoirs* **frequently top the bestseller list.** *Readers* **of all ages are finding them appealing.**

TOPIC CHAIN *Memoirs* **frequently top the bestseller list.** *They* **appeal to readers of all ages.**

In the revised version, the subject of the second sentence, *they*, refers to the subject of the previous sentence, *memoirs*; the new information about "readers of all ages" comes at the end, where it receives more emphasis (**37b**).

Examine your writing for awkward topic switches. Note that constructing a topic chain may mean using the passive voice, as in the last sentence of the revision that follows:

FREQUENT TOPIC SWITCHES *I* **have lived all my life in Brooklyn, New York.** *Park Slope* **is a neighborhood that has many different ethnic cultures.** *Harmony* **exists among the people there, even though it does not in many other Brooklyn neighborhoods.** *Several articles in the press* **have praised the Slope for its ethnic variety.**

REVISED WITH TOPIC CHAIN *Many different ethnic cultures* **flourish in Park Slope, Brooklyn, where I have lived all my life.** *These different cultures* **live together harmoniously there, even though they do not in many other Brooklyn neighborhoods. In fact,** *the ethnic variety* **of the Slope has often been praised in the press.**

EXERCISE 37.1 Use consistent subjects and topic chains. Write a revision of the following passage to avoid jarring and unnecessary shifts from one subject to another.

EXAMPLE:

Meiyuan Ding won the heavyweight division of the first

She competed in the summer 2000 Olympic Games in
Olympic women's weightlifting competition. Sydney, Australia
 ^ ⊙

~~hosted the Olympic Games where this event took place in the~~

~~summer of 2000.~~

    Weightlifter Cheryl Haworth hails from Savannah, Georgia. The bronze medal in the 75-kilograms-and-up class in women's weightlifting at the 2000 summer Olympics went to Haworth. Many people were surprised that the sixteen-year-old Haworth, who weighs 290 pounds and stands five feet nine inches tall, could be an Olympic medalist. Weighing more makes lifting heavier weights possible, so in this sport, size is actually an asset. The former American women's record fell when Haworth lifted 125 kilograms over her head, a weight she had never attempted to lift before the Olympic games. The combined total of the weights lifted for the bronze medal in the snatch and the clean and jerk competitions was 270 kilograms, nearly 600 pounds. Having a large body may not be every person's dream, but Haworth's being the third-strongest woman in the world is proof that bigger is sometimes better.

37b Place information at the end of a sentence for emphasis.

If you form a topic chain of old information, new information will come at the end of a sentence. Make your sentences end on a strong and interesting note, one that you want to emphasize. This technique helps keep your ideas flowing smoothly. Don't let a sentence trail off weakly.

WEAK
ENDING **Women often feel silenced by men, according to one researcher.**

REVISED **According to one researcher, women often feel silenced by men.**

WEAK
ENDING **Odysseus encounters Calypso, who tempts him with immortality, after he has resisted the Sirens.**

REVISED **After resisting the Sirens, Odysseus encounters Calypso, who tempts him with immortality.**

Cumulative and periodic sentences Cumulative (or loose) sentences begin with the independent clause and add on to it. Periodic sentences begin with words and phrases that lead to the independent clause, giving it more impact. The cumulative sentence is the norm in English prose. Use a periodic sentence to make a specific impact.

CUMULATIVE   *The experienced hunter stood stock still for at least five minutes,* **sweat pouring from his brow, all senses alert, waiting to hear a twig snap.**

PERIODIC   **Sweat pouring from his brow, all senses alert, waiting to hear a twig snap,** *the experienced hunter stood stock still for at least five minutes.*

EXERCISE 37.2 Emphasize information.
Revise the following sentences as needed to emphasize the important information.

EXAMPLE:

     According to a 1997 study, the
~~The~~ human sleep cycle can be disrupted after many weeks in
       ⊙
space, ~~according to a 1997 study.~~

1. Human beings follow circadian rhythms that regulate the body according to a twenty-four-hour schedule under normal circumstances.

2. In 1997, an American astronaut at the *Mir* space station measured his own body temperature and recorded his level of alertness and the amount and quality of his sleep in order to research the effect on the body of months in space.

3. The temperature of the human body normally falls when a person sleeps and rises again just before the person wakes, as sleep researchers have known for years.

4. However, after four months in space, the American astronaut's body temperature remained the same at all times, he was not

sleepy at bedtime, and he woke often and rarely dreamed, the astronaut found.

5. Space travelers may need to find a way to trick their bodies into retaining circadian rhythms, say the creators of the astronaut study.

37c Explore options for connecting ideas: coordination, subordination, and transitions.

When you write sentences containing two or more clauses (**16e**), consider where you want to place the emphasis. Decide whether to give each clause equal weight or to subordinate one or more ideas in a complex sentence (see **16f**).

Coordination   You give two or more clauses equal emphasis when you connect them with a coordinating conjunction—*and, but, or, nor, so, for,* or *yet* (see **16a**). (For more on clauses, see **16e** and **16f**.)

┌─── independent clause ──┐   ┌─── independent clause ───
▶ **The bus trip was long, and the seats seemed more**

───────────────────────────────────
uncomfortable with every mile.

┌─── independent clause ──┐   ┌─── independent clause ───┐
▶ **The bus trip was long, but we managed to enjoy it.**

Subordination   When you use subordinating conjunctions (**16e**) such as *when, if,* or *because* to connect clauses, you give one idea more importance by putting it in the independent clause.

▶ **Brillo pads work well. I don't give them as gifts.**
 [Two independent clauses: equal importance]

┌──────── dependent clause ───────┐   ┌─── independent clause ───┐
▶ **Although Brillo pads work well, I don't give them as gifts.**
 [The focus is on the notion of what makes a suitable gift.]

Note how subordinating a different idea can change meaning and emphasis: *Although I don't give Brillo pads as gifts, they work well.*

▶ We cannot now end our differences. At least we can help make the world safe for diversity. [Two independent clauses: statements of equal importance]

┌─────────── dependent clause ───────────┐ ┌─
▶ If we cannot now end our differences, at least we can help
┌────────── independent clause ──────────┐
make the world safe for diversity.   —John F. Kennedy

[Two clauses connected by *if*, setting up a condition under which the independent clause holds true]

Transitional expressions Use words such as *however, therefore,* and *nevertheless* (known as *conjunctive adverbs*; see **16a**) and phrases such as *as a result, in addition,* and *on the other hand* to signal the logical connection between independent clauses (for a list of transitional expressions, see **5e**). A transitional expression can move around in its own clause—yet another stylistic option for you to consider.

▶ He made a lot of money; however, his humble roots were always evident.

▶ He made a lot of money; his humble roots, however, were always evident.

▶ He made a lot of money; his humble roots were always evident, however.

The Key Points box summarizes the available connecting options.

KEY POINTS

Options for Connecting Clauses

COORDINATING CONJUNCTION	TRANSITIONAL EXPRESSION	SUBORDINATING CONJUNCTION
and (addition)	also, further, furthermore, moreover, in addition	
but, yet (contrast)	however, nevertheless, on the other hand	although, even though, whereas, while
or, nor (alternative)	instead, otherwise, alternatively	unless
so, for (result)	therefore, as a result, hence, consequently, thus, accordingly, then	because, as, since, so/such . . . that, now that, once

The following examples illustrate how the options may work.

▶ I often use pay phones. I have never seen the phone company emptying them.

▶ I often use pay phones, but I have never seen the phone company emptying them.

▶ Although I often use pay phones, I have never seen the phone company emptying them.

▶ I often use pay phones; however, I have never seen the phone company emptying them.

▶ I often use pay phones; I have, however, never seen the phone company emptying them.

Make your choice by deciding what you want to emphasize and seeing what structures you used in nearby sentences. If, for example, you used *however* in the immediately preceding sentence, choose some other option for expressing contrasting ideas.

Avoiding excessive coordination or subordination Too much of any one stylistic feature will become tedious to readers.

EXCESSIVE COORDINATION WITH *AND*	I grew up in a large family, and we lived on a small farm, and every day I had to get up early and do farm work, and I would spend a lot of time cleaning out the stables, and then I would be exhausted in the evening, and I never had the energy to read.
REVISED	Because I grew up in a large family on a small farm, every day I had to get up early to do farm work, mostly cleaning out the stables. I would be so exhausted in the evening that I never had the energy to read.
EXCESSIVE SUBORDINATION	Because the report was weak and poorly written, their boss, who wanted to impress the company president by showing her how efficient his division was, to gain prestige in the company, decided, despite the fact that work projects were piling up, that he would rewrite the report over the weekend.
REVISED	Because the report was weak and poorly written, their boss decided to rewrite it over the weekend, despite the fact that work projects were piling up. He wanted to impress the company president by showing her how efficient his division was; that was his way of gaining prestige.

EXERCISE 37.3 Use different options for connecting ideas.
In each of the following sentences, rewrite the two independent clauses as a single sentence, giving the information appropriate emphasis by using coordination, subordination, or a transitional expression. Then identify the method that you used.

EXAMPLE:

Environmental groups have often portrayed American Indians
     , but some
as conservationists. ~~Some~~ tribes feel that such portrayals are
       ^

simplistic and culturally insensitive. [coordination]

1. Environmentalists believe that drilling for oil in the Arctic National Wildlife Refuge would damage a wilderness area. They have also cast drilling for oil as a human rights issue.
2. The Gwich'in Indians rely on a caribou herd in the wildlife refuge. Drilling for oil on the caribou's calving ground could disrupt the herd and the tribe's way of life.
3. The Gwich'in are not categorically opposed to oil drilling on tribal lands. They have permitted an oil company to drill on their lands in Canada.
4. Many tribes around the United States have turned to allowing drilling for oil and gas, gambling, and even nuclear waste storage on their reservations in an effort to achieve economic independence. The Gwich'in are not alone in trying to use their land to make money.
5. The view of American Indians as stewards of the land may be based more on myth than on fact. Some feel that this view denies natives a place in the modern world.

EXERCISE 37.4 Avoid excessive coordination or subordination.
Eliminate excessive coordination or subordination.

EXAMPLE:

Isadora Duncan may have been one of the most riveting dancers
            her. Therefore,
in the world, but she never allowed anyone to film ~~her, so~~ dance
              ^

historians must rely on still photographs of her dancing, and

these can only offer tantalizing hints of what it must have been

like to see her perform.

1. Isadora Duncan developed modern dance and inspired early-twentieth-century audiences around the world with her riveting performances, and she continues to be an iconic figure.

2. Duncan came from a poor San Francisco family, but everyone in it was apparently convinced of Isadora's genius from her girlhood on, so when she was eighteen, she and her mother traveled east, and she worked briefly in theater before deciding that her talents lay in dance; by the time she was twenty-one, she had achieved some fame in New York and in New England by performing before wealthy and influential people, but after a hotel fire, the Duncans decided to travel to Europe, where Isadora soon achieved a reputation as one of the most exciting and charismatic figures on the stage.

3. Photographs of Duncan's performances indicate that she maintained an expressionless face so that audiences would pay attention to the movement of her hands, arms, legs, and feet, which she usually kept bare, and she did not leap high in the air, as a ballet dancer might, but instead used the floor a great deal, and her costumes were usually scanty and sometimes even shocking, although in general, audiences adored her.

4. Duncan had no love for ballet, which she once described as "living death," yet her arrival in St. Petersburg in 1904 greatly influenced the young Russian ballet choreographer Michel Fokine, and Russian ballet audiences loved Duncan as much as European dance fans had.

5. Many people who know little and care less about modern dance have still heard of Duncan, who lived a flamboyant life,

having many passionate affairs with great and near-great men, in addition to losing her two children in a tragic automobile accident, and her bizarre death remains one of the most noteworthy facts about her since she was strangled when the long scarf she was wearing became entangled in the wheel of the sports car in which she was riding.

37d Perhaps begin a sentence with *and* or *but*.

Sometimes writers choose to start a sentence with *and* or *but*, either for stylistic effect or to make a close connection to a previous, already long sentence:

▶ **You can have wealth concentrated in the hands of a few, or democracy. But you cannot have both.**

—Justice Louis Brandeis

People who consider *and* and *but* conjunctions to be used to join two or more independent clauses within a sentence may frown when they see these words starting a sentence. Nevertheless, examples of this usage can be found in literature from the tenth century onward, and sentences of this type occur in formal and academic writing. As with any stylistic device, it is wise not to use *and* or *but* too often at the beginning of sentences. And, given the difference of opinion on this usage, checking with your instructor may be a good idea, too.

37e Connect paragraphs.

Just as readers appreciate a smooth flow of information from sentence to sentence, they also look for transitions—word bridges—to move them from paragraph to paragraph. A new paragraph signals a shift in topic, but careful readers will look for transitional words and phrases that tell them *how* a new paragraph relates to the paragraph that precedes it. Provide readers with steppingstones; don't ask them to leap over chasms.

KEY POINTS

A Checklist for Connecting Paragraphs

1. Read your draft aloud. When you finish a paragraph, make a note of the point you made in the paragraph. Then, check your notes for the flow of ideas and logic.

2. Refer to the main idea of the previous paragraph as you begin a new paragraph. After a paragraph on retirement, the next paragraph could begin like this, moving from the idea of retirement to saving: *Retirement is not the only reason for saving. Saving also provides a nest egg for the unexpected and the pleasurable.*

3. Use adjectives like *this* and *these* to provide a link. After a paragraph discussing urban planning proposals, the next paragraph might begin like this: *These proposals will help. However, . . .*

4. Use transitions such as *also, too, in addition, however, therefore,* and *as a result* to signal the logical connection between ideas (**5e**).

REVIEW EXERCISE FOR SECTION 37 Make connections.

Revise the following passage to improve connections between ideas. As necessary, improve topic chains; add emphasis; include coordination, subordination, and transitions; eliminate excessive use of coordination and subordination; and connect paragraphs.

The Taliban rulers of Afghanistan fell from power in the fall of 2001. An interim government was formed to rule the war-torn country, and under the Taliban, the law had forbidden women to hold jobs, reveal their faces in public, or speak to men other than their relatives, and the interim government included a department devoted to women's affairs in a sign that times had changed in Afghanistan. Dr. Sima Samar was chosen as the minister for women's affairs. Dr. Samar earned a medical degree from Kabul University. Dr. Samar had spent years working from exile and from within Afghanistan to improve the conditions for women in her native country.

Dr. Samar had practiced medicine in refugee camps in Pakistan. She had helped to set up clinics and schools for women and girls inside Afghanistan, traveling frequently between Pakistan and her homeland. She was breaking Taliban law by giving women access to medical services and education. She believed that her work was worth the risk. "I've always been in danger, but I don't mind," she said in a BBC interview in December 2001.

Dr. Samar did not anticipate problems with any of the men who would work under her as she took her new post in the ministry for women's affairs. She told a reporter for the *New York Times* that she had goals for the ministry, and she expected the men working for her to help achieve the goals, and those goals included making sure that each woman in Afghanistan had "access to education, the right to vote, the right to go to work, to choose her spouse. All those things are the basic rights of human beings." Offering Afghan women even those basic rights after decades of war would be a difficult task for anyone. Dr. Samar did not turn away from the responsibility of ensuring women those rights when she was asked to serve her country through its interim government.

38 The Fourth C: Commit

Readers of academic prose in English usually expect writers to commit to an informed and interesting point of view (not necessarily to the dominant view) and to provide convincing reasons why that view is valid. For writers, commitment means researching and considering an issue, taking a position, and persuasively supporting that position (6a–6g). It means committing to a point of view and using an appropriate tone, so that readers feel they know what the writer's views are and where they come from. Readers want to feel they are in reliable hands.

According to E. B. White, coauthor of *The Elements of Style*, the original author William Strunk Jr. "scorned the vague, the tame, the colorless, the irresolute. He felt it was worse to be irresolute than to be wrong." This section focuses on ways to be bold and resolute.

38a Commit to critical thinking.

Critical thinking does not mean criticizing negatively. It means examining and analyzing information with an open mind. Whether you are writing a business analysis, an essay about literature, a scientific report, or a persuasive argument, committing to critical thinking is a necessary first step.

Develop a system of inquiry. Do not assume that because something is in print, it is accurate. A system of inquiry will lead you to use certain stylistic features in your writing: questions, reflective statements about the position of authors you read, and statements that point out an alternative view (introduced with transitional phrases such as *but, however, on the other hand,* and *this also indicates that . . .*). When you think critically, your writing takes on your own voice, your own stance. It becomes engaged and vital, a reflection of your thinking rather than a regurgitation of others' opinions. Following are suggestions to help you develop a style reflecting critical thinking skills. For more on critical thinking in reading, writing an essay, writing an argument, and writing a research paper, see sections **1, 6,** and **51.**

Write journal entries. When you read or research an issue, keep a journal of your responses to what you read. There, in your own ungraded writing, you can write summaries, make inferences (that is, draw conclusions from what you read), ask questions, challenge views, and reflect on the opinions of others.

Observe details. In your journal entries, e-mails, letters, conversations, and papers, develop your skill in observing and remembering details: the names of characters in a novel, the author of a magazine article, the main points in a lecture, and so on.

Ask questions. In spoken discussion, in the margins of books or articles, or in your journal, ask questions. Interact with ideas. As—or after—you read an article or listen to a lecture, write questions that you would like to see answered about the specific content covered. When confronting new information, ask yourself these questions:

What do I need to know to understand this information fully?

Where does this information come from?

What are the author's purpose and bias?

What evidence does the author provide? Do I find that evidence convincing?

How does this information fit with what I already know?

What else do I need to ask?

Look for assumptions and bias.   Writers often work to establish common ground with their readers (see **6e**). When you read, determine what that common ground is. Ask these questions:

> What audience is the writer writing for?
>
> Is the writer presenting facts or opinions?
>
> What does the writer assume about me, the reader?
>
> Do I feel comfortable with the writer's assumptions?

Understand other viewpoints, and consider alternatives. If you read an argument that you disagree with, do not automatically reject it or write it off as ridiculous. Try to understand why the writer holds the opinion, what the writer's background is, and what audience the writer is writing for. Such reflection can lead to concessive statements (those that yield to, grant, or acknowledge an opposing position) in your writing, such as "The author explains why he holds this view, and he does so convincingly for the small segment of the population he addresses. However, ..." Showing an understanding of alternative views can only strengthen the presentation of your opinions. Readers will know that you have read widely and considered the important issues.

Analyze and evaluate arguments.   Analyze how writers present information. If they classify information, do their categories cover all the material? If they compare and contrast, are their points solid or stretched? If they speculate about cause and effect, do they do a thorough job? Similarly, when you write and revise, consider your own presentation of information, and anticipate and address any objections or questions readers might have. As you evaluate other writers' logic, watch for flaws in your own logic, and construct your arguments with care.

38b   Commit to a point of view.

Your background reading, critical thinking, and drafting will help you discover and decide upon a perspective and thesis that seem correct to you (**3g**). Once you have made those decisions, commit to that point of view in your essay. When you are trying to persuade readers to accept your point of view, avoid the ambivalence and indecisiveness evident in words and phrases like *maybe, perhaps, it could be, it might seem,* and *it would appear.* Aim for language that reflects accountability and commitment: *as a result, consequently, believe, need, must.* Use the language of commitment, however, only after thoroughly researching your topic and satisfying yourself that your evidence is reliable and thorough and its presentation is convincing.

38c Commit to an appropriate tone.

Readers will expect the tone of your document to fit its purpose. The tone of your piece of writing reflects your attitude to your subject matter and is closely connected to your audience's expectations and your purpose in writing. If you were, for example, writing about a topic such as compensation for posttraumatic stress disorder suffered by families of victims of the World Trade Center attack on September 11, 2001, a serious, respectful tone would be appropriate.

For most academic writing, commit to an objective, serious tone, one that does not intrude upon the reader and take attention away from the ideas you are presenting. Avoid sarcasm, colloquial language, name-calling, or pedantic words and structures, even in the name of variety. Make sure you assign a special reading of a draft to the task of examining your tone; if you are reading along and a word or sentence strikes you as being unexpected and out of place, flag it for later. Since tone is really a function of how you anticipate readers' expectations, ask a tutor or friend to read your document and note for you any lapses in consistency of tone.

38d Commit to a confident stance.

Convey to readers an attitude of confidence in your own abilities and judgment. Readers will not be impressed by apologies. One student ended an essay draft this way:

Too
APOLOGETIC
I hope I have conveyed something about our cultural differences. I would like my reader to note that this is just my view, even if a unique one. Room for errors and prejudices should be provided. The lack of a total overview, which would take more time and expertise, should also be taken into account.

If you really have not done an adequate job of making and supporting a point, try to gather more information to improve the draft instead of adding apologetic notes. The student writer revised the ending after reading **5f** on conclusions.

REVISED
VERSION
The stories I have told and the examples I have given come from my own experience, but they illustrate clearly the idea that in one place and at one time,

cultural differences did not have to separate people but could bring them closer together. A diverse, multicultural society holds many potential benefits for all its members.

REVIEW EXERCISE FOR SECTION 38 Commit to a point of view and confident stance.

Underline places where you would advise the writer to consider revising to reflect commitment to critical thinking, a clear point of view, appropriate tone, and a confident stance. Revise any of the sentences that seem too ambivalent or apologetic.

EXAMPLE:

EBay ~~seems to provide~~ *provides* the kind of online community many

people want⊙ ~~of course, this is only one option.~~

1. The end of the dot-com boom drove many online companies out of business, but I believe that eBay, the online auction service, continued to thrive.

2. Although there may not be any concrete evidence to prove this, it could be that online shoppers could still feel that they were getting a bargain when they bid on eBay's merchandise.

3. Tough economic times did not stop me from bidding for items on eBay, but others might have had different experiences.

4. As a way of explaining eBay's popularity, writer Verlyn Klinkenborg argues that it would seem that eBay buyers and sellers love the idea of giving and getting feedback about transactions.

5. EBay's feedback system helps to make the transactions safe, but the real thrill of eBay, at least in some cases such as my own, might perhaps be the feeling shared by buyer and seller that each has gotten the best deal.

39 The Fifth C: Choose Your Words

Word choice, or *diction*, contributes a great deal to the effect your writing has on readers. Do not give readers puzzles to solve.

39a Word choice checklist

KEY POINTS

Word Choice: A Checklist for Revision

1. Underline words whose meaning or spelling you want to check and words that you might want to replace. Then spend some time with a dictionary and a thesaurus. **(39b)**

2. Look for words that might not convey exactly what you mean (*thrifty* vs. *stingy*, for example) or fit your audience's expectations, and look for vague words. **(39c)**

3. Check for the appropriateness of any colloquial, regional, ethnic, or specialized work terms. **(39d)**

4. Check figurative language for appropriateness, think about where a simile (a comparison) might help convey your meaning, and find original substitutes for any clichés. **(39e, 39g)**

5. Check for gender bias in your use of *he* and *she* and other words that show gender. **(39f)**

6. Look for language that might exclude or offend (such as *normal* to mean people similar to you). Build community with readers by eliminating disrespectful or stereotyping terms referring to race, place, age, politics, religion, abilities, or sexual orientation. **(39f)**

39b Use a dictionary and a thesaurus.

A good dictionary contains a wealth of information—spelling and definitions, syllable breaks, pronunciation, grammatical functions and features, word forms, etymology (word origins and historical development), usage, synonyms (words of similar meaning), and antonyms (words of opposite meaning). The following dictionary entry from *The American Heritage Dictionary of the English Language*, 4th edition, shows how much information is available. A "Usage Note" after this entry endorses using "She graduated from Yale in 1998" but notes that "She graduated Yale in 1998" was unacceptable to 77 percent of a usage panel.

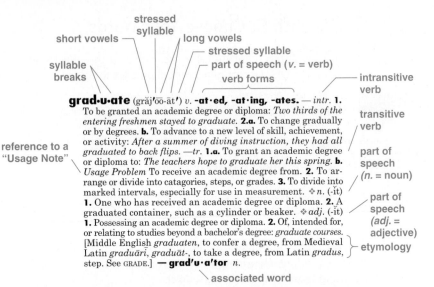

Use a dictionary to learn or confirm the *denotation*—the basic meaning—of a word. Some words that appear similar are not interchangeable. For example, *respectable* has a meaning very different from *respectful; emigrant* and *immigrant* have different meanings; and so do *defuse* and *diffuse, uninterested* and *disinterested,* and *principal* and *principle.* Also see section **33g** on words frequently misspelled.

A thesaurus is useful when you want to find alternatives to words that you know. Exercise caution, however, to make sure that the word you choose fits your context. Suppose you use the word *privacy* a few times and want an alternative in the sentence "She values the privacy of her own home." You could consult a thesaurus. The following entry, from Barbara Ann Kipfer, *Roget's Twenty-first Century Thesaurus,* provides synonyms listed alphabetically:

> **privacy** *n.* aloofness, clandestineness, concealment,
> confidentiality, isolation, one's space, penetralia,
> privateness, quiet, retirement, retreat, seclusion,
> separateness, separation, sequestration, solitude.

The word *aloofness* would not work as a replacement for *privacy* in the example sentence. *Seclusion* would probably be the best choice, but the thesaurus has no way of letting you know that. Using a thesaurus along with a dictionary allows you to find the exact word or words you need. You might, in the end, want to use two words to convey your meaning: "She values the *safety* and *seclusion* of her own home."

Thesaurus programs attached to word processing programs typically offer lists of synonyms but little guidance on *connotation*—the meaning associated with a word beyond its literal definition. While writing a sociology paper based on survey data, one student wanted an alternative to the word *average*, since she had already used it a few times in her paper. She checked *average* in a thesaurus program and found the alternative *mediocre* and then wrote, "The mediocre amount of time spent on the task was 45 minutes"—an inappropriate use of the word *mediocre*. A thesaurus alone is not enough. You also need to check a word in a dictionary that provides examples of usage. *The American Heritage Dictionary*, 4th edition, points out clearly the context for *mediocre*:

> *Mediocre* stresses the undistinguished aspect of what is average: *"The caliber of the students . . . has gone from mediocre to above average"* (Judy Pasternak).

EXERCISE 39.1   Use the dictionary.
Look up one of the following pairs of words in a comprehensive dictionary and in a thesaurus. Write a paragraph about what you learn. Report results to classmates.

uninterested, disinterested	proceed, precede
beside, besides	denote, connote
comprise, compose	carry, convey

39c   Use exact words and connotations.

When you write, use words that convey exactly the meaning you intend at the appropriate level of specificity and that meet readers' expectations of tone and level of formality.

Check for connotation.   Two words that have similar dictionary definitions (*denotation*) can also have additional positive or negative implications and emotional overtones (*connotation*). Readers will not get the impression you intend if you describe a person as *lazy* when you mean *relaxed*. Select words with appropriate connotations. Hurricanes *devastate* neighborhoods; construction workers *demolish* buildings. Writing "Construction workers devastated the building" would be inappropriate. Note how word choice can affect meaning:

VERSION 1   **The crowd consisted of young couples holding their children's hands, students in well-worn clothes, and activist politicians, all voicing support of their cause.**

VERSION 2   **The mob consisted of hard-faced workers dragging children by the hand, students in leather jackets and ragged jeans, and militant politicians, all howling about their cause.**

Make sure words convey specific meaning.   Notice the increasing concreteness and specificity in this list: *tool, cutting instrument, knife, penknife. Tool* is a general term; *penknife* is a specific term. Some words do little more than fill space because they are so abstract, general, and vague. Words such as the following signal the need for revision: *area, aspect, certain, circumstance, factor, kind, manner, nature, situation, thing.*

VAGUE   **Our perceptions of women's roles differ as we enter new *areas*. The girl in Kincaid's story did many *things* that are commonly seen as women's work.**

REVISED   **Our perceptions of women's roles differ as we learn more from what we *see, hear, read, and experience*. The girl in Kincaid's story did many *household chores* that are commonly seen as women's work. *She washed the clothes, cooked, swept the floor, and set the table.***

If you do not move away from the general and abstract, you will give readers too much imaginative leeway. "Her grandmother was shocked by the clothing she bought" leaves a great deal to readers' imaginations. What kind of clothing do you mean: a low-necked dress, high-heeled platform shoes, and black fishnet stockings, or a conservative navy blue wool suit? Choose words that convey exact images and precise information.

Check that your words fit the tone of your document.   Word choice conveys tone (see also **2d** and **38c**) as well as connotation and specificity. Note how the synonyms listed here convey different attitudes and varying degrees of formality:

> *child:* kid, offspring, progeny
>
> *friend:* pal, buddy, chum, mate, brother/sister, comrade
>
> *jail:* slammer, cooler, prison, correctional institution
>
> *angry:* ticked off, furious, mad, fuming, wrathful
>
> *computer expert:* geek, hacker, techie, programmer
>
> *threatening:* spooky, scary, eerie, menacing
>
> *fine:* cool, first-rate, excellent, superior

Some of these words—*kid, pal, slammer, ticked off, geek, spooky, cool*—are so informal that they would rarely if ever be appropriate in formal academic writing or business letters, though they would raise few eyebrows in journalism, advertising, or e-mail. Overuse of formal words—*progeny, comrade, wrathful*—on the other hand, could produce a tone that suggests a stuffy, pedantic attitude (see **39g**).

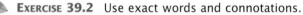

EXERCISE 39.2 Use exact words and connotations.
Write revisions, changing any words that are inexact or that have inappropriate connotations.

EXAMPLE:

American adults today are more likely than their parents were at

the same age to have their own ~~choppers~~. *teeth*

1. Better tooth care and fluoridated water are two of the reasons for falling rates of toothlessness among old people in North America.

2. Nutrition also plays a part in whether people hang on to their own teeth as they age.

3. The rate of toothlessness deviates from state to state, with Hawaii having the lowest rate of toothlessness among the elderly and West Virginia having the highest.

4. Rates of indigence—which can affect nutrition and dental care—and of smoking are probable reasons for these state-by-state variations in toothlessness.

5. Those who are better educated are also more likely to have their own teeth later in life, probably because education influences things like earnings.

39d Monitor the language of speech, region, and workplace.

The language of speech In a formal college essay, avoid colloquial language and slang. Do not enclose a slang expression in quotation marks to signal to readers that you know it is inappropriate. Instead, revise to reach an appropriate level of formality.

► The working conditions were "~~gross.~~"

inhumane.

► The sound of sirens ~~gets to me.~~

affects me powerfully

► The jury returned the verdict that the ~~guy~~ was guilty.

defendant

In formal writing, avoid colloquial words and expressions, such as *folks, guy, OK* or *okay, pretty good, cool, hassle, kind of interesting/nice, too serious of a problem* (*of* here is nonstandard), *a lot of, lots of, a ways away,* and *no-brainer.*

Regional and ethnic language Use regional and ethnic dialects in your writing only when you are quoting someone directly (*"Your car needs fixed," the mechanic muttered.*) or you know that readers will understand why you are using a nonstandard phrase.

► I bought ~~me~~ a camcorder.

myself

► He vowed that he wouldn't pay them ~~no never mind.~~

any attention

► They'~~re~~ here three years already.

have been

► She used to ~~could~~ run two miles, but now she's out of shape.

be able to

The language of the workplace People engaged in most areas of specialized work and study use technical words that outsiders perceive as jargon. A sportswriter writing about baseball will refer to *balks, twi-night double-headers, ERAs, brushbacks,* and *crooked numbers.* A linguist writing about language for an audience of linguists will use terms like *phonemics, sociolinguistics, semantics, kinesics,* and *suprasegmentals.* If you know that your audience is familiar with the technical vocabulary of a field, specialized language is acceptable. Avoid jargon when writing for a more general audience; if you must use technical terms, provide definitions that will make sense to your audience.

WORLDS OF WRITING
Dialect and Dialogue in Formal Writing

Note how Paule Marshall uses Standard English for the narrative thread of her story, while reproducing the father's Barbadian dialect and idioms in the dialogue, thus combining the formal and the informal, the academic and the personal into a rich whole:

> She should have leaped up and pirouetted and joined his happiness. But a strange uneasiness kept her seated with her knees drawn tight against her chest. She asked cautiously, "You mean we're rich?"
>
> "We ain rich but we got land."
>
> "Is it a lot?"
>
> "Two acres almost. I know the piece of ground good. You could throw down I-don-know-what on it and it would grow. And we gon have a house there—just like the white people own. A house to end all house!"
>
> "Are you gonna tell Mother?"
>
> His smile faltered and failed; his eyes closed in a kind of weariness. "How you mean? I got to tell she, nuh."
>
> "Whaddya think she's gonna say?"
>
> "How I could know? Years back I could tell but not any more."
>
> She turned away from the pain darkening his eyes.
>
> —Paule Marshall, *Brown Girl, Brownstones*

EXERCISE 39.3 Monitor word choices.
Revise to eliminate inappropriately colloquial language, regional or community dialect, nonstandard English, or workplace jargon. Some sentences may not need revision.

EXAMPLE:

difficulty
Organic farmers have a ~~rough time~~ protecting their corn crops from
                                    that has been genetically modified
genetic contamination by corn ~~produced through bioengineering~~
            wind and insects carry pollen from one plant
            to other plants that can be miles away.
because corn is open-pollinating.

1. A common agricultural genetic modification introduces *Bacillus thurengensis* into corn plants.

2. These bacteria bump off caterpillars; the bacteria, also called Bt, are sometimes spread on organic corn plants to rid them of corn borers and other destructive insects.

3. Organic farmers have been testing their corn crops for the presence of genetic modifications, and many of these guys are discovering that their crops have been contaminated by genetically modified corn grown up the road.

4. Some farmers are getting stuck with unsold corn, and others are selling it on the open market for less than half the price they would have gotten for a purely organic crop.

5. The problem of cross-pollination of genetically modified corn with organic corn—known as "genetic drift"—troubles many non-farmers as well.

6. A lot of other countries buy organic produce from the United States, and few of them countries allow genetically modified foods to cross their borders.

7. If genetically modified corn can contaminate organic corn naturally, pretty soon there won't be hardly any corn without genetic modifications, and exports of American corn will be greatly reduced.

8. Genetic drift also bugs people who believe that maintaining crops' genetic diversity is important to avoid massive crop failures caused by disease and pests.

9. Most of the dozens of unique corn types found in the world come from Central America.

10. Genetic drift has gotten to lots of the unique corn types in parts of Mexico that scientists have studied, and some folks fear that eventually there will be no untainted corn.

39e **Use figurative language for effect, but use it sparingly.**

Figures of speech can enhance your writing and add to imaginative descriptions, as in the following:

▶ [Tiger] Woods protects three-stroke leads **like a miser protecting the combination to his safe.**

—Clifton Brown, "A Challenge Becomes a Coronation"

Particularly useful are similes, analogies, and metaphors. A *simile* is a comparison in which both sides are stated explicitly and linked by the word *like* or *as*. A *metaphor* is an implied comparison in which the two sides are indirectly compared.

Simile: an explicit comparison with both sides stated

▶ America is *not like a blanket*—one piece of unbroken cloth, the same color, the same texture, the same size. America is more *like a quilt*—many pieces, many colors, many sizes, all woven and held together by a common thread.   —Rev. Jesse Jackson

▶ [Matt Drudge] is *like a kind of digital Robin Hood* among a corrupt and venal press.   —Joshua Quittner

▶ I hate and mistrust pronouns, every one of them *as slippery as a fly-by-night personal-injury lawyer.*   —Stephen King

Metaphor: an implied comparison, without *like* or *as*

▶ A foolish consistency is the hobgoblin of little minds.

—Ralph Waldo Emerson

▶ Some television programs are so much chewing gum for the eyes.   —John Mason Brown

Mixed metaphors   Take care not to mix metaphors.

▶ As she walked onto the tennis court, she was ready to sink or swim. [Swimming on a tennis court?]

▶ He is a snake in the grass with his head in the clouds.

[The two metaphors clash.]

▶ He was a whirlwind of activity, trumpeting defiance whenever anyone crossed swords with any of his ideas.

[The three metaphors—*whirlwind, trumpet, crossed swords*—obscure rather than illuminate.]

Be careful not to overdo figurative language so that it becomes tedious and contrived. For more on figurative language in literature, see **7f**.

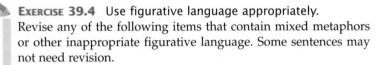

EXERCISE 39.4   Use figurative language appropriately.
Revise any of the following items that contain mixed metaphors or other inappropriate figurative language. Some sentences may not need revision.

EXAMPLE:

Grade inflation may have begun as a ~~salve to~~ students' self-
way to promote
esteem, but some professors believe that it has now become ~~a~~
~~tidal wave.~~ a self-perpetuating force.

1. Dr. Harvey C. Mansfield, a professor at Harvard University, recently argued that college students are too often allowed to coast easily along in the sea of courses and arrive in a harbor protected by unrealistically high grade point averages.

2. According to Mansfield's article in the *Chronicle of Higher Education*, half of the grades given at Harvard today are either *A*'s or *A*-minuses, so some professors, and even students, complain that there is no way to distinguish the cream from the chaff or to tell where students stand in relation to one another.

3. Faculty members who lack tenure are often handicapped in their grading because they know that good student evaluations can help them in the ceaseless competition for scarce teaching appointments.

4. Instructors who do not offer the carrot of *A*'s and *B*'s to students whose work is below par are likely to be bludgeoned with poor evaluations.

5. Mansfield wards off the minefield of grade inflation by keeping two grades for each student, an official inflated one that appears on the transcript and a privately communicated one that tells the student how well his or her work compared with that of other students in the class and with Dr. Mansfield's standards.

39f Avoid biased and exclusionary language.

You cannot avoid writing from perspectives and backgrounds that you know about, but you can avoid divisive terms that reinforce stereotypes or belittle other people. Be sensitive to differences. Consider the feelings of members of the opposite sex, minorities (perhaps more correctly labeled as "world majorities"), and special-interest groups. Do not emphasize differences by separating society into *we* (people like you) and *they* or *these people* (people different from you). Use *we* only to be truly inclusive of yourself and all readers. Be aware, too, of terms that are likely to offend. You don't have to be excessive in your zeal to be PC ("politically correct"), using *underachieve* for *fail*, or *vertically challenged* for *short*, but do your best to avoid alienating readers.

Gender   The writer of the following sentence edited it after a reader alerted him to gender bias in the perception of women's roles.

> Andrea
> ▶ Mrs. John Harrison, ~~married to a real estate tycoon and herself the bubbly, blonde~~ chief executive of a successful computer company, has expanded the business overseas.

Choice of words can reveal gender bias, too.

AVOID	USE
actress	actor
authoress	author
chairman	chair *or* chairperson
female astronaut	astronaut
forefathers	ancestors
foreman	supervisor
mailman	mail carrier
male nurse	nurse

AVOID	USE
man, mankind (meaning any human being)	person, people, our species, human beings, humanity
manmade	synthetic, artificial
policeman, policewoman	police officer
salesman	sales representative, salesclerk
veterans and their wives	veterans and their spouses

When using pronouns, too, avoid the stereotyping that occurs by assigning gender roles to professions.

▶ Before a surgeon can operate, he *or she* must know every detail of the patient's history.

Often it is best to avoid *he or she* by recasting the sentence or using plural nouns and pronouns.

▶ Before operating, a surgeon must know every detail of the patient's history.

▶ Before surgeons can operate, they must know every detail of the patients' history.

At times when the singular form is preferable, consider using *he* in one section of your manuscript and *she* in another, as long as you do not alternate within a paragraph. See **22e** for more on pronouns, gender, and the use of *he or she*.

Race Mention a person's race only when it is relevant. If you write "Attending the meeting were three doctors and an Asian computer programmer," you reveal more about your own stereotypes than you do about the participants in the meeting. In general, use the names that people prefer for their racial or ethnic affiliation. *The Columbia Guide to Standard American English* advises: "It is good manners (and therefore good usage) to call people only by the names they wish to be called." Consider, for example, that currently *African American* or *black* are preferred terms; *Native American* is preferred to *American Indian*; *Asian* is preferred to *Oriental*.

Place Avoid stereotyping people according to where they come from. Some British people may be stiff and formal, but not all are, and they certainly do not all play cricket, drink tea all day, and wear derbies (called "bowler hats" in England). Not all Germans eat sausage and drink beer; not all North Americans carry cameras and wear plaid shorts. Be careful, too, with the way you refer to countries and continents. The Americas include both North and South America, so you need to make the distinction. England, Scotland, Wales, and Northern Ireland make up the United Kingdom. In addition, shifts in world politics and national borders have resulted in the renaming of many countries: *Ceylon* became *Sri Lanka; Rhodesia* is now *Zimbabwe; Czechoslovakia* has been divided into the *Czech Republic* and *Slovakia. The Democratic Republic of the Congo* became *Zaire* in 1971, and then in 1997 the name changed back to *The Democratic Republic of the Congo.* Always consult a current atlas, almanac, or Web site.

Age   Avoid derogatory or condescending terms associated with age. Refer to a person's age or condition neutrally, if at all: not "a well-preserved little old lady" but "a woman in her eighties"; not "an immature sixteen-year-old" but simply "a teenager"; not "a middle-aged spinster" but "an unmarried woman."

Politics   Words referring to politics are full of connotations. Consider the positive and negative connotations of *liberal* and *conservative* in various election campaigns. Take care when you use words like *radical, left-wing, right-wing,* and *moderate.* How do you want readers to interpret them? Are you identifying with one group and implicitly criticizing other groups?

Religion   An old edition of an encyclopedia referred to "devout Catholics" and "fanatical Muslims." The new edition refers to both Catholics and Muslims as "devout," thus eliminating the bias of a sweeping generalization. Examine your use of the following: words that sound derogatory or exclusionary, such as *cult* or *fundamentalist;* expressions, such as *these people,* that emphasize difference; and even the word *we* when it implies that all readers share your beliefs.

Health and abilities   Avoid expressions such as *confined to a wheelchair* and *AIDS victim* so as not to focus on difference and disability. Instead, write *someone who uses a wheelchair* and *person with AIDS,* but only if the context makes it necessary to include the information. Do not unnecessarily draw attention to a disability or an illness. If the CEO of a huge fashion chain has Parkinson's disease, how relevant is that information to your account of the rise of the company in the stock market?

Sexual orientation   Mention a person's sexual orientation only if the information is relevant in context. To write that someone accused of stock market fraud was "defended by a homosexual lawyer" would be to provide gratuitous information. The sexual orientation of the attorney might be more relevant in a case involving discrimination against homosexuals. Since you may not know the sexual orientations of readers, do not assume it is the same as your own.

The word *normal* Be especially careful about using the word *normal* when referring to your own health, ability, or sexual orientation. Some readers might justifiably find that usage offensive.

EXERCISE 39.5 Avoid biased language.
In each of the following sentences, revise any biased or exclusionary language.

EXAMPLE:

~~The radical leftist~~ Aaron McGruder's comic strip offended some readers with its claim that the United States had helped to arm and train Osama bin Laden.

1. Some comic strips, such as *Doonesbury*, written by Garry Trudeau, and *The Boondocks*, created by the African American Aaron McGruder, can be considered political satires.

2. Many normal people have found *Doonesbury* offensive throughout its long history, for Trudeau has depicted premarital sex and drug use, championed women's libbers and peaceniks, and criticized politicians from Richard Nixon to George W. Bush.

3. In the fall of 2001, the main character in McGruder's comic strip argued that the ultra-conservative Reagan administration had aided Osama bin Laden and other fanatical Muslims fighting against the Soviet Union.

4. Many newspapers refused to carry McGruder's comic that day, and one female editor who claimed to be a fan of *The Boondocks* argued that the strip was inappropriate.

5. As newspaper comics have become more modern, comic strips feature single girls and dysfunctional families, but political issues that upset Midwestern readers are apparently still out of bounds.

39g Avoid pretentious language, tired expressions (clichés), and euphemisms.

Be aware that even formal academic writing should be clear. Don't think that a formal college essay has to be filled with big words and long complicated sentences. It certainly does not. In fact, the journal *Philosophy and Literature* sponsors an annual Bad Writing Contest, often "won" by renowned college professors. Convoluted writing is not necessarily a sign of brilliance or of an astonishingly powerful mind. It is usually a sign of bad writing. This passage from an essay on mimicry written by Professor Homi K. Bhabha, an academic now teaching at Harvard University, won second prize in the Bad Writing Contest in 1998:

> If, for a while, the ruse of desire is calculable for the uses of discipline soon the repetition of guilt, justification, pseudo-scientific theories, superstition, spurious authorities and classifications can be seen as the desperate effort to "normalize" formally the disturbance of a discourse of splitting that violates the rational, enlightened claims of its enunciatory modality.

Emily Eakin, a *New York Times* writer, calls this "indecipherable jargon" ("Harvard's Prize Catch, a Delphic Postcolonialist"). It is. Don't emulate it.

Distinguish the formal from the stuffy. Formal does not mean stuffy and pretentious. Writing in a formal situation does not require you to use obscure words and long sentences. Clear, direct expression works well in formal prose. Pretentious language makes reading difficult, as the following example shows.

> When a female of the species ascertains that a male with whom she is acquainted exhibits considerable desire to extend their acquaintance, that female customarily will first engage in protracted discussion with her close confidantes.

Simplify your writing if you find sentences like that in your draft. Here are some words to watch out for:

STUFFY	DIRECT	STUFFY	DIRECT
ascertain	find out	optimal	best
commence	begin	prior to	before
deceased	dead	purchase	buy
endeavor	try	reside	live
finalize	finish	terminate	end
implement	carry out	utilize	use

Avoid clichés. *Clichés* are tired, overly familiar expressions such as *hit the nail on the head, crystal clear, better late than never,* and *easier said than done.* They never contribute anything fresh or original. Avoid or eliminate them as you revise your early drafts.

▶ ~~Last but not least,~~ the article recommends the TeleZapper.
   Finally,

▶ My main ambition in life is not to make a fortune since I

   know that/ ~~as they say, "money is the root of all evil."~~
   having
   ~~Having~~ money does not lead automatically to a good life.

▶ For Baldwin, the problem never ~~reared its ugly head~~ until
   arose

   one dreadful night in New Jersey.

Joseph Epstein quotes a definition of a cliché and comments on the definition in a humorous way by using five clichés himself in his commentary (boldface added):

> In *On Clichés*, a Dutch sociologist named Anton C. Zijderveld defines a cliché thus:
>
> "A cliché is a traditional form of human expression (in words, thoughts, emotions, gestures, acts) which—due to repetitive use in social life—has lost its original, often ingenious heuristic power. Although it thus fails positively to contribute meaning to social interactions and communication, it does function socially, since it manages to stimulate behavior (cognition, emotion, volition, action), while it avoids reflection on meanings."
>
> This is a definition that doesn't, you might say, **throw the baby out with the bathwater**; it **leaves no stone unturned** while offering several **blessings in disguise**, and **in the final analysis** provides **an acid test**. You might say all this, that is, if you have an ear dead to the grossest of clichés.
> —Joseph Epstein, "The Ephemeral Verities," in *The Middle of My Tether*

Avoid euphemisms. *Euphemisms* are expressions that try to conceal a forthright meaning and make the concept seem more delicate, such as *change of life* for *menopause* or *downsized* for *fired.* Because euphemisms often sound evasive or are unclear, avoid them in favor of direct language. Similarly, avoid *doublespeak* (evasive expressions that seek to conceal the truth, such as *incendiary device* for *bomb*). Examples of such language are easy to find in advertising, business, politics, and some reporting. Do not equate formality with these roundabout expressions.

REVIEW EXERCISE FOR SECTION 39 Choose your words.
Revise the following passage as needed to correct inappropriate word choice.

Although Columbus is often cited as the first person to have landed in America, people of Norse descent on voyages from Iceland and Greenland must get the credit, for they came to this continent around the year 1000. Hale and hearty Viking seamen, whose methods of navigation were primitive, were sometimes blown off course as they sailed the North Atlantic, and on one such voyage a Viking named Bjarni Herjulfsson saw land even though he was far from his destination of Greenland. A few years later, Greenlander Leif Eriksson sailed west from his home so that he might ascertain the truth about Bjarni's stories. He found him a rocky island—probably Baffin Island—and named it Helluland, which means "Land of Stone." Leif also stopped at places he called Markland ("Land of Forest"), probably Labrador, and Vinland ("Land of Wine"), a still-unidentified island liberal with grapes. At the closure of his voyage, Leif established a camp in what is now Newfoundland; he collected timber there to take home to Greenland, where trees were scarce.

The Icelandic sagas, written two or three hundred years after these voyages, may not contain the truth, the whole truth, and nothing but the truth of the western explorations of these Vikings, but they yield tantalizing clues. Until 1960, however, there wasn't nobody knew for sure that Leif Eriksson had actually visited North America, let alone set up a camp there. In that year, a Norwegian explorer named Helge Ingstad sailed around the coast of western Canada looking for possible sites of Norse settlements. Ingstad talked to local yokels in Newfoundland, who directed him to L'Anse aux Meadows. For eight years, a noted female archaeologist, Anne Stine, led digs there, and L'Anse aux Meadows is now recognized as the only authenticated Viking site on the North American continent—the settlement founded by Leif Eriksson and used for a few years by other Vikings as a summer timber-gathering and trading site.

ESL

With the speed of travel and the rapid growth of instantaneous communication on the Internet, many parts of everyday life are becoming less insular and more global. Movies, radio, TV, telephones, Web communication, and e-mail allow many people in many parts of the world to be in constant touch with news, with personalities, and with cultures and customs many miles from where they live. Learning to write well often means learning to write for readers of many different linguistic and cultural backgrounds; it may also mean writing in more than one language and in more than one local version of a language. This section focuses on what learners of English need to know about the type of English commonly expected in academic settings in North America and known as *Standard English*.

40 Culture and Language

40a English and Englishes

At the same time as we are becoming more aware of diversity and other countries' languages and cultures, we are also experiencing an increase in the use of English. More than 350 million people speak English as their native language, and many more (estimated at more than a billion) use English as a common language spanning local dialects. They use it for special communicative, educational, and business purposes within their own communities. Given those figures, it is no surprise that English is the language most commonly used over the Internet, as shown in the pie chart on page 637. But it is not the whole story to emphasize the dominance of English in cyberspace. Languages are not fixed and static, and the users of English in their various locations adapt the language for their own uses. The concept of one English or a "standard" language is thus becoming more fluid, more focused on the situation and the readers than on one set of rules. Consequently, the English regarded as standard in North America is not necessarily standard in Australia, the United Kingdom, Hong Kong, Singapore, Indonesia, India, or Pakistan. Scholars see Englishes—varieties of English—in place of a monolithic English with an immutable set of rules. (See, for example, the Worlds of Writing box in **33a** for examples of words that differ in American English and British English.)

Varieties of English spoken in different geographical locations even have their own names: Spanglish (Spanish English), Singlish (Singaporean English), and Taglish (Tagalog English, spoken in the Philippines) are just a few examples of language varieties that have developed among multiethnic populations. In Singapore, for instance, the official languages of the multiethnic residents are Mandarin Chinese, Malay, Tamil, and English. But the English spoken by many has been adapted and appropriated to what some are now calling Singlish, a language meeting local needs. Examples of Singlish given in a *New York Times* article by Seth Mydans are these:

> It a bit the difficult.
>
> Because we a small country, cannot be not organized.
>
> Singlish same for everybody. Everybody speak.
>
> Got coffee or not? Got!
>
> You have milk, is it? Also have.
>
> —"Nations in Asia Give English Their Own Flavorful Quirks"

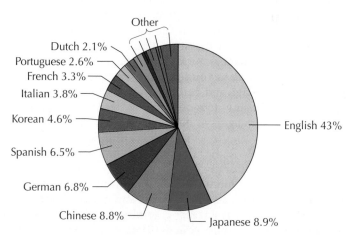

Other
Dutch 2.1%
Portuguese 2.6%
French 3.3%
Italian 3.8%
Korean 4.6%
Spanish 6.5%
German 6.8%
Chinese 8.8%
Japanese 8.9%
English 43%

Languages Used on the Internet (649 million users, March 2003)
Source: Global Reach <http://www.glreach.com/globstats/index.php3>

English is thus being reinvented around the world, sometimes to the dismay of academics and government officials, sometimes with the approval of citizens, who see the adaptation as an act of freedom, even rebellion. Mydans illustrates this when he reports the words of the Filipino poet Gemino Abad: "The English language is now ours. We have colonized it."

While colloquial speech is being adapted and other Englishes, including the English of the Internet, provide colorful global variations, the academic world of writing inevitably retains links to the concept of a standard language. To reach the expectations of the largest number of academic readers, standard vocabulary, syntax, and grammar still prevail. And it is useful for multilingual writers to concentrate on the standard language, which offers conventions and rules that are easier to grasp and apply than the multitude of variations in effect around the world.

40b English and ESL: difference, not deficit

Students in colleges in North America who grew up speaking another language are often called students of English as a Second Language (ESL), and the abbreviation is commonly used in college curricula, professional literature, and the press. However, the term is not really broad enough to include many individuals who grew up speaking languages other than English. Many so-called second-language students speak three or four languages besides English, depending on their lives and educational circumstances and the languages spoken at home. Along with being bilingual or multilingual, ESL students are frequently multicultural, equipped with all the knowledge and experience that those terms imply.

If your first language is not English, you may not be totally fluent yet in English, but as you learn, it is a good idea to see your knowledge of language and culture as an advantage rather than a problem. Unlike many monolingual writers (individuals who know only one language), you are able to know different cultures in an in-depth way and to switch at will among varied linguistic and rhetorical codes. Rather than having only one language, one culture, and one culturally bound type of writing, you have a broader perspective—more to think about, more to write about, more resources to draw on as you write, and far more comparisons to make among languages, writers, writing, and culture. You bring your culture with you into your writing, and as you do so, you help shape and reshape the culture of North America. The questions in the Key Points box will help you examine your unique situation.

Cultural, Rhetorical, and Linguistic Differences

Discuss these questions with members of your family or with friends who share your multicultural background:

1. What three features of your native culture are significantly different from features of North American culture? (These features might relate to customs, holidays, religion, relationships, the structure of family life and responsibility, growing up and adolescence, work and entertainment, or educational practices.) List them.

2. How have these three cultural issues affected you as a student and as a writer?

3. When you read articles, essays, and letters in your first language and in English, do you notice any differences in approach to the topic and in style? How would you characterize those differences?

4. How does your culture view references to classic texts and to the work of others? Does every reference to another writer's ideas have to be documented? Why or why not? (See **50a** for more on Western views of plagiarism.)

5. Write a paragraph in your native language about your experiences as a writer. What considerations occupied you as you wrote (for example, content, organization, grammar, punctuation)? How different are they from the considerations you have when you write in English?

6. List five linguistic features of English that cause you trouble when you write—problem areas in which you may make mistakes in sentence structure or grammar. Decide why you make mistakes in these areas: Are mistakes caused by the influence of your native language? Or do mistakes occur when you construct a hypothesis about English that turns out to be false (for example, "Many nouns form plurals by adding -s; therefore, the plural of *potato* is probably *potatos*"—but it is actually *potatoes*)?

7. For each of the five problem areas you have isolated, write down the corresponding usage in your native language. What does the comparison suggest about why these particular features of English cause you problems?

8. What variety of English did you learn when you first began to learn English? What have you noticed about it that might be different from other varieties of English?

Remember, also, that a good way to practice communicating in English is to join an e-mail discussion list on a topic that interests you. Read the postings and, when you feel confident enough, contribute your own ideas. For more on how to do this, see **11c.**

EXERCISE 40.1 Use ESL Web sites.
Access one of the Web sites recommended in the following TechNote and find two things that are particularly interesting or useful to you. Then go to the *Universal Keys* Web site <http://college .hmco.com/keys.html>, join the discussion list on "ESL Web sites," read some postings, and write a message making your own recommendations about the parts of the sites that interested you.

TECHNOTE Using ESL Web Sites

The Web sites listed here are useful to multilingual students.

ESL Resources, Handouts, and Exercises from Purdue University's Online Writing Lab: <http://owl.english .purdue.edu/handouts/esl/index.html>.

Activities for ESL Students: <http://a4ESL.org>.

This site, run by the *Internet TESL Journal,* offers crossword puzzles and quizzes, including bilingual quizzes in several languages.

Guide to Grammar and Writing: <http://ccc.commnet.edu/ grammar>

This is a Capital Community College site for students whose native language is not English. You will find information and quizzes on words, paragraphs, and essays. In addition, you can send in a question to the site's "Ask Grammar" section and someone will answer it. The Grammar Logs contain questions and answers and cover interesting points. ■

40c Multilingual writers at work

The following three samples are all from the writing of multilingual undergraduate college students in an ESL course or a first-year composition course.

1. Narrative giving an example of cultural difference: rough first draft, written quickly, with revisions

I came to the United States from Japan about three
and a half years ago to learn English and music
business. Five month ago, I interviewed with one of

executives in a record company for an internship, and got a position as a research assistant. On the very first day, I ~~had been~~ felt excited. I knew that something new would happen each day, and I also knew that I would learn a lot about American office customs and culture.

One day, I went to the office and started working on my task; listening to one of the demo tapes and searching for information that I could use for the proposal that my boss asked me to ~~help~~ write. A few hours later, the office manager asked me to come to a conference room. (That was the first time for me to enter the conference room.) *leave this out?* I saw the other workers ~~are~~ going to the same room. When I entered the room, I saw what I could not believe ~~that~~ I was seeing. There were chocolate and mint ice-cream cakes, a bottle of champagne, and some snacks on the middle of the table. A few minutes later, ~~one lady,~~ a woman who ~~is~~ was working in the public relations department, came into the room. Then everybody said together, "Happy Birthday, Grace," and some people set off crackers. It was a surprise birthday party in the middle of the working ~~time~~ day! Everybody, including Ben, a man from UPS, ate the ice cream cakes, some snacks and drank some champagne.

I was surprised too. I had never seen a surprise birthday party and could not ~~think about~~ imagine having ~~it~~ one at the office I used to work in Japan. There the atmosphere and relationship between bosses and subordinates in the office is quite strict and rigid. In Japan, it is hard to break the power relationship and create a family atmosphere ~~like family at offices.~~ in an office.

Mutsumi Nakagami, Japan

2. Passage from final draft of an analysis of an article (Mary Waters's article entitled "Names and Choice of Ancestry")

Here a student writer, Magdalena Wisniewska, uses a personal example to support Waters's contention that intermarriage and misidentification can cause problems with name identification.

To keep my Polish identity after getting married to an American, I kept my maiden name. This sometimes brings some problems to my everyday life when people ask my last name and I have to spell it for them and help them pronounce it. It is worth all the inconvenience, though. Knowing my name, people do not expect me to be a native speaker of English; they are interested in me and my background and experiences. Sometimes, when I hear my name pronounced as "Ms Waysnialska," I have to laugh, but I feel I am adapting to being American yet still being identified as Polish.

My husband has a German name, and having an accent similar to that of Germans, I know I would be regarded as German if I took his name. But I would not want to have a German name if I ever went back to Poland; I would then automatically be associated with Germany, which for some people is still our oppressor. Furthermore, "Shuler" (which in German is close to "student") does not have a positive meaning in Polish. It means "cheater" or "cardsharp." I would probably need to carry a sticky note on my forehead saying "I don't cheat and I don't play cards" in order to be treated seriously.

3. Excerpt from a research paper The following is an excerpt from a research paper with the thesis "Unfortunately, we all still have a long way to go before women can break the glass ceiling in the workplace." The writer, Angela Chan, introduced the topic and the thesis and then provided historical background. She did the editing after a conference with a group of classmates and with her instructor.

Virginia Woolf made a forceful statement to women of today about what it meant to be a woman in earlier times. In *A Room of One's Own,* she invented a supposed sister of Shakespeare, who was as young and talented ~~just like~~ as he was but instead of being offered the same opportunities to succeed, she was denied them because ~~of sex.~~ she was a woman. Her purpose in society was to fulfill three roles: daughter, wife, and mother.

As a respectful daughter, she could not disobey her parents; she had to excel in all arts of family life in preparation for her next role as a wife. If in any case circumstance? way? she refused that new role and "cried out that marriage was hateful to her, for that she was severely beaten by her father" (Woolf 8). As a submissive wife, she was to follow the orders of her husband and accommodate to his wants and desires. Finally, a nurturing mother, as writer Ellen Ross, ~~saw it~~ described, was "the fulcrum of adult women's identity" (201) because married women had no choice except to become mothers. As a A mother, a woman's solely responsibility was to attend to all the cries of her children and bring them up as healthy as the ~~kids~~ children next door. A woman's role in those times was to behave like the "silent, patient

```
root, which seems to have no life of its own and yet is
carrying the tree of mankind" (qtd. in Marx 23).
```

41 Language Learning and Error

41a Learning from errors

Even for learners who have been learning a new language or the conventions of a standard dialect for a while, errors are inevitable. They are not a sign of laziness or stupidity. Welcome and embrace your errors; study them; learn from them. Errors show language learning in progress. If you make no errors while you are learning to speak or write a new language, perhaps you are being too careful and using only what you know to be correct. Be willing to take risks and try new words, new expressions, new combinations. That is the way to expand your repertoire.

Keep a "Language Notebook." Write in it any new words and unusual structures that you find in your reading and your daily interactions. In addition, use a section of the notebook to record errors you make. Write both the sentence containing the error and the correction in the notebook. Consider why you made the error. Was it, for example, transfer from your native language, a guess, a careless mistake, or the employment of a hypothesis about English (such as "many verbs form the past tense with -ed; therefore, the past tense form of *swear* is probably *sweared*"—but it is actually *swore*)? Analyzing the causes of errors will help you understand how to edit them and avoid them in the future.

Readers are most likely to be disturbed by errors when the content and flow of ideas are not clear. A thoughtful, well-written essay that contains a few errors usually is preferable to a sloppy, flimsy piece of work that is grammatically flawless. Errors, however, do distract attentive readers, and you need to learn how to edit for accuracy. Sections **42–46** address some problems faced by language learners as they grapple with academic English. Consult those sections as you need to, along with the ESL Notes and Worlds of Writing boxes appearing throughout this book, which address not just Standard English but cultural variations and differences. Sections **16–24** offer help with common sentence problems faced by many writers, whether they speak one or more than one language.

41b Language guide to transfer errors

Errors in writing in a new language can occur when you are grappling with new subject matter and difficult topics. You concentrate on ideas and clarity, but because no writer can do everything at once, you fail to concentrate on editing.

The language guide here identifies several problem areas for multilingual and ESL writers. It shows grammatical features (column 1) of specific languages (column 2) that lead to an error when transferred to English (column 3), and an edited Standard English version (column 4). Of course, the guide covers neither all linguistic problem areas nor all languages. Rather, it lists a selection, with the aim of being useful and practical. Included in the guide are also references to Caribbean Creole (listed simply as "Creole"), a variety of English with features differing from Standard English. Use the guide to raise your awareness about your own and other languages.

If you think of a feature or a language that should be included in the guide, please write to the author at the publisher's address or send a message to the publisher's Web site at <http://college .hmco.com/keys.html>. This Web site also provides links to sites specifically designed for multilingual students.

LANGUAGE FEATURES	LANGUAGES	SAMPLE TRANSFER ERRORS IN ENGLISH	EDITED VERSION
ARTICLES (42c–42f)			
No articles	Chinese, Japanese, Russian, Swahili, Thai, Urdu	*Sun is hot.* *I bought book.* *Computer has changed our lives.*	*The sun is hot.* *I bought a book.* *The computer has changed our lives.*
No indefinite article with profession	Arabic, Creole, French, Japanese, Korean, Vietnamese	*He is student.* *She lawyer.*	*He is a student.* *She is a lawyer.*
Definite article with days, months, places, idioms	Arabic	*She is in the bed.* *He lives in the Peru.*	*She is in bed.* *He lives in Peru.*
Definite article used for generalization	Farsi, French, German, Greek, Portuguese, Spanish	*The photography is an art.* *The books are more expensive than the disks.*	*Photography is an art.* *Books are more expensive than disks.*
No article for generalization with singular noun	Creole	*Dog can be blind person's eyes.*	*A dog can be a blind person's eyes.*
Definite article used with proper noun	French, German, Portuguese, Spanish	*The Professor Brackert teaches in Frankfurt.*	*Professor Brackert teaches in Frankfurt.*

LANGUAGE FEATURES	LANGUAGES	SAMPLE TRANSFER ERRORS IN ENGLISH	EDITED VERSION
No definite article	Hindi, Turkish	*Store on corner is closed.*	*The store on the corner is closed.*
No indefinite article	Korean (uses *one* for *a*; depends on context)	*He ran into one tree.*	*He ran into a tree.*

VERBS AND VERBALS (43)

LANGUAGE FEATURES	LANGUAGES	SAMPLE TRANSFER ERRORS IN ENGLISH	EDITED VERSION
Be can be omitted.	Arabic, Chinese, Greek, Russian	*India more religious than Britain.* *She working now.* *He cheerful.*	*India is more religious than Britain.* *She is working now.* *He is cheerful.*
No progressive forms	French, German, Greek, Russian	*They still discuss the problem.* *When I walked in, she slept.*	*They are still discussing the problem.* *When I walked in, she was sleeping.*
No tense inflections	Chinese, Creole, Thai, Vietnamese	*He arrive yesterday.* *When I was little, I always walk to school.*	*He arrived yesterday.* *When I was little, I always walked to school.*
No inflections for person and number	Creole, Chinese, Japanese, Korean, Russian, Thai	*The singer have a big band.* *She work hard.*	*The singer has a big band.* *She works hard.*
Past perfect formed with *be*	Arabic	*They were arrived when I called.*	*They had arrived when I called.*
Different tense boundaries from English	Arabic, Chinese, Creole, Farsi, French	*I study here for a year.* *He has left yesterday.*	*I have been studying here for a year.* *He left yesterday.*
Different limits for passive voice	Creole, Japanese, Korean, Russian, Thai, Vietnamese	*They were stolen their luggage.* *My name base on Chinese characters.* *The mess clean up quick.* *A miracle was happened.*	*Their luggage was stolen.* *My name is based on Chinese characters.* *The mess was cleaned up quickly.* *A miracle (has) happened.*

LANGUAGE FEATURES	LANGUAGES	SAMPLE TRANSFER ERRORS IN ENGLISH	EDITED VERSION
No -*ing* (gerund) /infinitive distinction	Arabic, Chinese, Farsi, French, Greek, Portuguese, Spanish, Vietnamese	*She avoids to go.* *I enjoy to play tennis.*	*She avoids going.* *I enjoy playing tennis.*
Infinitive not used to express purpose	Korean	*People exercise for losing weight.*	*People exercise to lose weight.*
Overuse of progressive forms	Hindi, Urdu	*I am wanting to leave now.*	*I want to leave now.*

WORD ORDER AND SENTENCE STRUCTURE (44)

Verb precedes subject	Arabic, Hebrew, Russian, Spanish (optional), Tagalog	*Good grades received every student in the class.*	*Every student in the class received good grades.*
Verb-subject order in dependent clause	French	*I knew what would propose the committee.*	*I knew what the committee would propose.*
Verb after subject and object	Bengali, German (in dependent clause), Hindi, Japanese, Korean, Turkish	*. . . (when) the teacher the money collected.*	*. . . (when) the teacher collected the money.*
Coordination favored over subordination	Arabic	Frequent use of *and* and *so*	
Relative clause or restrictive phrase precedes noun it modifies	Chinese, Japanese, Korean, Russian	*The enrolled in college student . . .* *A nine-meter-high impressive monument . . .* *He gave me a too difficult for me book.*	*The student (who was) enrolled in college . . .* *An impressive monument that is nine meters high . . .* *He gave me a book that was too difficult for me.*

LANGUAGE FEATURES	LANGUAGES	SAMPLE TRANSFER ERRORS IN ENGLISH	EDITED VERSION
Adverb can occur between verb and object or before verb	French, Urdu (before verb)	*I like very much clam chowder.*	*I like clam chowder very much.*
		They efficiently organized the work.	*They organized the work efficiently.*
That clause rather than an infinitive	Arabic, French, Hindi, Russian, Spanish	*I want that you stay.*	*I want you to stay.*
		I want that they try harder.	*I want them to try harder.*
Inversion of subject and verb rare	Chinese	*She is leaving and so I am.*	*She is leaving, and so am I.*
Conjunctions occur in pairs	Chinese, Farsi, Vietnamese	*Although she is rich, but she wears simple clothes.*	*Although she is rich, she wears simple clothes.*
		Even if I had money, I would also not buy that car.	*Even if I had money, I would not buy that car.*
Subject (especially pronoun) can be omitted	Chinese, Italian, Japanese, Spanish, Thai	*Is raining.*	*It is raining.*
Commas set off a dependent clause	German, Russian	*He knows, that we are right.*	*He knows that we are right.*
No equivalent of *there is/ there are*	Japanese, Korean, Portuguese, Russian, Spanish, Thai (adverb of place and *have*)	*This article says four reasons to eat beans.*	*This article says [that] there are four reasons to eat beans.*
		In the garden has many trees.	*There are many trees in the garden.*

NOUNS, PRONOUNS, ADJECTIVES, ADVERBS (42a, 42b, 22, 23)

Personal pronouns restate subject	Arabic, Gujarati, Spanish	*My father he lives in California.*	*My father lives in California.*

LANGUAGE FEATURES	LANGUAGES	SAMPLE TRANSFER ERRORS IN ENGLISH	EDITED VERSION
No human/ nonhuman distinction for relative pronoun (who/which)	Arabic, Farsi, French, Russian, Spanish, Thai	*Here is the student which you met her last week.* *The people which arrived . . .*	*Here is the student [whom] you met last week.* *The people who arrived . . .*
Pronoun object included in relative clause	Arabic, Chinese, Farsi, Hebrew	*The house that I used to live in it is big.*	*The house [that] I used to live in is big.*
No distinction between subject and object forms of pronouns	Chinese, Gujarati, Korean, Spanish, Thai	*I gave the forms to she.*	*I gave the forms to her.* Or *I gave her the forms.*
Nouns and adjectives have same form.	Chinese, Japanese	*She is beauty woman.* *They felt very safety on the train.*	*She is a beautiful woman.* *They felt very safe on the train.*
No distinction between *he* and *she*, *his* and *her*	Bengali, Farsi, Gujarati, Thai	*My sister dropped his purse.*	*My sister dropped her purse.*
No plural form after a number	Creole, Farsi	*He has two dog.*	*He has two dogs.*
No plural (or optional) forms of nouns	Chinese, Japanese, Korean, Thai	*Several good book . . .*	*Several good books . . .*
No relative pronouns	Korean	*The book is on the table is mine.*	*The book that is on the table is mine.*
Different perception of countable/ uncountable	Japanese, Spanish	*I bought three furnitures.*	*I bought three pieces of furniture.* Or *I bought three chairs.*
		He has five chalk.	*He has five sticks of chalk.*
Adjectives show number.	Spanish	*I have helpfuls friends.*	*I have helpful friends.*
Negative before verb	Spanish	*Jack no like meat.*	*Jack does not like meat.*
Double negatives used routinely	Spanish	*They don't know nothing.*	*They don't know anything.* Or *They know nothing.*

EXERCISE 41.1 Identify transfer errors.
From samples of your writing marked by instructors, gather samples of transfer errors that you know you need to be aware of. Use your Language Notebook to keep a list of transfer errors that you make, with an edited version (see p. 643).

41c False friends (confusing cognates)

Turning to what you know as you grapple with writing in English can often be helpful, especially if your native language bears close similarities to English. But while the close linguistic connection may be helpful, you also have to beware of the traps of what are called "false friends," words and structures that seem to translate directly from your native language but in fact do not have the same meaning or connotation at all. Speakers of Spanish and Portuguese report being embarrassed when they tell a doctor they are suffering from constipation, only to realize that they are thinking of the word *constipado*, which in their language means "congestion from a cold." These false friends are numerous in several languages, especially European languages. Some common false friends in several languages are listed in the Worlds of Writing box that follows, but the list is far from complete. Keep your own list in your Language Notebook (p. 643) as you recognize the false friends your language generates.

WORLDS OF WRITING
False Friends

LANGUAGE	MEANING	ENGLISH COGNATE (FALSE FRIEND)	MEANING OF ENGLISH COGNATE
SPANISH			
adecuado	convenient	adequate	sufficient
asistir	attend	assist	help
embarazado	pregnant	embarrassed	self-conscious
formal	reliable	formal	adhering to form
librería	bookstore	library	place storing and lending books
pariente	relative	parent	mother or father
suburbio	slum	suburb	residential area close to a city

(continued)

(continued)

LANGUAGE	MEANING	ENGLISH COGNATE (FALSE FRIEND)	MEANING OF ENGLISH COGNATE
PORTUGUESE			
entender	understand	intend	plan
pretender	intend	pretend	assume falsely
tenente	lieutenant	tenant	occupant, rent payer
usar	wear	use	employ for a purpose
FRENCH			
actuellement	now, currently	actually	really
decevoir	disappoint	deceive	trick
demander	ask, request	demand	insist
large	wide	large	big
phrase	sentence	phrase	part of a sentence
sympathique	nice, friendly	sympathetic	understanding others' feelings
GERMAN			
also	therefore, well	also	too, in addition
bekommen	get, obtain	become	develop to be
GREEK			
agenda	notebook	agenda	plan, program for a meeting
cabaret	bar	cabaret	live entertainment, floor show
idiotic	private	idiotic	stupid
RUSSIAN			
salyut	show of fireworks	salute	gesture of respect
simpatichniy	nice, friendly	sympathetic	understanding others' feelings
JAPANESE			
konsento	electric outlet	consent	agreement, approval

Source of the information: Hunter College ESL students, supplemented by *Learner English* by Michael Swan and Bernard Smith (Cambridge: Cambridge University Press, 1991).

42 Nouns and Articles

42a Categories of nouns

Nouns in English fall into various categories.

Proper or common A *proper noun* names a unique person, place, or thing and begins with a capital letter: *Walt Whitman, Lake Superior, Grand Canyon, Vietnam Veterans Memorial, Tuesday.* A *common noun* names a general class of persons, places, or things and begins with a lowercase letter: *bicycle, furniture, plan, daughter, home, happiness.*

Countable or uncountable common nouns A *countable noun* can have a number before it (*one, two,* and so on) and has a plural form. Countable nouns frequently add *-s* to indicate the plural: *picture, pictures; plan, plans.* Use singular countable nouns after *a, an, the, this, that,* and singular quantity words (**21i**). Use plural countable nouns after *the, these, those,* and plural quantity words (**21i**).

An *uncountable noun* cannot be directly counted. It has no plural form: *furniture, advice, information.* Use uncountable nouns after *the, this, that,* and certain quantity words (**21i** and **42b**).

COMMON NOUNS

COUNTABLE	UNCOUNTABLE
machine, engine (machines, engines)	machinery
tool, hammer (tools, hammers)	equipment
bicycle, ship (bicycles, ships)	transportation
chair, desk (chairs, desks)	furniture
description, fact (descriptions, facts)	information
necklace, earring (necklaces, earrings)	jewelry
view, scene (views, scenes)	scenery
tip, suggestion (tips, suggestions)	advice
exercise, essay (exercises, essays)	homework

42b   Uncountable nouns

Some nouns are invariably uncountable and are listed as such in a language learners' dictionary such as *The American Heritage ESL Dictionary.* Learn the most common uncountable nouns and note the ones that end in *-s* but are nevertheless singular:

> *A mass made up of parts:* clothing, equipment, furniture, garbage, homework, information, jewelry, luggage, machinery, money, scenery, traffic, transportation
>
> *Abstract concepts:* advice, courage, education, fun, happiness, health, honesty, information, knowledge, success
>
> *Natural substances:* air, blood, cotton, hair, heat, ice, rice, sunshine, water, wood, wool
>
> *Diseases:* diabetes, influenza, measles
>
> *Games:* chess, checkers, soccer, tennis
>
> *Subjects of study:* biology, economics, history, physics

Follow these guidelines when using an uncountable noun:

1. Do not use a number, a plural word like *these* and *those,* or a plural quantity word (such as *many* or *several*) before an uncountable noun. An uncountable noun has no plural form.

   > *some*
   > ▶ She gave me ~~several~~ informations.

2. Do not use an uncountable noun with *a* or *an.*

   > ▶ Puerto Rico has ~~a~~ lovely scenery.

   Exceptions to this rule occur when the phrase *a little* or *a great deal of* is used.

   > ▶ He has a great deal of antique furniture.

   > ▶ She has a little modern furniture.

3. Always use a singular verb with an uncountable noun subject.

   > *is*
   > ▶ Their advice ~~are~~ useful.

4. Use the following before an uncountable noun:

   - no article (called the *zero article*) for a generalization: *Information is free.*

   - a singular word such as *this* or *that: This equipment is jammed.*

- a possessive (see **22b**): *His advice was useless.*
- a quantity word or phrase for nonspecific reference (see p. 435 in **21i**): *They gave us some advice. They gave us a little advice.*
- *the* for specific reference (**42d**): *The information we found was all wrong.*

5. Give an uncountable noun a countable sense—that is, indicate a quantity of it—by adding a word or phrase that indicates quantity. The noun itself will always remain singular: three pieces of *furniture,* two items of *information,* many pieces of *advice.*

6. Take into account the fact that the concept of countability varies across languages. Japanese, for example, makes no distinction between countable and uncountable nouns. In French, Spanish, and Chinese, the word for *furniture* is a countable noun; in English, it is not. In Russian, the word for *hair* is countable and is used in the plural.

7. Examine the context. Be aware that some nouns can be countable in one context and uncountable in another.

GENERAL CLASS (UNCOUNTABLE)

He loves *chocolate.* [All chocolate, in whatever form]

Time flies.

We all hang on to *life.*

He has red *hair.*

A COUNTABLE ITEM OR ITEMS

She gave him *a chocolate.* [One piece of candy from a box]

She then gave him *three chocolates.*

They are having *a good time.*

Try it *several times.*

He is leading *a hedonistic life.*

A cat is said to have *nine lives.*

There is a *long gray hair* on her pillow.

SPECIFIC REFERENCE

The chocolate you gave me is delicious. [Specific chocolate]

The time is ripe for action.

The life he is leading is hedonistic.

The hair in his wallet is from his son's first haircut.

KEY POINTS

**What to Use before an Uncountable Noun:
Summary Chart**

<u>YES</u>

Zero article	Furniture is expensive.
This, that	*This* furniture is tacky.
A possessive pronoun: *my, his, their*, and so on	*Their* furniture is modern.
Quantity word: *some, any, much, less, more, most, a little, a great deal (of), all, other*	She has bought *some* new furniture.

<u>NO</u>

A/an	The room needs a̶ new furniture.
Singular quantity word: *each, every, another*	All furniture E̶v̶e̶r̶y̶ furniture should be practical.
These, those	That furniture is T̶h̶o̶s̶e̶ furniture a̶r̶e̶ elegant.
Numerals: *one, two, three*, etc.	two pieces of furniture They bought t̶w̶o̶ f̶u̶r̶n̶i̶t̶u̶r̶e̶s̶.
Plural quantity words: *several, many, a few*	a little furniture She took only a̶ f̶e̶w̶ furniture with her to her new apartment.

EXERCISE 42.1 Use uncountable nouns correctly.

Correct any errors in the use of countable and uncountable nouns. Remember to check for subject-verb agreement when correcting errors.

EXAMPLE:

            paper   pieces   was
Until about 1810, p̶a̶p̶e̶r̶s̶ made from p̶i̶e̶c̶e̶ of cloth w̶e̶r̶e̶ used for printing books.

1. In most cases, the page of books made before 1840 is still flexible and well preserved.

2. Between 1840 and 1950, however, publishers began to use less expensive paper that was made from wood pulps instead of from cloth.

3. To turn wood into paper, manufacturers added acidic chemicals that could break down and soften the wood. The pages created from these paper still contained some of the acid.

4. The pages of many books printed between 1840 and 1950 are beginning to crumble into dusts because acid is eating away the wood fiber in the pages.

5. The Library of Congress, which owns a huge collection of books, has begun to soak books made with acid paper in chemical bath to remove any remaining acid from the pages; books treated in this way can last for another several hundred years.

42c Basic rules for articles

Articles are *a, an,* and *the.*

1. Use *the* whenever a reference to a common noun is specific and unique for both writer and reader (see **42d**).

   ▶ **He loves the museum that Rem Koolhaas designed.**

   [We know that the museum he loves is the specific one that Koolhaas designed.]

2. Do not use *a* or *an* with a plural countable noun.

   ▶ **They cited a̶ reliable surveys.**

3. Do not use *a* or *an* with an uncountable noun.

   ▶ **He gave a̶ helpful advice.**

4. Use *a* before a consonant sound: *a bird, a house, a unicorn.* Use *an* before a vowel sound: *an egg, an ostrich, an hour, an ugly vase.* Take

special care with the sounds associated with the letters *h* and *u*, which can have either a consonant or a vowel sound: *a housing project, an honest man, a unicorn, an uprising.*

5. To make a generalization about a countable noun, do one of the following:

- Use the plural form: *Lions are majestic.*
- Use the singular with *a* or *an*: *A lion is a majestic animal.*
- Use the singular with *the* to denote a classification: *The lion is a majestic animal.*

6. A countable singular noun can never stand alone, so make sure that a countable singular noun is preceded by an article or by a demonstrative pronoun (*this, that*), a number, a singular word expressing quantity, or a possessive.

> A (Every, That, One, Her) nurse
> ▶ ~~Nurse~~ has a difficult job.
>   ^

7. In general, though there are many exceptions, use no article with a singular proper noun (*Mount Everest*), and use *the* with a plural proper noun (*the Himalayas*). See **42f** for more examples.

42d *The* for a specific reference

When you write a common noun that both you and your readers know refers to one or more specific persons, places, things, or concepts, use the article *the.* You can make a specific reference to something outside the text or inside it.

Specific reference outside the text   References to specific people, places, things, or concepts outside the text point to something unique that both the writer and readers will know. In the following sentences, readers will not wonder which earth, sun, moon, door, or dog the writer means.

▶ **I study** *the* **earth, the sun, and the moon.**

[The ones in our solar system]

▶ **She closed** *the* **door.**

[Of the room she was in]

▶ **Her husband took** *the* **dog out for a walk.**

[The dog belonging to the couple, not any other dog]

Specific reference inside the text   A reference to a person, place, thing, or concept can also be made specific by identifying it within the text.

▶ *The* kitten that her daughter brought home had a distinctive black patch above one eye.

[The specific kitten is the one that was brought home.]

▶ Her daughter found *a* kitten. When they were writing a lost-and-found ad that night, they realized that *the* kitten had a distinctive black patch above one eye.

[The second mention is to a specific kitten identified earlier—the one her daughter had found.]

▶ He bought *the most expensive* bicycle in the store.

[A superlative makes a reference to one specific item.]

EXERCISE 42.2   Use articles, including *the*, correctly.
In each of the following sentences, correct any errors in article use.

EXAMPLE:

Many inactive people suffer from ~~the~~ depression.

1. Many scientific studies have proved that exercise helps the people sleep better and lose a weight.

2. A active lifestyle seems to improve not only a person's health but also his or her mood.

3. Endorphins, which are chemicals in human brain that are linked to feelings of well-being, increase when people get the enough exercise.

4. People who do not exercise are twice as likely as active people to suffer a symptoms of depression.

5. However, the scientists are not certain whether people do not exercise because they are depressed or whether they are depressed because they do not exercise.

42e Which article? Four basic questions

Multilingual writers often have difficulty choosing among the articles *a*, *an*, and *the* and the *zero article* (no article at all). Languages vary greatly in their representation of the concepts conveyed by English articles (see **41b**, Language guide to transfer errors).

The Key Points box lists four questions to ask about a noun to decide whether to use an article and, if so, which article to use.

KEY POINTS

Articles at a Glance: Four Basic Questions about a Noun

1. PROPER OR COMMON NOUN?
   ↓
   Singular: no
      article (zero article)
   Plural: *the*

2. SPECIFIC OR NONSPECIFIC REFERENCE?
   ↓
   the

3. UNCOUNTABLE OR COUNTABLE NOUN?
   ↓
   no article OR
   some, much,
   a little, etc.

4. PLURAL OR SINGULAR?
   ↓
   no article OR
   some, many,
   a few, etc.

                        a/an

You can use the questions to decide which article, if any, to use with the noun *poem* as you consider the following sentence:

▶ **Milton wrote** __?__ **moving poem about the blindness that afflicted him before he wrote some of his greatest works.**

1. Is the noun a proper noun or a common noun?

COMMON   **Go to question 2.**

2. Does the common noun refer to a specific person, place, thing, or idea known to both writer and readers as unique, or is the reference nonspecific?

NONSPECIFIC [*Poem* is not identified to readers in the same way that *blindness* is. We know the reference is to the blindness that afflicted Milton before he wrote some of his greatest works. However, there is more than one "moving poem" in literature, and Milton wrote more than one moving poem.]
Go to question 3.

3. Is the noun uncountable or countable?

COUNTABLE [We can say *one poem, two poems.*]
Go to question 4.

4. Is the noun plural or singular?

SINGULAR [The first letter in the noun phrase *moving poem* is *m,* a consonant sound.] **Use *a* as the article.**

Milton wrote *a* moving poem about the blindness that afflicted him before he wrote some of his greatest works.

42f Proper nouns and articles

Singular proper nouns: As a general rule, use with no article.

Names: *Stephen King, General Powell, Goh Chok Tong*

Continents: *South America, Asia, Africa*

Countries (one word): *Italy, Uganda, Greece, Thailand*

Regions, states, cities: *Tora Bora, Provence, Saskatchewan, Ohio, Rome, Cairo*

Mountains, lakes, and islands: *Mount St. Helens, Lake Temagami, Shelter Island*

Public places and local streets: *Golden Gate Park, Grand Army Plaza, Hollywood Boulevard, Avenue of the Americas*

Universities: *Cornell University, Oxford University, American University of Beirut*

Days and months: *Thursday, July*

Religions: *Islam, Catholicism*

There are, however, many exceptions, which you should note in your Language Notebook (p. 643) as you read.

EXCEPTIONS: SINGULAR PROPER NOUNS WITH *THE*

Proper nouns with a common noun and *of* as part of the name: *the University of Texas, the Fourth of July, the Museum of Modern Art, the Statue of Liberty*

Highways: *the New Jersey Turnpike, the Long Island Expressway*

Buildings: *the Eiffel Tower, the Prudential Building, the Sears Tower, the Empire State Building*

Bridges: *the Golden Gate Bridge, the Brooklyn Bridge*

Hotels and museums: *the Hilton Hotel, the Guggenheim Museum, the Louvre, the Palace of Science*

Countries named with a phrase: *the United Kingdom, the Dominican Republic, the People's Republic of China*

Parts of the globe and geographical areas: *the North Pole, the West, the East, the Riviera, the Ruhr*

Seas, oceans, gulfs, rivers, and deserts: *the Mediterranean Sea, the Atlantic Ocean, the Persian Gulf, the Yangtze River, the Mojave Desert*

Historical periods and events: *the Enlightenment, the October Revolution, the Cold War*

Groups: *the Taliban, the Chicago Seven, the IRA, the Mafia*

Titles: *the President of the United States, the Chancellor of the Exchequer, the Emperor of Japan*

Plural proper nouns: Use with *the* Examples are *the United States, the Great Lakes, the Himalayas, the Philippines, the Chinese* (people), the Americans, the Italians.

REVIEW EXERCISE FOR SECTION 42   Use nouns and articles correctly. In the following passage, correct any errors in article use.

Name of Emmanual "Toto" Constant may not be familiar to everyone in United States, but to Haitian immigrants in this country, he is familiar and controversial figure. Constant, the son of an powerful Haitian military leader, was raised as a aristocrat in the impoverished Caribbean nation. In 1991, he formed political party known as FRAPH. Purpose of FRAPH was to fight against return of exiled president Jean-Bertrande Aristide, whom most poor Haitians supported as a their leader. FRAPH men, armed with the machine guns and machetes, roamed country, terrorizing Aristide supporters with torture, rape, and murder. Constant encouraged Haitians to fear him, claiming that he had the voodoo powers. Observers from United Nations said that FRAPH had been "linked to assassinations and rapes," and a American military official in Haiti warned that FRAPH was turning into "a sort of Mafia."

Even after a American peacekeeping force helped Aristide return to power in the 1994, Toto Constant remained the powerful man in Haiti. He apparently cooperated with an American intelligence officers, revealing details about his group's terrorist activities. Somehow, Toto Constant got out of Haiti and migrated to the New York, where he lived in an Haitian immigrant neighborhood. Many of his neighbors recognized a face of Toto Constant.

In 2000, the most Haitian immigrants in New York wanted Toto Constant deported to Haiti. A trials were being held there to determine if he and other FRAPH members were guilty of the murder and torture. Although Constant did not return to Haiti, the Haitian court convicted him of murder and sentenced him to the life imprisonment. However, Constant remained free, and United States Immigration and Naturalization Service did not deport him. In 2001, after terror attacks on New York City, Haitians in a city demanded that the United States stop sheltering man who had terrorized his own people. Perhaps Constant does have the powerful connections to Central Intelligence

Agency, as some Haitian immigrants believe, for United States took no action against him. As 2001 ended, Constant was still the free man.

43 Verbs and Verb Forms

A clause needs a complete verb consisting of one of the five verb forms (**20a**) and any necessary auxiliaries. Some verb forms cannot serve as the complete verb of a clause; an -*ing* form, an infinitive (*to* + base form), and a past participle (ending in -*ed* for a regular verb) can never function as the complete verb of a clause. Because readers get so much information from verbs, they have a relatively low level of tolerance for error, so make sure you edit with care.

43a The *be* auxiliary

Inclusion (see also 20d) The *be* auxiliary must be included in a verb phrase in English, though in languages such as Chinese, Russian, and Arabic it can be omitted.

>   *are*
> ▶ They studying this evening.

>   *been*
> ▶ They have studying since dinner.

Sequence (see also 20d) What comes after a *be* auxiliary? You have two options:

1. The -*ing* form follows a form of *be* in the active voice.

> ▶ He *is sweeping* the floor.

2. The past participle follows a form of *be* in the passive voice.

> ▶ The floor *was swept* yesterday.

43b Modal auxiliary verbs: form and meaning

The modal auxiliary verbs are *will, would, can, could, shall, should, may, might,* and *must.* Note the following three important points.

1. The modals do not change form.
2. The modals never add an -*s* ending.

3. Modals are always followed by a base form without *to: could go, should ask, must arrive, might have* seen, *would be* sleeping.

▶ The committee must ~~to~~ vote tomorrow.

▶ The proposal might improve~~s~~ the city.

▶ The residents could disapprove~~d~~.

See also **20c**.

MEANINGS OF MODAL VERBS		
MEANING	PRESENT AND FUTURE	PAST
1. Intention	*will, shall*	*would*

▶ She *will* explain. ▶ She said that she *would* explain.

Shall is used mostly in questions: *Shall I buy that big green ceramic horse?*

2. Ability	*can (am/is/are able to)*	*could (was/were able to)*

▶ He *can* cook well. [He is able to cook well.]

▶ He *could* not read until he was eight. [He was not able to read until he was eight.]

Do not use *can* and *able to* together.

> am
▶ I ~~cannot~~ able to give you that information.
>   ^

3. Permission	*may, might, can, could*	*could, might*

▶ *May* I open the window? [*Might* or *could* is more tentative.]

▶ She said I *could* leave early.

4. Polite question	*would, could*

▶ *Would* you please pass the carrots?

▶ *Could* you possibly help me?

5. Speculation	*would, could, might*	*would* or *could* or *might* + *have* + past participle

▶ If I had time, I *would* bake a cake.

▶ If I had studied, I *might have* passed the test.

See also **20k**.

MEANINGS OF MODAL VERBS (continued)		
MEANING	PRESENT AND FUTURE	PAST
6. Advisability	*should*	*should* + *have* + past participle

▶ You *should* **go home and rest.**

▶ You *should have* **taken your medication.** [Implied here is "but you did not."]

7. Necessity (stronger than *should*)	*must* (or *have to*)	*had to* + base form

▶ He *must* **apply for a loan.** ▶ She *had* **to leave.**

8. Prohibition	*must* + *not*	

▶ You *must not* **leave until we tell you to.**

9. Expectation	*should*	*should* + *have* + past participle

▶ You *should* **receive the check soon.**

▶ You *should have* **received the check a week ago.**

10. Possibility	*may, might*	*might* + *have* + past participle

▶ They *might* **be at home now.**

▶ She *might have* **gone to the movies.**

11. Logical assumption	*must*	*must* + *have* + past participle

▶ She's late; she *must* **be stuck in traffic.**

▶ She *must have* **taken the wrong route.**

12. Repeated past action		*would* (or *used to*) + base form

▶ When I was a child, I *would* **spend hours drawing.**

EXERCISE 43.1 Use the *be* auxiliary and modal auxiliary verbs correctly.

Correct any errors in the use of the *be* auxiliary and modal auxiliaries.

EXAMPLE:

                      are   should
Young people who learning to play an instrument ~~would~~
practice if they want to improve.

Most people believe that musicians must to have talent in order to succeed. However, a 1998 study by British psychologist John Sloboda may indicates that the number of hours spent practicing affects musical ability more than inborn talent does. The study included musicians aged ten to sixteen years, from both public and private schools. Sloboda investigated how much each young musician practiced, whether parents and teachers involved in helping each musician improve, and how well each student scored on the British national music examination. Young musicians who had practicing most frequently were most successful on the exam; students whose parents and teachers working closely with them also received high scores. After looking at the exam results, Sloboda cannot help noticing that the students with the highest scores practiced eight hundred times more than the students with the lowest scores. Sloboda believes that individual differences in musical ability would be related to the amount students practice and the amount of support they get from teachers and parents. According to Sloboda's research, even people who do not believe they have musical talent became excellent musicians if they practiced hard enough.

43c The infinitive form after verbs and adjectives

Some verbs are followed by an infinitive (*to* + base form or base form alone). Some predicate adjectives also occur with an infinitive. Such combinations are highly idiomatic. You need to learn each one individually as you find it in your reading.

Verb + infinitive

           V   ⌐ Inf ⌐
▶ His father *wanted to rule* the family.

These verbs are commonly followed by an infinitive (*to* + base form):

agree	choose	fail	offer	refuse
ask	claim	hope	plan	venture
beg	decide	manage	pretend	want
bother	expect	need	promise	wish

Note any differences between English and your native language. For example, the Spanish word for *refuse* is followed by the equivalent of an *-ing* form.

▶ He refused ~~criticizing~~ the system.
             to criticize

Position of a negative In a verb + infinitive pattern, the position of the negative affects meaning. Note the difference in meaning that the position of a negative (*not, never*) can create.

▶ He did *not* decide to buy a new car. His wife did.

▶ He decided *not* to buy a new car. His wife was disappointed.

Verb + noun or pronoun + infinitive Some verbs are followed by a noun or pronoun and then an infinitive. See also **22a** for a pronoun used before an infinitive.

           V   pron. ┌ inf ┐
▶ The librarian *advised them to use* a better database.

Verbs that follow this pattern are *advise, allow, ask, cause, command, convince, encourage, expect, force, help, need, order, persuade, remind, require, tell, urge, want, warn.*

    Spanish and Russian use a *that* clause after verbs like *want.* In English, however, *want* is followed by an infinitive.

                 to
▶ Rose wanted ~~that~~ her son ~~would~~ become a doctor.

Make, let, and have After these verbs, use a noun or pronoun and a base form of the verb (without *to*).

▶ He *made his son practice* for an hour.

▶ They *let us leave* early.

▶ She *had her daughter wash* the car.

But note the past participle form of the verb in the corresponding passive voice structure.

▶ She usually *has the car washed* once a month.

Adjective + infinitive Some predicate adjectives are followed by an infinitive. The filler subject *it* often occurs with this structure.

infinitive

▶ **It is dangerous to hike alone in the woods.**

ADJECTIVES FOLLOWED BY INFINITIVE

anxious	(in)advisable	sorry
dangerous	likely	(un)fair
eager	lucky	(un)just
essential	powerless	(un)kind
foolish	proud	(un)necessary
happy	right	wrong
(im)possible	silly	

For the adjectives *easy, difficult,* and *hard,* see **46f.**

43d Verbs followed by an -*ing* verb form used as a noun

▶ **I *can't help laughing* at Jon Stewart's *Daily Show.***

The -*ing* form of a verb used as a noun is known as a *gerund*. The verbs that are systematically followed by an -*ing* form make up a relatively short and learnable list.

admit	discuss	practice
appreciate	dislike	recall
avoid	enjoy	resist
be worth	finish	risk
can't help	imagine	suggest
consider	keep	tolerate
delay	miss	
deny	postpone	

inviting

▶ **We considered ~~to invite~~ his parents.**
            ^

hearing

▶ **Most people dislike ~~to hear~~ cell phones at concerts.**
                    ^

Note that a negative comes between the verb and the -*ing* form:

▶ **During their vacation, they enjoy *not* getting up early every day.**

43e Verbs followed by either an infinitive or an *-ing* verb form

Some verbs can be followed by either an infinitive or an *-ing* verb form (a gerund) with almost no discernible difference in meaning: *begin, continue, hate, like, love, start.*

▶ **She loves** *cooking.*   ▶ **She loves** *to cook.*

The infinitive and the *-ing* form of a few verbs, however (*forget, remember, try, stop*), signal different meanings:

▶ **He remembered** *to mail* **the letter.** [An intention]

▶ **He remembered** *mailing* **the letter.** [A past act]

43f *-ing* and *-ed* verb forms used as adjectives

Both the present participle (*-ing* verb form) and the past participle (ending in *-ed* in regular verbs) can function as adjectives (see **20a** and **20h**). Each form has a different meaning: the *-ing* adjective indicates that the word modified produces an effect; the past participle adjective indicates that the word modified has an effect produced on it.

▶ **The** *boring* **cook served baked beans yet again.**

[The cook produces boredom. Everyone is tired of baked beans.]

▶ **The** *bored* **cook yawned as she scrambled eggs.**

[The cook felt the emotion of boredom as she did the cooking, but the eggs could still be appreciated.]

PRODUCES AN EFFECT	HAS AN EFFECT PRODUCED ON IT
amazing	amazed
amusing	amused
annoying	annoyed
boring	bored
confusing	confused
depressing	depressed
disappointing	disappointed
embarrassing	embarrassed
exciting	excited
interesting	interested
satisfying	satisfied

shocking	shocked
surprising	surprised
worrying	worried

Note: Do not drop the *-ed* ending from a past participle. Sometimes in speech it blends with a following *t* or *d* sound, but in writing the *-ed* ending must be included.

► I was surprise~d~ to see her wild outfit.

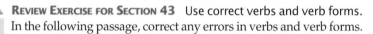
► The researchers were ~~worry~~ worried that the results were contaminated.

See also **20h**.

REVIEW EXERCISE FOR SECTION 43 Use correct verbs and verb forms. In the following passage, correct any errors in verbs and verb forms.

Can money makes people happy? A well-known proverb says, "Money can't buy happiness," but some people probably would to agree that money is important for a happy life. A survey by Andrew Oswald and Jonathan Gardner of the University of Warwick in England has investigating the connection between money and happiness for eight years. The results are not surprised. If people suddenly get money that they not expecting—from the lottery, for example—they generally feel more satisfying with their lives.

In general, according to the study, receiving about $75,000 must mean the difference between being fairly happy and being very happy. However, people who admitted to be miserable before they had money needed to get $1.5 million before they considered themselves happy. But Oswald and Gardner advise to recognize that the study is not finished. They not admit knowing whether the happiness from receiving unexpected money lasts for a long time.

People who do not expect getting a large amount of money can find other reasons not to despair. The researchers say that money is not the most important factor in whether a person is happy or not. People who married are happier than those who are not: the researchers estimate that a lasting marriage makes the partners as happy as an extra $100,000 a year can. Perhaps looking for love is as important as trying to make—or win—a large amount of money.

44 Word Order and Sentence Structure

Languages structure the information in sentences in many ways. For more on sentence structure, see **16c** and **19**.

44a Inclusion of a subject

In some languages, a subject can be omitted. In English, you must include a subject in every clause, even just a filler subject such as *there* or *it*.

there
▶ The director's business partners lost money, and were immediate effects on the share prices.

it
▶ He went bankrupt because was too easy to borrow money.

Do not use *it* to point to a long subject that follows.

▶ We can say that it does not matter the historical period of

the society.

44b Order of sentence elements

Expressions of time and place   Put adverbs and adverb phrases of time and place at the beginning or end of a clause, not between the verb and its direct object.

▶ The quiz show host congratulated |many times| |the winner.|

Descriptive adjective phrases   Put a descriptive adjective phrase after, not before, the noun it modifies.

▶ I would go to |known only to me| |places.|

Order of subject, verb, object   Languages differ in the order of appearance of the subject (S), verb (V), and direct object (DO) in a sentence. In English, the most commonly occurring sentence pattern is S + V + DO ("Children like candy"). See also **16c**.

Every   received good grades
▶ ~~Good grades received every~~ student in the class.

44c   Direct and indirect objects

Some verbs—such as *give, send, show, tell, teach, find, sell, ask, offer, pay, pass,* and *hand*—can be followed by both a direct object and an indirect object. The indirect object is the person or thing to whom or to which, or for whom or for which, something is done. It follows the verb and precedes the direct object (**16c**).

          ┌── IO ──┐ ┌── DO ──┐
▶ He gave his mother some flowers.

        IO ┌── DO ──┐
▶ He gave her some flowers.

An indirect object can be replaced with a prepositional phrase that *follows* the direct object.

          ┌── DO ──┐ prepositional phrase
▶ He gave some flowers to his mother.

Some verbs—such as *explain, describe, say, mention,* and *open*—are never followed by an indirect object. However, they can be followed by a direct object and a prepositional phrase with *to* or *for*.

                              to me
▶ She explained ~~me~~ the election process.

                        to us
▶ He described ~~us~~ the menu.

Note that *tell,* but not *say,* can take an indirect object.

        told
▶ She ~~said~~ him the secret.

EXERCISE 44.1 Correct errors in inclusion of a subject, order of elements, direct and indirect objects.

Correct any errors in the inclusion of a subject, in the order of elements, and in the use of direct and indirect objects. Some sentences may be correct.

EXAMPLE:

In the United States, more people are having ~~every year~~ plastic
                      every year   *there*
surgery even though are sometimes side effects from
        ^   ^

the surgery.

1. Cosmetic surgery had in the past a stigma, but now many people consider changing their appearance surgically.

2. In addition, the price of such surgery was once high, but it has declined in recent years.

3. In 2000, 7.4 million people had for one reason or another cosmetic surgery.

4. Were 370,000 African Americans among those 7.4 million patients, and African Americans represent a growing percentage of wanting plastic surgery people.

5. Cosmetic surgery gives to some people an improved self-image.

6. However, can be drawbacks to changing one's appearance.

7. Psychologists are concerned that some African American women reject their African features because they accept the most commonly seen in magazines standards of beauty.

8. Such women might say, for example, that it is a universal standard of beauty a narrow nose.

9. Some middle-class African Americans may also consider plastic surgery when they see that certain African American celebrities have changed their features.

10. Many psychologists say a patient considering cosmetic surgery that beauty comes from inside.

44d Direct and indirect (reported) quotations and questions

In a direct quotation or direct question, the exact words used by the speaker are enclosed in quotation marks. In a reported quotation or indirect question, the writer reports what the speaker said, and quotation marks are not used. Changes also occur in pronouns, time expressions, and verb tenses (**20j**).

▶ He said, "I have lost my notebook." *— direct quotation —*

▶ He said that he had lost his notebook. *— indirect quotation —*

▶ He asked, "Have you seen it?" *— direct question —*

▶ He asked if we had seen it. *— indirect question —*

Direct and indirect quotations Usually you must make several changes when you rewrite a direct quotation as an indirect quotation. You will do this often when you write college papers and report the views of others. Avoid shifts from direct to indirect quotations (**19d**).

TYPE OF QUOTATION	EXAMPLE
1. *Direct quotation* with quotation marks and present tense	The young couple said, "The price *is* too high."
Indirect quotation: no quotation marks; tense change (**20j**)	The young couple said that the price *was* too high.
2. *Direct quotation* with first person pronoun and present tense	He insisted, "I *understand* the figures."
Indirect quotation: change to third person pronoun; tense change (**20j**)	He insisted that *he understood* the figures.

3. *Direct quotation* of a command

"Cancel the payment," her husband said.

   Indirect quotation: verb + *to*

Her husband *said* [told her] *to* cancel the payment.

4. *Direct quotation* with expressions of time and place

The bankers said, "*We will* work on *this* deal *tomorrow.*"

   Indirect quotation: expressions of time and place not related to speaker's perspective; tense change **(20j)**; change to third person pronoun

The bankers said *they would* work on *that* deal *the next day.*

5. *Direct quotation* of spoken words and phrases

The clients said, "Well, no thanks; *we won't* wait."

   Indirect quotation: spoken words and phrases omitted *or* rephrased; tense change **(20j)**

The clients thanked the bankers but said *they would not* wait.

Direct and indirect questions When a direct question is reported indirectly, it loses the word order of a question and also loses the question mark. Sometimes changes in tense are necessary (see also **20j**).

DIRECT QUESTION
The buyer asked, "*Are* the goods ready to be shipped?"

INDIRECT QUESTION
The buyer asked if the goods *were* ready to be shipped.

DIRECT QUESTION
The boss asked, "What *are* they doing?"

INDIRECT QUESTION
The boss asked what they *were* doing.

DIRECT QUESTION
"Why *did* they *send* a letter instead of a fax?" her secretary asked.

INDIRECT QUESTION
Her secretary asked why they [*had*] *sent* a letter instead of a fax.

Use only a question word such as *why* or the words *if* or *whether* to introduce an indirect question. Do not use *that* as well.

▶ Her secretary asked ~~that~~ why they sent a letter instead of a fax.

DIRECT AND INDIRECT QUESTIONS

	INTRODUCTORY WORD	AUXILIARY VERB	SUBJECT	AUXILIARY VERB(S)	MAIN VERB AND REST OF CLAUSE
DIRECT	What	are	they		thinking?
INDIRECT Nobody knows	what		they	are	thinking.
DIRECT	Where	does	he		work?
INDIRECT I can't remember	where		he		works.
DIRECT	Why	did	she		write that poem?
INDIRECT The critic does not reveal	why		she		wrote that poem.
DIRECT		Have	the diaries	been	published yet?
INDIRECT The Web site does not say	if (whether)		the diaries	have been	published yet.
DIRECT		Did	the space program		succeed?
INDIRECT It is not clear	if		the space program		succeeded.

EXERCISE 44.2 Rewrite direct speech as reported speech.
Write the following sentences as indirect (reported) speech, making any necessary changes. In each case, use the given tag followed by *that, if,* or a question word.

EXAMPLE

"The soup is too spicy." (She complained)

She complained that the soup was too spicy.

1. "I cannot abide such pretentious prose." (The critic announced)
2. "Who is in charge?" (The mayor wanted to know)
3. "What is the square root of 2209?" (The contestant cannot work out)
4. "The economy will rebound." (The broker predicted)
5. "Will I lose all my savings?" (Investors constantly wonder)
6. "I understand the problems." (The candidate assured everyone)
7. "Who knows the answer?" (The game-show host asked)
8. "We will leave early tomorrow." (The guests hinted)
9. "Did my sweater shrink in the wash?" (Her son asked)
10. "We are going to a new French restaurant this evening." (The committee members said)

44e Dependent clauses with *although* and *because*

In some languages, a subordinating conjunction (such as *although* or *because*) can be used along with a coordinating conjunction (*but, so*) or a transitional expression (*however, therefore*) in the same sentence. In English, only one is used.

No	*Although* he loved his father, *but* he did not have much opportunity to spend time with him.
Possible Revisions	*Although* he loved his father, he did not have much opportunity to spend time with him.
	He loved his father, *but* he did not have much opportunity to spend time with him.

No	*Because* she had been trained in the church, *therefore* she was sensitive to the idea of audience.
Possible Revisions	*Because* she had been trained in the church, she was sensitive to the idea of audience.
	She had been trained in the church, *so* she was sensitive to the idea of audience.
	She had been trained in the church; *therefore*, she was sensitive to the idea of audience.

See **26e** for the punctuation of transitional expressions.

44f Unnecessary pronouns

Do not restate the simple subject of a sentence as a pronoun. See also **19i**.

▶ Visitors to the Statue of Liberty ~~they~~ have worn the steps down.

▶ The adviser who told me about dyslexia ~~he~~ is a man I will never forget.

In a relative clause introduced by *whom, which,* or *that,* do not include a pronoun that the relative pronoun has replaced. See also **24f**.

▶ The house that I lived in ~~it~~ for ten years has been sold.

REVIEW EXERCISE FOR SECTION 44   Use correct word order and sentence structure.
Correct any errors in word order or sentence structure.

Many people fear in China and Japan the number *four.* Is a good reason for this fear: in Japanese, Mandarin, and Cantonese, the word for *four* and the word for *death* are nearly identical. A study in the *British Medical Journal* suggests that cardiac patients from Chinese and Japanese backgrounds they may literally die of fear of the number four. According to the study, which looked at U.S. mortality statistics over a twenty-five-year period, Chinese and Japanese hospitalized for heart disease patients were more likely to die on the fourth day of the month. Although Chinese and Japanese cardiac patients across the country were all statistically more likely to die on that day, but the effect was strongest among Californian Chinese and Japanese patients. Is not clear why Californians are more at risk. However, one researcher suggested that because California's large Asian population includes many older people, the older generation may therefore teach to younger generations traditional beliefs.

Chinese and Japanese patients with other diseases they were no more likely to die on the fourth of the month than at any other time. White patients, whether they had heart disease or any other illness, they were no more likely to die on the supposedly unlucky thirteenth of the month than on any other day. Psychiatrist Jiang Wei of Duke University Medical School said, "She still didn't know the biological reason for the statistical effect" on Chinese and Japanese cardiac patients. David P. Phillips, the sociologist who conducted the study, said that the only explanation that makes sense is that the number four causes extra stress in Chinese and Japanese heart patients. More research may someday prove whether or not the stress on the fourth of the month it can be enough to kill.

45 Prepositions and Idiomatic Expressions

Prepositions appear in phrases with nouns and pronouns, and they also combine with adjectives and verbs in various ways. Learn the idioms one by one, as you come across them.

45a Idioms with three common prepositions

Learn the idiomatic uses of prepositions by writing them down in lists in your Language Notebook (see p. 643) when you come across them in your reading. Here is a start:

<u>IN</u>

in July	in Ohio
in 1999	in Milwaukee
in the morning	in the Bahamas
in the afternoon	in the cookie jar
in the evening	in the library stacks
in the drawer	singing in the rain
in the closet	in the United States

IN

in his pocket

in bed

in school

in class

in Spanish

in time (to participate
  in an activity)

in love

the letter in the
  envelope

ON

on the menu

on the library shelf

on Saturday

on 9 September 1999

on Union Street

on page 25

on the weekend

on the roof

a ring on her finger

an article on
  education

on the moon

on earth

on occasion

on time (punctual)

on foot

on the couch

knock on the door

the address on the
  envelope

AT

at 8 o'clock

at home

at a party

at night

at work

at the post office

EXERCISE 45.1 Use prepositions in their proper contexts.
In the following passage, fill in each blank space with the appropriate preposition, choosing among *in, on,* and *at.*

EXAMPLE:

People should save for retirement, but many workers resist
putting money ____*in*____ the bank for their future.

Everyone hopes to retire _____ some time _____ the

future. However, many people fail to invest for retirement, spend-

ing most of the money they earn _____ everyday expenses and

luxuries. The field of behavioral economics tries to explain why

people do not always make rational plans to save for the future.

Behavioral economists also work to find ways to convince people to save money and to get _____ a schedule that will allow them to retire. Although most people are reluctant to decrease the amount of money that is _____ their take-home pay, employers can often persuade workers to promise _____ advance to increase the percentage of the paycheck that they contribute to a retirement account. Many employees get an annual raise _____ work, and the increased contribution can take effect _____ the same time as the raise. In this way, people are likely to feel that they are _____ their way to a comfortable financial future without being forced to make ends meet _____ a smaller paycheck. Some people apparently need to play tricks _____ themselves to make sure that they make wise decisions.

45b Adjective + preposition

When you are writing, use a dictionary to check the specific prepositions used with an adjective.

▶ He is *afraid of* spiders.

▶ She was *interested in* bees.

Some common idiomatic adjective + preposition combinations are the following. Make your own lists to add to these.

ABOUT

anxious about	worried about
excited about	

OF

afraid of	guilty of
ashamed of	jealous of
aware of	proud of
capable of	suspicious of
fond of	tired of
full of	

<u>IN</u>

interested in

<u>TO/FOR</u>

grateful to (someone) for (something)

responsible to (someone) for (something)

<u>WITH</u>

content with

familiar with

patient with

satisfied with

45c Verb + preposition

Learn the following common idiomatic verb + preposition combinations.

apologize to (someone) for (an offense or error)

arrive in (a country or city); *arrive at* (a building or an event)

blame (someone) *for* (an offense or error)

complain about

concentrate on

congratulate (someone) *on* (success or good fortune)

consist of

depend on

explain (facts) *to* (someone)

insist on

laugh at

rely on

smile at

take care of

thank (someone) *for* (a gift or favor)

throw (an object) *at* (someone not expecting it)

throw (an object) *to* (someone waiting to catch it)

worry about

In your Language Notebook, keep a list of others you notice, and learn them.

EXERCISE 45.2 Use adjective + preposition, verb + preposition. In each of the following sentences, correct any errors in the choice of prepositions.

EXAMPLE:

about
Many Americans have been worried ~~from~~ the possibility of

of
biological terrorism, but some doctors are more afraid ~~from~~

the naturally caused influenza than any biological agent.

1. Although some Americans wanted to take antibiotics as a precaution against anthrax in the fall of 2001, the percentage of people who asked their doctors of flu shots at that time was no higher than normal.

2. Influenza has been responsible to the deaths of many healthy people in the past century, and doctors do not know when a dangerous strain of flu may appear.

3. Doctors in 1918 were unable to prevent the flu epidemic to killing millions of people around the world; more people died of the flu than as a result of World War I that year.

4. Many people may not be aware to the dangers of influenza.

5. Medical specialists are studying genetic samples from people who died with influenza in 1918 to try to find ways to prevent such a deadly flu from reoccurring.

45d Phrasal verbs

Prepositions and a few adverbs (such as *away* and *forward*) can combine with verbs in such a way that they no longer function as prepositions or ordinary adverbs. They are then known as *particles*. Only a few languages other than English—Dutch, German, and Swedish, for example—have this verb + particle (preposition or adverb) combination, which is called a *phrasal verb*. Examples of English phrasal verbs are *put off* and *put up with*.

The meaning of a phrasal verb is entirely different from the meaning of the verb alone. Note the idiomatic meanings of some common phrasal verbs.

break down [stop functioning]	run across [meet unexpectedly]
get over [recover from]	run out [become used up]
look into [examine]	take after [resemble]

Always check the meanings of such verbs in a specialized dictionary such as *The American Heritage English as a Second Language Dictionary*.

A particle can be followed by a preposition to make a three-word combination:

▶ She *gets along with* everybody.

[She is friendly toward everybody.]

Other three-word verb combinations are

catch up with [draw level with]	look forward to [anticipate]
look down on [despise]	put up with [endure]
look up to [admire]	stand up for [defend]

Position of direct objects with two-word phrasal verbs Some two-word transitive phrasal verbs are separable. The direct object of these verbs can come between the verb and the accompanying particle.

▶ She *put off* her dinner party.

[She postponed her dinner party.]

▶ She *put* her dinner party *off*.

When the direct object is a pronoun, however, always place the pronoun between the verb and the particle.

▶ She *put* it *off*.

Some commonly used phrasal verbs that follow that principle are listed here. They can be separated by a noun as a direct object; they must be separated when the direct object is a pronoun.

call off [cancel]	give up [surrender]	make up [invent]
fill out [complete]	leave out [omit]	turn down [reject]
find out [discover]	look up [locate]	turn off [stop]

Most dictionaries list phrasal verbs that are associated with a particular verb, along with their meanings and examples. Develop your own list of such verbs from your reading.

45e Preposition + *-ing* verb form used as a noun

The *-ing* verb form that functions as a noun (the *gerund*) frequently occurs after a preposition.

▶ They congratulated him *on winning* the prize.

▶ Sue expressed interest *in participating* in the fundraiser.

▶ He ran three miles *without stopping*.

▶ The cheese is the right consistency *for spreading*.

Note: Take care not to confuse *to* as a preposition with *to* used in an infinitive. When *to* is a preposition, it is followed by a noun, a pronoun, a noun phrase, or an *-ing* form, not by the base form of a verb.

⌐ infinitive ¬
▶ They want *to adopt* a child.

preposition + *-ing* form (gerund)
▶ They are looking forward *to adopting* a child.

Check which to use by testing a noun replacement:

▶ They are looking forward to parenthood.

Note also *be devoted to, be/get used to* (see **45f**).

45f The difference between *get used to* and *used to*

For multilingual writers of English, the distinction between *used to* + base form and *be/get used to* + *-ing* (gerund) is difficult.

▶ He *used to work* long hours. [He did in the past but doesn't anymore. The infinitive form follows *used* in this sense.]

▶ Air traffic controllers *are used to dealing* with emergencies.
  [They are accustomed to it. The *-ing* form follows *be/get used to*.]

EXERCISE 45.3 Use phrasal verbs, preposition + *-ing*, *get used to*, and *used to* correctly.
Correct any errors in the use of phrasal verbs, gerunds after prepositions, and the phrases *get used to* and *used to*.

EXAMPLE:

     used to be
AIDS ~~is used to being~~ a death sentence, but more people now
survive for years with the disease.

    Since scientists began to learn about AIDS more than twenty
years ago, many people have been counting up a cure for the disease. The cure has not yet been found, but today many people
with AIDS in this country used to live with the medications and
other treatments that allow them to having a reasonably healthy
life. In poorer countries, unfortunately, fewer people can look forward on living with AIDS, but AIDS researchers are excited about
a recent discovery in the central African country of Rwanda. In
Kigali, Rwanda's capital, a study has been following a group of
sixteen people who tested positive for HIV at least twelve years
ago but have neither taken medicine to treating the illness nor gotten sick. In most AIDS patients, the virus breaks out the immune
system; in many patients in the Rwandan study, however, the
virus shows an unusual mutation that seems to allow the body to
put the virus up with. Researchers do not yet know whether this
discovery will assist them in find a cure for the AIDS virus, but
every new piece of information in this puzzle may be helpful in
fight the disease.

REVIEW EXERCISE FOR SECTION 45 Use prepositions and
idiomatic expressions correctly.
Correct any errors in idiomatic structures with prepositions and
adverbs.

    How important is an American's cultural identity?
According to Walter Benn Michaels, the author of *Our America,*
people at the United States have been preoccupied of belonging

to a particular ethnic or racial group since the 1920s. In that time, some U.S. residents thought that too many immigrants were arriving to the country, and Congress strictly limited immigration in 1924. But other Americans during that decade wanted to find up more about their ancestors' culture and preserve their traditions; they were not happy at the idea that immigrants might change their customs at a new country. Although the Americans who were afraid about immigrants changing the country and the Americans who were interested in preserve different cultures did not agree with the issue of identity, both sides shared an interest on the subject.

More than seventy-five years later, the question on identity still concerns people in the United States, no matter what their political views are. Dr. Michaels argues that an emphasis on culture and diversity ends out putting people on groups according to their ancestry. Either people feel that Americans belong to a group based of their ethnic or racial background, or they feel that Americans all share the country's past and should all take pride of its accomplishments. At his book, Dr. Michaels asks, "Why should any past count as ours?" Although Americans—and people around the world—used to thinking of themselves as members of particular groups, Dr. Michaels argues that identity should not matter. He believes that Americans should take pride in to have their own accomplishments and stop worrying on the groups to which they belong.

46 Frequently Asked ESL Editing Questions

46a When do I use *no* and *not*?

Not is an adverb that negates a verb, an adjective, or another adverb. *No* is an adjective and therefore modifies a noun.

▶ She is *not* wealthy.   ▶ She is *not* really poor.

▶ The author does *not* intend to deceive the reader.

▶ The author has *no* intention of deceiving the reader.

46b What is the difference between *too* and *very*?

Both *too* and *very* intensify an adjective or adverb, but they are not interchangeable. *Too* indicates excess. *Very* indicates degree, meaning "extremely."

▶ It was *very* hot.

▶ It was *too* hot to sit outside. [*Too* occurs frequently in the pattern *too* + adjective or adverb + *to* + base form of verb.]

▶ The Volvo was *very* expensive, but he bought it anyway.

▶ The Volvo was *too* expensive, so he bought a Ford instead.

46c Does *few* mean the same as *a few*?

A few is the equivalent of *some*. *Few* is the equivalent of *hardly any*; it has more negative connotations than *a few*. Both expressions are used with countable plural nouns. Although *a* is not generally used with plural nouns, the expression *a few* is an exception.

some
▶ She feels fortunate because she has *a few* helpful colleagues.

hardly any
▶ She feels depressed because she has *few* helpful colleagues.

You might prefer to use only the more common *a few* and use *hardly any* in sentences in which the context demands *few*. Similar expressions used with uncountable nouns are *little* and *a little*.

⌐some⌐
► She has *a little* time to spend on work-related projects.

hardly any
► She has *little* time to spend on recreation.

EXERCISE 46.1 Use *no* and *not*, *too* and *very*, *few* and *a few* correctly.
Correct any errors in the use of *no* and *not*, *too* and *very*, or *few* and *a few*.

EXAMPLE:

not
A wildfire in a wilderness area is ~~no~~ necessarily a disaster.
        ^

1. Natural disasters such as fires, floods, and storms are usually seen as terrible events, but sometimes they have few positive results.

2. For example, a forest with many tall trees may be very dark for new plant growth, but fires can change the situation to allow sunlight to reach the ground.

3. A river that has no flooded for many years collects silt, which often means that a few fish can spawn.

4. Few human attempts to control disasters have been successful, and trying to ensure that not fire or flood can occur often means that fires and floods are more damaging when they do happen.

5. Although many ecologists have found it too difficult to stop trying to prevent natural disasters, they are now working instead to keep disasters from being too devastating.

46d How do I know when to use *been* or *being*?

In speech, these words often sound similar. In writing, it is absolutely necessary to distinguish them. See also **20d**, page 400.

Been   *Been* is the past participle of the verb *be.* Use it after auxiliaries *has, have,* and *had.* Follow *been* with an *-ing* form for the active voice and with the past participle form for the passive voice.

▶ It has *been* snowing. [Active]

▶ They have *been* indicted. [Passive]

Being   *Being* is the present participle *-ing* form of the verb *be.* Use it after a *be* auxiliary: *am, is, are, was, were.* In the active voice, *being* is followed by an adjective or a noun phrase.

▶ He is *being* pretentious. He is also *being* a bore. [Active]

In the passive voice, *being* is followed by a past participle.

▶ They are *being* watched. [Passive]

46e   How do I distinguish *most, most of,* and *the most?*

Most expresses a generalization, meaning "nearly all."

▶ *Most* Americans like ice cream.

When a word such as *the, this, these, that,* or *those* or a possessive pronoun (such as *my, their*) precedes the noun to make it specific, *most of* is used. The meaning is "nearly all of."

▶ I did *most of* this needlework.

▶ *Most of* his colleagues work long hours.

The most is used to compare more than two people or items.

▶ Bill is *the most* efficient of all the technicians.

46f   What structures are used with *easy, hard,* and *difficult?*

The adjectives *easy, hard,* and *difficult* cause problems for speakers of Japanese and Chinese. All of the following patterns are acceptable in English.

▶ It is *easy* for me to change a fuse.

▶ It is *easy* to change a fuse.

▶ To change a fuse is *easy* for me.

▶ To change a fuse is *easy.*

▶ Changing a fuse is *easy* for me.

▶ Changing a fuse is *easy.*

▶ I find it *easy* to change a fuse.

However, a sentence like the following needs to be edited in English into one of the patterns just listed or as shown here:

> think it is
▶ I ~~am~~ *easy* to change a fuse.
>   ^

46g How do I use *it* and *there* to begin a sentence?

Use *there* to indicate that something exists (or existed) or happens (or happened). See also **36b.**

> There
▶ ~~It~~ was a royal wedding in my country two years ago.

> There
▶ ~~It~~ is a tree on the corner of my block.

Use *it* for weather, distance, time, and surroundings.

▶ It is a long way to Tipperary.

▶ It is hot.

Use *it* also in expressions such as *it is important, it is necessary,* and *it is obvious,* emphasizing the details that come next. See also **36b.**

▶ It is essential for all of you to sign your application forms.

It or *there* cannot be omitted as a filler subject.

>   it
▶ As you can see, is dark out already.
>   ^

46h Which possessive pronoun do I use: *his* or *her*?

In some languages, the form of the pronoun used to indicate possession changes according to the gender of the noun that follows it, not according to the pronoun's antecedent. In French, for instance, *son* and *sa* mean, respectively, "his" and "her," the form being determined by the noun the pronoun modifies.

▶ **Marie et sa mère**   [Marie and her mother]

▶ **Pierre et sa mère**   [Pierre and his mother]

▶ **Pierre et son père**   [Pierre and his father]

In English, however, the gender of a possessive (*his*, *her*, or *its*) is always determined by the antecedent.

▶ **I met Marie and her mother.**   ▶ **I met Pierre and his mother.**

REVIEW EXERCISE FOR SECTION 46   Correct errors.
In the following passage, correct any errors.

In the 1970s, market researchers discovered that the most young children were unable to tell the difference between the television shows they watched and advertisements for products. Because of this discovery, it was an attempt in 1978 to put legal restrictions on television advertisements aimed at too young children, but advertisers objected. The industry of marketing to children has being growing steadily since then. Between 1978 and 1998, the amount of money directly spent by children age four to twelve increased from less than three billion dollars a year to almost twenty-five billion dollars, and is not end in sight. Researchers believe that children in that age group also convince their families to spend another two hundred billion dollars a year—such as when a young boy, for example, convinces her mother to purchase a more expensive computer than she might otherwise have bought. Marketers are easy to decide to target this young market—there is their job to aim at consumers who can be convinced and who will spend most money.

However, few other groups have also helped marketers figure out the best way to target a too young audience. Many child psychologists are now been asked to join market-research firms to provide information about how to reach children more effectively. Some members of the American Psychological Association lobbied their organization in 2002 to discipline APA members who have helped advertisers target children, but the APA has no taken action yet. The most psychologists feel that the marketers and their advisers have being allowed very much freedom to appeal to children who cannot make informed decisions about products, but the situation does no seem likely to change.

Finding, Using, Documenting Sources

You think you might have West Nile virus or Lyme disease, and you try to find out what the symptoms are and the best way to treat them. That's research. You want to buy a digital camera, but you are not sure about the features, brands, and prices. You order catalogs, talk to salespeople, go to stores, try out cameras, ask friends what they recommend, read consumer magazines, and roam the Web. That's research. You have a bet with a friend that tea contains as much caffeine as coffee, so you go to an encyclopedia or to Ask Jeeves! and find out you are wrong. That's research, too. When you do research, you begin by identifying a need to find information.

When an instructor in one of your courses assigns a research paper, you engage in similar activities, but in a more systematic and formal way. You find out what the issues are, focus on one important issue, formulate a research question about that issue, and then attempt to find an answer or answers to that question, considering the opinions of experts who have studied the question. The answer then becomes the thesis (claim or main idea) of your research paper (see **3g** and **47g**).

Research—finding information for a purpose—is the basis of what is called "information literacy." Here is the Association of College and Research Libraries' description of what that literacy entails, from <http://www.ala.org/acrl/ilintro.html>. This Web site also contains useful information on standards, performance indicators, and outcomes for "information literate students."

Information literacy forms the basis for lifelong learning. It is common to all disciplines, to all learning environments, and to all levels of education. It enables learners to master content and extend their investigations, become more self-directed, and assume greater control over their own learning. An information literate individual is able to

- determine the extent of information needed
- access the needed information effectively and efficiently
- evaluate information and its sources critically
- incorporate selected information into one's knowledge base
- use information effectively to accomplish a specific purpose
- understand the economic, legal, and social issues surrounding the use of information, and access and use information ethically and legally

Part VIII
Using Sources to Write a Research Paper

RESEARCH

Note: Exercises for Part VIII appear on the *Universal Keys* Web site at <college.hmco.com/keys.html>.

47 Planning

47a The requirements of the task

For a college research assignment, find out what the demands of the assignment are:

- length
- due date
- purpose
- audience
- information to be included
- recommended approaches
- number and types of sources
- documentation style
- manuscript format and document design
- presentation: paper versus screen

If you are relatively new to research paper writing, let your instructor know; ask for advice and for sample papers from previous semesters. For advice on writing research papers in the various disciplines, turn to **51e.** You can also turn to sample papers and excerpts included throughout this book to see how other students have tackled their assignments:

Papers in English courses (humanities)—MLA style: **6k, 7j, 52f**

Papers in sociology and psychology courses (social sciences)—
 APA style: **8d, 53f**

Papers in history, art history, and linguistics (humanities)—
 Chicago style: **8b, 55f**

Papers in biology and computer science (sciences)—CBE/CSE
 style: **8c, 54f**

47b The organization of the task

Research brings a heavy load, in more than one way. You will collect and carry around books, papers, notes, and drafts. If there is ever a time in your life when you need to be organized, this is it. If

KEY POINTS

Overview of the Research Process

1. Start early and plan. Allot time to tasks. Fill out the schedule in **47c**, copy it, and put it right next to a copy of the assignment in a place where you can look at it every day.

2. Don't be afraid to ask questions of your instructor or librarians. No questions are "silly questions" if you need to know the answer to proceed. All instructors and librarians expect students to feel somewhat bewildered by the size and scope of the task. They know how to help and are glad to help.

3. Gather the tools that you will need: disks, ink for your printer, a pack of paper, a notebook, index cards, highlighting pens, folders, paperclips, money or a prepaid card for the library photocopier, a stapler, and self-stick notes.

4. Do the following to get started, though not necessarily in this order (see the sections listed for more details):

   - Make sure you understand the requirements (**47a**).
   - Plan which sources to begin with: primary or secondary (**47d**).
   - Select or narrow a topic (**3f, 47f**).
   - Compose a purpose statement (**47e**), a research question, and a tentative working thesis (**47f**).

5. Find and evaluate sources (**48, 49**), make notes (**50e**), and prepare a working bibliography (**50f**).

6. Plan your paper and write an outline (**3i**) and a draft (**51d**).

7. Evaluate the draft and get feedback (**4c, 4d**).

8. Revise your draft for ideas and organization—as many times as necessary (**51d**).

9. Prepare a list of works cited (**52c, 53c, 54c, 55d,** or **56c**).

10. Edit, proofread, and design the format of your paper (**4i, 16–24, 10g**).

you work mostly on paper, buy several folders of different colors and label them for each part of your research. Keep your research for, say, an English course separate from your notes for a chemistry course. Make a schedule (see **47c**) and look at it every day to make sure you are on track. In addition, make a list of what to do next.

A research notebook Researchers find a research notebook handy, either a paper version or a handheld computer notebook. When an idea occurs to you or you see or hear something relevant to your topic, you can jot down notes. Keep a dated research log so that you keep track of what you find, where, and when. Keep your pencil and notebook next to your bed, too, for those night-time flashes of insight. Make sure that both on paper and in your computer documents you indicate clearly which words and ideas come from what you find in your source materials and which words and ideas are your own. See **50** for more on the importance of avoiding plagiarism.

Computer files Use your computer not just for writing but for organizing your work.

 TECHNOTE How to Organize Computer Files

1. In the Save As window, click on Create New Folder and name it "Research Project."

2. Save in that folder all the files you create pertaining to research: notes on sources, freewriting and brainstorming, ideas for a topic and research question, thesis possibilities, outline, numbered drafts, working bibliography, works-cited list, and so on.

3. If a folder gets unwieldy, move some files into new folders and rename the first, so that you have a system such as "My Drafts," "Notes from Sources," and "Works Cited." ■

47c Making a tentative schedule

Get started as early as you can. As soon as a project is assigned, set a tentative schedule, working backwards from the date the paper is due and splitting your time so that you know when you absolutely must move on to the next step. On the next page is a sample time block schedule that you can use and adapt. You will find in reality that several tasks overlap and the divisions are not neat. If you finish a block before the deadline, move on and give yourself more time for the later blocks.

The amount of time suggested in the sample schedule assumes that your instructor gives the assignment five weeks before the paper is due. You will need to recalculate the time allotted to each block of activities if more or less time is available. This schedule is also available online at <http://college.hmco.com/keys.html> for you to print or save.

RESEARCH SCHEDULE

Starting date:
Date final draft is due:

Block 1: Getting started
Understand the requirements.
Select a topic or narrow a given topic.
Determine the preliminary types of sources to use.
Do preliminary research to discover the important issues.
Organize research findings in computer files.
Write a purpose statement.

1 week. Complete by _____

Block 2: Reading, researching, and evaluating sources
Find and copy print and online sources.
Annotate and evaluate the sources.
Write summaries and paraphrases and make notes.
Set up a working bibliography.

1 week. Complete by _____

Block 3: Planning and drafting
Formulate a working thesis.
Write a proposal and/or a scratch outline.
Write a first draft.

1 week. Complete by _____

Block 4: Evaluating the draft and getting feedback
Put the draft away for a day or two—but continue collecting useful sources.
Outline the draft and evaluate its logic and completeness.
Plan more research as necessary to fill any gaps.
Get feedback from instructor and classmates.

1 week. Complete by _____

Block 5: Revising, preparing list of works cited, editing, presenting
Revise the draft.
Prepare a list of works cited.
Design the format of the paper.
Edit.
Proofread the final draft.

1 week. Complete by _____
(final deadline for handing in)

47d Basic, primary, and secondary sources

Even at the very beginning of the research process, consider the types of sources you are likely to use as you work on your project. See **48** for more on finding specific print and online sources.

Basic sources to get you started Tools such as encyclopedias and general or specialized reference works can help you choose or focus a topic. Because they provide an overview of the issues involved in a complex topic and some may also provide extensive bibliographies of other useful sources, these encyclopedias can also help you develop your research and formulate a research proposal if you are asked to provide one.

Caution: Use encyclopedias only as a way to start investigating your subject, but do not rely on them for most of your project.

Here are some basic tools for initial explorations. Some, such as the first one listed, are available to everyone online. Others may be available free online only though your local library, your college library system, or your Internet service provider.

ENCYCLOPEDIAS TO GET YOU STARTED

General	*Columbia Encyclopedia* <http://www.bartleby.com> *Encyclopaedia Britannica*
Art	*Encyclopedia of World Art*
Biology	*Encyclopedia of the Biological Sciences*
Business	*International Encyclopedia of Business and Management*
Chemistry	*Encyclopaedia of Chemistry*
Communications	*International Encyclopedia of Communications*
Computer science	*Encyclopedia of Computer Science* *McGraw-Hill Circuit Encyclopedia*
Economics	*Encyclopedia of American Economic History*
Education	*Encyclopedia of Educational Research*
Engineering	*McGraw-Hill Encyclopedia of Engineering*
English literature	*Oxford Companion to English Literature*

Environmental science	*Encyclopedia of the Environment*
Ethnic studies	*Gale Encyclopedia of Multicultural America*
Film	*International Encyclopedia of Film*
Geography	*Encyclopedia of World Geography*
Geology	*Encyclopedia of Earth System Science*
History	*Encyclopedia of American History*
Linguistics	*Cambridge Encyclopedia of Language*
Mathematics	*CRC Concise Encyclopedia of Mathematics*
Music	*New Grove Dictionary of Music and Musicians*
Nursing	*Encyclopedia of Nursing Research*
Philosophy	*Encyclopedia of Philosophy*
Physics	*Encyclopedia of Physics*
Political science	*International Handbook of Political Science*
Psychology	*Encyclopedia of Psychology*
Religion	*Encyclopedia of Religion*
Sciences	*McGraw-Hill Encyclopedia of Science and Technology*
Sociology	*Encyclopedia of Sociology*
Women's studies	*Women's Studies Encyclopedia*

Primary sources Primary sources are the firsthand, raw, or original materials that researchers study and analyze:

historical documents	works of literature
journals and letters	live performances
memoirs	your own case study
autobiographies	your own scientific experiment
government documents	interviews you conduct
speeches	questionnaires you devise
news reports	
works of art	

The use of such primary sources can lend an original note to your research and bring readers new information.

Conducting interviews Interview people who have expert knowledge of your topic, perhaps faculty members, public officials, or business people. You need to plan ahead so that your interview takes place when you already feel at ease with your topic and know a lot about it. The purpose of the interview should be to reinforce points you have in mind and to add specific details to the evidence you can provide. Interviews add to library research; they do not replace it.

Once you have a firm idea of where your research is headed, you can plan a good set of interview questions. However, try to make the interview like a conversation. Avoid marching through your questions one by one, as if working from a checklist. And do not stick so closely to your script that you fail to follow up on good leads in your respondent's replies.

Observe interview etiquette. Call ahead of time to schedule the interview. If you want to use a tape recorder (doing so is a good idea because then you will not have to try to scribble down every word), ask permission first, and check the functioning of your tape recorder beforehand. Make note of the date, time, and place of the interview, be punctual, and send the person you interview a thank-you note afterwards. It is also courteous to send a copy of your write-up of the interview for the interviewee to peruse and approve.

Administering questionnaires Designing useful questionnaires is tricky, since much depends on the number and sample of respondents you use, the types of questions you ask, and the methods you employ to analyze the data. Embark on questionnaire research only if you have been introduced to the necessary techniques in a college course or have consulted experts in this area.

Secondary sources Secondary sources are analytical works that comment on and interpret other works, such as primary sources. Examples include the following:

- reviews
- interpretive works
- biographies
- critical studies
- accounts of interviews
- analyses of literary or artistic works or live performances
- commentaries on current and historical events
- class lectures and discussions
- electronic discussions

47e Statement of purpose

To focus your ideas and give yourself something to work with, write a simple statement of purpose after you have done some preliminary research (see **2a** and **3i**). This statement may become more developed or even later change completely, but it will serve to guide your first steps in the process. Here is an example (see the paper in **52f**):

> The purpose of this documented paper is to persuade general adult readers that historical films—such as Amadeus—should give precedence to a good story over historical accuracy because readers expect entertainment rather than education when they go to the movies.

As you progress with your research, you can develop your simple statement into a proposal and then an outline (**3i, 51c**).

47f From topic to research question to working thesis

At the planning stage, you may not move far beyond establishing a topic and forming a research question. For this, you will turn to sources (see especially **48b** and **48c** for sources to use to select and narrow a topic). Move toward a research question and a working thesis as soon as you can, so that then your search for sources is guided and productive. The secret is to be flexible. If a topic, a question, or a working thesis appears to be not producing good results, be prepared to find a new topic, question, or working thesis. That is why it is essential to start work early.

Searching for a good topic Try these tools and techniques to help yourself find a good topic—usually a more productive approach than staring at the ceiling hoping for a good idea.

- Look through your college textbooks in various fields for issues worth exploring.
- Consult general and specialized encyclopedias (see **47d** for a list). These sources sketch out the important issues and provide bibliographies for further reading.
- Browse the Web and subject directories (see the TechNote that follows) by searching for the keywords that interest you. You may find material that illuminates new issues or new sides of an issue.
- Use the *Library of Congress Subject Headings* (LCSH—in the Reference section of your library) to get ideas for topics and

the books available on those topics and to learn the terminology used to search catalogs and databases. For instance, in a search for information on "doping in sports," the LCSH would provide the search term "anabolic steroids" and many narrower related terms. See more on LCSH in **48e**.

- Talk, listen, and write. Talk to classmates and your instructors about possible topics. Listen to people around you: what topics engage their interest? Above all, carry your research notebook with you and jot down any good ideas and leads.

TechNote How to Find Topics on the Web

1. Log on to the *Librarians' Index to the Internet* <http://lii.org> or, for general-interest topics, commercial search directories such as Yahoo! <http://www.yahoo.com>, AltaVista <http://www.altavista.com>, or Google <http://www.google.com>. See **48f**.

2. Find a subject area that interests you, such as Education, Literature, Health, Sports, Politics, Business, or Science. A click on a specific subject area will produce lists of many different topics within that category.

3. Keep clicking on a topic until you narrow the search to one that interests you and is appropriate for your assignment.

Keep the search for a topic in mind as you go about your daily life. Think to yourself, "What would I like to know more about? What am I curious about?" Reading a magazine, watching TV, and thinking about the things that really matter to you—all these simple everyday activities can generate ideas for research. Carry a notebook and pencil or computer notebook with you so that you can jot down every idea that seems promising.

Selecting a topic   Select your own topic with two criteria in mind:

1. Does the topic interest you? Your topic should engage and sustain not only readers' interests but your own. Readers recognize a bored writer who is simply going through the motions.

2. Is the topic appropriate (for example, in terms of the assignment, length, materials available)? Check with your instructor.

Narrowing a topic   You may need to narrow a topic so that it is manageable for the number of pages you intend to write. Narrow by limiting place, time, or issues you will address.

TOO BROAD	NARROWED
Parkinson's disease	Current treatments for Parkinson's disease
Pollution	Remedies for PCBs in U.S. rivers
Genetic engineering	The hazards of genetically altered foodstuffs
Computers	Health issues of computers
Popular music	The appeal of hip-hop to the young

To find a narrow enough topic, you may have to do background reading to discover the important issues. Even if you begin with what you think is a clear response to your topic, make sure you explore any historical background or complexity that you may have overlooked. Spend time looking at what others have said about the issues before you settle on a direction for your research.

If your instructor assigns a topic, make sure you understand the terms used in the assignment, such as *analyze, interpret,* and *argue* (see **9b** for definitions). You may also have to narrow a subject area your instructor assigns to a manageable topic for a short paper.

Moving from topic to question Being assigned a topic or finding an interesting topic and narrowing it gets you on your way, but it is just a beginning. For example, one student, Claudia Esteban, decided to write on automobile safety. She then needed to decide what aspect of this topic to investigate. Here is her brainstorming list on the topic of automobile safety:

```
Child seats
Air bags
Seat belts
SUVs
Restrictions on drinking
Punishments for driving while intoxicated
Speeding
Using a cell phone while driving
```

Esteban then did some preliminary reading and research to find out which areas offered useful material. From the narrowed list of topics she framed two possible research questions and concentrated on discovering what material was available in these two areas:

```
What effects would increasing the speed limit on
   highways to 75 mph have?
What measures would make SUVs less dangerous on the
   roads?
```

Designing a research question For a full-scale research paper, design a research question that gets at the heart of what you want to discover. Your question should contain concrete keywords that you can search (see **48d**) and not rely heavily on general terms or abstractions. The answer you find as you do research is likely to become your thesis. If you find huge amounts of material on your question and realize that you would have to write a book (or two) to cover all the issues, narrow your question.

Questions needing narrowing

1. How important are families? (too broad: important to whom and for what? no useful keywords to search)
2. What problems does the Internet cause? (too broad: what types of problems? what aspects of the Internet?)
3. What are the treatments for cancer? (too wide-ranging: volumes could be and have been written on this)
4. Should prayer be encouraged in schools? (difficult to discuss without relying on personal and religious conviction)

Revised questions

1. In what ways does a stable family environment contribute to an individual's future success?
2. Should Internet controls be established to protect individual privacy?
3. For which types of cancer are the success rates of radiation therapy highest?
4. If prayer is allowed in schools, how can a multicultural policy be maintained?

A research question will give you a sense of direction. Frequently, as you read and take notes, you will have in mind a tentative response to your question. Sometimes that hypothesis will be confirmed. Sometimes, though, your research will reveal issues you have not previously considered and facts that are new to you, so you will refine, adapt, or even totally change your working thesis (see **3g** and **6c** for more on a working thesis). If after a few days of research you either cannot find enough material on your topic or discover that all the information is dated, flimsy, or biased, waste no more time. Turn immediately to another topic and formulate a new research question. (See **49** on evaluating sources.)

Formulating a working thesis As you do your preliminary work of examining the task, planning which types of sources to use, and moving toward a topic, you will probably have in mind the point you want to make in your paper. If your research question is "Should Internet controls be established to protect individual privacy?" you probably favor either a "yes" or "no" answer to your question. At this point, you will formulate a working thesis in the form of a statement of opinion, which will help drive the organization of your paper.

> Internet controls to protect individual privacy should be established.

Or Internet controls to protect individual privacy should not be established.

KEY POINTS

Writing a Working Thesis

1. Make sure the thesis is a statement. A phrase or a question is not a thesis: "Internet controls" is a topic, not a thesis statement. "Are Internet controls needed?" is a question, not a thesis statement.

2. Make sure the thesis statement is not merely a statement of fact: "NUA Internet Surveys estimate that 513.41 million people were online as of August 2001" is a statement that cannot be developed and argued. A statement of fact does not let readers feel the need to read on to see what you have to say.

3. Make sure the thesis statement does more than announce the topic: "This paper will discuss Internet controls." Instead, your thesis statement should give information about or express an opinion on the topic: "Service providers, online retailers, and parents share the responsibility of establishing Internet controls to protect an individual's privacy."

4. Above all, be prepared to change and refine your thesis as you do your research and discover what your topic entails.

When you have a working thesis, your research becomes more focused. You look for material that relates to your thesis. If you find none, you can revise your thesis. If you find huge amounts of material, that is a signal for you to refine your thesis to make it more narrow and more focused on specific issues. Then you are ready to find sources and evaluate their relevance and reliability (**48** and **49**). As you read and make notes, you may find that your initial working thesis—"Internet controls should be established to protect individual privacy"—is too broad, and you may decide to narrow it: "Parents need to establish controls to protect their family's privacy on the Internet."

48 Finding Sources

48a Library and Web: a merger

In a search for sources, you are not faced with the choice of either going to a library for print materials or turning on a computer to find online sources. You can do your computer search in a library or by accessing a library or database from a remote location by using a password; your search can help you find traditional print materials as well as Internet sources. In addition, a visit to the library will give you access not only to books, print articles, and special collections but also to the collection of the online databases the library subscribes to. The amount of information available in all formats can be overwhelming, so be sure to ask librarians for help. They have expertise and can direct you to relevant sources to help you search efficiently. Many print materials have accompanying Web sites and links; Web sites provide access to print materials such as newspaper and periodical articles and even complete books. The Web, aptly named, has woven itself into the fabric of our lives.

Providing access to reference works, complete texts, and reliable sources such as databanks of scholarly articles, the Internet can be seen as a virtual library, available at the click of a mouse. The Internet provides a means of access to what were once seen as traditional print sources and to information that exists only online.

Using the Internet as a means to access information can lead you to many sources once viewed as traditional—reference works, books, scholarly articles, newspaper reports, government documents, and other traditional reference works, as well as to many reputable sources available only online, such as scholarly online journals and professional sites. Check at your library reference desk and on your library's Web page to find out which scholarly reference works and databases are available to you online and which Web sites might be particularly pertinent to your topic.

However, not everything you need is going to be available to you from your home computer. Your search will not be comprehensive if you limit yourself to generally available online sources. Do not neglect the print and online resources provided by your library. Apart from giving you access to the world of books, the library can extend your search choices for other resources, too. Get to know your library, its layout, and what its holdings include: What CD-ROMs does it own? What online databases and indexes does it subscribe to? Does it provide online access to the full text of scholarly articles? The greatest resource of all is the reference librarian, who can direct you to valuable sources, a service not available from America Online (AOL). Never be afraid to ask for a librarian's help.

Consider where you are likely to find the most appropriate sources for your topic. For tracing historical development or looking back to the past, scholarly articles, books, and primary documents such as diaries, memoirs, and speeches are your best bet. For contemporary political or cultural issues, you will probably search newspapers, magazines, Web sites, and online discussion groups. If in doubt about whether time spent in the library or time at your home computer will be more productive for your topic, get advice from your instructor or a reference librarian.

Searching for, evaluating, and recording source information are crucial parts of research. Each is discussed here in sequence, but in reality you will be searching, evaluating, and recording all through the process of writing a research paper. In particular, as you search for sources, be sure to keep full records of the sources you find and may use. See **50e** on how best to do this.

48b Basic reference works: bibliographies, biographical sources, directories, dictionaries, and others

The reference section of your college or local library is a good place to gather basic information. Reference books cannot be taken home, so they are in the library at all times. Also, more and more reference works are being made generally available online, so the accessibility of material from a library or home computer increases.

Reference works provide basic factual information and lead to other sources. However, use the same caution with other reference works as with encyclopedias—use them to get started with basic information, and then quickly move beyond them. (See **48c–48g** for details on finding sources other than basic reference works.)

Bibliographies (also known as *guides to the literature*) You can find lists of books and articles on a subject in bibliographies such as the following (this is a highly selective list):

Bibliographies in American History, Science and Engineering Literature

Books in Print

Books on Early American History and Culture, 1991–1995: An Annotated Bibliography

Foreign Affairs Bibliography

Guide to Sources of Educational Information

Japanese Business

MLA International Bibliography of Books and Articles on the Modern Languages and Literature

New Cambridge Bibliography of English Literature
Political Science Bibliographies

Biographical sources For background information on people's
lives, turn to biographical reference sources.

General	*Who's Who*
	Dictionary of American Biography
	Biography Index: A Cumulative Index to Biographic Material in Books and Magazines
	Authors Resources at <http://www.ipl.org/ref/RR/static/hum60.10.00.html>
Art	*Lives of the Painters*
Education	*Biographical Dictionary of American Educators*
Ethnic studies	*African American Biographies*
	Chicano Scholars and Writers
Literature	*Contemporary Authors*
	Dictionary of Literary Biography
Psychology	*Biographical Dictionary of Psychology*
Sciences	*American Men and Women of Science*
	Dictionary of Scientific Biography
Women's studies	*Notable American Women*

Directories Directories provide lists of names and addresses of
people, companies, and institutions. These are useful for setting up
interviews and contacting people when you need information.
Examples are *Jane's Space Directory* and *Communication Media in
Higher Education: A Directory of Academic Programs and Faculty in
Radio-Television-Film and Related Media.*

Dictionaries For etymologies, definitions, synonyms, and spelling,
consult *The American Heritage Dictionary of the English Language*, 4th
edition, *Oxford English Dictionary* (multiple volumes—useful for
detailed etymologies and usage discussions), *Facts on File* specialized
dictionaries, and other specialized dictionaries such as *Dictionary of
Literary Terms* and *Dictionary of the Social Sciences.*

Dictionaries of quotations For a rich source of traditional quotations, go to *Bartlett's Familiar Quotations* at <http://www.bartleby
.com/100/>; for more contemporary quotations, searchable by
topic, go to *The Columbia World of Quotations* at <http://www
.bartleby.com/66/>. Also, consult specialized dictionaries of quota-

tions, such as volumes devoted to chess, law, religion, fishing, women, and Wall Street.

Collections of articles of topical interest and news summaries *Opposing Viewpoints* series, *CQ (Congressional Quarterly)* weekly reports, *Facts on File* publications, and *CQ Almanac* are available in print and online by subscription. *Newsbank* provides periodical articles on microfiche, classified under topics such as "law" and "education," and *SIRS (Social Issues Resources Series)* appears in print and online.

Statistics and government documents Among many useful sources are *Statistical Abstract of the United States, Current Index to Statistics, Handbook of Labor Statistics, Occupational Outlook Handbook,* U.S. Census publications (print and online), *GPO Access, UN Demographic Yearbook, Population Index,* and *Digest of Educational Statistics.*

Almanacs, atlases, and gazetteers For population statistics and boundary changes, see *The World Almanac, Countries of the World,* or *Information Please.* For locations, descriptions, pronunciation of place names, climate, demography, languages, natural resources, and industry, consult *Columbia-Lippincott Gazetteer of the World* and the *CIA World Factbook* series, both available in print and online.

General critical works Read what scholars have to say about works of art and literature in *Contemporary Literary Criticism,* and in *Oxford Companion* volumes (such as *Oxford Companion to Art* and *Oxford Companion to African American Literature*).

48c Indexes, databases, and informational Web sites

Indexes Indexes of articles appearing in periodicals will start you off in your search for an article on a specific topic. Print indexes, such as *Readers' Guide to Periodical Literature,* will list works published before 1980. More recent publications are listed in online indexes, such as *Applied Science and Technology Index, Engineering Index,* and *Art Index.* An index will provide a complete citation: author, title, periodical, volume, date, and page numbers, often with an abstract. That information will narrow your search. Then you have to locate the periodical in a library and find the actual article.

Online databases Online databases provide a variety of types of data based on a variety of time periods. *PsycINFO,* for example, lists article abstracts from 1887 to the present; other databases are far less comprehensive in their time span. An online library or museum catalog is a database, providing information about the institution's collection. Some databases function as an online index (such as *Readers' Guide Abstracts, Wilson Business Abstracts, General Science Abstracts, ERIC, Humanities Abstracts, Sociological Abstracts*) providing only basic bibliographic information about where and when a source was published, along with an abstract. Others, known as full-text databases (such as *EBSCOhost Academic Search Premier, Dialog, InfoTrac,* and *Lexis-Nexis*), provide the publication information along with the full text of the article, available for downloading, printing, or e-mailing to yourself right from your computer. Netlibrary provides the full text of books. You can also access databases devoted to statistics (such as Bureau of Labor Statistics Data at <http://www.bls.gov/data/home.htm> or Census Bureau figures at <http://www.census.gov/>) or to images, such as works of art, at <http://www.getty.edu/>.

For basic information on authors and literary works, turn to *InfoTrac Literature Resource Center.* Try *J-Stor* for pre-1980 sources; the database is not as vast as others but it does provide access to older materials. For ethnic magazines and newspapers, *Ethnic Newswatch* is the database to turn to.

Your library houses print and CD-ROM indexes and databases and subscribes to some online; others are accessible through online library catalogs or Web links. See **48g** for lists of general and specialized indexes and databases available online.

Informational Web sites Some Web sites contain vast amounts of information and useful links to other sites. Always bookmark any sites you find useful so you can return to them easily. Examples: *The WWW Virtual Library* (covers basic sources in many academic disciplines) at <http://vlib.org/>; the University of Minnesota *Research Quickstart* site, with basic resources for research by subject, at <http://research.lib.umn.edu>; and, for the humanities, *Voice of the Shuttle* at <http://vos.ucsb.edu>.

48d Keyword searches

Use keywords to search for any material stored electronically—on the Web, in library catalogs, in CD-ROM databases, or in online subscription services. Keyword searching is especially effective for finding material in journal and newspaper articles in databases such as *EBSCOhost, InfoTrac, Lexis-Nexis,* and specialized subject-area databases because a computer can search not only titles but also abstracts (when available) or full articles.

Keywords are vital for your Web searches. Spend time thinking of the keywords that best describe what you are looking for. If a search yields thousands of hits, try requiring or prohibiting terms and making terms into phrases (see the Key Points box). If a search yields few hits, try different keywords or combinations of keywords, or try another search engine. In addition, try out variant spellings for names of people and places: *Chaikovsky, Tchaikovsky, Tschaikovsky.*

KEY POINTS

Doing a Keyword Search

1. *Know the search engine's system.* Use the Search Tips or Help link to find out how to conduct a search. Search engines vary. Some search for any or all of the words you type in, some need you to indicate whether the words make up a phrase, and some allow you to exclude words or search for alternatives.

2. *Use Boolean terms to narrow or expand a search.* Some advanced searches operate on the Boolean principle, which means that you use the "operators" *AND, OR,* and *NOT* in combination with keywords to define what you want the search to include and exclude. Imagine that you want to find out if and how music can affect intelligence. The search term *music AND intelligence* would find sources in the database that include both the word *music* and the word *intelligence* (the overlap in the circles below).

music   intelligence

Parentheses can aid in searches, too. The search term *music AND (intelligence OR learning)* would expand the search. You would find sources in the database that include both the word *music* and also the word *intelligence* or the word *learning.*

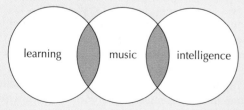
learning   music   intelligence

(continued)

(continued)

In Boolean searches, *AND* and *NOT* narrow the search: *chicken AND salmonella; dolphins NOT Miami; OR* expands the search: *angiogram OR angioplasty.* Not all databases and search engines use this system. MetaCrawler, for instance, asks simply if you want to include *any* or *all* of the search terms, or use *all* the terms as a phrase. Always check the instructions with each search engine or database.

3. *Use a wildcard character to truncate a term and expand the search.* A wildcard allows you to use at the end of a phrase a character that indicates that more letters can be attached. Common wildcard characters are * and ?. The truncated search term *addict** will produce references to *addict, addicts, addiction, addictive,* and so on.

4. *Narrow a search by grouping words into phrases.* Often, you can use double quotation marks—"Michael Jackson"—or parentheses—(Michael Jackson)—to surround a search term and group the words into a phrase. *Michael Jackson* entered as a term without such quotation marks or parentheses would produce references to other Michaels—Johnson and Jordan, for instance—and to other Jacksons—Stonewall Jackson, Jackson Pollock, and so on.

5. *Learn how to require or prohibit a term to narrow a search.* Many search engines allow you to use a symbol such as + (plus) before a term that must be included in the document indexed; a − (minus) symbol prohibits a term: + "Civil War" − Gettysburg. Some search engines use these symbols in place of the *AND* and *NOT* of Boolean searching.

6. *Take advantage of the "proximity" search feature if available.* Some search engines—AltaVista is one—let you indicate when you want your search terms to occur close to each other in the text. Check in the Help or Tips file to determine whether the engine you are using has this feature. Proximity is indicated in various ways in various search engines. *NEAR* or *ADJ* (adjacent) are common: "Virginia Woolf" *NEAR* "Bloomsbury group" would search for the two phrases near each other in the text.

Use the results to help tailor and refine your search. If your search produces only one useful source, look at the terms used in that one source and its subject headings and search again, using those terms maybe with a different search engine. Above all, be flexible. Each search engine indexes only a portion of what is available on the Web. Once you find a promising reference to a source that is not available online in full text, check whether your library owns the book or journal. If your search yields a source available only on microfilm or microfiche, you might need a librarian's help to learn how to use the reading machines and how to make copies.

48e Searching for books and print periodical articles

Types of search   When you use library catalogs or periodical databases, decide whether to search by T (title), A (author), S (subject), or K (keyword). Exact wording and exact spelling are essential for all these searches. Use keyword searching (**48d**) when searching for material that is electronically stored, whether in a library catalog, on a CD-ROM, in a database, or on a Web page. For subject searching, you need to know the specific subject headings the catalogers used to identify and classify material.

Subject headings   To find an appropriate search term for a subject, consult a reference source such as *Library of Congress Subject Headings,* or ask a librarian for help. For example, you won't find "cultural identity" or "social identity" in *Library of Congress Subject Headings,* but you can look up "culture" and find a list of thirty-one narrower topics (NT), such as "language and culture" and "personality and culture."

Culture
  [CB]
  [GN400–GN406 (Primitive)]
  [HM101 (Sociology)]
    UF   Cultural sociology
           Sociology of culture
    BT   Historical sociology
    RT   Civilization
           Education
           Learning and scholarship
    NT   Acculturation
           Biculturalism
           Buddhism and culture
           Christianity and culture
           Classification—Books—Culture
           Cognition and culture
           Communication and culture
           Cross-cultural studies
           Cultural lag

Cultural policy
Culture diffusion
Educational anthropology
Fascism and culture
Guilt and culture
Hinduism and culture
Intellectual life
Intercultural communication
International relations and culture
Language and culture
Material culture
Personality and culture
Philistinism
Political culture
Politics and culture
Psychoanalysis and culture
Religion and culture
Self-culture
Social evolution
Socialism and culture
Subculture
World Decade for Cultural Development, 1988–1997

The abbreviations can help you in your search. The codes at the beginning of the entry (CB, GN, and HM) refer to Library of Congress classification numbers (that is, call numbers). You can use these to go to open stacks and browse the area to find books on a topic. The codes on the left of the entry help you in a search: UF means "Used For" and provides alternative subject terms, BT stands for "Broader Topic," RT for "Related Topic," and NT for "Narrower Topic." All of these can be useful to you in your subject searches, as well as being suggestive of specific topics to address in writing.

In addition, these subject headings show related terms, which can suggest ways to narrow or broaden a topic and can help you in other subject searches, particularly in electronic keyword searches. *Bilingualism*, for example, takes you to topics such as "air traffic control," "code-switching," and "language attrition." An entry in a library catalog or a database will also appear with subject descriptors, so if you find one good source, use its subject classifications to search further. Subject headings are usually linked, so you can follow links that are relevant, and this may help you narrow your search.

Another way to find the subject headings relevant to your topic is to do a keyword search and note the subject headings attached to items you find that are useful to you. For example, a search in a library database for books on plants nearing extinction could begin with the keywords *threatened species*. These keywords produce a series of items, including the following screen, which provides subject terms to help with further searching: *endangered plants, plant conservation,* and *legumes.*

Details (long view)

Your Search: **Anywhere in record = threatened species**
Displaying Record: **2 of 39**

Title:	Sensitive joint-vetch : a threatened species.
Published:	<Washington, D.C.> : U.S. Fish & Wildlife Service, <1999>
Description:	<6> p. : ill., map ; 22 x 11 cm.
Subject:	Endangered plants --United States. Plant conservation --United States. Legumes --United States.
Other Authors:	U.S. Fish and Wildlife Service.
Distinctive title:	Sensitive joint vetch
Notes:	Cover title. Shipping list no.: 99-0376-P. "August 1999"--P. <4> of cover.

If your college library does not own a book or periodical you want, ask a librarian about interlibrary loan, a system that allows you to locate and order books from another library. This option is helpful, of course, only if you begin your search early.

Finding print books   Books are a valuable resource for research. Reputable publishers will review the content and decide to publish only when they are convinced the material is accurate and responsible. Books present a far more thorough overview and in-depth investigation of a topic than an article does. For eBooks, see page 724.

Call number   The call number tells you where a book is located in the library stacks (the area where books are shelved). Write this number down immediately if a book looks promising, along with the book's title and author(s) and publication information (**50e**). Many catalogs identify the floor on which the book is located. Write that information down to save time later.

If a library has open stacks, you will be able to browse through books on a similar topic on the same shelf or on one nearby. In a library with closed stacks, you need the call number to direct a library staff member to locate the book for you. Most college libraries use the Library of Congress classification system, which arranges books according to subject area and often the initial of the author's last name and the date of publication. The Library of Congress call number determines where a book is shelved in the library.

Information in the catalog The screens of electronic catalogs vary from one system to another, but most screens contain the following information:

- the name of the system you are using
- the details of your search request and of the search, such as the number of records found
- the number of pages (or screens) that the record covers
- a list of commands that the system uses
- a blinking cursor, where you type the command for what you want to do next

---

Details (long view)

Your Search: Author = Crawford James
Displaying Record: **18 of 97**

Author:	Crawford, James, 1949-
Title:	Bilingual education : history, politics, theory, and practice /
Published:	Trenton, N.J. : Crane Pub. Co., c1989.
Description:	204 p. : ill. ; 23 cm.
Subject:	Education, Bilingual --United States.
Notes:	Includes index. Bibliography: p. <179>-192.

Location	Call Number	Note	Summ
Baruch Stacks	LC 3731 .C73 1989		

The screen shown here tells you that the book is available on a shelf of the main library stacks. It provides all the essential information you will need to document the source at the end of your paper: author, title, place of publication, publisher, and date of publication. In addition, it lets you know the number of pages in the book and shows that the book contains illustrations (*ill.*), a bibliography, and an index—all useful research tools.

Once you find a book that seems to be related to your topic, you do not have to read the whole book to use it for your paper. Learn what you can from the catalog entry; then skim the table of contents, chapter headings, and bibliography. Your best timesaver is the index. Turn to it immediately and look up some keywords for your topic. Read the section of the book in which references to your topic appear; take notes; annotate a photocopy of the relevant pages (**50e**). A book's bibliography and references are useful, too. The author has done research, and this can help you in your search. It is a good idea to make a copy of the title page and the page on which the copyright notice appears. If you find nothing remotely connected to your research question, do not cite the book as a resource, even though you looked at it.

Books in Print *and alternatives*   If you want to find a book or to check on bibliographical details, use *Books in Print* (available in print and online). If your library does not subscribe to the online version, you can use for no charge the Amazon.com site at <http://www.amazon.com> or any other large commercial online book-seller's site to look up the details of a book.

Finding periodical articles   Find articles in periodicals (works issued periodically, such as scholarly journals, magazines, and newspapers) by using a periodical index. Use electronic indexes for recent works, print indexes for earlier works, especially for works written before 1980. Check which services your library subscribes to and the dates the indexes cover. Indexes may provide abstracts; some, such as *Lexis-Nexis Academic Universe, InfoTrac, EBSCOhost,* and *OCLC FirstSearch,* provide the full text of articles. (See also **48c** for more on indexes and databases.)

Search methods are similar to those in book searches. If the periodical index does not provide the full text, you will need to find out first whether your library owns the periodical and then in which form it is available: in files, in bound volumes, or in film form with pages shown in a strip (microfilm) or on a sheet (microfiche), which you will need to read with a special machine. The catalog for your library will tell you on the screen which issues are available in your library and in which format and location.

To search for articles in a full-text database that a library subscribes to, follow the search directions in the database. Generally, you will be able to search by author, title, or keyword (see **48d**), and you will be able to refine your search by type of source or date.

48f   Online searches and search engines

URLs   If you already know the Web address (the Uniform Resource Locator or URL) of a useful site, type it exactly, paying attention to spaces (or, more often, lack of spaces), dots, symbols, and capital or lowercase letters. Just one small slip can prevent access. Whenever you can, copy and paste a URL from a Web source so that you do not make mistakes in typing. If you ever get a message saying "site not found," check your use of capitals and lowercase letters (and avoid inserting spaces as you type an address), and try again. You may find that the site is no longer available. See **11b** for more on e-mail and Web addresses.

Browsers, search engines, meta search engines, subject directories, and virtual libraries If you do not know the exact Web site you want, you need to use search tools. Some search the whole Web for you; some search selected sites; some search only the first few pages of a document; still others search only a specific site, such as a university library system or a noncommercial organization, or they search other search engines (these are called *meta search engines*). Make sure you try all types to find information on your topic.

Your Web browser, probably Netscape, Internet Explorer, AOL, or the newer Mozilla, will give you access to search engines and other resources that do for you most of the work of rapidly searching Web sites. Note that the Internet Explorer browser offered through AOL does not have the same capability to access complex sites as a stand-alone version of the browser. You can, however, use AOL as a portal to take you to a full version of Netscape or Internet Explorer. Whichever browser you use, spending time searching (and playing) is the best way to become familiar with reliable search tools, the types of searches they do best, and the system they use for searching. You may find the following search tools useful. If one does not provide good results, try another.

- AltaVista <http://www.altavista.com> is a comprehensive search tool using keywords. It is a good tool for serious academic research. Its database is huge, more than 500 million Web pages and Usenet groups, so you need to be precise with your search terms. It can also search for images and for audio and video files. AltaVista allows you to check the reliability of a site by doing a reverse search to find out who else is linking to it. It can also provide translations.

- Argus Clearinghouse <http://www.clearinghouse.net> provides links to virtual (that is, online) libraries, subject guides, and search engines.

- Ask Jeeves! <http://www.ask.com> responds to a question, such as "Does tea contain more caffeine than coffee?"

- CataList <http://www.lsoft.com/lists/listref.html> catalogs discussion lists using Listserv software, which offers Web interface.

- Google Groups <http://groups.google.com> searches Usenet groups by topic and presents its findings in reverse chronology. It can be difficult to evaluate the credentials of contributors and the accuracy of information, but the correspondence gives a sense of the issues people are interested in.

- Excite <http://excite.com> searches by concept as well as by keyword, so it finds not only documents containing your search terms but also documents related to the same idea. When a search retrieves a list of documents, you can look for the document that seems to be what you want and initiate a new search based on the features that one document exhibits.

- Google <http://www.google.com> (the favorite of many academics) searches more than 675 million Web pages and other search engines. It organizes and ranks results by the numbers of links to a site.

- iLor <http://www.ilor.com> has results similar to Google's but offers different options and a listing of findings that Google does not offer.

- Infomine <http://infomine.ucr.edu/> provides scholarly resources in social sciences, humanities, and general reference, selected and annotated.

- Internet Public Library <http://www.ipl.org> is run by librarians. It includes a guide to home pages and a Reference Center, which allows you to e-mail a question about a research project to librarians and receive a reply in a few days.

- Kovacs Directory of Scholarly and Professional E-Conferences <http://www.kovacs.com/> includes links to online journals, discussion lists, Usenet groups, and real-time conferencing programs.

- Liszt <http://www.liszt.com> catalogs over 90,000 discussion lists.

- MetaCrawler <http://www.metacrawler.com> provides a subject directory, and it searches many of the best search engines: AltaVista, Excite, Lycos, Infoseek, Google, WebCrawler, and others.

- WWW Virtual Library <http://vlib.org> is useful for finding sources in a large number of academic disciplines.

- Yahoo! <http://www.yahoo.com> is a subject index and directory of the Web, organized hierarchically. You can keep narrowing down your subjects, or you can also use specific keywords. Such a tool is particularly useful when you are trying to decide what to write about.

TechNote List of Search Engines

For a detailed list of search engines and their search options, see The Search Tools Chart by the Infopeople Project at <http://infopeople .org/search/chart.html>. ■

48g Searching for materials available online

The Internet can take you to many sources formerly accessible only if you went to a library and dug through shelves and bound volumes of periodicals. Newspaper and magazine articles from ten years ago, scholarly journal articles, news commentary, statistical information —all are available. You will find vast resources, current material, and frequent updates—all without leaving your computer. However, the democratic nature of the Internet means that many Web pages have no editorial control and can therefore be mindless and inaccurate (see **49d**). As you plan your research, consider which Internet resources described in this section might be the most trustworthy and appropriate for your topic. A reference librarian can help you decide. As you do the research, remember to keep track of your sources and record all the necessary information. See **50e** for ways to do this.

 TechNote Tutorial on Web Research

For a tutorial on how to use the Web for research, go to the Widener University Wolfgram Memorial Library site *Using the Web for Research* <http://www2.widener.edu/Wolfgram-Memorial-Library/ pyramid/goals2.htm>. The *Search Engine Watch* site also provides useful tips and an annotated list of search engines and directories <http://www.searchenginewatch.com>. ■

Online library catalogs and home pages of libraries and universities The Web gives you access to the online resources of many libraries (actual and virtual) and universities, which are good browsing sites. Some useful sites follow:

- *Library of Congress* <http://lcweb.loc.gov> provides lists of links (with descriptions) of Internet search tools, as well as access to subject guides, government resources, online library catalogs, and Internet tutorials.
- *LibWeb* <http://sunsite.berkeley.edu/Libweb> offers information on library holdings in over 100 countries.
- *New York Public Library* <http://www.nypl.org/index.html> allows searching of its vast online catalog.

- *Smithsonian Institution Libraries* <http://www.sil.si.edu/> provides a catalog and tools for the researcher, including links to databases and e-journals.

Online indexes and databases Online databases and citation indexes owned or leased by libraries can be accessed in the library itself. Many libraries also make the databases they subscribe to available on the Internet through their home pages. For example, many libraries provide online access to the following:

- databases of abstracts in specific subject areas, such as *ERIC* (for education), *PAIS* (for public affairs), *PsycINFO* (for psychology), and *Sociofile* (for the social sciences)
- databases of full texts of articles published from 1980, such as *InfoTrac: Expanded Academic ASAP* (see **48i** for a sample search), *Lexis-Nexis Academic Universe*, *EBSCOhost*, and *OCLC FirstSearch*
- databases of abstracts of general, nonspecialized magazine articles, such as the Wilson *Readers' Guide to Periodical Literature*

Frequently, though, access to databases in university library Web sites is limited to enrolled students who have been assigned a password. Check with your college library to see which databases are available online in the library only and which are available on the Web. NoodleLinks provides a useful *Database of Academic Bibliographies* at <http://noodletools.com/noodlelinks/>.

Online magazines and journals Online magazines and journals are proliferating. Here are some examples:

- *Slate* <http://www.slate.com>
- *Salon* <http://www.salon.com>
- *Early Modern Literary Studies* <http://purl.oclc.org/emls/emlshome.html>
- *Postmodern Culture* <http://jefferson.village.virginia.edu/pmc>
- *Sociological Research Online* <http://www.socresonline.org.uk>

Some online journals are available free; some allow you to view only the current issue at no cost. Many, however, require a subscription through your library computer network or a personal subscription.

Online texts Literary texts that are out of copyright and in the public domain are increasingly available online for downloading. The following are useful sites to consult, although the versions of texts you see may not always be authoritative:

- *Project Bartleby* <http://www.bartleby.com>
- *Project Gutenberg* <http://www.promo.net/pg/index.html>
- *University of Virginia's Electronic Text Center* <http://etext.lib .virginia.edu>

EBooks   Many books are becoming available as eBooks, either to be read online at a computer or downloaded and read in an eBook reader. An eBook offers several advantages:

- You can read online or you can check a book out and return it—without ever having to go to a library.
- You can bookmark your place and return to it at any time.
- You can click on a word to look up its meaning in the online dictionary included in the program.
- You can open several eBooks at the same time.
- You can use the search capability, which is much quicker and more reliable than flipping back through the pages of a print book to find a reference to a name or term that you only vaguely remember.

NetLibrary.com is one of the companies offering eBooks. If your library subscribes to its database, make sure you check its offerings when you are looking for a book.

Online news sites   The Web sites of major newspapers, magazines, and television networks provide up-to-date news information; some offer archived information but often only to subscribers. See, for example, *The New York Times on the Web* <http://www.nytimes.com> and *CNN Interactive* <http:www.cnn.com>.

Nonprofit research sites   Many nonprofit sites offer valuable and objective information. For example, see *Public Agenda Online* <http://www.publicagenda.org>, *American Film Institute* <http:// www.afi.com>, and *San Francisco Bay Bird Observatory* <http://www.sfbbo.org/index.html>.

Web pages and hypertext links   Many universities and research institutes provide information through their own Web home pages, with hypertext links that take you with one click to many other sources. Try, for example, <http://www.refdesk.com> for more than twenty thousand links to reference works and informational sites. Individual Web pages can provide useful information, too, but need careful evaluation, since anyone can publish anything on the Web (**49d**).

E-mail discussion lists   With e-mail, you have access to many discussion groups. Messages go out to a list of people interested in specific topics. Without charge, you can join a list devoted to a topic of interest (see **11c** for how to join a list and participate in a list). These discussion lists number more than ninety thousand, according to Liszt at <http://www.liszt.com>, a catalog of lists. However, most of the lists are not refereed or monitored, so you have to evaluate carefully any information you find (**49d**). Listserv, Listproc, and Majordomo are the common list programs, accessed through e-mail. The Hypernews tool at <http://www.hypernews.org>, which sponsors independent Web discussions on specific themes (threads), also allows you to read and contribute to the discussions.

Usenet newsgroups   Usenet newsgroups are open e-mail discussions on a wide variety of topics, linked under a common address. These newsgroups are different from discussion lists in that you do not have to join a list to read and contribute messages. Newsgroup mailings are not forwarded to your e-mail mailbox; you access them with newsreader programs such as the one provided by AOL (in AOL, click on Internet, then on Newsgroups), Netscape Messenger, or Outlook Express or by searching on <http://groups.google.com>. Addresses begin with terms like *rec.* (recreation), *sci.* (science), *soc.culture* (cultural environment in various countries and locations), *biz.* (business), *comp.* (computing), and *alt.* (alternatives—a variety of topics) and then indicate the subject matter: *alt.alien.visitors; biz.comp.accounting; comp.ai.nat-lang; rec.arts.movies.production.* See **11c** for more on newsgroups.

Other interactive sources   Other interactive e-mail sources of information are "buddy lists" such as those offered by AOL; Web forums and bulletin board services provided by business and academic sites; and real-time spaces for interaction such as chat rooms, MUDs (multiuser domains), and MOOs (multiuser domains, object-oriented). However, evaluating the reliability of someone's contribution to interactive discussion can be difficult.

48h   A student's search

Audrey Fort searched for print and online sources to do research for a paper about the connections between music and intelligence. Each search will vary, but your overall process will probably resemble Fort's. Consider different types of sources, and tailor your search to the time you have available.

Step 1: Topic Fort began with the idea that she wanted to write about music, specifically about the new field that examines the nervous system in relation to music—the field called neuromusicology. That idea had been suggested to her by a section in the textbook assigned for her music appreciation course.

Step 2: Research question First, Fort went to encyclopedias and the *Readers' Guide to Periodical Literature* database of general articles; she read several articles, discussed the issues with her music instructor, and on the basis of information she had discovered, formulated some research questions: Does the new field of neuromusicology offer us insights into emotions, behavior, health, and intelligence? Does such scientific application affect our enjoyment of music?

Step 3: College library catalog for articles and books Fort began her research by finding article abstracts in her college library catalog database and finding the print articles in the library in bound volumes or on microfilm. Several of the articles she found were published in newspapers or popular magazines such as *Newsweek* and *Psychology Today,* so she broadened her search to find a scholarly article (see **49b**) in *Social Forces.* The bibliography accompanying this article also led her to books on the topic, which she checked out of the library, skimmed, and made notes on.

Step 4: Online subscription database Fort then ran a search on an online database her college subscribed to. In *InfoTrac: Expanded Academic ASAP,* using the keywords *music AND intelligence,* she was able to find abstracts and full-text articles of academic studies, and she marked three articles to download from the first ten hits of sixty-five hits. But after reading the full text of each, she found only one of them (by Larkin) useful enough to include in her paper. One citation on the extended *InfoTrac* list referred her to an abstract of an article in the journal *Nature.* She went back to her college library to locate the full text in a bound journal and decided to use that source in her paper. See page 727 for the InfoTrac list.

Step 5: Formation of working thesis Fort felt she had explored the topic in enough breadth and depth to understand the issues involved and to formulate a tentative thesis. She wrote a working thesis to guide her future research: *The scientific examination of responses to music threatens the mystery of music and our enjoyment of it.*

Step 6: Internet research To discover more material on the topic, Fort turned to two Internet search engines. Using AltaVista, she typed

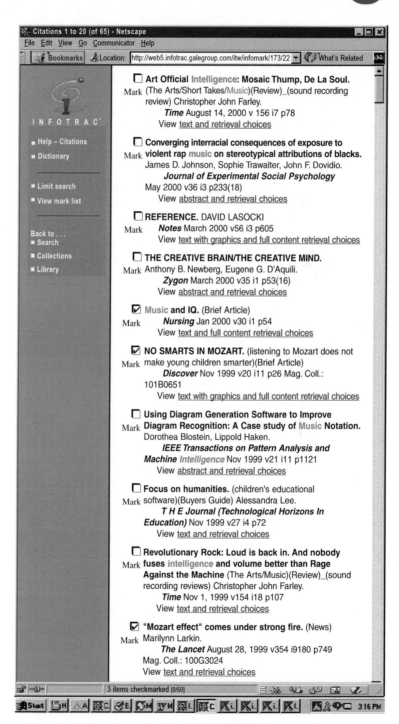

in *neuromusicology + intelligence,* and AltaVista came up with over two million hits. Aghast, Fort quickly realized that she had put the plus sign only before the last term, not the first. A new search using *+ neuromusicology + intelligence* instructed the search engine to find only documents containing both terms. The result was three hits, as shown below. Fort knew that the search engines get revenue from advertising, so she wisely ignored the clutter on the screen from the ads. She copied and saved the URL of the third hit, an article in an online journal. She eventually used this article in her paper.

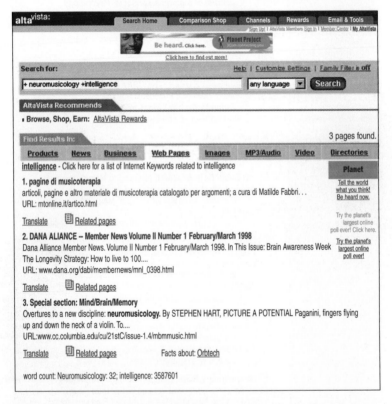

Step 7: Another search engine As an alternative, Fort began a new search on MetaCrawler. She typed only the two words (this engine requires only the words, with no symbols or connecting words) and hit the button for *all* rather than *any,* telling MetaCrawler to search first for documents containing all the terms listed, then for documents containing one term. This search produced twenty-one results (see the first few hits on the next screen capture), though some of these were off the track. The Central Intelligence Agency site, pro-

duced in response to the search term *intelligence*, obviously would not offer much about music.

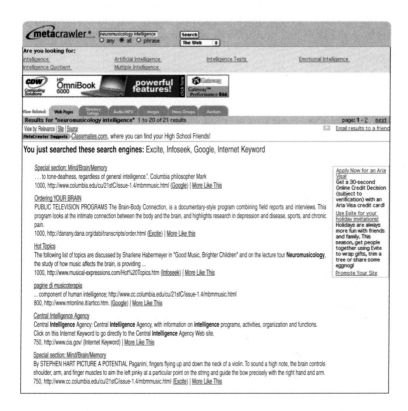

Fort followed some of the promising-looking links. One that both search engines had found took her to the Columbia University site of an online journal containing an article by Stephen Hart called "Overtures to a New Discipline: Neuromusicology." Another useful source found in the MetaCrawler search was an announcement of a book by Sharlene Habermeyer called *Good Music, Brighter Children.* Fort decided to include the two sources in her paper. Several of the sites identified by the search engines also provided links to other useful sites. Habermeyer's site, for instance, included a page on recent research.

Throughout the searches, Fort made print copies or saved online material, evaluated the reliability of sources (see **49c** and **49d**), kept a working bibliography (**50f**), and made careful notes. Armed with solid research findings, she was able to confirm her thesis—though she later revised the wording—and to support it with a great deal of evidence from her sources. She reworded her thesis, created a scratch outline (**3i**), making note of the specific details gleaned from her research, wrote a draft, obtained feedback from classmates and her instructor, and drafted and revised her paper several times. You can read her final draft on the Web site: <http://college.hmco.com/keys.html>.

49 Evaluating Sources

Finding sources is only half the battle. The other half is finding good, relevant sources. How can you tell which sources to use and which to reject? Use the following guidelines.

49a How to read source material critically

It is always difficult to write about something if you don't know much about it. Reading, understanding, and synthesizing your sources (putting them together to form your own ideas and opinions) are important activities in the process of research. A quick scan is never enough.

Spend time reading your sources carefully, thinking about them, questioning them, and writing about them. If you read critically, you will generate ideas of your own as you read. Reading critically does not mean criticizing a writer's views, though it may sometimes include that. Rather, it means reading with an open, questioning mind, examining the writer's assumptions and biases, and scrutinizing the evidence the writer provides.

KEY POINTS

Guidelines for Critical Reading of Research Sources

1. Ask questions about the credentials and reputation of the author and the place of publication. What do you learn about the writer's purpose and the audience whom the author is addressing? Make sure you subject any material you find on Web pages to especially careful scrutiny. (**49d**)

2. Ask questions about the ideas you read. An easy way to do this is to write your annotations in the margin. If you find yourself thinking "But . . ." as you read, go with that sense of doubt and make a note of what troubles you.

3. Be on the lookout for assumptions that may be faulty. If you are reading an article on home-schooling and the writer favors home-schooling because it avoids subjecting students to vio-

lence in schools, the unstated assumption is that all schools are violent places. For more on the logic of argument, see **6.**

4. Ascertain whether the ideas the writer expresses are current and timely—or is that not important for the topic?

5. Make sure the writer's evidence is adequate and accurate. For example, if the writer is making a generalization about all Chinese students based on a study of only three, you have cause to challenge the generalization as resting on inadequate evidence.

6. Note how the writer uses language. For instance, does the writer denigrate the views of others with phrases such as "right- [or left-] wing extremism," "unpatriotic dogma," or "laughably inept policies"?

7. Be alert for sweeping generalizations, bias, and prejudice: "Atheists are evil." "Women want to stay home and have children." "Men love to spend Sundays watching sports."

Do your reading when you can write—not on the treadmill or while watching TV. Note any questions, objections, or challenges on the page, on self-stick notes, on index cards, in a response file on your computer, or in a double-entry journal (see **3a**). Your critical responses to your reading will provide you with your own ideas for writing.

 TechNote Information on the Home Page of an Internet Site

Before you devote time to reading and taking notes from a Web site, always check the home page to find out about the purpose, intended audience, and bias of the site. Not all sites present information objectively and logically. See also **49d.** ■

49b How to recognize a scholarly article

Learn to distinguish scholarly from nonscholarly articles. A scholarly article is not something you are likely to find in a magazine in a dentist's office. A scholarly journal is refereed—that is, other scholars read all the articles and approve them for publication.

Just looking at the cover of the journal, noting the length of the article and the length of each paragraph, and scanning the beginning and end of the article should help make the distinction between a scholarly and a nonscholarly periodical obvious.

See pages 732–734 for examples of what a scholarly journal looks like.

Cover of a scholarly journal

TEACHERS OF ENGLISH TO SPEAKERS OF OTHER LANGUAGES, INC.

TESOL QUARTERLY

VOLUME 34 / NUMBER 3 / AUTUMN 2000

KEY POINTS

What a Scholarly Article Does

A scholarly article

1. refers to the work of other scholars (look for in-text citations and a bibliographical list of works cited, footnotes, or endnotes)

2. names the author and usually describes the author's credentials

3. includes notes, references, or a bibliography, and may include an abstract

4. deals with a serious issue in depth

5. uses academic or technical language for informed readers

6. appears in journals that do not include colorful advertisements or eye-catching pictures (a picture of two stunning models is an indication that you are not looking at a scholarly article)

Table of contents of a scholarly journal

Volume 34, Number 3 □ Autumn 2000

REVIEWS

Computers and Pedagogy   617

New Ways of Using Computers in Language Teaching
Tim Boswood (Ed.)

CALL: Media, Design and Applications
Keith Cameron (Ed.)

WorldCALL: Global Perspectives on Computer-Assisted Language Learning
Robert Debski and Mike Levy (Eds.)

CALL Environments: Research, Practice, and Critical Issues
Joy Egbert and Elizabeth Hanson-Smith (Eds.)

Computer-Assisted Language Learning: Context and Conceptualization
Mike Levy

Network-Based Language Teaching: Concepts and Practice
Mark Warschauer and Richard Kern (Eds.)

Computers and Talk in the Primary Classroom
Rupert Wegerif and Peter Scrimshaw (Eds.)
Reviewed by Leo van Lier

Language, Literacy, Politics, and Access   625

Literacy, Access, and Libraries Among the Language Minority Population
Rebecca Constantino (Ed.)

Language and Politics in the United States and Canada: Myths and Realities
Thomas Ricento and Barbara Burnaby (Eds.)

Dialects in Schools and Communities
Walt Wolfram, Carolyn Temple Adger, and Donna Christian
Reviewed by Johnnie Johnson Hafernik

Information for Contributors   631
     Editorial Policy
     General Information for Authors
TESOL Membership Application

Pages from *TESOL Quarterly* 34(3) copyright 2000 by TESOL Inc. Reproduced by permission of TESOL Inc. in the format Trade Book via Copyright Clearance Center.

When you read scholarly articles, scan any section headings, read the abstract and any section headed "Summary" or "Conclusions," and skim for the author's main idea to find out whether the article addresses your topic. If you are working on a topic related to current events, you probably will need to consult newspapers, magazines, and online sources as well as or in place of scholarly journals. Two print publications describe the intended audience of magazines and provide information about whether articles are peer reviewed:

- William A. Katz and Linda Sternberg Katz, *Magazines for Libraries: For the General Reader and School, Junior College,*

Article abstract and first page of a scholarly article

L2 Literacy and the Design of the Self: A Case Study of a Teenager Writing on the Internet

WAN SHUN EVA LAM
University of California
Berkeley, California, United States

This article presents a case study that uses ethnographic and discourse analytic methods to examine how electronic textual experiences in ESL figure in the identity formation and literacy development of the learner. First, the article reviews some recent work in literacy studies, L2 learning, and computer-mediated communication to provide a conceptual basis for studying discursive practices and identity formation in L2 learning. The results of a case study of a Chinese immigrant teenager's written correspondence with a transnational group of peers on the Internet then show how this correspondence relates to his developing identity in the use of English. This study develops the notion of textual identity for understanding how texts are composed and used to represent and reposition identity in the networked computer media. It also raises critical questions on literacy and cultural belonging in the present age of globalization and transborder relations.

Current research on L2 literacy (e.g., McKay, 1993, 1996; Kern, 1995) has demonstrated the contextual nature of literacy practices and raised questions about how literacy experiences in a nonnative language influence the identity formation of the learner. The relation between identity and literacy development in TESOL warrants critical examination in the present age of globalization as "virtual communities" emerge on the Internet and cultural products, symbols, and images circulate transnationally. How do communities on the Internet act as contexts for L2 literacy use and development? What kinds of textual forms and cultural discourses are used and developed in these literacy practices? How are learners' identities in the L2 constructed through networked computer media? These are some of the questions that guided this study.

In this article, I introduce constructs from L2 literacy research and communication studies to develop a conceptual basis for studying literacy development in ESL in the contexts created through electronic

Distinguishing scholarly articles in general databases Some databases are specialized and will yield only research articles (or only abstracts) published in scholarly journals. Other databases, such as *EBSCOhost, Dialog,* and *InfoTrac,* are more general, including pop-

Article last page and references (APA style)

positioning in other target languages to challenge and expand their notion of that standard as they are learning it. In this way, the development of literacy or multiple literacies in ESL may become not only an opportunity for gaining access to the standard language or dominant discourses but also a creative process of self-formation in light of diverse practices and ways of representing human experiences.

ACKNOWLEDGMENTS

I thank Claire Kramsch for her insights and mentorship throughout the evolution of this article. I am grateful to Mark Warschauer and two anonymous reviewers for their very helpful comments on earlier drafts of this article, and to the editor of *TESOL Quarterly* for her continual support. My deep appreciation goes to Almon, who generously shared his work and experiences with me during this study and beyond.

THE AUTHOR

Wan Shun Eva Lam is a PhD candidate in the language, literacy, and culture division of the Graduate School of Education at the University of California, Berkeley. Her areas of specialization are literacy theory, language and culture, and the role of bilingual development in L2 learning.

REFERENCES

Atkinson, D. (1999). TESOL and culture. *TESOL Quarterly, 33,* 625–654.

Auerbach, E. R., & Paxton, D. (1997). "It's not the English thing": Bringing reading research into the ESL classroom. *TESOL Quarterly, 31,* 237–261.

Barton, D., Hamilton, M., & Ivanic, R. (2000). *Situated literacies: Reading and writing in context.* London: Routledge.

Baym, N. K. (1995). The emergence of community in computer-mediated communication. In S. G. Jones (Ed.), *Cybersociety: Computer-mediated communication and community* (pp. 138–163). Thousand Oaks, CA: Sage.

Baynham, M. (1995). *Literacy practices: Investigating literacy in social contexts.* London: Longman.

Bays, H. (1998, January). Framing and face in Internet exchanges: A socio-cognitive approach. *Linguistic Online, 1.* Retrieved June 6, 2000, from the World Wide Web: http://viadrina.euv-frankfurt-o.de/~wjournal/bays.htm.

Bruner, J. (1986). *Actual minds, possible worlds.* Cambridge, MA: Harvard University Press.

Bruner, J. (1990). *Acts of meaning.* Cambridge, MA: Harvard University Press.

Carey, J. W. (1988). *Communication as culture: Essays on media and society.* London: Unwin Hyman.

Christie, F. (1999). Genre theory and ESL teaching: A systemic functional perspective. *TESOL Quarterly 33,* 759–763.

Cope, B., & Kalantzis, M. (Eds.). (1993). *The powers of literacy: A genre approach to teaching writing.* Pittsburgh, PA: University of Pittsburgh Press.

Cope, B., & Kalantzis, M. (Eds.). (2000). *Multiliteracies: Literacy learning and the design of social futures.* London: Routledge.

ular magazines as well as serious and scholarly periodicals. You can search for scholarly articles by opting to find refereed articles; these are articles that have been approved by an editorial board. Such a process guarantees a scholarly article. However, when you find and click on an article in a database, you have none of the distinguishing signs of the journal type and format to help you make decisions about the article's level of academic seriousness and scholarly approach. At first glance, all articles in a database look alike. Use the guidelines in the Key Points box to help yourself make decisions.

KEY POINTS

Recognizing a Scholarly Article in a Full-Text Database

1. Look at the length: scholarly articles tend to be longer than others.

2. Turn to the end of the article and look for a bibliographical list of references.

3. At the beginning or end of the article, look for information about the author: academic affiliation, research interests, publications, and so on.

4. Consider the length and substance of the paragraphs; journalistic articles tend to have shorter paragraphs than scholarly articles. The paragraphs of a scholarly article usually will have a clear topic and supporting evidence.

5. Examine the language used. If you come across words like *guys* and *OK* and expressions like "Snap out of it," you have found a piece of journalism.

6. If you cannot make up your mind about the type of article, follow up on the source journal. Find it in a library and examine the cover, table of contents, and statement of purpose.

 TECHNOTE Web Site for Distinguishing Types of Articles

The Cornell University Web site *Distinguishing Scholarly Journals from Other Periodicals* at <http://www.library.cornell.edu/okuref/research/skill20.html> provides definitions and examples of four categories of periodical literature: scholarly, substantive news and general interest, popular, and sensational. ◼

49c How to evaluate works originating in print

Before you make detailed notes on a book or an article that began its life in print, be sure it will provide suitable information to help answer your research question.

Print books Check the date of publication, notes about the author, table of contents, and index. Skim the preface, introduction, chapter headings, and summaries to give yourself an idea of the information contained in the book and of the book's theoretical basis and perspective. Do not waste time making detailed notes on a book that deals only tangentially with your topic or on an out-of-date book (unless your purpose is to discuss and critique its perspective or examine a topic historically). Ask a librarian or your instructor for help in evaluating the appropriateness of sources you discover. If your topic concerns a serious academic issue, readers will expect you to consult books and not limit your references to popular magazines, newspapers, and Internet sources.

Periodical articles in print   Take into account the type of periodical, any organization with which it is affiliated, and the intended audience. Differentiate among the following types of articles (listed in descending order of reliability, with the most reliable first):

- scholarly articles (see **49b**)
- articles, often long, in periodicals for nonspecialist but serious, well-educated readers, such as the *New York Review of Books, Atlantic Monthly, Economist, Scientific American,* and *Nation*
- shorter articles, with sources not identified, in popular magazines for a general audience, such as *Ebony, Time, Newsweek, Parents, Psychology Today,* and *Vogue*
- articles with dubious sources, written for sensational tabloid magazines, such as *National Enquirer, Globe,* and *Star*

Newspaper articles   The *New York Times, Washington Post,* and *Los Angeles Times,* for example, provide mostly reliable accounts of current events, daily editorial comments, and reviews of books, films, and art. Be aware that most newspapers have political leanings, so reports of and comments on the same event may differ.

KEY POINTS

Questions to Evaluate a Print Source

1. *What does the work cover?* It should be long enough and detailed enough to provide adequate information.
2. *How objective is the information?* The author and publisher or periodical should not be affiliated with an organization that has an ax to grind—unless, of course, your topic entails examining the ax, reading critically, and making comparisons with other points of view.
3. *How current are the views?* Check the date of publication. The work should be up to date if you need a current perspective.

(continued)

(continued)

4. *How reputable are the publisher and author?* The work should be published by a reputable publisher in a source that is academically reliable, not one devoted to gossip, advertising, propaganda, or sensationalism. Check *Books in Print* or *Literary Market Place* for details on publishers. The author should be an authority on the subject. Find out what else the author has written (in *Books in Print* or at <http:www.amazon.com>) and what his or her qualifications are as an authority.

49d How to evaluate sources originating on the Internet

What makes the Internet so fascinating is that it is wide open, free, and democratic. Anyone can "publish" anything, and thousands or millions can read it. For scholars looking for information and well-presented, informed opinion, however, the Internet can pose a challenge. The following signals should indicate that a source is relatively objective and academically acceptable:

- An article in a CD-ROM or online subscription database (*InfoTrac, EBSCOhost, FirstSearch,* or *Lexis-Nexis,* for example) has been previously published in print, so you can use the criteria for print works (**49c**) to evaluate it, knowing that an article published in a reputable periodical is a valid source for a research paper.

- An article in an online journal sponsored by a professional organization or university probably has been refereed for content and accepted as meeting certain standards. Go to the journal's submission requirements to check this.

- A Web source sponsored by a government organization (.gov) or an accredited university (.edu) has probably been through a review process. Check on how recently the source has been updated.

49e How to develop junk antennae

To evaluate works devised specifically for the Internet, use the strategies in the Key Points box to help yourself separate the informational from the junk.

Be aware that site ratings of "excellent" given by search engines and directories may be based not on reliability of content but on other criteria, such as humor and attractiveness of graphics. In short, with Web sources, give each one a *careful evaluation*.

Developing Your Junk Antennae

1. *Scrutinize the domain name of the URL.* Informational Web pages tend to come from .gov and .edu addresses. Nonprofit organizations (.org) provide interesting mission statements. With .com ("dot com") sources, always assess whether the source provides information or self-promotion.

2. *Check the home page.* Always take the link from a Web site to its home page for information about the author, the sponsor, the purpose, and the date of posting. You can also discover site aims and sponsors by progressively deleting backwards parts of the URL up to the first slash.

3. *Assess the originator of an .edu source.* Is the educational institution or a branch of it sponsoring the site? A tilde (~) followed by a name in the URL indicates an individual posting from an academic source. Try to ascertain whether the individual is a faculty member or a student.

4. *Discover what you can about the author.* Look for a list of credentials, a home page, a résumé, or Web publications. In Google, use the author's name as a search term to see what the author has published on the Internet or who has cited the author.

5. *Investigate the purposes of a Web page author or sponsor.* Objectivity and rationality are not necessarily features of all Web pages. You may come across propaganda, hate sites, individuals purporting to have psychic powers, religious enthusiasts, and extreme political groups. The sponsor of a site may want to persuade, convert, or sell. Go to the home page and to linked sites and, in addition, note any postal or e-mail address or phone number you can use to get more information about the page and the sponsor. Even if the message is not pointedly biased and extreme, be aware that most authors write from some sense of conviction or purpose. Look for alternative points of view, too.

6. *Evaluate the quality of the writing.* A Web page filled with spelling and grammatical errors should not inspire confidence. If the language has not been checked, the ideas probably have not been given much time and thought, either. Don't use such a site as a source. Exceptions are discussion lists and Usenet postings. They are written and posted quickly, so even if they contain errors, they can also contain useful ideas to stimulate thinking on your topic.

(continued)

(continued)

7. *Follow the links.* See whether the links in a site take you to authoritative sources. If the links no longer work (you will get a 404 message: "Site Not Found"), the home page with the links has not been updated in a while—not a good sign.

8. *Check for dates, updates, ways to respond, and ease of navigation.* A recent date of posting or recent updating, information about the author, ways to reach the author by e-mail, regular mail, or phone, a clearly organized site, easy navigation, and up-to-date links to responsible sites are all indications that the site is well managed and current.

 TechNote Information on Evaluating Sources

Useful information on evaluating sources is available at the Widener University (Chester, PA) site at <http://www2.widener.edu/Wofgram-Memorial-Library/webevaluation/webeval.htm> and at a site called *Thinking Critically about World Wide Web Resources*, prepared by a UCLA librarian, <http://www.library.ucla.edu/libraries/college/help/critical/index.htm>. ■

50 Using Sources

Once you have found useful sources for your paper, you then need to know how to record the information and use your sources to support your points. It is especially important to know how to cite any source that you refer to, summarize, paraphrase from, or quote from, so that you avoid plagiarizing. First, though, understand what plagiarism is and how careful documentation can steer you clear of it.

50a What is plagiarism?

The word *plagiarize* is derived from a Latin verb meaning "to kidnap," and kidnapping or stealing someone else's ideas and presenting them as your own is regarded as a serious offense in Western academic culture and public life. Any of the following are regarded as plagiarizing:

- presenting the work of others as your own work
- downloading material from the Internet without any acknowledgment

- using the ideas or words you find in a print or Web source without acknowledging where those ideas or words come from

- forgetting to add a citation to ideas and words that are not your own

In short, plagiarizing is seen as stealing somebody else's words and ideas. It can be done intentionally; it can also occur unintentionally (as some writers have claimed), as a result of sloppy research and acknowledgment. Either way, intentional or not, plagiarizing is a serious offense. Avoid it by always using your own work and always documenting a source.

 TECHNOTE A Web Site on Plagiarism

For more on the topic of plagiarism, see the Georgetown University Web site *What Is Plagiarism?* at <http://www.georgetown.edu/honor/plagiarism.html>. ▓

50b What is documentation?

The need to acknowledge and document sources is not merely academic pickiness. It is a service to readers. When you document a source, you provide readers with exact details about where to find the reference, the fact, or the quotation. (For a book, for example, you need to supply information about who wrote it, what the title is, the publisher, the place of publication, and the date of publication.) Then it will be quick and easy for interested readers to locate the exact source that you found.

Readers may want to find all or some of your sources for any of the following reasons: you have made them curious and they want to read more; they want to explore the topic in greater depth; they find it hard to believe that a source says what you say it says, so they want to read it for themselves. When you write, you are expected to provide all the necessary information in an organized system of documentation. In addition, you do yourself a service, too, every time you cite and document sources, because when you acknowledge ideas and words that you have found in the works of reputable authors, you bolster your own case. Readers are far more likely to treat your claim seriously and heed your argument if you show that you can support it with documented evidence, instead of presenting it as something you happened to think of in a random moment or something you heard from a friend. Readers will be impressed by a judicious use of sources, both those that support your claim and those that run counter to it—which you, of course, will refute. Such an approach reveals a thoroughness that readers find impressive and convincing. From the beginning, then, treat source material and the documenting of it as an aid to your argument.

Research and clear documentation open a channel of communication between you and your readers. They learn what your views are and what has influenced those views. They will assume that anything not documented is your original idea and your wording. So if you even accidentally present someone else's actual words or ideas as if they were your own, readers might suspect you of plagiarizing. Look at the following examples and how they handle and acknowledge (or not) the original source.

ORIGINAL SOURCE

Chip explained that he had been "mentally perturbed" the weekend before the paper was due, and that the essay he had written failed to meet his high standards. But I sensed that Chip felt that he had made a choice akin to having a pizza delivered. He had procrastinated on an assignment due the next day, had no time left in which to prepare his work from scratch, and had to get on to those pressing matters that shape the world of an 18-year-old. He dialed his Internet service provider, ordered takeout, and had it delivered.

—Ellen Laird, "Internet Plagiarism: We All Pay the Price"

NO DOCUMENTATION (PLAGIARIZED)

```
Students sometimes feel caught by the pressure of time
and that leads them to plagiarize. The way they take
material from an online source is like simply ordering a
takeout pizza.
```

CLEAR DOCUMENTATION

```
Students sometimes feel caught by the pressure of time
and that leads them to plagiarize. Ellen Laird compares
the way they take material from an online source to
simply ordering a takeout pizza (5).
```

[The student includes Laird's article in her list of works cited at the end of the essay.]

50c How to avoid plagiarizing

Avoiding plagiarism begins with accurate recording and careful management of source material so that you do not end up confused about which parts of your notes contain your ideas and which are derived from the works of others.

KEY POINTS
How to Avoid Plagiarizing

1. Make a record of each source, so that you have all the information you need for appropriate documentation.

2. Set up a working annotated bibliography.

3. Take notes from the sources, with a systematic method of indicating quotation, paraphrase, and your own comments. For example, use quotation marks around quoted words, phrases, sentences, and passages; introduce a paraphrase with a tag, such as "Laird makes the point that . . ."; in your notes about a source, write your own comments in a different color. Then, later, you will see immediately which ideas are yours and which come from your source.

4. Never include in your own essay a passage, an identifiable phrase, or an idea that you have copied from someone else's work without acknowledging and documenting the source.

5. Never use exactly the same sequence of ideas and organization of argument as your source.

6. When you use a single key word from your source or three or more words in sequence from your source, use the appropriate format for quoting and documenting.

7. Always cite the source of any summary or paraphrase. Not only exact words but also ideas need to be credited.

8. Never simply substitute synonyms for a few words in the source or move a few words around.

9. Never use in your paper passages that have been written or rewritten by a friend or a tutor.

10. Never buy, find, download from the Internet, or "borrow" a paper or a section of a paper that you turn in as your own work.

Acknowledging your sources not only gives credit where it is due but also shows how much research you have done. The first step is careful recording of source information and precise note-taking (**50d** and **50e**). The second step is careful acknowledging and citing of sources in your paper and listing the sources you have used. Sections **52–56** show you how to use five different styles of citation and documentation: MLA, APA, CBE/CSE, *Chicago,* and *Columbia.* Once you have recorded the basic information about each source, you will be able to use it in whatever documentation style your instructor or discipline requires.

WORLDS OF WRITING
Ownership Rights across Cultures

The Western view takes seriously the ownership of words and text. It respects both the individual as author (and authority) and the originality of the individual's ideas. Copyright laws define and protect the boundaries of intellectual property. However, even the Western world acknowledges that authors imitate and borrow from others' work, as Harold Bloom notes in *The Anxiety of Influence*. In some cultures, memorization and the use of classic texts are common in all walks of life. And worldwide, the ownership of language, texts, and ideas is being called into question by the democratic, interactive nature of the Internet. In short, therefore, plagiarism is not something universal and easy to define. Nevertheless, in Western academic culture, basic ground rules exist for the "fair use" of other writers' work without payment, but acknowledging the source of borrowed material is always necessary.

50d What to cite and document

When you do refer to a source in your work, carefully cite and document it. Systematically provide information about the author, title, publication data, page numbers, Internet address, dates—whatever is available (see **50f** for the information you need to collect). You provide such documentation so that readers can locate your sources and turn to them for further information. (See **52–56** for guides to specific systems of documentation.) You also document sources so there will be no question about which words and ideas are yours and which belong to other people.

KEY POINTS
What to Cite

1. Cite all facts, statistics, and pieces of information unless they are common knowledge and are accessible in many sources.

2. Cite exact words from your source, enclosed in quotation marks.

3. Cite somebody else's ideas and opinions, even if you restate them in your own words in a summary or paraphrase.

4. Cite each sentence in a long paraphrase (if it is not clear that all the sentences paraphrase the same original source).

Note how James Stalker, in his article "Official English or English Only," does not quote directly but still cites the source of the specialized facts:

> By 1745 there were approximately 45,000 German speakers in the colonies, and by 1790 there were some 200,000, nine per cent of the population (Anderson 80).

Citation is not necessary for facts regarded as common knowledge, such as the dates of the Civil War; facts available in many sources, such as authors' birth and death dates and chronological events; or allusions to folktales that have been handed down through the ages. When you are in doubt about whether a fact is common knowledge, cite your source.

 TECHNOTE The Instability of Internet Information

The Internet is democratic in its approach to knowledge; information there is plentiful, readily available, and free. The Internet's interactive nature means that issues get discussed and worked over by many people (look at an online discussion group or Usenet newsgroup to see examples), so ideas are often generated by collaboration with others. In addition, the information out there is constantly changing. The source material you find today might disappear by tomorrow. The bounty, collaborative nature, and flux of online information mean that you have to be especially careful as you do Internet research and record information. Again, when in doubt, even if you are using information from a discussion list to which you have contributed, always keep a copy of the source on disk or in print and cite your source in your essay. ■

50e Keeping track of sources and taking notes

The first step toward avoiding plagiarism is keeping track of what your sources are and which ideas come from your sources and which from you. You will find that one of the frustrating moments for you as a researcher occurs when you find some notes about an interesting point you read but you cannot remember where you found the passage or who wrote it or whether your notes represent an author's exact words. You can spend hours in tedious retracing of your steps. Avoid this frustration by keeping track as you go along. However rushed you are or however little time you have, this saving and recording of source material is essential. See **50f** for details on exactly what type of information to record about each source.

Use the Bookmarks or Favorites feature. Many browsers have a Bookmarks or Favorites feature that allows you to compile and save a list of useful sites you have visited. You can then easily revisit these sites by simply clicking on the bookmark. Bookmarks can be deleted later when you no longer need them. If you work on a networked computer in a lab where you cannot save your work on the hard drive, save your bookmarks to your own bookmark file on a diskette. (In Netscape, go to Bookmarks/Edit Bookmarks/File/ Open Bookmark File, and specify the location to save the file. In Internet Explorer, go to File/Import and Export, and export your "Favorites" to a diskette file.)

Record URL and date of access. Note that bookmarking will not always last with a long URL, such as URLs of online subscription services. To be safe, also use the Copy and Paste features to copy the URL on your hard drive or diskette, along with the date on which you access the source. As a last resort, copy the URL by hand, but take care to get it exactly right: every letter, symbol, and punctuation mark is important.

TECHNOTE Keeping a Bookmark or Favorites File on the Internet

If you do most of your writing in a college computer lab, you may not be able to use the Bookmark or Favorites feature of the browser. In that case, try the free bookmark service on the Internet at <http://www.blink.com>. ∎

Highlight, copy, and paste. As you read material on the Web, most reasonably powerful computers allow you to highlight a passage you find, copy it, and then paste it into a file on your own disk. Make sure that you indicate clearly in your new document that you have included a direct quotation: use quotation marks or a bigger font along with an author/page citation. Save as much information as you can about the original document in your working bibliography.

Make photocopies of sources. Photocopying print articles and printing or downloading online articles allow you to devote research time to locating relevant sources and taking notes from reference works and books; you can take the copies of articles with you and use them when you are unable to be in the library. A quick way to make a copy of an Internet source or material in an online database is to e-mail it to yourself: in Netscape, go to File/Send Page; in Internet Explorer, use File/Send. This is often easier and cheaper than printing out at the library. As soon as you have time, though, evaluate the usefulness of your copies by highlighting and commenting on relevant sections or by taking notes.

Annotate and take careful notes. Printing and saving from online sources make a source text available for you to annotate. You can interact with the author's ideas, asking questions, writing comments, and jotting down your own ideas. Here is an editorial from the *Boston Globe* that student Martin Matos found in an online database that his college library subscribed to. He had been reading articles related to free speech and the Columbine High School tragedy, and he used the search terms "Columbine," "threat," and "punishment" as he continued browsing to narrow his topic. He decided that the *Globe* article would be helpful to narrow his topic to the issue of free speech in high school assignments. He then copied and printed the article, read it again, and annotated it as he read.

Punishing Assignment

Find other articles about other threats?   Threats made by students have become dynamite. After last year's tragic shooting at Columbine High School in Colorado, officials have become fiercely vigilant, trying to save lives. But in some cases—including a recent one at Boston Latin Academy— it is important to ask if school punishments exceed the offenses. *Is this a public or a private school? Would it make a difference?*

The exact wording of the assignment could be revealing.   Boston Latin's case is a murky one. Students in an English class who had been studying William Faulkner were asked to write a Southern Gothic tale using details about characters and their community, according to Boston Public School spokeswoman Tracy Lynch. Junior Charles Carithers turned in a story *Oh wow!* about a student who kills his English teacher with a chain saw. It read more like the capsule summary of a slasher film that could take place in Anytown, USA. School officials determined that the story was a threat to do bodily harm, in part because the story's characters were similar to Carithers and his teacher. Carithers faces a three-day suspension.

    Officials were right to respond. Red flags, no matter how small, demand attention. And students must recognize that in today's environment, comments about killing someone are a serious matter.

Good point to consult with the student.   Carithers should be asked about his intentions, however. Making the story's victim an English teacher certainly seems

like a deliberate affront to a real person. But given the nature of
the assignment, suspension may be an overreaction.

Find the
ACLU
source
on Web?

The American Civil Liberties Union has sided with
Carithers, arguing that Superintendent Thomas Payzant should
nullify the suspension. A better step would be to let the appeals
process roll forward. In mid-May an appeals officer will be
brought in from outside the school. No action on the proposed
suspension will occur until after that.

*A nicely
balanced
point of
view.*

Find out
the
outcome
of the
appeal.

The appeal will address the Carithers case, but, more
important, it will give Boston Latin Academy a chance to
rethink and refine its procedures. This is an invaluable opportunity since the school and the system will undoubtedly face
this issue in the future. Boston Latin Academy's wise vigilance
could be strengthened by this experience.

*Do other
sources
also
regard
this as
"wise
vigilance"?*

—Editorial, *Boston Globe* 28 Apr. 2000: A22

Annotating is useful for comments, observations, and questions.
You will also need to make notes when you do not have a copy that you
can write on or when you want to summarize, paraphrase, and make
detailed connections to other ideas and other sources. Write notes on
the computer, on legal pads, in notebooks, or on index cards—whatever
works best for you. Index cards—each card with a heading and only
one note—offer the advantage of flexibility: you can shuffle and reorder
them to fit the organization of your paper. In notes written separately,
always include the author's name, a short version of the title of the
work, and any relevant page number whenever you summarize, paraphrase, or quote. Include full bibliographical information in your working bibliography. (See **50g** for Matos's summary of the *Boston Globe* editorial.) Then when you start to write your paper, you will have at your
fingertips all the information necessary for a citation.

50f Setting up a working bibliography

From the first steps of your research, keep accurate records of each
source in a working bibliography. Record enough information so that
you will be able to make up a list of references in whichever style of
documentation you choose, though not all the points of information
you record will be necessary for every style of documentation. Use
the following templates as guides for what to record, but be aware
that with online sources, especially, much of the information may not
be available. Essential information for an online source is always the

URL and the date on which you access the material. Always make a note of that information. The templates are available for printing and filling out at <http://college.hmco.com/keys.html> (click on Downloadable Forms).

PRINT BOOK

1. Author(s), editor(s), translator(s) : last name, first name
2. Title and subtitle
3. Publication information

   place of publication

   name of publishing company

   year of publication
4. If available, volume number or edition number
5. Call number (see **48e**)

Hint: Photocopy the title page and the copyright page, where the first four items of information are available.

PRINT ARTICLE

1. Author(s), editor(s) translator(s): last name, first name
2. Title and subtitle
3. Name of periodical
4. Publication information
   a. For a periodical

      volume number

      issue number

      date of publication

      inclusive page numbers of article
   b. For an article in a book

      title of book, name of editor

      publisher, place, and year of publication

      inclusive page numbers of article

Hint: Photocopy the table of contents of the periodical or anthology.

ELECTRONIC OR ONLINE SOURCE

1. Author(s), editor(s), translator(s): last name, first name
2. Title and subtitle of work
3. Any print publication information (as for a book or an article)

4. Name of site (for example, title of online periodical or Web site, database, name of discussion list or forum, home page, subject line of e-mail message)

5. Electronic publication information, as available, for

   a CD-ROM: version number

   a document in a database: document access number

   an article in an online journal: volume, issue number, and date of publication

   a Web site: date of online publication or latest update

   electronic or online material: number of paragraphs, but only if paragraph numbers actually appear on the screen

6. Compiler or sponsor of Web site or distributor of CD-ROM

7. For an e-mail message or discussion list posting: name of sender, subject line, date of posting, name of discussion list, your date of access

8. MOST IMPORTANT! For any Web source, the date when you access the source and the complete URL

Hint: Save to disk, e-mail yourself a copy, or print out an online source. For a printout of a Web document, you can set your computer so that the URL appears on the printout, along with the date on which you print the document (the date of access). If you are saving information in a computer program, use the Copy and Paste functions to copy the URL accurately into your own document.

Keep your list of sources in a form that you can work with to organize them alphabetically, add and reject sources, and add summaries and notes. Note cards and computer files have the advantage over sheets of paper or a research journal. They don't tie you to page order. (See **50g** for examples of note cards.)

KEY POINTS

Ways to Set Up a Working Bibliography

Choose which of the following methods best suits your work habits and learning style.

1. Use 3" x 5" index cards, one for each source, to record the essential information.

2. Use the templates (available for printing or downloading) on the Web site for this book: <http://college.hmco.com/keys.html>.

3. Use a computer file to record information and begin each entry with the last name of the author. That way, you can use the Table/Sort Text feature to alphabetize the entries when you are ready to work on your list of works cited.

4. Use a computer software program such as TakeNote! to provide computer note cards. Some bibliography programs will use the information you provide in specified categories to prepare lists in different styles, such as MLA and APA.

5. Use a software program to help with researching, recording sources, and formatting a bibliography. See <http://www.endnote.com/EN4infor.htm> for more information on this program that formats your references in the style you designate. Or use the Termperfect CD that formats the header, the title, and the works-cited entries of your MLA paper. For information, see <http://www.termperfect.com>.

6. Try out the free service at NoodleBib, which promises to simplify "the process of creating and editing MLA-style bibliographies": <http://noodletools.com/noodlebib/index.php>.

Annotating the working bibliography   If you need to prepare an annotated bibliography, one that summarizes the contents of each source, write a brief summary on the back of the index card or hardcopy template. Or if you are using a computer to record information, keep a separate file for the summaries you will need for an annotated bibliography.

Here are entries from an annotated bibliography on ichthyology, the study of fishes:

Long, John A. The Rise of Fishes: 500 Million Years of
   Evolution. Baltimore: Johns Hopkins UP, 1995.
   Highly readable book on fossils, combining a large and colorful art program with stories by the author (a specialist
   in vertebrate paleontology, Western Australian Museum, Perth)
   about his interesting fieldwork around the world.

Maisey, John G. Discovering Fossil Fishes. New York: Holt, 1996.
   Well-illustrated and informative overview of fish evolution,
   notable for its discussion of a recent movement (cladistics)
   to change the longstanding fish classification system.

In addition, see **8b** for an entry in an annotated bibliography done in preparation for the MLA paper by Jared Whittemore shown in **52f**.

50g Summarizing and paraphrasing

Summary Summaries are useful for giving your reader basic information about the work you are discussing. To summarize a source or a passage in a source, select only the main points as the author presents them, without your own commentary or interpretation. Be brief, and use your own words at all times. To ensure that you use your own words, do not have the original source in front of you as you write. Read, understand, and then put the passage away before writing your summary. If you find that you must include some particularly apt words from the original source, put them in quotation marks.

Use summaries in your research paper to let readers know the gist of the most important sources you find. When you include a summary in a paper, introduce the author or the work to indicate where your summary begins. At the end of the summary, give the page numbers you are summarizing. Do not include page numbers if you are summarizing the complete work or summarizing an online source; instead, indicate where your summary ends and your own ideas return (see **50i**). When you write your paper, provide full documentation of the source in the list of works cited at the end.

As Martin Matos was working on his essay on students' rights to free speech, he recorded on a 3″ × 5″ index card for his working bibliography the following entry on the article in **50e:**

"Punishing Assignment." Editorial. Boston Globe 28 Apr. 2000 : A22 . Academic Universe. Lexis-Nexis. City U of New York Lib. New York, NY. 20 Nov. 2001 <http:// web.lexis-nexis .com/ universe>.

He then wrote notes in a computer file he named "Creativity and free speech." The heading of each note referred directly to the first word on the bibliography card.

```
"Punishing"                                      Summary
A student in a Boston school fulfilled a writing
assignment by writing a gruesome story. He was
subsequently told that he would be suspended from school
for three days. While the school's procedures can be seen
as "wise vigilance," suspension should not occur until
the student has a chance to appeal.
```

Matos could also have handwritten the same summary on a 4" × 6" index card. (See <http://rwc.hunter.cuny.edu/writing/on-line/notetaki.html> for more on using note cards.)

Paraphrase When you need more details than a summary provides, paraphrasing offers a tool. Use paraphrase more often than you use quotation. A paraphrase uses your words and your interpretations of and comments on the ideas you find in your sources. Many instructors feel that if you cannot paraphrase information, then you probably do not understand it. So paraphrase serves the purpose of showing that you have absorbed your source material.

A paraphrase is similar in length to the original material— maybe somewhat longer. In a paraphrase, present the author's argument and logic, but be very careful not to use the author's exact words or sentence structure.

KEY POINTS
How to Paraphrase

1. Keep the source out of sight as you write a paraphrase, so you will not be tempted to use any of the sentence patterns or phrases of the original.

2. Do not substitute synonyms for some or most of the words in an author's passage. This practice will result in plagiarism.

3. Use your own sentence structure as well as your own words. Your writing will still be regarded as plagiarized if it resembles the original in sentence structure as well as in wording.

4. Do not comment or interpret: just tell readers the ideas that the author of your source presents.

5. Check your text against the original source to avoid inadvertent plagiarism.

6. Cite the author (and page number if a print source) as the source of the ideas, introduce and integrate the paraphrase, and provide full documentation. If the source does not name an author, cite the title.

When Michelle Guerra was writing a paper on the English-only controversy (whether languages other than English should be banned in schools and government offices and publications) and looking for the history of the issue, she came across the following source.

ORIGINAL SOURCE

If any language group, Spanish or other, chooses to maintain its language, there is precious little that we can do about it, legally or otherwise, and still maintain that we are a free country. We cannot legislate the language of the home, the street, the bar, the club, unless we are willing to set up a cadre of language police who will ticket and arrest us if we speak something other than English.

—James C. Stalker, "Official English or English Only,"
English Journal 77 (Mar. 1988): 21

You can use common words and expressions such as *language, street,* or *free country* and recognized technical terms such as *language group* without quotation marks. But if you use more unusual expressions from the source ("precious little that we can do"; "cadre of language police"), enclose them in quotation marks. In Guerra's first attempt at paraphrase on a note card, she does not quote, but words and structure closely resemble the original.

PARAPHRASE TOO SIMILAR TO THE ORIGINAL

```
Stalker                              Paraphrase, p. 21
As Stalker points out, if any group of languages, Greek
or other, decides to keep its language, there is not much
any of us can do, with laws or not, and still claim to
be a free country. We cannot pass legislation about the
language we speak at home, on the street, or in
restaurants, unless we also want to have a group of
special police who will take us off to jail if they hear
us not speaking English (21).
```

Guerra cites the page number of the source, using the MLA style of parenthetical documentation. Documentation, however, is not a guarantee against plagiarism. Guerra's wording and sentence structure follow the original too closely. When classmates and her instructor pointed this out to her, she then revised the paraphrase by keeping the ideas of the original but using different wording and sentence structure.

REVISED PARAPHRASE

```
Stalker                              Paraphrase, p. 21
Stalker points out that in a democracy like the United
States, people of all ethnic and language backgrounds are
always free to speak their own language without any
interference. It is not feasible to have laws against the
uses of a language because it certainly would not be
possible to enforce such laws in homes, on the streets,
and in public places (21).
```

50h Quoting

To make a paper your own, rather than a cutting and pasting of quotations, rely on paraphrase of your sources rather than quoting. Readers do not want to read pages of quotations, one after another. They want to read what you have to say about what you have read. Your voice should be the dominant voice in the paper.

However, when an author says something in a particularly clever or dramatic way, you may want to quote his or her words directly. Highlight or make a note of quotations that could be useful in your paper; make sure that you use words and punctuation exactly as in the original. If you are downloading information and writing notes on a computer, you can use a different font size or style—such as large or bold type—to download the passage from the source and put it within quotation marks. Then you will see at a glance which words are not yours when you cut and paste them into your essay.

Readers should immediately realize why you quote a particular passage and what the quotation contributes to the ideas you want to convey. They should also learn who said the words you are quoting and, if the source is a print source, on which page of the original work the quotation appears. Then they can look up the author's name (or the title of the work if no author is named) in the list of works cited at the end of your paper and find out exactly where you found the quotation.

The Modern Language Association (MLA) format for citing a quotation from an article by one author is illustrated in this section and in section **52.** See **53–56** for examples of citations of sources in APA and other styles of documentation.

Deciding what and when to quote   Quote when you use the words of a well-known authority or when the words are particularly striking. Quote only when the original words express the exact point you want to make and express it succinctly and well. Otherwise, paraphrase. When you consider quoting, ask yourself: Which point of mine does the quotation illustrate? Why am I considering quoting this particular passage? Why should this particular passage be quoted rather than paraphrased? What do I need to tell readers about the author of the quotation?

Quoting the exact words of the original   To understand how to deal with quotations in your paper, consider an article Martin Matos found (available both in print and online) and the quotations he used as he was working on his paper on students' rights to free speech:

> Late last month, Charles Carithers got an English assignment: Write "a vivid horror story" about a mysterious person in the community who had a "shocking" secret in his past. So the 11th-grader at Boston Latin Academy, a competitive-admissions public school, wrote about a student athlete (which he is) who went after his English teacher with a chain saw.

> The teacher saw details that hit too close to home. Charles got a three-day suspension. The school is defending the action, and Charles's mother is appealing it.

> In the current climate of jitters in schools across the United States, chainsaw murders might not be the best topic for an essay. But assignments that open the door to writing about chainsaw murders might not be all that inspired, either. Adults can say that they weren't as prone to writing about such gore in their day, or that horror is more effective when less crudely rendered. But high-schoolers don't think like adults—and they are routinely doused with ridiculously crude and gory films like "Scream" (1, 2, and 3) and "I Know What You Did Last Summer," all of which Charles said he pondered as he created his opus. (As did perhaps a peer—not suspended—whose protagonist murdered children and cut them up for fertilizer.)

> It seems like a "teachable moment" that engendered a hard-line response. And such debacles happen across the US. Why no open discussion of what's acceptable? Or specifics: a horror story, children, but no guns or chain saws allowed. Or, show me the difference between horror and tension.

Assignments can't be created in a cultural vacuum—and no
one should expect the results to be, either.

—Amelia Newcomb, "Suspense and Suspension,"
Christian Science Monitor, 2 May 2000, 13

Any words you use from a source must be included in quotation
marks and quoted exactly as they appear in the original, with the
same punctuation marks and capital letters. Do not change pronouns
or tenses to fit your own purpose, unless you enclose changes in
square brackets (see the examples that follow).

NOT EXACT QUOTATION

```
Newcomb reports that Charles Carithers wrote an essay
about "someone in his community with a secret in his past."
```

EXACT QUOTATION, WITHOUT CITATION

```
Newcomb reports that Charles Carithers wrote an essay
"about a mysterious person in the community who had a
'shocking' secret in his past."
```

EXACT QUOTATION, WITH CITATION

```
Newcomb reports that Charles Carithers wrote an essay
"about a mysterious person in the community who had a
'shocking' secret in his past" (13).
```

Note that if your quotation includes a question mark or exclamation
point, you must include it within the quotation. Your sentence period
then comes after your citation.

```
Newcomb wonders, "Why no open discussion of what's
acceptable?" (13).
```

Quoting part of a sentence   You can make sure that quotations
make a point and are not just dropped into your essay if you integrate
parts of quoted sentences into your own sentences. When it is obvious
that parts of the quoted sentence have been omitted at the beginning
or end of the quotation, you do not need to use ellipsis dots.

```
Reporter Amelia Newcomb wonders about the influence of
"ridiculously crude and gory films."
```

Omitting words in the middle of a quotation   If you omit as
irrelevant to your purpose any words or passages from the middle of
a quotation, signal the omission with the ellipsis mark, three dots
separated by spaces. To make it clear that the ellipsis is your addition

and not part of the original text, you can place the dots within square brackets (in MLA style). See **30c** for more on brackets and **30e** for more on ellipsis dots.

> According to Newcomb, a high school teacher asked students
> to write about a "mysterious person ... who had a
> 'shocking' secret in his past." ⌐____Or [. . .]

Omitting words at the end of a quotation If you omit the end of the source's sentence at the end of your own sentence, and your sentence is not followed by a page citation, signal the omission with three ellipsis dots following the sentence period—four dots in all. Then close the quotation marks.

> With resignation, Newcomb concedes that "such debacles
> happen. . . ."

When you include a page citation for a print source, place it after the closing quotation marks and before the final sentence period.

> With resignation, Newcomb concedes that "such debacles
> happen . . ." (13).

Omitting a sentence or a line of poetry Use a sentence period followed by three dots if you omit a complete sentence (or more) when the omission is preceded and followed by complete sentences.

> Most teachers would agree that "chainsaw murders might
> not be the best topic for an essay.... But highschoolers
> don't think like adults," as Newcomb aptly reminds us (13).

Use a line of dots if you omit a whole line of a poem (see **30e** for an example).

Adding or changing words If you add any comments or explanations in your own words, or if you change a word in the quotation to fit it grammatically into your sentence, enclose the added or changed material in square brackets. Generally, however, it is preferable to rephrase your sentence because bracketed words and phrases make sentences difficult to read.

NO: DIFFICULT TO READ **Newcomb wonders whether we as adults were not "as prone to writing about such gore [in a high school essay assignment] in [our] day."**

YES: CLEARER **Newcomb wonders whether we as adults just were not "as prone to writing about such gore" in our high school essays.**

Quoting longer passages   If you quote more than three lines of poetry or four typed lines of prose, do not use quotation marks. Instead, begin the quotation on a new line, and indent the quotation one inch (or ten spaces) from the left margin in MLA style, or indent it half an inch (five spaces) from the left margin if you are using APA style. Double-space throughout the quotation. Do not indent from the right margin. You can establish the context for a long quotation and integrate it effectively into your text if you state the point that you want to make and name the author of the quotation in your introductory statement.

Author mentioned in introductory statement

Newcomb lays some blame on the teacher and uses sentence fragments to make a strong point about the way the teacher neglected to discuss the specifics of the assignment:

Quotation indented one inch or ten spaces

It seems like a "teachable moment" that engendered a hard-line response. And such debacles happen across the U.S. Why no open discussion of what's acceptable? Or specifics: a horror story, children, but no guns or chain saws allowed. Or show me the difference between horror and tension. (13)

No quotation marks at beginning or end of indented quotation

Page citation (only for a print source) after period

Note: With a long indented quotation, the citation follows the end punctuation of the quotation. Do not add any punctuation after the citation.

Avoiding a string of quotations   Use quotations, especially long ones, sparingly, and only when they bolster your argument. Readers do not want to read a list of snippets from the works of other writers. They want your analysis of your sources, and they are interested in the conclusions you draw from your research. Never let one quotation follow another in your essay. Readers will wonder where you have disappeared to and why they are reading a string of other people's voices. If you find yourself writing something such as *The author also says,* "..." or *The author goes on to say,* "...", see that as a danger signal for a string of quotations—and revise.

Fitting a quotation into your sentence   When you quote, use the exact words of the original, and make sure that those exact words do not disrupt the flow of your sentence and send it in another direction. A sentence that includes a quotation must not slide off the tracks into a mixed construction (**19a**), as the following "No" examples do.

No | Newcomb says that a teacher suspending a student for writing a gory essay, "such debacles happen across the US."

Yes | Newcomb says that the teacher who suspended a student was influenced by the contemporary climate since "such debacles happen across the US."

No | I wonder if Newcomb is biased when she claims that some "assignments that open the door to writing about chainsaw murders."

Yes | I wonder if Newcomb is biased when she claims that some "assignments . . . open the door to writing about chainsaw murders."

KEY POINTS

Using Quotations: A Checklist

Examine a draft of your paper and ask questions about each quotation you have included.

1. Why do you want to include this quotation? How does it support a point you have made?
2. What is particularly remarkable about this quotation? Would a paraphrase or a combination of paraphrase and quotation be better?
3. Does what you have written in the quotation exactly match the words and punctuation of the original?
4. Have you told readers the name of the author of the quotation or, if your source does not identify the author, have you cited the title?
5. Have you included the page number of the quotation for a print source?
6. How have you integrated the quotation into your own passage? Will readers know whom you are quoting and why?
7. What verb have you used to introduce the quotation?
8. Are there any places where you string quotations together, one after another? If so, revise. Look for quotation marks closing and then immediately opening again. Also look for phrases such as "X goes on to say . . ."; "X also says . . ."; "X then says . . . ."

9. Have you indented any quotations longer than four lines of type—with no added quotation marks?

10. Have you used long quotations sparingly?

50i Introducing source material and indicating the boundaries of a citation

When you provide a summary, paraphrase, or quotation to support one of the points in your paper, set up the context. Don't just drop in the material as if it came from nowhere. Think about how to introduce and integrate the material into the structure of your paper.

No   **Teachers might feel that Internet plagiarism is just too easy and that students plagiarize too easily by downloading material just like ordering takeout and "having a pizza delivered" (Laird 5).** [If this is your first mention of Laird, readers may wonder who the author is, what the context is, and how the quotation is relevant.]

YES   **Teachers might feel that Internet plagiarism is just too easy and that students plagiarize too easily by downloading material. In fact, college teacher Ellen Laird compares this practice to the ease of ordering takeout and "having a pizza delivered" (5).** [You would cite the original source fully in your works-cited list.]

Introducing source material   If you quote a complete sentence or if you paraphrase or summarize a section of another work, it is advisable to prepare readers for your summary, paraphrase, or quotation by mentioning the author's name in an introductory phrase, rather than just adding a parenthetical citation. In your first reference to the work, give the author's full name. To further orient readers, you can also include a brief statement of the author's expertise or credentials and thesis, so readers understand why this is an important source for you to cite. Here are some useful ways to introduce source material:

X has pointed out that

X, in a seminal article on the topic, has made it clear that

X makes it clear from the evidence she provides that

X uses the evidence to suggest that

According to the expert opinion of X,

In 1999, X, the vice president of the corporation, declared

Varying the introductory verb The introductory verbs *say* and *write* are clear and direct. For more nuances, though, consider using verbs that offer shades of meaning, such as *acknowledge, agree, argue, ask, assert, believe, claim, comment, contend, declare, deny, emphasize, insist, note, observe, point out, propose, speculate, suggest.*

Indicating the boundaries of a citation Naming an author or title in your text tells readers that you are citing ideas from a source, and citing a page number at the end of a summary or paraphrase lets them know where your citation ends. However, for one-page print articles and for Internet sources, a page citation is not necessary, so indicating where your comments about a source end is harder to do. You always need to indicate clearly where your summary or paraphrase ends and where your own comments take over. Convey the shift to readers by commenting on the source in a way that clearly announces a statement of your own views. Use expressions such as *it follows that, X's explanation shows that, as a result, evidently,* or *clearly* to signal the shift.

UNCLEAR CITATION BOUNDARY

> **According to a Sony page on the Web, the company has decided to release *Mozart Makes You Smarter* as a cassette on the strength of research indicating that listening to Mozart improves IQ. The products show the ingenuity of commercial enterprise while taking the researchers' conclusions in new directions.**
>
> [Does only the first sentence refer to material on the Web page, or do both sentences?]

REVISED CITATION, WITH SOURCE BOUNDARY INDICATED

> **According to a Sony page on the Web, the company has decided to release *Mozart Makes You Smarter* as a cassette on the strength of research indicating that listening to Mozart improves IQ. Clearly, Sony's plan demonstrates the ingenuity of commercial enterprise, but it cannot reflect what the researchers intended when they published their conclusions.**

Another way to indicate the end of your citation is to include the author's or authors' name(s) at the end of the citation instead of introducing the citation with the name.

UNCLEAR CITATION

> **For people who hate shopping, Web shopping may be the perfect solution. Jerome and Taylor's exploration of "holiday hell" reminds us that we get more choice from online vendors than we do**

when we browse at our local mall because the online sellers, unlike mall owners, do not have to rent space to display their goods. In addition, one can buy almost anything online, from CDs, cassettes, and books to cars and real estate.

REVISED CITATION, WITH SOURCE BOUNDARY INDICATED

For people who hate shopping, Web shopping may be the perfect solution. An article exploring the "holiday hell" of shopping reminds us that we get more choice from online vendors than we do when we browse at our local mall because the online sellers, unlike mall owners, do not have to rent space to display their goods (Jerome and Taylor). In addition, one can buy almost anything online, from CDs, cassettes, and books to cars and real estate.

51 Writing the Research Paper

51a Putting yourself in your paper

You have done hours, days, maybe weeks of research. You have found useful sources. You have a working bibliography and masses of photocopies, printouts, and notes. You have worked hard to analyze and synthesize all your material. You have made a scratch outline. Now comes the time to write your draft.

Get mileage out of your sources. Let readers know about the sources that support your point effectively. Don't mention an author of an influential book or long, important article just once and in parentheses. Let readers know why this source adds so much weight to your case. Tell about the expert's credentials, affiliations, and experience. Tell readers what the author does in the work you are citing. A summary of the work along with a paraphrase of important points may also be useful to provide context for the author's remarks and opinions. Show readers that they should be impressed by the heavyweight opinions and facts you present.

Synthesize your sources—don't string them. Never get so involved in your mountains of notes and copies of sources that you include everything you have read and string it all together. Large amounts of information are no substitute for a thesis with relevant support. Your paper should *synthesize* your sources, not just tell about them, one after the other. When you synthesize, you connect the ideas in individual sources to create a larger picture, to inform yourself about the topic, and to establish your own ideas on the topic. So leave plenty of time to read through your notes, think about what you have read, connect with the material, form responses to it, take into account new ideas and opposing arguments, and find connections among the facts and the ideas your sources offer. Avoid sitting down to write a paper at the last minute, surrounded by library books or stacks of photocopies. In this scenario, you might be tempted to lift material, and you will produce a lifeless paper. Remember that the paper is ultimately *your* work, not a collection of other people's words, and that your identity and opinions as the writer should be evident.

As you gather information and take notes, always remember to relate your notes to your research question and working thesis. All the notes on your source materials should contribute something to the issue you are researching. As you read and prepare to summarize, to paraphrase, or to record a quotation, ask yourself, "Why am I telling readers this? How does it relate to my topic, my research question, or my thesis?" Those questions should determine the type of notes you take. Then, when you review your notes later, consider what you know about the authors and whether you share their perspectives on the issue and find their evidence convincing. List the ideas and arguments that emerge from your research, and group various authors' contributions according to the points they make.

51b Driving the organization with ideas, not sources

Let your ideas, not your sources, drive your paper. Resist the temptation to organize your paper in the following way:

1. What points Smith makes
2. What points Jones makes
3. What points Fuentes makes
4. What points Chiu makes
5. What points Jackson and Hayes make in opposition
6. What I think

That organization is driven by your sources, with the bulk of the paper dealing with the views of Smith, Jones, and the rest. Instead, let your points of supporting evidence determine the organization:

THESIS

1. First point of support: what evidence I have to support my thesis and what evidence Fuentes and Jones provide

2. Second point of support: what evidence I have to support my thesis and what evidence Smith and Fuentes provide

3. Third point of support: what evidence I have to support my thesis and what evidence Chiu, Smith, and Jones provide

4. Opposing viewpoints of Jackson and Hayes

5. Common ground and refutation of those viewpoints

6. Synthesis

 ESL NOTE   Cultural Conventions about Texts

Be aware that the conventions regarding the use of source materials, especially classic texts, differ from culture to culture. When you are writing in English, readers will expect you to propose and explain your ideas and not to rely too heavily on classic well-known texts from thinkers in the field. ■

To avoid producing an essay that reads like a serial listing of summaries or references ("Crabbe says this," "Tyger says that," "Tyger also says this"), spend time reviewing your notes and synthesizing what you find into a coherent and convincing statement of what you know and believe. Do the following:

- Make lists of good ideas your sources raise about your topic.
- Look for the connections among those ideas: comparisons and contrasts.
- Find links in content, examples, and statistics.
- Note connections between the information in your sources and what you know from your own experience.

If you do this, you will take control of your material instead of letting it take control of you.

51c Making use of an outline

Some people—those who find their way into a paper as they write it—like to make a rough scratch outline of the points of the paper before they begin to write; then, once they have a draft on paper, they try to make a detailed sentence outline of what they have written to check the completeness and logic of the draft. Other people like to prepare a detailed outline before they start to write—but these are usually the people who have done a great deal of research and have planned the paper before they begin to write. Whichever type of researcher you are, make sure that you do at some point pause to make an outline, especially if your paper is long and your topic complex. It will help you avoid gaps and repetition and will give you a way to see how well you take readers from one point to the next and how well all your points connect with your thesis. See **3i** for examples of a scratch outline and a formal sentence outline. Here is an outline Jared Whittemore made for his research paper on community colleges. He highlighted the key words in his thesis and developed each point in turn in his essay. You can read the fifth draft of his paper in **52f**.

Thesis: With their policy of open access, community colleges provide exceptional opportunities especially to students from low-income families, minorities, those with inadequate primary and secondary schooling, and women.

Support I: Historically, community colleges have provided open access.
  A. Statistics in California
  B. Statistics in the U.S.

Support II: Community colleges help low-income students.
  A. Examples of costs
    1. California
    2. Texas
    3. Florida
  B. Cost of community college vs. four-year college

Support III: Minorities especially can benefit from a community college opportunity.
  A. Statistics for public and private two-year colleges
  B. Statistics for two-year and four-year colleges
  C. Statistics on race nationwide
  D. Statistics on race in California; example of student

Support IV: Community colleges help students with limited academic skills.
  A. Preparation for a four-year school
  B. Preparation for work
  C. Preparation for older students' lives

Support V: Community colleges provide women with opportunities.
  A. Increased earning power for women
  B. Lifestyle change for returning women

51d Guidelines for writing research paper drafts

WHAT NOT TO DO

1. Do not expect to complete a polished draft at one sitting.

2. Do not write the title and the first sentence and then panic because you feel you have nothing left to say.

3. Do not constantly imagine your instructor's response to what you write.

4. Do not worry about coherence—a draft by nature is something that you work on repeatedly and revise for readers' eyes.

5. Do not necessarily begin at the beginning; do not think you must first write a dynamite introduction.

WHAT TO DO

1. Wait until you have a block of time available before you begin writing a draft of your paper.

2. Turn off the phone, close the door, and tell yourself you will not emerge from the room until you have written about six pages.

3. Promise yourself a reward when you meet your target—a refrigerator break or a trip to a nearby ice cream store, for instance.

4. Assemble your copy of the assignment, your thesis statement, all your copies of sources, your research notebook and any other notes, your working bibliography, and your proposal or outline.

5. Write the parts you know most about first.

6. Write as much as you can as fast as you can. If you only vaguely remember a reference in your sources, just write what you can remember—but keep writing, and don't worry about gaps:

   ```
   As so and so (who was it? Jackson?) has observed, malls are
   taking the place of city centers (check page reference).
   ```

7. Write the beginning—the introduction—only after you have some ideas on paper that you feel you can introduce.

8. Write at least something on each one of the points in your outline. Start off by asking yourself: What do I know about this point, and how does it support my thesis? Write your answer to that in your own words without worrying about who said what in which source. You can check your notes and fill in the gaps later.

9. Write until you feel you have put down on the page or screen your main points and you have made reference to most of your source material.

Now here is the hard part. Do not go back over your draft and start tinkering and changing—at least not yet. Congratulate yourself on having made a start and take a break, a long one. Put your draft in a drawer and do not look at it for at least a few days. In the meantime, you can follow up on research leads, find new sources, and continue writing ideas in your research log.

51e Writing research papers in the disciplines

When you write research papers in different disciplines such as sociology, physics, psychology, art history, and English, you not only use different sources and different systems of documentation, but you may also approach the research and the writing in ways that fit the conventions of the discipline. This section outlines approaches to researched writing in the humanities, the natural sciences and mathematics, and the social sciences.

The cultures of the disciplines Each discipline has a culture and conventions. People who write, research, and teach in a discipline form sets of expectations about how articles and papers will be written. When you take a course in a new discipline that requires research, use the strategies in the Key Points box to get acquainted with its ways of thinking and operating.

KEY POINTS

The Cultures of the Academic Disciplines

Each discipline has its own culture and its own expectations of the people who practice in the discipline and write about it. When you take a course in a new discipline, use the following strategies to get acquainted with its ways of thinking and operating.

1. Listen carefully to lectures and discussion; note any specialized vocabulary.
2. Read the assigned textbook and note the conventions that apply in writing about the field.
3. Subscribe to e-mail discussion lists (**11c**) in the field so that you can see what issues people are concerned about.
4. When given a writing assignment, make sure you read samples of similar types of writing in that discipline.
5. Talk with your instructor about the field, its literature, and readers' expectations.

Before you begin work on a research project, try to find out as much as you can about the following:

- the types of data you should gather: primary or secondary sources, print or Web?

- the standard sources in the field to consult for reliable information

- the design of the paper: headings, title page, graphics?

- the documentation style preferred: MLA, APA, CBE/CSE, *Chicago, Columbia,* or other?

- the terminology specific to the field

- the type of language in common use: active or passive voice? first or third person?

See **8a** for examples of writing in different disciplines.

Writing research papers in the humanities and arts   A great deal of research in the humanities and arts consists of examining texts—written texts as well as the texts of artistic creation and performance. You may, for instance, need to examine poems, novels, short stories, films, plays, works of art, or advertisements to explore their history, their connections to their time, their values, and their meaning. When you do research in the humanities and the arts, you may be called on to consult both primary and secondary sources. Using secondary sources such as critical works will help you set the art, literature, or issues you discuss in context and will show you the reactions and interpretations of others. Research generally will consist of examining and analyzing original works, people's actions, and significant issues, along with exploring critical works to discover reactions to those original works, actions, and issues.

Do the following whenever appropriate when you write research papers in literature, language, philosophy, art, communications, music, or theater. History, too, is sometimes categorized with the humanities; otherwise, it is placed within the social sciences.

- Consult primary sources, such as original works of literature, radio and television programs, original documents, and informational Web sites, or attend original performances, such as plays, films, poetry readings, and concerts.

- For works written before 1980, be sure to do extensive library research for print sources. The Web will yield more material on current works or works in the news.

- Form your own interpretations of works.

- Use secondary sources (works of criticism) only after you have formed your own interpretations and established a basis for evaluating the opinions expressed by others.

- Look for patterns and interpretations supported by evidence, not for one right answer to a problem.

- Use the present tense to refer to what writers have said (*Emerson points out that . . .*). See **20f**.

- Use MLA guidelines (**52**) or *Chicago Manual of Style* (**55**) for documentation style. See **51f** for useful resources for research in art, architecture, classics, communications, ethnic studies, history, literature, music, philosophy, religion, and women's studies.

Writing about literature is common in research papers in the humanities. See **7** for more on writing about literature.

Writing research papers in the natural sciences, applied sciences, medicine, and mathematics Research in the natural sciences (astronomy, biology, zoology, geography, geology, physics, chemistry), applied sciences (engineering, computer science), medicine, and mathematics has much less to do with reading, analyzing, interpreting, and commenting than research in the humanities does. The individual writer's feelings, reactions, interpretations, and responses are not so important. Rather, exact accounts of firsthand experiments and observations are the order of the day. The writer's responses take second place to the careful observation and recording of experimental data. Do the following when you write a research paper in the natural sciences, medicine, or mathematics.

- Report firsthand original experiments and calculations.

- Be exact, complete, and precise in all descriptions.

- Present a hypothesis, detailed experimental methods, and detailed numerical and statistical results.

- Discuss the results in the light of procedural problems, previous experiments, and future directions.

- Provide supporting tables, graphs, and charts to illustrate the findings.

- Refer to secondary sources in the introductory section of your paper, a section sometimes called "Review of the Literature."

- Avoid personal anecdotes.

- Use the present perfect tense to refer to what researchers and writers have reported in published works (*Brown has said that . . .*).

- Use the passive voice more frequently than in other types of writing (**20l**).
- Be prepared to write according to a set format, using sections with headings. (For lab reports, see **8c**.)
- Use APA (**53**) or CBE/CSE (**54**) documentation style, or follow specific style manuals in scientific areas.

Writing research papers in the social sciences   The social sciences (for example, anthropology, business, economics, political science, psychology, and sociology) examine the forms and processes that contribute to the construction of society and social institutions. Researchers observe and examine the behavior of people in groups by careful observation and note-taking, by interviewing, or by using questionnaires. Tools often used to help with observation are cameras, tape recorders, movie cameras, Web cams, and so on. Do the following when you write a research paper.

- Examine research studies in the field, evaluate their methodology, compare and contrast results with those of other experimental procedures, and draw conclusions based on the empirical evidence uncovered.
- Look for accurate, up-to-date information, and evaluate it systematically against stated criteria.
- Use the first person (*I* and *we*) less frequently than in the humanities.
- Use the present perfect tense to refer to what researchers and writers have reported (*Smith's study has shown that . . .*).
- Use the passive voice as appropriate when reporting on scientific and experimental procedures (for example, *The stimulus was repeated* in place of *I repeated the stimulus*).
- Where possible and appropriate, present graphs, charts, and tables to illustrate your data and support your conclusions.
- Use APA documentation style (**53**) or ask your instructor what is recommended.

51f   Research paper resources in 27 subject areas

This selective list of frequently used reference works in print, print and electronic indexes, and Web sites was compiled with the help of twenty-one college librarians from eighteen colleges in thirteen states. These resources are particularly useful for alerting you to the culture of the different disciplines, providing background information, and pointing you in the right direction for further research. Browse freely, and remember to ask a librarian for advice if you have trouble finding a source or need a specific piece of information.

 TECHNOTE Links from the Web Site for *Universal Keys for Writers*

The Web site for this book at <http://www.college.hmco.com/ keys.html> duplicates and expands this list, keeping it up to date and providing direct links to all the nonsubscription online reference sites. From the *Universal Keys for Writers* home page click on Web Links, then on Links across the Curriculum. From there, you can click on an online source in, say, business or engineering, and you will be taken right there. Sources with no URL given may also be available in online databases accessible in a library. Check with your librarian as to the availability of these sources. ■

ART AND ARCHITECTURE

American Museum of Photography: <http://www.photographymuseum .com>

Art Abstracts (online and CD-ROM)

Art History Resources on the Web: <http://witcombe.bcpw.sbc .edu/ARTHLinks.html>

Art Index (print, online, and CD-ROM)

Arts and Humanities Citation Index

Avery Index to Architectural Periodicals (online and CD-ROM)

Bibliography of the History of Art

Contemporary Artists

Dictionary of Art (known as *Grove's*) (print and online)

Encyclopedia of World Art

Getty Institute: <http://www.getty.edu>

Lives of the Painters

Local and Global Internet Resources for Art Historians and Art History Students: <http://www.wisc.edu/arth/otherresources .html>

Metropolitan Museum of Art Time Line: <http://www.metmuseum .org/toah/splash.htm>

Oxford Companion to Art

World Wide Arts Resources: <http://wwar.com>

BIOLOGY

Biological Abstracts: BIOSIS (print, online, and CD-ROM)

Biological and Agricultural Index (print, online, and CD-ROM)

BioView.com: <http://www.biolinks.com>

Cell and Molecular Biology Online: <http://cellbio.com>

Encyclopedia of Bioethics

Encyclopedia of Human Biology

Encyclopedia of the Biological Sciences

Gray's Anatomy

Henderson's Dictionary of Biological Terms

Tufts University Biology Research Guide: <http://ase.tufts.edu/biology/bio14v2>

WWW Virtual Library: Biosciences: <http://mcb.harvard.edu/Biolinks.html>

Zoological Record: Internet Resource Guide for Zoology (by BIOSIS): <http://www.biosis.org.uk/free_resources/resource_guide.html>

BUSINESS

ABI Inform Index (online and CD-ROM)

Bureau of Labor Statistics: <http://www.bls.gov>

Business Abstracts (online, full text)

Business and Industry (database with full texts of articles): <http://library.dialog.com/bluesheets/html/bl0009.html>

Business Dateline (CD-ROM database of full-text articles from business journals)

Business Periodicals Index (print, online, and CD-ROM)

Encyclopedia of American Business History and Biography

Gale Business and Company Resource Center: <http://www.galegroup.com>

Hoover's Handbook of World Business

International Encyclopedia of Business and Management

Monthly Labor Review

MSU-Ciber International Business Resources on the WWW (Michigan State University): <http://ciber.bus.msu.edu>

Prentice Hall Encyclopedic Dictionary of Business Terms

Ward's Business Directory of U.S. Private and Public Companies

CHEMISTRY

American Chemical Society ChemCenter: <http://www
.chemcenter.org>

Beilstein Handbook of Organic Chemistry

Chemical Abstracts (online and CD-ROM, from the American
Chemical Society)

Chemicool Periodic Table: <http://www-tech.mit.edu/Chemicool/
index.html>

ChemInfo (Chemical Information Sources): <http://www.indiana
.edu/~cheminfo>

Chemistry Virtual Library Resources: Links for Chemists: <http://
www.liv.ac.uk/Chemistry/Links/links.html>

CRC Handbook of Chemistry and Physics

Encyclopedia of Chemical Terminology

Kirk-Othmer Encyclopedia of Chemical Technology

Macmillan Encyclopedia of Chemistry

NIST (National Institute of Standards and Technology) *Webbook*
(physical properties for thousands of substances): <http://
webbook.nist.gov>

Ullman's Encyclopedia of Industrial Chemistry

CLASSICS

Chronology of the Ancient World

Classical Scholarship: An Annotated Bibliography

Concise Oxford Companion to Classical Literature

DCB: Database of Classical Bibliography (CD-ROM)

Internet Classics Archive: <http://classics.mit.edu>

Library of Congress Resources for Greek and Latin Classics:
<http://www.loc.gov/rr/main/alcove9/classics.html>

Perseus Project: <http://www.perseus.tufts.edu>

COMMUNICATIONS AND MEDIA

ABC-CLIO Companion to the Media in America

American Communication Association: <http://www.uark.edu/
~aca>

ComAbstracts (print and online)

ComIndex (print and CD-ROM index of articles)

Encyclopedia of Rhetoric and Composition

International Encyclopedia of Communications

International Women's Media Foundation: <http://www.iwmf.org>

Kidon Media-Link: <http://www.kidon.com/media-link/index.shtml>

News Resource: <http://newo.com>

Telecom Information Resources: <http://china.si.umich.edu/telecom/telecom-info.html>

Webster's New World Dictionary of Media and Communications

WWW Virtual Library: Communications and Media: <http://vlib.org/Communication.html>

COMPUTER SCIENCE

ACM Guide to Computing Literature (print, online, and CD-ROM)

Association for Computing Machinery: <http://www.acm.org>

Computer Abstracts

Encyclopedia of Computer Science

History of the Internet: A Chronology, 1843 to the Present (ed. Christos Moschovitis)

Information Resources for Computer Science: <http://www.library.ucsb.edu/subj/computer.html>

Microcomputer Abstracts (online by subscription)

MIT Laboratory for Computer Science: <http://www.lcs.mit.edu>

Virtual Computer Library: <http://www.utexas.edu/computer/vcl>

WWW Virtual Library: Computing: <http://vlib.org/Computing.html>

ECONOMICS

Dictionary of Economics

Econlit (online by subscription)

Gale Encyclopedia of U.S. Economic History (ed. Thomas Carson)

PAIS (Public Affairs Information Service) database (print, online, and CD-ROM)

Prentice Hall Encyclopedic Dictionary of Business Terms

Social Sciences Citation Index: <http://www.hwwilson.com>

WWW Virtual Library: Resources in Economics: <http://www.hwwilson.com>

EDUCATION

Ask ERIC (Educational Resources Information Center; supplies indexes such as *Current Index to Journals in Education* and *Resources in Education*): <http://www.askeric.org/>

Dictionary of Education

Education Index: <http://www.educationindex.com>

Education Virtual Library: <http://www.csu.edu.au/education/library.html>

Encyclopedia of Educational Research

Higher Education Research Institute, UCLA: <http://www.gseis.ucla.edu/heri/heri.html>

International Encyclopedia of Education

Michigan Electronic Library: Education: <http://mel.lib.mi.us/education/education-index.html>

National Center for Education Statistics: <http://nces.ed.gov>

U.S. Department of Education: Other Educational Resources: <http://www.ed.gov/about/organizations.jsp>

ENGINEERING

Applied Science and Technology Index (print and online)

Compendex/Engineering Index (online by subscription)

Engineering Library at Cornell University: <http://www.englib.cornell.edu>

McGraw-Hill Encyclopedia of Engineering

WWW Virtual Library: Engineering: <http://vlib.org/Engineering.html>

ENVIRONMENTAL STUDIES

Dictionary of the Environment

Encyclopedia of Environmental Science

Environmental Encyclopedia

Environmental Science: Working with the Earth

Facts on File Dictionary of Environmental Science

National Library for the Environment: <http://www.cnie.org/nle>

Scripps Institution of Oceanography: <http://www.sio.ucsd.edu>

Sourcebook on the Environment: A Guide to the Literature

Toxic Air Pollution Handbook

United Nations Environment Programme: <http://www.unep.org>

US Environmental Protection Agency: <http://www.epa.gov/>

WWW Virtual Library: Earth Science: <http://vlib.org/EarthScience
.html>

ETHNIC STUDIES

Chicano Scholars and Writers

Encyclopedia of Asian History

Gale Encyclopedia of Multicultural America (ed. Robert von
Dassanowsky)

Harvard Encyclopedia of American Ethnic Groups

Historical and Cultural Atlas of African Americans

Native Web: <http://www.nativeweb.org>

Oxford Companion to African American Literature

WWW Virtual Library: Migration and Ethnic Relations:
<http://www.ercomer.org/wwwvl>

GEOGRAPHY

Companion Encyclopedia of Geography

Encyclopedia of World Geography

Geographical Abstracts (online and CD-ROM)

U.S. Census Bureau: U.S. Gazetteer: <http://www.census.gov/
cgi-bin/gazetteer>

WWW Virtual Library: Geography: <http://geography.pinetree.org>

GEOLOGY

AGI (American Geological Institute): <http://www.agiweb.org>

Encyclopedia of Earth System Science

GeoRef (electronic index produced by American Geological
Institute): <http://www.agiweb.org/georef>

Glossary of Geology and Earth Sciences

Macmillan Encyclopedia of Earth Sciences

New Penguin Dictionary of Geology

USGS (United States Geological Survey): <http://www.usgs.gov>

USGS Library: <http://www.usgs.gov/library>

HISTORY

Dictionary of Medieval History (Scribner)

Don Mabry's Historical Text Archive: <http://historicaltextarchive
.com/>

Encyclopedia of American History

Great Events from History series

Historical Abstracts and America: History and Life from ABC-CLIO (print and online): <http://www.abc-clio.com>

WWW Virtual Library: History Central Catalogue: <http://www.ukans .edu/history/VL>

LINGUISTICS

Applied Linguistics WWW Virtual Library: <http://alt.venus .co.uk/VL/AppLingBBK/welcome.html>

Cambridge Encyclopedia of Language (ed. David Crystal)

Cambridge Encyclopedia of the English Language (ed. David Crystal)

Center for Applied Linguistics: <http://www.cal.org>

Linguistics: A Guide to the Reference Literature (ed. Anna L. DeMiller)

Oxford Companion to the English Language (ed. Tom McArthur)

LITERATURE

Complete Works of Shakespeare: <http://the-tech.mit.edu/ Shakespeare>

Dictionary of Literary Biography

MLA International Bibliography of Books and Articles on the Modern Languages and Literature (online and CD-ROM)

New Cambridge Bibliography of English Literature

Oxford Companion to Contemporary Authors

Project Bartleby (complete texts of books no longer in copyright): <http://www.bartleby.com>

Victorian Women Writers Project: <http://www.indiana.edu/ ~letrs/vwwp>

Voice of the Shuttle: <http://vos.ucsb.edu>

MATHEMATICS AND STATISTICS

American Mathematical Society MathSciNet (index and abstracts of articles): <http://www.ams.org/mathscinet>

CRC Concise Encyclopedia of Mathematics (ed. Eric Weisstein)

HarperCollins Dictionary of Mathematics

Mathematical Reviews (print and online)

Statistical Abstract of the United States (Government Printing Office: print and online): <http://www.census.gov/statab/www>

University of Tennessee Math Archives: <http://archives.math.utk.edu>

WWW Virtual Library: Statistics: <http://www.stat.ufl.edu/vlib/statistics.html>

MUSIC

Baker's Biographical Dictionary of Musicians

Classical USA: <http://classicalusa.com>

Indiana University Worldwide Internet Music Resources: <http://www.music.indiana.edu/music_resources>

International Index to Music Periodicals

New Grove Dictionary of Music and Musicians

New Harvard Dictionary of Music

New Oxford History of Music

RILM Abstracts of Musical Literature (online and CD-ROM)

Thematic Catalogues in Music: An Annotated Bibliography Including Printed, Manuscript, and In-Preparation Catalogues

The Music Index (CD-ROM)

WWW Virtual Library: Classical Music: <http://www.gprep.pvt.k12.md.us/classical/catalog.html>

WWW Virtual Library: Music: <http://www.vl-music.com>

NURSING

Allnurses.com: <http://allnurses.com>

American Nurses Association Nursing World: <http://www.nursingworld.org>

Cambridge World History of Human Disease

Culture and Nursing Care

Dorland's Illustrated Medical Dictionary

Encyclopedia of Nursing Research

Gray's Anatomy

Health Web: <http://healthweb.org/>

National Institute of Nursing Research: <http://www.nih.gov/ninr>

Nursing Net: <http://www.nursingnet.org>

PHILOSOPHY

American Philosophical Association: <http://www.udel.edu/apa>

Cambridge Dictionary of Philosophy

Guide to Philosophy on the Internet: <http://www.earlham.edu/~peters/philinks.htm>

Handbook of Western Philosophy

Internet Encyclopedia of Philosophy: <http://www.utm.edu/research/iep>

Oxford Companion to Philosophy

Philosopher's Index

Philosophy in Cyberspace: <http://www-personal.monash.edu.au/~dey/phil>

Routledge History of Philosophy

PHYSICS

American Institute of Physics: <http://www.aip.org>

American Physical Society: <http://www.aps.org>

Encyclopedia of Physics (ed. Rita Lerner and George L. Trigg)

Macmillan Encyclopedia of Physics

Physics Abstracts (online and CD-ROM)

Physics Today: <http://www.physicstoday.org>

WWW Virtual Library: Physics: <http://vlib.org/Physics.html>

POLITICAL SCIENCE

American Statistics Index

Congressional Quarterly Weekly Reports

International Handbook of Political Science

International Political Science Abstracts

PAIS (Public Affairs Information Service) database (online and CD-ROM)

Political Handbook of the World (Annual)

Political Science Links: <http://www.loyola.edu/dept/politics/polilink.html>

Political Science Resources on the Web: <http://www.lib.umich.edu/govdocs/polisci.html>

The White House: <http://www.whitehouse.gov>

THOMAS: Legislative Information on the Internet: <http://thomas.loc.gov>

United Nations: <http://www.un.org>

U.S. Census Bureau: The Official Statistics: <http://www.census.gov>

PSYCHOLOGY

American Psychological Association: <http://www.apa.org>

CyberPsychLink: <http://cctr.umkc.edu/user/dmartin/psych2
.html>

Encyclopedia of Psychology: <http://www.psychology.org>

Handbook of Practical Psychology

Psychological Abstracts

PsycInfo (database of online abstracts)

The Social Psychology Network, Wesleyan University: <http://www
.socialpsychology.org>

WWW Virtual Library: Psychology: <http://www.clas.ufl.edu/
users/gthursby/psi/>

RELIGION

Academic Info: Religious Studies: <http://www.academicinfo
.net/Religion.html>

Anchor Bible Dictionary

ATLA Religion Database

Encyclopedia of Religion (print and CD-ROM)

Encyclopedia of the American Religious Experience

Encyclopedia of World Religions

New Interpreter's Bible

Religion Index

*Wabash Center Guide to Internet Resources for Teaching and Learning
in Theology and Religion:* <http://www.wabashcenter.wabash
.edu/Internet/front.htm>

SOCIOLOGY

CIA Factbook: <http://www.odci.gov/cia/publications/factbook/
index.html>

Data on the Net: <http://odwin.ucsd.edu/idata>

Encyclopedia of Sociology (ed. Rhonda J. Montgomery)

Firstgov (U.S. Government site): <http://firstgov.gov>

Handbook of Sociology (ed. Neil Smelser)

International Encyclopedia of the Social and Behavioral Sciences (print
and online)

Public Agenda (public opinion data): <http://www.publicagenda.org/>

Social Sciences Abstracts (print and online)

Sociological Abstracts: <http://www.socabs.org>

Sociological Tour through Cyberspace: <http://www.trinity.edu/~mkearl/index.html>

Statistical Abstract of the United States: <http://www.census.gov/statab/www/>

Statistical Resources on the Web: <http://www.lib.umich.edu/govdocs/stats.html>

U.S. Census Bureau: <http://quickfacts.census.gov/qfd>

WWW Virtual Library: Sociology: <http://vlib.org/SocialSciences.html>

WOMEN'S STUDIES

ABC-CLIO Guide to Women's Progress in America

Encyclopedia of Feminism

Feminism and Women's Studies: <http://eserver.org/feminism/index.html>

Gender Studies Page: <http://vos.ucsb.edu/browse.asp?id=2711>

Handbook of American Women's History

Notable American Women

Women in the World

Women's Studies Encyclopedia

WWW Virtual Library: Women's History: <http://www.iisg.nl/~womhist/vivalink.html>

Part IX
Documenting Sources: MLA Style

AT A GLANCE: INDEX OF MLA STYLE FEATURES

MLA

You need to document the sources of your information, not only in research papers but also in shorter essays in which you mention only a few books, articles, or other sources to illustrate a point or support your case. Section **52** provides information on the system commonly used to document sources in the humanities, the Modern Language Association (MLA) system, as recommended in Joseph Gibaldi, *MLA Handbook for Writers of Research Papers,* 6th ed. (New York: MLA, 2003), in Joseph Gibaldi, *MLA Style Manual,* 2nd ed. (New York: MLA, 1998), and on the MLA Web site at <http://www.mla.org>.

Be accurate and consistent when you follow any documentation style. With the MLA style of citing author and page number, learn the basic principles (**52a**), and use the detailed examples in **52c** and **52d** for help with citations and links to the list of references. Do not try to rely on memory; instead, always look up instructions and follow examples.

52 MLA Style of Documentation

52a Two basic features of MLA style

KEY POINTS

Two Basic Features of MLA Style

1. *In the text of your paper,* include the following information each time you cite a source:
   the *last name*(s) of the author or authors (or the title of the work if no author is named), along with the *page number*(s) where the information is located, unless the source is online or only one page long.
   See **52b** for examples.

2. *At the end of your paper,* include a list, alphabetized by authors' last names (or by title if no author is named) of all the sources you refer to in the paper. Begin the list on a new page and title it "Works Cited." See **52d** for sample entries.

Illustrations of the two basic features

a. Reference to a book, with author named in your sentence and page number given in parentheses

> Historian David McCullough paints a vivid picture of the army's retreat from Boston: "The British had been out-witted, humiliated. The greatest military power on earth had been forced to retreat by an army of amateurs; it was a heady realization" (76).

b. Reference to a book, with author named in parentheses and page number given

> The army retreated from Boston in disarray: "The British had been outwitted, humiliated. The greatest military power on earth had been forced to retreat by an army of amateurs; it was a heady realization" (McCullough 76).

c. Listing of book in your works-cited list

> McCullough, David. John Adams. New York: Simon, 2001.

d. Reference to an article in an online database (no page number)

For his admiring depiction of John Adams, McCullough has
been accused of "pandering to the highly renumerative
national yearning for heroes" and depriving readers of
"the critical lessons in liberty and democracy that every
history of the Early Republic should teach" (Rosenfeld).

e. Listing of the review in an online database as it appears in your works-cited list

Rosenfeld, Richard N. "The Adams Tyranny." Rev. of John
Adams, by David McCullough. Harper's Sept. 2001: 82-86.
Academic Search Premier. EBSCOhost. City U of New York
Lib., New York, NY. 28 Mar. 2002 <http://search.epnet.com/
direct.asp?an=5043467&db=aph>.

52b MLA author/page style for in-text citations

For all MLA in-text citations, identify the author, if the name is available. If the source does not name an author, give the title; but beware
that a source with no named author may not be reliable. Give the
page number of a print work in parentheses at the end of your text
sentence if the work is more than one page long. Do not write "p.,"
"pp.," or the word *page*. Put the sentence period after the closing
parenthesis. Cite inclusive page numbers as follows: 35–36; 257–58;
100–01; 305–06; 299–300. For online sources, see **52d,** item 30.

A. One author, named in your introductory phrase The first
time you mention an author (or authors) whose work you discuss in
detail in your text or make several references to, give the full name
and, if useful to readers, a brief statement about expertise or credentials. Thereafter, use the author's last name only.

┌— author —┐
The sociologist Ruth Sidel's interviews with young women
┌— quotation —┐
provide examples of what Sidel sees as the "impossible
┌——— page number
dream" (19).——period

When a quotation ends the sentence, as in that example, close the quotation marks before the parentheses, and place the sentence period after

the parentheses. (This rule differs from the one for undocumented writing, which calls for a period *before* the closing quotation marks.) See **52d**, item 1, to see how this work appears in a works-cited list.

When a quotation includes a question mark or an exclamation point, also include a period after the citation:

```
                                      question mark
    Mrs. Bridge wonders, "Is my daughter mine?"
             period
    (Connell 135).
```

B. Author not named in your text   If you do not mention the author while introducing the reference, include the author's last name in the parentheses before the page number, with no comma between them.

```
    Many young women, from all races and classes, have taken

    on the idea of the American Dream, however difficult it

                                  author and page
                                 ┌── numbers ──┐
    might be for them to achieve it (Sidel 19-20).
```

C. Two or more authors   For a work with two or three authors, include all the names, either in your text sentence or in parentheses.

```
    (Lakoff and Johnson 42)

    (Hare, Moran, and Koepke 226-28)
```

For a work with four or more authors, use only the first author's name followed by "et al." (*Et alii* means "and others.") See **52d**, item 2.

```
    Some researchers have established a close link between

    success at work and the pleasure derived from community

    service (Bellah et al. 196-99).
```

D. Author with more than one work cited   You can include the author and title of the work in your text sentence.

```
    Alice Walker, in her book In Search of Our Mothers'

    Gardens, describes revisiting her past to discover more

    about Flannery O'Connor (43-59).
```

If you do not mention the author in your text, include in your parenthetical reference the author's last name, followed by a comma, an abbreviated form of the title, and the page number.

```
    O'Connor's house still stands and is looked after by a

                   comma┐  abbreviated title    ┌page number
                        ┌─────────────┐
    caretaker (Walker, In Search 57).
```

E. Work in an anthology Cite the author of the included or reprinted work (not the editor of the anthology) and the page number in the anthology. The entry in the works-cited list will include the title of the article, its inclusive page numbers, and full bibliographical details for the anthology: title, editor(s), place of publication, publisher, date. See **52d,** items 5 and 6, for examples.

```
Des Pres asserts that "heroism is not necessarily a
romantic notion" (20).
```

F. Work quoted in another source Use "qtd. in" (for "quoted in") in your parenthetical citation, followed by the last name of the author of the source in which you find the reference (the indirect source) and the page number where the reference appears. List the indirect source in your list of works cited. In the following example, Smith would be included in the list of works cited, not Britton.

```
We generate words unconsciously, without thinking about
them; they appear, as James Britton says, "at the point of
utterance" (qtd. in Smith 208).
```

G. Reference to an entire work and not to one specific page If you are referring not to a quotation or idea on one specific page, but rather to an idea that is central to the work as a whole, use the author's name alone. Include the work in your works-cited list.

```
We can learn from diaries about people's everyday lives
and the worlds they create (Mallon).
```

H. One-page work If an article is only one page long, cite the author's name alone; include the page number in your works-cited list (**52d,** item 22).

I. No author or editor named in source In your text sentence, give the complete title to refer to the work. In parentheses, use a short title to refer to the work. See **52d,** item 8.

```
According to Weather, one way to estimate the Fahrenheit
temperature is to count the number of times a cricket
chirps in 14 seconds and add 40 (18).
```

```
Increasing evidence shows that glucosamine relieves the
symptoms of arthritis (PDR Family Guide 242).
```

J. Electronic and Internet sources Electronic database material and Internet sources, which appear on a screen, have no stable page numbers that apply across systems or when printed. Only sources accessed in PDF (portable document format) files will preserve and show the page numbers of an original print source. If your source as it appears on the screen includes no text divisions, numbered pages, or numbered paragraphs, simply provide the author's name. In the first mention, it is common practice to establish the expertise or credentials of authors or the authority of your source. If no author's name is given, refer to the title.

```
Science writer Stephen Hart describes how researchers
Edward Taub and Thomas Ebert conclude that for musicians,
practicing "remaps the brain."
```
> Online source has no numbered pages or paragraphs.

With no page number to indicate the end of a citation, be careful to define where your citation ends and your own commentary takes over. See **50i** for more on defining the boundaries of a citation.

If possible, locate online material by the internal headings of the source (for example, *introduction, chapter, section*). Give paragraph numbers only if they are supplied in the source and you see them on the screen (use the abbreviation "par." or "pars."). If paragraph numbers do appear, include the total number of numbered paragraphs in your works-cited list (see **52d,** item 35).

```
Hatchuel discusses how film editing "can change points of
view and turn objectivity into subjectivity" (par. 6).
```

```
Film editing provides us with different perceptions of
reality (Hatchuel, par. 6).
```

To cite an online source with no author, give the title of the Web page or the posting. Then begin your works-cited entry with the name of the site (see **52d,** item 40).

```
A list of frequently asked questions about documentation
and up-to-date instructions on how to cite online
sources in MLA style can be found on the association's
Web site (Modern Language Association).
```

K. Other nonprint sources For radio or TV programs, interviews, live performances, films, computer software, recordings, and other nonprint sources, include only the title or author (or, in some cases, the interviewer, interviewee, director, performer, or producer, and so on, corresponding to the first element of the information you provide in the entry in your list of works cited). (See **52d,** item 59.)

```
Some writers and directors can take a lesson from seeing
what Copenhagen does with three chairs and three actors
talking about physics.
```

```
It takes an extraordinary director to make a success
from three chairs and three actors talking about physics
(Blakemore).
```

L. Work by a corporation, government agency, or other organization Give the complete name of the organization in the introductory passage, or give a shortened form in parentheses.

```
                ┌──────────── full name ────────────┐
The College Entrance Examination Board (CEEB) assures
students that the test "better reflects the type of work
you will do when you get to college" (4).
```

```
Students are assured that the tasks on the SAT closely
resemble the tasks they will be expected to perform in
college (College Board 4).
                    └────────────┘
                     shortened name
```

See **52d,** item 9, for an example of a corporation as author in the works-cited list.

For a work by a government agency, if you do not know the name of the author or editor of the report, include in your passage the name of the agency as you list it in your works-cited list.

```
According to statistics prepared by the United States
Department of Education in 2000, students in four-year
public colleges paid an average tuition cost of $2617
(346).
```

See **52d,** item 10, for an example of the above in the works-cited list.

M. Two authors with the same last name Include each author's first initial or the whole first name if the authors' initials are the same.

```
A writer can be seen as both "author" and "secretary" and
the two roles can be seen as competitive (F. Smith 19).
```

N. Multivolume work Indicate the volume number, followed by a colon, a space, and the page number. List the number of volumes in your works-cited list. (See **52d,** item 12.)

```
Barr and Feigenbaum note that "the concept of translation
from one language to another by machine is older than
the computer itself" (1: 233).
```

O. More than one work in a citation Separate two or more works with semicolons. However, avoid making a parenthetical citation so long that it disrupts the flow of your text. Consider adding a footnote or an endnote to provide lists of additional source material, as in the second example here.

> The links between a name and ancestry have been noted
> before (Waters 65; Antin 188).

> Many writers and researchers have discussed the links
> between a name and ancestry.[1]

For the use of footnotes and endnotes in MLA documentation, see **52e.**

P. Lecture, speech, or personal communication such as a letter, an interview, e-mail, or a conversation In your text, give the name of the lecturer or person you communicated with. In your works-cited list, list the type of communication after the author or title (see **52d,** items 49 and 53).

> According to George Kane, a vice president at Learning
> Network, Inc., online courses are more convenient, and
> often less expensive, than courses in actual classrooms.

Q. Literary works: fiction, poetry, and drama For well-known works published in several different editions, include information so readers may locate material in whatever edition they are using.

For a novel Give the chapter or section number in addition to the page number in the edition you used: (104; ch. 3).

For a poem Give line numbers, not page numbers: (lines 62–73). Subsequent line references can omit the word *lines.* Include up to three lines of poetry sequentially in your text, separated by a slash with a space on each side (/) (see **30d**). For four or more lines of poetry, begin on a new line, indent the whole passage one inch from the left, double-space throughout, and omit quotation marks from the beginning and end of the passage (see **50h**).

For classic poems, such as the Iliad Give the book or part number, followed by the line numbers, not page numbers: (8.21–25).

For a play For dialogue, set the quotation off from your text, indented one inch with no quotation marks, and write the name of the character speaking in all capital letters, followed by a period. Indent subsequent lines of the same speech another quarter inch (three spaces). For a classic play, one published in several different editions (such as plays by William Shakespeare or Oscar Wilde), omit page numbers and cite in parentheses the act, scene, and line numbers of the quotation, in Arabic numerals. In your works-cited list, list the bibliographical details of the edition you used.

> Shakespeare's lovers in <u>A Midsummer Night's Dream</u> appeal
> to contemporary audiences accustomed to the sense of
> loss in love songs:
>> LYSANDER. How now, my love! Why is your cheek so pale?
>>> How chance the roses there do fade so fast?
>> HERMIA. Belike for want of rain, which I could well
>>> Beteem them from the tempest of mine eyes.
>> LYSANDER. Ay me! for aught that ever I could read,
>>> Could ever hear by tale or history,
>>> The course of true love never did run smooth;
>>> (1.1.133-39)

For a new play available in only one published edition, such as a play by Wendy Wasserstein, cite author and page numbers as you do for other MLA citations.

For Shakespeare, Chaucer, and other literary works Abbreviate titles cited in parentheses, such as the following: *Cym.* for *Cymbeline*; *Temp.* for The *Tempest*; *2H4* for *Henry IV, Part 2*; *MND* for *A Midsummer Night's Dream: GP* for the *General Prologue*; *PrT* for *The Prioress's Tale*; *Aen.* for *Aeneid*; *Beo.* for *Beowulf*; *Prel.* for Wordsworth's *Prelude*.

R. The Bible Give book, chapter, and verse(s) in your text—Genesis 27.29—or abbreviate the book in a parenthetical citation (Gen. 27.29). Do not underline the title of a book in the Bible or the word *Bible* itself. Include an entry in your works-cited list only if you do not use the King James Version as your source.

S. Two or more sequential references to the same work If you rely on several quotations from the same page within one of your paragraphs, one parenthetical reference after the last quotation is enough, but make sure that no quotations from other works intervene. If you are paraphrasing from and referring to one work several times in a paragraph, mention the author in your introductory phrase; cite the page number at the end of a paraphrase and again if you paraphrase from a different page. Make it clear to a reader where paraphrase ends and your own comments take over (**50i**).

T. A long quotation Indent by one inch a quotation of four or more lines, without enclosing the quotation in quotation marks. See **50h** for an example.

52c Guidelines for the MLA works-cited list

The references you make in your text to sources are very brief—usually only the author's last name and a page number—so they allow readers to continue reading without interruption. For complete information about the source, readers can use your brief in-text citation as a guide to the full bibliographical reference in the list of works cited at the end of your paper.

Features of the list Before you begin to prepare your list, familiarize yourself with the basic features of MLA style. For examples of an MLA works-cited list in students' papers, see **6k, 7j,** and **52f.**

KEY POINTS

Setting Up the MLA List of Works Cited

1. *What to list* List only works you actually cited in the text of your paper, not works you read but did not mention, unless your instructor requires you to include all the works you consulted as well as those mentioned in your text.

2. *Format of the list* Begin the list on a new numbered page after the last page of the paper or any endnotes. Center the heading (Works Cited) without quotation marks, underlining, or a period. Double-space throughout the list. Do not add space between entries.

3. *Organization* Do not number the entries. List works alphabetically by author's last name. Begin each entry with the author's name, last name first (or the corporate name or the title of the work if no author is stated). Omit titles ("Dr.") or degrees, but include a suffix like "Jr." or a Roman numeral, as in "Patterson, Peter, III." Use normal order—first name first—for the names of authors after the first name. List works with no named author by the first main word of each entry (**52d,** item 26).

4. *Indentation* To help readers find an author's name and to clearly differentiate one entry from another, indent all lines of each entry, except the first, one-half inch (or five spaces). A

word processor can provide these "hanging indents" (see **10c** for how to format hanging indents).

TECHNOTE Indentation in Online Writing

If you intend to publish on the Internet, it is often preferable to use no indentation at all (HTML does not support hanging indents well). Instead, follow each bibliographical entry with a line space.

5. *Periods* Separate the main parts of each entry—author, title, publishing information—with a period, followed by one space.

6. *Capitals* Capitalize all words in titles of books and articles except the coordinating conjunctions; the articles, *a, an, the; to* in an infinitive; and prepositions (such as *in, to, for, with, without, against*)—unless they begin or end the title or subtitle.

7. *Underlining or italics* Underline the titles of books and the names of journals and magazines as in the examples in this section. You may use italics instead if your instructor approves and if your printer makes a clear distinction from regular type.

TECHNOTE Avoiding Underlining in Online Texts

If you write for publication on a World Wide Web site, avoid underlining titles of books and journals, because underlining is a signal for a hypertext link. Use italics or consult your instructor or editor. If you write for e-mail publication, use _ and _ before and after the text you would normally underline (**34b**).

8. *Month* When citing articles in journals, newspapers, and magazines, abbreviate all months except May, June, and July. For the abbreviations to use, see page 797.

9. *Publisher* Use a short form of the name of book publishers (*Random*, not *Random House; Columbia UP*, not *Columbia University Press*). See page 797 for some common abbreviations. For place of publication when more than one office is mentioned, list only the first city mentioned on the title page.

10. *Page numbers* Give inclusive page numbers for articles and sections of books. Do not use "p." ("pp.") or the word *page* (or *pages*) before page numbers in any reference. For page citations over 100 and sharing the same first number, use only the last two digits for the second number (for instance, 683–89, but 798–805). For an unpaginated print work, write "n. pag."

Order of entries in the list of works cited

Alphabetical order Alphabetize entries in the list of authors' last names. Note the following:

- Alphabetize by the exact letters in the spelling: *MacKay* precedes *McHam.*
- Let a shorter name precede a longer name beginning with the same letters: *Linden, Ronald* precedes *Lindenmayer, Arnold.*
- With last names using a prefix such as *le, du, di, del,* and *des,* alphabetize by the prefix: *LeBeau, Bryan F.*
- When *de* occurs with French names of one syllable, alphabetize under *d: De Jean, Denise.* Otherwise, alphabetize by last name: *Maupassant, Guy de.*
- Alphabetize by the first element of a hyphenated name: *Sackville-West, Victoria.*
- Alphabetize by the last name when the author uses two names without a hyphen: *Thomas, Elizabeth Marshall.*

No author named For a work with no author named, alphabetize by the first word in the title other than *A, An,* or *The* (see **52d,** items 8 and 26).

Several works by the same author(s) For all entries after the first, replace the name(s) of the author(s) with three hyphens followed by a period, and alphabetize according to the first significant word in the title. If an author serves as an editor or translator, put a comma after the three hyphens, followed by the appropriate abbreviation ("ed." or "trans."). If, however, the author has coauthors, repeat all authors' names in full and put the coauthored entry after all the single-name entries for the author.

> Goleman, Daniel. <u>Vital Lies, Simple Truths</u>. New York:
>   Simon, 1996.
>
> ---. <u>Working with Emotional Intelligence</u>. New York:
>   Bantam, 2000.
>
> Goleman, Daniel, Paul Kaufman, and Michael L. Ray.
>   "The Art of Creativity." <u>Psychology Today</u> Mar./Apr.
>   1992: 40-47.

Authors with the same last name Alphabetize by first names: *Smith, Adam* precedes *Smith, Frank.*

Abbreviations for months When you give the date of a journal or newspaper article or of an online source, spell out the months May, June, and July in full. Otherwise, use the following abbreviations:

Jan.	Feb.	Mar.	Apr.	Aug.
Sept.	Oct.	Nov.	Dec.	

Abbreviations for names of publishers Shorten the names of publishers.

- Omit any articles: *A, An, The.*
- Omit abbreviations such as *Co.* and *Inc.*
- Give only first name if name of company consists of several last names: *Little,* not *Little, Brown and Company, Inc.*
- If the publisher's name includes a first and last name, give only the last name: *Abrams,* not *Harry N. Abrams.*
- Use abbreviations: *Acad.* for *Academy, Assn.* for *Association.*
- Use *UP* for *University Press: U of Chicago P, Cambridge UP.*
- Use abbreviations that will be familiar to your readers: *MLA, GPO*

Some sample abbreviations:

Basic Books	Basic
Department of Education	Dept. of Educ.
The Feminist Press at the City University of New York	Feminist
Government Printing Office	GPO
Houghton Mifflin Co.	Houghton
National Center for Education Statistics	Natl. Center for Educ. Statistics
Simon and Schuster, Inc.	Simon

52d Examples of entries in MLA list of works cited

Print books and parts of books On the title page of a book and on the copyright page, you will find the information you need for an entry. Use the most recent copyright date. Use a shortened form of the publisher's name; usually one word is sufficient: *Houghton* (not *Houghton Mifflin*); Basic (not *Basic Books*). For university presses, use the abbreviations "U" and "P" (no periods).

1. Basic form for a book with one author

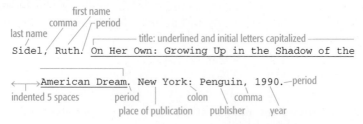

2. Book with two or more authors

Use authors' names in the order in which they appear in the book. Separate the names with commas. Reverse the order of only the first author's name.

```
                    second author's name
          comma         not reversed
Lakoff, George, and Mark Johnson. Metaphors We Live By.
    Chicago: U of Chicago P, 1980.
```

For a work with four or more authors, either list all the names or use only the first author's name followed by "et al." (Latin for "and others").

```
Bellah, Robert N., et al. Habits of the Heart: Individualism
    and Commitment in American Life. Berkeley: U of
    California P, 1985.
```

3. Edited book

Use the abbreviation "ed." or "eds.," preceded by a comma, after the name(s) of the editor or editors.

```
Gates, Henry Louis, Jr., ed. Classic Slave Narratives.
    New York: NAL, 1987.
```

For a work with four or more editors, use only the name of the first, followed by a comma and "et al."

4. Author and editor

When an editor has prepared an author's work for publication, list the book under the author's name if you cite the author's work. Then, in your listing, include the name(s) of the editor(s) after the title, introduced by "Ed." for one or more editors. "Ed." here stands for "edited by."

```
  ── author of letters ──┐                    ┌─name of editor─┐
Bishop, Elizabeth. One Art: Letters. Ed. Robert Giroux.
    New York: Farrar, 1994.
```

If you cite a section written by the editor, such as a chapter introduction or a note, list the source under the name of the editor

```
┌─name of editor─┐  editor                   ┌── author of letters ──┐
Giroux, Robert, ed. One Art: Letters. By Elizabeth Bishop.
    New York: Farrar, 1994.
```

5. One work in an anthology (original or reprinted) For a work included in an anthology, first list the author and title of the included work. Follow this with the title of the anthology, the name of the editor(s), publication information (place, publisher, date) for the anthology, and then, after the period, the pages in the anthology covered by the work you refer to.

author of article
or chapter

Des Pres, Terrence. "Poetry and Politics." The Writer

means
"edited by"

name of editor
of anthology

in Our World. Ed. Reginald Gibbons. Boston:

Atlantic Monthly, 1986. 17-29.

inclusive page numbers of article or chapter

Nye, Naomi Shihab. "My Brother's House." The Riverside
Reader. 6th ed. Ed. Joseph F. Trimmer and Maxine
Hairston. Boston: Houghton, 1999. 171-81.

If the work in the anthology is a reprint of a previously published scholarly article, supply the complete information for both the original publication and the reprint in the anthology.

Gates, Henry Louis, Jr. "The Fire Last Time." New Republic
1 June 1992: 37-43. Rpt. in Contemporary Literary
Criticism. Ed. Jeffrey W. Hunter. Vol. 127. Detroit: Gale,
2000. 113-19.

6. More than one work in an anthology, cross-referenced If you refer to more than one work from the same anthology, list the anthology separately, and list each essay with a cross-reference to the anthology. Alphabetize in the usual way. The following examples show references to two different articles in the same anthology edited by Gibbons. The two articles are listed and cross-referenced to the anthology.

title of
author of article | article in anthology

Des Pres, Terrence. "Poetry and Politics." Gibbons
17-29.

editor of anthology

page numbers of article

editor of anthology | title of anthology

Gibbons, Reginald, ed. The Writer in Our World. Boston:
Atlantic Monthly, 1986.

author of article | title of article in anthology

Walcott, Derek. "A Colonial's-Eye View of America."

editor of anthology page numbers of article
Gibbons 73-77.

7. *Reference book* For a well-known reference book, give only the edition number and the year of publication. When entries in a dictionary or an encyclopedia are arranged alphabetically, omit page numbers.

"Multiculturalism." <u>Columbia Encyclopedia</u>. 6th ed. 2000.

8. *Book with no author named* Put the title first. Do not consider the words *A, An,* and *The* when alphabetizing the entries. The following entries would be alphabetized under *P* and *W*.

<u>The PDR Guide to Natural Medicines and Healing Therapies</u>.
     New York: Three Rivers-Random, 1999.

<u>Weather</u>. New York: Discovery-Random, 1999.

9. *Book by a corporation or some other organization* Alphabetize by the name of the corporate author. If the publisher is the same as the author, include the name again as publisher.

College Entrance Examination Board. <u>Index of Majors and
     Graduate Degrees 2000</u>. New York: College Entrance
     Examination Board, 1999.

10. *Government publication* If no author is named, begin the entry with the name of the federal, state, or local government, followed by the agency. *GPO* stands for "Government Printing Office."

United States. Dept. of Educ. Office of Educ. Research and
     Improvement. Natl. Center for Educ. Statistics. <u>Digest of
     Education Statistics, 2000</u>. Washington: GPO, 2001.

11. *Translated book* After the title, include "Trans." for "Translated by" followed by the name of the translator, first name first.

Grass, Günter. <u>Novemberland: Selected Poems, 1956-1993</u>.
     Trans. Michael Hamburger. San Diego: Harcourt, 1996.

12. *Multivolume work* If you refer to more than one volume of a multivolume work, indicate the number of volumes (abbreviated "vols.") after the title.

Barr, Avon, and Edward A. Feigenbaum, eds. <u>The Handbook of
     Artificial Intelligence</u>. 4 vols. Reading: Addison,
     1981-86.

If you refer to only one volume of a work, limit the information in the entry to that one volume.

Feigenbaum, Edward A., and Paul R. Cohen, eds. <u>The Handbook
     of Artificial Intelligence</u>. Vol. 3. Reading: Addison, 1985.

13. Book in a series   Give the name of the series after the book title.

Connor, Ulla. <u>Contrastive Rhetoric: Cross-Cultural Aspects of Second Language Writing</u>. Cambridge Applied Linguistics Series. New York: Cambridge UP, 1996.

14. Book published under publisher's imprint   State the names of both the imprint (the publisher within a larger publishing enterprise) and the larger publishing house, separated by a hyphen.

Richards, Thomas. <u>The Meaning of</u> Star Trek. New York: Anchor-Doubleday, 1999.

15. Foreword, preface, introduction, or afterword   List the name of the author of the book element cited, followed by the name of the element, with no quotation marks. Give the title of the work; then use "By" to introduce the name of the author of the book (first name first). After the publication information, give inclusive page numbers for the book element cited.

Hemenway, Robert. Introduction. <u>Dust Tracks on a Road: An Autobiography</u>. By Zora Neale Hurston. Urbana: U of Illinois P, 1984. ix-xxxix.

16. Republished book   After the title, give the original date of publication. Then cite information about the current publication.

Walker, Alice. <u>The Color Purple</u>. 1982. New York: Pocket, 1985.

17. Edition after the first   After the title, give the edition number, using the abbreviation "ed."

Raimes, Ann. <u>Keys for Writers</u>. 3rd ed. Boston: Houghton, 2002.

18. Book title including a title   Do not underline a book title that is part of the source title. (However, if the title of a short work, such as a poem or short story, is part of the source title, enclose it in quotation marks.)

Hays, Kevin J., ed. <u>The Critical Response to Herman</u>

book title not
┌underlined┐
<u>Melville's</u> Moby Dick. Westport: Greenwood, 1994.

19. Dissertation   For an unpublished dissertation, follow the title (in quotation marks) with "Diss." and the university and date.

Hidalgo, Stephen Paul. "Vietnam War Poetry: A Genre of Witness." Diss. U. of Notre Dame, 1995.

Cite a published dissertation as you would a book, with place of publication, publisher, and date, but also include dissertation information after the title (for example, "Diss. U of California, 1998.").

If the dissertation is published by University Microfilms International (UMI), underline the title and include "Ann Arbor: UMI," the date, and the order number at the end of the entry.

Diaz-Greenberg, Rosario. <u>The Emergence of Voice in Latino</u>
     <u>High School Students</u>. Diss. U of San Francisco, 1996. Ann
     Arbor: UMI, 1996. 9611612.

If you cite an abstract published in *Dissertation Abstracts International* (*DAI*), give the relevant volume number and page numbers.

Hidalgo, Stephen Paul. "Vietnam War Poetry: A Genre of Witness."
     Diss. U of Notre Dame, 1995. <u>DAI</u> 56 (1995): 0931A.

Examples of MLA entries: print articles   The conventions for listing print articles depend on whether the articles appear in newspapers, popular magazines, or scholarly journals. For distinguishing scholarly journals from other periodicals, see **49b.** In all cases, omit from your citation any introductory *A, An,* or *The* in the name of a newspaper, magazine, or scholarly journal. For page citations over 100 and sharing the same first number, use only the last two digits for the second number (for instance, 528–39, but 598–605).

20. *Article in a scholarly journal: pages numbered consecutively through issues of a volume*   For journals with consecutive pagination through a volume (for example, the first issue of volume 1 ends with page 174, and the second issue of volume 1 begins with page 175), give only the volume number and year.

Korotayev, Andrey, and Dmitri Bondarenko. "Polygyny
     and Democracy: A Cross-Cultural Comparison."
     <u>Cross-Cultural Research</u> 34 (2000): 190–206.
                         volume number   year

21. *Article in a scholarly journal: each issue paged separately*   For journals in which each issue begins with page 1, include the issue number after the volume number, separated from the volume number by a period, or include the issue number alone if no volume number is given.

Ginat, Rami. "The Soviet Union and the Syrian Ba'th
     Regime: From Hesitation to <u>Rapprochement</u>."
     <u>Middle Eastern Studies</u> 36.2 (2000): 150–71.
                    volume number   issue number

22. *Article in a magazine*   For a magazine published every week or biweekly, give the complete date: date (numeral), month (abbreviated if necessary—see **52c**), and year, in that order, with no commas between them. For a monthly or bimonthly magazine, give only the month and year. In either case, do not include volume and issue numbers. If the article is no longer than one page, give that page number. If the article covers two or more consecutive pages, list inclusive page numbers.

Roston, Eric. "How Much Is a Living Wage?" <u>Time</u> 8 Apr. 2002:
    52-54.

Bry, David. "Hard Time." <u>Vibe</u> Apr. 2002: 110-16.

Rauch, Jonathan. "Seeing around Corners." <u>Atlantic</u>
    Apr. 2002: 35.

        article only one page long

23. Article in a newspaper Omit an initial *The* in a newspaper title. Include the date after the newspaper title. For a newspaper that uses letters to designate sections, give the letter before the page number: "B9." For a numbered section, write, for example, "sec. 2: 23." See **52d,** item 37, for the online version of this article.

Krugman, Paul. "The Smoke Machine." <u>New York Times</u> 29 Mar.
    2002: A29.

24. Article that skips pages When an article does not appear on consecutive pages (the one by Boudette begins on page A1 and concludes on page A8), give only the first page number followed by a plus sign.

Boudette, Neal E. "A Holocaust Claim Cuts to the Heart of the
    New Germany." <u>Wall Street Journal</u> 29 Mar. 2002: A1+.

25. Review Begin with the name of the reviewer and the title of the review article, if these are available. After "Rev. of," provide the title and author of the work reviewed, followed by publication information for the periodical in which the review appears.

Alter, Robert. "Immodest Proposals." Rev. of <u>God, Gulliver, and</u>
    <u>Genocide: Barbarism and the European Imagination, 1492-</u>
    <u>1945</u>, by Claude Rawson. <u>New Republic</u> 11 Feb. 2002: 34-38.

26. Unsigned editorial or article Begin with the title. For an editorial, include the label "Editorial" after the title. In alphabetizing, ignore any initial *A, An,* or *The.*

"The Marriage Clock." Editorial. <u>New York Observer</u> 29 Apr.
    2002: 4.

"Oscars with Color." Editorial. <u>USA Today</u> 26 Mar. 2002: 14A.

27. *Letter to the editor* Write "Letter" or "Reply to letter of ..." after the name of the author.

Libby, Mark W. Letter. <u>Atlantic Monthly</u> Apr. 2002: 8.

Siddiqi, Shamim A. Letter. <u>Commentary</u> Feb. 2002: 3.

28. *Abstract in an abstracts journal* For abstracts of articles, provide exact information for the original work and add information about your source for the abstract: the title of the abstract journal, volume number, year, and item number or page number. (For dissertation abstracts, see **52d**, item 19.)

Van Dyke, Jan. "Gender and Success in the American Dance
    World." <u>Women's Studies International Forum</u> 19 (1996):
    535-43. <u>Studies on Women Abstracts</u> 15 (1997): item
    97W/081.

29. *Article on microform (microfilm and microfiche)* To cite sources that are neither in hard copy nor in electronic form, provide as much print publication information as is available along with the name of the microfilm or microfiche and any identifying features. Many newspaper and magazine articles published before 1980 are available only in microfiche or microfilm, so you will need to use this medium for historical research. However, be aware that such collections may be incomplete and difficult to read and duplicate clearly.

"War with Japan." Editorial. <u>New York Times</u> 8 Dec. 1941: 22. UMI
    University Microfilms.

Savage, David. "Indecency on Internet Faces High Court Test."
    <u>Los Angeles Times</u> 16 Mar. 1997. Newsbank: Law (1997):
    fiche 34, grid A6.

Examples of MLA entries: Internet and electronic sources

30. *General requirements* With the fast pace of change in the electronic world, standards are continually evolving for citing sources. For updated information on citing Internet sources in MLA style, refer to the MLA Web site at <http://www.mla.org>.

　　Whatever system of documentation you use, the basic question you need to ask is "What information do readers need in order to access the same site and find the same information I found?" Internet sites vary in the amount of information they provide, and with some you need to go to the home page or search the site to find information. Scroll to the end of a page—the author's name and the date of posting often lurk there.

Note: For all of your sources, you *must* provide the date when you found the material (your date of access) and the URL (or other access information for an online subscription database).

KEY POINTS
Citing Internet Sources

1. *Information to include* As a general rule, follow this pattern, including whatever items of information are relevant and available to you (**52d**, items 31–51).

   - author(s) or editor(s)
   - title of work
   - print publication information: name of periodical, details of publication, date of publication, and print page numbers
   - title of online page, project, journal, or database, underlined
   - online publication information: title of site, date of latest update, volume and issue number of online journal, name of online service, sponsor of site, or discussion list
   - date when you accessed the site
   - electronic address (URL)

2. *Dates* The last date in your source reference, immediately before the URL or keywords, should be the date when you accessed the material. Two dates might appear next to each other in a source reference, as in items 36 and 37, but both are necessary: the first, the date when the work was posted or updated electronically; the second, the date when you found the material.

3. *URL* Break a URL for a new line only after a slash. Never insert a hyphen into a Web address (a URL), and never split a protocol (for example, http://) across lines. When using MLA style, enclose a URL in angle brackets (< >).

4. *Page numbers only for print version* Include in your citation the range of page numbers for any version of the source if they are indicated in the source. For the electronic version, include page or paragraph numbers of the on-screen version only if they are indicated on the screen, as they will be in a PDF document (portable document format). Frequently they are not, so the page numbers on your printout of a source would not necessarily correspond to the page numbers on other printouts. When no

(continued)

(continued)

page or paragraph information for the online version appears on the screen, include no page numbers in your list of references. For how to cite unpaged online material in your text, see **52b,** item J. See also **50i** on how to indicate where your citation ends.

5. *Permissions* Request permission to use any graphics or e-mail postings you include in your paper, especially if you intend to post your paper on a Web site. Make this request via e-mail.

31. Work in an online database or subscription service Libraries subscribe to large information services (such as *InfoTrac, First Search, EBSCO, SilverPlatter, Dialog, SIRS,* and *Lexis-Nexis*) to gain access to extensive databases of online articles, as well as to specialized databases (such as *ERIC, Contemporary Literary Criticism,* and *PsycINFO*). You can use these databases to locate abstracts and full texts of thousands of articles.

The URLs used to access databases are useful only to those accessing them through a subscribing organization such as a college library or a public library. In addition, database URLs tend not to remain stable, changing day by day, so providing a URL at the end of your citation will not be helpful to your readers unless you know it will be persistent. Cite articles in library databases by providing the following information:

- last and first name of author(s)
- title of article, in quotation marks
- print information for the article (name of journal, underlined; date and pages, if the full range of pages is given online), or the starting page followed by a hyphen, space, and period (26- .)
- name of the database (underlined)
- name of the service providing the database (for example, *Lexis-Nexis, EBSCOhost, InfoTrac*)
- name of library system and location
- your date of access
- the URL of the document if it is persistent and not impossibly long, otherwise the URL of the search page or home page—or no URL at all
- a period at the end

If you provide that information, readers who have access to the database will then be able to retrieve the article you cite. The examples that follow show citations of a magazine article, a scholarly article, and a newspaper article accessed from different databases.

print publication
┌── information ──┐
Gray, Katti. "The Whistle Blower." Essence Feb. 2001: 148- .
            database   service   library
    Academic Search Premier. EBSCOhost. City U of New
                          date of access
    York Lib., New York, NY. 19 Oct. 2002 <http://search
      EBSCO database provides a persistent URL.
    .epnet.com/direct.asp?an=4011390&db=aph>.

Lowe, Michelle S. "Britain's Regional Shopping Centres: New
               volume and issue number for print version of scholarly article
    Urban Forms?" Urban Studies 37.2 (2000): 261- . Academic
    Search Elite. EBSCOhost. Brooklyn Public Lib., Brooklyn,
    NY. E-Resources. 20 Oct. 2002 <http://search.epnet.com/
    direct.asp?an=2832704&db=afh>.

Toplin, Robert Brent. "Cinematic History: A Defense of
    Hollywood." National Forum Spring 2000: 10- . Expanded
    Academic ASAP. InfoTrac. City U of New York Lib.,
                    URL of home page of service
    New York, NY. 13 Apr. 2002 <http://www.galegroup.com/>.

Weeks, Linton. "History Repeating Itself; Instead of
    Describing Our Country's Past, Two Famous Scholars
    Find Themselves Examining Their Own." Washington Post
    24 Mar. 2002: F01- . Academic Universe. Lexis-Nexis.
    City U of New York Lib., New York, NY. 3 Apr. 2002
    <http://web.lexis-nexis.com/>.
           URL of home page

If the service provider provides a direct link to a licensed database without displaying the URL, give the name of the database, the name of the subscription service or library, and your date of access. Specify any path or keywords that you used to access the source.

"Parthenon." The Columbia Encyclopedia. 6th ed. 2000. America
    Online. 12 July 2000. Keywords: Reference;
    Encyclopedias; Encyclopedia.com; Bartleby.com; Columbia
    Encyclopedia 6th ed.

Verdon, Mary E., and Leonard H. Sigal. "Recognition and
    Management of Lyme Disease." American Family Physician
    56.2 (1997). NOAH (New York Online Access to Health).
    Brooklyn Public Lib., Brooklyn, NY. 2 Apr. 2002. Path:
    Health topics; Lyme disease; Diagnosis and symptoms.

32. *Online book (eBook) or part of book*   Give whatever is available of the following: author, title, editor or translator (if applicable), print publication information, electronic publication information and date of electronic posting, date of access, and complete electronic address (URL).

```
                                              print publication
   ┌──── author ────┐  ┌──────── title of work ────────┐  ┌─ information ─┐
   Darwin, Charles. The Voyage of the Beagle. London: John

                                              date of electronic
   ┌────────────────┐  ┌──── title of database ────┐  ┌─ publication ─┐
   Murray, 1859. Oxford Text Archive. 28 Mar. 2000.

   ┌──────────────────── name of sponsor of site ────────────────────┐
   Arts and Humanities Data Service, Oxford U Computing

                date of              URL enclosed
   ┌────────┐  ┌─ access ─┐  ┌──── in angle brackets ────┐
   Services. 24 Mar. 2003 <http://ota.ahds.ac.uk>.
```

Green, Elna C. Southern Strategies. Chapel Hill:

     U of North Carolina P, 1997. NetLibrary.

     City U of New York Lib., New York, NY. 3 Apr. 2002

     <http://www.netlibrary.com/>.

33. *Online poem*

```
   ┌──── author ────┐  ┌ title of poem ┐  ┌ print source ┐  ┌────────────┐
   Levine, Philip. "What Work Is." What Work Is. New York:

   print publication                           date of electronic
   ┌─ information ─┐  ┌──────── title of database ────────┐  ┌─ updating ─┐
   Knopf, 1991. Internet Poetry Archive. 4 Apr. 2000.

             sponsor              date of
   ┌──────── of site ────────┐  ┌─ access ─┐
   U of North Carolina P. 24 Mar. 2003

   ┌──────────── URL enclosed in angle brackets ────────────┐
   <http://www.ibiblio.org/ipa/levine/work.html>.
```

34. *Article in a reference database*

```
                                   title of
                              ┌── electronic source ──┐  date of electronic update
   ┌─ title of article ─┐  ┌────────────────────────┐
   "Bloomsbury group." Columbia Encyclopedia. 6th ed. 2002.

                                              date of
   ┌──────────── title of database ────────────┐  ┌─ access ─┐
   Bartleby.com: Great Books Online. 24 Mar. 2003
```

     <http://www.bartleby.com/65/>.

35. Article in an online journal or newsletter Give the author, title of article, title of journal, volume and issue numbers, and date of issue. Include page or paragraph numbers only if pages or paragraphs are numbered in the source, as they are for the Hatchuel example. End with date of access and electronic address.

```
┌──── author ────┐   ┌──────── title of article ────────┐
Hatchuel, Sarah. "Leading the Gaze: From Showing to

     ┌───────────────────────────────────────────┐
     Telling in Kenneth Branagh's Henry V and Hamlet."

                name of            volume and
              ┌── online journal──┐ issue number  date of online
                                         ┌─┐      ┌ publication
     Early Modern Literary Studies 6.1 (2000):

     number of paragraphs      date of
     (numbered in the text)     access
     22 pars. 25 Mar. 2003 <http://www.shu.ac.uk/emls/06-1/
     hatchbra.htm>.

┌──── author ────┐   ┌──────── title of article ──────┐
Hart, Stephen. "Overtures to a New Discipline:

                              title of
     ┌──────────────────┐  ┌ online journal ┐ volume and issue numbers
     Neuromusicology." 21st Century 1.4 (July 1996).
                                         └── date of ──┘
     ┌ no numbered pages or paragraphs      electronic publication
     29 Apr. 2002 <http://www.columbia.edu/cu/21stC/
     └── date of ──┘
         access
     issue-1.4/mbmmusic.html>.
```

36. Article in an online magazine

```
Greenberg, David. "Explaining the Cult of Theodore
     Roosevelt." Slate 28 Mar. 2002. 29 Mar. 2002
     <http://Slate.msn.com/?id=2063795>.
```

37. Article in an online newspaper

```
Plate, Tom. "The Costs of a Ludicrous 'Defense.'" Los Angeles
     Times: LATimes.com 12 July 2000. 13 July 2000
     <http://www.latimes.com/news/comment/20000712/
     t000065479.html>.

Krugman, Paul. "The Smoke Machine." New York Times on the Web
     29 Mar. 2002. 31 Mar. 2002 <http://www.nytimes.com/2002/
     03/29/opinion/29KRUG.html>.
```

38. *Review, editorial, abstract, or letter in an online publication*
After author and title, identify the type of text: "Letter," "Editorial," "Abstract," or "Rev. of ..., by ...". Continue with details of the electronic source.

Delaney, Thomas. "Digital Keys 3.0 Online." Rev. of <u>Digital</u>
     <u>Keys 3.0</u>, by Ann Raimes. <u>TESL-EJ</u> 5.3 (Dec. 2001). 7 May
     2002 <http://www.writing.berkeley.edu/TESL-EJ/ej19/
     m3.html>.

39. *Scholarly project*

              title of   date of electronic
   ┌──── scholarly project ────┐ ┌──── editor ────┐ ┌──── update ────┐
  Perseus Digital Library. Ed. Gregory Crane. 14 Sept. 2001.

      sponsor   date of
      ┌────┐ ┌── access ──┐
    Tufts U. 9 May 2002 <http://www.perseus.tufts.edu>.

40. *Professional site*

                                      date of
   ┌──── title of professional site ────┐ ┌── update ──┐ ┌
  Modern Language Association. 17 Oct. 2001. Mod. Lang.

          ┌──── sponsor ────┐ ┌ date of access ┐
    Assoc. of America. 29 Mar. 2002 <http://www.mla.org>.

41. *Online government publication* Begin with the government agency, title of the work, and place and date of print publication. Follow this with the date of electronic posting or update, the date of access, and the URL.

United States. Dept. of Educ. Office of Educ. Research and
     Improvement. Natl. Center for Educ. Statistics. <u>Digest</u>
     <u>of Education Statistics, 2000</u>. Washington: GPO, 2001.
     Jan. 2001. 5 Feb. 2002 <http://nces.ed.gov/pubs2001/digest>.

42. *Linked site* If you connect to one site from another, include "Lkd." ("linked from") after the details of the source you cite, followed by the title of the document you originally accessed (in italics or underlined), along with any additional details necessary for linking. Follow this with the date of access and the URL.

"Morisot, Berthe." <u>WebMuseum, Paris</u> (30 Dec. 1995). Lkd.
     <u>AntePodium Links</u>, at "Gender Studies" and "Canadian
     Women's Studies Online." 15 June 2000
     <http://www.ruw.ac.nz/atp>.

43. Web page (course/personal) For a course home page, give name of instructor and course, the words **Course home page**, the dates of the course, the department and institution, and then your access date and the URL.

```
Raimes, Ann. Expository Writing. Course home page. Sept.
     2002-Dec. 2002. Dept. of English, Hunter Coll. 12 Dec.
     2002 <http://bb.hunter.cuny.edu>.
```

If the personal Web page has a title, supply it, underlined. Otherwise, use the designation "Home page."

```
Kuechler, Manfred. 10 Jan. 2002. Home page. 28 Mar. 2002
     <http://maxweber.hunter.cuny.edu/socio/faculty/
     kuech.html>.
```

44. Online posting to a discussion list, Web forum, chat group/ bulletin board, or Usenet newsgroup Give the author's name, title of document (as written in the subject line), the label "Online posting," and the date of posting. Follow this with the name of the discussion list or forum, date of access, and URL or address of discussion list. For a Usenet newsgroup, give the name and address of the group, beginning with the prefix "news."

DISCUSSION LIST

```
Peckham, Irvin. "Class origins." Online posting. 1 May 2000.
   name of discussion list        address of discussion list
        WPA-L. 6 May 2000 <WPA-L@asu.edu>.
```

To make it easier for readers to find the posting, refer whenever possible to one available in the list's archives or in Hypernews:

```
Peckham, Irvin. "Class origins." Online posting. 1 May 2000.
     WPA-L Archives. 6 Apr. 2002 <http://lists.asu.edu/
     archives/wpa-1.html>.
```

WEB FORUM

```
Reynolds, Don. "Airline security." Online posting.
     12 Apr. 2002. The Fray: Discussion Forum for
     Slate. 14 Apr. 2002 <http://slate.msn.com/
     ?id=3936&m=3331676>.
```

BULLETIN BOARD

```
Flores, Jason. "Scarlet Letter." Online posting. 23 Feb. 2002.
     Eng 120 Discussion Board on Blackboard course page.
     14 Apr. 2002 <http://online.cuny.edu:8001/bin/common/
     course.p1?course_id=266_1>.
```

                        title of
           ┌────────── posting ──────────┐
Kramer, Wayne. "'Crossing Over' on Ifilm.com." Online

            date of   name of
       ┌── posting ──┐   ┌──────── forum ────────
    posting. 28 Apr. 2000. LatinoLink Bulletin Board:

                            date of
    ┌─────────────────────┐ ┌── access ──┐ ┌─ URL ─┐
    Criminal Justice. 14 June 2000 <http://

    ┌─────────────────────────┐
    boards.Latinolink.com>.

USENET NEWS GROUP

Fontana, Richard. "Re: Pedantry." Online posting. 20 Mar. 2002.
       30 Mar. 2002 <news:alt.usage.english>.

A FORWARDED ONLINE POSTING

To cite a forwarded document in an online posting, include author, title, and date, followed by "Fwd. by" and the name of the person forwarding the document. End with "Online posting," the date of the forwarding, the name of the discussion group, date of access, and address of the discussion list.

Cooper, Sandi. "Defending Civilization." 16 Nov. 2001. Fwd. by
       Manfred Kuechler. Online posting. 16 Nov. 2001. Hunter-
       l. 20 Nov. 2001 <hunter-l@hunter.listserv.cuny.edu>.

45. Synchronous communication When citing a source from a chat room, a MUD (multiuser domain), or a MOO (multiuser domain, object-oriented), give the name of the person speaking or posting information, the type of event, title, date, forum, date of access, and electronic address. Refer to archived material whenever possible.

Day, Michael. Discussion of e-mail and argument.
       C-Fest 12. 19 June 1996. LinguaMOO. 9 Apr. 2002
       <http://lingua.ut.dallas.edu:7000/2007/>.

46. Work of art online

Kelly, Ellsworth. <u>Sculpture for a Large Wall</u>. 1957. Museum of
       Mod. Art, New York. 4 Apr. 2002 <http://www.moma.org/docs/
       collection/paintsculpt/recent/c467.htm>.

47. Television and radio programs online

Ardalan, Davar. "Muslim Women Breaking Down Barriers on the
       Web." <u>Weekend All Things Considered</u>. Natl. Public Radio.

23 Mar. 2002. <u>Cyber Islam: NPR Online</u>. 2 Apr. 2002
      <http://www.npr.org/programs/watc/cyberislam/
      fatima.html>.

48. Film or film clip online

Clinton, Bill. Address to California Institute of
      Technology on Science and Technology. 21 Jan. 2000.
      Caltech. 27 July 2000 <http://www.caltech.edu/events/
      PresVisit-MCP-LAN.ram>.

49. Personal e-mail message   Treat this form like a letter.

Kane, George. "Changing Times." E-mail to the author. 7 Apr.
      2002.

50. Other Internet sources   Identify online interviews, maps, charts, sound recordings, cartoons, and advertisements as you would sources that are not online (see items **54–62**), with the addition of electronic publication information, date of access, and the URL.

51. Electronic source medium not known   When you use a computer network to access information, you may not know whether the material is on the library's hard drive or on CD-ROM. In such a case, use the label "Electronic" for the medium, and give the name and sponsor of the network, followed by your date of access.

"Renaissance." 1996. <u>Concise Columbia Electronic
      Encyclopedia</u>. Electronic. Columbianet. Columbia U Lib.
      18 July 2000.

52. CD-ROM   Cite material from a CD-ROM published as a single edition (that is, with no regular updating) in the same way you cite a book, but after the title add the medium of publication (CD-ROM) and any version or release number.

Keats, John. "To Autumn." <u>Columbia Granger's World of Poetry</u>.
      CD-ROM. Rel. 3. New York: Columbia UP, 1999.

To cite an updated database on CD-ROM, include any print publication information, the name of the database, the label "CD-ROM," the name of the producer or distributor, and the electronic publication date.

Dowd, Maureen. "Spite or Art?" <u>New York Times</u> 23 Apr. 2000:
      11. <u>New York Times Ondisc</u>. CD-ROM. UMI-ProQuest, 2000.

Examples of MLA entries: other sources

53. *Lecture, speech, letter, personal communication, or interview* For a lecture or speech, give the author and title, if known. For a presentation with no title, include a label such as "Lecture" or "Address" after the name of the speaker. Also give the name of any organizing sponsor, the venue, and the date.

```
Diggs, Elizabeth. Lecture. New York U, New York. 9 Apr. 2002.
```

For a letter that you received, include the phrase "Letter to the author" after the name of the letter writer. For an interview that you conducted, indicate the type of interview ("Personal interview," "Telephone interview").

```
Rogan, Helen. Letter to the author. 3 Feb. 2002.

Gingold, Alfred. Telephone interview. 5 May 2002.
```

Cite a published letter as you would cite a work in an anthology. After the name of the author, include any title the editor gives the letter and the date. Add the page numbers for the letter at the end of the citation.

```
Bishop, Elizabeth. "To Robert Lowell." 26 Nov. 1951. One Art:
     Letters. Ed. Robert Giroux. New York: Farrar, 1994.
     224-26.
```

54. *Published or broadcast interview* For a print, radio, or TV interview that has no title, include the label "Interview" after the name of the person interviewed, followed by the bibliographical information for the source.

```
Lee, Spike. Interview. Charlie Rose. PBS. WNET, New York.
     29 Mar. 2002.
```

55. *Map or chart* Underline the title of the map or chart, and include the designation after that title.

```
Auvergne/Limousin. Map. Paris: Michelin, 1996.
```

56. *Film or video* List the title, director, performers, and any other pertinent information. End with the name of the distributor and the year of distribution.

```
Sunshine. Dir. Istvan Szabo. Perf. Ralph Fiennes. Paramount,
     2000.
```

When you cite a videocassette or DVD, include also the medium, the name of the distributor, and the date of the recording.

<u>Casablanca</u>. Dir. Michael Curtiz. Perf. Humphrey Bogart and
    Ingrid Bergman. Turner, 1943. DVD. MGM, 1998.

57. *Television or radio program* Give the title of the program; any
pertinent information about performers, writer, narrator, or director;
a series name, if applicable; the network; and the local station and
date of broadcast.

<u>Origins: Life on the Move</u>. Narr. Peter Coyote. The Shape of
    Life. PBS. WNET, New York. 2 Apr. 2002.

58. *Sound recording* List the composer or author, the title of the
work, the names of artists, the production company, and the date. If
the medium is not a compact disc, indicate the medium, such as
"Audiocassette," before the name of the production company.

Scarlatti, Domenico. <u>Keyboard Sonatas</u>. Andras Schiff, piano.
    London, 1989.

Walker, Alice. Interview with Kay Bonetti. Audiocassette.
    Columbia: American Audio Prose Library, 1981.

59. *Live performance* Give the title of the play, the author, pertinent
information about the director and performers, the theater, the location, and the date of performance. If you are citing an individual's
role in the work, begin your citation with the person's name.

<u>Copenhagen</u>. By Michael Frayn. Dir. Michael Blakemore. Perf.
    Philip Bosco. Royale Theater, New York. 16 May 2000.

Blakemore, Michael, dir. <u>Copenhagen</u>. By Michael Frayn. Perf.
    Philip Bosco. Royale Theater, New York. 16 May 2000.

60. *Work of art, slide, or photograph* List the name of the artist, the
title of the work (underlined), the name of the museum, gallery, or
owner, and the city.

Johns, Jasper. <u>Racing Thoughts</u>. Whitney Museum of Amer. Art,
    New York.

For a photograph in a book, give complete publication information,
including the page number on which the photograph appears.

Johns, Jasper. <u>Racing Thoughts</u>. Whitney Museum of Amer. Art,
    New York. <u>The American Century: Art and Culture 1950-
    2000</u>. By Lisa Phillips. New York: Norton, 1999. 311.

For a slide in a collection, include the slide number: "Slide 17," for
example.

61. *Cartoon* After the cartoonist's name and the title (if any) of the cartoon, add the label "Cartoon." Follow this with the usual information about the source, and give the page number.

```
Spiegelman, Art. "Duchamp Is Our Misfortune." Cartoon. New
    Yorker 25 Mar. 2002: 104.
```

62. *Advertisement* Give the name of the product or company, followed by the label "Advertisement" and publication information. If a page is not numbered, write "n. pag."

```
Altoids. Advertisement. Wired Mar. 2002: 22.
```

63. *Legal case* Give the name of the case with no underlining or quotation marks. Also give the volume number, name and page of the law report, the name of the court, and the year.

```
             volume   United States    court deciding case:
             number   Law Report       US Supreme Court

Roe v. Wade. 410 U.S. 209. U.S. Sup. Ct. 1973.
                  page number cited        year of decision
```

However, if you mention the case in your text, italicize or underline it: "Chief Justice Burger, in his concurring statement on the *Roe v. Wade* decision (209), noted that . . . ."

52e **When to use footnotes and endnotes**

With the MLA parenthetical style of documentation, use a footnote (at the bottom of the page) or an endnote (on a separate numbered page at the end of the paper before the works-cited list) only for notes giving supplementary information that clarifies or expands a point you make. You might use a note to refer to several supplementary bibliographical sources or to provide a comment that is interesting but not essential to your argument. Indicate a note with a raised number (superscript) in your text, after the word or sentence your note refers to. Begin the first line of each note one-half inch (or five spaces) from the left margin. Do not indent subsequent lines of the same note. Double-space endnotes. For footnotes, single-space within each footnote, but double-space between notes.

NOTE NUMBER
IN TEXT

Ethics have become an important part of many writing classes.[1]

52f

CONTENT ENDNOTE

five spaces ⎯⎯⎯ raised number followed by space

←⎯⎯→¹ For additional discussion of ethics in the classroom, see Stotsky 799–806; Knoblauch 15–21; Bizzell 663–67; Friend 560–66.

The *MLA Handbook* also describes a system of footnotes or endnotes as an alternative to parenthetical documentation of references.

52f Students' MLA papers

The first sample paper was written by Jared Whittemore in a required composition course at San Diego City College. Whittemore, the oldest of seven children, grew up in a military family, moving around often. When he graduated from a typical California high school in the San Francisco Bay Area in 1990, he knew that he wanted to go to college, but economically it was difficult. However, he had always wanted to be a firefighter, and most of the Fire Technology courses were offered at the community college level, where tuition was affordable for him. He enrolled in a local Bay Area junior college and began taking Fire Science classes, but after about a year, he was hired by a fire department. The demands of the job and of school courses were overwhelming, so he decided to postpone continuing his education. Now, he says, "Nearly twelve years later and after a move to Southern California, I am only one math class and one physical education class away from achieving my goal of getting an Associate Degree in Fire Protection Technology." He is now 29, engaged, and works as a firefighter with the Federal Fire Department in San Diego. Having attended three community colleges, he is enthusiastic about their mission and looks forward to achieving the goal he set himself twelve years ago—to finish his degree.

In his required composition course, Whittemore chose to write his research paper on a topic that is important to him. He wrote a proposal for the paper, prepared an extensive annotated bibliography (see an excerpt from it in **8b,** p. 183), drafted an outline (see **51c**), and wrote several drafts, refining his thesis and his supporting points as he did so. Here is his fifth draft.

Whittemore 1

Jared A. Whittemore

Professor K. Lim

English 101

14 March 2002

Community Colleges:

Providers of Opportunity

Community colleges open doors to a better life. Because of their small size, high level of accessibility, and low tuition fees, community colleges have been successful in providing postsecondary education to those who most need it. Four-year colleges do not provide access to all. Their doors are closed to students who cannot commit to or afford to pay for a full four-year education or who do not meet the standards of the entrance requirements. With their policy of open access, community colleges have provided exceptional opportunities, especially to students from low-income families, minorities, those with inadequate primary and secondary schooling, and women.

Such access is illustrated by the system of schools that has grown to be the California Community College system, originally set up to bridge the gap and smooth the transition between high school and four-year colleges. The schools were originally known as "junior colleges," offering an education comparable to thirteenth and fourteenth grades. In their early stages, the junior colleges were often looked upon as a daring experiment. Then in 1967, when Governor Ronald Reagan authorized the organization of the Board of Governors of the California Community Colleges, they began to be known as community colleges and to gain recognition as institutions of higher education. The original intent was make the colleges economically and geographically available to all residents of California who were high school graduates and at least eighteen years of age. Thirty-three years

---

Annotations:

1″

½″

Last name and page number on every page

Title centered, not underlined

No extra space below title

Double-spaced throughout

1″

Thesis statement

Paragraph indent ½″

Point I: history of open access

1″

Whittemore 2

later, in 2000, the Chancellor of the California
community colleges, Thomas Nussbaum, reports that
California has in five years increased the number of
students in the state's 108 community colleges by
260,000 students--"approximately twice the entire
undergraduate enrollment of the University of
California" (2000, 5) with the system serving 1.6
million students (2000, 2) and helping them achieve
self-reliance, self-improvement, and increased
productivity.

Community colleges provide opportunities for
further education not just in California but
across the country. The statistics assembled for
the annual Digest of Education Statistics, 2000
found that of the total number of 14,549,189 students
enrolled in degree-granting institutions in 1998,
5,516,444 (37.9%) of them were enrolled in two-year
colleges (United States, Dept. of Educ., table 179).
Community colleges are obviously filling a need for
many who want to continue their education beyond
high school.

While many students aim to improve their status
in life by getting vocational training in the
community colleges, others will choose a two-year
school for purely financial reasons. Particularly
benefiting from the community college system are those
who come from low-income families. Even with
scholarships available, the reality is that a four-
year college is geared to full-time students. However,
many students cannot afford not to work to make a
living while still attending school; they have to find
ways to improve their social status, and this is where
the community colleges have stepped in. Students
perceive the training offered by the colleges as a
means of escape from dependency on social welfare
programs, so much so that Robert McCabe, Senior Fellow
with the League for Innovation in the Community
College, claims that "community colleges are the key

Full name
for first
mention

Exact words
quoted

Year for
sources
with same
author
and title

Page
numbers
for a PDF
source

Statistics to
support
point of
access

Transition
to Point II:
Access for
low-income
students

to avoiding a national crisis by moving underprepared and dependent individuals into productive self-sufficiency" (23).

> Page number for a print source

    The state of California again provides striking evidence of this trend. California has the lowest average tuition and fees of all community colleges in the United States. For the 1999-2000 academic year, for example, the national average in-state tuition was $1,136. Students in Texas and Florida paid $895 and $1,330 respectively, while students in California community colleges paid only $317 (United States, Dept. of Educ., table 314). Beginning in the fall of 1999, California students paid just $12 per credit unit, far lower than the tuition rates in other states. In addition, students in California enjoyed a 7.7% drop in student fees between the 1997-98 and 1998-99 school year (<u>Higher</u>).

> Statistics to support point: California example

    Another overwhelming financial reason for attending a community college is the cost of tuition in comparison to public four-year colleges. For a four-year public institution in California, for instance in 1999-2000, the average cost of tuition alone was $2,617 (United States, Dept. of Educ., table 314). When we compare that to the community college tuition of $317, we see what a cost-effective alternative a community college provides for lower-income students.

> First word of article title with no author named

> Statistics: costs in two-year and four-year colleges

    Quite possibly the most conspicuous citizens to have enjoyed the benefits of community colleges are minorities. As early as 1973, Sidney Brossman, the first Chancellor of the California Community Colleges, and Myron Roberts, professor of English at Chaffey College, made this claim: "Community colleges have proven uniquely suited to meeting the educational needs of minority-group students in terms both of numbers of such students enrolled and of success achieved in the classroom" (9).

> Point III: access for minorities

    Minorities, a rapidly growing portion of the country's population, are largely turning to the public sector rather than the private for their

> Minorities in public colleges

Whittemore 4

college education, as the 1997 enrollment statistics in Table 1 show.

Table 1

Minority Enrollment at Degree-Granting Institutions, 1997 *Table caption*

	PUBLIC		PRIVATE	
	Minorities	Total enrolled	Minorities	Total enrolled
2-year	1,675,467	5,360,686	79,328	244,883
4-year	1,365,473	5,835,433	650,942	3,061,332
Total	3,040,940	11,196,119	730,270	3,306,215

Source: United States, Dept. of Educ., Office of Educ. Research *Source line included*
and Improvement, Natl. Center for Educ. Statistics, <u>Digest of
Education Statistics, 2000</u> (Washington: GPO, 2001) table 210.

These figures show that nationwide, in 1997, minorities formed 27% of total enrollment in public colleges, with higher figures for community colleges: 31% of total enrollment in two-year schools. In California, statistics tell an encouraging story. The student population in community colleges closely reflects the overall demographics of the state's population. Nussbaum reports on minority enrollment figures:

> As of 1995, the students attending our colleges *Long quotation indented one inch*
> rather closely mirrored the adult population of
> the state: Whites--45%, as compared with 55% in
> the population; African American--8%, as compared
> with 7% in the population; Hispanics--23%, as
> compared with 27% in the population; and Asian--
> 13%, as compared with 12% in the population.
> (1997, 4)

Community colleges can, therefore, provide a diverse, *Statistics on race*
multicultural experience to the students enrolled as

the numbers of minorities increase. And the numbers are increasing. For example, in the fall of 1999, of the 1.6 million students enrolled in California community colleges, Whites still make up the largest group--41.9%; Hispanics rank second with a percentage of 25% (13.1% of whom are Mexican, Mexican American, Chicano); Asians are the third largest group with a total of 11.8% enrolled (3.7% of Chinese origin); Blacks make up 7.4%; and the last ethnic group with substantial numbers is Filipinos, with 3.2% (CCC Statewide). It is interesting to note that white enrollees decreased by 22.5% between 1990 and 1999, with a dramatic increase in the enrollment of students of minority groups in that same time period. The largest increase has been in the Latino population, with an increase of 65.6%. Two other groups that have shown an increase in numbers are the Asian/Pacific Islanders, with an increase of 44.6%, and Blacks, with an increase of 8.7% (California Postsecondary Education Commission, Sec. 2-10C).

> Article title abbreviated

In addition to welcoming low-income students and minorities, community colleges offer significant education opportunities to students whose secondary education has been inadequate or interrupted and who require remedial education. Community colleges serve these students by providing a wide range of classes and programs to establish the basics in reading, writing, and mathematics. These programs can help ease students into the postsecondary education experience or prepare them for the workforce.

> Transition to Point IV: access for those needing remediation

Students who begin higher education with limited academic skills feel unprepared for the education demands of a four-year college and so turn to community colleges:

> Community colleges have been "second chance" institutions, providing courses and services that raise the level of literacy and prepare students for college-level work. The skills include reading, writing, basic math, thinking, and problem solving. (Community College League of California 5)

Whittemore 6

Students who might otherwise become frustrated, struggle, and ultimately fail in a four-year college that offers no programs designed for their specific need have discovered that they can flourish in a community college and then successfully transfer to a four-year school. The remedial courses provide knowledge and skills that secondary education has failed to provide. Community colleges have always had an interest in the successful articulation and transfer of students. Ray Giles, the director of special services at the Community College League of California, points out the recognition of the importance of this mission: "In 1989, remedial education was recognized by the legislature as a function of the community colleges."

However, some community college students in need of basic preparation courses have no intention of transferring into four-year institutions. Rather, they benefit from the remedial programs that bring them up to speed and allow them to be more competitive as they enter the workforce. Growing numbers of students are already in the workforce, but they attend community colleges seeking advancement in their jobs, new skills, or training to branch out to new careers. For this group of students, community colleges offer a wide range of occupational and technical programs. In our ever-changing hi-tech society, the task of training a technical workforce is one of the community colleges' basic missions. Many of these students already have associate degrees or even bachelor degrees but find it necessary to continue their education to be economically competitive or to seek new job opportunities in other career fields.

The "National Community College Snapshot" prepared by the American Association of Community Colleges shows that the average national age for community college students is approximately 29 years, suggesting an upsurge in students returning to community colleges in pursuit of marketability. Community colleges have made a

Preparation for a four-year school

No page number for an online source

Preparation for career advancement

commitment to continued workforce development, with a wide range of programs and schedules that accommodate students with busy family and work schedules. They offer intensive courses in the evenings and on weekends, with more and more online courses adding to flexibility in education for students with busy lives. In return, the community and businesses reap the benefits from the large numbers of educated students who are prepared to use their newly acquired education and skills to better themselves and become more productive.

One group that has especially responded to the offering of a wide and flexible range of courses and schedules is women. In 1997, women made up 57.6% of the total enrollment in public two-year institutions as opposed to only 40.3% in 1970 (United States, Dept. of Educ., table 179). In California, too, the statistics continue to show a steady increase: in 1990, the total enrollment for women in the fall term was 785,300, and by 1999 the fall term enrollment of women had grown to 799,438 (California Postsecondary Education Commission, Sec. 2-7C).

Many women have returned to college using the community colleges as a portal. In the past, women traditionally held the role of homemaker and were largely responsible for raising children. However, due to changes in economic needs and social attitudes, women see their roles more broadly defined. Women who attend community colleges see a dramatic rise in economic benefit. Ernest Pascarella, a professor at the University of Iowa, cites supporting statistics: "On average, women with associate degrees had about a 26 percent advantage over the annual earnings of their counterparts with a high school degree" (12).

Women who enroll in community colleges often do so after a life-changing event. They return to school after their children leave home, after divorces, or after being laid off from jobs. Many are also seeking to learn job skills, so they can contribute to their families' income. For all these reasons, women are

Point V: access for women

Page number in a print source

either enrolling for the first time or returning to
college in large numbers. The community colleges with
their wide variety of vocational programs are well
suited to help this large portion of the population
in their educational pursuits and play an integral
part in the improvements seen in the status of women
within society, such as higher pay and increased
opportunities for advancement.

Community colleges clearly play a major role in
providing a postsecondary education to wide-ranging
groups of individuals. These schools make higher
education available and accessible to all, making
their hopes and dreams reality. These dreams are
embodied by Cynthia Inda, who took remedial courses at
Santa Barbara City College. This is what she says
about her experience:

Example reinforces all the points about access

Without the opportunity to study at my local
community college, I probably wouldn't have gone
to college at all. My high school grades would
have sufficed to get me into a decent university,
but I didn't consider myself college material.
After all, none of my six brothers and sisters
had attended college, and most didn't even finish
high school. My parents have the equivalent of a
second-grade education, Mexican immigrants who do
not speak English; my mother worked as a maid
and my father as a dishwasher. But enrolling in
a community college was one of the smartest
decisions I ever made. Despite my slow start, I
learned the skills I needed to move ahead

Long quotation indented

Passage omitted from original

academically.... I also began to explore
educational alternatives. And transferring to a
reputable four-year university became my most
important goal." (qtd. in Nussbaum, 2000, 3)

Passage quoted as indirect source in Nussbaum

Inda thrived in the community college system and
went on to graduate magna cum laude from Harvard
University. Can anyone doubt that community colleges
truly provide a gateway to self-reliance, personal
improvement, higher education, and success?

Whittemore 9

Works Cited

Brossman, Sidney W., and Myron Roberts. <u>The California Community Colleges</u>. Palo Alto: Field Educ., 1973.

California Postsecondary Education Commission. <u>Student Profiles, 2000</u>. Nov. 2000.

<u>CCC Statewide Student Population: Fall 1999 Enrollments</u>. 3 Feb. 2001. California Comm. Colleges. 13 Feb. 2001 <http://misweb.cccco.edu/ mis/statlib/stw/studF99.htm>.

Community College League of California. <u>Achieving the Diversity Commitment: A Policy and Resource Paper of the California Community College Trustees</u>. Dec. 2000. 2 Mar. 2001 <http:// www.ccleague.org/pubs/policy/diversity.pdf>.

Giles, Ray. "Curriculum Changes Triggered by Changing Student Needs, Social Trends." <u>The News</u>. Comm. College League of California. Spring 2000. 3 Mar. 2001 <http://www.ccleague.org/pubs/ news00sp.htm>.

<u>Higher Education Update: 1998-99 State Appropriations for California Postsecondary Education, Update 98-6</u>. Oct. 1998. California Postsecondary Educ. Commission. 3 Mar. 2001 <http://www.cpec.ca.gov/ HigherEdUpdates/Update1998/UP98-6.ASP>.

McCabe, Robert H. "Can Community Colleges Rescue America?" <u>Community College Journal</u>. Apr./May 1999: 20-23.

"National Community College Snapshot." <u>About Community Colleges</u>. American Assoc. of Comm. Colleges. 11 Feb 1999. 3 Mar. 2001 <http://www.aacc.nche.edu/ Content/ContentGroups/Statistics/ Community_College_Snapshot.htm>.

Nussbaum, Thomas J. "The State of California Community Colleges Address, 1997." California Comm. College Chancellor's Office. Sept. 1997. 6 Feb. 2001 <http://www.cccco.edu/executive/chancellor/speeches/ sos0997.pdf>.

Title centered, not underlined

Indented ½"

Entries alphabetized, double-spaced throughout

Online source: date of access and URL

No author named: source listed by title

Print article: page range indicated

Whittemore 10

---. "The State of California Community Colleges
    Address, 2000." California Comm. College
    Chancellor's Office. 28 Sept. 2000. 13 Feb. 2001
    <http://www.cccco.edu/executive/chancellor/
    speeches/sos0900.pdf>.

Pascarella, Ernest T. "New Studies Track Community
    College Effects on Students." Community College
    Journal June/July 1999: 8-14.

United States. Dept. of Educ. Office of Educ. Research   Government
    and Improvement. Natl. Center for Educ.   publication
                                                          in print
    Statistics. Digest of Education Statistics, 2000.
    Washington: GPO, 2001.

The following paper was written by Jacob Radford, a student in
a required first-year writing course at Hunter College, City
University of New York. An avid fan of movies and of Mozart, he
chose his own topic for research, supplementing library and online
sources with personal e-mail correspondence with a film critic. This
is his final draft. Radford has decided to major in computer science.

1″

Radford 1

½″

Jacob Radford

Professor J. Knox

English 120

3 May 2002

Hollywood and Historical Accuracy

In the last decade the public has become captivated by "reality" entertainment, with docudramas, VR, and reality-based TV programs. The public has turned away from printed news publications in favor of visual media as a quick and action-oriented venue for information. The motion picture industry has replied with an increase of historically based biographical films. For moviegoers, these films raise the question of whether "public history" (Custen 12) is altered after Hollywood's depiction of events or people. What do we see when we see a movie: a version of historical reality or a director's fiction? Or what do we think we see? Some may accept a Hollywood movie about a historical event as showing the past, a director's version of what, after all, can only be interpreted. However, unless movies explicitly claim to be documentaries of history, we should recognize that they are conceived as art or entertainment, and in a commercial marketplace their stories are shaped for their audiences' enjoyment.

According to film critic Laura Clifford, recent films based on real people's lives, such as A Beautiful Mind, Iris, Erin Brockovich, Ali, and Pollock, run the gamut of accuracy. In some cases, the source material for the film, such as a written biography by a close relative, may be controversial, as in the film Iris, or the subject may have given approval to a screenplay that paints an overly favorable picture, which appears to be the case with A Beautiful Mind. In other films, such as Ali, public events depicted in the film can be documented as

Side annotations:

Last name and page number on every page

Title centered, not underlined

No extra space below title

Double-spaced throughout

Author and page number for a print source

Thesis

Paragraph indent ½″

Personal communication, listed in works cited

Background: biographical films vary in accuracy

1″

Radford 2

accurate, but private events must be recreated as speculation.

An examination of the film <u>Amadeus</u>, recently re-released to theaters, can shed light on the purposes of accuracy and entertainment. Most viewers are aware that <u>Amadeus</u> is concerned with a segment in the life of the composer Wolfgang Amadeus Mozart. Peter Shaffer, the co-author of the screenplay, describes his storyline as a "fantasia on events in Mozart's life" (qtd. in Kupferberg 240). The original film garnered popular acclaim and eight Academy Awards, including Best Screenplay, and the current re-release includes twenty minutes of restored scenes (Schaefer). <u>Amadeus</u> highlights a span of ten years and through careful consideration of costume and locale manages to construct a compelling vision of life during that era. It was filmed in the now divided and renamed Czechoslovakia, where the action takes place, so the period setting feels right. Local "extras" were also employed, eliminating Hollywood's typical backdrop of American faces from the set. Visually, everything seems accurate, but after examining the characters and events of the movie, we can see that they diverge from recorded history.

Mozart is portrayed in the movie as a childish, highly sexual, scandalous individual who could produce exceptional music without exceptional effort. While watching the movie, many are tempted to ask, "Was Mozart really like that?" and "Did that really happen?" In contrast to the way he is depicted in the movie, Mozart himself is quoted as saying that his masterpieces were attained through diligent study of other composers' works as well as through endless hours of composing (Schure). In the film, Mozart is also depicted as an alcoholic who is not able to support his family. In fact, however, during the time span that the movie deals with, Mozart was at the peak

Discussion of Amadeus: A. Background and setting

No page number here for a one-page source

B. Portrayal of Mozart

No page number for online source

of his wealth. He was in the top ten percent of Vienna's elite at the time, and by no means would he have been considered poor (Brown). Specific references to Mozart's drinking habits are elusive, although popular opinion is that he was not a drunk. He was wild and was known for his "playful and vulgar sides," and his word games and dirty language were prevalent in his personal communications, but he would never have acted bluntly or without courtesy and respect in public, as the film suggests (Schure). Here Peter Shaffer and his co-author and director Milos Forman strayed from recorded history, making their movie controversial in the process.

The writer and director also toyed with historical facts when they linked Mozart's fear that he was being poisoned with Salieri's dubious claim years later that he was Mozart's assassin. Then there is the mystery of the unknown man who commissioned a Requiem from Mozart just before his death--the perfect basis for a story. Mozart must have been an easy choice as a subject not only because of his fame, but also because his death was shrouded in mystery. During the 1790s, we now know, when people took ill for unknown reasons, poisoning was offered as a general explanation (Rosselli 154). But Salieri's claims to have poisoned Mozart are considered altogether impossible.

Although not a genius like Mozart, Salieri was a major composer, employed in a prestigious position, and wrote wonderful music that was true to the ideals of the period. He was in the favor of the emperor and was considered financially successful by his contemporaries (Rosselli 155; Kupferberg 118), so his portrayal in the movie as a mediocre musician is a twist on the facts.

C. Portrayal of Salieri

Another controversial element in the movie is Mozart's implied marital infidelity. While historians have speculated on possible affairs, they have never

D. Mozart's marriage

Radford 4

been corroborated (Brown). Mozart considered his father Leopold to be "next to God," and his wife Costanze to be next in line (Brown). This suggests a faithful husband who loved his wife, not a rambunctious youth who chased after women. It was probably not from lack of historical knowledge that the authors made these astounding adaptations, but from the need to make an entertaining movie for the general public.

Film, like other art forms, is made to be enjoyed by an audience. When people go to a movie today, they expect to be drawn into the story and engaged. Many factors contribute to the success of any movie in terms of mass appeal, but enjoyment is key. If the film is not widely appreciated, it will not be considered a success. Changes and embellishments are made to past events or people to keep the story compelling. Shaffer writes that they strayed from the facts in keeping with the "undeniable laws of drama" to captivate an audience (Shaffer 56). So while <u>Amadeus</u> was not written in Italian or German, as it should have been to be accurate, we can still learn from it and enjoy it. If you were to tell your life story, would you tell the exact truth--would you even be able to recall an exact truth--or would you embellish some areas, even just a little? Authors cut and edit the lives of their subjects, give us a story in a trim two hours, and try to keep everything believable while creating an interesting plot. Historical accuracy is only part of creating a movie, and if an inaccuracy doesn't harm the movie's success, then accuracy isn't vital.

The time setting and the audience's familiarity with the topic also contribute to the reaction to history on the screen. The more an audience is personally involved in and informed about a topic, the greater the importance of accuracy will probably be for the authors. Oliver Stone was resoundingly

Discussion of movie viewers' expectations

Expansion of thesis

Discussion of viewers' familiarity with topic: examples

criticized for his 1991 film <u>JFK</u>, his portrayal of events around the assassination of John F. Kennedy. Many viewers had seen the event occur on television, had watched hours of news broadcasts, and had formed their own opinions about the existence of a conspiracy theory; they were not ready to accept an interpretation that did not jibe with their own. Yet another factor in how much a work's accuracy will be criticized is how far back in history its events occurred. With <u>Amadeus</u>, which shows us an example from a few hundred years ago, people seem to be generally ignorant and not upset about errors. Yet there was a huge uproar concerning Martin Scorsese's 1988 film, <u>The Last Temptation of Christ</u>, because of the movie's depiction of Christ having an earthly vision in which he makes love to Mary Magdalene. People were shocked at the blasphemous characterization of Christ. Representing history even further back, <u>The Mummy</u> (1999) was allowed far more lenience than either of the other two, partly because the topic was so far back in history and partly because there are few who are concerned about specific details, whereas the Bible is familiar to many and is taken seriously.

When people are not aware of the true facts, they will believe in the history a movie creates if it does not conflict with their beliefs. Minor details are most often overlooked, the simple things that hardly matter to the nature of the story, like English being used in films about people who speak other languages. As people go to more and more films, letting others do the fact-finding for them, they allow films to guide their knowledge of events. In George F. Custen's book <u>Bio/Pics</u>, John E. O'Connor emphasizes that "even well-educated Americans are learning most of their history from film and television" (7), while student journalist Jessica Emerson points out that it is difficult to show that people who extracted history from the movies actually "relied on the movies for historical education."

It is not a movie's or the author's job to educate viewers about history; that job belongs to the historians. One historian, David Brown, actually states that dramas create interest in a subject and a desire for more knowledge found in books (Goodale 13). If I found a story interesting, I would probably do research on the material, as I am doing with Mozart right now. But historian Steven Gillan has found the opposite: some of his students have regarded the movie <u>JFK</u> as a work of nonfiction and cited it as a source of information on Kennedy for their term papers (Goodale 13). Even the historians cannot agree on some details of history, as shown by their comments on Mozart's funeral. Many think that Salieri was a mourner at his funeral (Brown), others that he was a pallbearer (Freeman 26), still others that he did not even attend the funeral (Rosselli 158). Such disputes among historians over supposed facts reveal that historical accounts are themselves only interpretations. How can we know what really happened when any details can be questioned? Someone will always scrutinize movies for their accuracy, even a blockbuster movie made solely to entertain, but who can determine exactly where accuracy lies? That is what history does--it interprets and fleshes out the sketchy objective facts we have at our disposal.

Movies that lay no claims on the truth have no obligation to society other than to be enjoyable. No one should expect gospel truth on the silver screen. Let the buyer beware: the book you are reading or the movie you are watching reflects the opinions of the person who created it. Any work is ultimately an interpretation of the facts. Says Laura Clifford, "All biopics take dramatic license to some degree; otherwise they'd be dramatic recreations, or the

Discussion of movies and history

Reinforcement of thesis

filmmaker would make a documentary." We have a need to blend fact and fiction to make something more enticing, something that Robert Toplin calls "faction," even when it may upset some people who consider that this melding tarnishes their idea of an event or person. Yet their own original view on the subject is only their interpretation, sometimes a globally accepted one, but still an interpretation.

In this light we can reexamine <u>Amadeus</u> and say that Shaffer offers a wonderful story of Salieri in a maddened state perceiving the past in a distorted way. I like to think that Salieri could have felt so inferior to Mozart that for years he wished he could have eliminated Mozart, until finally he went insane and believed that he had actually eliminated him. This version is not what historians believe to be the truth, but it could have been what Salieri believed to be the truth. After all, we all take what we can out of the movies, as out of real life.

Concluding thoughts—back to <u>Amadeus</u>

Radford 8

Works Cited

Amadeus. Dir. Milos Forman. Perf. Tom Hulce, F. Murray
        Abraham. Warner, 1984.

Brown, A. Peter. "*Amadeus* and Mozart: Setting the Record
        Straight." <u>The American Scholar</u> 61.1 (1992). <u>The
        Mozart Project</u>. 13 Apr. 2002
        <http://www.mozartproject.org/essays/brown.html>.

Clifford, Laura. "Opinion on Recent Biopics." E-mail to
        the author. 26 Apr. 2002.

Custen, George F. <u>Bio/Pics</u>. New Brunswick: Rutgers UP,
        1992.

Emerson, Jessica. "Artistic Integrity of the Cinema
        Must Be Respected." <u>Daily Trojan</u> 2 Nov. 2000: 4-6.
        U of Southern California. 3 Apr. 2002
        <http://www.usc.edu/student-affairs/dt/V141/
        N46?02-artis.46v.html>.

Freeman, John. W. "The Real Salieri." <u>Opera News</u> 28 Mar.
        1998: 26- . <u>Academic Search Premier</u>. EBSCOhost.
        City U of New York Lib., New York, NY. 9 Apr. 2002
        <http://search.epnet.com/direct.asp?an=380240&db=aph>.

Goodale, Gloria. "History according to Hollywood."
        <u>Christian Science Monitor</u> 28 Sept. 2001: 13.
        <u>Academic Search Premier</u>. EBSCOhost. City U of New
        York Lib., New York, NY. 9 Apr. 2002 <http://search
        .epnet.com/direct.asp?an=5239252&db=aph>.

<u>JFK</u>. Dir. Oliver Stone. Perf. Kevin Costner. Warner, 1991.

Kupferberg, Herbert. <u>Amadeus: A Mozart Mosaic</u>. New York:
        McGraw, 1986.

Rosselli, John. <u>The Life of Mozart</u>. New York: Cambridge
        UP, 2000.

Schaefer, Stephen. "<u>Amadeus</u> Features Notable Additions."
        <u>Boston Herald</u> 19 Apr. 2002: S17.

Schure, K. A. 1997. <u>Amadeus</u>. 1997. 1 Nov. 2001
        <http://www.geocities.com/Vienna/Strasse/2915/
        amadeus.html>.

Title
centered
not
underlined

Entries
alphabetized

Personal
communication

Online
source:
date of
access and
URL

Article in
subscription
database

Film

Radford 9

Shaffer, Peter. "Making the Screen Speak." <u>Film Comment</u>
    Sept./Oct. 1984: 50-51+. <u>UMI University Microfilms</u>.

Toplin, Robert Brent. "Cinematic History: A Defense of
    Hollywood." <u>National Forum</u> 81.2 (2001): 10- .
    <u>Academic Search Elite</u>. EBSCOhost. Brooklyn
    Public. Lib., Brooklyn, NY. 10 Apr. 2002 <http://
    search.epnet.com/direct.asp?an=4514003&db=afh>.

Article
skips
pages

Part X
Documenting Sources: APA, CBE/CSE, *Chicago*, and *Columbia* Styles

In Part X, you will find descriptions of documentation systems other than the MLA system. Section **53** focuses on the style recommended for the social sciences by the *Publication Manual of the American Psychological Association*, 5th ed. (Washington, DC: Amer. Psychological

Assn., 2001), and on the Web site for the APA *Publication Manual* at <http://www.apastyle.org>. It includes a sample of a student's paper written in APA style. Section **54** describes the citation-sequence style recommended by the Council of Biology Editors/Council of Science Editors (CBE/CSE). Section **55** describes the endnote and footnote styles recommended in *The Chicago Manual of Style*, 14th ed. (Chicago: U of Chicago P, 1993), for writing in the humanities; it is sometimes used as an alternative to MLA style. Section **56** outlines the system recommended in *The Columbia Guide to Online Style* (New York: Columbia UP, 1998) and at <http://www.columbia.edu/cu/cup/cgos> for citing online sources in the humanities and sciences.

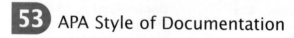

53 APA Style of Documentation

AT A GLANCE: INDEX OF APA STYLE FEATURES

53a Two basic features of APA style

KEY POINTS

Two Basic Features of APA Style

1. *In the text of your paper*, include these two pieces of information (if they are available) each time you refer to a source:

   • the last name(s) of the author(s)
   • the year of publication *(continued)*

(continued)

For quotations, paraphrase, and reference to a specific idea, also include the page number of a print source or any visible paragraph number or section location for an online source.

2. *At the end of your paper*, include on a new numbered page a list entitled "References," double-spaced and arranged alphabetically by authors' last names (or title if no author is named), the date in parentheses, and other bibliographical information. See **53d** for examples of what to include in an APA-style reference list.

Illustrations of the two basic features

a. A reference in the text of the paper, with author, year, and page number for a specific reference

```
In Australia, as in many parts of the world, improvements
in information technology are generating collaborative
work (Ellyard, 1998, p. 70).
```

b. The entry in the references list

```
Ellyard, P. (1998). Ideas for the new millennium.
     Melbourne: Melbourne University Press.
```

53b APA author/year style for in-text citations

A. One author   If you mention the author's last name in your own sentence, include the year in parentheses directly after the author's name.

```
   author    year
Wilson (1994) has described in detail his fascination
with insects.
```

(See **53d**, item 1, to see how this work appears in a reference list.)

If you do not name the author in your sentence, include both the name and the year, separated by a comma, in parentheses.

```
The role of the Educational Testing Service (ETS) in
designing, evaluating, and promoting the test has been
harshly criticized (Owen, 1985).
                    author  comma  year
```

If you use a direct quotation, a paraphrase, or a reference to a specific idea in a work, help readers locate the passage by including in parentheses the abbreviation "p." or "pp." followed by a space and the page number(s). Separate items within parentheses with commas.

```
Memories are built "around a small collection of
dominating images" (Wilson, 1994, p. 5).
```
                             comma comma page number
                                           with a quotation

If the reference is to an online source with no page numbers indicated, use a paragraph number or section number if it appears on the screen. This will help readers locate the reference (see **53b**, item H, for an example). If no section headings or paragraph numbers are visible, omit a reference to an exact location; readers will be able to use a browser to search for key words in the reference.

B. More than one author   For a work by two authors, name both in the order in which their names appear on the work. Within parentheses, use an ampersand (&) between the names, in place of *and*.

```
Kanazawa and Still (2000) in their analysis of a large
set of data show that the statistical likelihood of
being divorced increases if one is male and a secondary
school teacher or college professor.
```

```
Analysis of a large set of data shows that the
statistical likelihood of being divorced increases if
one is male and a secondary school teacher or college
professor (Kanazawa & Still, 2000).
```
                             ampersand in parentheses

(See **53d**, item 13, to see how this work appears in a reference list.)
    For a work with three to five authors or editors, identify all of them the first time you mention the work. In later references, use only the first author's name followed by "et al." (Latin for "and others") in place of the other names.

```
Jordan, Kaplan, Miller, Stiver, and Surrey (1991) have
examined the idea of self.
```

```
Increasingly, the self is viewed as connected to other
human beings (Jordan et al., 1991).
```

(See **53d**, item 2, to see how this work appears in a reference list.)
    For six or more authors, use the name of the first author followed by "et al." both for the first mention and in a parenthetical citation.

C. Author with more than one work published in one year
Identify each work with a lowercase letter after the date: (Zamel, 1997a, 1997b). Separate the dates with a comma. The reference list will contain the corresponding letters after the dates of each work. (See **53c** for how to order the entries in the list of references.)

D. Work in an anthology In your text, refer to the author of the work, not to the editor of the anthology. In the reference list, give the author's name, title of the work, and bibliographical details about the anthology, such as the editor, title, publisher, and date (**53d**, item 4).

> Seegmiller (1993) has provided an incisive analysis of the relationship between pregnancy and culture.

E. Work cited indirectly in a secondary source Give the author or title of the original work preceded by "as cited in" to indicate that you are referring to a work mentioned in the work of another author. List the secondary source in your list of references. In the following example, *Smith* will appear in the list of references; *Britton* will not.

> The words we use simply appear, as Britton says, "at the point of utterance" (as cited in Smith, 1982, p. 108).

F. An entire work or an idea in a work Use only an author and a year to refer to a complete work; for a paraphrase or a comment on a specific idea, a page number is not required but is recommended.

G. No author identified If no author is named, use the complete title if it is short (capitalizing major words) or a few words for the title in parentheses, along with the year of publication.

> According to *Weather* (1999), one way to estimate the Fahrenheit temperature is to count the number of times a cricket chirps in 14 seconds and add 40.

> Increasing evidence shows that glucosamine relieves the symptoms of arthritis (*The PDR Family Guide*, 1999).

(See **53d**, item 5, to see how the latter work is listed.)

H. Electronic or other Internet source Give author, if available, or title, followed by the year of electronic publication or of the most recent update. As online sources have no page numbers (unless they are PDF—portable document format—documents), provide as much information as you can to help readers find a quotation, paraphrase, or specific idea. For instance, provide a paragraph number, preceded by "para." or the symbol ¶; or provide a visible heading and the number of the paragraph in that section.

> The end of Branagh's *Hamlet* presents a "centrifugal development of the original play" (Hatchuel, 2000, ¶5).

```
Krause and Shaw posit three reasons that the results of
their study are important (2000, Conclusion section, para. 1).
```

Sometimes, however, no location markers will appear on the screen, so you will be able to provide only the author's name and year. Whatever the case, always provide the date on which you access the material.

Be wary of citing e-mail messages (personal, bulletin board, discussion list, or Usenet group) because these are not peer reviewed or easily retrievable. If you need to cite an e-mail message, cite from an archived list whenever possible (see examples in **53d**, item 31); otherwise, cite the message in your text as a personal communication (**53b**, item O), but do not include it in your list of references.

I. Entire Web site   Give the complete URL in the text of your paper. Do not list the site in your list of references.

```
Research on the "Mozart effect" has generated an
institute with a Web site providing links to research
studies (http://www.mindinst.org).
```

J. Nonprint source   For a film, television or radio broadcast, recording, or other nonprint source, include in your citation the name of the originator or main contributor (such as the writer, interviewer, director, performer, or producer) or an abbreviated title if the originator is not identified, along with the year of publication—for example, "(Morris, 1993)." (See **53d**, item 33, to see how this work appears in a reference list.)

K. Work by a corporation, group, or government agency   In the initial citation, use the organization's full name; in subsequent references, use an abbreviation if one exists.

```
One of the defenders of the appropriateness of the SAT
                     ┌──────── first mention: full name ────────┐
is its creator, the College Entrance Examination Board

(CEEB). The claim is that "the SAT has been changed
                         abbreviation in citation
                                       ╲
because education has changed" (CEEB, 1993, p. 4).
```

L. Two authors with the same last name   Include the authors' initials, even if the publication dates of their works differ.

```
F. Smith (1982) has often described a writer as having
two competitive roles: author and secretary.
```

(For the order of entries in the list of references, see **53c**.)

M. Multivolume work   In your citation, give the publication date of the volume you are citing: (Barr & Feigenbaum, 1982). If you refer to more than one volume, give inclusive dates for all the volumes you cite: (Barr & Feigenbaum, 1981–1986). (See **53d**, item 8, for how this work appears in a reference list.)

N. More than one work in a citation   List the sources in alphabetical order, separated by semicolons. List works by the same author chronologically (earliest source first) or by the letters *a, b,* and so on, if the works were published in the same year.

> Criticisms of large-scale educational testing abound
> (Crouse & Trusheim, 1988; Nairn, 1978, 1980; Raimes, 1990a,
> 1990b; Sacks, 2000).

O. Personal communication, such as a conversation, a letter, an e-mail message, an unarchived electronic discussion group posting, or an interview   Mention these only in your paper; do not include them in your list of references. Give the last name and initial(s) of the author of the communication and the exact date of posting.

> According to Dr. C. S. Apstein, Boston University School
> of Medicine, research in heart disease is critical to the
> well-being of society today (personal communication,
> January 7, 2002).

P. A classic work of literature   If the date of publication of a classic work is not known, use in your citation "n.d." for "no date." If you use a translation, give the year of the translation, preceded by "trans." You do not need a reference list entry for the Bible or ancient classic works. Just give information about book and line numbers in your text.

Q. Long quotation   If you quote more than forty words of prose, do not enclose the quotation in quotation marks. Start the quotation on a new line, and indent the whole quotation one-half inch or five spaces from the left margin. Do not indent from the right margin. Double-space the quotation.

53c Guidelines for the APA list of references

Setting up the APA list of references   The APA *Publication Manual* and Web site provide guidelines for submitting professional papers for publication, and many instructors ask students to follow those guidelines to prepare them for advanced work. This section follows APA guidelines. Check with your instructor, however, as to specific course requirements for the reference list. See page 846 for a discussion of format and indentation.

KEY POINTS

Setting Up the APA List of References

1. *What to list* List only the works you cited (quoted, summarized, paraphrased, or commented on) in the text of your paper, not everything you read.

2. *Format* Start the list on a new numbered page after the last page of text or notes. Center the heading "References," without quotation marks, not underlined or italicized, and with no period following it. Double-space throughout the list.

3. *Organization* List the works alphabetically, by last names of primary authors. Do not number the entries. Begin each entry with the author's name, last name first, followed by an initial or initials. Give any authors' names after the first in the same inverted form, separated by commas. Do not use "et al." List works with no author by title, alphabetized by the first main word.

4. *Date* Put the year in parentheses after the authors' names. For journals, magazines, and newspapers, include also month and day, but do not abbreviate the names of the months.

5. *Periods* Use a period and one space to separate the main parts of each entry.

6. *Indentation* Use hanging indents of five to seven spaces or one-half inch.

7. *Capitals* In titles of books and articles, capitalize only the first word of the title or subtitle and any proper nouns or adjectives.

8. *Italics* Italicize the titles of books, but do not italicize or use quotation marks around the titles of articles. For magazines and journals, italicize the publication name, the volume number, and the comma. Italicize the names of newspapers.

9. *Page numbers* Give inclusive page numbers for articles and sections of books, using complete page spans ("251–259"). Use the abbreviation "p." or "pp." only for newspaper articles and sections (such as chapters) of books.

10. *Publisher* Do not abbreviate the name of the publisher. Give state (abbreviated) as well as city except for major cities.

Order of entries in the reference list

Alphabetical order Alphabetize letter by letter. Treat *Mac* and *Mc* literally, by letter.

MacKay, M.	D'Agostino, S.
McCarthy, T.	De Cesare, P.
McKay, K.	DeCurtis, A.

A shorter name precedes a longer name beginning with the same letters, whatever the first initial: *Black, T.* precedes *Blackman, R.*

For a work with no known author, list by the first word in the title other than *A, An*, or *The*.

Alphabetize numerals according to their spelling: 5 ("five") will precede 2 ("two").

Several works by the same author List the author's name in each entry. Arrange entries chronologically from past to present. Entries published in the same year should be arranged alphabetically by title and distinguished with lowercase letters after the date (*a, b*, and so on). Note that entries for one author precede entries by that author but written with coauthors.

Goleman, D. (1996a, July 16). Forget money; nothing can buy
    happiness, some researchers say. *The New York Times*,
    p. C1.

Goleman, D. (1996b). *Vital lies, simple truths*. New York: Simon
    & Schuster.

Goleman, D. (2000). *Working with emotional intelligence*. New
    York: Bantam.

Goleman, D., Kaufman, P., & Ray, M. L. (1992, March-April). The
    art of creativity. *Psychology Today, 25*, 40-47.

Authors with the same last name List alphabetically by first initial: *Smith, A.* precedes *Smith, F.*

Format and indentation

Underlining or italics? The fifth edition of the APA *Publication Manual* includes instructions that "take advantage of the nearly universal use of sophisticated word processors." It recommends that authors use italics (not underlining) to represent text that would eventually be converted to italics in print.

Hanging indents in the list of references The APA guidelines specify hanging indents for manuscript and final copy. A hanging indent sets the first line of each item in the reference list at the left margin, with subsequent lines of the entry indented five to seven spaces or one-half inch.

Klein, D. F. (1995). Response to Rothman and Michels on placebo-controlled clinical trials. *Psychiatric Annals, 25*, 401–403.

Rothman, K. F., & Michels, K. D. (1994). The continuing unethical use of placebo controls. *New England Journal of Medicine, 331*, 394–398.

However, the fifth edition of the *Publication Manual* also notes that if a word processing program makes it difficult to achieve a hanging indent, then a paragraph indent (first line of entry indented five spaces) is acceptable. In either case, the usage should be consistent throughout.

53d Examples of entries in APA list of references

Print books and parts of books

1. Book with one author   You will find the information you need on the title page and the copyright page of the book. Use the most recent copyright date. Include both the city and the state of publication if the name of the city is not familiar. Give the publisher's name in a short but intelligible form, spelling out *University* and *Press* but omitting *Co.* and *Inc.*

periods
last name   initials
comma   year in parentheses
                              title and period italicized
                      period

Wilson, E. O. (1994). *Naturalist*. Washington: Island Press.
        publisher   final period   place of   colon
                                        publication

2. Book with two or more authors   List all authors' names in the order in which they appear on the book's title page. Reverse the order of each name: last name first, followed by initials. Do not use "et al." Separate all names with commas, and insert an ampersand (&) before the last name.

────────── all names reversed ──────────   ampersand

Jordan, J. V., Kaplan, A. G., Miller, J. B., Stiver, I. P., &

Surrey, J. L. (1991). *Women's growth in connection: Writings from the Stone Center*. New York: Guilford Press.
indented
5 spaces

3. *Edited book* Use "Ed." or "Eds." for one or more editors, in parentheses.

Denmark, F., & Paludi, M. (Eds.). (1993). *Psychology of women: A handbook of issues and theories*. Westport, CT: Greenwood Press.

4. *Work in an anthology or reference book* List the author, date of publication of the edited book, and title of the work. Follow this with "In" and the names of the editors (not inverted), the title of the book, and the page numbers (preceded by "pp.") of the work in parentheses. End with the place of publication and the publisher. If you cite more than one article in an edited work, include full bibliographical details in each entry.

names of editors
⌐—— not reversed ——⌐
Seegmiller, B. (1993). Pregnancy. In F. Denmark & M. Paludi (Eds.), *Psychology of women: A handbook of issues and theories* (pp. 437–474). Westport, CT: Greenwood Press.

For a well-known reference book with unsigned alphabetical entries, give only the edition number and year of publication. When articles are arranged alphabetically in an encyclopedia or a dictionary, omit page numbers.

Multiculturalism. (2000). In *Columbia Encyclopedia* (6th ed.).

For a reference book with an editorial board, list the name of the principal editor.

5. *Book with no author identified* Put the title first. Ignore *A, An,* and *The* when alphabetizing. Alphabetize the following under *P.*

The PDR family guide to natural medicines and healing therapies. (1999). New York: Three Rivers-Random House.

6. *Book by a corporation or some other organization* Give the name of the corporate author first. If the publisher is the same as the author, write "Author" for the name of the publisher.

College Entrance Examination Board. (1999). *Index of majors and graduate degrees 2000*. New York: Author.

7. *Translated book* In parentheses after the title of the work, give the initials and last name of the translator, followed by a comma and "Trans."

name of translator not reversed
Jung, C. G. (1960). *On the nature of the psyche* (R. F. C. Hull, Trans.). Princeton, NJ: Princeton University Press.

8. *Multivolume work* When you refer to several volumes in a work of more than one volume, give the number of volumes after the title, in parentheses. The date should indicate the range of years of publication, when appropriate.

Barr, A., & Feigenbaum, E. A. (1981–1986). *The handbook of artificial intelligence* (Vols. 1–4). Reading, MA: Addison-Wesley.

9. *Foreword, preface, introduction, or afterword* List the name of the author of the book element cited. Follow the date with the name of the element, the title of the book, and, in parentheses, the page numbers on which the element appears.

Weiss, B. (Ed.). (1982). Introduction. *American education and the European immigrant, 1840–1940* (pp. xi–xxviii). Urbana: University of Illinois Press.

10. *Republished book* After the author's name, give the most recent date of publication. At the end, in parentheses add "Original work published" and the date. In your text citation, give both dates: (Smith, 1793/1976).

Smith, A. (1976). *An inquiry into the nature and causes of the wealth of nations.* Chicago: University of Chicago Press. (Original work published 1793)

11. *Technical report* If the report has a number, state it in parentheses after the title.

Breland, H. M., & Jones, R. J. (1982). *Perceptions of writing skill* (Rep. No. 82-4). New York: College Entrance Examination Board.

For reports from services such as ERIC or NTIS, give a report number after the title, and any document retrieval number in parentheses, with no period at the end.

Avery, P. G. (2001, December 1). Developing political tolerance (Report No. EDO-SO-2001-10). Bloomington, IN: ERIC Clearinghouse for Social Studies/Social Science Education. (ERIC Document Reproduction Service No. ED458186)

12. *Dissertation or abstract* For a manuscript source, give the university and year of the dissertation and the volume and page numbers of *DAI*.

Salzberg, A. (1992). Behavioral phenomena of homeless women in San Diego county (Doctoral dissertation, United

States International University, 1992). *Dissertation Abstracts International, 52*, 4482.

For a microfilm source, also include in parentheses at the end of the entry the university microfilm number. For a CD-ROM source, include after the title the label "CD-ROM" in brackets followed by a period. Then name the electronic source of the information and the *DAI* number.

Examples of APA entries: Print articles

13. Article in a scholarly journal: pages numbered consecutively through issues of a volume Give only the volume number and year for journals with consecutive pagination through a volume (for example, the first issue of volume 1 ends on page 174, and the second issue of volume 1 begins on page 175). Italicize the volume number and the following comma as well as the title of the journal. Do not use "p." or "pp." with page numbers. Do not abbreviate months. For the title of an article, use capital letters only for the first word of the title and subtitle (if any) and for proper nouns. See **49b** on recognizing a scholarly journal.

no quotation marks around
article title

Kanazawa, S., & Still, M. C. (2000). Teaching may be

journal title, volume number,
and commas italicized

hazardous to your marriage. *Evolution and Human*

Behavior, 21, 185–190.
no "p." or "pp." before page numbers

14. Article in a scholarly journal: Each issue paged separately For journals in which each issue begins with page 1, include the issue number—in parentheses but not in italics—immediately after the volume number.

Ginat, R. (2000). The Soviet Union and the Syrian Ba'th
regime: From hesitation to *rapprochement. Middle
Eastern Studies, 36*(2), 150–171.
issue number not in italics

15. Article in a magazine Include the year and month or month and day of publication in parentheses. Italicize the magazine title, the volume number, and the comma that follows; then give the page number or numbers.

year, month

Perina, K. (2002, March/April). Battling for benefits.
Psychology Today, 35, 64–66.
volume number, italicized

16. Article in a newspaper In parentheses, include the month and day of the newspaper after the year. Give the section letter or number before the page, where applicable. Use "p." and "pp." with page numbers. Do not omit *The* from the title of a newspaper.

Boudette, N. E. (2002, March 29). A Holocaust claim cuts to the heart of the new Germany. *The Wall Street Journal*, pp. A1, A8.

17. Article that skips pages When an article appears on discontinuous pages, give all the page numbers, separated by commas, as in item 16.

18. Review After the title of the review article, add in brackets a description of the work reviewed and identify the medium: book, film, or video, for example.

Alter, R. (2002, February 11). Immodest proposals. [Review of the book *God, Gulliver, and genocide: Barbarism and the European imagination, 1492-1945,* by Claude Rawson]. *The New Republic, 226,* 34-38.

19. Unsigned editorial or article For a work with no author named, begin the listing with the title; for an editorial, add the label "Editorial" in brackets.

The marriage clock. [Editorial]. (2002, April 29). *The New York Observer*, p. 4.

20. Letter to the editor Put the label "Letter to the editor" in brackets after the date or the title of the letter, if it has one.

Libby, M. W. (2002, April). [Letter to the editor]. *The Atlantic Monthly, 289*, 3.

Examples of APA entries: Internet and other electronic sources The American Psychological Association supplements the fifth edition of its *Publication Manual* with a style Web site <http://www.apastyle.org> offering examples, periodic updates, tips, and the opportunity to ask questions. Provide as many of the following elements as you can when citing Internet and electronic sources.

- name of author(s), if available
- date of work ("n.d." if no date is available)
- title of work (article, report, Web document or site, abstract, subject line of e-mail message), with additional necessary information added in brackets: [*letter to the editor, data file,* etc.]

- print publication information (such as name of journal, volume number, page numbers)
- a retrieval statement containing the date you retrieved the information (month, day, year, with comma after day and after year) and the name of the database or the Internet address (URL) of the specific document you refer to, not just the home page
- a period at the end of the entry—but no period if the entry ends with a URL

The URL must be exact. Use the Copy function to copy it from the address window in your browser (making sure you have turned off automatic hyphenation—in Microsoft Word, for example, by going to Tools/Language/Hyphenation), and then use the Paste function to paste the URL into your document.

If you are given the option of downloading a document in HTML or in PDF format, be aware that the latter (for which you need the Acrobat Reader software, downloadable free) will show you page numbers and all the features of the original print document.

21. Work in an electronic database Many universities, libraries, and organizational Web sites subscribe to large searchable databases, such as *InfoTrac, EBSCO, Lexis-Nexis, OCLC, SilverPlatter, WilsonWeb, Dialog*, and *SIRS*. These databases provide access to large numbers of published, scholarly abstracts and full-text articles. In addition, available both online and on CD-ROM are specialized databases such as *ERIC, PsycINFO*, and *PAIS* (Public Affairs Information Service). However or wherever you access a source from an electronic database, cite it as in the following example:

Goldstein, B. S. C., & Harris, K. C. (2000). Consultant
    practices in two heterogeneous Latino schools.
    The School Psychology Review, *29*, 368-377. Retrieved
    May 20, 2002, from WilsonWeb Education Full Text
    database.

If an item number or accession number is provided, you have the option of including it at the end in parentheses. With the item number, the preceding entry would look like this:

Goldstein, B. S. C., & Harris, K. C. (2000). Consultant
    practices in two heterogeneous Latino schools. *The
    School Psychology Review*, *29*, 368-377. Retrieved May

20, 2002, from WilsonWeb Education Full Text database
(200002685300).

For citing the same source accessed from the same database in PDF
format, see item 24.

22. *Newspaper article retrieved from database or Web site*
Newspaper articles, as well as journal articles, are often available
from several sources, in several databases and in a variety of formats, such as on CD-ROM, in a university online subscription database, or on a Web site. The two examples here show references to the
same article, accessed first via an online database and then via a
CD-ROM.

Wade, N. (2000, May 9). Scientists decode Down syndrome
        chromosome. *The New York Times,* p. F4. Retrieved
        May 17, 2002, from Lexis-Nexis Academic Universe
        database.

Wade, N. (2000, May 9). Scientists decode Down syndrome
        chromosome. *The New York Times*, p. F4. Retrieved
        September 18, 2000, from UMI ProQuest database.

The following example shows a newspaper article accessed from a
Web site:

Brody, J. (2002, May 14). The color of nutrition: Fruits and
        vegetables. *The New York Times*. Retrieved May 20, 2002,
        from http://www.nytimes.com

23. *Online abstract*   For an abstract retrieved from a database or
from a Web site, begin the retrieval statement with the words
"Abstract retrieved" followed by the date and the name of the database or the URL of the Web site.

Zadra, A., & Donderi, D. C. (2000, May). Nightmares and bad
        dreams: Their prevalence and relationship to
        wellbeing. *Journal of Abnormal Psychology, 109*, 273-
        281. Abstract retrieved May 21, 2002, from http://
        www.apa.org/journals/abn/500ab.html#11

24. *Online article, based on a print source*   If you read a print article
in electronic form, unchanged from the original and with no additional commentary (such as an article you access in PDF—portable
document format), cite the article as you would a print article, with
the addition of the label "Electronic version" in brackets after the title

of the article. The following citation is to the same source in the *WilsonWeb* database as shown in item 21, but the source was accessed in PDF instead of HTML format.

Goldstein, B. S. C., & Harris, K. C. (2000). Consultant
    practices in two heterogeneous Latino schools.
    [Electronic version]. *The School Psychology Review, 29,*
    368-377.

If information such as page numbers or figures is missing from the electronic version or if the document has other alterations, give full retrieval information, with date of retrieval and the URL:

Krause, N., & Shaw, B. A. (2000, December). Role-specific
    feelings of control and mortality. *Psychology and
    Aging, 15,* 617-626. Retrieved May 19, 2002, from
    http://www.apa.org/journals/pag/pag154617.html

25. Article in an online journal, no print source

Holtzworth-Munroe, A. (2000, June). Domestic violence:
    Combining scientific inquiry and advocacy.
    Prevention & Treatment, 3. Retrieved May 16, 2002,
    from http://journals.apa.org/prevention/volume3/
    pre0030022c.html

26. Article in an online site, no author identified

Gold medal awards. (2000, September). *APA Monitor, 31*(8).
    Retrieved September 11, 2000, from http://www.apa.org/
    monitor/apfnews.html

27. Entire Web site
Give the complete URL in the text of your paper, not in your list of references. For an example see **53b**, item I.

28. Document on a Web site, no author identified
Italicize the title of the document (the Web page). Alphabetize by the first major word of the title.

APAStyle.org: Electronic references. (2001, August 3).
    Retrieved May 22, 2002, from http://www
    .apastyle.org/elecref.html

29. Document on a university site
Italicize the title of the document. In the retrieval statement, give the name of the university (and the

department or division if it is named). Follow this with a colon and the URL.

McClintock, R. (2000, September 20). *Cities, youth, and technology: Toward a pedagogy of autonomy.* Retrieved May 21, 2002, from Columbia University, Institute for Learning Technologies Web site: http://www.ilt.columbia.edu/publications/cities/cyt.html

30. Technical report on government agency site

United States. Department of Education. Office of Educational Research and Improvement. National Center for Education Statistics. (2001, January). *Digest of education statistics, 2000.* Retrieved May 20, 2002, from http://nces.ed.gov/pubs2001/digest

31. Contributions to electronic mailing lists
Make sure that you cite only scholarly and retrievable e-mail communications. Cite a personal e-mail message in the body of your text as "personal communication," and do not include it in your list of references (see **53b,** item O). For messages posted to discussion lists and newsgroups, put the following information in your list entry, but only if the material is scholarly and the list maintains archives:

> Name of author or authors. (Date of posting: year, month, day). Subject line or "thread" of message [message number, if available]. Message posted to [electronic address of newsgroup or discussion group]

Gracey, D. (2001, April 6). Monetary systems and a sound economy [Msg 54]. Message posted to http://groups.yahoo.com/group/ermail/message/54

Peckham, I. (2000, May 1). Class origins. Message posted to WPA-L electronic mailing list, archived at http://lists.asu.edu

Examples of APA entries: other sources

32. Personal communication (conversation, letter, e-mail message, or interview)
Cite a personal communication only in your text. (See **53b,** item O.) Do not include it in your list of references.

33. Film, recording, or video Identify the medium in brackets after the title.

Spiegel, S. (Producer), & Kazan, E. (Director). (1954). *On the waterfront* [Motion picture]. United States: Columbia TriStar.

Morris, E. (Director). (1993). *A brief history of time* [Videocassette]. Hollywood: Paramount.

34. Television or radio program

Coyote, P. (Narrator). (2002, April 2). *Origins: Life on the move* [Television series]. New York: WNET.

35. Computer software

Movie Magic Screenwriter (Version 4.5) [Computer software]. (2000). Burbank, CA: Storymind.

53e Notes, tables, and figures

Notes In APA style, you can use content notes to amplify or explain information in your text. Number notes consecutively with superscript numerals. After the list of references, attach a separate page containing your numbered notes and headed "Footnotes." However, it is better to include all important information in your text, not in footnotes. Use notes sparingly.

Tables Place tables on a separate page after any notes. Number each table and provide a heading.

Figures Place figures at the end of your paper, after the references and after any notes or tables. Provide first a separate page with the caption for each figure, then the figures themselves, numbered. See page 864 for examples of figures in Todd Kray's paper.

53f Student paper, APA style

The paper that follows was written by Todd Kray for an introductory college course in experimental psychology. Kray worked for almost twenty years as a musician and songwriter before returning to college. He eventually majored in biology. For this paper, his instructor asked for adherence to APA guidelines for student papers. Check with your instructor to see whether your title page should strictly follow APA guidelines, as this one does, or whether it should be modified to include the course name, instructor's name, and date.

Running head and page number on every page

5 spaces

Absolute Auditory Thresholds⟵→1⟵⟶

1" margin

Running head: ABSOLUTE AUDITORY THRESHOLDS

Absolute Auditory Thresholds
in College Students
Todd Kray
Hunter College of the City University of New York

Centered title, writer's name, and writer's affiliation

Absolute Auditory Thresholds   2

Heading centered

Abstract

Seventeen college students participated in an auditory experiment, collecting data while working in pairs. In the experiment, absolute auditory thresholds were established and compared to "normal" thresholds. This study discusses details and plots results on two graphs for one pair of students: one 20-year-old female, and one 37-year-old male. While results paralleled the "norm" at many frequencies (125Hz, 250Hz, 500Hz, 1000Hz, 2KHz, 4KHz, and 8KHz), strong evidence for high frequency loss was discovered for the older of the two participants. Environmental conditions and subject fatigue were also seen to be influences on determining auditory thresholds.

Passive voice common in accounts of research

Results summarized

Absolute Auditory Thresholds 3

Absolute Auditory Thresholds
in College Students

Title centered, not underlined

For decades, the branch of psychophysics known as psychoacoustics has concerned itself with the minimum amount of Sound Pressure Level (SPL) required for detection by the human ear. An early landmark study by Sivian and White (1933) examined loudness thresholds by measuring minimum audible field (MAF) and minimal audible pressure (MAP) and found that the ear was not as sensitive as had been reported in earlier studies by Wien (as cited in Sivian & White, 1933). Parker and Schneider (1980) tested Fechner's and Weber's laws, both of which concern themselves with measuring changes in physical intensity and the psychological experiences of those changes (Ansburg, 2000) and determined that loudness is a power function of intensity, which was consistent with Fechner's assumption.

1″ margin

Date after citation

Ampersand within parentheses

Author and year in parentheses

An experiment was designed to utilize the method of limits, which establishes the absolute sensitivity (threshold) for a particular sound, to test auditory thresholds in college students and compare them to the "norm." Each threshold is determined by presenting the tone at a sound level well above threshold, then lessening it in discrete intervals until the tone is no longer perceived by the participant (Gelfand, 1981). The present study predicts that, according to Gelfand's (1981) summary of the research on normal hearing, college students' thresholds would be described as "normal."

Hypothesis

Method

Main heading centered

Participants

Subheading italicized

Seventeen college students in an introductory experimental psychology course participated in the experiment. The median age of the 5 males and 12

Details of participants

1″ margin

Absolute Auditory Thresholds   4

females was 24, with ages ranging from 20 to 37 years old. None of the participants claimed to be aware of any significant hearing loss, and none claimed to have ever participated in this or a similar experiment before. All appeared to be in good overall physical and mental condition, though no formal testing was done in these areas.

Apparatus

Specialized equipment described

Pure tones were generated by a B&K waveform generator. The intensity of the tones was controlled by a Hewlett-Packard 350D attenuator. Tones were gated on and off by a push-button-controlled, light-dependent resistor. This provided for a gradual "ramping" on and off of sound. The tones were presented to the subject through a pair of Koss PRO/99 headphones. The headphones were calibrated at all test frequencies on a Kemar dummy head with a 6 cc coupler.

Passive voice common in description of experiment

Procedure

Participants worked in pairs to run and participate in the experiment. In each pair, one participant controlled the waveform generator and attenuator while the other faced away from the tester toward the wall. Participants had been instructed to choose an order of frequencies prior to taking the test. They then administered the tests to each other, trading "roles" after one block of attenuated tones for each frequency was completed. On the first day of testing, the method of limits was utilized to determine a baseline threshold for each frequency. Seven frequencies were generated: 125Hz, 250Hz, 500Hz, 1000Hz, 2KHz, 4KHz, and 8KHz.

The tests were administered in small cubicles that were quiet but not soundproof. Participants had been instructed to use their "good ear." Tones were heard monophonically, through one side of the headphones.

Details of procedure

Absolute Auditory Thresholds   5

Eight blocks were run for each frequency, 4
ascending and 4 descending, in a semirandomized order
determined by the experimenter to help ensure accurate
responses rather than the participant being able to
"guess it out." Participants were instructed to say
"yes" after each audible tone for a descending block,
until they could no longer hear the tone, at which
point they would say "no" and that particular block
would end. For an ascending block, participants were to
say "no" for each ascending tone that they could not
hear, until the first tone they heard, at which point
they would say "yes" and that block would be complete.
Each response was recorded on a sheet of paper by the
experimenter, handwritten.

Results

For this pair of participants, 2 audiograms
were plotted to display dB SPL (decibel sound
pressure level) thresholds for Subject A and Subject
B. Threshold ranges for the subjects in one pair were
quite different from each other. Subject A's ranged
from 5.9 dB to 39.3 dB (Fig. 1); Subject B's ranged
from 2.7 dB to 26.6 dB (Fig. 2), resulting in a more
"normal" curve than the one for Subject A.

Discussion

Subject B's absolute threshold levels somewhat
resemble those of "normal" hearing, as reported by
Gelfand (1981) with a peculiar loss of sensitivity at
2 KHz and extreme sensitivity at 8 KHz. While loss
of sensitivity is not uncommon for those who have had
prolonged exposure to loud sounds, such as listening
to a Walkman being played at the maximum level or
attending rock concerts frequently, it seems odd that
Subject B, who claimed not to possess these conditions,
would experience a loss of sensitivity at 2 KHz,
particularly at age 20. In the light of that, it seems
even stranger that Subject B would have sensitivity

Main heading centered

References to figures at end of paper

Results evaluated with respect to hypothesis

Unusual results analyzed

greater than the norm at both 4KHz and 8KHz. However,
the fact that both subjects had elevated thresholds at
2KHz could lead to the suspicion of faulty apparatus.

Causes of results considered

Subject A seems to be a classic example of
somebody who would be prone to loss of sensitivity at
higher frequencies. He had constant exposure to loud
sounds as a result of over 2 decades spent playing in
rock bands, frequently attending rock concerts, wearing
a Walkman often in his youth, working in extremely loud
nightclubs, and working in recording studios. In
addition, he is currently 37 years old and may be
experiencing the first symptoms of Presbyacusia--
hearing loss at high frequencies due to aging. Subject A
showed an extreme loss of sensitivity at 2 KHz (again,
apparatus could be at fault here) and the loss at 4 KHz
seems real when compared to Gelfand's (1981) norm.

Details of causes

Auditory testing over the years has provided us
with no easy answers regarding absolute threshold.
Many of the articles cited in this study provide more
questions than conclusions. Sivian and White (1933)
inquired as to whether ear sensitivity was determined
by the actual physiological construction of the ear or
if air as a transmitter was responsible. It would be
helpful to test for this in the future.

Study related to prior research

The tests themselves were problematic as well.
It is easy to wind up with a masked threshold if
thresholds are not measured in absolute silence--not
always an easy condition to create. Even under the
best conditions that could be achieved in this
experiment, demand characteristics and experimenter
effects were unavoidable. The dial of the attenuator
clicked loudly when turned, providing very definite
clues that attenuation levels were being changed. In
addition, the test, which took several hours to
complete, caused subjects to feel fatigued and
restless, making it difficult to concentrate at times.

Future research suggested

Problems with research procedures discussed

Absolute Auditory Thresholds   7

Despite these hurdles, the experiment produced
reasonable estimates for absolute auditory thresholds
for college students and a reasonable estimate for a
person experiencing symptoms of high-frequency loss
due to abuse to the ear in the form of prolonged and
excessive exposure to high volume.

Results
related to
hypothesis

New page for
references,
double-spaced

Absolute Auditory Thresholds   8

References

Ansburg, P. (2000, April 24). *Fechner's law* [Lecture
notes]. Retrieved March 15, 2001, from
http://clem.mscd.edu/-ansburg/sensationperception/
splecchpt2.htm

Organized
alphabetically

Gelfand, S. A. (1981). *Hearing: An introduction to
psychological and physiological acoustics.* New
York: Marcel Dekker.

Year in
parentheses
after author

Hanging
indents
(see **53c**)

Parker, S., & Schneider, B. (1980). Loudness and
loudness discrimination. *Perception and
Psychophysics, 28,* 398–406.

Sivian, L. J., & White, S. D. (1933). Minimum audible
sound fields. *The Journal of the Acoustical
Society of America, 4,* 288–321.

Italics
extend
through
volume
number and
commas

Absolute Auditory Thresholds   9

Figure Captions

Figure 1. Comparison of thresholds for "normal" and
Sub. A.

Figure 2. Comparison of thresholds for "normal" and
Sub. B.

Figure 1

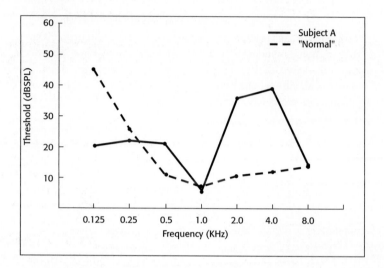

Figure 2

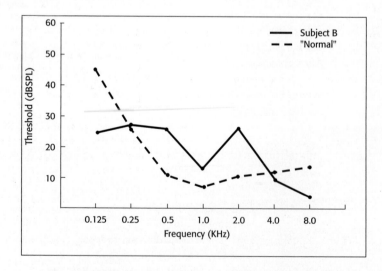

54 CBE/CSE Style of Documentation

AT A GLANCE: INDEX OF CBE/CSE STYLE FEATURES

This section outlines the documentation style recommended by the Council of Biology Editors (CBE)—recently renamed "Council of Science Editors"(CSE)—for all scientific disciplines in *Scientific Style and Format: The CBE Manual for Authors, Editors, and Publishers*, 6th ed. (New York: Cambridge UP, 1994). For online citations, the Council of Science Editors refers authors to the system presented on the Web site of the National Library of Medicine (NLM) at <http://www.nlm.nih.gov/pubs/formats/internet.pdf>. *Scientific Style and Format* recommends two systems of documentation, one an author/year system similar to the APA system, the other a citation-sequence system that numbers and lists sources in the order in which they are mentioned in the paper. This section (**54**) gives details for using the latter system.

54a Two basic features of CBE/CSE citation-sequence style

Always check with your instructor about documentation style guidelines. Some may not specify one particular style but will ask you to select a style and use it consistently. For CBE/CSE citation-sequence style, follow these guidelines.

KEY POINTS

Two Basic Features of CBE/CSE Citation-Sequence Style

1. *In the text of your paper,* number each reference with a superscript in a smaller size than the type for the text, or place the reference number on the line within parentheses. Numbers run sequentially through your paper. Use the same number for a source you have previously cited; do not renumber it for the second and subsequent mentions.

2. *At the end of your paper,* list the references by number, in the order in which you first cite them in your paper. Do not alphabetize the entries. Begin the list on a new page and title it "References" (see **54e**).

54b CBE/CSE in-text citations

Use superscript numbers or numbers enclosed within parentheses to refer readers to the numbered list of references at the end of your paper.

Illustrations of in-text citations

a. Reference number in your text

SUPERSCRIPT NUMBER
One summary of studies of the life span of the fruit fly[1] has shown . . .

PARENTHETICAL NUMBER
One summary of studies of the life span of the fruit fly (1) has shown . . .

b. Items listed numerically, not alphabetically, in your list of references

1. Kowald A, Kirkwood TB. Explaining fruit fly longevity. Science 1993;260:1664-5.

c. References to more than one entry in the reference list

SUPERSCRIPT Two studies of the life span of the fruit fly[1, 2]
NUMBER   have shown that . . .

PARENTHETICAL Several studies of the life span of the fruit
NUMBER   fly (1–4) have shown that . . .

For the listed entries that the numbers refer to, see **54e**.

54c Guidelines for the CBE/CSE list of references

KEY POINTS

Setting Up the CBE/CSE List of References

1. After the last page of your paper, attach the list of references, headed "References" or "Cited References."

2. Number the works consecutively in the order in which you first mention them in your paper. Invert all authors' names, and use the initials of first and middle names. Use no punctuation between last names and initials, and leave no space between initials.

3. Begin each entry with the note number followed by a period and a space. Do not indent the first line of each entry. Align the second and subsequent lines of an entry below the first letter on the previous line.

4. Do not underline or use quotation marks for the titles of articles, books, or journals and other periodicals.

5. Capitalize only the first word of a book title or article title and any proper nouns.

6. Abbreviate titles of journals, publishers, and organizations.

7. Use a period between major divisions of each entry.

8. Use a semicolon and a space between the name of the publisher and the publication date of a book. Use a semicolon with no space between the date and the volume number of a journal.

9. For books, give the total number of pages, followed by a space and "p." For journal articles, give inclusive page spans, using digits in the second number that are *not* included in the first: 135–6; 287–93; 500–1.

(continued)

(continued)

10. For online sources, provide author, title, any print publication information, online publication date or latest update, your date of access, and the URL. NLM guidelines, however, give a strong recommendation that "the user produce a print or other copy when possible for future reference" (iii).

54d Examples of entries in CBE/CSE list of references

Print books and parts of books

1. Book with one author

no punctuation ⌐— title not underlined, only first word capitalized ———⌐

initials with no periods between

2. Finch CE. Longevity, senescence and the genome.

abbreviated   semicolon
⌐— publishing terms —⌐   /   number of pages in book

Chicago: Univ Chicago Pr; 1990. 922 p.

If an author's first and middle names are hyphenated, include the hyphen between the initials: *Muller H-G*. Otherwise, include no punctuation and no space: *Finch CE*.

2. Book with two or more authors

⌐— all authors' names inverted —⌐

8. Ferrini AF, Ferrini RL. Health in the later years.
2nd ed. Dubuque (IA): Brown & Benchmark; 1993. 470 p.
state abbreviation   semicolon after publisher

3. Edited book

9. Baxevanis AD, editor. Bioinformatics: a practical guide to the analysis of genes and proteins. 2nd ed. New York: Wiley-Interscience; 2001. 432 p.

4. Chapter in an edited anthology

16. Seegmiller B. Pregnancy. In: Denmark F, Paludi M, editors. Psychology of women: a handbook of issues and theories. Westport (CT): Greenwood Press; 1993. p 437-74.
no period when not at end of entry

5. Book with corporation or organization as author

14. Chemical Bond Approach Project. Chemical systems. St. Louis: McGraw-Hill; 1964. 772 p.

Examples of CBE/CSE entries: Print articles and audiovisual materials

6. Article in a scholarly journal

1. Kowald A, Kirkwood TB. Explaining fruit fly longevity.

no spaces in information
┌— about journal —┐
Science 1993;260:1664-5.
volume number

In a journal paginated by issue, include the issue number in parentheses after the volume number.

7. Article in a newspaper or magazine

13. Altman LK. Study prompts call to halt a routine eye operation. NY Times 1995 Feb 22;Sect C:10.

Sect stands for section number.

8. Article with no author identified   Begin with "[Anonymous]." Follow this with the title.

9. Editorial   After the title, insert "[editorial]."

10. Audiovisual materials   Begin the entry with the title, followed by the medium in brackets, such as "[filmstrip]" or "[videocassette]". Then include the author (if known), producer, place, publisher, and date. Include a description, such as number of cassettes, length, color or black and white, and accompanying material. End with a statement of availability, if necessary.

7. AIDS in Africa: living with a time bomb [videocassette]. Princeton: Films for the Humanities and Sciences; 1991. 33 min, sound, color, 1/2 in.

Examples of CBE/CSE entries: electronic and online sources

11. Electronic journal article with a print source   Cite as for a print journal article, and include the type of medium in brackets after the journal title. Include any document number, the accession date "[cited (year, month, date)]," and an availability statement with the URL.

12. Jones, CC, Meredith, W. Developmental paths of psychological health from early adolescence to later adulthood. Psych and Aging [Internet] 2000 [cited 2002 May 3];15(2):351-360. Available from: http://www.apa.org/journals/pag/pag152351.html

12. Electronic journal article with no print source   If no print source is available, provide an estimate of the length of the document in pages, paragraphs, or screens. Place the information in square brackets, such as "[about 3 p.]," "[about 15 paragraphs]," or "[about 6 screens]."

6. Holtzworth-Munroe, A. Domestic violence: Combining
   scientific inquiry and advocacy. Prev and Treatment
   [serial on the Internet], 2000 June 2 [cited 2002 May
   12];3 [about 6 pages]. Available from: http://journals
   .apa.org/prevention/volume3/pre0030022c.html

13. Article in an electronic database   After author, title, and print publication information, give the name of the database, the designation in square brackets "[database on the Internet]," any date of posting or modification, or the copyright date. Follow this with the date of access, the approximate length of the article, the URL, and any accession number.

15. Mayor S. New treatment improves symptoms of Parkinson's
    disease. Brit Med J 2002 324(7344):997. In: EBSCOhost
    Health Source: Nursing/Academic Edition [database on the
    Internet]; c2002 [cited 2002 May 14]. [about 1 screen].
    Available from: http://ehostvgw17.epnet.com; Accession No.:
    6609093.

14. Internet home page   Give author (if available) and title of page followed by "[Internet]." Follow this with any available information about place of home page publication and sponsor, and then include date of publication or copyright date, along with any update. End with your date of citation and the URL.

11. Anemia and iron therapy [Internet]. Hinsdale (IL):
    Medtext, Inc.; c1995-2002 [cited 2002 May 15]. Available
    from: http://www.hdcn.com/ch/rbc/

15. Posting to a discussion list   After the author's name and the subject line of the message, give information about the discussion list, including name of list, place and sponsor, if available; year, date, and time of posting; date of citation; and approximate length of the posting. End with an availability statement of the address of the discussion list or the archive.

10. Bishawi AH. Summary: hemangioendothelioma of the larynx.
    In: MEDLIB-L [discussion list on the Internet]. [Buffalo
    (NY): State Univ of NY]; 2002 May 6, 11:25am [cited 2002
    May 15]. [about 4 screens]. Available from:
    MEDLIBL@LISTSERV.ACSU.BUFFALO.EDU

54e Sample CBE/CSE list of references

The following list of references for a paper on "Research Findings and Disputes about Fruit Fly Longevity" uses the CBE/CSE sequential numbering system. Note the use of abbreviations and punctuation.

Fruit fly longevity   17

References

1. Kowald A, Kirkwood TB. Explaining fruit fly longevity. Science 1993;260:1664-5.

2. Finch CE. Longevity, senescence and the genome. Chicago: Univ Chicago Pr; 1990. 922 p.

3. Carey JR, Liedo P, Orozco D, Vaupel JW. Slowing of mortality rates at older ages in large medfly cohorts. Science 1992;258:457.

4. Skrecky D. Fly longevity database. In Cryonet [discussion list on the Internet]. 1997 June 22, 7:23 pm [cited 2002 May 8]. [about 12 screens]. Available from: http://www.cryonet .org/archive/8339

5. Vaupel JW, Carey JR. Compositional interpretations of medfly mortality. Science 1993 June 11;1666-8. In: InfoTrac Searchbank: InfoTrac Expanded Academic ASAP [database on the Internet] [cited 2002 May 3]. [about 6 screens]. Available from: http://web4.infotrac .galegroup.com/; Accession No.: A14023382.

54f Student paper excerpt, CBE/CSE style

For a paper in an experimental biology course, with further research funded by the Parkinson's Disease Foundation Summer 2000 Fellowship, student Jennifer Martinez investigated experimental studies of Parkinson's disease. She used the CBE/CSE citation-sequence style of documentation and followed APA format guidelines (**53**) since the CBE Manual supplies no manuscript instructions. She included a title page, numbered as page 1, with the essay title, running head, her name, name of course and instructor, and date; see example on page 857. Here are her abstract and first and last page.

Abstract

Ubiquitin/Proteasome Pathway   2

Abstract

The human brain consists of billions of cells, known as neurons. Once these neurons die, they cannot be regenerated. In neurological disorders, such as Parkinson's disease (PD), an area of the brain known as the substantia nigra is depleted of neurons that are responsible for controlling muscle movement. The etiology of the disorder is not yet known. One mechanism postulated to be involved in the loss of neuronal cells in PD is a dysfunction of the ubiquitin/proteasome pathway. This pathway removes short-lived and abnormal proteins from the cell. The proteins to be removed are first tagged with a chain of a small protein called ubiquitin, which is recognized by the proteasome, the machinery that breaks down the proteins into small fragments. Proteins that are not rapidly removed from the cell tend to cluster and are unable to be broken down or degraded. These clusters or intracellular aggregates remain in the cell and may contribute to cell death. In PD, these intracellular inclusions, known as Lewy bodies, are found in neurons. There are two forms of PD: (1) familial, caused by genetic factors, and (2) sporadic, caused by environmental factors. The focus of this paper is to review the most recent findings relating PD with a dysfunction of the ubiquitin/proteasome pathway. In addition, the role played by intracellular proteins such as vimentin, parkin, alpha-synuclein, and cyclooxygenase 2 in formation of PD Lewy bodies is discussed based on recent experimental studies. The results of this investigation showed that the proteins vimentin, parkin, alpha-synuclein, and cyclooxygenase 2 were found to be associated with these inclusions.

Running head and page number on every page (Title page is page 1.)

Technical language in scientific paper

First page of paper

The Role of the Ubiquitin/Proteasome Pathway in
Parkinson's Disease

Proteolysis is the breakdown or degradation of
proteins and is an important cellular event involving
tightly regulated removal of unwanted proteins and
retention of those that are essential. The
ubiquitin/proteasome pathway plays an important role
in the intracellular quality control process by
degrading mutated or abnormally folded proteins to
prevent their accumulation as intracellular
aggregates. Proteolysis by the ubiquitin/proteasome
pathway involves two major steps: ubiquitination
followed by degradation. A de-ubiquitination step also
plays an important role in this pathway (1).

Ubiquitin (Ub) is a small peptide consisting of 76
amino acids and is abundant in all eukaryotic cells
(1). Covalent attachment of ubiquitin to proteins targets
them for degradation. Once ubiquitinated, proteins do
not accumulate in cells since the Ub/proteasome pathway
degrades them. Proteins become ubiquitinated by a series
of four enzymatic reactions: the ATP dependent
activation of ubiquitin by Ub-activating enzymes (E1),
binding of activated ubiquitin to Ub-conjugating
enzymes (E2), the covalent conjugation of ubiquitin to
the protein substrate by Ub-ligases (E3), and the
formation of a polyubiquitin chain by the elongation
factor E4. Polyubiquitination acts as a tag for
recognition by the 26S proteasome for protein
degradation. The 26S proteasome consists of two main
particles, the 19S regulatory particle and the 20S
catalytic particle. The 19S particle has a lid and
base arrangement. The lid contains ATPases and
deubiquitinating enzymes, whereas the base contains
polyub-binding subunits. The 20S particle is a cylinder-
shaped complex with a catalytic core. The hydrolysis of
peptide bonds occurs in this core particle (1,2).

Numbered reference to first source

Second reference to first numbered source

List of references

References

Entries aligned under first word of entry

1. Figueiredo-Pereira ME, Rockwell P. The ubiquitin/proteasome pathway in neurological disorders. In: Banik NL, Lajtha A, editors. Proteolysis in the pathophysiology of neurodegenerative disease. New York: Kluwer/Plenum; 2000. Forthcoming.

2. Wigley WC, Fabunmi RP, Lee MG, Marino CR, Muallem S, Demartino G-N, Thomas PJ. Dynamic association of proteasomal machinery with the centrosome. J Cell Biol 1999;145(3):481-90.

3. Update on Parkinson's disease [Internet]. Leawood (KA): Am Acad of Family Physicians; 1999 Apr 14 [cited 2000 Sep 22]. Available from: http://www.aafp.org/afp/990415ap/2155.html

4. Research news: Parkinson's disease [Internet]. Bethesda (MD): Nat Human Genome Research Inst; [cited 2000 Sep 15]. Available from: http://www.nhgri.nih.gov/DIR/LGDR/PARK/about_parks.html

5. Parkinson's disease—-hope through research [Internet]. Bethesda (MD): Nat Inst of Neurological Disorders and Stroke; updated 2000 July 1 [cited 2000 Sep 22]. Available from: http://www.ninds.nih.gov/health_and_medical/pubs/parkinson_disease_htr.htm

6. Johnson JA, Ward CL, Kopito RR. Aggresomes, a cellular response to misfolded proteins. J Cell Biol 1998;143(7):1883-98.

References on new numbered page

No italics or underlining in list

55 *Chicago* Style of Documentation

AT A GLANCE: INDEX OF *CHICAGO* STYLE FEATURES

The Chicago Manual of Style, 14th ed. (Chicago: U of Chicago P, 1993), describes a system in which sources are documented in footnotes or endnotes. This system is used widely in the humanities, especially in history, art history, literature, and the arts. For a *Chicago*-style paper, include an unnumbered title page, and number the first page of your text as page "2." Guidelines for student papers based on *Chicago* style can be found in Kate L. Turabian, *A Manual for Writers of Term Papers, Theses, and Dissertations,* 6th ed. (Chicago: U of Chicago P, 1996).

Because the author/year citation style also recommended in the *Chicago Manual of Style* is similar to the APA style, this section focuses on the *Chicago* recommendation for endnotes and footnotes.

55a Two basic features of *Chicago* style

KEY POINTS

Two Basic Features of *Chicago* Endnotes and Footnotes Style

1. Place a superscript numeral at the end of the quotation or the sentence in which you mention source material; place the number after all punctuation marks except a dash.

2. List all endnotes—single-spaced, but double-spaced between notes, unless your instructor prefers double-spaced throughout—on a separate numbered page at the end of the paper, and number the notes sequentially, as they appear in your paper. Your word processing program will automatically place footnotes at the bottom of each page (Insert/Footnote). See **55e**, page 884, for examples. Also see **10c**.

Illustrations of the two basic features

a. Reference to a book in your paper

> Historian David McCullough paints a vivid picture of the army's retreat from Boston: "The British had been out-witted, humiliated. The greatest military power on earth had been forced to retreat by an army of amateurs; it was a heady realization."[3]

b. Listing of book and page number of quotation in your note

> 3. David McCullough, *John Adams* (New York: Simon and Schuster, 2001), 76.

55b *Chicago* in-text citations and notes

Use the following format, and number your notes sequentially.

> George Eliot thought that Eliot was a "good, mouth-filling, easy to pronounce word."[5]

First note for a source

author's name
in normal order

title italicized, all
important words capitalized

5. Margaret Crompton, *George Eliot: The Woman*

comma   page number

(London: Cox and Wyman, 1960), 123.

Note referring to the immediately preceding source   In the second reference to the immediately preceding source, use "Ibid." (Latin *ibidem*, meaning "in the same place") instead of repeating the author's name and the title of the work. All the details except the page number must be the same as in the previous citation. If the page number too is the same, omit it following "Ibid."

6. Ibid., 127.

However, avoid a series of "ibid." notes, which is likely to irritate your reader. Instead, place page references within your text: *As Crompton points out (127), . . .*

Any subsequent reference to a previously cited source   For a reference to a previously cited source, but not to the one immediately before, do not use "Ibid," but give the author and page number.

18. Crompton, 124.

55c Guidelines for *Chicago* endnotes and footnotes

KEY POINTS

Setting Up *Chicago* Endnotes and Footnotes

1. In the list of endnotes, place each number on the line (not as a superscript), followed by a period and one space. For footnotes, word processing software will often automatically make the number a superscript number—just be consistent with whatever format you use.

2. Indent the first line of each entry three or five spaces. Single-space within a note and double-space between notes, unless your instructor prefers double-spacing throughout.

3. Use the author's full name, not inverted, followed by a comma and the title of the work. Italicize titles of books and periodicals (or underline—but be consistent), and put quotation marks around article titles.

4. Capitalize all words in the titles of books, periodicals, and articles except *a, an, the*, coordinating conjunctions, *to* in an infinitive, and prepositions. Capitalize any word that begins or ends a title or subtitle.

(continued)

(continued)

5. Follow a book title with publishing information in parentheses followed by a comma and the page number(s), with no "p." or "pp." Follow an article title with the journal or newspaper name and pertinent publication information (volume, issue, date, page numbers). Do not abbreviate months.

6. Separate major parts of the citation with commas, not periods.

7. For online sources, provide the URL after "available from," and end with the date on which you accessed the source.

55d Examples of entries in *Chicago* notes

Print books and parts of books

1. Book with one author

9. Judith Thurman, *Isak Dinesen: The Life of a Storyteller* (New York: St. Martin's Press, 1982), 80.

2. Book with two or three authors

7. George Lakoff and Mark Johnson, *Metaphors We Live By* (Chicago: University of Chicago Press, 1980), 22.

3. Book with four or more authors

For a book with four or more authors, use only the name of the first author followed by "et al." (for "and others").

13. Randolph Quirk et al., *A Comprehensive Grammar of the English Language* (London: Longman, 1985).

4. Book with no author identified

14. *Chicago Manual of Style*, 14th ed. (Chicago: University of Chicago Press, 1993), 369.

5. Book with editor or translator

5. John Updike, ed., *The Best American Short Stories of the Century* (Boston: Houghton Mifflin, 1999).

Use "trans." for a translator.

6. Author's work quoted in another work

17. E. M. Forster, *Two Cheers for Democracy* (New York: Harcourt, Brace & World, 1942), 242, quoted in Phyllis Rose, *Woman of Letters, A Life of Virginia Woolf* (New York: Oxford University Press, 1978), 219.

Examples of entries in *Chicago* notes: Print articles and audiovisual materials

7. Article in an edited volume

> 3. Terrence Des Pres, "Poetry and Politics," in *The Writer in Our World*, ed. Reginald Gibbons (Boston: Atlantic Monthly Press, 1986), 25.

8. Article in a scholarly journal, continuously paged through issues of a volume
For journals paged continuously through issues of a volume (for example, if issue 1 ends on page 189, issue 2 of the same volume begins with page 190), give only the volume number and year, not the issue number.

> 25. William W. Cook, "Writing in the Spaces Left," *College Composition and Communication* 44 (1993): 21.

9. Article in a scholarly journal, each issue paged separately
When each issue of a journal is paged separately, with each issue beginning with page 1, include "no." and the issue number after the volume number.

> 16. Rami Ginat, "The Soviet Union and the Syrian Ba'th Regime: From Hesitation to *Rapprochement*," *Middle Eastern Studies* 36, no. 2 (2000): 150–71.

10. Article in a magazine
Include the month for monthly magazines and the complete date for weekly magazines.

> 2. Marc Cooper, "Arizona: The New Border War," *Nation*, 17 July 2000, 22.

11. Article in a newspaper
Include the complete date, the edition, if relevant, and the section number. Do not include the word *the* in the name of a newspaper. A page number is optional. It can be prefaced with "p." if section and/or column numbers are also provided (see endnotes 3 and 6 in the student paper in **55f** for examples).

> 15. Barry Levinson, "Telling Complex Stories Simply," *New York Times*, 26 April 2002, sec. E, p. 1.

If the city is not part of the newspaper title, include it in parentheses: *Times* (London).

12. Review of book, play, or movie

> 21. Robert Alter, "Immodest Proposals," review of *God, Gulliver, and Genocide: Barbarism and the European Imagination, 1492-1945*, by Claude Rawson, *New Republic*, 11 February 2002, 34–38.

13. Film, filmstrip, slide, videocassette, DVD, or audiocassette
End the note with an indication of the type of medium, such as *film, filmstrip, slide, videocassette,* or *audiocassette.*

```
    10. Citizen Kane, prod., written, and dir. Orson
Welles, 119 min., RKO, 1941, film.
```

Examples of entries in *Chicago* notes: electronic and online sources

14. Article obtained through a computer service (ERIC, NTIS)

```
    19. James C. Stalker, "Slang Is Not Novel," paper
presented at a meeting of the American Association for
Applied Linguistics, Long Beach, California, 1995, 8, ERIC,
ED 392 251.
```

15. Online book

```
    16. Mary Wollstonecraft Shelley, Frankenstein or The
Modern Prometheus [book online] (London: Dent, 1912),
Oxford Text Archive; available from http://ota.ahds.ac.uk;
accessed 23 May 2002.
```

16. Article in an online database   After any available print information, give the name of the database; the URL and other retrieval information; and the date you accessed the material.

```
    23. Geoffrey Bent, "Vermeer's Hapless Peer," North
American Review 282 (1997), InfoTrac: Expanded Academic
ASAP; available from http://www.infotrac.galegroup.com;
accessed 8 January 2001.
```

17. Government publication online

```
    4. Department of Labor, "Labor Department Responds to
Disaster Relief Effort" [government publication online],
22 May 2002; available from http://www.dol.gov/_sec/programs/
responds.htm; accessed 22 May 2002.
```

55e Sample *Chicago* endnotes and bibliography

Check whether your instructor wants you to include a list of works cited or a bibliography of works consulted in addition to notes. A bibliography begins on a new, numbered page after the endnotes. List entries alphabetically, by authors' last names. Include full names, inverted, not just initials. Indent all lines three or five spaces except the first line of each entry. Single-space entries and double-space between entries. Separate the major parts of each entry with a period and one space.

Excerpts of some endnotes and bibliography from a student's paper on the seventeenth-century Dutch painter Pieter de Hooch follow.

Notes

    1. Peter Sutton, *Pieter de Hooch: Complete Edition, with a Catalogue Raisonné* (Ithaca, N.Y.: Cornell University Press, 1980), 44.

    2. Wayne E. Franits, "The Depiction of Servants in Some Paintings by Pieter de Hooch," *Zeitschrift für Kunstgeschichte* 52 (1989): 560.

Bibliography

Bent, Geoffrey. "Vermeer's Hapless Peer." *North American Review* 282 (1997). InfoTrac: Expanded Academic ASAP. Available from http://www.infotrac.galegroup.com; accessed 8 January 2001.

Botton, Alain de. "Domestic Bliss: Pieter de Hooch Exhibition." *New Statesman* 9 October 1998: 34–35.

Franits, Wayne E. "The Depiction of Servants in Some Paintings by Pieter de Hooch." *Zeitschrift für Kunstgeschichte* 52 (1989): 559–66.

Glueck, Grace. "A Loving Home Life, Right Down to the Nits." *New York Times*, 8 January 1999, sec. E, p. 40.

Sutton, Peter. *Pieter de Hooch: Complete Edition, with a Catalogue Raisonné*. Ithaca, N.Y.: Cornell University Press, 1980.

55f Student paper, *Chicago* style (endnote and footnote styles)

A paper with endnotes Eva Hardcastle wrote the following research paper for a writing course with a focus on language use. The class had been discussing slang and Standard English, and she chose to expand the discussion by doing research on slang dictionaries. Her instructor asked for endnotes to be double-spaced.

SLANG DICTIONARIES:
MIRRORING OUR FLEXIBLE USE OF LANGUAGE

EVA HARDCASTLE

ENGLISH 218
PROFESSOR MARINO
APRIL 22, 2002

SLANG DICTIONARIES:

MIRRORING OUR FLEXIBLE USE OF LANGUAGE

The reference section of every library contains one or more slang dictionaries.[1] At first it is puzzling to consider why slang dictionaries are published and how they are used. People who use slang do not get it out of a slang dictionary, do not check the spelling of slang, and do not look up the meaning of an unfamiliar slang expression they may hear used by a friend or coworker. Close examination of slang dictionaries, however, suggests that these works reflect the flexible ways people shift back and forth between informal and formal speech. On one hand, we often communicate in a standardized way, so we can be clearly understood and can successfully fit into the larger society. On the other hand, we often talk in many diverse and free-style ways, so we can express our individuality and belong to various sub-groups within society. Slang dictionaries convey the message that both types of speech have validity and historical interest.

Slang exists largely in relation to what it is not--it is not Standard English. James Stalker makes this point as he summarizes colleagues' attempts to date the beginning of slang:

> Lighter (1994) maintains that we cannot really label words as being slang before c. 1660, the Restoration period, because "standard" English did not exist before that time, hence the concept of slang could not exist before that time, although cant, criminal jargon, could. Partridge (1954) seems to agree. Slang arose as a response to Standard.[2]

In-group slang is informal, irreverent, and edgy, while Standard English is formal, respectful, and mainstream. Slang dictionaries make these distinctions clear, neatly translating slang into Standard English and highlighting the difference between the two in a non-judgmental way.

These dictionaries let a reader know, for instance, that in Australia *narky* means "upset," that in the Royal Air Force *pukka gen* means "trustworthy information," or

Superscript number for first endnote

Thesis

3

that in England in 1811 *Pompkin* meant "A man or woman of Boston in America; from the number of pompkins raised and eaten by the people of that country."[3] With slang words and their definitions each presented in this straightforward, neutral manner, it is easy to see both as valid ways of expressing oneself, depending on one's choices, aims, priorities, audience, time period, and context.[4]

Interestingly, many people have always felt strongly that Standard English needs to be championed as the only way to communicate. Other people have always felt equally strongly that English must be appreciated and preserved in all its natural exuberance and variety. Tom McArthur, a scholar of global English, writes, for instance, about early "dialectologists," who "pursued their cataloging and commentary under the vast shadow of standardization . . . and so worked with a sense of urgency."[5] Clearly slang dictionary writers are more aligned with this second group, valuing slang's idiosyncrasies. But slang dictionary writers also approve highly of Standard English, as found in their prefaces and definitions. Both slang and Standard English have their place, slang dictionaries seem to say, and are worthy of attention and preservation.[6]

In *Democratic Eloquence*, Kenneth Cmiel considers how nineteenth-century citizens of America wrestled with slang, "the riff-raff of language."[7] Americans were famous for being able to use language in colorful, casual ways, but they actively questioned the role of slang in a democracy. They wondered whether slang was a good thing, embodying friendliness, independence, self-confidence, and a democratic disregard for class distinctions, or a bad thing, indicating boorishness, low sensibility, incivility, poor education, and an embarrassing lack of culture and refinement. Or was it both? People were ambivalent, in other words. Cmiel writes:

4

Americans were pulled in contradictory directions. The new expressive decorum encouraged informal speech, and slang, dialect, and familiarity all contributed to moments of egalitarianism. Popular education, however, encouraged refined and elegant prose.[8]

Cmiel follows the debate in newspapers, grammar guides, speeches, and dictionaries of the day. In the mid-nineteenth century, regular dictionaries condemned slang as vulgar and low, leaving most of it entirely out. By the 1880s and into the twentieth century, not only do more slang dictionaries appear, but the next generation of general dictionaries includes more slang words. As the editors of Funk and Wagnall's *Standard* (1890) put it in their preface to their new edition: "The question that should control the lexicographer is not, should the word be in the English language? But *is it*?"[9] Expressing this nonjudgmental philosophy, long, new, academic-style slang dictionaries appear. They document in great detail that people in all walks of life and occupations use slang sometimes and that a person sometimes talks freely or rudely, sometimes more delicately. For example, in one slang dictionary is the slang expression "Blue o'clock in the morning," followed by the definition, "Pre-dawn, when black sky gives way to purple. Suggestive of rollicking late hours."[10] Both parts of this entry seem like fine uses of language, and the mind goes happily back and forth between them. That back-and-forth mirrors how we vary our mode of communication according to mood, audience, and situation.

So, finally, what is the purpose of slang dictionaries? Some slang dictionary prefaces say that their purpose is to preserve a national language and national pride.[11] Some say their purpose is to "help ESL students learn informal English as it is spoken or heard on TV."[12] Some dictionaries of technical terms such as computer slang can have a practical, job-training

5

aspect.[13] But mostly slang dictionaries seem to celebrate the quirkiness of slang. They present old slang, such as *frisk* for search or *racket* for noise (both from c. 1780) and newer slang, such as *24/7* for *constantly* (from c. 2000), and in the process make clear that people move easily back and forth between the slang and Standard English, usually without any dictionary at all.

NOTES

1. Examples include Eric Partridge, *A Dictionary of Slang and Unconventional English*, 7th ed., ed. Paul Beale (London: Routledge and Kegan Paul, 1984); Harold Wentworth and Stewart Berg Flexner, *Dictionary of American Slang* (New York: Crowell, 1975); Jonathan Lighter, *Random House Historical Dictionary of American Slang*, 2 vols. (New York: Random House, 1994–97).

2. James C. Stalker, "Slang Is Not Novel," paper presented at a meeting of the American Association for Applied Linguistics, Long Beach, California, 1995, 8, ERIC, ED 392 251.

3. Pete Alfano, "Australian for Olympics," *Fort Worth Star Telegram*, 10 September 2000, Sports, p. 13; Eric Partridge, *Dictionary of Slang and Unconventional English*, 5th ed. (New York: Macmillan, 1961), 1103; Francis Grose, *Lexicon Balatronicum: A Dictionary of the Vulgar Tongue: A Dictionary of Buckish Slang, University Wit, and Pickpocket Eloquence* (London: Jones, 1811; reprint, Chicago: Follett, 1971).

4. This concept is discussed in Harvey Daniels, *Famous Last Words: The American Language Crisis Reconsidered* (Carbondale: Southern Illinois University Press, 1983), 68. In his chapter "Nine Ideas about Language," Idea 5 is "Speakers of all languages employ a range of styles and a set of subdialects or jargons."

6

5. Tom McArthur, *The English Languages* (Cambridge, U.K.: Cambridge University Press, 1998), xiv. See also Tom McArthur, *Living Words: Language, Lexicography, and the Knowledge Revolution* (Exeter: University of Exeter Press, 1998), 37. Here McArthur calls the pro-diversity group "permissivists."

6. In an interview (Janny Scott, "That All-American Dictionary Adds an All-American Coach," *New York Times*, 19 August 2000, sec. A, p. 1), dictionary editor Jesse Sheidlower echoes this point: "You can be interested in slang or dialect or things that people call ungrammatical, but still think that there is a formal way of speech. . . . Our entire conversation has been conducted in a relatively formal standard English despite the fact that I know a lot of words that will make people's hair crawl."

7. Kenneth Cmiel, *Democratic Eloquence: The Fight over Popular Speech in Nineteenth-Century America* (New York: William Morrow, 1990), 127–28.

8. Ibid., 90.

9. Quoted in Cmiel, 224.

10. J. Redding Ware, *Passing English of the Victorian Era: A Dictionary of Heterodox English, Slang, and Phrase* (London: Routledge, 1909), 38.

11. S. B. Flexner, introduction to Wentworth and Flexner, viii.

12. David Burke, *Street Talk: Slang Used in Popular American Television Shows* (Berkeley: Optima, 1992), viii.

13. See, for examples, Constance Hale, ed., *Wired Style: Principles of English Usage in the Digital Age* (San Francisco: Hard Wired Books, 1996), 35–58; and University of Wisconsin-Platteville, "Computer Slang Glossary"; available from http://www.uwplatt.edu/~disted/general/glossary.htm; accessed 20 April 2002.

A paper with footnotes   Word processing commands make it easy to present a paper with footnotes in place of endnotes. Going to Insert/Footnote in Microsoft Word, for example, allows you the option of choosing a footnote or an endnote for each number inserted in your document. When you add or delete material, footnotes automatically adjust. What follows is the first page of Eva Hardcastle's essay with notes as footnotes.

SLANG DICTIONARIES:

OUR FLEXIBLE USE OF LANGUAGE

~~~~erence section of every library contains
~~ more slang dictionaries.[1] At first it is
puzzling to consider why slang dictionaries are
published and how they are used. People who use slang
do not get it out of a slang dictionary, do not check
the spelling of slang, and do not look up the meaning
of an unfamiliar slang expression they may hear used
by a friend or coworker. Close examination of slang
dictionaries, however, suggests that these works
reflect the flexible ways people shift back and forth
between informal and formal speech. On the one hand,
we often communicate in a standardized way, so we can
be clearly understood and can successfully fit into
the larger society. On the other hand, we often talk
in many diverse and free-style ways, so we can express
our individuality and belong to various subgroups
within society. Slang dictionaries convey the message
that both types of speech have validity and
historical interest.

Slang exists largely in relation to what it is
not--it is not Standard English. James Stalker makes
this point as he summarizes colleagues' attempts to
date the beginning of slang:

> Lighter (1994) maintains that we cannot really
> label words as being slang before c. 1660, the
> Restoration period, because "standard" English did
> not exist before that time, hence the concept of
> slang could not exist before that time, although

---

[1]Examples include Eric Partridge, *A
Dictionary of Slang and Unconventional English*,
7th ed., ed. Paul Beale (London: Routledge and
Kegan Paul, 1984); Harold Wentworth and Stewart
Berg Flexner, *Dictionary of American Slang* (New
York: Crowell, 1975); Jonathan Lighter, *Random
House Historical Dictionary of American Slang*, 2
vols. (New York: Random House, 1994-97).

56 CGOS (*Columbia Guide to Online Style*) Style of Documentation

AT A GLANCE: INDEX OF CGOS STYLE FEATURES

Two Basic Features (56a), 890

In-Text Citations (56b), 890

Guidelines for CCGOS Bibliographic List: Humanities and Sciences (56c), 891

Examples of Entries (56d):

World Wide Web (WWW) Sites, 893
1. Web site, 893
2. Web site, revised or modified, 893
3. Web site maintained by an individual, 893
4. Web site by a group or organization, 894
5. Web site, corporate, 894
6. Web site, government, 895
7. Web site, no author listed, 895
8. Web site, printed book, available online, 895
9. Web site, online article, 896
10. Web site, article from a news service, 896
11. Web site, article from an archive, 896
12. Web site, with frames, 897
13. Web site, graphic or audio file, 897

E-mail, Discussion Groups (Listservs), and Newsgroups, 898
14. Personal e-mail, 898
15. Listserv, 898
16. Newsgroup, 898
17. Message from an archive, 899
18. Material from a gopher site, 899
19. Material from a file transfer protocol (FTP) site, 900
20. Material from a Telnet site, 900

Online Reference Sources and Databases, 900
21. Encyclopedia or reference article, online, 900
22. Material from a CD-ROM, 901
23. Material from an online database, 901

Other Sources, 902
24. Synchronous Communications (MOOs/MUDs/LANs) Sites, 902
25. Software, 902

Student Paper Excerpt (56e), 902

Columbia Guide to Online Style, by Janice Walker and Todd Taylor (New York: Columbia UP, 1998), is designed for use with existing documentation formats in the humanities (MLA and *Chicago*) and the sciences (APA and CBE/CSE). It provides a thorough treatment for citing online sources, both in your text and in the list of biblio-graphic citations. CGOS provides regular updates at <http://www.columbia.edu/cu/cup/cgos>.

56a Two basic features of CGOS style

KEY POINTS

Two Basic Features of CGOS Style

1. Cite sources in your paper by following the guidelines of MLA, APA, CBE/CSE, or *Chicago*. Whenever possible, identify the author in your text (rather than in a parenthetical citation). You will not be able to provide page numbers for sources accessed online.

2. In your list of references, for all online sources follow the exam-ples of CGOS style for the humanities or sciences. Always give the URL, followed by the date on which you access the materials.

Not all instructors require students to use CGOS style for online sources, especially when a style of documentation has updated its recommendations on citing Internet sources. Always check with your instructor regarding accepted documentation formats.

56b CGOS in-text citations

In most cases, in-text (or parenthetical) citations will include the last name of the author of a source and a page number (for MLA style) or the author's last name, a date of publication, and a page number for a quotation (for APA style). However, in a majority of electronic sources, some or all of this information may be missing. Therefore, for such sources, only the author's name need be put in the paren-theses. If you provide the author's name in the body of your paper before a quotation or paraphrase, no additional citation is needed. Remember that an author may be a person or an organization.

```
Science writer Stephen Hart claims that neuromusicology
is being hailed as a "new discipline."

Neuromusicology is being hailed as a "new discipline" (Hart).
```

For sources such as listservs or e-mails, if you do not have the author's name, you may use the screen name (nickname or alias) of the author:

```
In a posting dated March 15, 2002 on the WPA Listserv,
jlang argues . . .
```

Often, though, no author will be listed for a Web site. In such cases, as with other documentation formats, include a shortened form of the title of the site.

> Some of the themes in rock music that many parents and critics point to as potentially harmful include "advocating and glamorizing abuse of drugs and alcohol" and "explicit lyrics presenting suicide as an 'alternative' or 'solution'" ("Influence of Rock Music").

Occasionally, you may even find a site with no obvious title. In such situations, include the file name of the site.

When citing a source using an author/year system like APA, you will need to cite the year of the Web site's publication (either its original publication or its most recent updating). Use only the year, even if a month and date are provided.

> Science writer Stephen Hart (2000) claims that neuromusicology is being hailed as a "new discipline."
>
> Neuromusicology is being hailed as a "new discipline" (Hart, 2000).

When dealing with sites in which no date is given, you can use the date you accessed the site, using the date/month/year pattern.

> Some of the themes in rock music that many parents and critics point to as potentially harmful include "advocating and glamorizing abuse of drugs and alcohol" and "explicit lyrics presenting suicide as an 'alternative' or 'solution'" ("Influence of Rock Music," 31 May 2001).

Remember, though, your goal as a writer is to keep your citations as unobtrusive as possible, so that your readers are not distracted by the citations.

56c Guidelines for entries in CGOS bibliographic list: humanities and sciences

CGOS can be used to cite sources for a "Works Cited" page in MLA format or a "References" page in APA (and CBE/CSE) format. This style can also be adapted for use in creating *Chicago*-style footnote or endnote citations. For the humanities (MLA and *Chicago*) approach and the sciences (APA or CBE/CSE) approach, list the following basic elements in a bibliographic citation.

HUMANITIES

- author's last name, first name
- title of document (if given), using capital letters for each important word and quotation marks around the entire title

- title of complete work (if applicable and available), using capital letters for each important word and italics for the entire title
- file or version number (if applicable and available)
- document date or date of last revision (if different from access date)
- electronic address (provide the complete Web address and access path)
- date of access, placed in parentheses and followed by a period

SCIENCES

- author's last name, initials
- document date (if different from access date), in parentheses
- title of document (if given), using a capital letter only for the first word in the title and in the subtitle; do not use quotation marks around the entire title
- title of complete work (if applicable and available), using a capital letter only for the first word in the title and in the subtitle; use italics for the entire title
- file or version number (if applicable and available)
- edition or date of last revision, if applicable; place in parentheses
- electronic address (provide the complete Web address and access path)
- date of access, placed in parentheses and followed by a period

NOTES FOR LISTING INFORMATION

- If no person's name is listed, use the name of the organization or company, or the author's alias.
- If no author is given, start your citation with the title of the site.
- If the source was previously published in print, give the date of publication as you would for other formats. If not, note when the site was posted or updated, if such information is provided.
- The electronic address is perhaps the most crucial piece of information in citing online sources. Therefore, it is important that you type the address and access path accurately or, better still, copy the URL from the source and paste it into your list. Do not place site addresses in angle brackets (< >).

Like other formats, CGOS recommends indenting all but the first line of each bibliographic entry. However, if you publish your paper online, such hanging indents may cause formatting problems. In such cases, it may be preferable to use no indentation at all; instead, separate each entry by skipping a line. Check with your instructor.

56d Examples of entries in CGOS bibliographic list: humanities and sciences

World Wide Web (WWW) Sites

1. Web site For a basic Web site, put the title of any particular page on that site in quotation marks when using MLA or *Chicago* styles. For APA style, capitalize the first word in the name of the page, along with any proper names; do not put the page's name in quotation marks. For all styles, the name of the site itself should be italicized.

HUMANITIES   Kuhl, Ken. "Fast Food Facts Fast Facts." *Fast Food
                Facts*. 2000. http://www.kenkuhl.com/fastfood/
                fastfacts.shtml (23 Aug. 2002).

SCIENCES   Kuhl, K. (2000). Fast food facts fast facts. *Fast
                food facts*. http://www.kenkuhl.com/fastfood/
                fastfacts.shtml (23 Aug. 2002).

2. Web site, revised or modified If the site lists a date on which it was updated or modified, list that date as you would the usual copyright date.

HUMANITIES   Walker, Janice R., and Todd Taylor. "Updates." *The
                Columbia Guide to Online Style*. Rev. 17 May
                2002. http://www.columbia.edu/cu/
                cup/CGOS/idx_update.html (19 May 2002).

SCIENCES   Walker, J. R., & Taylor, T. (2002, May 17). Updates.
                The Columbia Guide to Online Style. Rev.
                http://www.columbia.edu/cu/cup/CGOS/
                idx_update.html (19 May 2002).

3. Web site maintained by an individual Many Web sites have individuals who are hired to update the site's links, information, and other details. If such an individual is named on the site, you can list that individual first, if you wish to focus attention on his or her work, or list the site first, then mention him or her (use such abbreviations as *maint.* for "maintained by" or *comp.* for "compiled by"). Of course, if the person who maintains the site is not listed, you need not include this information.

HUMANITIES   College of DuPage Sci-Fi/Fantasy Club. "Schedule
              of Events." *CODCON VII: Oh No, Not Again!* Maint.
              Jim Allen. 2002. http://www.geocities.com/
              scificod (5 Apr. 2002).

              Allen, Jim, maint. College of DuPage Sci-Fi/Fantasy
              Club. "Schedule of Events." *CODCON VII: Oh No,
              Not Again!* 2002. http://www.geocities.com/
              scificod (5 Apr. 2002).

SCIENCES   College of DuPage Sci-Fi/Fantasy Club. (2002).
              Schedule of events. *CODCON VII: Oh No, Not
              Again!* Maint. Jim Allen. http://www.geocities
              .com/scificod (5 Apr. 2002).

              Allen, J., maint. (2002). College of DuPage Sci-
              Fi/Fantasy Club. Schedule of events. *CODCON
              VII: Oh No, Not Again!* http://www.geocities.com/
              scificod (5 Apr. 2002).

4. Web site by a group or organization   For sites sponsored by an organization or group, treat the group as the author of the site.

HUMANITIES   American Fibromyalgia Syndrome Association.
              "Twenty-Two Research Projects Funded." *The
              American Fibromyalgia Syndrome Association,
              Inc.* 2002. http://afsafund.org/research.htm (23
              Mar. 2002).

SCIENCES   American Fibromyalgia Syndrome Association. (2002).
              Twenty-two research projects funded. *The
              American Fibromyalgia Syndrome Association,
              Inc.* http://afsafund.org/research.htm (23 Mar.
              2002).

5. Web site, corporate   For sites sponsored by a corporation, treat the corporation as the author. If the site's name is different from the corporate author, include the name of the site (in italics) after the title of the page.

HUMANITIES   Wizards of the Coast, Inc. "Events." Rev. 23 May
              2002. http://www.wizards.com/default
              .asp?x=welcome/events (23 May 2002).

SCIENCES   Wizards of the Coast, Inc. (2002, May 23). Events.
Rev. http://www.wizards.com/default.asp?x=welcome/
events (23 May 2002).

6. Web site, government   Treat the government agency as the author.
If the site is regularly updated, in MLA/*Chicago* styles you need not
list a date for the site, but you should still give the date you accessed
it. In APA style, even if the site is regularly updated, you should still
include the year following the agency's name.

HUMANITIES   Federal Bureau of Investigation. "Crackdown on
Identity Fraud." *FBI Home Page.* http://www
.fbi.gov/page2/idtheft.htm (21 May 2002).

SCIENCES   Federal Bureau of Investigation. (2002). Crackdown
on identity fraud. *FBI Home Page.*
http://www.fbi.gov/page2/idtheft.htm (21 May 2002).

7. Web site, no author listed   If no author (individual, group, corporation, or government agency) is indicated for a site, start your entry
with the name of the site or the name of the page you are referencing
on that site.

HUMANITIES   "Influence of Rock Music and Videos on Young
People." 2001. http://www.vicnet.net
.au/vicnet/health/Rockmusicfactsheet.html
(31 May 2001).

SCIENCES   Influence of rock music and videos on young
people. (2001). http://www.vicnet.net
.au/vicnet/health/Rockmusicfactsheet.html
(31 May 2001).

8. Web site, printed book, available online   In this situation, provide
the same information (if available on the site) as you would if citing
a printed book. If a separate title for the electronic version is given,
follow with that, as well as any electronic publication information
(such as editor, date posted, Web address, and so on). Finish by citing the date accessed.

HUMANITIES   Melville, Herman. *Moby Dick, or, The Whale.* 1851.
Project Gutenberg. July 2001. http://promo.net/
cgi-promo/pg/t9.cgi (2 Apr. 2002).

SCIENCES   Melville, H. (1851). *Moby Dick, or, the whale.*
Project Gutenberg. July 2001. http://promo.net/
cgi-promo/pg/t9.cgi (2 Apr. 2002).

9. Web site, online article Articles available online follow a pattern similar to articles in print: provide the name of the author (if given), the title of the article (for humanities style, in quotation marks), the title of the online journal (in italics), the volume number for the article (for sciences style, also in italics), the issue number of the journal (if given), then the date of publication, followed by the Web address and the date of access.

HUMANITIES Hart, Stephen. "Overtures to a New Discipline: Neuromusicology." *21st Century* 1.4 (1996). http://www.columbia.edu/cu/21stC/ issue-1.4/mbmmusic.html (3 Nov. 2000).

SCIENCES Hart, S. (1996). Overtures to a new discipline: Neuromusicology. *21st Century* *1*(4). http://www.columbia.edu/cu/21stC/ issue-1.4/mbmmusic.html (3 Nov. 2000).

10. Web site, article from a news service For articles from online news services or online newspapers, cite the author of the article first (if no author is listed, use the name of the news source or organization, if given). Next, provide the title of the article (in quotation marks for humanities style), the name of the online newspaper or news service, the date of publication (if different from the date of access), the Web address, and the date of access.

HUMANITIES Tobin, Kate. "Cosmic Impact Could Have Started Dinosaur Age." *CNN.com.* 16 May 2002. http://www.cnn.com/2002/TECH/space/05/16/asteroid .dinosaurs/index.html (22 May 2002).

SCIENCES Tobin, K. (2002, May 16). Cosmic impact could have started dinosaur age. *CNN.com.* http://www.cnn.com/ 2002/TECH/space/05/16/asteroid.dinosaurs/ index.html (22 May 2002).

11. Web site, article from an archive Give the same information as you would for a print article (author, title, date, journal, and so on); then give the name of the archive site of the source, the Web address, and the date of publication.

HUMANITIES Trainor, Jennifer Seibel, and Amanda Godley. "After Wyoming: Labor Practices in Two University Writing Programs." *College Composition and Communication* 50.2 (1998): 153-81. *College Composition and Communication Online Archives.* http://www.ntce.org/ccc/2/50.2/art1.html (14 Feb. 2001).

SCIENCES   Trainor, J. S., & Godley, A. (1998). After
Wyoming: Labor practices in two university
writing programs. *College Composition
and Communication 50*(2): 153-181. *College
Composition and Communication Online
Archives.* http://www.ntce.org/ccc/2/50.2/art1.html
(14 Feb. 2001).

12. Web site, with frames   Occasionally you will encounter material on a Web site presented from other Web sites, where you are not able to find the original Web address of that material. In such cases, provide the author, title, and other available publication information first; then list the site where the frame(s) appear. Provide the Web address, followed by a blank space, and identify the link(s) needed to access that particular site. Follow this information with your date of access.

HUMANITIES   "Morisot, Berthe." *Webmuseum, Paris*. 30 Dec. 1995.
AntePodium Links. http://www.ruw.ac.nz/atp
Morisot (15 Jun. 2000).

SCIENCES   Morisot, Berthe. (1995, December 30). *Webmuseum,
Paris. AntePodium links.* http://www.ruw.ac.nz/atp
Morisot (15 Jun. 2000).

13. Web site, graphic or audio file   Here you have two options: you can either cite the graphic or audio file on its own, using its own Web address, or you can cite it as part of the Web page on which it appears. In either case, provide the name of the artist (if given) and the title of the piece. Then, for the graphic itself, provide the Web address and date of access. To cite it as part of a Web page, include the title of the page and the Web address of the page, followed by the date of access.

HUMANITIES   Brueghel, Pieter the Elder. "Landscape with the
Fall of Icarus." c. 1558. http://www.uiuc.edu/
maps/poets/s_z/williams/icarus.jpg (12 May
2002).

         Brueghel, Pieter the Elder. "Landscape with
the Fall of Icarus." c. 1558. In Nicolas
Pioch, "Bruegel, Pieter the Elder."
Webmuseum, Paris. 22 June 1996.
http://www.ibiblio.org/wm/paint/auth/bruegel
(12 May 2002).

SCIENCES   Brueghel, P. (c. 1558). Landscape with the fall of
Icarus. http://www.uiuc.edu/maps/poets/s_z/
williams/icarus.jpg (12 May 2002).

Brueghel, P. (c. 1558). Landscape with the fall of
Icarus. In N. Pioch, Bruegel, Pieter the elder.
Webmuseum, Paris. 22 Jun. 1996.
http://www.ibiblio.org/wm/paint/auth/bruegel (12
May 2002).

E-mail, Discussion Groups (Listservs), and Newsgroups

14. Personal E-mail Provide the name (or alias or nickname) of the author and the title of the message (normally found in the Subject line), placed in quotation marks (for humanities style only). Insert the phrase "Personal e-mail" and then give the date of access (most often, the date of receipt). For sciences styles, you may also need to include (after the name of the author) the date the message was sent, if different from the date of access. Also, the phrase "personal email" (no hyphen) follows within brackets. In either style, do not give the e-mail address of the author.

HUMANITIES   Bustin, Martha. "CGOS section of handbook."
Personal email. (22 May 2002).

SCIENCES   Bustin, M. CGOS section of handbook. [Personal
email]. (22 May 2002).

15. Listserv For postings to listservs or other such online discussion groups, provide the name (or alias) of the author of the message, followed by the subject heading of the posting. Next, provide the date of the posting (if different from the date of access), the address of the listserv or discussion group, and your date of access. Remember that for sciences style, the date of posting (if different from the date of access) comes after the author's name.

HUMANITIES   Kramer, Wayne. "'Crossing Over' on Ifilm.com." 28 Apr.
2000. *LatinoLink Bulletin Board: Criminal Justice.*
http://boards.latinolink.com (14 Jun. 2000).

SCIENCES   Kramer, W. (2000, April 28). "Crossing over" on
Ifilm.com. *LatinoLink Bulletin Board: Criminal
Justice.* http://boards.latinolink.com (14 Jun. 2000).

16. Newsgroup Citing postings from newsgroups works much the same as citing postings to listservs: give the name or alias of the author (if provided), the subject line of the posting, the date the message was posted (if not the same as the date accessed). In sciences style, this information will be placed after the author's name and followed by the address of the newsgroup and the date of access.

HUMANITIES St. John, Ian. "Re: Please Explain Antarctic Ice
     Shelf Consequences." 16 May 2002.
     http://news.talk.environment (22 May 2002).

SCIENCES St. John, I. (2002, May 16). Re: Please explain
     Antarctic ice shelf consequences.
     http://news.talk.environment (22 May 2002).

17. Message from an archive For e-mail discussion messages saved to an archive, provide the name of the author, the message title, the date the message was posted, and the address of the list (if available). Then list the name (if given) of the archive, its Web address, and any other information (such as a link) needed to access the message, followed by the date of access.

HUMANITIES Kishore. "Connection Exception." *Archives of*
     RMI-USERS@Java.Sun.Com. 31 Oct. 2001.
     http://swjscmail1.java.sun.com/cgi.bin/wa?A1=Ind01
     10&L=rmi-users#11 (11 Jan. 2002).

SCIENCES Kishore. (2001, October 31). Connection exception.
     Archives of RMI-USERS@Java.Sun.Com.
     http://swjscmail1.java.sun.com/cgi.bin/
     wa?A1=Ind0110&L=rmi-users#11 (11 Jan. 2002).

Information Available Using Gopher, FTP, and Telnet Protocols

18. Material from a gopher site Provide the name of the author (if given), followed by the title of the file or article. Next, if applicable and available, give the title of the complete work from which the article or file comes (in italics), followed by the publication date and any other publication information provided (remember: the publication date comes after the author's name in sciences style). Finally, list the full address, beginning with the protocol *gopher* and including all information needed to access the file, followed by the date of access.

HUMANITIES United States. Dept. of the Army. *Israel Army Area*
     Handbook. 1994. gopher://gopher.umsl
     .edu/00/library/govdocs/armyahbs/aahb6/
     aah60000%09%09%2B (20 Apr. 2001).

SCIENCES U.S. Department of the Army. (1994). *Israel Army*
     Area Handbook. gopher://gopher.umsl.edu/
     00/library/govdocs/armyahbs/aahb6/
     aah60000%09%09%2B (20 Apr. 2001).

19. *Material from a File Transfer Protocol (FTP) site* Provide the name
of the author (if given), followed by the title of the file or article. Next, if
applicable and available, give the title of the complete work from which
the article or file comes (in italics), followed by the publication date and
any other publication information provided (remember: the publication
date comes after the author's name in sciences style). Finally, list the full
address, beginning with the protocol *ftp* and including all information
needed to access the file, followed by the date of access.

HUMANITIES   Hawthorne, Nathaniel. *The House of the Seven*
                  Gables. 1851. The Project Gutenberg etext of
                  The House of the Seven Gables, by Nathaniel
                  Hawthorne. Etext #77. August 1993. *Project*
                  Gutenberg. ftp://ftp.sudval.org/gutenberg/
                  etext93/7gabl10.txt (25 Jun. 2001).

SCIENCES   Hawthorne, N. (1851). *The house of the seven*
                  gables. The Project Gutenberg etext of *The*
                  house of the seven gables, by Nathaniel
                  Hawthorne. (Etext #77). (August 1993).
                  Project Gutenberg. ftp://ftp.sudval.org/
                  gutenberg/etext93/7gabl10.txt (25 Jun. 2001).

20. *Material from a Telnet site* Provide the name of the author (if
given), followed by the title of the file or article. Next, if applicable and
available, give the title of the complete work from which the article or
file comes (in italics), followed by the publication date and any other
publication information provided (remember: the publication date
comes after the author's name in sciences style). Finally, list the full
address, beginning with the protocol *telnet* and including all information needed to access the file; be sure to set off any commands from the
address with a blank space. Follow this with the date of access.

HUMANITIES   United States. Dept. of Labor. "Davis-Bacon
                Wage Determination Database." *FEDWORLD:*
                National Technical Information Service.
                telnet://fedworld.gov (22 May 2002).

SCIENCES   U.S. Department of Labor. (2002). Davis-Bacon
                wage determination database. *FEDWORLD:*
                National technical information service.
                telnet://fedworld.gov (22 May 2002).

Online Reference Sources and Databases

21. *Encyclopedia or reference article, online* For online encyclopedias
like *Encarta* or *Britannica Online*, as well as other online reference
works, such as dictionaries, almanacs, handbooks, and the like,

provide the name of the author, if given; if no author is listed, start with the title of the entry or article. Follow this with the title (in italics) of the encyclopedia or reference work, including any publication information (both electronic and, if applicable, print versions) and the date of publication (in sciences style, the date will come after the author's name). Provide the name of the subscription service, if applicable and available; then conclude with the full address (including any paths or directories needed to reach the article) and your date of access.

HUMANITIES "Mental Disorder." *Encyclopædia Britannica*. 2002.
           http://www.search.eb.com/eb/article?eu=118186 (23
           Mar. 2002).

SCIENCES Mental disorder. (2002). *Encyclopædia britannica*.
          http://www.search.eb.com/eb/article?eu=118186 (23
          Mar. 2002).

22. Material from a CD-ROM   Provide the name of the author or editor (if an editor, include the abbreviation *Ed.* in parentheses after the name); then give the name of the article or part of the disk being used, followed by the title of the CD-ROM (in italics). Conclude with the version number (preceded by the word *Version*) in parentheses, followed by the city of publication, publisher, and date of publication (in sciences style, put the date of publication after the author's name). No date of access needs to be provided.

HUMANITIES Raimes, Ann. "The Structure of the Argument."
           Digital Keys. (Version 3.0). Boston: Houghton,
           2002.

SCIENCES Raimes, A. (2002). The structure of the argument.
          Digital Keys. (Version 3.0). Boston: Houghton.

23. Material from an online database   For citing articles or other material from an online database such as *InfoTrac Expanded Academic, Expanded Academic SIRS Researcher, CQ Researcher*, and others, provide all the information you would if citing the original print version, such as a magazine or journal article (refer to the appropriate style guide for examples). Follow this information with the name of the database (italicized); then give the file or article number (for sciences style, place this number in parentheses) or, if unavailable, the full electronic address, and the date of access in parentheses.

HUMANITIES Lowe, Michelle S. "Britain's Regional Shopping
           Centres: New Urban Forms?" *Urban Studies* 37
           (Feb. 2000). *Infotrac: Expanded Academic ASAP*.
           Article A61862666. (14 Jan. 2001).

SCIENCES   Lowe, M. S. (2000, February). Britain's regional
            shopping centres: New urban forms? *Urban
            Studies* 37(2). *Infotrac: Expanded Academic ASAP*
            (Article A61862666). (14 Jan. 2001).

Other sources

24. Synchronous communications (MOOs/MUDs/LANs) sites
Begin with the name or alias of the author (if available); then list
either the type of communication (such as a personal interview) or, if
a synchronous conference, the title of the session, if given. Follow this
information with the site title (in italics), the full address (including
the proper protocol), and end with the date of access.

HUMANITIES Brin and Thomas. Personal interview. *Dare to Dream
            MOO.* telnet://moo.cmoo.com:9911 (15 May 2002).

SCIENCES   Brin and Thomas. (2002). Personal interview. *Dare
            to Dream MOO.* telnet://moo.cmoo.com:9911 (15 May
            2002).

25. Software   To cite from a software program or video game, give
the name (either individual or corporation), if provided, followed by
the name of the program or game (in italics). If applicable, and not
already included in the title of the program, include the version
number and all publication information, including the date of publication (if given; remember, the date will come after the author's
name in the sciences style). Note also that for sciences style, the version number is placed in parentheses, followed (in brackets) by a
phrase identifying the type of software cited. You need not provide
a date of access.

HUMANITIES Interplay Entertainment Corp. *Starfleet Command,
            Volume II: Empires at War.* Version 2.0.0.2.
            Irvine, CA: Interplay Entertainment Corp., 2000.

SCIENCES   Interplay Entertainment Corp. (2000). *Starfleet
            command, volume II: Empires at war.* (Version
            2.0.0.2) [Computer game]. Irvine, CA: Interplay
            Entertainment Corp.

56e Student paper excerpt, CGOS style

Cara McCauley wrote the following paper (its first and last pages are
shown here) for a first-year writing course at the College of DuPage
in Glen Ellyn, Illinois. She used CGOS guidelines for citing and documenting online sources in the humanities. The documentation of
print sources follows MLA guidelines.

First page of paper

McCauley 1

Cara McCauley
Professor J. Allen
English 103
15 May 2002

Freedom to Fight: Frederick Douglass
and the Civil War

Frederick Douglass was one of the greatest abolitionists in American history. He was an African American born into slavery but found a way to become educated at a time when such a thing was taboo for anyone of his race. By the age of twenty-one, he had bought his freedom, and he then made it his business to bring freedom to all other African Americans. Philip Foner and Yuval Taylor, editors of *Frederick Douglass: Selected Speeches and Writings*, note that, through his many speeches and publications, "Douglass changed American history. For, more than any other African-American, it was he who was responsible for the downfall of slavery, for the enlistment of men of his race in the Union army," and for helping the American people realize what few gains the Civil War had brought to blacks in the South (xi). Douglass's work for the antislavery movement, particularly during the Civil War, changed the face of the nation.

During the election year of 1860, Douglass campaigned for the Republican Abraham Lincoln because the Republicans were against the spread of slavery into the new territories, but when Lincoln won, many of the Southern states would not accept the results of the election; in 1860 and 1861, South Carolina, Georgia, Florida, Mississippi, Alabama, Louisiana, and Texas seceded from the Union to form the Confederate States of America (Thomas). As the secession movement progressed, Douglass saw only "one ray of hope for the cause--Lincoln's inauguration" (Foner and Taylor 432).

Citation of print source, with page number (MLA style)

Thesis

Citation of online article: no page number

List of works cited

Works Cited

"The Fight for Equal Rights: Black Soldiers in the Civil War." US National Archives and Records Administration. 1999. http://www.nara.gov/ education/teaching/usct/home.html (22 Apr. 2002).

Online article with no author named

Foner, Philip S., and Yuval Taylor, eds. *Frederick Douglass: Selected Speeches and Writings.* Chicago: Lawrence Hill-Chicago Review, 1999.

"Frederick Douglass." http://www.americancivilwar.com/ colored/frederick_douglass.html (24 Apr. 2002).

Library of Congress. "Frederick Douglass: Abolitionist Leader." *America's Story.* http://www.americaslibrary.gov/pages/ aa_douglass_leader_1.html (20 Apr. 2002).

Online reference article

"North Star." *The Revolutionary Era: African American Soldiers in the American Revolution.* http://memory.loc.gov/ammem/ aaohtml/exhibit/aopart2b.html (29 Apr. 2002).

Online article with no author named

Thomas, Sandra. "The Civil War Years." *A Biography of the Life of Frederick Douglass.* http://www.history.rochester.edu/class/douglass/ part4.html (29 Apr. 2002).

Chapter in online book

Glossaries

57. Glossary of Usage   58. Glossary of Grammatical Terms

57 Glossary of Usage

Listed in this glossary are words that are often confused *(affect/effect, elicit/illicit)*, misspelled *(alright, it's/its)*, or misused *(hopefully)*. Also listed are nonstandard words *(irregardless, theirself)* and colloquial expressions *(a lot, OK)* that should be avoided in formal writing. For an extensive list of commonly confused words and their definitions, see **33h.**

a, an   Use *an* before words that begin with a vowel sound (the vowels are *a, e, i, o,* and *u*): *an apple, an hour* (begins with silent *h*). Use *a* before words that begin with a consonant sound: *a planet, a yam, a ukelele, a house* (begins with pronounced *h*).

accept, except, expect   *Accept* is a verb: *She accepted the salary offer. Except* is usually a preposition: *Everyone has gone home except my boss. Expect* is a verb: *They expect to visit New Mexico on vacation.*

adapt, adopt   *Adapt* means "to adjust" and is used with the preposition *to*: *Some people adapt slowly to the work routine after college. Adopt* means "to take into a family" or "to take up and follow": *The couple adopted a three-year-old child. The company adopted a more aggressive policy.*

adverse, averse   *Adverse* is an adjective describing something as hostile, unfavorable, or difficult. *Averse* indicates opposition to something and usually takes the preposition *to*. *The bus driver was averse to driving in the adverse driving conditions.*

advice, advise   *Advice* is a noun: *Take my advice and don't start smoking. Advise* is a verb: *He advised his brother to stop smoking.*

affect, effect   In their most common uses, *affect* is a verb, and *effect* is a noun. To *affect* is to have an *effect* on something: *Pesticides can affect health. Pesticides have a bad effect on health. Effect,* however, can be used as a verb meaning "to bring about": *The administration hopes to effect new health care legislation. Affect* can also be used as a noun in psychology, meaning "a feeling or emotion."

aggravate   *Aggravate* is a verb meaning "to make worse." Avoid using *aggravate* as a synonym for "irritate," "annoy," or "exasperate." *My sister was being quite annoying, and her whining was only aggravating the situation.*

ain't   Slang for "am not," "is not," and "are not." Avoid.

all ready, already   *All ready* means "totally prepared": *The students were all ready for their final examination. Already* is an adverb meaning "by this time": *He has already written the report.*

all right, alright   *All right* is standard. *Alright* is nonstandard.

all together, altogether   *All together* is used to describe acting simultaneously: *As soon as the boss had presented the plan, the managers spoke up all together. Altogether* is an adverb meaning "totally," often used before an adjective: *His presentation was altogether impressive.*

allude, elude   *Allude* means "to refer to": *She alluded to his height. Elude* means "to avoid": *He eluded her criticism by leaving the room.*

allusion, illusion   The noun *allusion* means "reference": *Her allusion to his height made him uncomfortable.* The noun *illusion* means "false idea": *He had no illusions about being Mr. Universe.*

almost, most   Do not use *most* to mean *almost: Almost* [not *Most*] *all my friends are computer literate.*

alot, a lot of, lots of   *Alot* is nonstandard. *A lot of* and *lots of* are regarded by some as informal for *many* or *a great deal of: They have performed many research studies.*

aloud, allowed   *Aloud* is an adverb meaning "out loud": *She read her critique aloud. Allowed* is a form of the verb *allow: Employees are not allowed to participate in the competition.*

ambiguous, ambivalent   *Ambiguous* is used to describe a phrase or act with more than one meaning: *The ending of the movie is ambiguous; we don't know if the butler really committed the murder. Ambivalent* describes lack of certainty and the coexistence of opposing attitudes and feelings: *The committee is ambivalent about the proposal for restructuring the company.*

among, between   Use *between* for two items, *among* for three or more: *I couldn't decide between red or blue. I couldn't decide among red, blue, or green.*

amoral, immoral   *Amoral* can mean "neither moral nor immoral" or "not caring about right or wrong," whereas *immoral* means "morally wrong": *Some consider vegetarianism an amoral issue, but others believe eating meat is immoral.*

amount, number   *Amount* is used with uncountable expressions: *a large amount of money, work, or effort.* Number is used with countable plural expressions: *a large number of people, a number of attempts.* See **42b** ESL.

an   See *a.*

and   *And* should be used as a conjunction only, never to mean *to.* For example, not Try and find me but Try to find me.

ante-, anti-   *Ante-* is a prefix meaning "before," as in *anteroom. Anti-* means "against" or "opposite," as in *antiseptic* or *antifreeze.*

anxious, eager Avoid using these words interchangeably. *Anxious* should be used only if anxiety is involved, as a synonym for *nervous* or *worried*. *Eager* should be used to mean "keenly interested" or "looking forward" and is usually followed by an infinitive: *She was anxious about getting her shot and was eager to leave the doctor's office.*

any more, anymore *Any more* refers to quantity; *anymore* means "from now on": *He doesn't want any more pecan pie, because he doesn't like it anymore.*

anyone, any one *Anyone* is a singular indefinite pronoun meaning "anybody": *Can anyone help me? Any one* refers to one from a group and is usually followed by *of* + plural noun: *Any one* [as opposed to any two] *of the suggestions will be considered acceptable.*

anyplace The standard *anywhere* is preferable.

anyway, anywhere, nowhere; anyways, anywheres, nowheres *Anyway, anywhere,* and *nowhere* are standard forms. The others, ending in *-s,* are not.

apart, a part *Apart* is an adverb: *The old book fell apart.* "A part" is a noun phrase: *I'd like to be a part of that project.*

as, as if, like See *like.*

as regards, in regard to See *in regard to.*

assure, ensure, insure All three words mean "to make secure or certain," but only *assure* is used in the sense of making a promise: *He assured us everything would be fine. Ensure* and *insure* are interchangeable, but only *insure* is commonly used in the commercial or financial sense: *We wanted to ensure that the rate we paid to insure our car against theft would not change.*

at Avoid ending a question with *at:* <u>not</u> *Where's the library at?* <u>but</u> *Where's the library?*

awful Avoid using *awful* to mean "bad" or "extremely": <u>not</u> *He's awful late* <u>but</u> *He's extremely late.*

a while, awhile *A while* is a noun phrase: *a while ago; for a while. Awhile* is an adverb meaning "for some time": *They lived awhile in the wilderness.*

bad, badly *Bad* is an adjective, *badly* an adverb. Use *bad* after linking verbs (such as *am, is, become, seem*): *They felt bad after losing the match.* Use *badly* to modify a verb: *They played badly.*

bare, bear *Bare* is an adjective meaning "naked": the *bare* facts, a *bare*-faced lie. *Bear* is a noun (the animal) or a verb meaning "to carry" or "to endure": *He could not bear the pressure of losing.*

barely Avoid creating a double negative (such as *can't barely type*). *Barely* should always take a positive verb: *She can barely type. They could barely keep their eyes open.* See *hardly.*

because, because of *Because* is a subordinating conjunction used to introduce a dependent clause: *Because it was raining, we left early. Because of* is a two-word preposition: *We left early because of the rain.*

being as, being that Avoid. Use *because* instead: *Because* [not *Being as*] *I was tired, I didn't go to class.*

belief, believe *Belief* is a noun: *She has radical beliefs. Believe* is a verb: *He believes in an afterlife.*

beside, besides *Beside* is a preposition meaning "next to": *Sit beside me. Besides* is a preposition meaning "except for": *He has no assistants besides us. Besides* is also an adverb meaning "in addition": *I hate horror movies. Besides, there's a long line.*

better See *had better.*

between See *among.*

born, borne These are both past participle forms of the verb *bear,* but *born* has the sense of "given birth," while *borne* means "supported" or "endured": *I was born in 1980 in an ambulance on the way to the hospital. The weight of the arch is borne by two huge concrete pillars.*

breath, breathe The first word is a noun, the second a verb: *Take three deep breaths. Breathe in deeply.*

bring, take Use *bring* to suggest carrying something from a farther place to a nearer one, and *take* for any other transportation: *First bring me a cake from the store, and then we can take it to the party.*

bust *Bust* is nonstandard slang. Avoid using it as a verb or a form of *burst.*

but Avoid inserting *but* before *that* and *what* in instances where it does not belong: *I don't doubt that* [not *don't doubt but that*] *they will be on time.*

can, may *Can* should be used in reference to ability or capacity, while *may* is used to denote permission: *May I speak with you a moment? Can you hear me?* See **43b** ESL.

can't barely This expression is nonstandard. See *barely.*

can't hardly This expression is nonstandard. See *hardly.*

capitol, capital A *capitol* is a building where the legislature meets. *Capital* can refer to a city that is the seat of government: *The capitol is located within the capital. Capital* can also refer to the top of a column, and—as both noun and adjective—to wealth or to uppercase: *He admired the Corinthian capitals in the church aisle. He lost capital in the Enron crash. He made a large capital investment in a risky company.* Use a capital letter for a proper noun.

censor, censure The verb *censor* refers to editing or removing from public view. *Censure* means to criticize harshly. *The new film was censored for graphic content, and the director was censured by critics for his irresponsibility.*

cite, site, sight *Cite* means "to quote or mention"; *site* is a noun meaning "location"; *sight* is a noun meaning "view": *She cited the page number in her paper. They visited the original site of the abbey. The sight of the skyline from the plane produced applause from the passengers.*

compare to, compare with Use *compare to* when implying similarity: *They compared the director to Alfred Hitchcock.* Use *compare with* when examining similarities or differences: *She wrote an essay comparing Hitchcock with Orson Welles.*

complement, compliment As verbs, *complement* means "to complete or add to something," and *compliment* means "to make a flattering comment about someone or something": *The wine complemented the meal. The guests complimented the hostess on the fine dinner.* As nouns, the words have meanings associated with the verbs: *The wine was a fine complement to the meal. The guests paid the hostess a compliment.*

compose, comprise *Compose* means "to make up"; *comprise* means "to include": *The conference center is composed of twenty-five rooms. The conference center comprises twenty-five rooms.*

conscience, conscious *Conscience* is a noun meaning "awareness of right and wrong." *Conscious* is an adjective meaning "awake" or "aware." *Her conscience troubled her after the accident. The victim was still not conscious.*

continual, continuous *Continual* implies repetition; *continuous* implies lack of a pause: *The continual interruptions made the lecturer angry. Continuous rain for two hours stopped play.*

could care less This expression is often used but is regarded by some as nonstandard. In formal English, use it only with a negative: *They could not care less about their work.*

could of Incorrect usage. See *have*.

council, counsel A *council* is a group formed to consult, deliberate, or make decisions. *Counsel* is advice or guidance. *The council was called together to help give counsel to the people. Counsel* can also be a verb: *We counseled the students to withdraw from the course.*

credible, creditable, credulous *Credible* means "believable": *The jury found the accused's alibi to be credible and so acquitted her. Creditable* means "deserving of credit": *A B+ grade attests to a creditable performance. Credulous* means "easily taken in or deceived": *Only a child would be so credulous as to believe that the streets are paved with gold.* See also *incredible, incredulous.*

criteria, criterion *Criteria* is the plural form of the singular noun *criterion: There are many criteria for a successful essay. One criterion is sentence clarity.*

curricula, curriculum *Curricula* is the plural form of *curriculum.* All the departments have well-thought-out curricula, but the English Department has the best curriculum.*

custom, customs, costume All three words are nouns. *Custom* means "habitual practice or tradition": *a family custom. Customs* refers to taxes on imports or to the procedures for inspecting items entering a country: *go through customs at the airport.* A *costume* is "a style of dress": *a Halloween costume.*

dairy, diary The first word is associated with cows and milk, the second with daily journal writing.

desert, dessert *Desert* can be pronounced two ways and can be a noun with the stress on the first syllable (*the Mojave Desert*) or a verb with the stress on the second syllable: *When did he desert his family?* The noun *desert* means "a dry, often sandy, environment." The verb *desert* means "to abandon." *Dessert* (with stress on the second syllable) is the sweet course at the end of a meal.

device, devise *Device* is a noun: *He said they needed a device that could lift a car. Devise* is a verb: *She began to devise a solution to the problem.*

differ from, differ with To *differ from* means "to be unlike": *Lions differ from tigers in several ways, despite being closely related.* To *differ with* means to "disagree with": *They differ with each other on many topics but are still good friends.*

different from, different than Standard usage is *different from: She looks different from her sister.* However, *different than* appears frequently in speech and informal writing, particularly when *different from* would require more words: *My writing is different than* [in place of *different from what*] *it was last semester.*

discreet, discrete *Discreet* means "tactful": *Be discreet when you talk about your boss. Discrete* means "separate": *They are researching five discrete topics.*

disinterested, uninterested *Disinterested* means "impartial or unbiased": *The mediator was hired to make a disinterested settlement. Uninterested* means "lacking in interest": *He seemed uninterested in his job.*

dive, dived Be sure to use *dived* for the past tense of the verb *dive. Dove* is nonstandard.

do, due *Do* is a verb. Do not write "*Do* to his absences, he lost his job"; instead use the two-word preposition *due to* or *because of.*

drag, dragged Use *dragged* for the past tense of the verb *drag. Drug* is nonstandard.

drown, drowned The past tense of the verb *drown* is *drowned; drownded* is not a word: *He almost drowned yesterday.*

due to the fact that, owing to the fact that Wordy. Use *because* instead: *They stopped the game because* [not *due to the fact that*] *it was raining.*

each, every These are singular pronouns; use them with a singular verb. See also **21i** and **22d**.

each other, one another Use *each other* with two; use *one another* with more than two: *The twins love each other. The triplets all love one another.*

eager See *anxious.*

effect See *affect.*

e.g. Use *for example* or *for instance* in place of this Latin abbreviation.

either, neither *Neither* is the negative form of *either.* Always use *nor* with *neither. Either Jill or Bob will be here tomorrow, but neither of them will stay long. Neither Joe nor Ed has a reason to come.*

elicit, illicit *Elicit* means "to get or draw out": *The police tried in vain to elicit information from the suspect's accomplice. Illicit* is an adjective meaning "illegal": *Their illicit deals landed them in prison.*

elude See *allude.*

emigrate, immigrate *Emigrate from* means "to leave a country"; *immigrate to* means "to move to another country": *They emigrated from Ukraine and immigrated to the United States.* The noun forms *emigrant* and *immigrant* are derived from the verbs.

eminent, imminent *Eminent* means "well known and noteworthy": *an eminent lawyer. Imminent* means "about to happen": *an imminent disaster.*

enough Refrain from overuse of *enough: We were lucky* [not *We were lucky enough*] *to survive.*

ensure See *assure.*

enthused Avoid *enthused* as nonstandard and use *enthusiastic* instead: *The audience became enthusiastic* [not *enthused*] *when the band came back for an encore.*

etc. This abbreviation for the Latin *et cetera* means "and others." Do not let a list trail off with *etc.*: not *They took a tent, a sleeping bag, etc.* but *They took a tent, a sleeping bag, cooking utensils, and a stove.*

every, each See *each.*

everyday, every day *Everyday* (one word) is an adjective meaning "usual": *Their everyday routine is to break for lunch at 12:30. Every day* (two words) is an adverbial expression of frequency: *I get up early every day.*

except, expect See *accept.*

explicit, implicit *Explicit* means "direct": *She gave explicit instructions. Implicit* means "implied": *A tax increase is implicit in the proposal.*

farther, further Both words can refer to distance: *She lives farther (further) from the campus than I do. Further* also means "additional" or "additionally": *The management offered further incentives. Further, the union proposed new work rules.*

female, male   Use these words as adjectives, not as nouns in place of *man* and *woman*: *There are only three women* [not *females*] *in my class. We are discussing female conversational traits.*

few, a few   For the distinction, see **46c** ESL.

fewer, less   Formal usage demands *fewer* with plural countable nouns *(fewer holidays)*, *less* with uncountable nouns *(less sunshine)*. However, in informal usage, *less* with plural nouns commonly occurs, especially with *than: less than six items, less than ten miles, fifty words or less.* In formal usage, *fewer* is preferred.

first, firstly   Avoid *firstly, secondly*, and so on when listing reasons or examples. Instead, use *first, second.*

flammable, inflammable, nonflammable   Both *flammable* and *inflammable* mean the same thing: able to be ignited easily. *Nonflammable* means "unable to be ignited easily." *Dry wood is flammable* <u>or</u> *Dry wood is inflammable. Asbestos is nonflammable.*

flaunt, flout   *Flaunt* means "to show [something] off" or "to display in a proud or boastful manner." *Flout* means "to defy or to show scorn for": *When she flaunted her jewels, she flouted good taste.*

former, latter   These terms should be used only in reference to a list of two people or things: *We bought lasagna and ice cream, the former for dinner and the latter for dessert.* For more than two items, use *first* and *last: I had some pasta, a salad, and ice cream; though the first was very filling, I still had room for the last.*

get married to, marry   These expressions can be used interchangeably: *He will get married to his fiancée next week. She will marry her childhood friend next month.* The noun form is *marriage: Their marriage has lasted thirty years.*

go, say   Avoid replacing the verb *say* with *go*, as this is nonstandard usage: *Jane says* [not *goes*] *"I'm tired of this game."*

good, well   *Good* is an adjective; *well* is an adverb: *If you want to write well, you must use good grammar.* See **23a.**

got   Avoid using *got* in place of the verb *have* to refer to ownership: *I have* [not *got*] *a brown dog. John has a black one.*

had better   Include *had* in Standard English, although it is often omitted in advertising and in speech: *You had better* [not *You better*] *try harder.*

hanged, hung   Both words are the past tense of *hang*; however, *hanged* should be used only when referring to a method of execution, and *hung* is used for all other meanings: *The rope still hung from the gallows. The executioner hanged five men there in one year.*

hardly   This is a negative word. Do not use it with another negative: <u>not</u> *He couldn't hardly walk* <u>but</u> *He could hardly walk.*

have, of   Use *have*, not *of*, after *should, could, may, might,* and *must*: *They should have* [not *should of*] *appealed.* See **20d**.

height   Note the spelling and pronunciation: <u>not</u> *heighth*.

heroin, heroine   Do not confuse these words. *Heroin* is a drug; *heroine* is a brave woman. *Hero* may be used for an admirable person of either sex.

hisself   Nonstandard; instead use *himself*.

hopefully   This word is an adverb meaning "in a hopeful manner" or "with a hopeful attitude": *Hopefully, she e-mailed her résumé.* Avoid using *hopefully* in place of *I hope that*: <u>not</u> *Hopefully, she will get the job* <u>but</u> *I hope that she will get the job.*

illicit, elicit   See *elicit*.

illusion, allusion   See *allusion*.

immigrate, emigrate   See *emigrate*.

imminent, eminent   See *eminent*.

immoral   See *amoral*.

implicit, explicit   See *explicit*.

imply, infer   *Imply* means "to suggest in an indirect way": *He implied that further layoffs were unlikely. Infer* means "to guess" or "to draw a conclusion": *I inferred that the company was doing well.*

in, into   The preposition *in* indicates location, while *into* indicates movement or change: *Billy thought his mother was in the garage, so he went into the kitchen to take a cookie.* Avoid using *into* as a synonym for "interested in": *I am really into this movie.*

incredible, incredulous   *Incredible* means "difficult to believe": *The violence of the storm was incredible. Incredulous* means "skeptical, unable to believe": *They were incredulous when he told them about his daring exploits in the whitewater rapids.*

infamous   *Infamous* is an adjective meaning "notorious."   Avoid using it as a synonym for "not famous": *Blackbeard's many exploits as a pirate made him infamous along the American coast.*

inflammable   See *flammable*.

in regard to, as regards   Use one or the other. Do not use the nonstandard *in regards to*.

install, instill   To *install* is to "set in position for use" or "establish." To *instill* is to "implant": *She would not have been able to install the fixture if her parents hadn't instilled in her a sense of craftsmanship.*

insure   See *assure*.

irregardless   Nonstandard; instead use *regardless*: *He selected a major regardless of the preparation it would give him for a career.*

it's, its The apostrophe in *it's* signals not a possessive but a contraction of *it is* or *it has*. *Its* is the possessive form of the pronoun *it*: *The city government agency has produced its final report. It's available upon request.* See also **28f**.

kind, sort, type In the singular, use each of these with *this* and a singular noun: *this type of book*. Use in the plural with *these* and a plural noun: *these kinds of books*.

kind of, sort of Do not use these to mean "somewhat" or "a little." *The pace of the baseball game was somewhat [not kind of] slow.*

knew, new *Knew* is the past tense of the verb *know. New* is an adjective meaning "not old."

later, latter *Later* is used in reference to time; *latter* refers to the second of two named items. See *former, latter*.

leave, let Avoid interchanging these verbs. *Leave* means "depart" and *let* means "permit" or "allow."

lend, loan *Lend* is a verb, and *loan* is ordinarily used as a noun: *Our cousins offered to lend us some money, but we refused the loan.*

less, fewer See *fewer*.

lie, lay Be sure not to confuse these verbs. *Lie* does not take a direct object; *lay* does. See **20c**.

like, as, as if In formal usage, *as* and *as if* are subordinating conjunctions and introduce dependent clauses: *She walks as her father does. She looks as if she could eat a big meal. Like* is a preposition and is followed by a noun or pronoun, not by a clause: *She looks like her father.* In speech, however, and increasingly in writing, *like* is often used where formal usage dictates *as* or *as if*: *She walks like her father does. He looks like he needs a new suit.*

likely, liable *Likely* means "probably going to," while *liable* means "at risk of" and is generally used to describe something negative: *Eddie plays the guitar so well he's likely to start a band. If he keeps playing that way, he's liable to break a string. Liable* also means "responsible": *The guitar manufacturer cannot be held liable.*

literally Avoid overuse: *literally* is an adverb meaning "actually" or "word for word" and should not be used in conjunction with figurative expressions such as *she was driving me crazy* or *he was bouncing off the walls. Literally* should be used only when the words describe exactly what is happening: *He was so scared his face literally went white.*

loan See *lend, loan*.

loose, lose *Loose* is an adjective meaning "not tight": *This jacket is comfortable because it is so loose. Lose* is a verb (the past tense form and past participle are *lost*): *Many people lose their jobs in a recession.*

lots of, alot, a lot of See *alot.*

man, mankind Avoid using these terms, as they are gender-specific. Instead, use *people, human beings, humankind, humanity,* or *men and women.*

marital, martial *Marital* is associated with marriage, *martial* with war.

may See *can.*

may be, maybe *May be* consists of a modal verb followed by the base form of the verb *be; maybe* is an adverb meaning "perhaps." If you can replace the expression with *perhaps,* make it one word: *They may be there already, or maybe they got caught in traffic.*

may of Incorrect usage. See *have.*

media, medium *Media* is the plural form of *medium: Television and radio are both useful communication media, but his favorite medium is the written word.*

might of Incorrect usage. See *have.*

most, almost See *almost.*

must of Incorrect usage. See *have.*

myself Use only as a reflexive pronoun *(I told them myself)* or as an intensive pronoun *(I myself told them).* Do not use *myself* as a subject pronoun: not *My sister and myself won* but *My sister and I won.*

neither See *either.*

nonflammable See *flammable.*

nowadays All one word. Be sure to include the final -*s.*

nowhere, nowheres See *anyway.*

number, amount See *amount.*

of a Do not use *of a* after an adjective: not *She's not that good of a player* but *She's not that good a player.*

off, off of Use only *off,* not *off of: She drove the car off* [not *off of*] *the road.*

oftentimes Do not use. Prefer *often.*

OK, O.K., okay Reserve these forms for informal speech and writing. Choose another word in a formal context: not *Her performance was OK* but *Her performance was satisfactory.*

one another See *each other.*

oral, verbal These two adjectives are often interchanged. Strictly speaking, *oral* should be used to mean "spoken," while *verbal* is used more broadly to mean "pertaining to words": *The telephone is used for oral communication. Fax machines and e-mail are modern forms of verbal communication technology.*

owing to the fact that See *due to the fact that.*

passed, past *Passed* is a past tense verb form: *They passed the deli on the way to work. He passed his exam. Past* can be a noun *(in the past)*, an adjective *(in past times)*, or a preposition *(She walked past the bakery)*.

people, persons Use *people* to refer to a general group, and *persons* to refer to a collection of individuals: *Although many people saw the crime happen, it will still be hard to find the person or persons responsible.*

personal, personnel *Personal* is an adjective meaning "individual," while *personnel* is a noun referring to employees or staff: *It is my personal belief that a company's personnel should be treated like family.*

phenomena, phenomenon *Phenomena* is the plural form of the noun *phenomenon: Outer space is full of celestial phenomena, one spectacular phenomenon being the Milky Way.*

plus Do not use *plus* as a coordinating conjunction or a transitional expression. Use *and* or *moreover* instead: *He was promoted, and* [not *plus*] *he received a bonus.* Use *plus* as a preposition meaning "in addition to": *His salary plus his dividends placed him in a high tax bracket.*

precede, proceed *Precede* means "to go or occur before": *The Roaring Twenties preceded the Great Depression. Proceed* means "to go ahead": *After you pay the fee, proceed to the examination room.*

pretty Avoid using *pretty* as an intensifying adverb. Instead use *really, very, rather,* or *quite: The stew tastes very* [not *pretty*] *good.* Often, however, the best solution is to avoid using any adverb: *The stew tastes good.*

principal, principle *Principal* is a noun *(the principal of a school)* or an adjective meaning "main" or "most important": *His principal motive was monetary gain. Principle* is a noun meaning "standard or rule": *He always acts on his principles.*

quite, quiet Do not confuse the adverb *quite,* meaning "very," with the adjective *quiet* ("still" or "silent"): *We were all quite relieved when the audience became quiet.*

quote, quotation *Quote* is a verb. Do not use it as a noun. Use *quotation: The quotation* [not *quote*] *from Walker tells the reader a great deal.*

real, really *Real* is an adjective; *really* is an adverb. Do not use *real* as an intensifying adverb: *She acted really* [not *real*] *well.*

reason is because Avoid *the reason is because.* Instead, use *the reason is that* or rewrite the sentence. See **19f.**

regardless See *irregardless.*

respectable, respectful, respective *Respectable* means "presentable, worthy of respect": *Wear some respectable shoes to your interview. Respectful* means "polite or deferential": *Parents want their children to be respectful to adults. Respective* means "particular" or "individual": *The friends of the bride and the groom sat in their respective seats in the church.*

respectfully, respectively *Respectfully* means "showing respect": *He bowed respectfully when the queen entered. Respectively* refers to items in a list and means "in the order mentioned": *Horses and birds gallop and fly, respectively.*

rise, raise *Rise* is an intransitive verb: *She rises early every day. Raise* is a transitive verb: *We raised alfalfa last summer.* See **20c.**

sale, sell *Sale* is a noun: *The sale of the house has been postponed. Sell* is a verb: *They are still trying to sell their house.*

set, sit *Set* should not be used in place of *sit,* as *set* must always take an object. *He was sitting in his favorite chair* (<u>not</u> *He was setting in his favorite chair*). *When she came in, she sat down* (<u>not</u> *When she came in, she set down*). Conversely, *sit* should not be used in place of *set: Set the bags down there* (<u>not</u> *Sit the bags down there*). See **20c.**

should of Incorrect usage. See *have.*

since Use this subordinating conjunction only when time or reason is clear: *Since you insist on helping, I'll let you paint this bookcase.* Unclear: *Since he got a new job, he has been happy.*

site, sight, cite See *cite.*

someplace Prefer the standard *somewhere.*

sometimes, sometime, some time The adverb *sometimes* means "occasionally": *He sometimes prefers to eat lunch at his desk.* The adverb *sometime* means "at an indefinite time": *I read that book sometime last year.* The noun phrase *some time* consists of the noun *time* modified by the quantity word *some: After working for Honda, I spent some time in Brazil.*

sort, type, kind See *kind.*

sort of, kind of See *kind of.*

stationary, stationery *Stationary* is an adjective meaning "not moving" (*a stationary vehicle*); *stationery* is a noun referring to the paper on which you write letters.

stayed, stood Do not confuse these forms. *Stayed* is the past tense form of *stay; stood* is the past tense form of *stand.*

supposedly Use this, not *supposably: She is supposedly a great athlete.*

take See *bring.*

taught, thought Do not confuse these verb forms. *Taught* is the past tense and past participle form of *teach; thought* is the past tense and past participle form of *think: The students thought that their professor had not taught essay organization.*

than, then *Then* is a time word; *than* must be preceded by a comparative form: *bigger than, more interesting than.*

that See *who.*

their, there, they're   *Their* is a pronoun indicating possession; *there* indicates place or is used as a filler in the subject position in a sentence; *they're* is the contracted form of *they are*: *They're over there, guarding their luggage.*

theirself, theirselves, themself   Nonstandard; instead use *themselves.*

threat, treat   These words have different meanings: *She gave the children some cookies as a treat. The threat of an earthquake was alarming.*

thru   Nonstandard. Use *through.*

thusly   Incorrect form of *thus.*

to, too, two   Do not confuse these words. *To* is a sign of the infinitive and a common preposition; *too* is an adverb meaning "also"; *two* is the number: *She is too smart to agree to report to two bosses.*

undoubtedly   This is the correct word, <u>not</u> *undoubtably.*

uninterested, disinterested   See *disinterested.*

unique   The adjective *unique* means "the only one of its kind" and therefore should not be used with qualifying adjectives like "very" or "most": *His recipe for chowder is unique* [not *most unique* or *quite unique*]. See **23h.**

used to, get (become) used to   These expressions share the common form *used to.* But the first, expressing a past habit that no longer exists, is followed by the base form of a verb: *He used to wear his hair long.* (Note that after *not,* the form is *use to: He did not use to have a beard.*) In the expression *get (become) used to, used to* means "accustomed to" and is followed by a noun or an *-ing* form: *She couldn't get used to driving on the left when she was in England.* See also **45f** ESL.

verbal   See *oral.*

way, ways   Use *way* to mean "distance": *He has a way to go. Ways* in this context is nonstandard.

wear, were, we're, where   *Wear* is a verb; *were* is a past tense form of *be; we're* is a contraction of *we are; where* is a relative pronoun, a subordinating conjunction, or a question word. *Hikers wear bells. Bears were roaming. We're afraid. I don't know where the bears are.*

weather, whether   *Weather* is a noun; *whether* is a conjunction: *The weather will determine whether we go on the picnic.*

well, good   See *good.*

who, whom, which, that   See **24a** and **24g.**

whose, who's   *Whose* is a possessive pronoun: *Whose goal was that? Who's* is a contraction of *who is* or *who has: Who's the player whose pass was caught? Who's got the ball?*

would of   Incorrect usage. See *have.*

your, you're   *Your* is a pronoun used to show possession. *You're* is a contraction of *you are: You're wearing your new shoes today, aren't you?*

58   Glossary of Grammatical Terms

absolute phrase   A phrase consisting of a noun followed by a participle (*-ing* or past participle) and modifying an entire sentence: *Flags flapping in the wind,* the stadium looked bleak. **16d.**

acronym   A pronounceable word formed from the initials of an abbreviation: *NATO, MADD, NOW.* **32b.**

active voice   Attribute of a verb when its grammatical subject performs the action that the verb describes: The dog *ate* the cake. **20l, 36c.** See also *passive voice.*

adjective   The part of speech that modifies a noun or pronoun: A *happy* child. She is *happy.* **16a, 23.** See also *comparative; coordinate adjective; superlative.*

adjective clause   A dependent clause beginning with a relative pronoun (*who, whom, whose, which,* or *that*) and modifying a noun or pronoun: The writer *who won the prize* was elated. Also called a *relative clause.* **16e, 24.**

adverb   The part of speech that modifies a verb, an adjective, or another adverb. Many adverbs end in *-ly:* She ran *quickly.* He is *really* successful. The children were *well* liked. **16a, 23.** See also *comparative; conjunctive adverb; frequency adverb; superlative.*

adverb clause   A dependent clause that modifies a verb, an adjective, or an adverb and begins with a subordinating conjunction: He left early *because he was tired.* **16e, 18c, 19g, 26c.**

agent   The person or thing doing the action described by a verb in the active voice: *His sister* won the marathon. **20l, 36c.**

agreement   The grammatical match in person, number, and gender between a verb and its subject or between a pronoun and its antecedent (the word the pronoun refers to): The *benefits continue; they are* pleasing. The *benefit continues; it is* pleasing. **21, 22d.**

antecedent   The noun that a pronoun refers to: *My son who* lives nearby found a *kitten. It* was black and white. **22c, 22d, 24a.**

appositive phrase   A phrase occurring next to a noun and used to describe it: His father, *a factory worker,* is running for office. **16d, 22a, 26d.**

article   *A, an* (indefinite articles), or *the* (definite article). Also called a *determiner.* **42c ESL, 42d ESL, 42e ESL.**

aspect   Nature of the relationship between the action of a verb and time. Aspects are perfect, progressive, and perfect progressive. **20a, 20e.**

auxiliary verb   A verb that joins with another verb to form a complete verb. Auxiliary verbs are forms of *do, be,* and *have,* as well as the modal auxiliary verbs. **20d.** See also *complete verb; modal auxiliary verb.*

base form   The dictionary form of a verb, used in an infinitive after *to: see, eat, go, be.* **20a.**

clause A group of words that includes a subject and a verb. A clause is not necessarily a complete sentence. **16b, 16e, 16f.** See also *dependent clause; independent clause.*

cliché An overused, predictable expression: *as cool as a cucumber.* **39g.**

collective noun A noun naming a collection of people or things that are regarded as a unit: *team, jury, family.* For agreement with collective nouns, see **21g, 22d.**

comma splice The error that results when two independent clauses are incorrectly joined with only a comma. **18g.**

common noun A noun that does not name a unique person, place, or thing. **16a, 42a ESL.** See also *proper noun.*

comparative The form of an adjective or adverb used to compare two people or things: *bigger, more interesting.* **23h.** See also *superlative.*

complement A *subject complement* is a word or group of words used after a linking verb to refer to and describe the subject: Harry looks *happy.* An *object complement* is a word or group of words used after a direct object to complete its meaning: They call him a *liar.* **16c, 21d.**

complete verb All the words of a verb phrase that together indicate person, number, tense, and aspect. Some verb forms, such as *-ing* (present) participles and past participles, are nonfinite verbs (see *finite verb*) and require auxiliary verbs showing person, number, and tense in order to become complete verbs. *Going* and *seen* are not complete or finite verbs; *are going, has been seen,* and *should have been seen* are complete. **18d, 20a, 20d.**

complex sentence A sentence that has one independent clause and one or more dependent clauses: *He wept when he won the marathon.* **16f.**

compound adjective An adjective formed of two or more words often connected with hyphens: a *well-constructed* house. **23d, 33j.**

compound-complex sentence A sentence that has at least two independent clauses and one or more dependent clauses: *She works in Los Angeles, but her husband works in San Diego, where they both live.* **16f.**

compound noun A noun formed of two or more words: *toothbrush, merry-go-round.* **16a, 33j.**

compound predicate A predicate consisting of two or more verbs and their objects, complements, and modifiers: He *whistles and sings in the morning.* **16c, 18e, 19h.**

compound sentence A sentence that has two or more independent clauses: *She works in Los Angeles, but her husband works in San Diego.* **16f.**

compound subject A subject consisting of two or more nouns or pronouns and their modifiers: *My uncle and my aunt* are leaving soon. **16c, 21h, 22a.**

conditional clause   A clause introduced by *if* or *unless*, expressing conditions of fact, prediction, or speculation: *If we earned more*, we would spend more. **20k.**

conjunction   The part of speech used to link words, phrases, or clauses. **16a, 16e, 21h, 26b.** See also *coordinating conjunction; correlative conjunctions; subordinating conjunction.*

conjunctive adverb   A transitional expression used to link two independent clauses. Some common conjunctive adverbs are *moreover, however,* and *furthermore.* **5e, 16a, 16e, 26e, 37c.**

connotation   The meanings and associations suggested by a word, as distinct from the word's denotation, or dictionary meaning. **39c.**

contraction   The shortened form that results when an apostrophe replaces one or more letters: *can't* (for *cannot*), *he's* (for *he is* or *he has*), *they're* (for *they are*). **28d.**

coordinate adjective   One of two or more evaluative adjectives modifying the same noun or pronoun. When coordinate adjectives appear in a series, their order can be reversed, and they can be separated by *and*. Commas are used between coordinate adjectives: the *comfortable, expensive car*. **23f, 26g.**

coordinating conjunction   The seven coordinating conjunctions are *and, but, or, nor, so, for,* and *yet*. They connect sentence elements that are similar in type and equal in weight: He couldn't call, *but* he wrote a letter. **16a, 16e, 26b, 37c.**

coordination   The connection of two or more ideas to give each one equal emphasis: *Sue worked after school,* so *she didn't have time to jog.* **37c.**

correlative conjunctions   A pair of conjunctions joining equivalent elements. The most common correlative conjunctions are *either . . . or, neither . . . nor, both . . . and,* and *not only . . . but also: Neither* my sister *nor* I could find the concert hall. **16a, 19j.**

countable noun   A common noun that has a plural form and can be used after a plural quantity word (such as *many* or *three*): one *book*, three *stores*, many *children*. **42a ESL, 42e ESL.**

dangling modifier   A modifier that fails to modify the noun or pronoun it is intended to modify: not *Turning the corner*, the lights went out but *Turning the corner, we* saw the lights go out. **19c.**

demonstrative pronoun   The four demonstrative pronouns are *this, that, these,* and *those: That* is my glass. **21j.**

denotation   A word's dictionary meaning. See also *connotation.* **39b, 39c.**

dependent clause   A clause that cannot stand alone as a complete sentence and needs to be attached to an independent clause. A dependent clause begins with a subordinating word such as *because, if, when, although, who, which,* or *that: When it rains,* we can't take the children outside. **16e, 26c, 37c.**

diction Choice of appropriate words and tone. **33h, 39.**

direct object The person or thing that receives the action of a verb: They ate *cake* and *ice cream*. **16c, 44c** ESL. See also *transitive verb; voice*.

direct quotation A person's words reproduced exactly and placed in quotation marks: *"I won't be home until noon,"* she said. **19d, 29b, 44d** ESL, **50h.**

double negative The use of two negative words in the same sentence: He does *not* know *nothing*. This usage is nonstandard and should be avoided: *He does not know anything. He knows nothing.* **23g.**

ellipsis Omission of words from a quotation, indicated by three dots: "I pledge allegiance to the flag . . . and to the republic for which it stands. . . ." **30e, 50h.**

etymology The origin of a word. **39b.**

euphemism A word or phrase used to disguise literal meaning: She is *in the family way* [meaning "pregnant"]. **39g.**

faulty predication The error that results when subject and verb do not go together logically: not The *decrease* in stolen cars *has diminished* in the past year but The *number* of stolen cars *has decreased* in the past year. **19e.**

figurative language The use of unusual comparisons or other devices to draw attention to a specific meaning. See *metaphor; simile*. **7f, 39e.**

filler subject *It* or *there* used in the subject position of a clause, followed by a form of *be: There are* two elm trees on the corner. **21e, 36b, 46g** ESL.

finite verb A verb form that indicates person, number, and tense. *Sing* and *sang* are finite verbs; *singing, sung*, and *to sing* are not. **16a.**

first person The person speaking or writing: *I* or *we*. **22a.**

fragment A group of words that is punctuated as if it were a sentence but is grammatically incomplete because it lacks a subject or a predicate or begins with a subordinating word: *Because it was a sunny day.* **18a–18f.**

frequency adverb An adverb that expresses time (such as *often, always*, or *sometimes*). It can be the first word in a sentence or be used between the subject and the main verb, after an auxiliary verb, or as the last word in a sentence. **23e.**

fused sentence See *run-on sentence*.

gender Classification of a noun or pronoun as masculine (*Uncle John, he*), feminine (*Ms. Torez, she*), or neuter (*book, it*). **22a, 46h** ESL.

generic noun A noun referring to a general class or type of person or object: A *student* has to write many *papers*. **22d.**

gerund The *-ing* verb form used as a noun: *Walking* is good for the health. **16d, 21f, 43d** ESL, **43e** ESL. See also *verbal*.

helping verb See *auxiliary verb*.

homonym Word that is pronounced the same as another word but has a different meaning: *bear* (animal), *bear* (carry), *bare* (naked). **33h.**

imperative mood Verb mood used to give a command: *Follow* me. **16a, 16b.**

indefinite pronoun A pronoun that refers to a nonspecific person or thing: *anybody, something*. **21i, 22d.**

independent clause A clause that has a subject and predicate and is not introduced by a subordinating word. An independent clause can function as a complete sentence: *Birds sing. The old man was singing a song. Hailing a cab, the woman used a silver whistle.* **16e, 27b, 37c.**

indicative mood Verb mood used to ask questions or make statements. It is the most common mood. **16a, 16b.**

indirect object The person or thing to whom or to which, or for whom or for which, an action is performed. It comes between the verb and the direct object: He gave his *sister* some flowers. **16c, 44c** ESL. See also *transitive verb*.

indirect question A question reported by a speaker or writer, not enclosed in quotation marks: They asked *if we would help them*. **19d, 44d** ESL.

indirect quotation A description or paraphrase of the words of another speaker or writer, integrated into a writer's own sentence and not enclosed in quotation marks: He said *that they were making money*. **19d, 44d** ESL, **50h.**

infinitive The base form, or dictionary form, of a verb, preceded by *to*: *to see, to smile*. **16d, 43c** ESL, **43e** ESL.

infinitive phrase An infinitive with its objects, complements, or modifiers: *To wait for hours* is unpleasant. He tries hard *to be punctual*. **16d.**

intensive pronoun A pronoun ending in *-self* or *-selves* and used to emphasize its antecedent: They *themselves* will not attend. **22h.**

interjection The part of speech that expresses emotion and is able to stand alone: *Aha! Wow!* Interjections are seldom appropriate in academic writing. **16a.**

interrogative pronoun A pronoun that introduces a direct or indirect question: *Who* is that? I don't know *what* you want. **21l, 22i.**

intransitive verb A verb that does not take a direct object: Exciting events *have occurred*. He *fell*. **16c, 20a, 20l.** See also *transitive verb*.

inverted word order The presence of the verb before the subject in a sentence; used in questions or for emphasis: *Do you expect* an award? Not only *does she do* gymnastics, but she also wins awards. **16c, 21e, 36b.**

irregular verb A verb that does not form its past tense and past participle with *-ed: sing, sang, sung; grow, grew, grown.* **20b.**

linking verb A verb connecting a subject to its complement. Typical linking verbs are *be, become, seem,* and *appear:* He *seems* angry. A linking verb is intransitive; it does not take a direct object. **16c, 22a, 23c.**

main verb The part of a verb that carries meaning. It can be a finite verb (*drives, drove*) or a form occurring after auxiliaries: would have been *driving.* **16a, 20a, 20d.**

mental activity verb A verb not used in a tense showing progressive aspect: *prefer, want, understand:* <u>not</u> He *is wanting to leave* <u>but</u> He *wants* to leave. **20e.**

metaphor A figure of speech implying a comparison but not stating it directly: a *gale* of laughter. **7f, 39e.**

misplaced modifier An adverb (particularly *only* and *even*) or a descriptive phrase or clause positioned in such a way that it modifies the wrong word or words: <u>not</u> She showed the ring to her sister *that her aunt gave her* <u>but</u> She showed her sister the ring *that her aunt gave her.* **19b.**

mixed structure An error involving a sentence with two or more types of structures that clash grammatically: *By doing* her homework at the last minute *caused* Meg to make many mistakes. **19a, 19f.**

modal auxiliary verb The nine modal auxiliaries are *will, would, can, could, shall, should, may, might,* and *must.* They are followed by the base form of a verb: *will go, would believe.* Modal auxiliaries do not change form. **20d, 43b** ESL.

modifier A word or words used to describe another noun, adverb, verb, phrase, or clause: He is a *happy* man. He is smiling *happily.* **23.**

mood The mood of a verb tells whether the verb states a fact (*indicative:* She *goes* to school); gives a command (*imperative: Come* back soon); or expresses a condition, wish, or request (*subjunctive:* I wish you *were* not leaving). **16a, 20a, 20k.** See also *imperative mood; indicative mood; subjunctive mood.*

nonrestrictive phrase or clause A phrase or clause that adds extra or nonessential information to a sentence and is set off with commas: His report, *which he gave to his boss yesterday,* received enthusiastic praise. **24d, 26d.**

noun The part of speech that names a person, place, thing, or idea. Nouns are proper or common and, if common, countable or uncountable. **16a, 32a, 42a** ESL. See also *collective noun; common noun; compound noun; countable noun; generic noun; noun clause; proper noun; uncountable noun.*

noun clause A dependent clause that functions as a noun: I like *what you do*. **16e**.

number The form of a noun or pronoun that indicates whether it is singular (one person, place, thing, or idea) or plural (more than one). **21a, 22d**.

object of preposition The noun or pronoun (along with its modifiers) that follows a preposition: on *the beach*. **16d, 45e** ESL.

paragraph A group of sentences set off in a text, usually on one topic. **5, 10g**.

parallelism The use of coordinate structures that have the same grammatical form: She likes *swimming* and *playing* tennis. **5e, 19j**.

participle phrase A phrase beginning with an *-ing* verb form or a past participle: The woman *wearing a green skirt* is my sister. *Baffled by the puzzle*, he gave up. **16d, 19c**. See also *verbal*.

particle A word (frequently a preposition or adverb) that combines with a verb to form a phrasal verb, a verb with an idiomatic meaning: get *over*, take *after*. **45d** ESL.

passive voice Attribute of a verb when its grammatical subject is the receiver of the action that the verb describes: The book *was written* by my professor. **20l, 36c**. See also *active voice*.

past participle A verb form that in regular verbs ends with *-ed*. The past participle needs an auxiliary verb or verbs to function as the complete verb of a clause: *has chosen, was cleaned, might have been told*. The past participle can function alone as an adjective. **20a, 20b, 20d, 20h, 43f** ESL.

perfect progressive tense forms Verb tenses that show actions in progress up to a specific point in present, past, or future time. For active voice verbs, use forms of the auxiliary *have been* followed by the *-ing* form of the verb: *has/have been living, had been living, will have been living*. **20e**.

perfect tense forms Verb tenses that show actions completed by present, past, or future time. For active voice verbs, use forms of the auxiliary *have* followed by the past participle of the verb: *has/have arrived, had arrived, will have arrived*. **20e**.

person The form of a pronoun or verb that indicates whether the subject is doing the speaking (first person, *I* or *we*); is spoken to (second person, *you*); or is spoken about (third person, *he, she, it*, or *they*). **21a, 22a**.

phrasal verb An idiomatic verb phrase consisting of a verb and a preposition or adverb called a particle: *put off, put up with*. **45d** ESL.

phrase A group of words that lacks a subject or predicate and functions as a noun, verb, adjective, or adverb: *under the tree, has been singing, amazingly simple*. **16d**. See also *absolute phrase; appositive phrase; infinitive phrase; participle phrase; prepositional phrase*.

possessive   The form of a noun or pronoun that indicates ownership. Possessive pronouns include *my, his, her, their, theirs*, and *whose: my* boat, *your* socks. The possessive form of a noun is indicated by an apostrophe or an apostrophe and *-s: Mario's* car, the *children's* nanny, the *birds'* nests. **21k, 22b, 28a, 28b.**

predicate   The part of a sentence that contains the verb and its modifiers and that comments on or makes an assertion about the subject. To be complete, a sentence needs a subject and a predicate. **16b, 16c, 19e.**

prefix   Letters attached to the beginning of a word that change the word's meaning: *un*necessary, *re*organize, *non*stop. **33j.**

preposition   The part of speech used with a noun or pronoun in a phrase to indicate time, space, or some other relationship. **16a, 24f, 45** ESL. The noun or pronoun is the object of the preposition: *on the table, after dinner, to her.* Examples of prepositions:

about	among	between	for	near	past	under
above	around	by	from	of	since	until
across	at	despite	in	off	through	up
after	before	down	inside	on	till	with
against	behind	during	into	out	to	within
along	below	except	like	over	toward	without

prepositional phrase   A phrase beginning with a preposition and including the object of the preposition and its modifiers: The head *of the electronics company* was waiting *for an hour.* **16d, 18b, 45** ESL.

present participle   The *-ing* form of a verb, showing an action as being in progress or continuous: They are *sleeping.* Without an auxiliary, the *-ing* form cannot function as a complete verb but can be used as an adjective: *searing* heat. When the *-ing* form is used as a noun, it is called a gerund: *Skiing* can be dangerous. **19b, 20a, 20f.** See also *verbal.*

progressive tense forms   Verb tenses that show actions in progress at a point or over a period of time in past, present, or future time. They use a form of *be* + the *-ing* form of the verb: They *are working;* he *will be writing.* **20e, 20f, 20g.**

pronoun   The part of speech that takes the place of a noun, a noun phrase, or another pronoun. Pronouns are of various types: personal *(I, they);* possessive *(my, mine, their, theirs);* demonstrative *(this, that, these, those);* intensive and reflexive *(myself, herself);* relative *(who, whom, whose, which, that);* interrogative *(who, which, what);* and indefinite *(anyone, something).* **16a, 21i, 21j, 21k, 22, 24a.**

pronoun reference   The connection between a pronoun and its antecedent. Reference should be clear and unambiguous: The *lawyer* picked up *his* hat and left. **22c.** See also *agreement.*

proper noun   The capitalized name of a specific person, place, or thing: *Golden Gate Park, University of Kansas*. **16a, 32a, 42f** ESL. See also *common noun*.

quantity word   A word expressing the idea of quantity, such as *each, every, several, many*, and *much*. Subject-verb agreement is tricky with quantity words: *Each* of the students *has* a different assignment. **21i**. See also *agreement*.

reflexive pronoun   A pronoun ending in *-self* or *-selves* and referring to the subject of a clause: They incriminated *themselves*. **22h**.

regular verb   Verb that ends with *-ed* in its past tense and past participle forms. **20a**.

relative clause   See *adjective clause*.

relative pronoun   A pronoun that introduces a relative clause: *who, whom, whose, which, that*. **24a**.

restrictive phrase or clause   A phrase or clause that provides information essential for identifying the word or phrase it modifies. A restrictive phrase or clause is not set off with commas: The book *that is first on the bestseller list* is a memoir. **24d, 26j**.

run-on sentence   The error that results when two independent clauses are not separated by a conjunction or by any punctuation: not *The dog ate the meat the cat ate the fish* but *The dog ate the meat; the cat ate the fish*. Also called a *fused sentence*. **18g, 18h**.

second person   The person addressed: *you*. **22a, 22g**.

shifts   Inappropriate switches in grammatical structure, such as from one tense to another, from statement to command, or from indirect to direct quotation: not *Joan asked whether I was warm enough and did I sleep well* but *Joan asked whether I was warm enough and slept well*. **19d, 20i**.

simile   A figure of speech that makes a direct comparison: She has a laugh *like a fire siren*. **7f, 39e**.

simple tense forms   Verb tenses that show present, past, or future time with no perfect or progressive aspects: they *work*, we *worked*, she *will work*. **20e, 20f, 20g**.

split infinitive   An infinitive with a word or words separating *to* from the base verb form: *to successfully complete*. This structure has become acceptable. **19b**.

Standard English   "The variety of English that is generally acknowledged as the model for the speech and writing of educated speakers." This *American Heritage Dictionary*, 4th edition, definition warns that the use of the term is "highly elastic and variable" and confers no "absolute positive evaluation." **1c**, Introduction to Part IV, **17**.

subject The noun or pronoun that performs the action of the verb in an active voice sentence or receives the action of the verb in a passive voice sentence. To be complete, a sentence needs a subject and a verb. **16c, 18d, 19i, 44a** ESL.

subjunctive mood Verb mood used in conditions and in wishes, requests, and demands: I wish he *were* here. She demanded that he *be* present. **20k.**

subordinate clause See *dependent clause.*

subordinating conjunction A conjunction used to introduce a dependent adverb clause: *because, if, when, although, since, while.* **16e, 18c, 37c.**

suffix Letters attached to the end of a word that change the word's function or meaning: gentle*ness*, humor*ist*, slow*er*, sing*ing*. **33f.**

superlative The form of an adjective or adverb used to compare three or more people or things: *biggest; most unusual; least effectively.* **23h, 42d** ESL. See also *comparative.*

synonym A word that has the same or nearly the same meaning as another word: *quick, rapid; stanza, verse; walk, stroll; shiny, sparkling.* **39b.**

tense The form of a verb that indicates time. Verbs change form to distinguish present and past time: he *goes;* he *went.* Various structures are used to express future time, mainly *will* + the base form, or *going to* + the base form. Closely associated with time is *aspect* (perfect and progressive), which expresses the relation between the action of the verb and past, present, and future time. **20a, 20e.** See *aspect;* see also *perfect progressive tense forms; perfect tense forms; progressive tense forms; simple tense forms.*

third person The person or thing spoken about: *he, she, it, they,* or nouns. **21a, 21b, 22a.**

topic chain Repetition of key words or related words throughout a passage to aid cohesion. **20l, 37a.**

transitional expression A word or phrase used to connect two independent clauses. Typical transitional expressions are *for example, however,* and *similarly:* We were able to swim today; *in addition,* we took the canoe out on the river. A semicolon frequently connects the two independent clauses. **5e, 26e, 27b.**

transitive verb A verb that needs a direct object to complete its meaning in the active voice: Dogs *chase* cats. **20c, 20l.** See also *direct object; intransitive verb; voice.*

uncountable noun A common noun that cannot follow a plural quantity word (such as *several* or *many*), is never used with *a* or *an*, is used with a singular third person verb, and has no plural form: *furniture, happiness, information.* **16a, 21f, 42b** ESL.

verb The part of speech that expresses action or being and tells what the subject of the clause is or does. The complete verb in a clause might require auxiliary or modal auxiliary verbs to complete its meaning. **16a, 20, 43** ESL. See also the following entries for more specific information:

active voice	*linking verb*	*predicate*
agreement	*main verb*	*present participle*
aspect	*mental activity verb*	*progressive tense forms*
auxiliary verb	*modal auxiliary verb*	*regular verb*
base form	*mood*	*simple tense forms*
complete verb	*passive voice*	*subjunctive mood*
compound predicate	*past participle*	*tense*
indicative mood	*perfect progressive tense*	*transitive verb*
infinitive	*forms*	*verb chain*
intransitive verb	*perfect tense forms*	*voice*
irregular verb	*phrasal verb*	

verbal A form that is derived from a verb but is nonfinite: it cannot function as the main verb of a clause. The three types of verbals are the infinitive, the *-ing* participle, and the past participle. **16a, 20a, 43** ESL, **46d** ESL.

verb chain Combination of an auxiliary verb, a main verb, and verbals: She *might have promised to leave;* they *should deny having helped* him. **43** ESL.

voice The form of a verb that indicates whether the subject acts or is acted on. In the active voice, the subject acts: *He is painting the door.* In the passive voice, the subject is acted on: *The door is being painted.* **20l, 36c.** See also *transitive verb.*

zero article The lack of an article (*a, an,* or *the*) before a noun. Uncountable nouns are used with the zero article when they make no specific reference. **42b** ESL, **42c** ESL, **42e** ESL.

Photo Credits

Credits *(continued from copyright page iv)*

Grossman, Lawrence K. "Why Local TV News Is So Awful." *Columbia Journalism Review* 34.4 (Nov./Dec. 1997): 21.

Hirsch, E. D., Jr. *Cultural Literacy: What Every American Needs to Know.* New York: Vintage, 1988. 63.

Hölldobler, Bert, and Edward O. Wilson. *Journey to the Ants.* Cambridge, MA: Harvard University Press, 1994. 29.

Kinsley, Michael. "Consuming Gets Complicated." *Washington Post* 23 November 2001: A43.

Krucoff, Carol. "A Walk a Day." *Saturday Evening Post* May/June 2000: 12.

LaRoche, Loretta. *Life Is Not a Stress Rehearsal.* New York: Broadway, 2001. 82.

Mallon, Thomas. *A Book of One's Own: People and Their Diaries.* New York: Ticknor and Fields, 1984. 1.

Markoff, John. "A Computer Scientist's Lament: Grammar Has Lost Its Technological Edge." *New York Times* 15 April 2002: C4.

McArthur, Tom. "The English Languages?" *English Today* 11 (July 1987): 11. Figure ("Circle of World English"). Reprinted with the permission of Cambridge University Press.

McMurtry, Larry. *Walter Benjamin at the Dairy Queen.* New York: Simon and Schuster, 1999. 81–82.

Mendelson, Cheryl. *Home Comforts.* New York: Scribner, 1999.

Microsoft Word 2000. Screen shot, reprinted by permission from Microsoft Corporation.

Munson, Ronald. "The Donor's Right to Take a Risk." *New York Times* 19 January 2002: A19.

Myers, B. R. "A Reader's Manifesto." *Atlantic Monthly* July/August 2001: 104.

Nielsen, Jakob. *Designing Web Usability.* Indianapolis: New Riders, 1999. 33, 168.

Nye, Naomi Shihab. "Maintenance." *The Georgia Review* (Spring/Summer 1990): 219–227.

Olsen, Tillie, *Silences.* New York: Dell, 1983. 23.

Orman, Suze. *The Courage to Be Rich: Creating a Life of Material and Spiritual Abundance.* New York: Riverhead, 1999. 244.

Orwell, George. "Politics and the English Language." *In Front of Your Nose—1945–1950: The Collected Essays, Journalism and Letters of George Orwell.* Vol. 4. Eds. Sonia Orwell and Ian Angus. New York: Harcourt, 1968. 133.

Quindlen, Anna. "Parental Rites." *Thinking Out Loud.* New York: Random, 1993. 57.

Reader's Digest Association. *How to Do Just About Anything.* Pleasantville, NY: Reader's Digest Association, 1986. 289.

Reed, Ishmael. "America: The Multinational Society." *Writin' Is Fightin'.* New York: Atheneum, 1990. 1. Copyright © 1990 by Atheneum.

Reichl, Ruth. *Tender at the Bone: Growing Up at the Table.* New York: Broadway, 1999. 95.

Ridley, Matt. *Genome.* New York: Perennial-HarperCollins, 2000. 28–29.

Rose, Phyllis. *Parallel Lives: Five Victorian Marriages.* New York: Knopf, 1986. 106.

Sigmund, Karl, Ernst Fehr, and Martin A. Nowak. "The Economics of Fair Play." *Scientific American,* January 2002: 83. Copyright © 2002 by Scientific American, Inc. All rights reserved.

Tannen, Deborah. *You Just Don't Understand.* New York: Ballantine, 1990. 226.

Walker, Alice. Foreword. *Zora Neale Hurston: A Literary Biography.* By Robert E. Hemenway. Urbana: U of Illinois P, 1977. xvi.

Ward, Geoffrey C. *The Civil War: An Illustrated History.* New York: Knopf, 1990. 12.

Welty, Eudora. *One Writer's Beginnings.* New York: Warner, 1985. 68.

Wilentz, Sean. "The Father-and-Son Presidencies." *New York Times* 16 August 2001: A23.

Yahoo Search page: education. Reproduced with permission of Yahoo! Inc. © 2000 by Yahoo! Inc. Yahoo! and the Yahoo! Logo are trademarks of Yahoo! Inc.

Part II   Brooks, Gwendolyn. "We Real Cool." *Blacks.* Chicago: Third World Press, 1991. Copyright 1991 by Gwendolyn Brooks Blakely. Reprinted by permission of the Estate of Gwendolyn Brooks.

Dickinson, Emily. "A Certain Slant of Light." *The Poems of Emily Dickinson.* Ed. Thomas H. Johnson. Cambridge, MA: The Belknap Press of Harvard. Reprinted by permission of the publishers and the Trustees of Amherst College. Copyright © 1951, 1955, 1979 by the President and Fellows of Harvard College.

Dove, Rita. "Rosa." *On the Bus with Rosa Parks.* New York: Norton, 1999. Copyright © 1999 by Rita Dove. Reprinted by permission of W. W. Norton and Company.

Dowd, Maureen. "Leave It to Hollywood." *New York Times* 16 August 1997: sec.1: 26.

Drummond, Sean P. A., et al. "Altered Brain Response to Verbal Learning Following Sleep Deprivation." *Nature* 10 February 2000: 655–658.

Frost, Robert. "Stopping by Woods on a Snowy Evening." *The Poetry of Robert Frost.* Ed. Edward Connery Lathem. New York: Henry Holt and Co., 1979. Copyright © 1923 by Henry Holt and

Company, Inc., © 1951 by Robert Frost, © 1969 by Henry Holt and Company. Reprinted by permission of Henry Holt and Company, LLC.

Gallop-Goodman, Gerda. "Please Don't Hang Up." *American Demographics* 23.5 (2001): 28. Chart ("Do Not Disturb"). Some data from Pitney Bowes. Reprinted by permission of *American Demographics*.

Hoeksema-van Orden, Claudia Y. D., Anthony W. K. Gaillard, and Bram P. Buunk. "Social Loafing under Fatigue." *Journal of Personality and Social Psychology* 75 (1998): 1179–1190.

Hung, Jenny. "Surviving a Year of Sleepless Nights." *Newsweek* 20 September 2000: 9. All rights reserved. Reprinted by permission.

King, Martin Luther, Jr. "I Have a Dream." Reprinted by arrangement with the Heirs to the Estate of Martin Luther King, Jr. c/o Writers House, Inc. as agent for the proprietor. Copyright 1963 by Martin Luther King, Jr., copyright renewed 1991 by Coretta Scott King.

Moore, Gerald. Letter. *The Independent* 3 July 2001: 13. Reprinted by permission of the author.

Rothstein, Richard. "Lessons: Food for Thought? In Many Cases, No." *New York Times* 1 August 2001.

Part III Arnold, Raymond J. Résumé. *Contemporary Business Communication.* 5th ed. Scot Ober. Boston: Houghton, 2003.

Bolles, Richard Nelson. *What Color Is Your Parachute?* Berkeley: Ten Speed Press, 2000. 218–219.

Bookbuilders of Boston. Newsletter. *Pages.* Summer 2000.

Carlsbad Caverns National Park Chat page <http://www.carlsbad.caverns.national-park.com/wwwboard/carlchat.htm>.

City University of New York. CUNY sample Web page, using course management system Blackboard. Microsoft Internet Explorer screen shot reprinted by permission from Microsoft Corporation.

Crossen, Cynthia. Newsletter. *Booked.* July 2002.

Gomez, Aurelia. Résumé, job application letter, electronic résumé format, cover e-mail, follow-up letter. *Contemporary Business Communication.* 5th ed. Scot Ober. Boston: Houghton, 2003.

Horizons Initiative. Brochure. Boston: Horizons Initiative, 90 Cushing Ave., Dorchester, MA 02125.

Impulse Dance. Flyer. "The Studio."

Kuechler, Manfred. Dept. of Sociology, Hunter College. "Computer Access Survey" Spring 2001. Pie charts ("Internet/Web Experience #1, 2").

Lilly Careers. Web page. *Contemporary Business Communications.* 5th ed. Scot Ober. Boston: Houghton, 2003.

Marsh, Allison. Web pages. <http://www.student.richmond.edu/2001/amarsh/public_html/>. Allison Marsh's Web Pages are reprinted with her permission.

Massachusetts Division of Medical Assistance. Brochure. "What Is MassHealth?" Boston: Massachusetts Executive Office of Health and Human Services.

Microsoft Word 2000. Screen shots reprinted by permission from Microsoft Corporation.

National Telecommunications and Information Administration. "Falling through the Net: Toward Digital Inclusion. A Report on Americans' Access to Technology Tools." <http://www.ntia.doc.gov/ntiahome/fttn00/Falling.htm#31>. (5 February 2002). Table ("Percent of U.S. Households with Internet Access by Education of Householder, 1998 and 2000").

---. "Falling through the Net: Toward Digital Inclusion. A Report on Americans' Access to Technology Tools." October 2000. <http://www.ntia.doc.gov/ntiahome/fttn00/Falling.htm#f11>. Bar graph ("Percent of U.S. Households with Internet Access by Education of Householder, 1998 and 2000").

Ober, Scot. "Employment Communication." *Contemporary Business Communication.* 5th ed. Boston: Houghton, 2003. Copyright © 2003 by Houghton Mifflin Company. Reprinted with permission.

Quinn, Mary Rose. "Saugus Public Library." PowerPoint slides and narrative.

Rahman, Yousef. "Working in the Public/Private Sector." PowerPoint slide. Office of Management and Budget, 75 Park Place, New York, NY, 10007.

Raimes, Emily. "New York City." PowerPoint slide.

Sax, L. J., et al. *An Overview of the 2000 Freshman Norms.* Los Angeles Higher Education Research Institute, UCLA, January 2001 <http://www.gseis.ucla.edu/heri/heri.html>. (22 July 2002). Graphs ("Freshman Interest in Politics, 1966–2000"; "Declining Interest in Medical and Health Careers: 1971–2000, Men and Women"). Reprinted by permission of Higher Education Research Institute, UCLA, January 2001.

White, Sebastian F. G. Web pages. <http://students.alfred.edu/~whitesf>. Sebastian F. G. White's Web Pages are reprinted with his permission.

The Winter's Tale. Flyer. Harvard University. April 2002.

Part IV   Raban, Jonathan. *Bad Land: An American Romance.* New York: Vintage, 1997. 77.
Rodriguez, Richard. *Hunger of Memory.* Boston: David Godine, 1981. 11.
Rosenblatt, Roger. "The Downside of Talking to the Dead." *Time* 9 July 2001: 100.
Trillin, Calvin. "A Traditional Family." *Too Soon to Tell.* New York: Warner, 1995. 63–64.

Part V   *The American Heritage Dictionary of the English Language.* 4th ed. Definition of "graduate."
Copyright © 2000 by Houghton Mifflin Company.
Croce, Arlene. *The Fred Astaire and Ginger Rogers Book.* New York: Dutton, 1987. 66.
Larkin, Philip. "Toads." *The Less Deceived, Philip Larkin: Collected Poems.* Ed. Anthony Thwaite.
London: Marvell, 1989. By permission of the Marvell Press, England and Australia.
Morales, Aurora Levins. "Class Poem." *Getting Home Alive.* Eds. Aurora Morales and Rosario
Morales. Ithaca: NY: Firebrand. 45–47. Copyright 1986 by Aurora Levins Morales. Used with
permission from Firebrand Books, Ithaca, NY.
Sidel, Ruth. *On Her Own: Growing Up in the Shadow of the American Dream.* New York: Penguin,
1990. 27.
Thomas, Lewis. "Notes on Punctuation." *The Medusa and the Snail.* New York: Viking, 1974.
125–129.

Part VI   Eakin, Emily. "Harvard's Prize Catch, a Delphic Postcolonialist." *New York Times* 17
November 2001: A15.
Epstein, Joseph. "The Ephemeral Verities." *The Middle of My Tether.* New York: Norton, 1983.
42–43.
Kipfer, Barbara Ann. Entry on "privacy." *Roget's Twenty-first Century Thesaurus.* New York: Phillip
Lieff/Dell, 1992. 653.
Marshall, Paule. *Brown Girl, Brownstones.* New York: Feminist Press, 1981. 12.
Mitchell, Elvis. "The Sorcerer's Apprentice." *New York Times* 16 November 2001: E1.

Part VII   Global Reach, Global Internet Statistics. <http://www.glreach.com/globstats/index
.php3>. Pie chart ("Online Language Populations").
Mydans, Seth. "Nations in Asia Give English Their Own Flavorful Quirks." *New York Times*
1 July 2001: 1.

Part VIII   Alta Vista Search page: + neuromusicology + intelligence. Reprinted by permission of
Alta Vista Company, Palo Alto, CA.
City University of New York. Library catalog (CUNY PLUS) details for "Sensitive joint-vetch."
Instructional Screen Images from Expanded Academic ASAP. Reprinted by permission of
The Gale Group.
---. Library catalog (CUNY PLUS) screen for Crawford, James. Instructional Screen Images from
Expanded Academic ASAP. Reprinted by permission of The Gale Group.
Houghton Mifflin. *A Guide for Authors.* © 1998 by Houghton Mifflin Company. Used with permission.
Laird, Ellen. "Internet Plagiarism: We All Pay the Price." *Chronicle of Higher Education* 13 July 2001: 5.
MetaCrawler search page: neuromusicology intelligence. © InfoSpace, Inc. All rights reserved.
InfoSpace, their designs, and related marks are the intellectual property of InfoSpace, Inc.
Netscape/Infotrac Search page: music and intelligence. Netscape Communication browser window
copyright © 1999 Netscape Communications Corporation. Used with permission.
Newcomb, Amelia. "Suspense and Suspension." *Christian Science Monitor* 2 May 2000: 13.
Reproduced with permission. Copyright © 2000 *Christian Science Monitor.* All rights reserved.
Online at <http://csmonitor.com>.
"Punishing Assignment." Editorial. *The Boston Globe* 28 April 2000. Reprinted by permission.
Stalker, James. "Official English or English Only." *English Journal* 77 (March 1988): 20–21.
TESOL Quarterly (Teachers of English to Speakers of Other Languages). 34.3 (Autumn 2000).

Index

Note: An asterisk (*) refers to a glossary entry.

A

LIST OF BOXES AND NOTES